McGraw-Hill Ryerson

MathLinks 8

Authors

Bruce McAskill
B.Sc., B.Ed., M.Ed., Ph.D.
Mathematics Consultant
Victoria, British Columbia

Wayne Watt
B.Sc., B.Ed., M.Ed.
Mathematics Consultant
Winnipeg, Manitoba

Stella Ablett
B.Sc., B.Ed., M.Ed.
Mulgrave School, West
  Vancouver (Independent)
British Columbia

Blaise Johnson
B.Sc., B.Ed.
School District 45 (West
  Vancouver)
British Columbia

Greg McInulty
B.Sc., B.Ed.
Edmonton Public Schools
Alberta

Tricia Perry
B.Ed.
St. James-Assiniboia School
  Division
Manitoba

Michael Webb
B.Sc., M.Sc., Ph.D.
Mathematics Consultant
Toronto, Ontario

Rick Wunderlich
B.Ed.
School District 83 (North
  Okanagan/Shuswap)
British Columbia

Chris Zarski
B.Ed., M.Ed.
Evergreen Catholic Separate
  Regional Division No. 2
Alberta

Assessment/Pedagogy Consultants

Bruce McAskill
B.Sc., B.Ed., M.Ed., Ph.D.
Mathematics Consultant
Victoria, British Columbia

Wayne Watt
B.Sc., B.Ed., M.Ed.
Mathematics Consultant
Winnipeg, Manitoba

Chris Zarski
B.Ed., M.Ed.
Evergreen Catholic Separate
  Regional Division No. 2
Alberta

Aboriginal Consultant

Cheryl Makokis
Edmonton Public Schools
Alberta

Gifted Consultant

Robert Wong
Edmonton Public Schools
Alberta

Literacy and Numeracy Consultant

Ian Strachan
Calgary Board of Education
Alberta

Problem Solving, Mental Math, and Estimation Consultant

Greg McInulty
Edmonton Public Schools
Alberta

Special Education Consultant

Joanne Aldridge
Edmonton Public Schools
Alberta

Technology Consultant

Ted Keating
Thompson Rivers University
British Columbia

ESL Consultant

Maureen Sims
Special Education and
  ESL Teacher
Toronto, Ontario

Advisors

Ralph Backé
The Winnipeg School Division
Manitoba

Eric Balzarini
School District 35 (Langley)
British Columbia

Sandra Harazny
Regina Roman Catholic
Separate School Division No. 81
Saskatchewan

Erv Henderson
Mathematics Consultant
Saskatchewan

Emily Kalwarowsky
Edmonton Catholic Separate
School District No. 7
Alberta

Wanda Lloyd
Calgary Roman Catholic
Separate School District No. 1
Alberta

Tony May
West Point Grey Academy
  (Independent)
British Columbia

James McConville
School District 43 (Coquitlam)
British Columbia

Enzo Timoteo
Mathematics Consultant
Edmonton, Alberta

McGraw-Hill Ryerson

Toronto   Montréal   Boston   Burr Ridge, IL   Dubuque, IA   Madison, WI   New York
San Francisco   St. Louis   Bangkok   Bogotá   Caracas   Kuala Lumpur   Lisbon   London
Madrid   Mexico City   Milan   New Delhi   Santiago   Seoul   Singapore   Sydney   Taipei

COPIES OF THIS BOOK MAY BE OBTAINED BY CONTACTING:

McGraw-Hill Ryerson Ltd.

WEB SITE:
http://www.mcgrawhill.ca

E-MAIL:
orders@mcgrawhill.ca

TOLL-FREE FAX:
1-800-463-5885

TOLL-FREE CALL:
1-800-565-5758

OR BY MAILING YOUR ORDER TO:
McGraw-Hill Ryerson
Order Department
300 Water Street
Whitby, ON L1N 9B6

Please quote the ISBN and title when placing your order.

McGraw-Hill Ryerson
MathLinks 8

ISBN-13: 978-0-07-097338-1
ISBN-10: 0-07-097338-5

http://www.mcgrawhill.ca

4 5 6 7 8 9 10 TCP 3 2 1 0 9 8

Printed and bound in Canada

Care has been taken to trace ownership of copyright material contained in this text. The publishers will gladly accept any information that will enable them to rectify any reference or credit in subsequent printings.

Statistics Canada information is used with the permission of Statistics Canada. Users are forbidden to copy the data and redisseminate them, in an original or modified form, for commercial purposes, without permission from Statistics Canada. Information on the availability of the wide range of data from Statistics Canada can be obtained from Statistics Canada's Regional Offices, its World Wide Web site at *http://www.statcan.ca*, and its toll-free access number 1-800-263-1136.

MATH PUBLISHER: Linda Allison
PROJECT MANAGER: Helen Mason
CONTENT MANAGER: Jean Ford
DEVELOPMENTAL EDITORS: Susan Till, Janice Dyer, Rosemary Tanner, Rita Vanden Heuvel
MANAGER, EDITORIAL SERVICES: Crystal Shortt
SUPERVISING EDITOR: Shannon Martin
COPY EDITOR: Linda Jenkins, Red Pen Services
PHOTO RESEARCH & PERMISSIONS: Linda Tanaka
EDITORIAL ASSISTANT: Erin Hartley
EDITORIAL COORDINATOR: Jennifer Keay, Christine Arnold
MANAGER, PRODUCTION SERVICES: Yolanda Pigden
PRODUCTION COORDINATOR: Paula Brown
INTERIOR DESIGN: Pronk & Associates
COVER DESIGN: Valid Design & Layout
ART DIRECTION: Tom Dart, First Folio Resource Group, Inc.
ELECTRONIC PAGE MAKE-UP: Tom Dart, Luciano Sebastion De Monte, Kim Hutchinson, Lesley Rouse, Adam Wood, First Folio Resource Group, Inc.
COVER IMAGE: Corbis Canada

Acknowledgements

There are many students, teachers, and administrators who the publisher, authors, and consultants of MathLinks 8 *wish to thank for their thoughtful comments and creative suggestions about what would work best in their classrooms. Their input and assistance have been invaluable in making sure that the Student Resource and its related Teacher's Resource meet the needs of students and teachers who work within the Western and Northern Canadian Protocol Common Curriculum Framework.*

We would like to thank the Grade 8 students of Wilson Middle School, Lethbridge, Alberta, Principal, Craig Brack, and teachers, Nancy Bridal, and Irene Dersch, for their help in coordinating the photography sessions.

Aboriginal Reviewer
Paul Paling
School District 52 (Prince Rupert)
British Columbia

Inuit Reviewer
Christine Purse
Mathematics Consultant
British Columbia

Métis Reviewer
Greg King
Pembina Hills Regional Division
   No. 7
Alberta

Reviewers
Lisa Allen
Regina School District 4
Saskatchewan

Ryan Bailey
Northern Lights School Division
   No. 69
Alberta

Tammy Baydock
St. James-Assiniboia School Division
Manitoba

Linda Benson
Seven Oaks School Division 10
Manitoba

Scott Carlson
Golden Hills School Division No. 75
Alberta

Kelly Choy
Yukon Education
Yukon

Dale Cooper
Edmonton Public Schools
Alberta

Nicolas Curci
Louis Riel School Division
Manitoba

Brad Epp
School District 73 (Kamloops/
   Thompson)
British Columbia

Victor Epp
School District 5 (Southeast
   Kootenay)
British Columbia

Shelly Fletcher
St. James-Assiniboia School Division
Manitoba

Barb Gajdos
Calgary Roman Catholic Separate
   School District No. 1
Alberta

Domenico Gallo
Elk Island Catholic Separate
   Regional Division No. 41
Alberta

Laurie Gatzke
Regina School District 4
Saskatchewan

Lauri Goudreault
Holy Family Catholic Regional
   Division No. 37
Alberta

Gord Grams
Foothills School Division No. 38
Alberta

Doug Jonasson
The Pembina Trails School Division
Manitoba

Heather Jones
St. James-Assiniboia School Division
Manitoba

Jeff Krar
Calgary Science School
   (Independent)
Alberta

Luc Lerminiaux
Regina School District 4
Saskatchewan

Miles MacFarlane
Seven Oaks School Division 10
Manitoba

Martin Mazurek
Evergreen Catholic Separate
   Regional Division No. 2
Alberta

Marg McDonough
Mathematics Consultant
British Columbia

Jim Mennie
Mathematics Consultant
British Columbia

Merry Nenadov
Calgary Board of Education
Alberta

David Noonan
Elk Island Catholic Separate
  Regional Division No. 41
Alberta

Margo Perry
Edmonton Catholic Schools
Alberta

Donna Prato
Edmonton Public Schools
Alberta

Christine Prystenski
St. James-Assiniboia School Division
Manitoba

Nancy Reyda
St. James-Assiniboia School Division
Manitoba

Tom Sherbrook
Winnipeg School Division No. 1
Manitoba

Robert Shkrobot
Edmonton Public Schools
Alberta

Bill Slevinsky
St. Albert School District No. 6
Alberta

Ian Strachan
Calgary Board of Education
Alberta

Maureen Switzer
St. James-Assiniboia School Division
Manitoba

Kandel Vick
Grande Yellowhead Regional
  Division No. 35
Alberta

Greg Woitas
Calgary Roman Catholic Separate
  School District No. 1
Alberta

Anthony Yam
School District No. 41 (Burnaby)
British Columbia

Shannon Zanni
Regina School District 4
Saskatchewan

Field Testers

Amy Bado
Evergreen Catholic Separate
  Regional Division No. 2
Alberta

Ryan Bailey
Northern Lights School Division
  No. 69
Alberta

Linda Benson
Seven Oaks School Division 10
Manitoba

Nicolas Curci
Louis Riel School Division
Manitoba

Victor Epp
School District 5 (Southeast
  Kootenay)
British Columbia

Shelly Fletcher
St. James-Assiniboia School Division
Manitoba

Patrick Giommi
St. Margaret's School (Independent)
British Columbia

Sandra Harazny
Regina Roman Catholic Separate
  School Division No. 81
Saskatchewan

Blaise Johnson
School District 45 (West Vancouver)
British Columbia

Emily Kalwarowsky
Edmonton Catholic Separate School
  District No. 7
Alberta

Jeff Krar
Calgary Science School
  (Independent)
Alberta

Blair Lloyd
School District 73 (Kamloops/
  Thompson)
British Columbia

Patti Lovallo
Edmonton Public Schools
Alberta

Wanda Lloyd
Calgary Roman Catholic Separate
  School District No. 1
Alberta

Cheryl Makokis
Edmonton Public Schools
Alberta

Martin Mazurek
Evergreen Catholic Separate
  Regional Division No. 2
Alberta

David Noonan
Elk Island Catholic School Regional
  Division No. 41
Alberta

Christine Prystenski
St. James-Assiniboia School Division
Manitoba

Fariyal G. Samson
Calgary Board of Education
Alberta

Robert Shkrobot
Edmonton Public Schools
Alberta

Bill Slevinsky
St. Albert School District No. 6
Alberta

Edward Suderman
School District 45 (West Vancouver)
British Columbia

Rick Wunderlich
School District 83 (North
  Okanagan/Shuswap)
British Columbia

Shannon Zanni
Regina School District 4
Saskatchewan

Contents

A Tour of Your Textbook

Chapter Opener

Each chapter begins with a two-page spread which introduces you to what you will learn in the chapter.

Foldables™

Each chapter includes a Foldable to help you organize what you are learning and keep track of what you need to work on. Instructions on where and how to record information on the Foldable will help you use it as a study tool.

Math Link

Each chapter introduces a Math Link that helps you connect math and your own personal experiences. You will often revisit the Math Link at the end of a lesson. This is an opportunity for you to build concepts and understanding. The Wrap It Up! at the end of each chapter gives you an opportunity to demonstrate your understanding of the chapter concepts.

Numbered Sections

The numbered sections often start with a visual to connect the topic to a real setting. The purpose of this introduction is to help you make connections between the math in the section and the real world, or to make connections to what you already know.

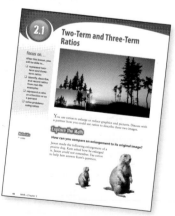

A three-part lesson follows.

- An activity is designed to help you build your own understanding of the new concept and lead toward answers to the key question.

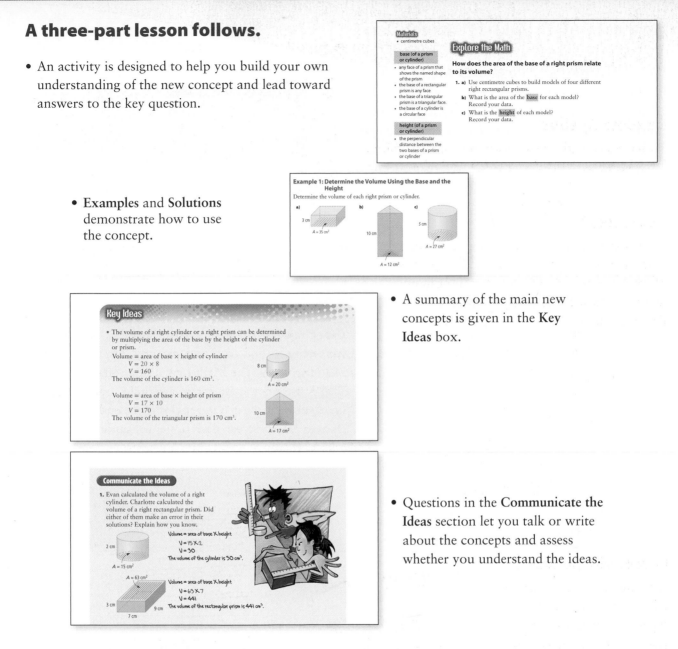

- **Examples** and **Solutions** demonstrate how to use the concept.

- A summary of the main new concepts is given in the **Key Ideas** box.

- Questions in the **Communicate the Ideas** section let you talk or write about the concepts and assess whether you understand the ideas.

Check Your Understanding

- **Practise:** These are questions to check your knowledge and understanding of what you have learned.

- **Apply:** In these questions, you need to apply what you have learned to solve problems.

- **Extend:** These questions may be more challenging and may make connections to other lessons.

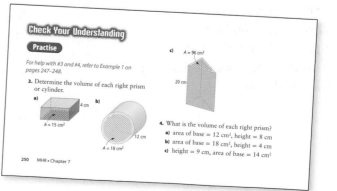

How does *MathLinks 8* help you learn?

Understanding Vocabulary

Key Words are listed on the Chapter Opener. Perhaps you already know the meaning of some of them. Great! If not, watch for these terms the first time they are used in the chapter. The meaning is given close by in the margin.

A **Literacy Link** at the beginning of each chapter provides tips to help you read and interpret the chapter content.

Other **Literacy Links** throughout the chapter assist you in reading and interpreting items in math. These tips will help you in other subjects as well.

Understanding Concepts

The **Explore the Math** activities are designed to help you construct your own understanding of new concepts. The key question tells you what the activity is about. Short steps, with illustrations, lead you to make some conclusions in the **Reflect on Your Findings** question.

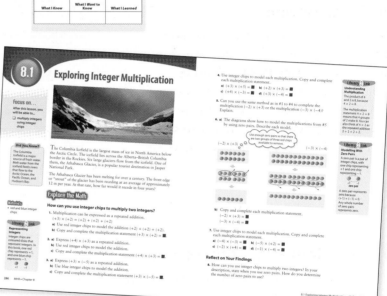

The **Examples** and their worked **Solutions** include several tools to help you understand the work.

- Notes in a thought bubble help you think through the steps.
- Sometimes different methods of solving the same problem are shown. One way may make more sense to you than the other.
- **Problem Solving Strategies** are pointed out.
- Calculator key press sequences are shown where appropriate.
- Most Examples are followed by a **Show You Know**. These questions help you check that you understand the skill covered in the Example.

The exercises begin with **Communicate the Ideas**. These questions focus your thinking on the **Key Ideas** you learned in the section. By discussing these questions in a group, or doing the action called for, you can see whether you understand the main points and are ready to begin the **Check Your Understanding**.

The first few questions in the **Check Your Understanding** can often be done by following one of the worked Examples.

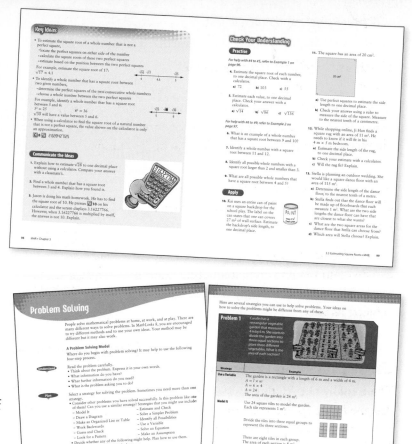

Problem Solving

At the beginning of the student resource there is an overview of the four steps you can use to approach **Problem Solving**. Samples of problem solving strategies are shown. You can refer back to this section if you need help choosing a strategy to solve a problem. You are also encouraged to use your own strategies.

Mental Math and Estimation

This **Mental Math and Estimation** logo does one of two things:

1. It signals where you can use mental math and estimation.
2. It provides useful tips for using mental math and estimation.

You could also determine 1.5% of $20 000 as:

30% of 20 000 is 6000.
3% of 20 000 is 600.
1.5% of 20 000 is 300.

Other Features

Did You Know?

Did You Know?
The Columbia Icefield is a major source of fresh water. Melt water from the icefield feeds rivers that flow to the Arctic Ocean, the Pacific Ocean, and Hudson's Bay.

These are interesting facts related to math topics you are learning.

History Link

In Roman times, the term *centurion* was used to describe an officer in the Roman Legion who was in charge of 100 soldiers. There was one centurion *per cent*, meaning there was one centurion per 100 soldiers. What other English words do you know that include *cent*?

Subject Links

This feature links the current topic to another subject area.

Web Links

WWW Web Link
To generate tessellations on the computer, go to www.mathlinks8.ca and follow the links.

You can find extra information related to some questions on the Internet. Log on to **www.mathlinks8.ca** and you will be able to link to recommended Web sites.

Chapter Review *and* Practice Test

There is a **Chapter Review** and a **Practice Test** at the end of each chapter. The chapter review is organized by section number so you can look back if you need help with a question. The test includes the different types of questions that you will find on provincial tests: multiple choice, numerical response, short answer, and extended response.

Cumulative Review

To help you reinforce what you have learned, there is a review of the previous four chapters at the end of Chapters 4, 8, and 12. Each of these special reviews is followed by a Task.

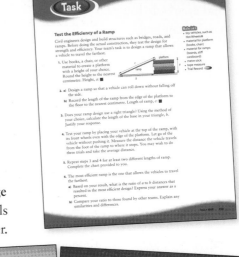

Task

These tasks require you to use skills from more than one chapter. You will also need to use your creativity.

Math Games *and* Challenge in Real Life

The last two pages of each chapter provide **Math Games** and a **Challenge in Real Life**. **Math Games** provide an interesting way to practise the skills you learned during the chapter. Most games can be played with a partner. Some can be played with a larger group. Enjoy them with your friends and family. The **Challenge in Real Life** provides an interesting problem that shows how the math you learned in the chapter relates to jobs, careers, or daily life.

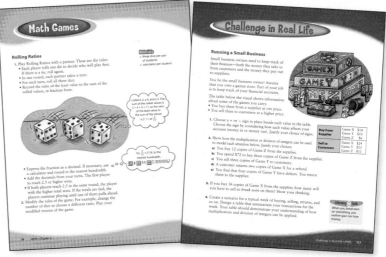

Answers

Answers are provided for all Practise, Apply, Extend, and Review questions. Sample answers are given for questions that have a variety of possible answers or that involve communication. If you need help, read the sample and then try to give an alternative response. Answers are omitted for the Math Link questions and for Practice Tests because teachers may use these questions to assess your progress.

Glossary

Refer to the illustrated **Glossary** at the back of the student resource if you need to check the exact meaning of mathematical terms.

Problem Solving

People solve mathematical problems at home, at work, and at play. There are many different ways to solve problems. In *MathLinks 8*, you are encouraged to try different methods and to use your own ideas. Your method may be different but it may also work.

A Problem Solving Model

Where do you begin with problem solving? It may help to use the following four-step process.

Understand

Read the problem carefully.
- Think about the problem. Express it in your own words.
- What information do you have?
- What further information do you need?
- What is the problem asking you to do?

Plan

Select a strategy for solving the problem. Sometimes you need more than one strategy.
- Consider other problems you have solved successfully. Is this problem like one of them? Can you use a similar strategy? Strategies that you might use include:
  - Model It
  - Draw a Diagram
  - Make an Organized List or Table
  - Work Backwards
  - Guess and Check
  - Look for a Pattern
  - Estimate and Check
  - Solve a Simpler Problem
  - Identify all Possibilities
  - Use a Variable
  - Solve an Equation
  - Make an Assumption
- Decide whether any of the following might help. Plan how to use them.
  - tools such as a ruler or a calculator
  - materials such as grid paper or a number line

Do It!

Solve the problem by carrying out your plan.
- Use mental math to estimate a possible answer.
- Do the calculations.
- Record each of your steps.
- Explain and justify your thinking.

Look Back

Examine your answer. Does it make sense?
- Is your answer close to your estimate?
- Does your answer fit the facts given in the problem?
- Is the answer reasonable? If not, make a new plan. Try a different strategy.
- Consider solving the problem a different way. Do you get the same answer?
- Compare your methods with those of your classmates.

Here are several strategies you can use to help solve problems. Your ideas on how to solve the problems might be different from any of these.

Problem 1

Carolin has a rectangular vegetable garden that measures 4 m by 6 m. She wants to divide the garden into three equal sections to plant three different vegetables. What is the area of each section?

Strategy	Example
Use a Variable	The garden is a rectangle with a length of 6 m and a width of 4 m. $A = l \times w$ $A = 6 \times 4$ $A = 24$ The area of the garden is 24 m².
Model It	Use 24 square tiles to model the garden. Each tile represents 1 m². Divide the tiles into three equal groups to represent the three sections. There are eight tiles in each group. The area of each section is 8 m².
Use a Variable	The garden is a rectangle with a length of 6 m and a width of 4 m. $A = l \times w$ $A = 6 \times 4$ $A = 24$ The area of the garden is 24 m². Let S represent the area of each section. S = area of garden ÷ number of sections $S = 24 \div 3$ $S = 8$ The area of each section is 8 m².

Problem 2

Amil is downloading some software. It has taken 56 s to complete $\frac{1}{4}$ of the download.

What is the total time that the download will likely take?

Strategy	Example
Solve an Equation	Let t represent the total time required to complete the download. $\frac{1}{4}$ of the total time is 56 s. The equation that models this situation is $\frac{t}{4} = 56$. $$\frac{t}{4} = 56$$ $$\frac{t}{4} \times 4 = 56 \times 4 \qquad \text{Multiply both sides of the equation by 4.}$$ $$t = 224$$ The download will take about 224 s, or 3 min and 44 s. *There are 60 s in 1 min.*
Estimate and Check	Estimate that 56 s is close to 60 s, which is 1 min. $\frac{1}{4}$ of the download takes about 1 min. Multiply by 4 to estimate the total download time. $1 \times 4 = 4$ The total download will likely take about 4 min. Check: $56 \times 4 = 224$ The download will take about 224 s, or 3 min and 44 s. The estimate and the calculated values are close.

Problem 3

A teacher is playing a guessing game with her class. Her clue is "After a reflection in each axis of a Cartesian plane, a point is in quadrant II. What quadrant did the point start in?" What is the solution?

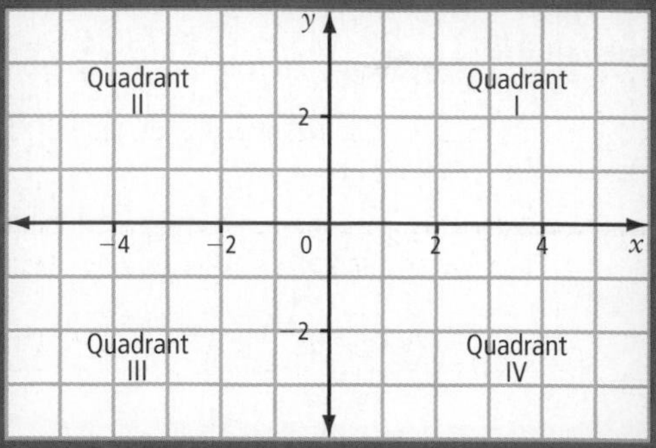

Strategy	Example
Identify all Possibilities	The point can be reflected in x-axis and then in the y-axis or it can be reflected in the y-axis and then the x-axis. After the two reflections, the point lies in quadrant II. So, the possible starting quadrants are quadrants I, III, or IV. List all the possibilities, using quadrants I, III, and IV as the starting quadrants.

Starting in Quadrant I

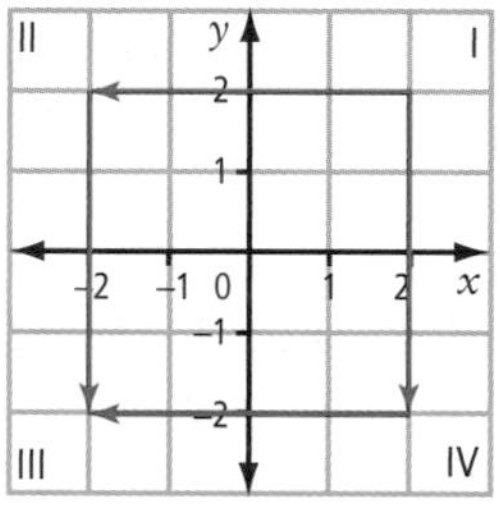

Both possibilities result in quadrant III as a final position.

Starting in Quadrant III

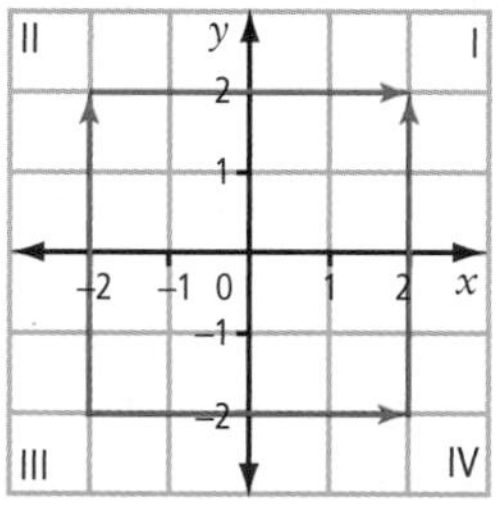

Both possibilities result in quadrant I as a final position.

Starting in Quadrant IV

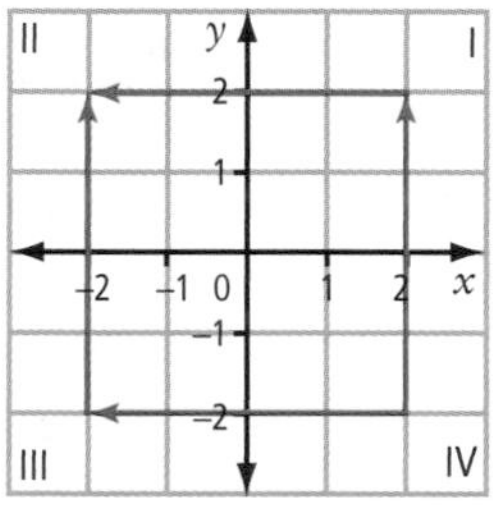

Both possibilities result in quadrant II as a final position.

The point started in quadrant IV.

Work Backwards	Use the final position of quadrant II as the starting quadrant and work backwards. Both possibilities result in quadrant IV. The point started in quadrant IV.

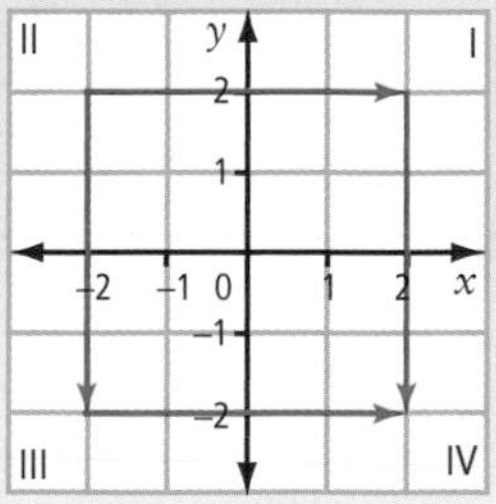

<table>
<tr><td>**Problem 4**</td><td>Sharon's family owns and operates a small restaurant. They have many small square tables and stacking chairs. What is the greatest number of people that can be seated when 10 tables are put together?</td></tr>
</table>

Strategy	Example

Make an Assumption

Draw a Diagram

Make an Organized List or Table

Look for a Pattern

Assume that only one person can sit along each side of a table.

Diagram	Number of Tables	Number of People
	1	4
	2	6
	3	8
	4	10

When 10 tables are put together in a line,
$4 + 2 \times 9$ people can be seated.
This is 22 people.

> The table shows a pattern. One table seats four people. With each extra table, two more people can be seated.

Identify all Possibilities

Consider other possible arrangements.

When 3 tables are put together in an L-shape, 8 people can be seated. This is the same as when the tables are in a line.

When 4 tables are put together to form a square, 8 people can be seated. This is less than when the tables are in a line.

Other arrangements of tables cannot seat more people than when the tables are arranged in a line. So, the greatest number of people that can be seated when 10 tables are put together is 22 people.

Representing Data

Data surrounds you everywhere you turn. It is up to you to identify and compare daily information. Have you considered how athletic statistics are determined, how newspaper and magazine surveys are supported, or how industries use information to predict sales?

A graph is a visual way of displaying data. There are many decisions to make when you create a graph. What type of graph will you use? What portion of the data will you display? How will the display communicate your message?

What You Will Learn

- ❏ to compare how different graphs represent the same data
- ❏ to identify the advantages and disadvantages of different graphs
- ❏ to explore how data can be misrepresented
- ❏ to justify using a specific graph to represent data

20

Position:
Forward

Height:
5'10"

Weight:
171 lbs.

Born:
8/12/78
Shaunavon, SK

® Registered trademark
of Hockey Canada/
® Marque déposée de
Hockey Canada

HAYLEY WICKENHEISER

Team Canada Career

GP	G	A	PTS	PIM
168	109	131	240	216

Wickenheiser led the National Women's Team in scoring with 17 points at the 2006 Winter Games in Torino, capturing the second Gold Medal of her career. She was also the Most Valuable Player at the 2002 Winter Games in Salt Lake City. In 2004-05, she captured the inaugural WWHL Cup with the Calgary Oval X-Treme and was the first player to score 100 goals for Canada at the international level.

©2006 In The Game, Inc. Made in Canada

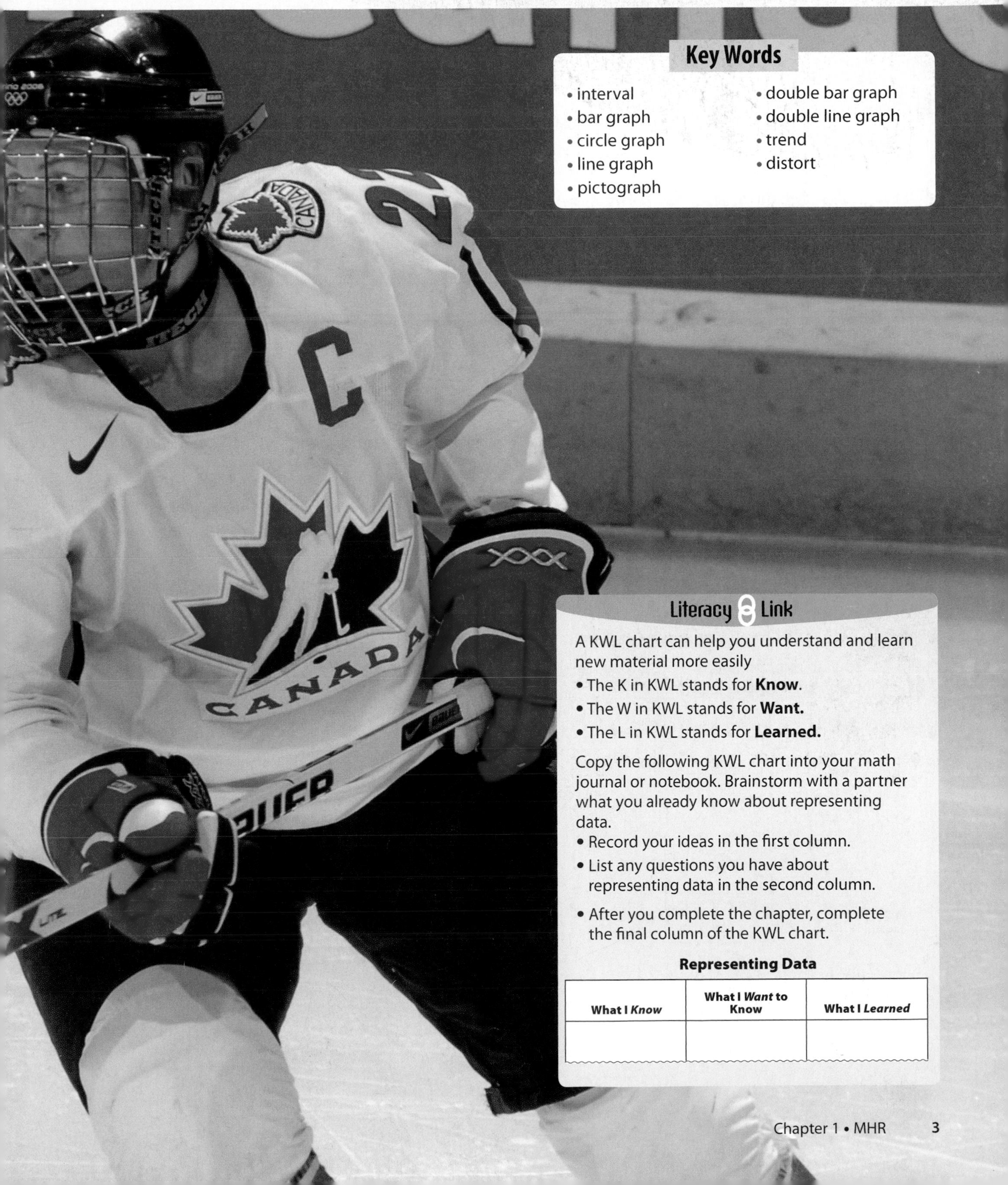

- interval
- bar graph
- circle graph
- line graph
- pictograph
- double bar graph
- double line graph
- trend
- distort

Literacy ⬡ Link

A KWL chart can help you understand and learn new material more easily

- The K in KWL stands for **Know**.
- The W in KWL stands for **Want**.
- The L in KWL stands for **Learned.**

Copy the following KWL chart into your math journal or notebook. Brainstorm with a partner what you already know about representing data.

- Record your ideas in the first column.
- List any questions you have about representing data in the second column.

- After you complete the chapter, complete the final column of the KWL chart.

Representing Data

What I *Know*	What I *Want* to Know	What I *Learned*

Making the Foldable

- 11 × 17 sheet of paper
- ruler
- stapler
- several sheets of notebook paper cut into quarters or large index cards
- scissors (optional)

Step 1 Fold an 11 × 17 sheet of paper into thirds lengthwise.

Step 2 Label the outside of your Foldable as shown.

Step 3 Unfold the paper. Fold the bottom edge upward approximately 8 cm. Staple the outer edges and along each crease to make three pockets.

Step 4 Label each section and pocket as shown.

Step 5 Label the back of the Foldable as shown.

Using the Foldable

Use the back of the Foldable for your answers to the Math Link introduction on page 5.

As you work through each section of Chapter 1, make notes about examples and Key Ideas on quarter sheets of paper or index cards and put them in the appropriate pocket. Place your responses to the Math Link for each section in the same place.

Write the Key Words above the appropriate pocket.

Keep track of what you need to work on. Check off each item as you deal with it.

As you think of ideas for the Wrap It Up!, record them on the back of the Foldable.

MATH LINK

Music Industry

Music producers sell hundreds of millions of recordings each year. Although music is popular, predicting the sales of a new release can be challenging due to new technology. Will a new release be a hit or a flop? Music producers collect information to help them predict sales. For example, is the artist new? Is the artist currently touring? Who does the music appeal to? How could you organize the information that music producers gather?

1. The circle graph shows the music preferences of young Canadian adults between the ages of 14 and 19.

   a) What was the favourite type of music? What is the least favourite type of music?

   b) Research the music preferences of young adults between the ages of 14 and 19 in your province or territory. Does this circle graph provide a good representation of preferences where you live? Explain.

Music Preferences in Young Canadian Adults (Ages 14 to 19)

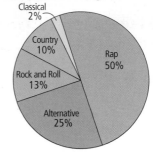

- Classical 2%
- Country 10%
- Rap 50%
- Rock and Roll 13%
- Alternative 25%

2. The double bar graph shows Canadian sales of music in different formats.

   a) What were the sales for DVDs in 2006?

   b) Compare the sales for CDs in 2006 and 2007.

   c) How do you see this data changing over time? Explain your reasoning.

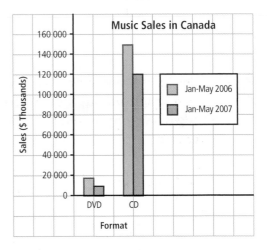

Music Sales in Canada

Jan-May 2006
Jan-May 2007

Sales ($ Thousands)

Format: DVD, CD

3. The table shows the music market shares for several music producers.

Music Producer	Market Share (%)
Sony BMG	26
Universal Music Group	32
Warner Music Group	15
EMI Group	9
Independent Labels	18

   a) Represent the data using a bar graph and a circle graph.

   b) Which graph do you prefer? Explain.

In this chapter, you will collect, analyse, and display data about the music industry. What is your favourite type of music?

Advantages and Disadvantages of Different Graphs

How tall are the students in your class? Is everyone nearly the same height? Or are the heights spread out? What is the most common height for the boys and the girls?

Explore the Math

Materials
• metre stick
• chalk or masking tape
• ruler
• grid paper (optional)
• coloured pencils

What are the best ways to display a large quantity of data?

1. Work in groups of three or four. To the nearest centimetre, measure and record the height of each member of your group.

2. Record the results for the entire class on the board. Include the height and gender of each student.

interval
• the spread between the smallest and the largest numbers in a range of numbers

3. Decide on an **interval**, and then organize the data into groups. You may wish to use 10 cm as the interval for the height of students in your class. Round the shortest height down to the nearest 10 cm. For example, if the shortest height is 122 cm, start the first interval at 120 cm. Develop a frequency table using the model below.

Interval	Tally	Frequency
120 to 129 cm		
130 to 139 cm		

> A frequency table lists items and uses tally marks to record the number of times each item occurs.

4. Display your data using a graph of your choice.

5. a) Compare the information on your graph with that of other groups. How does the type of graph you used affect the amount and the type of information it displays?

   b) List advantages and disadvantages of the type of graph you used.

6. Separate the data into two categories. For example, you might compare boys and girls.

7. Choose one type of graph to display both sets of data.

8. a) Compare the data on the two graphs that you made.

   b) List advantages and disadvantages of the type of graph you used in step 7.

   c) Compare the information on your second graph with that of other groups. Did you reach the same conclusions? Explain.

Reflect on Your Findings

9. How might you decide which graph is best for representing a large quantity of data?

Literacy Link

Types of Graphs

Bar Graph

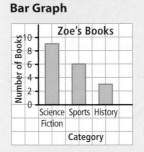

Line Graph

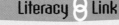

Circle Graph

Double Bar Graph

Double Line Graph

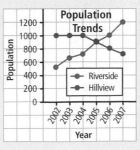

Pictograph

Did You Know?

Many cultures have their own version of pizza with unique toppings. For example, Canadian pizza toppings may include bacon, pepperoni, and mushrooms. In India, pizza toppings include ginger, paneer, which is a form of cottage cheese, and chicken tikka.

Example 1: Compare Two Graphs

During one weekend, the owners of Pascal's Pizzeria recorded how they received pizza orders and then presented the data using a circle graph and a pictograph.

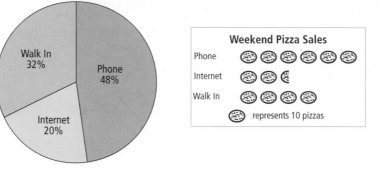

a) How many more pizzas were ordered by phone than on the Internet? Which graph shows this more clearly? Explain.

b) Almost half of the total number of orders came by phone. Which graph shows this more clearly? Explain.

c) Which graph better shows the number of pizzas ordered by Internet? Justify your choice.

d) Would a line graph be a useful way to display the data? Explain why or why not.

e) What other type of graph could be used to display the data?

Solution

a) There were 35 more pizzas ordered by phone than on the Internet.

   The pictograph uses symbols to compare the number of pizza orders from the phone, the Internet, and walk ins. The pictograph shows more clearly that there were more than twice as many phone orders as Internet orders.

b) The circle graph shows that 48% of the pizzas were ordered by phone. The circle graph shows this more clearly because almost half of the circle is shaded to represent phone orders.

c) The pictograph shows the number of pizzas ordered by Internet better than the circle graph. The pictograph uses 2.5 pizza symbols to represent the orders from the Internet.

Since each symbol represents 10 pizzas, then $2.5 \times 10 = 25$ pizzas.

You would have to perform extra calculations to determine the number of pizzas ordered by Internet using the information on the circle graph.

For example, the circle graph shows that 20% of the 125 pizzas were ordered on the Internet. You can find the number of pizzas by calculating 20% of the total number of pizzas.

Since $20\% = 0.2$, then $0.2 \times 125 = 25$ pizzas.

d) A line graph would not be useful since the data do not show changes over time. You need to use a graph that compares data in different categories.

e) A bar graph could also have been used to compare data about pizza orders.

Show You Know

The graphs show the number of each variety of apple sold in a fruit stand.

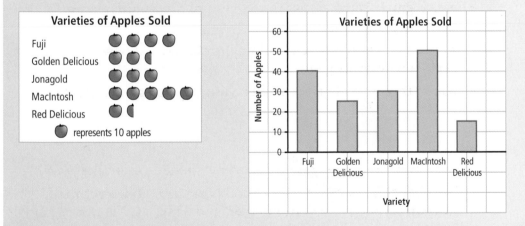

a) In your opinion which graph is easier to read? Justify your choice.

b) Would a line graph be a useful way to display the data? Explain why or why not.

c) What other type of graph could be used to display the data?

Example 2: Representing Data

History 🔗 Link

The Stanley Cup was originally called the Dominion Hockey Challenge Cup. It was donated by Lord Stanley of Preston, a Governor General of Canada, and was first awarded in 1893 to Montréal.

During the 2005–2006 hockey season, the Edmonton Oilers advanced to the Stanley Cup finals. In regular season play, two of their top three players were Shawn Horcoff (born in Trail, BC) and Jarret Stoll (born in Melville, SK). Here are the statistics for their previous three regular seasons with the Oilers.

Horcoff (Centre)

Season	Games Played	Goals	Assists	Total Points
1	78	12	21	33
2	80	15	25	40
3	79	22	51	73

Stoll (Centre)

Season	Games Played	Goals	Assists	Total Points
1	4	0	1	1
2	68	10	11	21
3	82	22	46	68

a) Use a double bar graph to display the data.

b) Which player shows the most improvement in total points?

c) Total points are used to assess a player's worth. Take a look at the number of games Horcoff and Stoll played. Is this a fair way to assess a player's worth?

d) Would two circle graphs be effective to display the data? Explain.

Solution

a)

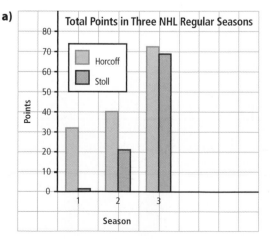

b) Stoll shows the most improvement in total points over three seasons.

c) Total points are not a fair way to assess a player's worth. The graph does not take into account the number of games that each centre played during the regular season. The number of games that Stoll played increased over the three seasons, whereas the number of games that Horcoff played stayed approximately the same each season.

d) No, two circle graphs are less effective. Each circle graph shows the percent of points scored in each season compared with the total number of points scored over three seasons. It is difficult to compare the total points of the two players.

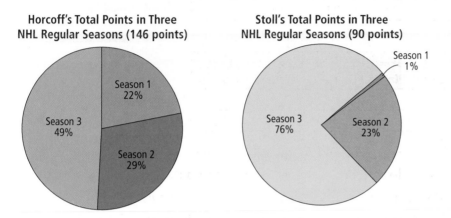

**Horcoff's Total Points in Three
NHL Regular Seasons (146 points)**

Season 1
22%

Season 3
49%

Season 2
29%

**Stoll's Total Points in Three
NHL Regular Seasons (90 points)**

Season 1
1%

Season 3
76%

Season 2
23%

Show You Know

Jenna surveyed students in grade 8 in her school to determine their favourite team sports.

a) Choose one type of graph to display the data.

b) Graph the data.

c) Give one advantage of using your choice of graph.

Sports	Frequency
Basketball	24
Volleyball	20
Soccer	45
Baseball	25
Hockey	32
Other	4
Total	150

- Data can be presented using bar graphs, double bar graphs, circle graphs, line graphs, and pictographs.
- Different graphs may provide different information and display certain types of data better.

  - Bar graphs are best for comparing data across categories.

    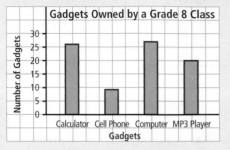

  - Double bar graphs are best for comparing two sets of data across categories.

    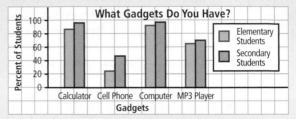

  - Circle graphs are best for comparing categories to the whole using percents. The sum of the percents in a circle graph is 100%.

    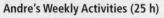
    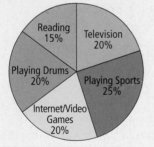

  - Line graphs are best for showing changes in data over time.

    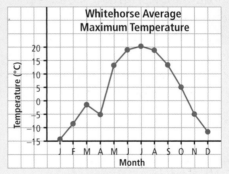

  - Pictographs are best for comparing data that can be easily counted and represented using symbols.

1. Flora wants to use a graph to summarize movie ticket sales for two movies, and make a prediction for future sales. Which graph should she use—the double line graph or the double bar graph? Explain why.

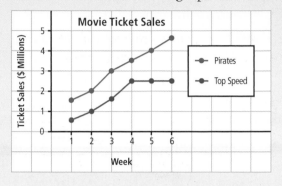

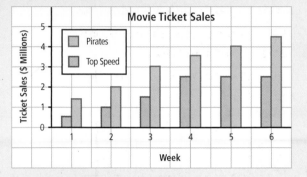

2. Wes surveyed 60 students to determine which type of computer game is the most popular. Wes decided to display the data in a bar graph. Bonnie suggested that a circle graph would be more useful for displaying the data. Who made a better choice? Explain.

Type of Game	Votes
Quest	15
Role-play	20
Simulation	9
Strategy	16
Total	60

3. How are a bar graph and a pictograph similar? How are they different? What type of data is each useful for displaying? Share your answer with a classmate.

Check Your Understanding

Practise

For help with #4 to #6, refer to Example 1 on pages 8–9.

4. Ravi recorded his spending for one month. He displayed the data in a circle graph and a pictograph.

   a) How much more does Ravi spend on food than on movies? Which graph shows this more clearly? Explain.

   b) Ravi spends half of his money on food and clothing. Which graph shows this more clearly? Explain.

   c) Describe one advantage and one disadvantage of using each graph.

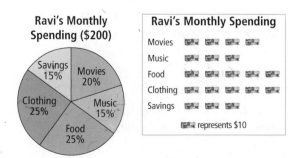

5. The piano that Sara, Ann, and Min use is available for 40 h of practice every week. The graphs show how they divide the practice time.

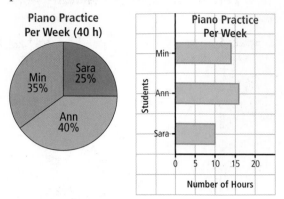

a) What information does each graph provide?

b) Write and answer one question about the data that can be answered from the circle graph.

c) Write and answer one question about the data that can be answered from the bar graph.

6. For a science fair experiment, Mitchell measured the height of a plant every Monday for four weeks. He displayed the data in a line graph and a pictograph.

Week	1	2	3	4
Plant Height (cm)	20	40	60	90

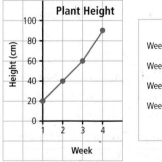

a) What information does each graph provide?

b) Between which two weeks did the plant grow at the same rate?

c) Between which two weeks did the plant change the most in height? Which graph shows this more clearly?

d) Describe one advantage and one disadvantage of using each graph.

For help with #7 and #8, refer to Example 2 on pages 10–11.

7. The table shows the heights of two friends measured over time.

	Lewis		Andrea
Age	**Height (cm)**	**Age**	**Height (cm)**
2	40	2	40
4	60	4	60
6	70	6	80
8	100	8	110
10	120	10	130
12	145	12	150
14	165	14	160
16	175	16	160

a) Use a double bar graph and a double line graph to display the data.

b) How are the trends for Andrea and Lewis similar? How are they different?

c) Which graph do you think more clearly shows each student's height trend? Explain your choice.

d) Would two circle graphs be effective for displaying the data? Explain why or why not.

Literacy ⊖ Link

A *trend* is the general direction that a line graph is going.

8. The table shows the decibel levels of different sounds in the environment.

Sound	Level
Leaves rustling	20 dB
Whisper	30 dB
Heavy traffic	78 dB
Lawn mower	90 dB
Hockey game	104 dB
Thunder clap	120 dB
Stock car races	130 dB
Balloon pop	157 dB

a) Use a bar graph to display the data. What is one advantage of using a bar graph?

b) Could you use a line graph to display the data? Explain.

c) Could you use a circle graph to display the data? Explain.

d) Would a pictograph be an effective way to display the data? Explain why or why not.

Apply

9. The graphs show the categories of books that were signed out from a library over a year.

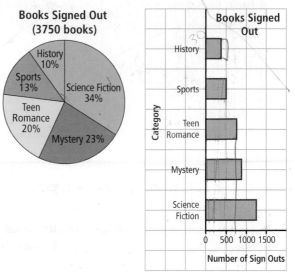

Books Signed Out (3750 books)

a) Estimate how many times more popular science fiction books are than history books.

b) Which graph helped you answer part a)? Why did you choose this graph?

c) Which category of book has approximately the same number of sign outs as history and sports books together? Show your thinking.

d) Which graph helped you answer part c)? Why did you choose this graph?

e) The library has $12 000 to spend on books based on their popularity. How much money should be spent for each category? Show your work.

f) Which graph did you use to answer part e)? Why did you choose this graph?

10. The pictograph shows the results of the election for the grade 8 representative on the students' council.

Grade 8 Representative

Ari ▦ ▦ ▦ ▦
Bai ▦ ▦ ▦ ▦ ▦ ▦
Niki ▦ ▦ ▦ ▦
Tuong ▦ ▦ ▦ ▦ ▦ ▦ ▦

▦ represents 10 votes

a) Draw a bar graph to show the data in the pictograph.

b) Does the pictograph or the bar graph more clearly show how students voted in this election? Explain your reasoning.

c) Would you recommend using a line graph to show the data? Explain.

d) Identify one advantage and one disadvantage of using a circle graph to show the data.

11. A store manager tracks jewellery sales for one month.

Week	Items Sold
1	14
2	25
3	39
4	65
Total	143

a) Use two different graphs to represent the data.

b) Compare the two graphs. Is one graph more effective in representing the data? Explain your reasoning.

c) Should the store continue to sell this jewellery? Explain your thinking.

12. A grade 8 class recorded the following percent scores on a Math test:

78 65 49 72 89 73 68 70 78 85
44 51 75 95 88 63 58 67 90 48
56 77 98 40 63 89 91 82 76 59

a) Organize the data into groups and develop a frequency table.

b) List the different graphs that could be used to display the data.

c) Which graph would most effectively display the test scores? Explain your choice.

13. A radio station was designing a web site for teen listeners. It surveyed 50 students from each of two schools to find out which features most interested students. Each student voted for the two features they most wanted to see on the web site.

School	Entertainment News	Music Downloads	Contests	Message Boards
Queen Elizabeth	40	45	5	10
Hillside	20	35	25	20

a) Choose one type of graph to represent the data. Explain your choice.

b) What two categories are the most important for students from Queen Elizabeth?

14. Janice surveyed ten friends about their favourite colour of Freezie™ to stock in the school store. She used this line graph to show the data.

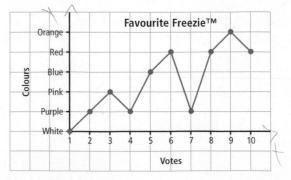

a) How could you improve this graph?

b) Why is using a line graph not a good choice in this case? Explain your reasoning.

15. Search various media, such as magazines, newspapers, and the Internet, for information about music or sports that has been represented in a graph. Print or cut out the graph. Glue or tape it into your notebook.

a) Write and answer two questions about the data in the graph.

b) Represent the data using a different kind of graph.

c) Write and answer two questions about the data that can be answered by your new graph. Your questions should be different from the ones you wrote in part a).

d) Compare the two graphs. Describe an advantage and a disadvantage of using each graph.

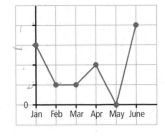

Extend

16. Here is an incomplete line graph.

a) Describe a scenario to represent the data on this graph. Then, complete the graph.

b) Draw another graph to show the data.

c) State one disadvantage of using each graph to show the data.

17. Prepare a survey question that would give you data that are appropriate to display in a circle graph.

a) How many different options does your question have? Is your question likely to have a different number of people responding to each option?

b) Explain why the circle graph is preferable to other graphs for displaying this data.

c) Prepare another survey question that would give you data that are appropriate to display in a different graph of your choice.

MATH LINK

Survey the students in your class about their favourite type of music from a list of five or six different types. Consider including the following choice on the survey: None of the above.

a) Record the data in a tally chart and create a frequency table.

b) Draw a graph of your data.

c) Explain an advantage and a disadvantage of using your graph format to display the data.

Misrepresenting Data

Kevin likes to stand in front of the fun house mirrors when he visits the World of Science. Someone looking at an image of Kevin in a curved mirror would know that it was distorted. How can you tell by looking at a graph if it has been distorted?

Literacy ⊖ Link

Distort means to change the appearance or twist the meaning of something in a way that is misleading.

Explore the Math

What are some ways to misrepresent data?

These two graphs display the same data in different ways.

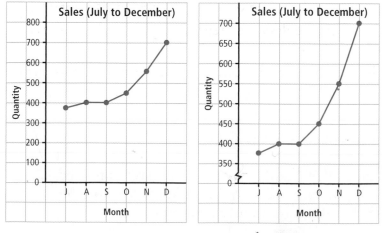

Graph A   Graph B

1. How are the graphs the same?

2. How are the graphs different?

3. Which graph gives a more accurate representation of the sales trend? Explain.

4. Change the scale of Graph B to go from 0 to 2000. Draw the new graph.

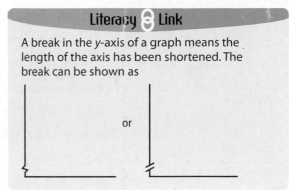

Literacy 🔗 Link

A break in the *y*-axis of a graph means the length of the axis has been shortened. The break can be shown as

or

Reflect on Your Findings

5. How can the scale on a graph affect the conclusions someone might make about the data?

Example 1: Distorting the Scale

Matthew's Math test scores are displayed on the bar graph.

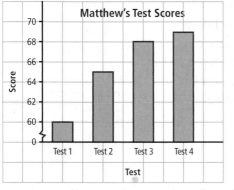

a) According to the graph, what did Matthew receive on each test?

b) From the graph, what appears to be true about Matthew's improvement over the four test scores? What part of the graph has been distorted to create this impression?

c) How should the graph be drawn to represent Matthew's progress more accurately?

d) What would be a more accurate conclusion about his improvement?

Solution

a) He received scores of 60, 65, 68, and 69.

b) The graph suggests that Matthew's test scores have improved significantly over the four tests. The break in the scale on the vertical axis creates this misleading impression.

c) The graph should be redrawn with a continuous scale that starts at zero. This would show that Matthew's test scores have improved, but not by as much as the first graph suggests.

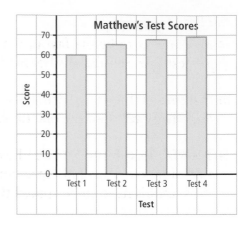

d) Matthew's test scores have improved a small amount over the last four tests. The greatest increase was from Test 1 to Test 2.

Show You Know

a) Explain how this graph could be misleading.

b) What conclusion does the graph suggest about the price of gas at the end of the day compared with the price at the beginning of the day?

c) Describe how to redraw the graph to represent the data more accurately.

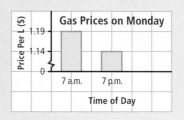

Example 2: Distorting the Visuals

a) From the pictograph, which pet seems to be the favourite? Explain.

b) From the pictograph, does it seem that more students like cats or dogs? Explain.

c) How should the pictograph be redrawn to represent the data more accurately?

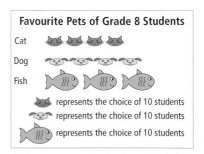

Solution

a) Fish appear to be the favourite pets because the line for fish is the longest one and the symbol for fish is much larger.

b) It seems as if more students like dogs than cats because the line for dogs is longer than the one for cats.

c) The pictograph should be redrawn so that each symbol is the same size, since each symbol represents the choice of ten students. Also, the symbols need to be spaced the same distance apart.

Show You Know

a) Explain how this graph could be misleading.

b) What conclusion does the graph suggest about favourite lunch specials?

c) How could you redraw the graph to represent the data more accurately?

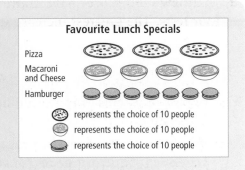

Favourite Lunch Specials

Pizza
Macaroni and Cheese
Hamburger

represents the choice of 10 people
represents the choice of 10 people
represents the choice of 10 people

Example 3: Distorting the Size of Bars

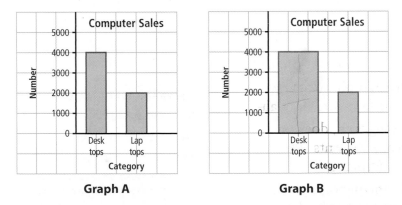

Graph A

Graph B

a) From Graph A, how many times more sales are there of desktops than laptops? Is this an accurate representation? Explain.

b) From Graph B, how many times more sales are there of desktops than laptops? How could Graph B be misleading?

Solution

a) Graph A shows sales of 4000 desktops and 2000 laptops. This is twice as many sales of desktops as laptops. The graph is an accurate representation of the data. The bar for desktops is twice as high as the bar for laptops.

> Recall that Area = *l* × *w*. In Graph B, the area of the desktops bar is four times as great as the laptops bar. This could suggest that desktop sales are four times as great as laptop sales.

b) Graph B shows sales of 4000 desktops and 2000 laptops. This is twice as many sales of desktops as laptops. The bar for desktops is twice as wide as the bar for laptops. Even though Graph B displays the same data as Graph A, the greater area of the first bar in Graph B suggests that the sales were much higher. The size of the first bar produces a misleading graph.

Show You Know

a) Explain how this graph could be misleading.

b) What conclusion does the graph suggest about the annual cost in 1997 compared with the annual cost in 2007?

c) Describe how to redraw the graph to represent the data more accurately.

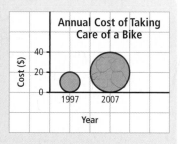

Key Ideas

- Misleading graphs can cause people to misinterpret the data and draw false conclusions.
- The format of a graph can be misleading. Misleading features include
  - distorting the scale

  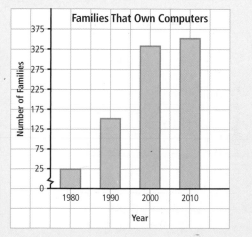

  - distorting the information by using visuals of different sizes

  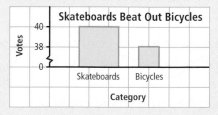

1. Travis recorded the following data about how he spends his day.

   a) How would you make a bar graph to help argue that Travis spends most of his time sleeping or going to school?

   b) How would you make a bar graph that Travis could use to argue that he spends almost as much time on homework as he does at school?

Activity	Time (h)
Chores	1
Eating	2.5
Homework	2.5
School	6.5
Sleep	7
Sports	2.5
TV	2
Total	24

2. a) Sophie surveyed her friends about their favourite flavour of ice cream. What information is missing on the graph?

   b) How could you present this data more accurately?

3. When might it be to someone's advantage to present distorted data? Share your answer with a partner.

Favourite Ice Cream

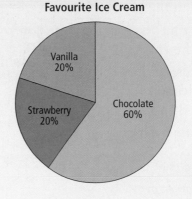

Vanilla 20%

Strawberry 20%

Chocolate 60%

Check Your Understanding

Practise

For help with #4 and #5, refer to Example 1 on pages 19–20.

4. Samantha recorded the temperature on a hot day. She displayed the data in a line graph.

   a) Explain how this graph could be misleading.

   b) What conclusion does the graph suggest about the changes in temperature?

   c) How should the graph be redrawn to make the data clearer?

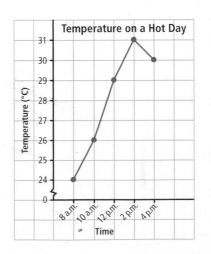

Temperature on a Hot Day

5. The election results for student council president were displayed in a bar graph.

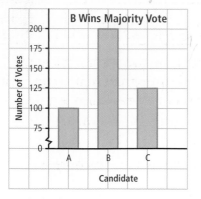

a) How many times taller does the bar for B appear than the bar for A?

b) How many times as great are the votes for B than the votes for A?

c) What conclusion does the graph suggest about the election results?

d) How could the graph be redrawn to make the data clearer?

Literacy ⊜ Link

Majority means more than 50%.

For help with #6 and #7, refer to Example 2 on pages 20–21.

6. a) From the pictograph, which fruit seems to sell the best? Explain.

b) Does it seem that more cherries were sold or more peaches? Explain.

c) How should the pictograph be redrawn to represent the data more accurately?

7. The graph in this advertisement shows the results of a taste test.

Move over Bonzo, The Big Cheese is in town!

| The Big Cheese | Bonzo Burger |
| 56% | 44% |

a) Which burger seems to be the favourite? Explain.

b) How is the graph misleading?

c) How should the graph be redrawn to represent the data more accurately?

For help with #8 and #9, refer to Example 3 on pages 21–22.

8. The graph shows the progress of friends who are playing a video game.

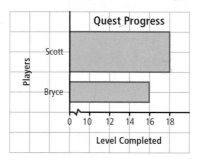

a) Explain how this graph could be misleading.

b) What conclusion does the graph suggest about Scott's progress compared with Bryce's progress?

c) Describe how to redraw the graph to represent the data more accurately.

9. The two graphs show the number of health bars sold by two students.

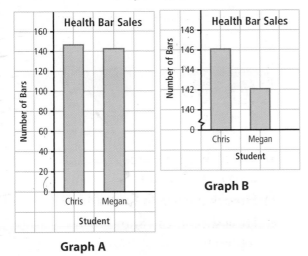

Graph A

Graph B

a) How are the two graphs different?

b) For each graph, what conclusion would you make about health bar sales?

c) Which graph gives a more accurate comparison of sales? Explain.

Apply

10. a) Explain how this graph is misleading.

b) From the graph, what conclusion can you make about the profits from January to June?

c) Draw a new graph using a vertical scale from 0 to 600. What conclusion can you now make about the profits from January to June?

11. Charles kept a record of his Math quiz scores for this term.

Quiz	1	2	3	4	5	6	7	8
Score (%)	65	66	69	70	75	72	77	80

a) He wants to make a distorted graph that will show a great improvement in his quiz scores. Draw such a graph.

b) Draw a new graph that displays the data more accurately.

c) How are the two graphs different?

12. a) Explain how this graph is misleading.

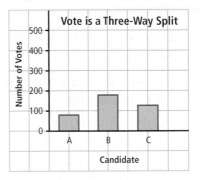

b) Based on the graph, what can you conclude about the outcome of the voting?

c) Does the data support the claim made in the title? If not, reword it to correct the misinformation.

13. a) The two circle graphs are meant to represent the same information. Does it appear that way? Explain.

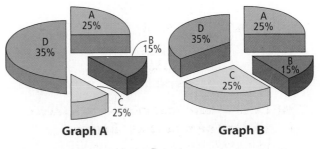

Graph A   **Graph B**

b) Identify the errors in Graph A.

14. Two grade 8 classes collected cans for the food drive. Ms. Chan's class brought in 100 cans. Mr. Rajwani's class brought in 200 cans. Luke made this graph to display the results.

Ms. Chan's class

Mr. Rajwani's class

a) How is this graph misleading?

b) Based on the graph, what can you conclude about the canned food drive?

c) Draw a different graph that is not misleading.

15. The grade 8 students voted on where to hold their year-end party. The results of the vote were presented in this graph.

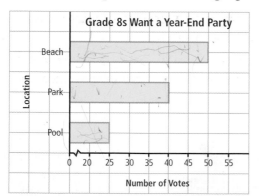

Grade 8s Want a Year-End Party

a) Based on the graph, how many times more popular was the beach than the pool?

b) Leah concluded that the majority of the students want to go to the beach. Is she correct? Explain.

c) Draw a new graph to represent the data more accurately.

16. An ice cream store developed the following graph to advertise its ice cream.

Cool Flavours

Dairy Tasty

$4.5 million $4.3 million

a) What ice cream store do you believe developed this graph? Explain.

b) How is the graph misleading?

17. A small town recorded crime statistics over the last six years.

Year	1	2	3	4	5	6
Number of Crimes	3	6	6	2	3	4

a) Make a bar graph to display the data.

b) Total the number of crimes for every two years. Make a new bar graph to display these data.

c) What can you conclude from the second bar graph? Do the data in the table support your statement? Explain.

d) How is the second graph misleading?

18. Grade 8 students were surveyed about their weekly use of a computer.

Time	Daily	2 to 6 days	Less than 2 days
Frequency	12	20	8

Draw a diagram to support an argument that Grade 8 students are not using the computer too often.

19. a) Which category on the graph does the government want the public to notice the most?

Provincial Budget 2008–2009

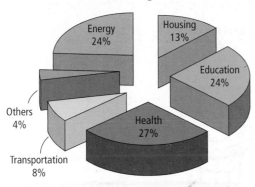

Energy 24%
Housing 13%
Education 24%
Others 4%
Health 27%
Transportation 8%

b) Explain how this graph could mislead people.

c) Draw a new graph to represent the data more accurately.

Extend

20. Prepare a survey question that requires making a choice from a list of several options.

a) Survey the students in your class. Record the data in a chart.

b) Make a graph that distorts the data.

c) Explain how your graph is misleading.

21. Paul's Pizza is a franchise that is starting a campaign to recapture pizza sales. The following graphs will be used to advertise their food products.

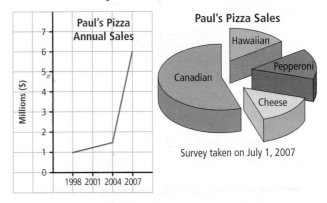

Paul's Pizza Annual Sales
Millions ($)
1998 2001 2004 2007

Paul's Pizza Sales
Hawaiian
Pepperoni
Canadian
Cheese
Survey taken on July 1, 2007

a) How might these graphs mislead people? List as many misleading features as you can.

b) Suggest ways to improve the graphs so that they are not misleading.

22. Search various media, such as magazines, newspapers, and the Internet, for an example of a graph that misleads people about a scientific topic. Print or cut out the graph. Glue or tape it into your notebook.

a) Draw a new graph to represent the data accurately.

b) Does your graph support the statement made in the original graph? Explain.

MATH LINK

Search the Internet, magazines, or newspapers for data about music sales for different artists. Choose an argument to make about the music sales.

a) Draw a graph that supports your argument about which artists are selling more than others.

b) How would you change your graph to support the opposite of your argument?

WWW Web Link

For information about music sales, go to www.mathlinks8.ca and follow the links.

Critiquing Data Presentation

Focus on...

After this lesson, you will be able to...

❏ explain how a graph is used to represent the data from a given situation

DNA Testing Helps Commercial Fishers

Thanks to DNA testing, B.C.'s commercial fishers can expect to catch as much as 90% of their quota of chinook salmon this year.

Since 2002, scientists have been using DNA testing to determine accurately where fish are originally from. As a result, fishery officials can better manage the fish stocks by setting specific harvest targets to protect the weaker stocks and allow more fishing of the stronger ones.

Between 1995 and 2001, fisheries used coded-wire tags inserted into salmon to estimate the populations of different runs of salmon. They used this information to limit the catch and the areas open to fishing for the following year. Using this method, only about 15% of the available quota was harvested in 2001.

Did You Know?

A *run* refers to a group of salmon that were hatched in the same place. During the salmon run, the fish swim back up rivers to their birthplace to spawn.

Literacy ⊖ Link

A *stacked bar graph* has bars stacked instead of side-by-side.

Tyler is presenting his current events report to his grade 8 Social Studies class. His report includes a newspaper article about chinook salmon and the bar graph shown. Does the bar graph support the story?

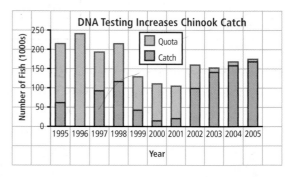

Explore the Math

Does the graph represent what it says it does?

1. Examine the graph about the chinook salmon catch. Why do you think the author used a stacked bar graph? Is it effective?

2. Decide if the graph is misleading.
   a) Examine the scales on the vertical and horizontal axes. What do you notice?
   b) How could you make the graph easier to understand?

3. The genetic testing of salmon began in 2002. The graph shows the quotas and catches since 1995. Use the graph and the information in the article to help answer the following questions.

a) What support is there for the idea that relying on coded-wire tags limited the catch of salmon?

b) What support is there for the idea that DNA testing has increased the chinook catch?

Reflect on Your Findings

4. What factors should you consider when you critique a graph for whether it represents a situation accurately?

Example: Critiquing a Graph

Bindi recorded the scores for two grade 8 classes that wrote the same test.

Class A (32 students)

Score (%)	Frequency
50–59	3
60–69	5
70–79	13
80–89	7
90–99	4

Class B (27 students)

Score (%)	Frequency
50–59	2
60–69	3
70–79	8
80–89	13
90–99	1

She decided to display the data on two circle graphs.

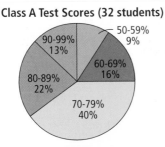
Class A Test Scores (32 students)

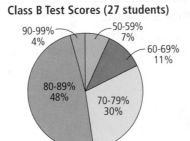
Class B Test Scores (27 students)

a) Why do you think Bindi used two circle graphs to display the data?

b) Are the graphs misleading? Explain.

c) State two conclusions that you can make based on the graphs.

d) Draw a double bar graph to display the data.

e) List the advantages and disadvantages of using a double bar graph to display the data.

Solution

a) There are more students in Class A than in Class B. By making circle graphs, Bindi can compare the percent of students who scored in each category. It would be less meaningful to compare the number of students who scored in each category.

b) The circle graphs are not misleading. Each sector of the graph is labelled with the category and percent, and the title includes the number of students in each class.

c) Two possible conclusions are:
- The majority of the students in both classes scored between 70% and 89%. A greater number of students in Class B scored between 70% and 89% than students in Class A.
- A total of 35% (11 students) in Class A scored over 80%. A total of 52% (14 students) in Class B scored over 80%. Therefore, a greater percent of students in Class B scored over 80% than students in Class A.

d)

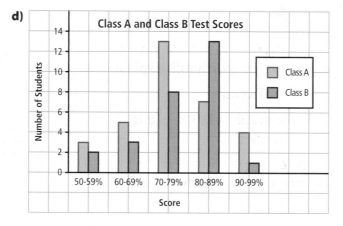

e) A double bar graph lets you compare the number of students who scored in each interval. It does not let you compare the percent of students who scored in each interval. Comparing the number of students in each interval is less meaningful in this case because the class sizes are not the same.

Show You Know

A group of teens picked pears during the pear harvest. The number of teens that picked each number of baskets is shown in the table.

The circle graph shows the percent of teens that picked each number of baskets.

Number of Baskets	Tally	Frequency
Three	|||	3
Four	ЖЖ	5
Five	ЖЖ ||||	9
Six	ЖЖ	5
Seven	|||	3

Baskets of Pears Picked (25 teens)

a) What is an advantage of displaying the data on a circle graph?

b) Is the graph misleading? Explain.

c) State two conclusions that you can make based on the graph.

- When critiquing a graph, it is important to consider several factors:
  - Graph type: Is the graph the best choice for displaying the data?
  - Graph format: Is the graph designed in a way that represents the data accurately?
  - Graph usefulness: Is the graph informative? Does the graph support a claim or an argument?

Communicate the Ideas

1. a) Is the pictograph an effective way to display the data about how students get to school? Explain.

b) Is the graph misleading? Explain.

c) How informative is the graph? How could it be made even more informative?

d) Suggest another type of graph to display the data. Give an advantage and a disadvantage of using this graph.

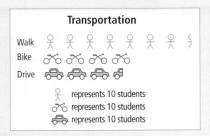

2. Danny made a graph to record his running times over a six-week period.

a) What can you conclude about Danny's performance from this graph?

b) How might this graph be misleading? How would you improve this graph?

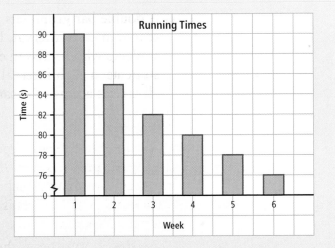

3. Your friend missed the lesson on critiquing graphs. Write her an explanation of how to critique graphs and why it is important to do so.

Practise

For help with #4 to #6, refer to the Example on pages 29–30.

4. Madison surveyed grade 8 students about which method they use most often to communicate with friends.

Means of Communication	Girls	Boys
Internet chat	13	11
In person	9	11
Telephone (land line)	7	5
Cell phone	1	3
Text messaging	2	2
E-mail	1	1
Total	33	33

She decided to make a double bar graph to display the data.

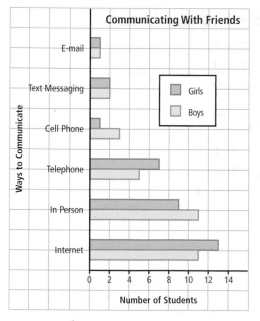

a) Why did Madison choose a double bar graph to display the data?

b) Is this graph misleading? Explain.

c) State two conclusions that you can make from this graph.

d) Why would you not represent the data in a double line graph?

5. a) Identify two conclusions you can make based on this double bar graph.

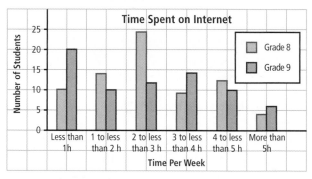

b) Is the graph misleading? Explain.

c) What improvements would you recommend for this graph?

d) What is one advantage of using a double bar graph to display the data?

e) Would another type of graph be more informative? Explain your reasoning.

6. a) What are two conclusions you can make based on this circle graph?

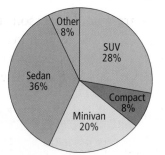

b) Is the graph misleading? Explain.

c) What is one advantage of using a circle graph to display the data?

d) Would another type of graph be more informative? Explain your reasoning.

7. The school web site posted a survey about the type of organization that grade 8 students would support if they had $1000 to donate. Each student was allowed to vote once. Colin made two graphs to display the data.

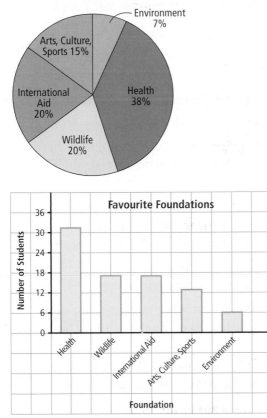

Favourite Foundations (85 votes)

Imagine that you are a spokesperson for a youth health foundation. Which graph would you use to encourage people to donate to your foundation? Explain why.

8. Truong recorded the sales of different colours of graphing calculators during the last month.

Colour	Number
Pink	45
Blue	56
Orange	25
Silver	35
Black	44
Total	205

He displayed the data in a bar graph.

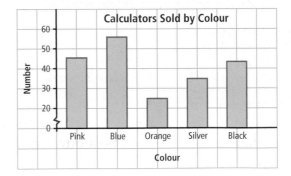

Calculators Sold by Colour

a) Why might Truong claim that blue calculators are about three times as popular as orange calculators? Is he correct? Explain.

b) Redraw the graph so it is more accurate. What conclusions can you make from the graph you drew?

c) Draw a circle graph to display the data.

d) Give an advantage of using a circle graph.

9. The director of a ski school tracked the snowboard rentals for one week.

Snowboard Type	Number
Freestyle	59
Freerider	138
Freecarve	49
Alpine	41
Total	287

a) Create a graph to display the data.

b) What conclusions can you make based on your graph?

c) Give an advantage of using the type of graph you made.

d) Exchange graphs with a classmate and critique each other's graph. What improvements can you make to your graph?

10. Chloe recorded the number of hours she spent on homework over the past six days.

She displayed the data in a circle graph.

Day	Hours
Monday	2
Tuesday	1
Wednesday	2.5
Thursday	1.5
Friday	0.5
Saturday	6
Total	13.5

Time Spent on Homework (13.5 h)

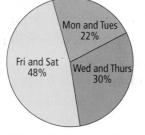

a) Chloe feels that the time she spends on homework has been increasing over the last six days. Why might she think so? Is she correct? Explain your reasoning.

b) Is Chloe's graph misleading? If yes, redraw the graph so it is more accurate.

c) What conclusions can you make based on the new graph?

d) Display the data in a bar graph.

e) What conclusions can you make based on the bar graph?

f) Is a bar graph a better way to display the data than a circle graph? Explain.

Extend

11. The two graphs show the same data about Manitoba's minimum wage.

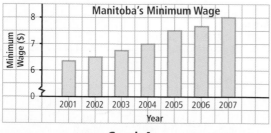

Graph A

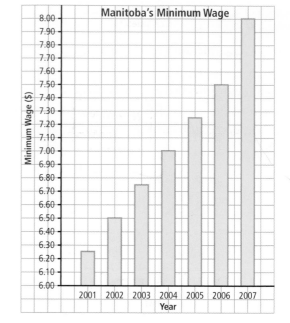

Graph B

a) Describe how each of the graphs is misleading.

b) Which graph would support a claim that wages have not increased much over time? Write a statement to support such a claim using the data.

c) Who would use Graph B to support a claim to the government about changing the minimum wage—an employer or an employee? Explain.

12. The graphs show the following sales for the first six months of the year for two car dealerships.

Month	Connor's Cars	Amy's Autos
January	12	1
February	15	8
March	20	11
April	3	10
May	5	13
June	2	14

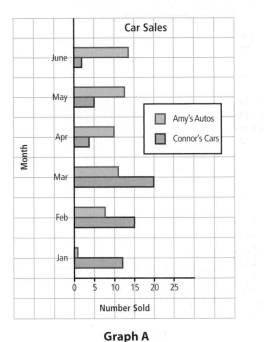

Graph A

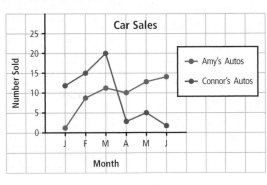

Graph B

a) Which graph did the manager of Connor's Cars likely develop? Explain.

b) What conclusions can you make based on the line graph?

MATH LINK

The organizers of a music concert are deciding between two performers as their headline attraction for a concert in December. The organizers want to use recording sales data to help make their decision. Consider the following graphs.

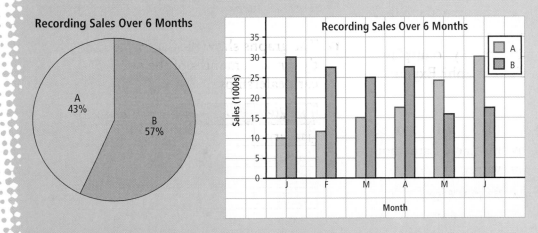

a) What information does each graph provide? Explain.

b) The organizers know they must attract a large crowd to cover expenses. Which performer would you select? Justify your answer.

① Chapter Review

Key Words

For #1 to #5, choose the letter that best matches each description.

1. best for comparing categories using percents

2. compares one set of data using horizontal or vertical bars

3. uses symbols to represent large quantities of data

4. shows changes in data over time

5. compares two sets of data across categories

A bar graph
B double bar graph
C line graph
D interval
E circle graph
F pictograph

1.1 Advantages and Disadvantages of Different Graphs, pages 6–17

6. The number of books in a classroom library is shown on these graphs.

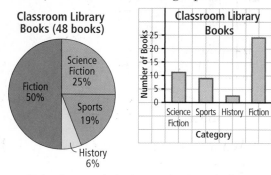

a) Which graph helps you decide how many more sports books than history books there are? Explain. Could the other graph help you answer the question? Explain.

b) Which graph would most help you decide how to spend $1000 on new books based on what the class has? How much money should be spent on each category? Show your work.

7. Michelle recorded data about how she spends time on a typical Saturday.

Activity	Time (h)
Chores	1.5
Eating	2
Homework	2.5
Sleep	9
Friends	3
Sports	4
TV	2
Total	24

a) List as many different ways to display the data appropriately as you can.

b) Choose and draw one type of graph to show the data.

c) State an advantage of the graph that you chose. State a disadvantage of one type of graph that you did not choose.

8. Describe a situation in which you would use each of the following to display data:

a) bar graph
b) double bar graph
c) circle graph
d) line graph

1.2 Misrepresenting Data, pages 18–27

9. The graph shows the number of electronic devices that grade 8 students own.

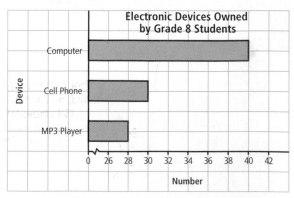

a) The graph shows that there are more computers than MP3 players and cell phones added together. Is this true? Describe how the graph is misleading.

b) Draw an accurate graph.

c) What conclusions can you make from your new graph?

10. The results of a pizza taste test showed that Mega Pizza was the favourite.

Mega Pizza
60%

a) How is this graph misleading?

b) Draw a new graph to represent the data more accurately.

Mr. Pizza
40%

11. Greg's company makes 2500 school lockers each day. Some lockers are rejected if they do not meet standards. The table shows the number of rejected lockers.

Day	Number Rejected
Monday	45
Tuesday	40
Wednesday	25
Thursday	30
Friday	35
Total	175

a) Greg wants to exaggerate the number of lockers rejected on Monday. Draw a graph to create this impression.

b) Make a new graph to represent the data accurately.

c) Explain how the two graphs are different.

1.3 Critiquing Data Presentation, pages 28–35

12. The graph represents data about which hand grade 8 students use to write.

a) What conclusions can you make from this graph?

b) Is the circle graph an appropriate way to present the data? Explain.

Right-Handed, Left-Handed, or Ambidextrous? (58 students)

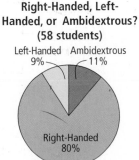

Left-Handed 9%
Ambidextrous 11%
Right-Handed 80%

c) What other way might you display the data? List an advantage of the graph you chose.

Literacy ⊜ Link

Someone who is *ambidextrous* is able to use both hands equally well.

13. Two television comedy shows are competing for sponsorship from an advertiser. The ratings for four seasons are shown in the table. The ratings are a percent of the total viewing audience.

Show	% Ratings			
	Season 1	Season 2	Season 3	Season 4
Laughing Out Loud	21	16	18	17
Open Mike Comics	12	13	14	15

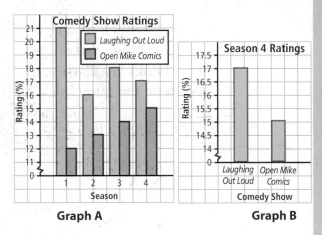

Graph A   Graph B

a) What rating information does each graph provide?

b) Suggest a catchy new title for each graph. Explain why you recommend each title.

c) Which graph do you think was created by the producer of *Open Mike Comics*? Explain.

d) Which graph do you think was created by the producer of *Laughing Out Loud*? Explain.

For #1 to #3, select the best answer.

1. Which type of graph is best used for comparing each category of data with the whole?

   A bar graph   **B** circle graph

   C line graph   **D** pictograph

2. Which type of graph is best used to compare the number of boys and girls born in each month of the year?

   A double bar graph

   B double line graph

   C two circle graphs

   D two pictographs

3. Energy bars cost 25¢ in 1985, 50¢ in 1995, and 75¢ in 2005. How is this graph misleading?

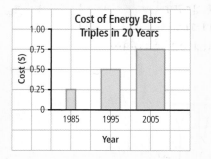

   A The intervals on the vertical scale are not equal.

   B The 2005 bar is three times taller than the 1985 bar.

   C The width of the bars varies.

   D The scale starts at 0.

Complete the statements in #4 and #5.

4. Symbols are used to represent data on a ▬▬▬ .

5. Zach wants to draw a graph to show changes over time. He should use a ▬▬▬ graph.

Short Answer

6. The graphs display population data of selected provinces.

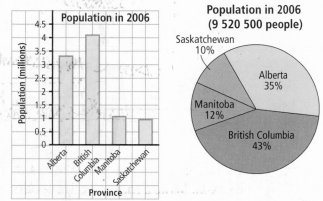

   a) Do both graphs provide the same information? Explain.

   b) Which graph best shows that Alberta's population is almost three times as great as the population of Manitoba? Explain.

7. Brenden recorded the results of a survey of grade 8s to determine their favourite choice of activity for the year-end field trip. His results are shown.

Activity	Votes
Bowling	17
Beach picnic	32
Inline skating	15
Movie	10
Total	74

   a) Display the data using a bar graph.

   b) Display the data using a circle graph.

   c) Which graph best displays the data? Explain.

8. One hundred grade 8 students were surveyed about their favourite ways to spend spare time.

Favourite Ways to Spend Time

Activity (y-axis): Other, Reading, Internet, Video or Computer Games, Sports, Television
Number of Students (x-axis): 0, 5, 10, 15, 20, 25, 30

a) State two conclusions you can make based on the graph. Write a more descriptive title.

b) Is the graph misleading? Explain.

c) Display the data using another graph of your choice.

d) Give an advantage or a disadvantage of representing the data on the new graph.

Extended Response

9. Use the data about ticket sales for a basketball game to create a bar graph. Use the same data to create another graph that is misleading. Explain how it is misleading.

Game	Ticket Sales
1	125
2	150
3	250
4	350
5	300

10. The following graph is partially completed.

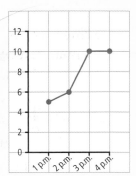

(y-axis: 0, 2, 4, 6, 8, 10, 12; x-axis: 1 p.m., 2 p.m., 3 p.m., 4 p.m.)

a) Describe a scenario to represent the data on this graph. Then, complete the graph.

b) Draw another graph to show the data.

c) Does each graph provide the same information? Explain.

d) Which graph best represents the information from the scenario that you created? Explain.

WRAP IT UP!

Suppose you are a reporter for the school's newspaper. Search the Internet, magazines, or newspapers for data about a topic related to the music industry. For example, you might want to use data about sales, favourite artists, attendance at tours, or popularity of different types of music.

a) Make a table that displays your data.

b) Decide on two different ways to represent the data by drawing one graph that represents the data accurately and another graph that misrepresents the data.

c) You have been asked to write articles that relate to each of your graphs. What will the headlines of your articles be? Explain your thinking.

Math Games

The Plot Thickens

Materials
• 2 dice per pair of students

1. Play The Plot Thickens with a partner. These are the rules:
   • Each player rolls one die to decide who will play first. If there is a tie, roll again.
   • For each turn, roll the two dice and add the values.
   • Record your total from each turn.

   > In my first four turns, I rolled totals of 7, 5, 11, and 7.
   >
   > ```
   >                     x
   >         x   x           x
   >   |---|---|---|---|---|---|---|---|---|---|---|
   >   2   3   4   5   6   7   8   9  10  11  12
   > ```

   > The total that I rolled five times was 6, so I scored six points for the round.

   • The first player to roll the same total five times wins the round.
   • The winner of the round scores the total that he/she rolled five times.
   • The player who loses a round plays first in the next round.
   • The first player to reach 20 points wins the game.

2. a) Suggest other ways of recording and displaying the data from The Plot Thickens.

   b) Play the game again. Record and display the data in a way you suggested.

3. Play modified versions of the game by using different numbers of dice or by determining products instead of sums.

Keep Your Community Green

Communities across Canada are concerned about the volume of waste they produce. As a result, many cities and towns have recycling programs. How well does your community do?

You be the researcher. Research data related to recycling in your community. Then, choose another Canadian community. Obtain recycling data from it too.

1. Compare the two sets of data and then represent the data in the following two different ways.

   a) Make one graph that misrepresents the data. For example, it could make it appear that your community is better at recycling when the other community is actually better.

   b) Make a second graph that accurately represents the data.

2. Write a brief news article for your community paper using the graphs that showcase your community.

2

Ratios, Rates, and Proportional Reasoning

Gail Greenough was born in Edmonton, Alberta, and was the first woman, the first Canadian, and the first North American to win the World Championship in Show Jumping in 1986. In show jumping, horse and rider jump a set course of obstacles. Ms. Greenough and her horse, Mr. T., worked together as one unit in a no-fault performance.

It takes excellent nutrition and training to win competitions. For example, a horse's rations contain nutrients that provide energy, protein, and vitamins and minerals in specific ratios that help maintain body weight and fitness. In training sessions, horse and rider work to improve on the speed at which they can complete a race course without errors. The skills with ratios, rates, and proportional reasoning that equestrians use play an important role in becoming a champion.

In this chapter, you will learn skills with ratios, rates, and proportional reasoning that will help you solve problems in a variety of different contexts.

What You Will Learn

- ☐ to express ratios using different notations
- ☐ to use ratios and rates in real-life examples
- ☐ to solve problems involving rates, ratios, and proportional reasoning

Key Words

- two-term ratio
- three-term ratio
- part-to-part ratio
- part-to-whole ratio
- rate
- unit rate
- unit price
- proportion

Literacy Link

A Frayer model can help you understand new terms. Copy the following Frayer model in your math journal or notebook. Make it large enough to write in each box. Record the following information for each new term.

- Write the term in the middle.
- Define the term in the first box. The glossary on pages 517–521 may help you.
- Write some facts in the second box.
- Give some examples in the third box
- Give some non-examples in the fourth box.

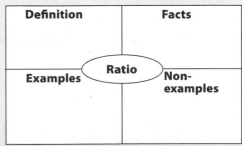

Definition	Facts
Examples	Non-examples

Ratio

Making the Foldable

Materials

- 11 × 17 sheet of paper
- ruler

Step 1

Fold an 11 × 17 sheet of paper into quarters lengthwise, and then into quarters widthwise.

Step 2

Divide each box in the What I Need to Work On and Wrap It Up! Ideas column in half horizontally. Label one side of your Foldable as shown.

	Key Words	Examples	What I Need to Work On / Wrap It Up! Ideas
2.1 Two-Term and Three-Term Ratios			
2.2 Rates			
2.3 Proportional Reasoning			

Step 3

Label the other side of your Foldable as shown.

	NOTES
2.1 Two-Term and Three-Term Ratios	
2.2 Rates	
2.3 Proportional Reasoning	

Using the Foldable

As you work through each section of Chapter 2, take notes on the appropriate side of your Foldable. Include information about the Key Words, examples, and Key Ideas.

Keep track of what you need to work on. Check off each item as you deal with it.

As you think of ideas for the Wrap It Up!, record them in the bottom box in each section of the What I Need to Work On and Wrap It Up! Ideas column.

MATH LINK

Multicultural Festival

Several Canadian cities celebrate a multicultural festival each year.

Winnipeg's Folklorama® is a multicultural festival extending over 14 days that involves more than 40 pavilions, each dedicated to a different cultural group or country. Visitors to each pavilion experience entertainment and food unique to that culture.

Imagine you are able to volunteer at a multicultural festival like Folklorama®.

1. Which pavilion would you select? Why did you select this pavilion?

2. There were 510 000 visitors to the 43 pavilions in a recent multicultural festival. Estimate the number of visitors you would expect to your pavilion. What assumptions did you make?

3. The ingredients for a dish at your pavilion cost $12.00. If the dish serves 30, what is the cost per person? What is the cost to serve your estimated number of visitors? Explain how you arrived at your answer.

4. Name two ethnic dishes that might be served at your pavilion. Estimate the cost of making one of these ethnic dishes for 10 visitors. How did you make your estimate?

5. Not everyone who visits a pavilion eats there. Estimate the number of visitors who eat at your pavilion. Then, estimate the ratio of visitors who eat to the total number of visitors to your pavilion. Express this ratio in three other ways.

In this chapter, you will use ratio, rate, and proportional reasoning to plan an international meal for you and nine of your friends. Your meal will include several different dishes from a culture of your choice. Which culture will you choose?

WWW Web Link

For more information about Folklorama®, go to www.mathlinks8.ca and follow the links.

Two-Term and Three-Term Ratios

After this lesson, you will be able to...

❏ represent two-term and three-term ratios
❏ identify, describe, and record ratios from real-life examples
❏ represent a ratio as a fraction or as a percent
❏ solve problems using ratios

You use ratios to enlarge or reduce graphics and pictures. Discuss with a partner how you could use ratios to describe these two images.

Explore the Math

Materials
• ruler

How can you compare an enlargement to its original image?

Jason made the following enlargement of a prairie dog. Kate asked how he enlarged it. Jason could not remember. Use ratios to help him answer Kate's question.

1. a) How might you compare the original photo to its enlargement? Share your method with a classmate.

   b) What might you compare on the two photos to give you a ratio?

   c) How many measurements would you need to make?

   d) Why would it be important to measure exactly the same parts of each photo?

2. Suggest a multiplier that Jason would have used to enlarge the photo of the prairie dog. How did you arrive at your answer? Compare your answer with those of your classmates.

Reflect on Your Findings

3. a) If the ratio comparing the image to the original is greater than one, what does this tell you?

   b) If the ratio comparing the image to the original is less than one, what does this tell you?

Example 1: Represent Ratios

A bag contains 20 marbles.

a) What is the **two-term ratio** of black to red marbles?

b) Compare the number of red marbles to the total number of marbles. Write the ratio as an equivalent fraction in lowest terms. $\frac{4}{20} = \frac{1}{5}$

c) What marbles are represented by the ratio $6:10$?

d) Write the **three-term ratio** comparing the red, purple, and black marbles. $4 : 6 : 10$

---

two-term ratio

- compares two quantities measured in the same units
- written as $a:b$ or a to b

blue : red is 6 : 4

---

three-term ratio

- compares three quantities measured in the same units
- written as $a:b:c$ or a to b to c

blue : red : brown is 6 : 4 : 2

Solution

a) *Method 1: Represent a Ratio Using a Drawing*

There are 10 black and 4 red marbles. The drawing shows the ratio.

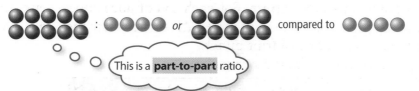

This is a **part-to-part** ratio.

Method 2: Represent a Ratio Using Symbols or Words

The ratio of black marbles to red marbles is 10:4 or 10 to 4.

b) There are 4 red marbles out of a total of 20 marbles.
The ratio can be expressed as 4:20.
A **part-to-whole ratio** can be expressed as a fraction.

$\dfrac{\text{red}}{\text{total}}$ is $\dfrac{4}{20}$

Write the fraction as an equivalent fraction in lowest terms.

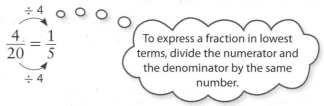

To express a fraction in lowest terms, divide the numerator and the denominator by the same number.

c) There are 6 purple marbles and 10 black marbles.
purple:black is 6:10

d) You can compare red, purple, and black marbles using a three-term ratio.

red:purple:black $= 4:6:10$
$= 2:3:5$

You can multiply or divide each term of a three-term ratio by the same number.

Strategies
Draw a Diagram

part-to-part ratio

- compares different parts of a group to each other
- 10:8 is the part-to-part ratio of brown to red beads.

part-to-whole ratio

- compares one part of a group to the whole group
- 5:23 is the part-to-whole ratio of blue to total number of beads.

Show You Know

Use the design to help answer the following questions.

a) What is the ratio of red tiles to total titles? Express the answer three different ways.
b) What could the ratio 4:6 represent?
c) What is the ratio of red to black to white tiles?

Example 2: Apply Ratios

Tamara has a recipe for fruit punch that calls for three cans of frozen orange juice concentrate, two cans of raspberry juice concentrate, and one can of lime juice concentrate. For each can of juice concentrate, the directions say to add three cans of water. All the cans are the same size. Tamara makes one recipe of fruit punch.

a) Copy and complete the following chart.

	Orange	Raspberry	Lime	Total
Juice Concentrate (cans)	3	2	1	6
Water (cans)	4	6	2	18
Total Punch (cans)				24

b) What is the ratio of orange juice to lime juice concentrate? Express the ratio two different ways.

c) What is the ratio of lime to orange to raspberry juice concentrate?

d) What is the ratio of water to juice concentrate?

e) How many cans of punch does the recipe make?

f) What is the ratio of orange, raspberry, and lime juice concentrate to total punch? Express the ratio as a fraction, a decimal, and a percent.

Solution

a)

	Orange	Raspberry	Lime	Total
Juice Concentrate (cans)	3	2	1	6
Water (cans)	$3 \times 3 = 9$	$2 \times 3 = 6$	$1 \times 3 = 3$	18
Total Punch (cans)				24

lime juice   water   water   water

Add three cans of water for one can of lime juice concentrate.

b) three cans of orange juice and one can of lime juice concentrate
The ratio of orange to lime juice concentrate is 3 : 1 or 3 to 1.

This is a part-to-part ratio.

c) one can of lime juice, three cans of orange juice, and two cans of raspberry juice concentrate
The ratio of lime to orange to raspberry juice concentrate is 1 : 3 : 2.

d) 18 cans of water, 6 cans of juice concentrate
The ratio of water to juice concentrate is 18 : 6 or 3 : 1.

$$\frac{18}{6} = \frac{3}{1}$$
$\div 6$ ... $\div 6$

e) 18 cans of water + 6 cans of juice concentrate = 24 cans of punch
One recipe makes 24 cans of punch.

f) 6 cans of juice concentrate, 24 cans of punch

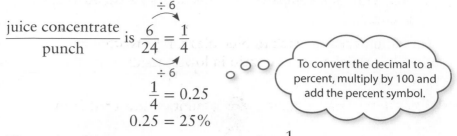

$$\frac{\text{juice concentrate}}{\text{punch}} \text{ is } \frac{6}{24} = \frac{1}{4}$$

$$\frac{1}{4} = 0.25$$

$$0.25 = 25\%$$

To convert the decimal to a percent, multiply by 100 and add the percent symbol.

The ratio of juice concentrate to punch is $\frac{1}{4}$, 0.25, or 25%.

Show You Know

A recipe for trail mix calls for three cups of mini pretzels, two cups of roasted soy chips, one cup of raisins, and one cup of sunflower seeds. You make two batches of trail mix.

a) What is the ratio of mini pretzels to raisins? Express the ratio two different ways.

b) What is the ratio of roasted soy chips to sunflower seeds?

c) How many cups of mix do two batches make?

d) What is the ratio of soy chips and sunflower seeds to total trail mix? Express the ratio as a fraction, a decimal, and a percent.

Key Ideas

- A part-to-part ratio compares different parts of a group.

  The ratio of red to black tiles is 6 : 3 or 6 to 3. The ratio in lowest terms is 2 : 1 or 2 to 1.

  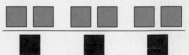

- A part-to-whole ratio compares one part of a group to the whole group.

  The ratio of red to total tiles is 6 : 12 or 6 to 12. The ratio in lowest terms is 1 : 2 or 1 to 2. One out of every two tiles is red.

  - A part-to-whole ratio can be written as a fraction, a decimal, and a percent.

    The ratio of $\frac{\text{red}}{\text{total}}$ is $\frac{6}{12}$ or $\frac{1}{2}$, 0.5, 50%.

- A three-term ratio compares three quantities measured in the same units.

  The ratio of red to black to blue tiles can be written as 6:3:3 or 6 to 3 to 3. The ratio in lowest terms is 2:1:1 or 2 to 1 to 1.

- A two-term ratio compares two quantities measured in the same units.

  The ratio of black to total tiles can be written as 3:12 or 3 to 12. The ratio in lowest terms is 1:4 or 1 to 4. One out of every four tiles is black.

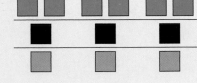

Communicate the Ideas

1. Janine wants to write the ratio of oranges to apples. How does she know whether to write 3:4 or 4:3?

2. Your friend missed the class when ratios were introduced. Use an example and draw a diagram to explain the difference between a part-to-part ratio and a part-to-whole ratio.

3. Give two examples of how ratios are used in daily life. Share your ideas with a classmate.

4. The fraction $\frac{2}{5}$ can be interpreted as two parts out of a total of five parts. Use a diagram to show an example of this part-to-whole ratio.

Check Your Understanding

Practise

For help with #5 to #8, refer to Example 1 on pages 47–48.

5. Write each ratio using ratio notation. Do not write the answers in lowest terms.
   a) $2 compared to $8.
   b) The width of the cover of this book compared to its length, in centimetres.
   c) In a class, 14 of 30 students are girls. What is the ratio of boys to girls to total students?
   d) Your age compared to that of a 28-year-old person.

6. Write each ratio in #5 as an equivalent ratio in lowest terms.

7. Write each ratio in fraction form. Do not write the answers in lowest terms.
   a) You spend $4 out of $10.
   b) A team won three games and lost six games. What is the ratio of games won to games played?
   c) A bag contains 12 red and 3 blue beads. Compare blue beads to total beads.
   d) A pond contains 27 guppies and 33 goldfish. What is the ratio of guppies to total fish?

8. Identify the missing number to make an equivalent fraction.

a) $\frac{1}{2} = \frac{\blacksquare}{8}$

b) $\frac{4}{5} = \frac{12}{\blacksquare}$

c) $\frac{2}{7} = \frac{\blacksquare}{21}$

d) $\frac{\blacksquare}{4} = \frac{3}{12}$

e) $\frac{21}{49} = \frac{3}{\blacksquare}$

f) $\frac{4}{\blacksquare} = \frac{12}{15}$

For help with #9 to #11, refer to Example 2 on pages 49–50.

9. Use the data about wins and losses on school teams to answer the questions.

Sport	Wins	Losses
Hockey	9	6
Volleyball	10	5
Baseball	12	8

a) Which sports have equivalent win–loss ratios? Show how you know.

b) What is the ratio of wins to total games played for hockey? Give your answer as a fraction, a decimal, and a percent.

10. Tyler counted 20 cars in the school parking lot. Of these, 6 were red, 4 were green, and 1 was yellow.

a) Draw a diagram to represent the situation.

b) How many cars were not red, green, or yellow?

c) What is the ratio of yellow to green to red cars?

d) What is the ratio of red to total cars? Express the ratio as a fraction and a percent.

11. What tiles could be represented by each of the following ratios?

a) 1 to 5

b) $1 : 6 : 5$

c) $\frac{1}{2}$

d) $\frac{11}{12}$

12. In a class of 32 students, there are 24 girls.

a) What is the boys to total students ratio? Express the ratio as a fraction and a percent.

b) What is the girls to boys ratio? Use ratio notation to express the ratio.

13. A soccer team played 28 games and won 4 out of every 7 games. There were no tied games.

a) How many games did they lose?

b) What was the team's win–loss ratio? Explain how you got your answer.

c) If this trend continues, how many losses would you expect the team to have once they have won 20 games?

14. Three eighths of the 96 adults in the McGregor clan are less than 150 cm tall.

a) Draw a diagram to represent the statement.

b) How many adults in the McGregor clan are less than 150 cm tall? Show your work using equivalent ratios.

c) How many adults are 150 cm or taller? Explain your thinking.

15. Diana and John are making three-cheese lasagna. The recipe calls for 100 g of Romano, 300 g of mozzarella, and 250 g of cottage cheese.

a) Write a ratio in lowest terms to compare the amounts of the three cheeses. State the order of the cheeses.

b) What amounts of Romano and cottage cheese do you need to make lasagna that contains 900 g of mozzarella cheese? Hint: Use equivalent ratios to help you.

16. Heather used a copier to make the following 50% reduction.

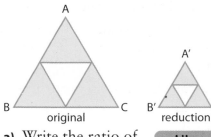

original

reduction

a) Write the ratio of the length of A′B′ compared to the length of AB.

b) Write the ratio of the length of A′C′ compared to the length of AC.

c) Use your knowledge of ratio and percent to explain the meaning of a 50% reduction.

> **Literacy Link**
> A′ is read as "A prime." A′ labels the point in the reduction that corresponds to point A.

17. There are 48 passengers on a transit bus. At the next stop, 16 passengers got off and 12 others got on the bus.

a) What is the ratio of the passengers who got off the bus compared to the original number on the bus? Show the ratio in lowest terms.

b) What is the ratio of the passengers who got on the bus at the stop compared to the new total then on the bus? Write your answer as a fraction, a decimal, and a percent.

18. The ratio of the width to the length of the Canadian flag is 1 : 2.

a) The flag on the cover of an atlas is 12 cm wide. How long is it?

b) A large flag outside a Calgary school is 3 m long. What is its width?

WWW Web Link

To practise solving ratio problems, go to www.mathlinks8.ca and follow the links.

19. The table gives the lengths of some rivers in Western Canada.

River	Length (km)
Churchill	1608
Fraser	1368
MacKenzie	1800
North Saskatchewan	1392
Thelon	904

a) Write a ratio in fractional form to compare the length of the Churchill River and the Mackenzie River. Express the ratio as a fraction in lowest terms.

b) Write a ratio in decimal form to compare the length of the North Saskatchewan River and the Fraser River. Express the ratio as a decimal correct to the nearest hundredth.

c) The calculator keying sequence that compares the length of the Thelon River and the Churchill River is

C 904 ÷ 1608 = 0.5621890547

Write the decimal to the nearest hundredth. What comparison statement can you make about the length of the two rivers?

20. A 30-kg bag of fertilizer is labelled 15–20–10. This means that it contains 15% nitrogen, 20% phosphorus, and 10% potassium by weight. How many kilograms of nitrogen, phosphorus, and potassium are in the bag?

> **Did You Know?**
>
> Fertilizer ratios indicate the percent of nitrogen, phosphorus, and potassium. This bag of fertilizer contains 15% nitrogen, 20% phosphorus, and 10% potassium by weight. The remaining 55% is made up of other micronutrients and filler.

21. A golden rectangle has a length to width ratio called the golden ratio, which is approximately 1.62.

a) Which of the following dimensions of rectangles are examples of golden rectangles?
- 24 m × 38.9 m
- 52 cm × 120.5 cm
- 348 mm × 565 mm

b) If the width of a golden rectangle is 6.4 m, what is its length? Give your answer to the nearest tenth of a metre.

Did You Know?

The golden rectangle is used often in art and architecture. For example, the front of the Parthenon, a temple in Athens, Greece fits into a golden rectangle.

22. The side view of a ramp is shown.

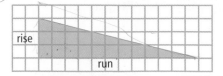

a) Express the ratio of rise to run in lowest terms. This ratio describes the slope of the ramp.

b) Express the slope ratio as a fraction, a decimal, and a percent.

c) Predict what effect each of the following would have on the slope of the ramp:
- increasing the rise
- decreasing the rise
- increasing the run
- decreasing the run

Did You Know?

The ratio $\frac{rise}{run}$ is called *slope*. Slope describes the steepness of roads, ramps, and ski runs.

WWW Web Link

For more information about the golden ratio in nature, architecture, art, poetry, and music, go to www.mathlinks8.ca and follow the links.

MATH LINK

Plan an invitation for your international meal. Create a logo as part of the front of the invitation. A logo is an identifying symbol used in advertising.

a) Design your logo using colours or measurements to show each of the following ratios

4:3   2:3:4

For example, if you use a rectangle in your logo, you could show that the length to width ratio is 4:3.

b) Draw the logo on a 36 cm² section of centimetre grid paper.

c) Identify the ratios used in your logo.

Rates

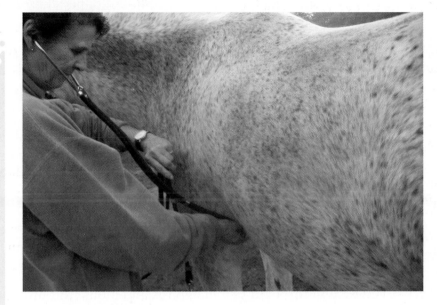

Trainers use technology to accurately and reliably monitor the heart rate of an equine competitor. Measuring the heart rate helps evaluate a horse's physical condition. The heart rate can be read at rest, during exercise, or during recovery after an event.

Heart rate is measured by counting the number of beats per minute. Note that a **rate** has two units. The units for heart rate are beats and minutes. Other common rates include growth rates and fuel efficiency rates. For example, a plant may grow 6 cm per month, and the fuel efficiency for a specific vehicle may be 6.8 L per 100 km.

What are some other rates you know about? What units are commonly used to measure these rates?

rate

• compares two quantities measured in different units
• $1.69 per 100 g or $1.69/100 g is a rate for purchasing bulk food
• 72 beats per minute or 72 beats/min is a heart rate

Explore the Math

How can you determine a conversion rate?

Work with a partner. You will need a chain of standard paper clips and a chain of jumbo paper clips.

Materials

• standard paper clips
• jumbo paper clips

1. Use the paper clip chains to measure the lengths of six different objects in the classroom. Record your data.

unit rate

- a rate in which the second term is one
- for example, 20 km/h and 64 beats/min

2. What two units of measure are you using?

3. How can you use your data to determine a multiplier that describes the number of standard paper clips to one jumbo clip? This multiplier is called a conversion rate.

Reflect on Your Findings

4. **a)** A conversion rate is sometimes called a unit rate. Explain why.

   b) Would the conversion rate for the number of jumbo clips for one standard clip be greater or less than one? Explain your thinking.

   c) Is the conversion rate between one jumbo clip and one standard clip always the same? Why or why not?

Example 1: Determine Unit Rates

Ruby-throated hummingbirds and monarch butterflies travel similar paths across the Gulf of Mexico. The distance is just over 800 km. It takes the hummingbird 18.5 h and the monarch butterfly 41.6 h to cross the Gulf.

a) Estimate the speed of the hummingbird and the butterfly.

b) Calculate the speed of the hummingbird and the butterfly. Give each answer to the nearest hundredth.

Solution

Speed = $\frac{\text{distance}}{\text{time}}$

	Hummingbird	**Butterfly**
a) Estimate speed.	$\frac{800 \text{ km}}{20 \text{ h}} = 40$ km/h	$\frac{800 \text{ km}}{40 \text{ h}} = 20$ km/h
b) Calculate speed.	$\frac{800 \text{ km}}{18.5 \text{ h}}$ [C] 800 [÷] 18.5 [=] 43.243243 The speed is 43.24 km/h.	$\frac{800 \text{ km}}{41.6 \text{ h}}$ [C] 800 [÷] 41.6 [=] 19.230769 The speed is 19.23 km/h.

The speed of the hummingbird is 43.24 km/h and the speed of the monarch butterfly is 19.23 km/h, to the nearest hundredth. The estimates suggest that these answers are reasonable.

A rate can be expressed as a fraction that includes the two different units. A rate cannot be expressed as a percent because a percent is a ratio that compares quantities expressed in the same units.

Show You Know

Determine the unit rate in each situation.
- **a)** Brandon runs 150 m in 25 s.
- **b)** Kira earns $88 for working 8 h.
- **c)** Cat food costs $9 for five cans.

Example 2: Compare Prices Using Unit Rates

Brett went to the grocery store to buy his favourite brand of orange juice. He found the following container sizes and prices. Which container of orange juice is the best buy?

414 mL	946 mL	1.89 L
$1.69	$2.99	$5.49

Solution

Calculate the **unit price** of each container of orange juice and then compare.

414 mL for $1.69

Unit price = $\dfrac{\text{cost}}{\text{volume}}$

$\qquad = \dfrac{\$1.69}{414 \text{ mL}}$

$\qquad = \$0.00408/\text{mL}$

C **1.69** ÷ **414** = 0.0040821

The unit price is $0.00408/mL or 0.408¢/mL.

$1 = 100¢
To convert dollars to cents, multiply by 100.

946 mL for $2.99

Unit price = $\dfrac{\text{cost}}{\text{volume}}$

$\qquad = \dfrac{\$2.99}{946 \text{ mL}}$

$\qquad = \$0.00316/\text{mL}$

C **2.99** ÷ **946** = 0.0031607

The unit price is $0.00316/mL or 0.316¢/mL.

1.89 L for $5.49

To compare unit prices, the numbers must be in the same units.

1 L = 1000 mL
1.89 L = 1000 × 1.89
= 1890 mL

Unit price = $\dfrac{\text{cost}}{\text{volume}}$

$\qquad = \dfrac{\$5.49}{1890 \text{ mL}}$

$\qquad = \$0.00290/\text{mL}$

C **5.49** ÷ **1890** = 0.0029048

The unit price is $0.00290/mL or 0.290¢/mL.

The unit price for the 1.89-L container is less than the unit prices of the other two containers. The best buy is the 1.89-L container for $5.49.

Show You Know

At Ed's Grocery, one brand of salsa is sold in the following container sizes. Which container of salsa is the best buy? Show your work.

Salsa 425 mL — $3.44   Salsa 642 mL — $6.29   Salsa 1.7 L — $15.49

- A rate is a comparison of two quantities measured in different units.

  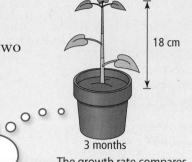

  18 cm

  - A rate can be expressed as a fraction that includes the two different units. A rate cannot be expressed as a percent because a percent is a ratio that compares quantities expressed in the same units.

  $$\text{Growth rate} = \frac{18 \text{ cm}}{3 \text{ months}}$$

  The plant grew 18 cm in 3 months.

  3 months

  The growth rate compares height (in centimetres) and time (in months).

- A unit rate is a rate in which the second term is one.

  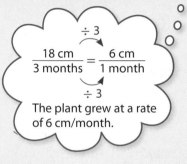

  $$\frac{18 \text{ cm}}{3 \text{ months}} = \frac{6 \text{ cm}}{1 \text{ month}}$$

  ÷ 3   ÷ 3

  The plant grew at a rate of 6 cm/month.

- A unit price is a unit rate that makes it easier to compare the cost of similar items.

  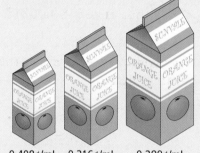

  0.408¢/mL   0.316¢/mL   0.290¢/mL

  0.290¢/mL < 0.316¢/mL < 0.408¢/mL
  The largest container is the best buy.

Communicate the Ideas

1. a) Give an example of a ratio using words and numbers from the table.

   b) What is a rate? Make up an example of a rate from the table.

   c) Convert the rate in part b) to a unit rate.

Bear	Birth Mass (kg)	Mass After 60 Days (kg)
Black	0.3	6.5
Polar	0.7	7.4

2. Two brands of canned dog food are on sale. Assume that the cans are the same size. Brand A costs $13.60 for eight cans and Brand B costs $8.75 for five cans. Explain how to find the unit price for Brands A and B. Explain how unit prices help you compare the cost of dog food.

3. a) Give two examples of rates that are common in every day life. Share your examples with a classmate.

b) What units measure each of the rates in part a)?

c) Explain why a rate cannot be expressed as a percent.

Check Your Understanding

Practise

For help with #4 to #6, refer to Example 1 on pages 56–57.

4. Determine the unit rate in each situation.

a) An orca swims 110 km in 2 h.

b) A Canada goose flies 800 km in 12.5 h.

c) Cathy plants 45 daffodils in 30 min.

5. What is the unit rate in each?

a) A blue whale eats 8 t of krill in 2 days.

b) The cruising speed of a blue whale allows it to travel 193 km in 10 h.

c) A bull moose bellows 15 times in $2\frac{1}{2}$ h.

6. Gina earns $78.00 for working 6 h. Asad makes $192.50 after working 14 h. Determine each person's unit rate of pay. Who has a greater hourly rate of pay?

For help with #7 to #9, refer to Example 2 on pages 57–58.

7. The table shows the price of different-sized packages of mixed nuts.

Nut Package	Mass	Price
1	300 g	$2.19
2	500 g	$3.09
3	700 g	$4.83

a) What is the unit price per 100 g for each package?

b) Which package is the best buy? Explain your choice.

8. Fraser is shopping for milk. It is available in three sizes.

$0.59 $1.09 $1.99

a) What is the unit price for each carton of milk?

b) What is the unit price per 100 mL for the l-L carton?

c) Which carton of milk is the best buy? Explain why.

9. Mala is shopping for honey. Her favourite brand is available in two sizes.

$2.79 $9.59

a) Estimate which is the better buy. Show your thinking.

b) Determine the better buy. Show your work.

Apply

10. Trevor rode his mountain bike 84 km in 3 h. Jillian rode 70 km in 2.5 h. Who is the faster cyclist? How do you know?

11. Shannon buys 12 granola bars for $9.96.

   a) Determine the price per bar. Give your answer in dollars and cents.

   b) Explain whether your answer in part a) is a ratio or a rate.

12. The rate at which glaciers melt is increasing globally. The Saskatchewan Glacier near Banff has receded 1.5 km in the last 75 years. The Peyto Glacier shown below receded 1320 m from 1923 to 1993. Which glacier had the greater annual rate of melting?

13. The table shows driving information for three drivers. Metric fuel consumption is measured in L/100 km, or litres per kilometre.

Driver	Distance (km)	Fuel Used (L)
Joe	400	28
Sarah	840	60
Martin	245	20

   a) What is the fuel consumption for Sarah's vehicle in litres per kilometre? Give your answer to four decimal places.

   b) How could you change the answer in part a) to express it in L/100 km?

   c) Which driver's vehicle had the lowest fuel consumption?

14. Conversion rates among currencies vary from day to day. The numbers in the table give the value in foreign currency of one Canadian dollar on one particular day.

Canadian	U.S.	Australian	European Union
1.00 dollar	0.8857 dollars	1.1527 dollars	0.6940 euros

   a) What was the value of $600 Canadian in euros?

   b) What was the value of $375 Canadian in U.S. dollars?

   c) What was the value of $450 Canadian in Australian dollars?

15. Cindy Klassen from Winnipeg, Manitoba, won five speed skating medals at the 2006 Olympics. As of March 2006, she held the world record in the 1000 m, the 1500 m, and the 3000 m distances. Her times are shown in the table.

Time (min : s)	Distance (m)
1 : 13.11	1000
1 : 51.79	1500
3 : 53.34	3000

   a) Express each time in seconds.

   b) What was Cindy's speed in metres per second for her 1500 m record?

   c) How far does she skate in 10 s for the 3000 m distance?

16. Twins, Daniel and Grace, take turns mowing the lawn. Last week Grace mowed the lawn in 45 min. This week Daniel mowed the lawn in 40 min.

a) What is the average mowing rate per hour for each twin? Give each answer to the nearest hundredth.

b) What is the difference between Daniel's and Grace's mowing rates?

17. The time it takes a planet to make one revolution of its axis is a day on that planet. Consider each planet to be a sphere. So, if you are standing on the equator of a planet, you are travelling in a circle as the planet spins on its axis. Use the table to find the rotation rate in kilometres per hour for each planet.

Planet	Radius at Equator (km)	Length of Day (h)
Venus	6 051	2 808
Earth	6 378	24
Saturn	60 268	10 233

The formula relating the circumference, C, of a circle to its radius is $C = 2 \times \pi \times r$.

18. Chad went to the bank to get some U.S. dollars for a trip to the Grand Canyon. He paid $500 Canadian and received $441.15 U.S.

a) What was the conversion rate for exchanging Canadian dollars to U.S. dollars? Give your answer to four decimal places. What does your answer represent?

b) How many U.S. dollars would Chad receive for $700 Canadian at the rate in part a)?

c) Two days later, Chad returned to the bank and converted the $441.15 U.S. back to Canadian dollars. He received only $492.25 Canadian. What was the bank's conversion rate on that day for exchanging U.S. dollars to Canadian dollars? Give your answer to four decimal places.

d) How many U.S. dollars would Chad receive for $700 Canadian at the rate in part c)?

19. Express 60 km/h in metres per second.

MATH LINK

Kheer is a traditional rice pudding made in India and Pakistan. Pakistani kheer tends to be thicker than the Indian version. Look at the recipe for kheer. If the original recipe serves four people, calculate the quantity of each ingredient you need to serve 10 people. Use ratios and rates to support your reasoning.

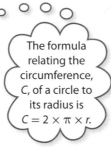

Kheer

Ingredients:
• 125 mL rice (basmati)   • 250 mL sugar
• 1 L milk   • 5 mL cardamom (or nutmeg)
• 50 mL raisins   • 50 mL almonds (slivered)

Method:
1. Wash rice well.
2. Boil milk and add rice. Simmer on low heat until rice is soft, stirring frequently to prevent sticking.
3. When the rice is cooked and the mixture gets a semi-thick creamy consistency, add sugar and stir well.
4. Remove from heat and add cardamom, slivered almonds, and raisins.
5. Serve warm or chilled.

2.3 Proportional Reasoning

Focus on...

After this lesson, you will be able to...

❏ solve problems using proportional reasoning

❏ use more than one method to solve proportional reasoning problems

When you go snowboarding or skiing, you use proportional reasoning to determine the correct length of ski or board for you to use. This involves using the ratio of your height to the length of the ski or board. To determine the correct width of the board so that your feet do not hang over, you use the ratio of the waist of the board, which is the narrowest part, to your boot size. Riders with small feet need narrower boards than riders with big feet.

When you draw a portrait in art class, you use proportional reasoning to figure out how large to make each facial feature in relation to the other features and how to align the features on the head.

Think about where you have made comparisons. Where might you have used proportional reasoning?

Explore the Math

How do you use proportional reasoning?

1. Copy the following table into your notebook. Put two rows under the column headings to record data for two typists.

Student	Number of Words	Time (min)
		4
		4

2. Work with a partner. Select a short story to type.

Materials

• computer access
• short story
• stopwatch
• sticky notes

Tech Link

You can use a word processing program to count the words for you.

3. Use a stopwatch and take turns to time each other's typing. The timer tells the typist when to begin and when to stop (after 4 min).

4. a) Type at a comfortable rate so you can avoid making many errors.

   b) After the time is up, mark your stopping place in the text using a sticky note.

   c) Count and record the total number of words typed in 4 min.

5. Trade roles and repeat step 4 to get data for your partner.

6. a) What is the four-minute typing rate for each typist?

   b) What is the unit rate for each typist?

Reflect on Your Findings

7. a) If each typist continued typing at the same rate, how many words could each person type in 1 h? Approximately how many pages is that?

   b) What other factors might affect how long it takes to type the entire story? Give an estimate of the time needed for each typist to type the story.

   c) How did you use a **proportion** to find your answer to part a)?

proportion

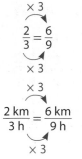

- a relationship that says that two ratios or two rates are equal
- can be written in fraction form:

$$\overset{\times 3}{\overgroup{\frac{2}{3}}} = \frac{6}{9}$$
$$\underset{\times 3}{\undergroup{\phantom{\frac{2}{3}}}}$$

$$\overset{\times 3}{\overgroup{\frac{2\ km}{3\ h}}} = \frac{6\ km}{9\ h}$$
$$\underset{\times 3}{\undergroup{\phantom{\frac{2\ km}{3\ h}}}}$$

Example 1: Solve a Rate Problem Using Proportional Reasoning

Electricity costs 11.58¢ for 2 kWh. How much does 30 kWh cost? Give your answer to the nearest cent.

Solution

Method 1: Use a Unit Rate

A cost of 11.58¢ for 2 kWh can be expressed as the rate $\frac{11.58¢}{2\ kWh}$.

Determine the unit rate.

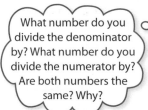

What number do you divide the denominator by? What number do you divide the numerator by? Are both numbers the same? Why?

$$\frac{11.58¢}{2\ kWh} = \frac{5.79¢}{1\ kWh}$$

Electricity costs 5.79¢ per kWh or 5.79¢/kWh.

30 kWh costs 30 × 5.79¢ = 173.7¢

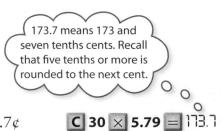

173.7 means 173 and seven tenths cents. Recall that five tenths or more is rounded to the next cent.

C 30 × 5.79 = 173.7

So, 30 kWh costs 174¢ or $1.74 rounded to the nearest cent.

Method 2: Use a Proportion

Make a proportion to show what you want to find.

$$\frac{11.58¢}{2 \text{ kWh}} = \frac{\blacksquare}{30 \text{ kWh}}$$

Solve the proportion.

$$\frac{11.58¢}{2 \text{ kWh}} = \frac{\blacksquare}{30 \text{ kWh}}$$

$11.58¢ \times 15 = 173.7¢$ C 11.58 × 15 = 173.7

What number do you multiply the denominator by? What number do you multiply the numerator by?

11.58¢ is about 12¢.
$12 \times 15 = (10 \times 15 + 2 \times 15)$
$= 150 + 30$
$= 180$
The answer will be about 180¢ or $1.80.

So, 30 kWh costs about 174¢ or $1.74.

Show You Know

There are 72 players on 8 baseball teams. Determine the number of players on 2 teams. Show how to find the answer more than one way.

Example 2: Solve a Ratio Problem Using Proportional Reasoning

A wildlife biologist wants to know how many trout are in a slough in Saskatchewan. He captures and tags 24 trout and releases them back into the slough. Two weeks later he returns and captures 30 trout and finds that 5 of them are tagged. He uses the following ratios to estimate the number of fish in the slough:

$$\frac{\text{fish recaptured with tags}}{\text{total fish recaptured}} = \frac{\text{fish caught and tagged}}{\text{total fish in slough}}$$

How many trout does he estimate are in the slough?

Solution

Method 1: Use a Proportion in Lowest Terms

$$\frac{\text{fish recaptured with tags}}{\text{total fish recaptured}} = \frac{\text{fish tagged}}{\text{total fish in slough}}$$

$\dfrac{5}{30} = \dfrac{24}{t}$ Set up the proportion using equal ratios.

$\dfrac{1}{6} = \dfrac{24}{t}$ Reduce $\dfrac{5}{30}$ to $\dfrac{1}{6}$.

$\overset{\times\,24}{\frown}$

$\dfrac{1}{6} = \dfrac{24}{t}$ Make equivalent ratios.

$\underset{\times\,24}{\smile}$

$t = 6 \times 24 = 144$

The biologist estimates there are 144 trout in the slough.

Literacy  **Link**

In Western Canada, a *slough* is a small lake or pond formed by rain or melted snow.

Did You Know?

Wildlife biologists can show that these ratios are equal if the fish population has an opportunity to mix before the recapture.

Strategies
Use a Variable

Method 2: Use the Original Proportion

How would you find the solution if you did not write $\frac{5}{30}$ in lowest terms?

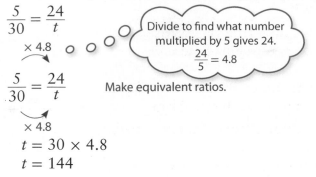

$$\frac{5}{30} = \frac{24}{t}$$

$\times 4.8$

Divide to find what number multiplied by 5 gives 24.

$$\frac{24}{5} = 4.8$$

$$\frac{5}{30} = \frac{24}{t}$$

Make equivalent ratios.

$\times 4.8$

$$t = 30 \times 4.8$$
$$t = 144$$

The biologist estimates there are 144 trout in the slough.

Show You Know

How much will a dozen erasers cost if three erasers cost 75¢?
Show how to find the answer in more than one way.

Key Ideas

- A proportion is a relationship that says that two ratios or two rates are equal.
  - A proportion can be expressed in fraction form:

  $\times 5$
  $$\frac{1}{2} = \frac{5}{10}$$
  $\times 5$

  $\div 3$
  $$\frac{60 \text{ sit-ups}}{3 \text{ min}} = \frac{20 \text{ sit-ups}}{1 \text{ min}}$$
  $\div 3$

- You can solve proportional reasoning problems using several different methods.

  A potato farmer can plant three potato plants per 0.5 m². How many potato plants can she plant in an area of 85 m²?

  - Use a unit rate. $\dfrac{3 \text{ plants}}{0.5 \text{ m}^2} = \dfrac{6 \text{ plants}}{1 \text{ m}^2}$ The unit rate is 6 plants/m².

    $$6 \times 85 = 510$$
    The farmer can plant 510 potato plants.

  - Use a proportion.

    $\times 170$
    $$\frac{3 \text{ plants}}{0.5 \text{ m}^2} = \frac{\blacksquare}{85 \text{ m}^2}$$
    $\times 170$

    Missing value is $3 \times 170 = 510$
    The farmer can plant 510 potato plants.

1. Explain the similarities and differences between a ratio, a rate, and a proportion. Give an example of each one.

2. Your friend missed the lesson on proportions. Explain how to use a proportion to solve this problem.
   Cheryl is selling marbles. What is the cost of seven marbles?

Marbles	2	3	4
Cost (¢)	70	105	140

3. a) Write a proportion based on the following scenario:
   Three balls cost $1.25. What is the cost of 12 balls?

   b) Solve the proportion.

Check Your Understanding

Practise

For help with #4 to #9, refer to Example 1 on pages 64–65.

4. Determine the unit rate.
   a) Three dinner rolls cost 99¢.
   b) Seven identical objects have a mass of 14 kg.

5. What is the unit rate in each?
   a) Two pens cost 94¢.
   b) Four blocks stacked one on top of the other are 24 cm high.

6. Delia was paid $35 for 5 h of babysitting. How much should she receive for 3 h? Use a unit rate to find the answer.

7. Solve #6 using a proportion. Show how to find the answer more than one way.

8. Determine the missing value.

   a) $\dfrac{2}{3} = \dfrac{\blacksquare}{15}$ b) $\dfrac{\blacksquare}{5} = \dfrac{14}{35}$

   c) $\dfrac{30}{45} = \dfrac{6}{\blacksquare}$ d) $\dfrac{3}{\blacksquare} = \dfrac{12}{36}$

9. Determine the missing value to make each rate equivalent. Include the units.

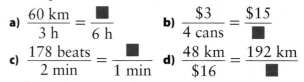

a) $\dfrac{60 \text{ km}}{3 \text{ h}} = \dfrac{\blacksquare}{6 \text{ h}}$ b) $\dfrac{\$3}{4 \text{ cans}} = \dfrac{\$15}{\blacksquare}$

c) $\dfrac{178 \text{ beats}}{2 \text{ min}} = \dfrac{\blacksquare}{1 \text{ min}}$ d) $\dfrac{48 \text{ km}}{\$16} = \dfrac{192 \text{ km}}{\blacksquare}$

For help with #10 to #14, refer to Example 2 on pages 65–66.

10. Set up a proportion for each situation.
    a) If 10 beans have a mass of 17 g, then 30 beans have a mass of 51 g.
    b) There are 13 boys for 15 girls in every classroom at Albany Middle School. If there are 65 boys in the school, then there are 75 girls.
    c) On a map, 1 cm represents 25 km. Kendra wants to ride her bike 160 km. This distance is 6.4 cm on the map.

11. A small gear turns 18 times in the same time that a large gear turns 4 times. How many times will the large gear turn if the small gear turns 54 times? Draw a diagram to help set up a proportion and solve the problem.

12. Set up a proportion for each situation using a variable. Do not find the answer.

   a) Walter makes his own oil and vinegar dressing. His recipe calls for 175 mL of olive oil and 50 mL of vinegar. What amount of vinegar does he need to mix with 300 mL of olive oil?

   b) A baseball player has a home run to strikeouts ratio of 3:17. How many home runs should he hit if he strikes out 187 times?

13. Two quarters have the same value as ten nickels. What is the value of five quarters in nickels?

14. Last night 30 cm of snow fell in 6 h. If it continues snowing at the same rate, how long will it take for 45 cm of snow to fall? Determine the answer two different ways.

Apply

15. Look at the pattern. Set up a proportion you could use to find the number of small squares in Figure 7.

Figure 1   Figure 2   Figure 3   Figure 4

16. A gardener takes a half hour to mow and weed a lawn that measures 20 m by 15 m. He charges $25 per hour. How much should the gardener receive for a lawn that measures 40 m by 30 m?

17. Fresh pickerel is advertised in a local market.

2 kg fresh pickerel
$17.60

1 kg = 1000 g

   a) How much will 6 kg of pickerel cost?

   b) Use a proportion to find the cost of 1600 g of pickerel.

18. At an amusement park, a new thrill ride was introduced. It costs $7.50 for 3 rides on the Wild Slider.

   a) What is the Wild Slider's unit rate per ride?

   b) At this rate, what would it cost for 18 rides on Wild Slider? Determine the answer two different ways.

19. Determine the missing value in each equivalent fraction.

   a) $\dfrac{3}{\blacksquare} = \dfrac{18}{24} = \dfrac{\blacksquare}{12}$

   b) $\dfrac{48 \text{ km}}{\$16} = \dfrac{144 \text{ km}}{\blacksquare} = \dfrac{\blacksquare}{\$64}$

20. A breakfast cereal contains corn, wheat, and rice in the ratio of 3 to 4 to 2. If a box of cereal contains 225 g of corn, how much rice does it contain?

21. David can saw a log into three pieces in 7 min. If he continues sawing at a constant rate, how long will it take him to saw a similar log into six pieces?

22. The height of an object compared to the length of its shadow is constant for all objects at any given time.

$$\frac{\text{tree height}}{\text{length of shadow}} = \frac{\text{student height}}{\text{length of shadow}}$$

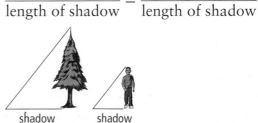

shadow   shadow

Use this information to help answer the following questions.

   a) If a 15-m tree casts a 9-m shadow, what is the height of a student who casts a 1.08-m shadow?

   b) If a 50-m tower has a shadow 16 m long, how long is the shadow of a student who is 1.5 m tall? Give your answer to the nearest centimetre.

23. According to the *Guinness Book of World Records*, the world's smallest horse is Thumbelina. Thumbelina is 42.5 cm tall and eats about 0.3 kg of food per day. A former world record holder ate food in the same proportion to its height. If it was 46.25 cm tall, how much did it eat? Give your answer to the nearest hundredth of a kilogram.

24. a) Describe a pattern you could use to find the next fraction in the following set of fractions. $\frac{1}{2}, \frac{2}{4}, \frac{3}{6}$

b) Describe a pattern you could use to find the next fraction in the following set of fractions. $\frac{5}{6}, \frac{10}{12}, \frac{15}{18}$

c) Choose any pair of fractions from part a) or part b). Multiply the numerator of one fraction by the denominator of the other fraction. Repeat for two other fractions in the same set. What do you notice about the two products?

d) What prediction could you make about the cross-products of any pair of equivalent fractions? Test your prediction on another pair of equivalent fractions.

Extend

25. Mark estimates that frogs eat six insects per hour and that dragonflies eat nine insects per hour. Assume a frog rests for 8 h each day and a dragonfly rests for 13 h each day. Neither eats while resting.

a) Determine the daily rate of insects eaten by a frog and a dragonfly. Which one eats more insects per day?

b) How many insects would a dragonfly eat in a week?

c) How many insects would a frog eat in August?

26. Two circles have radii with a ratio of 1 to 2. Use a diagram to help answer the following questions.

a) What is the ratio of their circumferences?

b) What is the ratio of their areas?

27. If $a:b = 4:5$, find the ratio of $5a:7b$.

28. The dosage of a certain medicine for a child is 2.5 mL for each 3 kg mass of the child. What is the dose, in millilitres, for a child with a mass of 16.5 kg?

MATH LINK

A horiatiki Greek salad has tomatoes, cucumbers, feta cheese, and olives. It does not contain any lettuce. Many cultures have similar salads. For example, ezme salatasi is a Turkish tomato-cucumber salad with red peppers and paprika, but without the feta and olives.

a) It costs $7.60 to make the horiatiki salad for 12 people. What is the unit price?

b) Choose and write down a recipe for a soup, a salad, or an appetizer that serves between 4 and 6 people. Record how much of each ingredient you will need to serve 10 people at your international meal.

Horiatiki Salata   Yield: 4 Servings

Ingredients:
- 3 to 4 tomatoes
- 1 cucumber
- 1 red onion
- 125 mL Kalamata olives
- 125 g feta cheese
- 250 mL dressing (olive oil, red wine vinegar, garlic, oregano, salt and pepper)

Key Words

For #1 to #5, choose the letter representing the example that best matches each term.

1. proportion
2. ratio
3. three-term ratio
4. unit price
5. unit rate

A $2.75 per tin

B $\frac{3}{5}$

C 5 students

D $\frac{7}{50} = \frac{14}{100}$

E 4:3:2

F 120 km in 2 h

G 27 km/h

2.1 Two-Term and Three-Term Ratios, pages 46–54

6. Use the square tile pattern to find each of the following:

   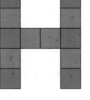

   a) ratio of red squares to blue squares

   b) blue squares:total squares

   c) two equivalent ratios for the answer in part b)

   d) percent of squares that are red

7. Look at the figure.

   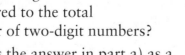

   a) What is the ratio of two-digit numbers in the red hexagon compared to the total number of two-digit numbers?

   b) Express the answer in part a) as a fraction in lowest terms.

   c) What is the ratio of two-digit numbers containing a 2 compared to the number of two-digit numbers in the red hexagon that contain a 2?

8. Stephanie counted 20 vehicles in a parking lot. Of these, five were silver, four were blue, two were red, and one was yellow.

   a) What is the ratio of yellow to red to silver vehicles?

   b) How many vehicles were not silver, blue, red, or yellow?

   c) What could the ratio 4 to 20 represent?

   d) What could 5:8 represent?

   e) Express the ratio of silver to total vehicles as a fraction and as a percent.

9. A football team won 10 of its 18 games and lost the rest.

   a) How many games did the team lose?

   b) What is the team's win–loss ratio?

10. Jan made the following enlargement.

    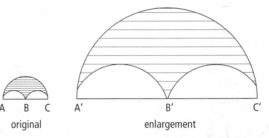

    original   enlargement

    a) What is the ratio of the length of A′B′ to the length of AB? Measure in millimetres.

    b) What is the ratio of the length of A′C′ to AC?

    c) What is the multiplier used in this enlargement?

2.2 Rates, pages 55–62

11. Determine a unit rate in each situation.

    a) Steven runs up 300 steps in 6 min.

    b) $3.60 is the price of 4 L of milk.

    c) A jet travels 2184 km in 3.5 h.

    d) A polar bear gains 450 kg in nine years.

12. Transportation increases the cost of groceries in Northern communities. Use the data about the cost of grocery items in Winnipeg and Little Grand Rapids to answer the questions.

Item	Cost in Winnipeg	Cost in Little Grand Rapids
3 kg bananas	$4.98	$13.95
Mini ravioli (720 mL)	$2.29	$5.49
Milk (1 L)	$1.39	$4.09

a) Give an example of a ratio.

b) Give an example of a rate.

c) What is the unit price for bananas in Winnipeg? in Little Grand Rapids? What is the difference in unit price for the two communities?

13. The table compares the typical monthly cost of electricity for several appliances.

Appliance	Time On (h)	Monthly Cost ($)
Fridge	240	12.11
Computer and monitor	120	4.26
Television	180	3.46
Treadmill	15	3.99

a) What is the hourly unit cost for each appliance? Give each answer to the nearest tenth of a cent.

b) Which appliance has the lowest rate of electricity consumption?

14. Shelly rode her mountain bike at a rate of 30 km/h for 2.5 h. Josh rode his mountain bike at a rate of 35 km/h for 1 h and then slowed down to 25 km/h for 1.5 h.

a) Who travelled farther in 2.5 h?

b) What is the difference in the distance travelled by the cyclists?

2.3 Proportional Reasoning, pages 63–69

15. Determine the missing value if each rate is equivalent. Give the unit for each.

a) $\dfrac{\blacksquare}{1 \text{ month}} = \dfrac{64 \text{ kg}}{4 \text{ months}}$

b) $\dfrac{\$84}{800 \text{ km}} = \dfrac{\blacksquare}{100 \text{ km}}$

c) $\dfrac{80 \text{ beats}}{2 \text{ min}} = \dfrac{720 \text{ beats}}{\blacksquare}$

16. Use a proportion to solve each question. Use a variable for the unknown quantity.

a) Three bars of soap cost $2.94. What is the cost of eight bars of soap?

b) On a map, 1 cm represents 150 km. On the map, how many centimetres represent a distance of 800 km?

17. A mass of 5 g stretches a rubber band by 15 mm. If the rubber band stretches at the same rate, find the following.

a) How much would a mass of 28 g stretch the rubber band? Give your answer to the nearest hundredth of a centimetre.

b) What mass would stretch a rubber band 32 mm?

c) What mass would stretch a rubber band 9.9 cm? Give your answer to the nearest tenth of a gram.

18. The height of an object compared to the length of its shadow is constant for all objects at any given time. Use this information and a drawing to help answer the following questions.

a) If a 20-m tower casts a 12-m shadow, what is the height of a tree with a shadow 3 m long?

b) If a 25-m building has a shadow 8 m long, how long is the shadow of a student who is 1.6 m tall? Give your answer to the nearest centimetre.

Practice Test

For #1 to #4, choose the best answer.

1. The ratio of Jared's stamps to Paulo's stamps is 4:7. If Jared has 36 stamps how many stamps does Paulo have?

A 21 **B** 63

C 84 **D** 99

2. A robot can make 27 toy cars in 9 min. Which of the following is the <u>unit rate</u> for this robot?

A 27 cars/9 min **B** 3 cars

C 3 cars per min **D** $\frac{1}{3}$ car/min

3. In the school choir, the ratio of girls to boys is 17:8. What percent of the school choir are boys?

A 8% **B** 17%

C 25% **D** 32%

4. The picture shows the ratio of the cost of a shirt to the cost of a hat and the ratio of the cost of the hat to the cost of a pair of jeans. What is the ratio of the cost of the shirt to the cost of the jeans?

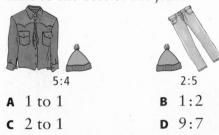

5:4   2:5

A 1 to 1 **B** 1:2

C 2 to 1 **D** 9:7

Complete the statements in #5 and #6.

5. A currency exchange requires $500 Canadian to receive $600 Australian. For $300 Canadian, you would receive ■ Australian.

6. Canadians buy five loaves of brown bread for every two loaves of white bread and one loaf of rye bread. A large bakery makes 20 000 loaves of brown bread. The bakery should make ■ loaves of white and ■ loaves of rye.

Short Answer

7. Randi made nine scarves from 4 m of fabric. How many scarves can she make from 28 m of the same fabric?

8. Tank A has a capacity of 20 L. It is half filled with maple syrup. The ratio of the volume of maple syrup in Tank A compared to the volume of maple syrup in Tank B is 2:5. How much maple syrup is in Tank B?

9. The circle graph shows the favourite pets for a class of 32 grade 8 students.

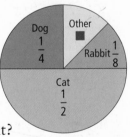

Favourite Pets

a) How many students selected a pet other than a dog, cat, or a rabbit?

b) Write a ratio to represent the number of students who selected a cat compared to a rabbit. Write an equivalent ratio.

10. The lengths of A, B, and C are in the ratio 8:2:3, respectively. The length of side C is 24 cm. What is the area of the top of the box?

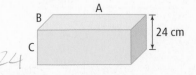

11. Kyra is shopping for ketchup. Her favourite brand is available in two sizes.

Ketchup 500 mL — $2.09

Ketchup 750 mL — $3.29

   a) Estimate which is the better buy. Show your work.

   b) Calculate to find the better buy. Show your work.

Extended Response

12. Peter runs 200 m in 30 s, while his sister Eva runs 300 m in 36 s.

   a) Who is the faster runner? Explain how you can tell.

   b) At the same rate, how far will each runner go in 2 min?

   c) How long should it take for each runner to travel 1 km? State any assumptions that you must make.

13. Each week, Karen earns $420 for 35 h of work at a factory. Her friend Liam makes $440 for 40 h of work at a store.

   a) Who has the greatest hourly rate of pay?

   b) How much does Liam earn in an 8-h shift?

14. The actual height of the goat shown here is 1.14 m. Measure the height of the goat in the picture in centimetres.

   a) What is the ratio of the height of the goat in the picture compared to the actual height of the goat? Explain what this ratio means.

   b) Use ratios to find the actual length of one of the mountain goat's horns. Show your work.

1 m = 100 cm

WRAP IT UP!

Plan an international meal that will serve 10 people. Include at least one dish from each of the following categories:
- a soup, salad, or appetizer
- a main course
- a dessert

Create your meal plan.

a) Finalize your invitation to the meal. Ensure that your logo design has an area of 36 cm² and uses colours or measurements to show each of the following ratios:

   4:3   2:3:4

b) Record your three recipes. Beside each recipe, write the amount of each ingredient you need to serve 10 people.

c) Justify your calculations for one recipe in part b).

d) Calculate the total cost of serving one of your dishes to your guests. Show your work.

WWW Web Link

To discover some international food recipes go to www.mathlinks8.ca and follow the links.

Math Games

Rolling Ratios

Materials
- three dice per pair of students
- calculator per student

1. Play Rolling Ratios with a partner. These are the rules:
   - Each player rolls one die to decide who will play first. If there is a tie, roll again.
   - In one round, each partner takes a turn.
   - For each turn, roll all three dice.
   - Record the ratio of the least value to the sum of the rolled values, in fraction form.

I rolled a 2, a 4, and a 5. The sum of the rolled values is $2 + 4 + 5 = 11$, so the ratio of the least value to the sum of the values is $2:11$ or $\frac{2}{11}$.

So, $\frac{2}{11} = 0.18$, to the nearest hundredth.

C **2** ÷ **11** = 0.181818182

   - Express the fraction as a decimal. If necessary, use a calculator and round to the nearest hundredth.
   - Add the decimals from your turns. The first player to reach 2.5 or higher wins.
   - If both players reach 2.5 in the same round, the player with the higher total wins. If the totals are tied, the players continue playing until one of them pulls ahead.

2. Modify the rules of the game. For example, change the number of dice or choose a different ratio. Play your modified version of the game.

Challenge in Real Life

Life of a Bush Pilot

Doug is a bush pilot who flies needed medical supplies and personnel to remote areas in the Northwest Territories. You be the flight planner. Calculate the distances and times for Doug's next flight plan.

Materials
- map of Northwest Territories per pair or small group
- ruler
- compass

1. To the nearest tenth of a centimetre, use a ruler to measure and record the distances on the map of the Northwest Territories between
   a) Hay River and Tuktoyaktuk
   b) Tuktoyaktuk and Paulatuk
   c) Paulatuk and Hay River

2. Write and solve a proportion to calculate the actual flying distances between
   a) Hay River and Tuktoyaktuk
   b) Tuktoyaktuk and Paulatuk
   c) Paulatuk and Hay River

3. Doug needs to fly some emergency serum from Yellowknife to Inuvik. He needs to do this flight in 4.5 h. What average cruising speed will you recommend that he use in kilometres per hour? Justify your suggestion mathematically.

4. Doug is based in Sachs Harbour. His usual cruising speed is 220 km/h. You have some clients who want to take a 2-h flight from Sachs Harbour. List all of the communities they can visit within two hours of flying time. Justify your answer.

Pythagorean Relationship

Many board games and puzzles include squares and triangles in their design. Checkers, chess, and SCRABBLE® have game boards made of squares. The game called Playing Leader, includes both squares and triangles in its game board design.

Squares and triangles are also important geometric figures in construction, art, and mathematics. There are many connections between squares and triangles in mathematics. In previous math courses, you have discovered some connections between these two shapes.

What You Will Learn

❑ to find the squares and square roots of whole numbers

❑ to estimate square roots of whole numbers

❑ to determine whether a triangle is a right triangle

❑ to apply the Pythagorean relationship to find missing dimensions of triangles and to solve problems

Literacy Link

You can use a Verbal Visual Chart (V VC) to help you learn and remember new terms.

Copy the blank V VC into your math journal or notebook and use it for the term *square*.

- Write the term in the first box.
- Draw a diagram in the second box.
- Define the term in the third box. The glossary on pages 517–521 may help you.
- In the fourth box, explain how you will remember the term and what it means. Consider using an example, a characteristic, a memory device, or a visual.

Term	Diagram
Definition	**How I Will Remember It**

Making the Foldable

Materials

- eight sheets of grid paper
- stapler
- ruler
- scissors

Step 1

Staple eight sheets of grid paper together along the top edge.

Step 2

Make a line 10.5 cm up from the bottom of the top page. Cut across the entire width of the page at this mark.

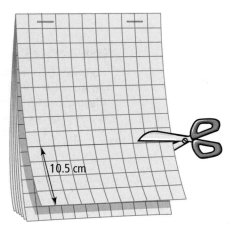

10.5 cm

Step 3

Make a line 9 cm up from the bottom of the second page. Cut across the entire page at this mark.

Step 4

In a similar manner, cut off 7.5 cm from the third page, 6 cm from the fourth page, 4.5 cm from the fifth page, 3 cm from the sixth page, and 1.5 cm from the seventh page.

Step 5

Label the tabs as shown.

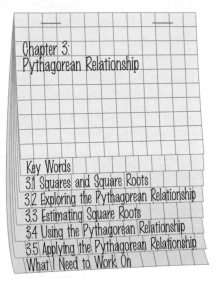

Chapter 3:
Pythagorean Relationship

Key Words
3.1 Squares and Square Roots
3.2 Exploring the Pythagorean Relationship
3.3 Estimating Square Roots
3.4 Using the Pythagorean Relationship
3.5 Applying the Pythagorean Relationship
What I Need to Work On

Using the Foldable

As you work through Chapter 3, define each Key Word on the first tab of your Foldable. Use a visual or example to help you remember each term.

Make notes about examples and Key Ideas under the appropriate tab.

On the last tab, make notes using the heading What I Need to Work On. Check off each item as you deal with it.

Use the back of the Foldable to list your ideas for the Wrap It Up!

MATH LINK

Game Design

Playing Leader is a peg board game. The board design for Playing Leader includes squares and triangles. In this game, two players compete against each other. One player controls 13 green pegs and the opponent controls the leader peg, which is a different colour. All of the pegs start at the top of the board and are moved one hole at a time along the lines on the board. The 13 green pegs may be moved left, right, or down. The leader peg may be moved left, right, up, or down. The green pegs try to surround the leader peg so that it cannot move to another position. The leader peg tries to capture all of the green pegs or advance to the bottom of the board. The leader peg captures a green peg by jumping over it to an empty space. Captured pegs are removed from the board.

Use a copy of the Playing Leader board to help answer the following questions.

1. Show how to place the 13 green pegs and one leader peg in such a way that the leader peg cannot move.

2. Moving one space at a time, what is the maximum number of moves you can make with one peg in a straight line vertically?

3. How many squares can you count on the board that do not overlap?

4. What words could you use to describe the triangles on the board, for example, *isosceles, equilateral, scalene, acute, right, obtuse*? Draw and label the triangle(s) to show why you used the words you did.

5. The horizontal or vertical distance between two peg holes is 5 cm. Determine the area of the game board in two different ways.

Compare your answers with those of a classmate.

At the end of the chapter, you will design a new board game that includes triangles and squares in the design.

Materials

- Playing Leader board
- coloured counters

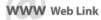

WWW Web Link

For more information about the game of Playing Leader, go to www.mathlinks8.ca and follow the links.

3.1 Squares and Square Roots

Focus on...

After this lesson, you will be able to...

❑ determine the square of a whole number

❑ determine the square root of a perfect square

The Pythagoreans were members of an academy of study that existed 2500 years ago. They created square numbers by arranging pebbles in equal numbers of rows and columns. Nine pebbles could be arranged in three rows and three columns. Nine is a square number because $3 \times 3 = 9$. The picture shows the first four square numbers that the Pythagoreans found: 1, 4, 9, and 16. How can you determine the next square number?

Literacy Link

A *square number* is the product of the same two numbers. $3 \times 3 = 9$, so 9 is a square number.

A square number is also known as a *perfect square*. A number that is not a perfect square is called a *non-perfect square*.

> **Did You Know?**
>
> Pythagoras (about 580–500 B.C.E.) was the leader of a group of academics called the Pythagoreans. They believed that patterns in whole numbers could help explain the universe.

Explore the Math

Materials

• square tiles

How can you identify a perfect square?

1. Use square tiles to make five rectangles with the dimensions shown.

What is the area of each rectangle?

Length (cm)	Width (cm)
5	3
8	2
9	1
4	3
9	4

2. Try to rearrange the tiles in each rectangle to make a square.

   a) Which rectangles can you make into squares?

   b) What is the side length of each square?

   c) How is the area of each square related to its side length?

3. a) Choose three perfect squares and three non-perfect squares.

   b) Express each number as a product of prime factors.

   c) For each number, how many times does each prime factor appear? Compare your results with a partner's results.

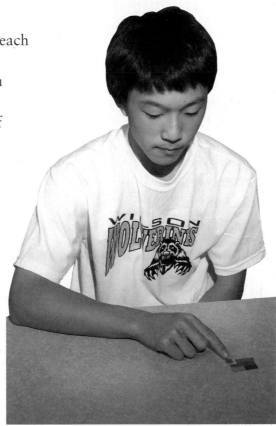

Literacy ❸ Link

Prime Numbers and Prime Factors

A *prime number* is a whole number greater than 1 that has only two factors: 1 and itself.

Prime factors are factors that are prime numbers.

For example, the prime factors of 10 are 2 and 5.

4. a) What do all of the perfect squares have in common?

   b) What do all of the non-perfect squares have in common?

Reflect on Your Findings

5. a) How can square tiles help you to determine if a number is a perfect square?

   b) How can prime factors help you to determine if a number is a perfect square?

Example 1: Identify Perfect Squares

a) Determine the prime factorization of the following numbers: 24, 36, 81.

b) Which of the numbers is a perfect square? Explain.

c) For each number that is a perfect square, draw the square and label its side length.

Different factor trees are possible to arrive at the same prime factorization.

Solution

a)

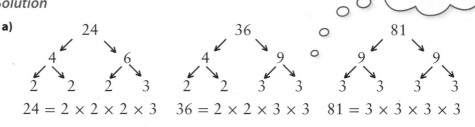

$$24 = 2 \times 2 \times 2 \times 3 \quad 36 = 2 \times 2 \times 3 \times 3 \quad 81 = 3 \times 3 \times 3 \times 3$$

b) To be a perfect square, each prime factor in the prime factorization must occur an even number of times. 36 and 81 are perfect squares because each prime factor occurs an even number of times.

$36 = 2 \times 2 \times 3 \times 3$ two factors of 2, two factors of 3
$81 = 3 \times 3 \times 3 \times 3$ four factors of 3

24 is not a perfect square because at least one of the prime factors occurs an odd number of times.

$24 = 2 \times 2 \times 2 \times 3$ three factors of 2, one factor of 3

c) To determine the side length of the squares, look at the product of prime factors for the area.

$36 = 2 \times 2 \times 3 \times 3$ $81 = 3 \times 3 \times 3 \times 3$

Rearrange the prime factors into two equal groups.

$36 = (2 \times 3) \times (2 \times 3)$
$36 = 6 \times 6$

$81 = (3 \times 3) \times (3 \times 3)$
$81 = 9 \times 9$

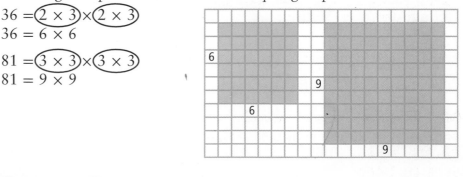

Show You Know

Write the prime factorization of each number. Which number is not a perfect square? Explain how you know.

a) 45   **b)** 100

Example 2: Determine the Square of a Number

Determine the area of a square picture with a side length of 13 cm.

Solution

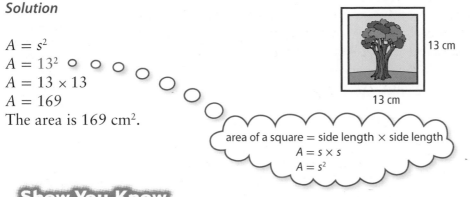

$A = s^2$
$A = 13^2$
$A = 13 \times 13$
$A = 169$
The area is 169 cm^2.

area of a square = side length × side length
$A = s \times s$
$A = s^2$

Strategies

Draw a Diagram

Show You Know

Determine the area of a square with a side length of 16 mm.

Literacy ⊖ Link

You can write a repeated multiplication like 13×13 as a square:
$13 \times 13 = 13^2$.
13^2 is read as thirteen squared.

Example 3: Determine the Square Root of a Perfect Square

Edgar knows that the square case for his computer game has an area of 144 cm^2. What is the side length of the case?

144 cm^2

Solution

Method 1: Use Inspection
To find the side length, determine what positive number when multiplied by itself equals 144.
$12 \times 12 = 144$
The **square root** of 144 is 12, or $\sqrt{144} = 12$.
The side length is 12 cm.

square root

• a number that when multiplied by itself equals a given value
• 6 is the square root of 36 because $6 \times 6 = 36$

Method 2: Use Guess and Check
Find the positive value for the blank boxes.
$\blacksquare \times \blacksquare = 144$
$10 \times 10 = 100$ Too low
$13 \times 13 = 169$ Too high
$12 \times 12 = 144$ Correct!
$\qquad 12 = \sqrt{144}$
The side length is 12 cm.

Literacy ⊖ Link

Reading Square Roots

The symbol for square root is $\sqrt{\ }$. Read $\sqrt{9}$ as the square root of 9, square root 9, or root 9.

Method 3: Use Prime Factorization

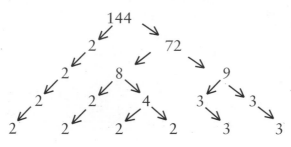

The prime factorization of 144 is $2 \times 2 \times 2 \times 2 \times 3 \times 3$.

Rearrange the prime factors into two equal groups.

$$144 = \overline{(2 \times 2 \times 3)} \times \overline{(2 \times 2 \times 3)}$$
$$144 = 12 \times 12$$
$$\sqrt{144} = 12$$

The side length is 12 cm.

Show You Know

Determine the side length of a square with an area of 196 cm².

Key Ideas

- The square of a number is the number multiplied by itself.
  $5 \times 5 = 25$, or $5^2 = 25$
- The square of a whole number is a perfect square. $2^2 = 4$
  So, 4 is a perfect square.
- The square of a number can be thought of as the area of a square.
  $4^2 = 16$
  The area is 16 cm².
- The square root of a number can be thought of as the side length
  of a square.
  $\sqrt{16} = 4$
  The side length is 4 cm.
- The square root of a value is a number that when multiplied by itself
  equals the value.
  $6 \times 6 = 36$, so $\sqrt{36} = 6$
- In the prime factorization of a perfect square, there is an even
  number of each prime factor.
  $36 = 2 \times 2 \times 3 \times 3$ two factors of 2, two factors of 3

$A = 16 \text{ cm}^2$ 4 cm

1. Explain how to square the number 7.

2. How would you use prime factorization to determine the square root of 225? Compare your answer with a classmate's.

3. The factors of 36 are 1, 2, 3, 4, 6, 9, 12, 18, and 36. Use words and/or diagrams to explain how you know which factor is the square root of 36.

4. Explain how squaring a number is the reverse of finding the square root of a number. Include an example with your explanation.

Check Your Understanding

Practise

For help with #5 to #8, refer to Example 1 on page 82.

5. a) Determine the prime factorization of 4.
   b) Is 4 a perfect square? Explain.
   c) Draw the square and label its side length.

6. A rectangle has an area of 64 m².
   a) Determine the prime factorization of 64.
   b) Is 64 a perfect square? Explain.
   c) Draw a square with that area and label its side length.

7. Write the prime factorization of each number. Identify the perfect squares.
   a) 42   b) 169   c) 256

8. Determine the prime factorization of each number. Which numbers are perfect squares?
   a) 144   b) 60   c) 40

For help with #9 to #12, refer to Example 2 on page 83.

9. What is the area of a square with each side length?
   a) 10   b) 16

10. Determine the area of a square with each side length.
    a) 20   b) 17

11. What is the square of each number?
    a) 9   b) 11

12. Determine the square of each number.
    a) 3   b) 18

For help with #13 to #16, refer to Example 3 on pages 83–84.

13. What is the side length of the square shown?

49 mm²

14. Determine the side length of a square with an area of 900 cm².

15. Evaluate.

a) $\sqrt{49}$ b) $\sqrt{64}$ c) $\sqrt{625}$

16. Determine the value.

a) $\sqrt{9}$ b) $\sqrt{25}$ c) $\sqrt{1600}$

Apply

17. A fridge magnet has an area of 54 mm². Is 54 a perfect square? Use prime factorization to find the answer.

18. A floor mat for gymnastics is a square with a side length of 14 m. What is the area of the floor mat in square metres?

19. The gym teacher told the students to run twice around the perimeter of the school field. The area of the square field is 28 900 m². What distance did the students run?

20. Adam's uncle has instructions for building a shed. One page of the instructions, shown below, is not very clear.

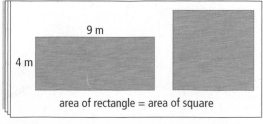

area of rectangle = area of square

a) What is the area of the rectangle?

b) What is the side length of the square?

21. Kate is going to put a patio in her backyard. The patio stones she is using each have an area of 1 m². She has created the rectangular design shown.

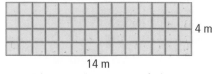

14 m

4 m

a) What is the area of the patio?

b) What are the dimensions of another rectangular patio she could build with the same area?

c) Kate decides to make a patio with the same area but she wants it to be a square with whole number side lengths. Is this possible? Explain your reasoning.

22. The world's largest city square is Tiananmen Square in Beijing, China. It has an area of 396 900 m².

a) What are the dimensions of the square?

b) If the square had dimensions of 629 m by 629 m, what would be the area?

c) If the square had an area less than 394 000 m² and greater than 386 000 m², what are all of the possible whole number dimensions that it could have?

23. A helicopter landing pad has a square shape. The area is 400 m². Use prime factorization to find the side length of the pad.

24. The first three triangular numbers are

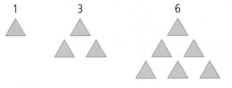

1   3   6

a) What are the next three triangular numbers?

b) Add together any two consecutive triangular numbers. What do you notice about the sums?

25. A square digital photo on the computer has an area of 144 cm².

a) What is the side length of the photo?

b) The photo is enlarged so that the side length is now 36 cm. What is the area of the enlarged photo?

c) How many times as large as the original area is the enlarged area?

Imagine your dog is 80 cm tall and your cat is 40 cm tall. How many times as tall as your cat is your dog? What operation did you perform?

d) How many times as large as the original side length is the enlarged side length?

e) Use what you know about the square root of a perfect square to identify the relationship between the numbers in parts c) and d).

26. a) Determine which of the following numbers are perfect squares: 10, 100, 1000, 10 000, 100 000.

b) State the square root of each perfect square.

c) Choose one of the numbers that is not a perfect square. Explain how you know that it is not a perfect square.

d) Describe a quick method for determining mentally if the numbers are perfect squares.

e) Use your method in part d) to decide if 1 000 000 000 is a perfect square.

27. a) Determine the square root of each number: 6400, 640 000, 64 000 000.

b) Describe a quick method for determining mentally the square root of each number in part a).

c) Explain why this method does not work for evaluating $\sqrt{640}$.

d) Use your method in part b) to evaluate $\sqrt{640\,000\,000\,000}$. Explain how you determined the answer.

MATH LINK

Chess is played on a square board. The board is made up of 32 white squares and 32 dark squares.

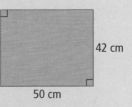

42 cm

50 cm

You decide to make your own chessboard. You are going to cut the board out of the 42 cm x 50 cm piece of wood shown.

Each square on the board will have whole number side lengths. The chess pieces fit on squares that are no smaller than 9 cm². What are all of the possible dimensions that your board could have?

Exploring the Pythagorean Relationship

Right triangles are found in art, construction, and many other objects. The sail for this sailboat is a right triangle. What makes this shape so special? You will explore some important properties of right triangles in this lesson.

Explore the Math

What is a relationship that applies to right triangles?

1. From a piece of centimetre grid paper, cut out three squares with the following dimensions:

6 cm × 6 cm   8 cm × 8 cm   10 cm × 10 cm

2. Arrange the squares to form Triangle 1 as shown. Tape the squares onto a sheet of paper. Label Triangle 1.

The length of side *a* is 6 cm, side *b* is 8 cm, and side *c* is 10 cm.

a

Triangle 1

c

b

3. Copy the table below into your notebook.

	Side	Side Length (cm)	Angle Opposite the Side (°)	Area of Square (cm²)	Right Triangle? (yes/no)
Triangle 1	a	6	37		
	b	8			
	c	10			
Triangle 2	a	5			
	b	7			
	c	10			
Triangle 3	a	5		25	
	b			144	
	c			169	

Literacy **Link**

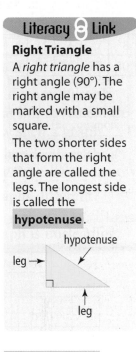

Right Triangle

A *right triangle* has a right angle (90°). The right angle may be marked with a small square.

The two shorter sides that form the right angle are called the legs. The longest side is called the **hypotenuse**.

4. Measure the angle opposite each side of Triangle 1 with a protractor.

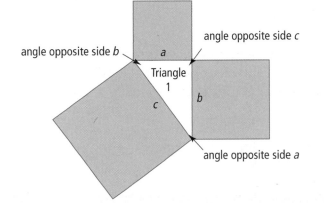

angle opposite side *c*

angle opposite side *b*

Triangle 1

angle opposite side *a*

hypotenuse

• the longest side of a right triangle
• the side opposite the right angle

5. In your table, record the angle measures to the nearest degree.

6. Complete the rest of the table for Triangle 1.

7. Repeat the above steps for Triangles 2 and 3 in the table.

Reflect on Your Findings

8. a) Which triangles are right triangles? How do you know?

b) For each right triangle, write an addition statement showing the relationship between the areas of the three squares.

c) For each right triangle, describe in words the relationship between the side lengths of the triangle.

Example 1: Describe Relationships in Right Triangles

a) What is the area of each square?

b) Which side is the hypotenuse of the triangle?

c) Write an addition statement showing the relationship between the areas of the three squares.

d) Describe, using words and symbols, the relationship between the side lengths of the triangle.

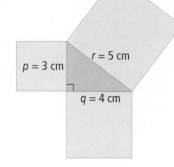

Solution

a)

$p = 3$ cm	$q = 4$ cm	$r = 5$ cm
$A = 3^2$	$A = 4^2$	$A = 5^2$
$A = 9$	$A = 16$	$A = 25$
The area is 9 cm².	The area is 16 cm².	The area is 25 cm².

b) Side r is the hypotenuse.

c) $9 + 16 = 25$

> This relationship is called the **Pythagorean relationship**.

d) The sum of the areas of the squares attached to legs p and q equals the area of the square attached to hypotenuse r.

For a right triangle with legs p and q and hypotenuse r, $p^2 + q^2 = r^2$.

Pythagorean relationship

- the relationship between the lengths of the sides of a right triangle
- The sum of the areas of the squares attached to the legs of a right triangle equals the area of the square attached to the hypotenuse.

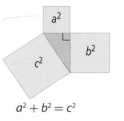

$a^2 + b^2 = c^2$

Show You Know

The sides of a right triangle are 9 cm, 12 cm, and 15 cm.

a) Sketch a picture of the triangle. Draw a square on each side of the triangle.

b) What is the area of each square?

c) Write an addition statement using the areas of the three squares.

Example 2: Identify a Right Triangle

A triangle has side lengths of 5 cm, 7 cm, and 9 cm.

a) What are the areas of the three squares that can be drawn on the sides of the triangle?

b) Is the triangle a right triangle? Explain your answer.

Solution

a) $5 \times 5 = 25$
The area is 25 cm².

$7 \times 7 = 49$
The area is 49 cm².

$9 \times 9 = 81$
The area is 81 cm².

b) Calculate the sum of the areas of the two smaller squares.
$25 + 49 = 74$
The sum of the areas is 74 cm². The sum does not equal the area of the large square. 74 cm² ≠ 81 cm²
The triangle is not a right triangle.

Show You Know

A triangle has side lengths of 12 cm, 16 cm, and 20 cm.

a) What are the areas of the three squares that can be drawn on the sides of the triangle?

b) Is the triangle a right triangle? Explain.

Key Ideas

- In a right triangle, the sum of the areas of the squares attached to the legs equals the area of the square attached to the hypotenuse.
- The Pythagorean relationship states that in a right triangle with sides s, t, and v, where side v is the hypotenuse, $v^2 = s^2 + t^2$.

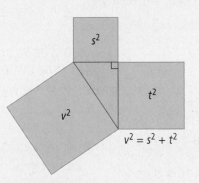

$v^2 = s^2 + t^2$

Communicate the Ideas

1. Describe, using words and symbols, the relationship among the areas of the three squares shown.

2. A triangle has side lengths of 7 cm, 11 cm, and 15 cm. Explain how you can determine whether or not it is a right triangle.

3. For the triangle shown, Kendra wrote the Pythagorean relationship as $r^2 = p^2 + q^2$. Is she correct? Explain.

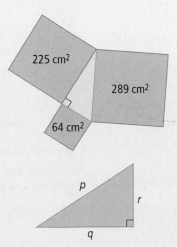

Practise

For help with #4 to #7, refer to Example 1 on page 90.

4. What are the areas of the three squares shown?

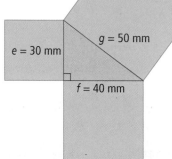

g = 50 mm
e = 30 mm
f = 40 mm

5. A right triangle has side lengths of 40 mm, 75 mm, and 85 mm.

a) Sketch the triangle. Draw a square on each side of the triangle.

b) What are the areas of the three squares?

c) Write an addition statement with the areas of the three squares.

6. a) Write an addition statement using the areas of these three squares.

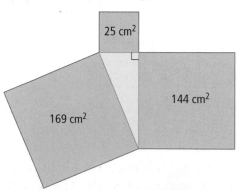

25 cm²

169 cm²

144 cm²

b) What is the side length of each square?

c) Describe, using words and symbols, the relationship between the side lengths of each square.

7. The sides of a right triangle measure 9 cm, 12 cm, and 15 cm.

a) What is the area of each square attached to the three sides of the right triangle?

b) Write an addition statement showing the relationship between the areas of the three squares.

c) Describe, using words and symbols, the relationship between the side lengths of each square.

For help with #8 to #11, refer to Example 2 on pages 90–91.

8. Is the triangle shown a right triangle? Explain your reasoning.

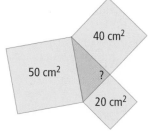

40 cm²
50 cm²
?
20 cm²

9. a) Calculate the areas of the three squares.

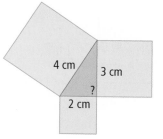

4 cm
3 cm
?
2 cm

b) Is this triangle a right triangle? Explain.

10. A triangle has side lengths of 120 mm, 160 mm, and 200 mm. Is the triangle a right triangle? Explain your reasoning.

11. The side lengths of a triangle are 5 cm, 6 cm, and 8 cm. Determine whether the triangle is a right triangle. Explain.

12. Use the Pythagorean relationship to find the unknown area of each square.

a)

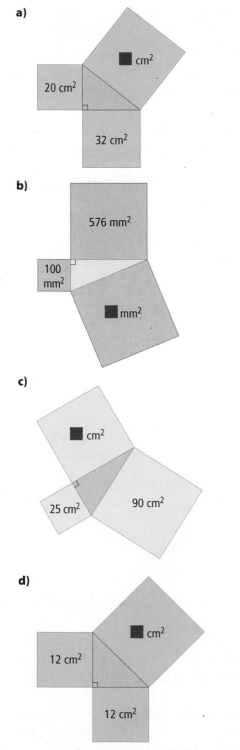

■ cm²

20 cm²

32 cm²

b)

576 mm²

100 mm²

■ mm²

c)

■ cm²

25 cm²

90 cm²

d)

■ cm²

12 cm²

12 cm²

13. A small triangular flower bed has a square stepping stone at each of its sides. Is the flower bed in the shape of a right triangle? Explain your reasoning.

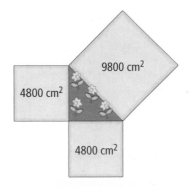

9800 cm²

4800 cm²

4800 cm²

14. Show whether each triangle in the table is a right triangle.

Triangle	Side Lengths (cm)
A	9, 12, 15
B	7, 8, 11
C	7, 24, 25
D	16, 30, 34
E	10, 11, 14

15. Construction workers have begun to dig a hole for a swimming pool. They want to check that the angle they have dug is 90°. They measure the diagonal as shown to be 9.5 m. Is the angle 90°? Explain your reasoning.

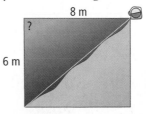

8 m

?

6 m

16. Baldeep is building a wooden box for storing coloured pencils. The box will have rectangular sides that are 12 cm wide and 20 cm long. Show how Baldeep can be sure the sides are rectangular, without using a protractor.

17. What is the area of the square that can be drawn on side c of each triangle?

a)
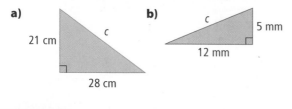
21 cm

c

28 cm

b)
c

5 mm

12 mm

Extend

18. The diagram is made of two right triangles and five squares.

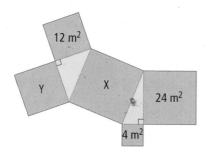

12 m²

Y

X

24 m²

4 m²

a) What is the area of square X?

b) What is the area of square Y?

19. A right triangle has a square attached to each side. Two of the squares have areas of 10 cm² and 15 cm². What are possible areas for the third square? Draw a sketch for each solution.

20. A right triangle has sides of 3 cm, 4 cm, and 5 cm. Attached to each side is a semi-circle instead of a square. Describe the relationship between the areas of the semi-circles.

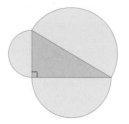

Literacy ⊖ Link

area of a circle $= \pi \times r^2$

21. An example of a Pythagorean triple is 3, 4, 5.

a) Multiply each number by 2. Show whether the resulting three numbers form a Pythagorean triple.

Did You Know?

A Pythagorean triple consists of three whole numbers that form the sides of a right triangle. For example, 3, 4, 5 make a Pythagorean triple because $3^2 + 4^2 = 5^2$.

b) Multiply each number in the triple 3, 4, 5 by a natural number other than 2. Show whether the results form a Pythagorean triple.

c) Is there any natural number that does not make a Pythagorean triple when 3, 4, 5 are multiplied by it? Explain.

MATH LINK

Identify the right triangle and three squares that complete this Pythagorean puzzle.

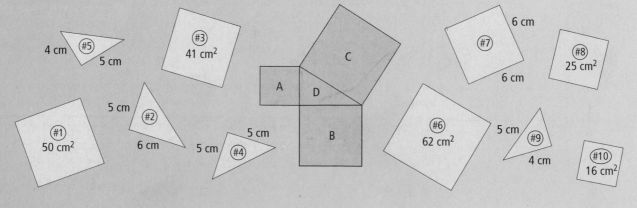

Estimating Square Roots

Focus on...

After this lesson, you will be able to...

- ☐ estimate the square root of a number that is not a perfect square
- ☐ identify a number with a square root that is between two given numbers

The picture shows three tatami mats that are used in judo. Can you think of a way to estimate the side length of the middle mat?

Explore the Math

How do you estimate a square root?

1. What is a reasonable estimate for the area of the middle mat in the picture?

2. What are the side lengths of the smallest and largest mats? Explain how you calculated these dimensions.

3. The number line below shows square roots of perfect squares. Copy the number line into your notebook. Complete the boxes.

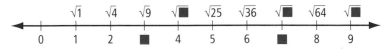

4. Use the number line to estimate the side length for the middle mat. Give your answer to one decimal place.

Reflect on Your Findings

5. a) Compare your estimate of the side length of the middle mat with a classmate's.

   b) Using a calculator, determine the square root of your estimate in #1. Give your answer to the nearest tenth. Compare this approximation to your estimate for the side length.

   c) Explain how you can use perfect squares to estimate a square root.

Example 1: Estimate the Square Root of a Number

Felicity wants to know if a wading pool will fit in a small space in her yard. She must estimate the side length of the square wading pool, which has an area of 7 m².

a) What is a reasonable estimate for the side length of the pool? Use perfect squares to estimate. Give your answer to one decimal place.

b) Use a calculator to approximate the side length of the pool, to the nearest tenth of a metre. Compare your estimate in part a) with the calculator's approximate answer.

Solution

a) The side length of the pool is the square root of 7.

The perfect squares on either side of 7 are 4 and 9.

Since 7 is closer to 9, the square root of 7 is closer to the square root of 9.

$\sqrt{9} = 3$
$\sqrt{7}$ will be a bit less than 3.
A reasonable estimate is 2.7 m.

Strategies

Estimate and Check

b) Approximate the square root of 7.

[C] 7 [√] 2.645751311

The answer to the nearest tenth of a metre is 2.6 m.
This answer is very close to the estimate of 2.7 m.

> This value is an approximation. The decimal portion of the exact answer continues forever. The calculator can display only ten digits. The square of the approximation shows that it is not an exact answer:
> $2.645751311^2 = 6.999999999658218721$
> ≈ 7

Show You Know

For each of the following, use perfect squares to estimate the square root to one decimal place. Check your answer with a calculator.

a) $\sqrt{18}$ **b)** $\sqrt{23}$ **c)** $\sqrt{35}$

Example 2: Identify a Number With a Square Root Between Two Numbers

a) What is a whole number that has a square root between 6 and 7?

b) How many whole numbers can you find that have a square root between 6 and 7? Show your work.

Solution

a) Determine the square of 6.

$6^2 = 36$

Determine the square of 7.

$7^2 = 49$

Draw a number line.

Find a value for ■ on the number line.
Choose any whole number between 36 and 49.
One possible whole number is 40.
$\sqrt{40}$ will have a value between 6 and 7.

Check:

C 40 √ 6.32455532

6.32455532 is between 6 and 7.
40 is a possible answer.

b) The possible answers are all of the whole numbers larger than 36 and smaller than 49:

37, 38, 39, 40, 41, 42, 43, 44, 45, 46, 47, 48

There are 12 whole numbers that have square roots between 6 and 7.

Show You Know

a) Identify a whole number with a square root between 8 and 9.

b) How many whole numbers can you find that have a square root between 8 and 9? Show your work.

Strategies

Estimate and Check

- To estimate the square root of a whole number that is not a perfect square,
  - locate the perfect squares on either side of the number
  - calculate the square roots of these two perfect squares
  - estimate based on the position between the two perfect squares

For example, estimate the square root of 17:
$\sqrt{17} \approx 4.1$

- To identify a whole number that has a square root between two given numbers,
  - determine the perfect squares of the two consecutive whole numbers
  - choose a whole number between the two perfect squares

For example, identify a whole number that has a square root between 5 and 6:
$5^2 = 25$ $6^2 = 36$
$\sqrt{30}$ will have a value between 5 and 6.

- When using a calculator to find the square root of a natural number that is not a perfect square, the value shown on the calculator is only an approximation.

  C 8 √   2.828427125

Communicate the Ideas

1. Explain how to estimate $\sqrt{28}$ to one decimal place without using a calculator. Compare your answer with a classmate's.

2. Find a whole number that has a square root between 3 and 4. Explain how you found it.

3. Jason is doing his math homework. He has to find the square root of 10. He presses √ 10 on his calculator and the screen displays 3.16227766. However, when 3.16227766 is multiplied by itself, the answer is not 10. Explain.

Practise

For help with #4 to #5, refer to Example 1 on page 96.

4. Estimate the square root of each number, to one decimal place. Check with a calculator.

a) 72   **b)** 103   **c)** 55

5. Estimate each value, to one decimal place. Check your answer with a calculator.

a) $\sqrt{14}$ **b)** $\sqrt{86}$ **c)** $\sqrt{136}$

For help with #6 to #9, refer to Example 2 on page 97.

6. What is an example of a whole number that has a square root between 9 and 10?

7. Identify a whole number with a square root between 11 and 12.

8. Identify all possible whole numbers with a square root larger than 2 and smaller than 3.

9. What are all possible whole numbers that have a square root between 4 and 5?

Apply

10. Kai uses an entire can of paint on a square backdrop for the school play. The label on the can states that one can covers 27 m² of wall surface. Estimate the backdrop's side length, to one decimal place.

11. The square has an area of 20 cm².

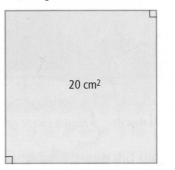

20 cm²

a) Use perfect squares to estimate the side length to one decimal place.

b) Check your answer using a ruler to measure the side of the square. Measure to the nearest tenth of a centimetre.

12. While shopping online, Ji Hun finds a square rug with an area of 11 m². He needs to know if it will fit in his 4 m × 5 m bedroom.

a) Estimate the side length of the rug, to one decimal place.

b) Check your estimate with a calculator.

c) Will the rug fit? Explain.

13. Stella is planning an outdoor wedding. She would like a square dance floor with an area of 115 m².

a) Determine the side length of the dance floor, to the nearest tenth of a metre.

b) Stella finds out that the dance floor will be made up of floorboards that each measure 1 m². What are the two side lengths the dance floor can have that are closest to what she wants?

c) What are the two square areas for the dance floor that Stella can choose from?

d) Which area will Stella choose? Explain.

14. Alex is thinking of a number.

The number has a square root between 7 and 8, and it is a multiple of 12.

a) What number could he be thinking of?

b) Is there more than one answer? Explain.

15. Order the following numbers from least to greatest: $7, \sqrt{46}, 5.8, \sqrt{27}, 6.3$.

16. A fitness centre will install a square hot tub in a 6 m × 6 m room. They want the tub to fill no more than 75% of the room's area.

a) What is the maximum area of the hot tub?

b) What dimensions, to a tenth of a metre, will the fitness centre order from the manufacturer? Explain.

17. Carmel wants to mount an 18 cm × 18 cm square picture on a square board that is four times the area of the picture.

a) What is the area of the picture?

b) What is the area of the board?

c) What are the dimensions of the board?

Extend

18. a) Evaluate $\sqrt{9}$.

b) Estimate the square root of your answer in part a), to one decimal place.

c) Use a calculator to check your estimate. Express your answer to the nearest hundredth.

d) How close is your estimate in part b) to your calculation in part c)?

19. Estimate $\sqrt{160\ 100}$. Explain how you determined your estimate.

20. What is the smallest natural number value for n if the solution for $\sqrt{56n}$ is also a natural number?

21. Determine two numbers that have a square root between 326 and 327, are divisible by 100, and are a multiple of 6.

MATH LINK

You have created a mini peg board game called Mind Buster. The square game board has a base area of 134 cm². You go to the store to get a box for storing the game. You find five boxes with the base dimensions shown.

a) Identify which boxes can store the game board. Explain.

b) Which box would you choose? Why?

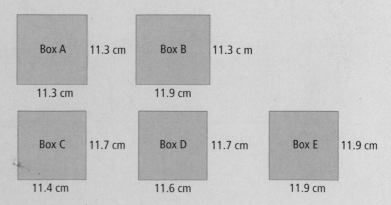

Box A — 11.3 cm — 11.3 cm

Box B — 11.3 cm — 11.9 cm

Box C — 11.7 cm — 11.4 cm

Box D — 11.7 cm — 11.6 cm

Box E — 11.9 cm — 11.9 cm

3.4

Using the Pythagorean Relationship

Focus on...

After this lesson, you will be able to...

❑ use the Pythagorean relationship to determine the missing side length of a right triangle

27 m

A baseball diamond is a square. How could you determine the distance from second base to home plate? How many different strategies can you develop?

Explore the Math

How do you determine the missing side length of a right triangle?

Materials
• centimetre grid paper
• ruler

1. On centimetre grid paper, draw a right triangle.

2. Describe two methods for finding the length of the hypotenuse of a right triangle.

Reflect on Your Findings

3. a) Describe a situation in which one method would be better to use than another.

b) Work with a partner to determine the distance from second base to home plate on a baseball diamond. Share your solution with another pair of classmates.

Example 1: Determine the Length of the Hypotenuse of a Right Triangle

Determine the length of hypotenuse c. Express your answer to the nearest tenth of a metre.

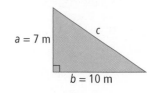
$a = 7$ m
c
$b = 10$ m

Solution

Use the Pythagorean relationship, $c^2 = a^2 + b^2$, where the length of the hypotenuse is c, and the lengths of the legs are a and b.

$c^2 = 7^2 + 10^2$
$c^2 = 49 + 100$
$c^2 = 149$
$c = \sqrt{149}$
$c \approx 12.2$

The length of the hypotenuse is approximately 12.2 m.

Show You Know

Determine the length of the hypotenuse for the right triangle, to the nearest centimetre.

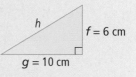
h
$f = 6$ cm
$g = 10$ cm

Example 2: Determine the Length of a Leg of a Right Triangle

What is the length of leg e of the right triangle?

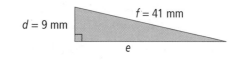
$d = 9$ mm
$f = 41$ mm
e

Solution

Use the Pythagorean relationship, $d^2 + e^2 = f^2$, where the length of the hypotenuse is f, and the lengths of the legs are d and e.

$9^2 + e^2 = 41^2$
$81 + e^2 = 1681$
$81 + e^2 - 81 = 1681 - 81$
$e^2 = 1600$
$e = \sqrt{1600}$
$e = 40$

Why do you subtract 81?

The length of the leg is 40 mm.

Show You Know

Determine the length of leg s of the right triangle.

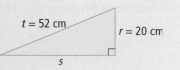
$t = 52$ cm
$r = 20$ cm
s

- The Pythagorean relationship can be used to determine the length of the hypotenuse of a right triangle when the lengths of the two legs are known.

$c^2 = a^2 + b^2$
$c^2 = 3^2 + 4^2$
$c^2 = 9 + 16$
$c^2 = 25$
$c = \sqrt{25}$
$c = 5$

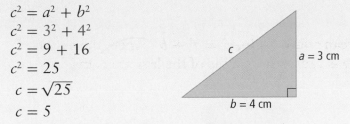

The length of hypotenuse c is 5 cm.

- The Pythagorean relationship can be used to determine the leg length of a right triangle when the lengths of the hypotenuse and the other leg are known.

$p^2 + q^2 = r^2$
$p^2 + 12^2 = 15^2$
$p^2 + 144 = 225$
$p^2 + 144 - 144 = 225 - 144$
$p^2 = 81$
$p = \sqrt{81}$
$p = 9$

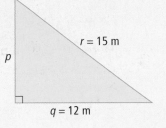

The length of leg p is 9 m.

Communicate the Ideas

1. Jack must determine the missing side length of a triangle. He decides to draw it and then measure it, as shown. Do you agree with the method that Jack is using? Explain.

2. Kira calculated the missing side length of the right triangle.

$y^2 = 5^2 + 13^2$
$y^2 = 25 + 169$
$y^2 = 194$
$y \approx 13.9$

The length of side y is approximately 13.9 cm.

$w = 5$ cm $x = 13$ cm y

Is Kira correct? If she is correct, explain how you know. If she is incorrect, explain the correct method.

Check Your Understanding

Practise

For help with #3 and #4, refer to Example 1 on page 102.

3. Determine the length of each hypotenuse.

a)
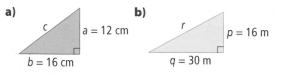
c, $a = 12$ cm, $b = 16$ cm

b)
r, $p = 16$ m, $q = 30$ m

4. What is the length of each hypotenuse? Give your answer to the nearest tenth of a centimetre.

a)
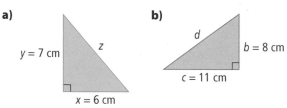
$y = 7$ cm, z, $x = 6$ cm

b)
d, $b = 8$ cm, $c = 11$ cm

5. a) What is the area of each square attached to the legs of the right triangle?

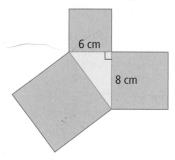
6 cm
8 cm

b) What is the area of the square attached to the hypotenuse?

c) What is the length of the hypotenuse?

For help with #6 and #7, refer to Example 2 on page 102.

6. Determine the length of the leg for each right triangle.

a)
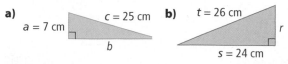
$a = 7$ cm, $c = 25$ cm, b

b)
$t = 26$ cm, r, $s = 24$ cm

7. What is the missing length of the leg for each triangle? Give your answer to the nearest tenth of a millimetre.

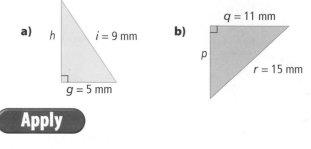

a)
h, $i = 9$ mm, $g = 5$ mm

b)
$q = 11$ mm, p, $r = 15$ mm

Apply

8. The side view of a ramp at a grocery store is in the shape of a right triangle. Determine the length of the ramp, to the nearest centimetre.

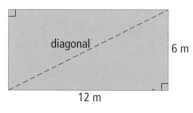
50 cm
200 cm

9. Tina wants to construct a path along the diagonal of her yard. What length will the path be? Express your answer to the nearest tenth of a metre.

diagonal
6 m
12 m

10. What is the minimum distance the player at third base has to throw the ball to get the runner out at first base? Express your answer to the nearest tenth of a metre.

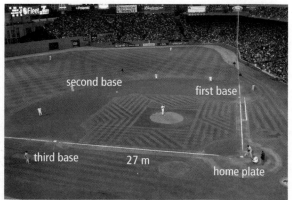
second base
first base
third base   27 m
home plate

11. The right triangle below has a square attached to its hypotenuse. What is the perimeter of the triangle? Give your answer to the nearest tenth of a centimetre.

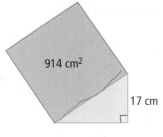

12. The hypotenuse of the triangle cuts the circle in half. What is the diameter of the circle? Express your answer to the nearest tenth of a centimetre.

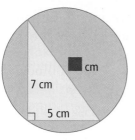

13. Determine the length of the base of the large triangle. Express your answer to the nearest tenth of a millimetre.

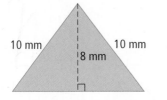

14. What are the lengths of b and c? Write your answer to the nearest tenth of a metre where appropriate.

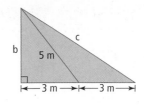

Extend

15. The coordinate grid shown was drawn on centimetre grid paper. What is the length of line segment AB? Express your answer to the nearest tenth of a centimetre.

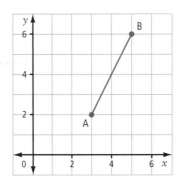

16. What is the length of the red diagonal in the box? Express your answer to the nearest tenth of a millimetre.

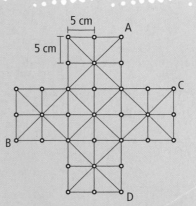

MATH LINK

For each of the following questions, express your answer to the nearest tenth of a centimetre.

a) What is the distance between A and B? Explain.

b) If you have to follow the lines on the game board, what is the shortest distance between C and D?

c) If you do not have to follow the lines on the game board, what is the shortest distance between C and D? Justify your answer.

Applying the Pythagorean Relationship

A ship leaves the Pacific coast of British Columbia and travels west for 10 km. Then, it turns and travels north. When the ship is 25 km from its starting point, how could you use the Pythagorean relationship to determine the distance the ship travelled north?

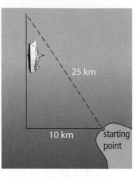

Explore the Math

How can you determine a distance using the Pythagorean relationship?

The diagram shows Sam's trip to school.

1. a) Work with a partner to determine how far his house is from the school.

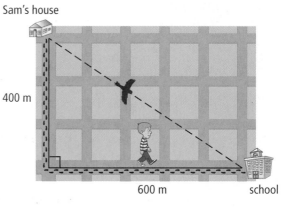

b) Share your answer with your classmates. Is there more than one possible answer? Explain.

2. a) What do you think the expression "as the crow flies" means?

b) How much farther does Sam travel than the crow? Show your method.

Reflect on Your Findings

3. Why is the path that the crow takes from Sam's house to the school difficult to measure directly?

Example 1: Determine Distances With Right Triangles

a) Anthony and Shalima are canoeing on a lake in Saskatchewan. There are two boat ramps on the lake. How far is it by canoe between the boat ramps?

b) How much farther is it for someone to travel by road from ramp A to ramp B than to canoe between the two ramps?

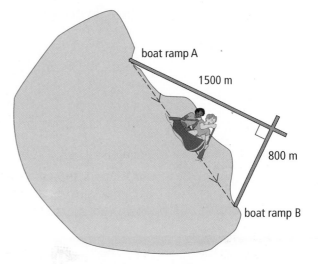

boat ramp A

1500 m

800 m

boat ramp B

Solution

a) The two roads leading from the boat ramps make the legs of a right triangle. The distance by canoe is the hypotenuse.

Let d represent the distance by canoe.

Use the Pythagorean relationship.
$d^2 = 1500^2 + 800^2$
$d^2 = 2\,250\,000 + 640\,000$
$d^2 = 2\,890\,000$
$d = \sqrt{2\,890\,000}$
$d = 1700$
The distance by canoe is 1700 m.

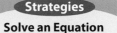

Strategies

Solve an Equation

Strategies

What other method could you use to solve this problem?

b) Determine the total distance by road between the boat ramps.
$1500 + 800 = 2300$
The total distance by road is 2300 m.

Determine the difference between the two distances.
$2300 - 1700 = 600$
It is 600 m farther to travel by road than by canoe between the boat ramps.

Show You Know

Refer to the opening paragraph and picture on page 106. A ship leaves the Pacific coast of British Columbia and travels west for 10 km. Then, it turns and travels north. If the boat is 25 km from its starting point, what distance did it travel north? Give your answer to the nearest tenth of a kilometre.

Example 2: Verify a Right Angle Triangle

Danelle is trying to install a corner shelf in her bedroom. Since the shelf does not fit properly, she thinks the two walls in her bedroom do not meet at a right angle. She measures a length of 30 cm along the base of each wall away from the corner. Then, she measures the hypotenuse to be 41 cm. Do the walls meet at a right angle? Explain.

Solution

Strategies

Draw a Diagram

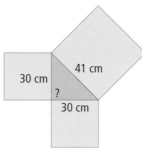

Strategies

What other method could you use to solve this problem?

Use the Pythagorean relationship to determine whether the triangle is a right triangle.

Determine whether the sum of the areas of the two smaller squares equals the area of the large square.

Left Side:
$$30^2 + 30^2 = 900 + 900$$
$$= 1800$$
The sum of the areas of the two smaller squares is 1800 cm².

Right Side:
$$41^2 = 1681$$
The area of the large square is 1681 cm².

$$1800 \text{ cm}^2 \neq 1681 \text{ cm}^2$$

The triangle is not a right triangle. The walls do not meet at a right angle.

Show You Know

A construction company is digging a rectangular foundation with a width of 17 m and a length of 20 m. To check that a corner is a right angle, a worker measures the diagonal length, which is 26.25 m. Is the corner a right angle? Explain.

- The Pythagorean relationship can be used to determine distances that might be difficult or impossible to measure.

$d^2 = 500^2 + 1200^2$
$d^2 = 250\,000 + 1\,440\,000$
$d^2 = 1\,690\,000$
$d = \sqrt{1\,690\,000}$
$d = 1300$

The hypotenuse is 1300 m.

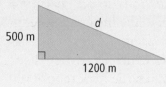

- The Pythagorean relationship can be used to show if a triangle is a right triangle.

Left Side:
$6^2 + 8^2 = 36 + 64$
$\qquad\quad = 100$
The sum of the areas of the two smaller squares is 100 cm².

Right Side:
$10^2 = 100$
The area of the large square is 100 cm².

$$100 \text{ cm}^2 = 100 \text{ cm}^2$$

The triangle is a right triangle.

Communicate the Ideas

1. Use an example from real life to explain how you can apply the Pythagorean relationship to calculate distance.

2. Ilana used the following method to determine whether the diagram shows a right triangle.

Left Side:
The large square is 61 cm.

Right Side:
$11 + 60 = 71$
The two smaller squares are 71 cm.

$61 \text{ cm} \neq 71 \text{ cm}$

The triangle is not a right triangle.

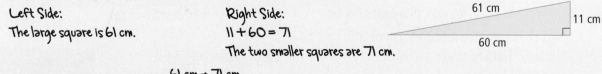

Is Ilana's method correct? If it is correct, explain how you know. If it is incorrect, explain the method Ilana should use.

Practise

For help with #3 and #4, refer to Example 1 on page 107.

3. Walter walks across a rectangular field in a diagonal line. Maria walks around two sides of the field. They meet at the opposite corner.

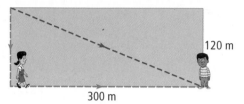

a) How far did Maria walk?

b) How far did Walter walk? Express your answer to the nearest metre.

c) Who walked farther? By how much?

4. Find the height of the pole where the guy wire is attached, to the nearest tenth of a metre.

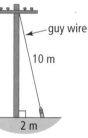

guy wire
10 m
2 m

For help with #5 and #6, refer to Example 2 on page 108

5. Martin measured a rectangle and wrote:

Width: 9 cm   Length: 22 cm   Diagonal: 23.8 cm

Could these measurements form a rectangle? Justify your answer.

6. You are asked to check the design plans for a baseball diamond. Is the triangle a right triangle? Explain.

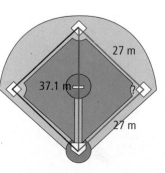

27 m
37.1 m
27 m

Apply

7. What is the height of the wheelchair ramp? Give your answer to the nearest tenth of a centimetre.

80 cm
79 cm

8. Shahriar knows that the size of a computer monitor is based on the length of the diagonal of the screen. He thinks that the diagonal is not as large as the ad says. Is he correct? Explain.

GREAT DEAL
42-cm monitor on sale!

25 cm
30 cm

9. A checkerboard is made of 64 small squares that each have a dimension of 3 cm × 3 cm. The 64 small squares are arranged in eight rows of eight.

a) What is the length of the diagonal of a small square? Give your answer to the nearest tenth of a centimetre.

b) What is the total length of the diagonal of the board? Give your answer to the nearest centimetre.

10. A gymnast requires a distance of 16 m for her tumbling routine. If the gymnast is competing on a 12 m × 12 m square mat, does she have enough room to do her routine safely? Explain your answer.

11. Johan has a 300-cm ladder that he leans up against a wall. The safety sticker on the side of the ladder shows that the bottom must be placed between 70 cm and 110 cm away from the wall. What are the minimum distance and maximum distance up the wall that the ladder can reach? Give your answers to the nearest tenth of a centimetre.

Extend

12. Sarah has a vegetable garden in the shape of a right triangle. She wants to put fencing all around it to keep the rabbits away.

a) What total length of fencing does she need? Give your answer to the nearest hundredth of a metre.

b) If fencing costs $2/m, what will be the total cost of the fencing?

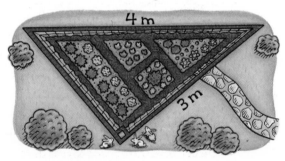

13. A cruise ship travels from Port Cassett north at a speed of 34 km/h for 2.5 h. Then it turns 90° and travels west at 30 km/h for 7.3 h. When it reaches Green Sea Island, how far is the ship from Port Cassett? Express your answer to the nearest kilometre.

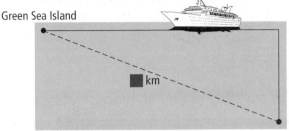

Green Sea Island

■ km

Port Cassett

14. The red square has a perimeter of 40 mm and the green square has an area of 4 mm². What is the shortest distance between A and B? Give your answer to the nearest tenth of a millimetre.

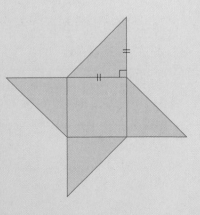

MATH LINK

The diagram shows the rough plans for a board game designed for a toy manufacturer. The board is composed of a square and four identical right triangles. Complete the plans by answering the following questions. Give your answers to the nearest tenth of a centimetre where appropriate.

a) If the central square has an area of 225 cm², what is the perimeter of the game board? Show how you know.

b) The game will be packaged in a box with a square base. Determine the minimum diagonal length of the base of the box.

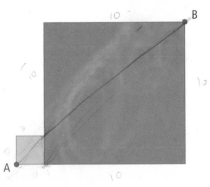

Key Words

For #1 to #5, write in your notebook the terms from the list that complete the sentences below.

hypotenuse   perfect square
prime factorization   Pythagorean relationship
square root

1. The ▮▮▮ ▮▮▮ of 36 is 6.

2. The number 25 is a ▮▮▮ ▮▮▮ because it is the product of the same two factors, $5 \times 5 = 25$.

3. In a right triangle, the longest side is known as the ▮▮▮.

4. If the sides of a right triangle are a, b, and c, and c is the longest side, the equation $c^2 = a^2 + b^2$ is known as the ▮▮▮ ▮▮▮.

5. The ▮▮▮ ▮▮▮ of 18 is $2 \times 3 \times 3$.

3.1 Squares and Square Roots, pages 80–87

6. Determine the square of each number.

    a) 6   **b)** 11   **c)** 25

7. Determine each square root.

    a) $\sqrt{49}$

    b) $\sqrt{256}$

    c) $\sqrt{100\,000\,000}$

8. Lisa needs at least 17 m² of fabric to make curtains. Is this square piece of fabric large enough? Show your work.

4 m

3.2 Exploring the Pythagorean Relationship, pages 88–94

9. A triangle has squares on each of its sides.

    a) Is the triangle a right triangle? Explain.

    b) What is the length of each of the three sides?

36 cm²

16 cm²

?

16 cm²

10. Is the triangle a right triangle? Explain.

$v = 15$ cm

$w = 36$ cm

$x = 39$ cm

11. The table shows the side lengths of four triangles. Which triangles are right angled?

Triangle	Side x	Side y	Side z
A	9	12	15
B	5	6	7
C	12	35	37
D	30 000	40 000	50 000

3.3 Estimating Square Roots, pages 95–100

12. Cliffmount School is creating invitations for its 50th anniversary celebration. There are three possible designs.

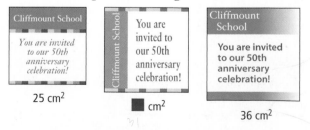

25 cm²   ▮ cm²   36 cm²

    a) What is a possible whole number area for the middle invitation?

b) What is the side length of the smallest one? the largest one?

c) What is an estimate for the side length of the middle invitation? Express your answer to one decimal place.

d) With a calculator, use the area in part a) to check the side length in part c). Give your answer to the nearest tenth of a centimetre.

13. Use the number line to answer the following questions.

a) What is an estimate for $\sqrt{10}$? Give your answer to one decimal place.

b) Is $\sqrt{6}$ closer to 2 or 3? Explain.

c) A calculator shows that the approximate square root of a certain whole number is 3.61. What is a reasonable value for this whole number? Explain.

3.4 Using the Pythagorean Relationship, pages 101–105

14. Find the missing side length of each triangle.

a)

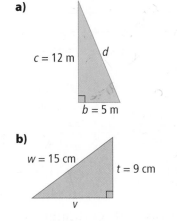

$c = 12$ m
d
$b = 5$ m

b)

$w = 15$ cm
$t = 9$ cm
v

15. The coordinate grid shown was drawn on centimetre grid paper. Answer the following questions to the nearest tenth of a centimetre where appropriate.

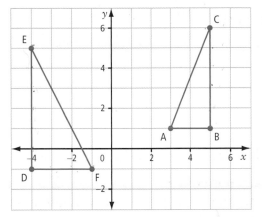

a) What is the length of the hypotenuse in △ABC? in △DEF?

b) What is the perimeter of △DEF?

3.5 Applying the Pythagorean Relationship, pages 106–111

16. A 4-m ladder is being used for a production of *Romeo and Juliet*. The bottom of the ladder will be placed 1 m from the base of Juliet's house. Will the ladder reach the window? Show your work.

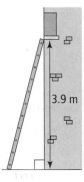

3.9 m

17. Yosef wants to buy a hutch. It must fit in the 90° corner of his dining room. Yosef measures as shown. What should his measurement be? Give your answer to the nearest tenth of a centimetre.

70 cm
70 cm

3 Practice Test

For #1 to #5, choose the best answer.

1. Which number is a perfect square?

   A 10   **B** 20

   C 50   **D** 100

2. What is the side length of the square in the diagram?

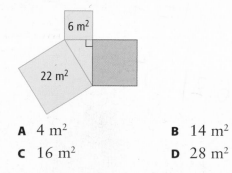

81 mm²

   A 6 mm   **B** 9 mm

   C 12 mm   **D** 18 mm

3. A square has a side length of 7 cm. What is the area of the square?

   A 14 cm²   **B** 21 cm²

   C 28 cm²   **D** 49 cm²

4. A right triangle has squares on each of its sides. What is the area of the blue square?

6 m²

22 m²

   A 4 m²   **B** 14 m²

   C 16 m²   **D** 28 m²

5. The value of $\sqrt{51}$ is closest to which whole number?

   A 7   **B** 8

   C 49   **D** 51

Complete the statements in #6 and #7.

6. For a right triangle with sides a, b, and c, the Pythagorean relationship is $c^2 = a^2 + b^2$. The variable that represents the length of the hypotenuse is ■.

7. A square has an area of 53 cm². When you calculate the side length of the square, to the nearest tenth, the answer is ■.

Short Answer

8. The legs of a right triangle measure 3 cm and 7 cm.

   a) Use a calculator to determine the approximate length of the hypotenuse, to the nearest tenth of a centimetre.

   b) Explain why the length is an approximation both before and after you round the answer.

9. The rectangular pool at Wild Water World has a length that measures 15 m and a diagonal that measures 17 m. A float line divides the shallow end and deep end. What is the length of the float line?

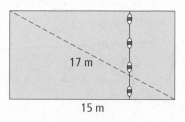

17 m

15 m

10. a) Identify a whole number that has its square root between 7 and 8.

   b) How many whole numbers have a square root between 7 and 8? Identify these whole numbers.

11. Use the Pythagorean relationship to determine whether a triangle with sides of 14 mm, 48 mm, and 50 mm is a right triangle. Show your work.

12. Josie skated diagonally across a rectangular ice rink. Han is skating along two sides of the rink and has just reached the first corner. How much farther does he have to skate to meet up with Josie?

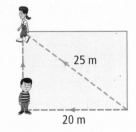

25 m

20 m

Extended Response

13. Determine the perimeter of △ABC.

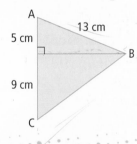

A

13 cm

5 cm

B

9 cm

C

14. A carpenter's square is a tool in the shape of a right triangle. Joe thinks there may be something wrong with the one he bought. Determine whether the carpenter's square shown is a right triangle. Explain your reasoning.

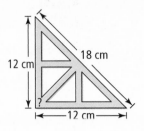

12 cm

18 cm

12 cm

15. The prime factorization of 15 876 is $2 \times 2 \times 3 \times 3 \times 3 \times 3 \times 7 \times 7$.

a) How can you use prime factorization to determine that 15 876 is a perfect square?

b) Use a calculator to check that 15 876 is a perfect square. Show your work.

c) Explain how you can calculate $\sqrt{15\,876}$ using its prime factors.

WRAP IT UP!

Create a game of your own. Include squares and right triangles in the game board. Write rules for your game.

The design of your board or the way you play your game needs to cover the following concepts:
- calculating the square of a number
- calculating the square root of a perfect square
- estimating the square root of a non-perfect square
- using the Pythagorean relationship to determine if a triangle is a right triangle
- determining the missing side length of a right triangle

Show how you have covered the concepts.

Math Games

It's Prime Time

Materials
• 2 dice per pair of students

1. Play It's Prime Time! with a partner. These are the rules:
   • Each player rolls one die to decide who will play first. If there is a tie, roll again.
   • For each turn, roll one die twice. The result of the first roll gives the first digit of a two-digit number. The result of the second roll gives the second digit of the number. For example, if you roll a 5 and then a 2, your number is 52.
   • Determine the prime factorization of the two-digit number. For example, the prime factorization of 52 is $2 \times 2 \times 13$.
   • Determine the sum of the factors in the prime factorization. This sum is your score for the turn. For instance, for a roll of 52, your score is 17 points.
   • Score zero points for the turn if the two-digit number is a prime number. For example, if you roll 41, which is a prime number, your score is zero.
   • Score ten bonus points for the turn if the two-digit number is a perfect square. For instance, if you roll 16, which is a perfect square, your score is 18 points.
   • The first player to reach 100 points wins.

$2 + 2 + 13 = 17$

The prime factorization of 16 is
$2 \times 2 \times 2 \times 2$.
$2 + 2 + 2 + 2 = 8$
Adding the 10 bonus points gives a score of 18 points.

2. Play a different version of the game by modifying the rules as follows:
   • For each turn, roll both dice together.
   • Record the results in either order to make the two-digit number. For example, if you roll a 2 and a 4, you can choose either 24 or 42 as your two-digit number.
   • Award points and decide the winner in the same way as before.

Challenge in Real Life

Building a Staircase

Carpenters are well known for their skill in mental math. By studying the blueprint of a house plan, they are able to build many parts of the house such as walls, floors, and stairs.

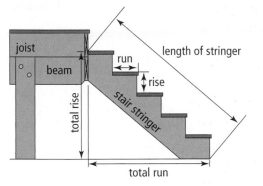

You be the carpenter! Your task is to calculate the length of a stringer for a staircase. The staircase has five steps. Each step has a rise of 18 cm and a run of 24 cm.

1. What is the total rise of the staircase?

2. What is the total run of the staircase?

3. Using the Pythagorean relationship, calculate the length of a piece of wood needed to make the stringer.

4. A retirement residence wants you to build a number of step stools for its residents. Each step stool should be two steps high. Each step should have a rise of 13 cm and a run of 26 cm.
   a) Design and label a step stool.
   b) To the nearest centimetre, calculate the length of stringer needed for the stool.

4

Understanding Percent

Water is crucial to the health of Earth and to your own health. About 71% of Earth's surface is covered by water. Of all the water on Earth, 97.5% is salt water, and the remaining 2.5% is fresh water. About 70% of the fresh water is permanently frozen. Only about 0.007% of all water on Earth is fresh water that is accessible for direct human use.

The human body is 60% water. To maintain a healthy balance, it is recommended that humans drink plenty of water each day. Maintaining adequate body water content during illness contributes significantly to the recovery process.

In this chapter, you will use percents to explore and learn more about the world's most valuable liquid—water. Think of some facts you already know about water. How are percents used to describe these facts?

What You Will Learn

- ❏ to describe a situation where a percent may be more than 100%, may be between 0% and 1%, or contains a fractional portion
- ❏ to use grids to represent percents that are between 0% and 1%, and those that are greater than 100%
- ❏ to find the percent represented by a given shaded region on a grid and record it in decimal, fraction, and percent form
- ❏ to convert between percents, fractions, and decimals
- ❏ to solve problems involving percents and combined percents

Literacy Link

You can use a concept map to visually organize your understanding of a math concept such as percent.

Copy the concept map below into your math journal or notebook. Make each shape large enough to write in. Write what you already know about percents.

- Definition: What is a percent?
- Comparisons: What can you compare percents to?
- Facts: What are some facts or characteristics you know about percents?
- Examples: What are some examples of percents?

Share your ideas with a classmate. You may wish to add to or correct what you have written.

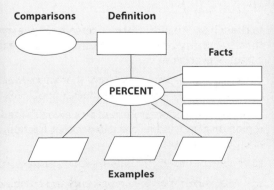

Making the Foldable

Materials

- three sheets of notebook paper
- ruler
- stapler
- three hundred grids
- scissors
- transparent tape or glue

Step 1

Collect three sheets of paper and place them 2 cm apart. Keep the edges straight.

Step 2

Fold the top edge of the paper. Stop 2 cm from the bottom edge of the top sheet. This makes all tabs the same size. Staple together along the fold.

2 cm

Step 2

Label the tabs as shown.

Chapter 4:
Understanding Percent
4.1 Representing Percents
4.2 Fractions, Decimals, and Percents
4.3 Percent of a Number
4.4 Combining Percents
What I Need to Work On

Step 3

Cut out three hundred grids. Tape or glue them, side by side, inside the flap of Section 4.1.

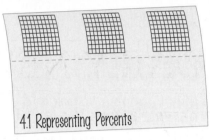

4.1 Representing Percents

Using the Foldable

As you work through Chapter 4, make notes about Key Words, examples, and Key Ideas under the appropriate tab. Use the hundred grids to show what you learn about percents in section 4.1.

On the last tab, make notes for the heading What I Need to Work On. Check off each item as you deal with it.

Use the back of the Foldable to record your ideas for the Wrap It Up!

MATH LINK

Water Conservation

Conserving water is a key step to making a difference to the world's fresh water supply.

Read the following article.

THE DAILY NEWS

Rainforest Town Suffers Water Shortages

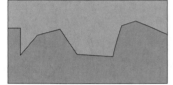

Residents and businesses in Tofino, a small seaside town on Vancouver Island, have been asked to restrict their water use. This popular resort town attracts 15 000 to 20 000 visitors a day during the summer, doubling water consumption rates. The old water reservoir is not large enough to deal with such demands.

Rather than shut down the popular resort, residents have been asked to restrict their water usage, including no watering of gardens and lawns, or washing of sidewalks, driveways, and vehicles. Ironically, this seaside town is one of the wettest places in Canada, receiving more than three metres of precipitation each year. Most of the rain falls during the winter, however.

1. Why might Tofino need to restrict water use?

2. Why might other communities have water restrictions?

3. What kinds of water restrictions might there be?

4. If you usually shower for 20 min, what percent of water would you save by showering for 1 min less?

5. What percent savings in water might there be if you change from a 10 L/min showerhead to an 8.5 L/min showerhead?

In this chapter, you will use percents to learn about one of our most valuable resources—water. What ways can you think of to conserve water at home and at school?

Representing Percents

After this lesson, you will be able to...

❏ **show percents that are between 0% and 1%**

❏ **show percents that are greater than 100%**

❏ **show percents involving fractions**

People often read nutrition labels on food products to determine the **percent** of the recommended daily value (RDV) of nutrients the food contains. By reading these labels you can make wiser food choices to help maintain a healthy lifestyle.

The nutrition label on a certain brand of grape juice says that one 250-mL glass of juice contains 130% of the RDV of Vitamin C, 2% of the RDV of iron, and 1% of the RDV of sodium. Half a glass would contain 65% of the RDV of Vitamin C, 1% of the RDV of iron, and $\frac{1}{2}$% of the RDV of sodium. You have seen how to represent a percent like 65% on a grid. How might you use grids to represent 130% or $\frac{1}{2}$%?

---

percent

- means *out of 100*
- another name for hundredths
- 65% means 65 out of 100 or $\frac{65}{100}$ or 0.65.

Explore the Math

How can you represent percents on a grid?

1. a) The hundred grid shows 100%. How many squares are shaded?

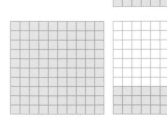

b) Explain how the following diagram shows 130%.

c) Shade hundred grids to show 350%. How many squares did you shade?

Materials

- hundred grids
- coloured pencils

2. a) Shade a hundred grid to show half of 100%. How many squares did you shade? What percent of the whole grid do the shaded squares represent?

b) Shade a hundred grid to show half of your answer to part a). How many squares did you shade? What percent of the whole grid do the shaded squares represent?

c) Shade a hundred grid to show half of your answer to part b). How many squares did you shade? What percent of the whole grid do the shaded squares represent?

d) How does the type of number represented by the percent value in part c) differ from the types of numbers in parts a) and b)? Explain why.

3. The circled square represents 1% on the hundred grid shown.

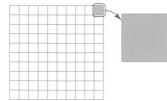

a) What fraction of the enlarged square would you need to shade to show half of 1%? What percent of the whole grid would your shaded portion represent?

b) What fraction of a 1% square would you need to shade to represent $\frac{3}{4}$%?

c) What fraction of a 1% square would you need to shade to represent 0.37%?

Reflect on Your Findings

4. Describe how to use grids to represent the following types of percent values.

a) percents greater than 100%

b) percents between 0% and 1%

c) percents containing a mixed number greater than 1%

Example 1: Determine the Percent Represented on a Grid

One completely shaded grid represents 100%. What percent does each diagram represent?

a)

b)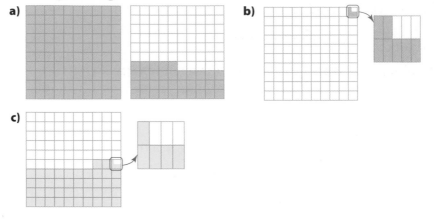

c)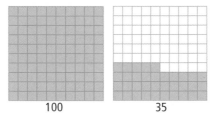

Solution

a) Each grid is divided into 100 squares. A completely shaded grid represents 100%.

The first grid is completely shaded. There are 100 squares shaded.

In the second grid, there are three full rows of ten shaded and five squares shaded in the fourth row. There are 35 squares shaded.

There are a total of 135 squares shaded.

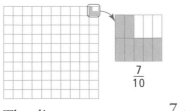

100   35

This diagram represents 135%.

b) Since a portion of only one square of a hundred grid is shaded, the percent represented is between 0% and 1%. You can *zoom in* on the partially shaded square and count the number of shaded parts. The enlarged diagram shows seven out of a total of ten parts shaded.

The shading represents $\frac{7}{10}$ or 0.7 of 1% of the whole diagram.

$\frac{7}{10}$

The diagram represents $\frac{7}{10}$% or 0.7%.

c) The diagram shows 42 squares shaded plus a portion of another square.

You can *zoom in* on the partially shaded square to determine the fraction that is shaded.

The enlarged diagram shows $\frac{5}{8}$ shaded.

The shading represents $\frac{5}{8}$ of 1% of the whole diagram.

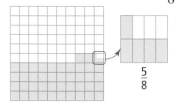

$\frac{5}{8}$

The diagram represents $42\frac{5}{8}\%$.

Show You Know

One completely shaded grid represents 100%. What percent does each diagram represent?

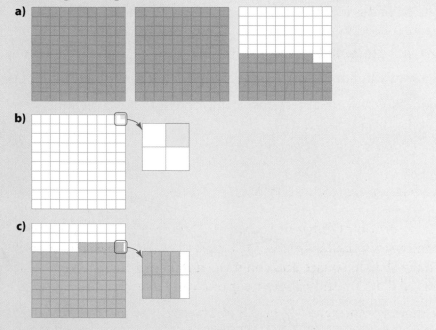

a)

b)

c)

Example 2: Represent Percents on a Grid

Represent the percent in each statement on a grid.

a) An orange juice container shows that one 250-mL serving contains 120% of the recommended daily value of Vitamin C.

b) A significant portion of the world's fresh water is found in Canada, but Canada has only 0.5% of the world's population.

c) A credit card company charges an interest rate of $18\frac{3}{4}\%$ on unpaid balances.

Solution

a) Since 120% is greater than 100%, more than one hundred grid is needed.

You can represent 100% by completely shading one grid. You can represent 20% by shading 20 squares of a second hundred grid.

b) 0.5% is a **fractional percent** between 0% and 1%. *Zoom in* on one square of a hundred grid. Since 0.5 represents $\frac{1}{2}$, divide the enlarged square into two equal sections. Shade one of the two sections.

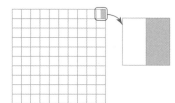

c) $18\frac{3}{4}\%$ is a fractional percent between 1% and 100%.

Use one hundred grid.

Shade 18 squares to represent 18%.

Shade $\frac{3}{4}$ of another square to represent $\frac{3}{4}\%$.

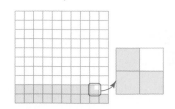

Represent each percent on a grid.

a) 180%   **b)** 0.6%   **c)** $12\frac{3}{8}\%$

Key Ideas

- To represent a percent, you can shade squares on a grid of 100 squares called a hundred grid. One completely shaded grid represents 100%.

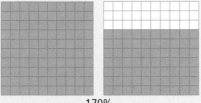

45%

- To represent a percent greater than 100%, shade more than one grid.

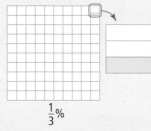

170%

- To represent a fractional percent between 0% and 1%, shade part of one square.

$\frac{1}{3}\%$

- To represent a fractional percent greater than 1%, shade squares from a hundred grid to show the whole number and part of one square from the grid to show the fraction.

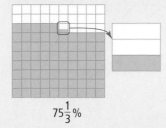

$75\frac{1}{3}\%$

Communicate the Ideas

1. Use hundred grids and words to describe the similarities and differences between a percent less than 1%, a percent between 1% and 100%, and a percent greater than 100%.

2. **a)** You are asked to show a classmate how to use hundred grids to show 243%. How do you explain which squares need shading?

   b) Explain how you would represent $25\frac{1}{4}\%$ on a grid.

3. Shindi commented to a friend that "some percents would be easier to show if we shaded the parts that were not included in the percent." Explain what she means. Which percents are easier to show using Shindi's method? Why?

Check Your Understanding

Practise

For help with #4 and #5, refer to Example 1 on pages 124–125.

4. One full grid represents 100%. What percent does each diagram represent?

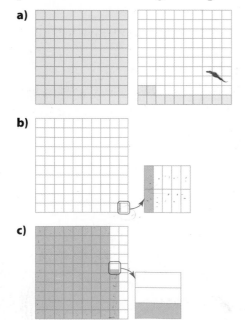

5. What percent is represented by each diagram if a completely shaded grid represents 100%?

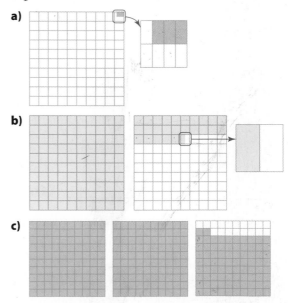

For help with #6 and #7, refer to Example 2 on page 126.

6. Represent each percent on a grid.

   a) 125%   **b)** $10\frac{1}{2}\%$ **c)** 0.4%

   d) 262%   **e)** $\frac{7}{8}\%$ **f)** 45.6%

7. Represent the percent in each statement on a grid.

a) Attendance at the fall fair increased by 3.2% this year.

b) The average mass of a Singapura cat is about 0.13% of the mass of a Siberian tiger.

c) The length of the Yukon River is about 230% of the length of the Fraser River.

8. How many hundred grids are needed to show each of the following percents?

a) 300%   **b)** 466%   **c)** 1200%

Apply

9. Give two examples where a percent greater than 100% might be found in everyday life.

10. Why might a scientist studying water pollution work with percents less than one?

11. The land area of Alberta is about 113% of the land area of Saskatchewan. Use hundred grids to show how the land area of Alberta compares with the land area of Saskatchewan.

12. A 250-mL glass of milk contains 30% of the recommended daily value of calcium. Use a hundred grid to show how many glasses of milk you would need to drink to get 100% of the daily value of calcium.

Extend

13. a) Use a calculator to convert $\frac{1}{3}$ to a decimal. How could $\frac{1}{3}$% be shown using a hundred grid?

b) Why are percents involving repeating decimals sometimes difficult to show on a hundred grid?

14. a) If 200 squares were used instead of 100 squares to represent 100%, how would you show 0.25%?

b) If 400 squares were used instead of 100 squares to represent 100%, how would you show 0.75%?

15. Show how hundred grid(s) could be used to represent a very small percent, such as 0.000 0125%.

16. Suppose one large square represents 100%. The square is divided into smaller equal-sized pieces.

a) If there are 1000 pieces, what percent do 17 pieces represent?

b) If there are two large squares each divided into ten smaller pieces, what percent do 13 pieces represent?

c) If the large square is divided into eight smaller pieces, show how to represent $87\frac{1}{2}$% and $56\frac{1}{4}$%.

MATH LINK

Use hundred grids to represent the following data.

97.5% of Earth's Water is Salt Water

2.5% of Earth's Water is Fresh Water

0.04% of Fresh Water Found in Earth's Atmosphere

$\frac{3}{10}$% of Fresh Water Found in Lakes and Rivers

0.007% of Fresh Water Accessible for Drinking Water

Fractions, Decimals, and Percents

The period was not bad with 90% of the shots saved by the home team goalie. The second period saw 150% as many shots on goal, yet an amazing 0.9333 save performance held the home team in the game. But, how many ways can you spell disaster? In the third period, the home team goaltender let in two easy goals for a dismal 66⅔% of shots on goal stopped.

Sports commentators often use statistics to report on the performance of a goalie. Commentators often change the way the information is presented to make it sound more interesting.

How did the sports commentator use the information from the following table in the report on the goalie's performance?

Goalie Statistics				
Period	Shots on Goal	Saves	Goals Against	Save Percent
1	10	9	1	90%
2	15	14	1	$93\frac{1}{3}$%
3	6	4	2	$66\frac{2}{3}$%

Explore the Math

How are percents related to fractions and decimals?

1. a) What fraction of this figure is shaded?

   b) Rewrite your fraction with a denominator of 100.

   c) Express the fraction shaded as a decimal.

   d) What percent of the figure is shaded?

2. Suppose you want to shade one half as many sections as in #1. Show the area that will be shaded on a new diagram. How much of the diagram will you shade? Express your answer as a fraction, a decimal, and a percent.

3. Suppose you want to shade three times as many sections as in #1. If one large square represents one whole, how many squares will you need to draw to show this situation? How many squares will you shade? Express your answer as a fraction, a decimal, and a percent.

Reflect on Your Findings

4. a) How are the decimal, percent, and fraction representations of a number the same? How are they different?

   b) Which representations do you prefer to work with? Why?

Example 1: Convert Fractions to Decimals and Percents

Convert each fraction to a decimal and a percent.

a) $\dfrac{1}{20}$ **b)** $\dfrac{71}{200}$ **c)** $\dfrac{9}{8}$

Solution

a) Percent means out of 100. So, $\dfrac{1}{20} = \dfrac{x}{100}$.

You could represent this using a hundred grid.

5 of 100 squares are coloured.

So, $\dfrac{1}{20} = \dfrac{5}{100}$. That is 5% or 0.05.

Sometimes you interpret $\dfrac{1}{20}$ as $1 \div 20 = 0.05$.

0.05 can be expressed as 5%.

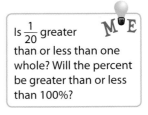

Is $\dfrac{1}{20}$ greater than or less than one whole? Will the percent be greater than or less than 100%?

b) $\dfrac{71}{200} = \dfrac{x}{100}$

   $x = 35.5$

How do you know x = 35.5?

That is 35.5% or 0.355.

You could interpret $\dfrac{71}{200}$ as $71 \div 200 = 0.355$.

0.355 can be expressed as 35.5%.

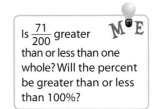

Is $\dfrac{71}{200}$ greater than or less than one whole? Will the percent be greater than or less than 100%?

c) $\dfrac{9}{8}$ can be expressed as $\dfrac{8}{8} + \dfrac{1}{8} = 1 + \dfrac{1}{8}$.

One whole represents 100%.

You know that $\dfrac{1}{4}$ represents 25%. So, $\dfrac{1}{8}$ represents 12.5%.

$\dfrac{9}{8}$ can be expressed as $100\% + 12.5\% = 112.5\%$.

You could also interpret $\dfrac{9}{8}$ as $9 \div 8 = 1.125$.

1.125 can be expressed as 112.5%.

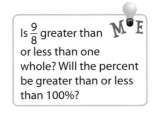

Is $\dfrac{9}{8}$ greater than or less than one whole? Will the percent be greater than or less than 100%?

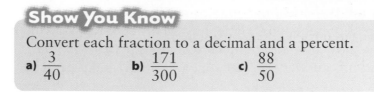

Show You Know

Convert each fraction to a decimal and a percent.

a) $\dfrac{3}{40}$ b) $\dfrac{171}{300}$ c) $\dfrac{88}{50}$

Example 2: Convert Decimals to Percents and Fractions

Convert each decimal to a percent and a fraction.

a) 3.26   b) 0.125   c) 0.0032

Solution

a) Use hundred grids.

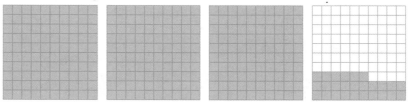

$3.26 = 3$ full hundred grids plus 26 squares

That is $\dfrac{326}{100} = 326\%$.

$3.26 = 3\dfrac{26}{100}$ or $3\dfrac{13}{50}$.

Since 13 is a prime number, $3\dfrac{13}{50}$ is in lowest terms.

$\dfrac{326}{100}$ can also be expressed as $\dfrac{163}{50}$ or $3\dfrac{13}{50}$ in lowest terms.

> What would you divide into both the numerator and denominator of $\dfrac{326}{100}$ to get $\dfrac{163}{50}$?

b) $0.125 = \dfrac{125}{1000}$ since the 5 is in the thousandths place.

0.125 can also be expressed as $\dfrac{12.5}{100}$ or 12.5%.

$\dfrac{125}{1000} = \dfrac{1}{8}$

> What factors of 125 divide evenly into 1000?

> How do you know $\dfrac{125}{1000}$ and $\dfrac{12.5}{100}$ are equivalent?

c) $0.0032 = \dfrac{32}{10\,000}$ since the 2 is in the ten thousandths place.

0.0032 can also be written as $\dfrac{0.32}{100}$ or 0.32%.

$\dfrac{32}{10\,000} = \dfrac{2}{625}$

> What factors of 32 divide evenly into 10 000?

> How do you know that $\dfrac{32}{10\,000}$ and $\dfrac{0.32}{100}$ are equivalent?

Show You Know

Convert each decimal to a percent and a fraction.

a) 0.0064   b) 0.268   c) 5.98

Example 3: Convert Percents to Fractions and Decimals

Convert each percent to a decimal and a fraction.

a) 160% **b)** 0.35% **c)** $25\frac{3}{5}\%$

Solution

a) You could represent 160% using hundred grids.

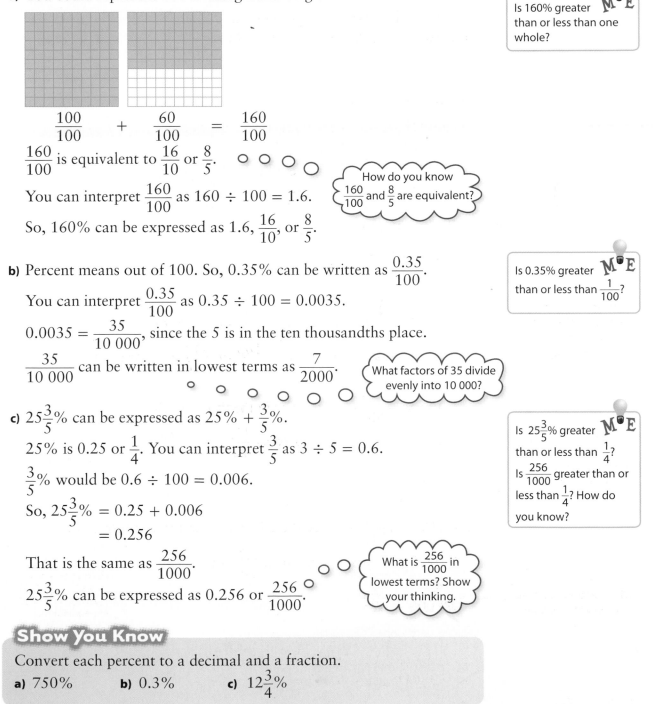

$$\frac{100}{100} \quad + \quad \frac{60}{100} \quad = \quad \frac{160}{100}$$

$\frac{160}{100}$ is equivalent to $\frac{16}{10}$ or $\frac{8}{5}$.

You can interpret $\frac{160}{100}$ as $160 \div 100 = 1.6$.

So, 160% can be expressed as 1.6, $\frac{16}{10}$, or $\frac{8}{5}$.

> Is 160% greater than or less than one whole?

> How do you know $\frac{160}{100}$ and $\frac{8}{5}$ are equivalent?

b) Percent means out of 100. So, 0.35% can be written as $\frac{0.35}{100}$.

You can interpret $\frac{0.35}{100}$ as $0.35 \div 100 = 0.0035$.

$0.0035 = \frac{35}{10\,000}$, since the 5 is in the ten thousandths place.

$\frac{35}{10\,000}$ can be written in lowest terms as $\frac{7}{2000}$.

> Is 0.35% greater than or less than $\frac{1}{100}$?

> What factors of 35 divide evenly into 10 000?

c) $25\frac{3}{5}\%$ can be expressed as $25\% + \frac{3}{5}\%$.

25% is 0.25 or $\frac{1}{4}$. You can interpret $\frac{3}{5}$ as $3 \div 5 = 0.6$.

$\frac{3}{5}\%$ would be $0.6 \div 100 = 0.006$.

So, $25\frac{3}{5}\% = 0.25 + 0.006$

$\qquad\qquad = 0.256$

That is the same as $\frac{256}{1000}$.

$25\frac{3}{5}\%$ can be expressed as 0.256 or $\frac{256}{1000}$.

> Is $25\frac{3}{5}\%$ greater than or less than $\frac{1}{4}$?
> Is $\frac{256}{1000}$ greater than or less than $\frac{1}{4}$? How do you know?

> What is $\frac{256}{1000}$ in lowest terms? Show your thinking.

Show You Know

Convert each percent to a decimal and a fraction.

a) 750% **b)** 0.3% **c)** $12\frac{3}{4}\%$

Example 4: Determine a Percent

For the past century, the north magnetic pole has been drifting across the Canadian Arctic. Prior to the 1970s, the magnetic pole was drifting at an average speed of 10 km/year. Since the 1970s, the speed at which the magnetic pole has been drifting has increased to about 50 km/year. The circumference of Earth is approximately 40 000 km.

a) What percent is the current speed of the original speed?

b) The circumference of Earth is approximately 40 000 km. At 50 km/year, what percent of Earth's circumference will the pole drift in one year?

Solution

a) The current speed is 50 km/year.
The original speed is 10 km/year.

Divide to find what percent the current speed is of the original speed.

$$\frac{50}{10} = 5$$

Percent means out of 100. So, $5 = \frac{500}{100}$.

So, $5 = 500\%$

The current speed is 500% of the original speed.

b) The circumference of Earth is 40 000 km.
The distance the pole drifts in one year is 50 km.

The amount of Earth's circumference travelled in one year is represented by

$$\frac{50}{40\ 000} = \frac{1}{800}$$

$$= 0.001\,25$$

$0.00125 = 0.125\%$

At 50 km/year, the pole will drift 0.125% or $\frac{1}{8}\%$ of Earth's circumference in one year.

> 0.125 is equivalent to the fraction $\frac{1}{8}$.

Show You Know

Suppose that the speed at which the pole is drifting increased to 75 km/year.

a) What percent is 75 km/year of the original speed?

b) At 75 km/year, what percent of 40 000 km would the pole drift in one year?

- Fractions, decimals, and percents can be used to represent numbers in various situations.
- Percents can be written as fractions and as decimals.

$$\frac{1}{2}\% = 0.5\% \qquad\qquad 150\% = \frac{150}{100}$$
$$0.5\% = \frac{0.5}{100} \qquad\qquad\qquad = 1.5 \text{ or } 1\frac{1}{2}$$
$$\qquad\quad = 0.005$$

$$42\frac{3}{4}\% = 42.75\%$$
$$42.75\% = \frac{42.75}{100}$$
$$\qquad\quad = 0.4275$$

Communicate the Ideas

1. Kaitlyn and Jordan are converting 0.003 to a percent. Who is correct? Show how you know.

   Kaitlyn: Jordan:
   $0.003 = 3\%$ $0.003 = 0.3\%$

2. Which number does not have the same value as the other three? Explain your reasoning.

   $\frac{12}{5}$ 2.4   250% $\frac{60}{25}$

3. Teammates Mark and Jonas are discussing the outcome of a game. Mark says their team scored 500% as many goals as the other team and Jonas says they scored five times as many goals as the other team. Can they both be correct? Explain how you know.

Check Your Understanding

Practise

For help with #4 and #5, refer to Example 1 on page 131.

4. Convert each fraction to a decimal and a percent.

   a) $\frac{1}{250}$ b) $\frac{81}{200}$ c) $\frac{7}{5}$

5. Rewrite each fraction as a decimal and a percent.

   a) $\frac{51}{30}$ b) $\frac{21}{200}$ c) $\frac{3}{500}$

For help with #6 and #7, refer to Example 2 on page 132.

6. Convert each decimal to a percent and a fraction.

   a) 0.0072   b) 0.548   c) 3.45

7. Change each decimal to a percent and a fraction.

a) 0.256 b) 0.0005 c) 6.5

For help with #8 and #9, refer to Example 3 on page 133.

8. Convert each percent to a decimal and a fraction.

a) 248% b) 0.56% c) $75\frac{3}{4}\%$

9. Express each percent as a decimal and a fraction.

a) $5\frac{9}{10}\%$ b) 550% c) 0.8 %

10. Copy and complete the following table. The first row is completed for you.

Percent	Fraction	Decimal
165%	$\frac{165}{100}$	1.65
a) 230%		
b) 0.38%		
c) 19.9%		

11. Express the shaded portion of each diagram as a fraction, a decimal, and a percent.

a)

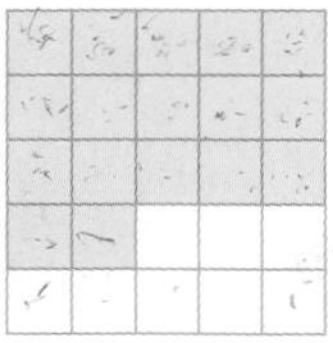

b)

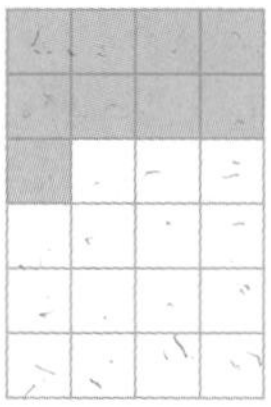

12. If one completely shaded grid represents one whole, express the shaded portion of each diagram as a fraction, a decimal, and a percent.

a)

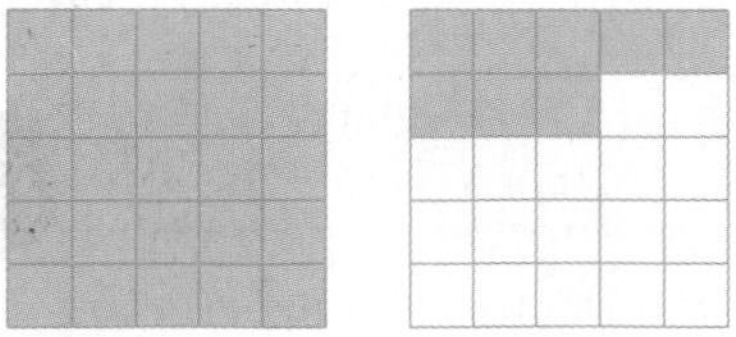

b)

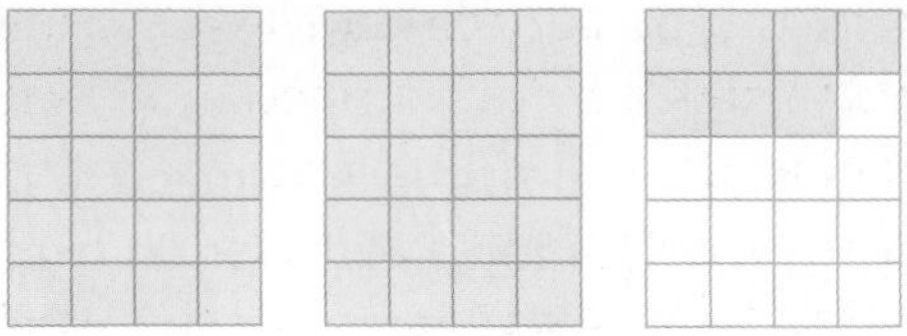

Apply

For help with #13 and #14, refer to Example 4 on page 134.

13. Several years ago Claire bought the first issue of a popular comic book for $10. At a recent auction, it sold for $200. What percent is the new value of the comic book of the price several years ago?

14. A snack contains 0.9 g of fat. Suppose that in one day, Shaun consumed a total of 40 g of fat, including the snack. What percent of Shaun's total fat consumption does the snack represent? What is this percent as a decimal and as a fraction?

15. Use hundred grids to help place the following numbers in ascending order.

145%, $\frac{5}{8}\%$, 1.32, 0.65, 33.5%, 0.6%

16. A miner found 12 g of gold in a 2700-g sample of ore. What percent of the sample is gold, to the nearest tenth of a percent? What is the percent as a repeating decimal and as a fraction in lowest terms?

Literacy Link

A repeating decimal contains a digit or group of digits that repeat forever. You can write a repeating decimal using bar notation.

$0.333\ 33\ldots = 0.\overline{3}$ $0.454\ 545\ldots = 0.\overline{45}$

17. A fundraising coordinator is preparing an advertising flyer for an upcoming event. She wants to use either a fraction or a decimal number to represent each of the percents in the following statements. Decide whether a fraction or a decimal number is better and rewrite each statement using your chosen representation. Justify your choices.

a) Ticket sales are 130% of what they were at this time last year.

b) We are already at $60\frac{1}{2}$% of our target and we just started!

c) We have managed to cut our costs by 0.75%.

18. A fisheries worker recorded the following species and numbers of fish passing by a fish counter. Copy and complete the following table.

Species	Number	Percent of Total	Fraction of Total	Decimal Equivalent
Chinook	143			
Coho	122			
Steelhead	2			

19. Over five years, the circulation of a magazine increased from 25 000 copies to 150 000 copies. What percent is the new circulation of the circulation five years ago? What is this percent as a decimal and as a fraction?

20. Kim's resting heart rate was 75 beats per minute. A trainer advised Kim to have a portion of her workout at 90 beats per minute and a portion at 125 beats per minute, but not to exceed 150 beats per minute. Express each heart rate compared to the resting heart rate as a percent, a fraction, and a decimal.

Extend

21. Copy and complete the first three rows of the table. Use the patterns in the first three rows to complete the last two rows.

Percent	Decimal	Fraction
a) 1000		
b)	5.00	
c)		$\frac{5}{2}$
d)		
e)		

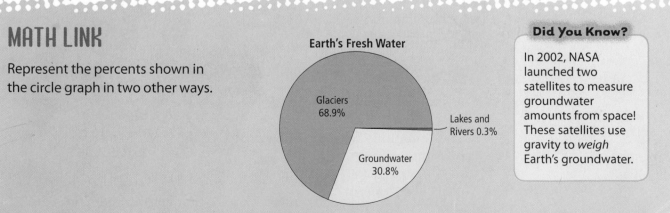

MATH LINK

Represent the percents shown in the circle graph in two other ways.

Earth's Fresh Water

Glaciers 68.9%

Lakes and Rivers 0.3%

Groundwater 30.8%

4.3 Percent of a Number

Focus on...

After this lesson, you will be able to...

- ❏ solve problems that involve percents less than 1%
- ❏ solve problems involving percents greater than 100%
- ❏ solve problems involving fractional percents

You often use percents to make comparisons and help make decisions.

A fundraising team is raising money for a relief organization. The team wants to use their profits for several purposes.

How could the team use percents to decide how much money to donate for each purpose?

Literacy ⊖ Link

Profit is the amount of money left over after all expenses are paid.

Explore the Math

How can you solve problems involving percents?

Last year the fundraising team ran a school store and made $50\frac{1}{2}$% profit. The school store usually has total sales of about $10 000 per year.

1. a) How much is 50% profit?

b) How much is 1% profit?

c) How much is $\frac{1}{2}$% profit?

d) How much is $50\frac{1}{2}$% profit?

2. The committee wants to donate 10% of the store profits for providing food.

a) What is 10% of the profit calculated in #1d)?

b) How could you determine 10% of a number mentally? Explain.

3. The committee knows that access to clean drinking water is critical in preventing serious illness. They would like to donate 20% of their profits for providing clean drinking water. How could you determine 20% of the profits mentally using your answer to #2?

4. Oral rehydration therapy (ORT) is a simple yet inexpensive medicine designed to fight dehydration.

   a) If it costs $0.10 to prepare 1 L of ORT solution, how many litres of ORT can be prepared using the money from the $\frac{1}{2}$% portion of the store profits?

   b) If the average adult needs about 4 L of ORT for adequate rehydration, how many adults can be treated using the $\frac{1}{2}$% profit?

Reflect on Your Findings

5. How can you use mental math techniques to help you find the percent of a number?

Did You Know?

Oral rehydration therapy (ORT) is a mixture of water, salt, and sugar. It is used to restore necessary water content to people who have become dehydrated because of illness or a lack of proper drinking water. What do you think is the purpose of the salt and the sugar?

Example 1: Use Mental Math to Find the Percent of a Number

Use mental math to determine each of the following.

   a) 150% of $5   **b)** 0.1% of $1000   **c)** $1\frac{1}{2}$% of $20 000

Solution

   a) 150% is 100% + 50%.
   100% of 5 is 5.
   50% is half of 100%.

   Use halving to find 50% of 5.
   Half of 5 is 2.5.

   150% of 5 is 5 + 2.5.
   5 + 2.5 = 7.5

   So, 150% of $5 is $7.50.

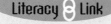

Literacy Link

Halve means divide by two.
Double means multiply by two.

   b) To determine 0.1% of $1000, divide repeatedly by tens.
   100% of 1000 is 1000.
   10% of 1000 is 100.
   1% of 1000 is 10.
   0.1% of 1000 is 1.

   So, 0.1% of $1000 is $1.

Strategies

Look for a Pattern

You could also **M E** determine 1.5% of $20 000 as:

30% of 20 000 is 6000.

3% of 20 000 is 600.

1.5% of 20 000 is 300.

c) Divide repeatedly by tens to reach 1%, and then divide by two.

100% of 20 000 is 20 000.

10% of 20 000 is 2000.

1% of 20 000 is 200.

$\frac{1}{2}$% of 20 000 is 200 ÷ 2.

200 ÷ 2 = 100

$1\frac{1}{2}$% of 20 000 is 200 + 100.

200 + 100 = 300

So, $1\frac{1}{2}$% of $20 000 is $300.

Show You Know

Use mental math to determine each of the following.

a) 350% of $10

b) 0.1% of $5000

c) $2\frac{1}{10}$% of $20 000

Example 2: Calculate the Percent of a Number

a) A survey showed that $\frac{1}{4}$% of 800 students use inline skates to get to school. How many of the 800 students in a school use inline skates to get to school?

b) $30\frac{3}{4}$% of 400 students surveyed said they own a cell phone. How many of the students own a cell phone?

c) Adele invested $40.12 in a savings plan at the beginning of the year. By the end of the year her investment was worth 120% of its original value. How much was her investment worth, to the nearest cent?

Literacy Link

In math, the word of often means to multiply.

10% of 800 is 80. **M E**

1% of 800 is 8.

$\frac{1}{4}$% of 800 is 2.

Solution

a) Determine $\frac{1}{4}$% of 800.

$\frac{1}{4}$% = 0.25%

Divide by 100 to write the percent as a decimal.

0.25 ÷ 100 = 0.0025

0.0025 of 800 = 0.0025 × 800   **C** .0025 **×** 800 **=** 2.
                = 2

So, two students out of 800 students used inline skates to get to school.

b) Determine $30\frac{3}{4}\%$ of 400.

Since $\frac{3}{4}\%$ is 0.75%, $30\frac{3}{4}\% = 30.75\%$.

Divide by 100 to write the percent as a decimal.

$30.75 \div 100 = 0.3075$

0.3075 of $400 = 0.3075 \times 400$ <kbd>C</kbd> **.3075** <kbd>×</kbd> **400** <kbd>=</kbd> `123.`

$\qquad\qquad\qquad = 123$

So, 123 of the 400 students own a cell phone.

> 10% of 400 is 40. **M E**
> 30% of 400 is 120.
> 1% of 400 is 4.
> $\frac{1}{4}\%$ of 400 is 1.
> $\frac{3}{4}\%$ of 400 is 3.
> $30\frac{3}{4}\%$ of 400 is $120 + 3$.
> $120 + 3 = 123$

c) Determine 120% of $40.12.

Divide by 100 to write the percent as a decimal.

$120 \div 100 = 1.2$

1.2 of $40.12 = 1.2 \times 40.12$ <kbd>C</kbd> **1.2** <kbd>×</kbd> **40.12** <kbd>=</kbd> `48.144`

$\qquad\qquad\quad \approx 48.14$

So, 120% of $40.12 is $48.14.

> To the nearest cent means to the nearest hundredth of a dollar.

> 100% of 40.12 is **M E**
> 40.12.
> 10% of 40.12 is 4.012.
> 20% of 40.12 is 8.024.
> 120% of 40.12 is
> $40.12 + 8.024$.
> $40.12 + 8.024 = 48.144$

Show You Know

Determine the percent of each number.

a) 160% of $53.27

b) $\frac{3}{4}\%$ of 135

c) $55\frac{8}{10}\%$ of 500

Key Ideas

- You can use mental math strategies such as halving, doubling, and dividing by ten to find the percents of some numbers.
- To calculate the percent of a number, write the percent as a decimal and then multiply by the number.

$12\frac{1}{2}\%$ of $50 = 0.125 \times 50$
$\qquad\qquad\quad = 6.25$

> $12\frac{1}{2}\% = 12.5\%$
> $\qquad\quad = 0.125$

Communicate the Ideas

1. Explain to a classmate how you could use mental math to find each of the following.

   a) 300% of 40   **b)** 0.5% of 120   **c)** $10\frac{1}{2}\%$ of 80

2. Describe two ways to find 6% of 120.

Practise

For help with #3 and #4, refer to Example 1 on pages 139–140.

3. Use mental math to determine each of the following.
   a) 300% of 2000
   b) $1\frac{1}{4}$% of 60
   c) 0.1% of 40

4. Use mental math to find the following.
   a) 20% of 60
   b) 250% of 400
   c) $10\frac{1}{2}$% of 100

For help with #5 and #6, refer to Example 2 on pages 140–141.

5. Determine the percent of each number. Give your answer to the nearest hundredth.
   a) $\frac{2}{5}$% of 325
   b) $15\frac{1}{4}$% of 950
   c) 175% of $125.50

6. What is the percent of each number? Give your answer to the nearest hundredth.
   a) $\frac{5}{8}$% of 520
   b) $75\frac{2}{5}$% of 200
   c) 250% of $76.50

Apply

7. Two hundred tickets are being sold for a school draw.
   a) What is your chance of winning with one ticket? Express your answer as a percent.
   b) How many tickets would you need to purchase to have a 2.5% chance of winning?

8. The original price of a jacket was $84.00. A store manager marked the price down by $25\frac{1}{2}$%. By how much was the price reduced?

9. The highest point in Canada is Mount Logan, which is in the Yukon Territory. Mount Logan is 159% as high as the highest point in Alberta, Mount Columbia. The elevation of Mount Columbia is 3747 m. What is the elevation of Mount Logan?

10. When water freezes, its volume increases by approximately 10%.
   a) By how much does the volume of 750 mL of water increase when it freezes?
   b) What is the volume of ice created?

11. The area of Canada is approximately 9 984 670 km². The area of Manitoba is about $6\frac{1}{2}$% of the area of Canada. What is the area of Manitoba to the nearest square kilometre?

12. A manufacturer of electric hybrid vehicles claims its vehicle will travel 200% as far as its regular vehicle on a full tank of gas. If the regular vehicle travels an average of 550 km on a full tank, how far will the hybrid go?

13. Suppose a real estate agent receives 5% commission on the first $200 000 of a house's selling price, and 6% on the remaining amount.

a) What does *commission* mean?

b) If a house sells for $345 000, how much commission does the real estate agent make on the sale of the house?

Extend

14. 4% of 100 is the same as 8% of what number? Explain how you arrived at your answer.

15. A new video gaming system was auctioned on the Internet. The starting bid was $100. The second bid was 135% of the first bid. The third bid was 257% of the second bid. There were then five more bids, each $10\frac{1}{2}$% over the previous bid. The winning bid came with only seconds left and was only 0.1% greater than the previous bid. What was the winning bid? What assumptions did you make to arrive at your answer?

16. Josephine scored 12 baskets out of 30 shots in her first basketball game this year. Her scoring average was then 40%. The next game, she made ten shots and raised her scoring average for both games to 50%. How many of the ten shots in the second game were baskets?

MATH LINK

Water conservation is very important to protect local fresh water supplies.

a) Research at least three ways that your home, school, and community could reduce water consumption.

b) Develop three water math problems that ask how much water you might save if you used some of these ways of conserving.

WWW Web Link

Did you know that a swimming pool cover can help reduce water loss by evaporation by 90%? To find data and tips on conserving water, go to www.mathlinks8.ca and follow the links.

4.4 Combining Percents

Focus on...

After this lesson, you will be able to...

☐ solve problems involving combined percents

Literacy Link

PST means provincial sales tax. PST varies by province.

GST means goods and services tax. GST is the same across Canada.

Jesse and Jenna have $55 to purchase prizes for a school fundraiser. The items cost $49.99 plus 5% GST and 7% PST. Do you think they will have enough money?

When they reach the cashier, they discover that the store has a one-day sale—they only have to pay 50% of the tax. How much tax do you think they will have to pay?

Explore the Math

How can you combine percents?

1. A store advertises 40% off. You purchase an item regularly priced at $100.

   SALE **40%** OFF REGULAR PRICES

   a) What is the discount for the item?

   b) What is the sale price of the item?

   c) What percent of the original price are you paying?

   d) How are the percent discount and the percent of the original price related? Use a grid to explain your answer.

   e) How could you estimate the price of something that has a 40% discount?

2. Suppose GST is 5% and PST is 7%. You purchase an item for $100.

   a) Represent the GST and the PST on a hundred grid.

   b) How much is the GST? the PST?

   c) How much tax do you pay altogether?

   d) What is your total tax as a percent of $100? How does this percent value compare to the sum of the percent values for GST and PST?

   e) What decimal could you multiply $100 by to find the total cost including tax?

3. Suppose an item regularly priced at $200 is on sale for 10% off. PST is 7% and GST is 5%.

   a) Write a multiplication expression to show how to determine the price of the item with the 10% discount applied.

   b) Write a multiplication expression to show how to determine the total amount of tax on the item in part a).

   c) What is the total cost of the item including tax?

4. Caroline purchased a sweatshirt originally priced at $50. It was on sale for 25% off. The PST where she lives is 5%. The GST is 5%.

   a) What is the cost of the sweatshirt before tax?

   b) Caroline used the single expression 10% of 75% of $50 to determine the total amount of tax. Explain why Caroline's expression is correct.

Reflect on Your Findings

5. a) Describe two ways that you can calculate the total tax on an item.

   b) Which method do you prefer to use? Explain why.

Example 1: Combined Percents

Suppose GST is 5% and PST is 7%. Calculate the total tax and total cost of a sound system that is priced at $250.

Solution

Method 1: Calculate the Taxes Separately
The GST is 5%.
5% is 0.05.
Multiply by the price to determine the amount of GST.
$0.05 \times 250 = 12.5$
The amount of GST is $12.50.

Did You Know?

In Saskatchewan, PST is 5%. In Alberta there is no PST. The city of Lloydminster, Saskatchewan, is half in Alberta!

A provincial law states that no PST is paid in the whole city. What might be a reason for the law?

The PST is 7%.
7% is 0.07.
Multiply by the price to determine the amount of PST.
$0.07 \times 250 = 17.5$
The amount of PST is $17.50.

Add the two tax amounts.
$12.50 + 17.50 = 30.00$.
The total tax is $30.00.
Total Cost = Cost of Item + Total Tax
$$= 250.00 + 30.00$$
$$= 280.00$$
The total cost of the sound system is $280.00.

Literacy Link

You can combine percents by adding individual percent values together.

Method 2: Combine the Tax Percents First
The GST is 5%. The PST is 7%.
The combined tax is 5% + 7% or 12%.
Convert the percent to a decimal.
$12\% = 0.12$
Multiply by the price to determine the total amount of tax.
$0.12 \times 250 = 30$
The total tax is $30.00.

Total Cost = Cost of Item + Total Tax
$$= 250.00 + 30.00$$
$$= 280.00$$
The total cost of the sound system is $280.00.

Method 3: Combine the Cost and Tax Percents
You could use a percent greater than 100% to find the total cost.
The cost of the sound system is 100%.
The PST is 7%.
The GST is 5%.
The cost of the sound system expressed as a percent of the original cost is 100% + 7% + 5% or 112%.
Convert the percent to a decimal.
$112\% = 1.12$
Multiply by the price to determine the total cost.
$1.12 \times 250 = 280$
The total cost of the sound system is $280.00.

Show You Know

A backpack costs $35. Use the method of your choice to find the total cost of the backpack if GST is 5% and PST is 6%. Use another method to check your work.

Example 2: Percent of a Percent

Sports R Us offers a 10% off discount one day and then an additional 10% off the sale price the next day. Sports Galore offers a 20% discount on one day only. Keifer wants to buy a new goalie mask that has a regular price of $200 at both stores.

a) Which store gives the better buy? Explain your reasoning.

b) What single percent discount is equivalent to a discount of 10% one day followed by an additional discount of 10% off the sale price the second day?

Solution

a) *Sports R Us*

The discount on the first day is 10% of $200.

10% of 200 = 0.10 × 200
= 20

Subtract to find the discount price.

200 − 20 = 180

The discount price on the first day is $180.

The discount on the sale price the second day is 10% of $180.

10% of 180 = 0.10 × 180
= 18

Subtract to find the discount price.

180 − 18 = 162

The discount price after the second day is $162.

Sports Galore

The discount is 20% of $200.

20% of 200 = 0.20 × 200
= 40

Subtract to find the discount price.

200 − 40 = 160

The discount price is $160.

Sports Galore gives a better buy than Sports R Us. The 10% discount followed by another 10% discount is not the same as a 20% discount because the discount on the second day is only 10% of $180 and not 10% of $200.

b) The original price is $200.

The selling price after two 10% discounts at Sports R Us is $162.

Subtract to find the total amount of the discount.

200 − 162 = 38

The total amount of the discount is $38.

Determine what percent the total discount is of the original price.

$$\frac{38}{200} = 0.19$$

The total discount is 19% of the original price.

A 19% discount is less than the single discount of 20% offered by Sports Galore.

What is the final sale price at each store? Which is a better buy? Explain your thinking.

Store A: 50% off one day only

Store B: 25% off one day followed by 25% off the reduced price the second day

Key Ideas

- Percents can be combined by adding to solve problems. $5\% + 7\% = 12\%$
- To calculate the increase in a number,
  - You can add the combined percent amount to the original number.

    12% of $100 = 0.12 \times 100 = 12$

    $100 + 12 = 112$

  - You can multiply the original number by a single percent greater than 100.

    112% of $100 = 1.12 \times 100$

    $= 112$

- Percents of percents can be used to determine amounts that result from consecutive percent increases or decreases.

Communicate the Ideas

1. Draw a diagram to show how you could represent the cost of a $100 item with and without tax.

2. Your friend shows you how to calculate the cost of an item including tax using several steps. You tell her that you can do the calculation in one step. Show how you would do this.

3. Kyle says that a population increase of 15% one year followed by an increase of 10% the next year is the same as a population increase of 25% over two years. Is Kyle correct? Explain your reasoning.

Check Your Understanding

Practise

For help with #4 and #5, refer to Example 1 on pages 145–146.

4. Chris purchased the following items:
   - 2 binders at $4.99 each
   - 1 math set for $3.99
   - a backpack for $19.99

   Find the total cost including 5% GST and 7% PST.

5. Ravi purchased 3 DVDs for $19.99 each. Find the total cost for the DVDs including 5% GST and 6% PST.

For help with #6 and #7, refer to Example 2 on page 147.

6. A store discounted items by 50% off the original price one week. The following week an additional 10% was taken off the already reduced price. The regular price of a CD player was $85.00. What is the reduced price in the second week?

7. A herd of 100 caribou was moved to a new location. The population increased by 10% the first year and then increased by 20% the second year.

   a) Find the population after the second year.

   b) Explain why there was not a 30% increase in population over the two years.

8. Copy and complete the following table. Use 5% GST and the percent of PST applicable to where you live.

Item Purchased	Price	Total Tax	Total Cost
a) Boots	$119.99		
b) Pants	$89.99		
c) Gloves	$39.99		
d) Helmet	$189.99		

Apply

9. Arjay was thinking of buying a car worth $23 000, but delayed purchasing the car for a year. During that year, the cost of the car increased by 3.2%.

   a) What was the price of the car when Arjay purchased it?

   b) What was the total cost of the car including 5% GST and 5% PST?

10. What is the total cost for four tires that sell for $85 each, plus 5% GST and a 1.5% environment tax?

11. A student is awarded a $1000 scholarship and places it in an account that pays 3% simple interest per year.

   a) What is the total value of the scholarship amount at the end of the second year?

   b) What is the single percent increase in value of the scholarship after two years?

12. Simon Whitfield of Victoria, British Columbia, won the men's triathlon at the Sydney Olympics. The race consisted of a 1.5-km swim in Sydney Harbour, a 40-km bike ride through Sydney and a 10-km run.

   a) What percent of the race distance is each component? Express your answer to the nearest tenth of a percent.

   b) What percent of the race distance is spent on land? Express your answer to the nearest tenth of a percent.

Extend

13. A ski jacket has been marked down on three occasions, first 20% off, then 25% off the new price, and finally 50% off the previous price. What is the overall percent saved?

14. The selling price of a DVD player is 35% more than its cost. It is sold at a discount of 20% off the selling price. How much does the store still gain?

MATH LINK

a) In one day, a dripping faucet wastes about 25 L of water. A regular toilet flush uses 6 L of water per flush. If you flush your toilet 30 times a day, what percent of the water used by your toilet is wasted by the dripping faucet?

b) $\frac{3}{10}$% of the world's fresh water is held in rivers and lakes. Approximately 9% of that water is used for industry and may be returned to the environment polluted. What percent of the world's fresh water is used by industry?

Key Words

Unscramble the letters for each puzzle. Use the clues to help you solve the puzzles.

1. R C E E T N P

   ▆▆▆▆▆ means *out of 100*.

2. C R A T F I O L N A

   A ▆▆▆▆ percent is a percent that includes a portion of 1%.

3. M C N O B D E I

   Percents that are added together are ▆▆▆▆ percents.

4.1 Representing Percents, pages 122–129

4. How many hundred grids are needed to show each of the following percents?

   a) 101%   b) 589%   c) 1450%

5. What percent does each diagram represent? One completely shaded grid represents 100%.

   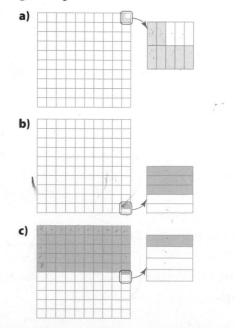

   a)

   b)

   c)

d)

6. Use hundred grids to represent each percent.

   a) 110%   b) $\frac{1}{10}\%$ c) $7\frac{7}{8}\%$

   d) 172.5%   e) 0.75%   f) 500%

7. Use hundred grids to show

   a) 0.4%   b) 12%   c) 115%

8. Represent the percent in each statement on a hundred grid.

   a) 79.1% of all students are right-handed.

   b) The average person in Canada uses about 223% as much water per day as the average person in France.

   c) The school enrollment increased by 0.8% this year.

4.2 Fractions, Decimals, and Percents, pages 130–137

9. Copy and complete the following table. The first row is done for you.

Fraction	Decimal	Percent
$1\frac{2}{5}$	1.4	140%
a)	0.115	
b)		$23\frac{3}{4}\%$
c) $\frac{3}{200}$		
d)	3.85	

10. A coach asked the team to give 110%.

   a) What is this value as a fraction and as a decimal number?

   b) What does this statement mean to you?

11. Express each percent as a decimal number and as a fraction. Rewrite each sentence using either the decimal or fraction form.

   a) Kyle scored 95.5% on a practice test.

   b) The store's sales increased by 140%.

   c) By getting your car tuned up, you can reduce emissions by $\frac{9}{10}$%.

4.3 Percent of a Number, pages 138–143

12. Determine the following. Write your answer to the nearest tenth.

   a) 115% of 230

   b) $80\frac{3}{4}$% of 50

   c) 500% of 0.02

   d) $\frac{1}{10}$% of 800

   e) $63\frac{4}{5}$% of 12 000

   f) 0.05% of 1 000 000

13. A photocopier increased a diagram to 250% of its original size. What is the enlarged length of the diagram if its original length was 2.5 cm?

14. Julia borrowed $100 from her brother. Her brother charged her $5\frac{1}{2}$% interest per month on the loan. She paid him back after one month. How much interest did she pay?

15. A forester recorded the following data on tree types.

Tree Species	Number of Trees
Fir	567
Pine	324
Larch	156
Cedar	89
Hemlock	678

   a) What is the total number of trees recorded?

   b) What percent of the total does each tree species represent?

4.4 Combining Percents, pages 144–149

16. The cost of an airline ticket is $289.50. Added to this cost is 5% GST, 7% PST, 1% airport improvement fee, and $\frac{3}{4}$% booking fee. What is the total cost of the ticket?

17. One year, the towns of Cedarville and Pinedale each had the same population of 1200. Over the next two years, the population of Cedarville increased by 8% one year and 7% the next year. Over the same two years, the population of Pinedale increased by 15%.

   a) Did the population of each town increase by the same amount? Explain.

   b) What was the new population of each town?

4 Practice Test

For #1 to #5, choose the best answer.

1. What is 0.0235 as a percent?

   A 2.35%   B 0.235%

   C 0.0235%   D 0.002 35%

2. What is 135% as a decimal?

   A 0.135   B 1.35

   C 13.5   D 135

3. What is $66\frac{2}{3}\%$ as a fraction?

   A $\frac{1}{3}$ B $\frac{1}{2}$

   C $\frac{2}{3}$ D $\frac{3}{4}$

4. What is $\frac{1}{8}$ as a percent?

   A 0.0125%   B 0.125%

   C 1.25%   D 12.5%

5. A bicycle is on sale for 10% off the original price of $420.00. When it does not sell, the store reduces the sale price by another 5%. What is the final sale price of the bicycle?

   A $357   B $359.10

   C $378.50   D $405

Complete the statements in #6 and #7.

6. One completely shaded grid represents 100%. The hundred grids shown represent ■%.

7. One completely shaded grid represents 100%. The hundred grid shown represents ■%.

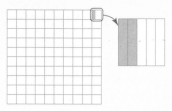

Short Answer

8. Use hundred grids to represent the following percents.

   a) 0.1%

   b) 35%

   c) 102%

9. Convert each of the following:

   a) 15% to a decimal and a fraction in lowest terms

   b) 1.24 to a percent and a fraction in lowest terms

   c) $\frac{13}{25}$ to a decimal and a percent

10. Suppose a real estate agent receives 5% commission on the first $250 000 of a house's selling price and 7% on the remaining amount. If a house sells for $423 000, how much commission does the real estate agent make on the sale of the house?

11. A census recorded the population of a town at 50 000. The population of the town increased by 0.7% in each of the next two years. What was the population at the end of the two years? Round your answer to the nearest whole number.

12. Helen bought a scooter for $64.98 plus 5% GST and 7% PST.

a) How much tax did she pay altogether?

b) What was the total price of the scooter?

Extended Response

13. During a magazine drive, the school drama club receives 25% of the sales as commission for the first $5000 worth of magazine subscriptions sold. The parent committee agrees to donate to the club an additional 125% of the total commission earned by the club.

a) How much commission will the club earn if members sell $6000 worth of subscriptions?

b) How much will the parent committee donate to the club?

c) How much will the club receive from the magazine drive altogether?

14. An Arctic ice study found that in the summer, 70% of an ocean region was ice covered. The study also predicted the region's ice would be reduced by 6% per year.

a) What percent of the region will be ice covered after the first year? Express your answer to the nearest tenth of a percent.

b) What percent of the region will be ice covered after the third year? Express your answer to the nearest tenth of a percent.

c) How many years will pass before less than one half of the region is covered by ice?

WRAP IT UP!

Use the information about water that you have gathered in the Math Links throughout this chapter to help you develop a water conservation plan that identifies at least five ways you could conserve fresh water. For each suggestion, estimate how much water you would use before the conservation method and how much you would save using the conservation method (in volume and in percent). Record your total savings as a percent of the original estimated water consumption.

Present your plan in the form of a newspaper article, cartoon strip, or another format of your choice.

Math Games

Number Match

In the card game Number Match, players take turns flipping cards until the last two cards flipped are equal in value. The 52 number cards include whole numbers, fractions, decimals, and percents. You will need to identify matching values expressed in different forms. For example, $\frac{6}{5}$, $\frac{12}{10}$, 1.2, 20% of 6, and 120% all have the same value.

These are the rules for Number Match:

- Play the game with a partner.
- One player shuffles the cards.
- With the deck face down, each player draws a card. The player with the higher-value card is Player 1. The player with the lower-value card is Player 2. If the two cards have the same value, try again.
- Player 1 again shuffles the cards and deals all of them, face down. Each player gets 26 cards to put in their stack.
- Beginning with Player 2, the players take turns flipping the top card from their stack.
- If the top two flipped cards have the same value, the first player to say "match" wins all the flipped cards and places them on the bottom of their stack.
- If a player says "match" when the top two flipped cards do not match, the other player wins all the flipped cards.
- The first player to run out of cards loses the round.
- Play as many rounds as you choose to decide who wins the game.

Materials
- deck of Number Match cards per pair of students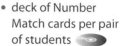

Challenge in Real Life

The Buying and Selling Game

When did you last buy something? If you are like many people, you probably buy things regularly.

How often have you been the seller? Many people are involved in selling things, either in their job or as volunteers selling such items as decorations, flowers, or popcorn for a community organization.

As in real life, in this challenge you will be both the seller and the buyer.

Materials
- coloured pencils or markers
- Seller's Record
- Buyer's Record

Sellers	Buyers
You be the seller. Your goal is to sell as much as you can. Decide what you will sell. Make a poster or advertising flyer that shows five items, their cost, and any discount. • Each item must be discounted a different amount, with a minimum of 20% off. • GST and any PST for your area should be added to the selling price. Make up a record sheet to keep track of your sales.	You be the buyer. Your goal is to buy items worth $500. You must buy at least one item from each seller. Make up a record sheet to show who you are buying from, what you buy from each person, and the final purchase total. Remember to subtract any discount and add any tax. Keep a running total of your purchases. You want to spend as close to $500 as you can, without going over $500.

Chapters 1-4 Review

Chapter 1 Representing Data

1. What kinds of information does each graph best represent?

   a) bar graph
   b) double bar graph
   c) circle graph
   d) line graph

2. Five hundred people were asked what types of food they liked. They were allowed to give more than one answer.

Type of Food	Preference
Aboriginal	325
Chinese	400
French	250
East Indian	275
Italian	450
Mexican	350

   a) State one advantage of using a pictograph to display the data.

   b) Use a pictograph to represent the data.

   c) Explain why you should not use a line graph to display the data.

3. The double bar graph shows the monthly sales for two video game systems.

   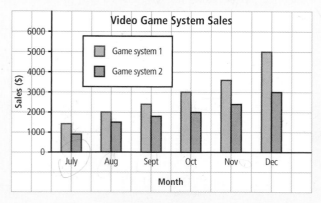

   a) List three things the double bar graph tells you.

b) Use the data from the double bar graph to make a double line graph.

c) List two things the double line graph tells you.

d) Which graph more clearly shows the month with the biggest increase in game system 1 sales and the month with the biggest increase in game system 2 sales? Explain your reasoning.

e) Describe one strength and one limitation of each graph for comparing sales.

4. Eighty grade 8 students were asked to name one item they would want to have with them on a long car trip. The results are displayed in a pictograph.

   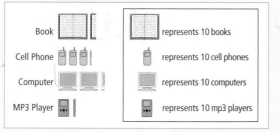

   a) Describe how this graph is misleading.

   b) Redraw the pictograph so it is not misleading.

   c) Display the data in a circle graph.

   d) What is one advantage of using a circle graph to display the data?

5. Calvin recorded his pulse rate for 5 min while he was riding his bike.

Time (min)	0	1	2	3	4	5
Pulse Rate (beats per min)	65	78	92	110	110	112

   a) Create a graph to display the data. You may wish to use a spreadsheet to create your graph.

b) What conclusions can you make based on your graph?

c) What is an advantage of using the type of graph you made?

d) Exchange graphs with a classmate and critique each other's graph. What improvements can you make to your graph?

Chapter 2 Ratios, Rates, and Proportional Reasoning

6. Three eighths of the students in a class of 32 students are boys.

a) How many students are boys?

b) What is the ratio of girls to total students? Express the ratio as a fraction and a percent.

c) What is the ratio of girls to boys? Use ratio notation to express your answer.

7. The makers of Purr 'n' Chew cat food want to price their cat food so that it costs just less than their main competitor, Happy Kitty. A 5-kg bag of Happy Kitty cat food costs $12.99. What is the maximum price that Purr 'n' Chew should charge for their 4-kg bag of cat food? Explain how you found this price.

8. Two brands of noodles are shown. The noodles are of the same quality.

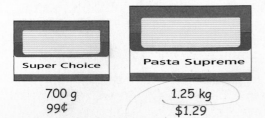

Super Choice
700 g
99¢

Pasta Supreme
1.25 kg
$1.29

a) Without calculating, which do you think is the better buy? Explain.

b) Calculate the unit price per 100 g for each brand.

c) Which is the better buy? Explain your choice. Compare it with your prediction.

d) Explain why estimating unit costs is useful when grocery shopping.

9. Use the information in the chart to help answer the questions.

Vehicle	Distance (km)	Fuel Used (L)
1	190	20.2
2	460	44.7
3	800	85

a) What is the fuel consumption for each vehicle in L/100 km? Give your answers to the nearest hundredth.

b) Which vehicle has the lowest fuel consumption? How do you know?

10. Use a proportion to solve each question. Use a variable for the unknown quantity.

a) Three lemons cost 96¢. What is the cost of eight lemons?

b) On a map, 1 cm represents 125 km. How many centimetres represent a distance of 550 km?

11. Four quarters has the same value as 20 nickels. How many nickels equals the value of five quarters?

Chapter 3 Pythagorean Relationship

12. Determine the squares of the following numbers.

a) 8   **b)** 13   **c)** 17   **d)** 80

13. Determine the square root of each perfect square.

a) 121   **b)** 900   **c)** 49   **d)** 256

14. Identify the perfect square that lies on either side of each value.

   a) 42   **b)** 139   **c)** 200

15. Estimate the square root of each number. Give your answer to one decimal place.

   a) 58   **b)** 140   **c)** 6   **d)** 29

16. Which value is the closest approximation to $\sqrt{90}$? Show how you know.

   9, 10, 9.2, 9.5, 9.8

17. Show whether 11 cm, 60 cm, and 61 cm can be the measurements for the sides of a right triangle.

18. Sarah has a rectangular corral for her horses. She wants to put new rail fencing all around the corral.

   a) What total length of fencing will she need? Give your answer to one decimal place.

   b) If rail fencing costs $15/m, what will be the total cost of the fencing before tax? Give your answer to the nearest dollar.

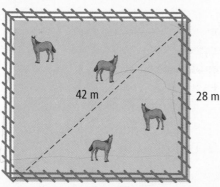

42 m   28 m

19. What is the distance from A to B?

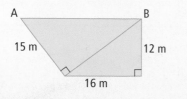

A   B

15 m   12 m

16 m

Chapter 4 Understanding Percent

20. The front sprocket of a mountain bike is 155% as large as one of the rear sprockets. Use hundred grids to show how the front sprocket compares to the rear sprocket.

21. A 1-kg ore sample contains 9 g of copper. Use a hundred grid to show the percent of copper in the ore sample.

22. In a recent survey, $66\frac{2}{3}\%$ of people liked ice cream.

   a) Express this percent as a decimal and as a fraction.

   b) If 900 people were surveyed, how many do not like ice cream?

23. A credit card charges 18.9% simple interest per year. How much interest is charged on an outstanding balance of $150 for one year?

24. The number of caribou in a particular herd was monitored over a two-year period. The first year, the size of the herd was estimated at 20 000. The second year, the herd was estimated to be 90% of its original size. What was the approximate size of the herd in the second year?

25. The cost of a downloaded album is $10.99. Added to this cost is a 10% before-tax processing fee, 5% GST, and 7% PST. What is the total cost of the album?

26. The number of bacteria in a colony grows 200% every 20 min.

   a) If a cut on a finger contains 100 bacteria, how many bacteria are present after 1 h?

   b) A new antibiotic is applied 1 h after the cut. The antibiotic kills $75\frac{1}{2}\%$ of the bacteria every second. How many bacteria are left after the first second?

Task

Test the Efficiency of a Ramp

Civil engineers design and build structures such as bridges, roads, and ramps. Before doing the actual construction, they test the design for strength and efficiency. Your team's task is to design a ramp that allows a vehicle to travel the farthest.

1. Use books, a chair, or other material to create a platform with a height of your choice. Round the height to the nearest centimetre. Height, a: ■

2. **a)** Design a ramp so that a vehicle can roll down without falling off the side.
   b) Record the length of the ramp from the edge of the platform to the floor to the nearest centimetre. Length of ramp, c: ■

3. Does your ramp design use a right triangle? Using the method of your choice, calculate the length of the base in your triangle, b. Justify your response.

4. Test your ramp by placing your vehicle at the top of the ramp, with its front wheels even with the edge of the platform. Let go of the vehicle without pushing it. Measure the distance the vehicle travels from the foot of the ramp to where it stops. You may wish to do three trials and take the average distance.

5. Repeat steps 3 and 4 for at least two different lengths of ramp. Complete the chart provided to you.

6. The most efficient ramp is the one that allows the vehicles to travel the farthest.
   a) Based on your result, what is the ratio of a to b distances that resulted in the most efficient design? Express your answer as a percent.
   b) Compare your ratio to those found by other teams. Explain any similarities and differences.

Materials

- toy vehicles, such as Hot Wheels®
- material for platform (books, chair)
- material for ramps (boards, stiff cardboard)
- metre stick
- tape measure
- Trial Record

Surface Area

A skyline is a view of the outline of buildings or mountains shown on the horizon. You can see skylines during the day or at night, all over the world. Many cities have beautiful skylines. City planners have to consider much more than just how the skyline will look when they design a city.

In the skyline shown in the picture, what shapes do you see? What three-dimensional objects can you identify?

In this chapter, you will learn how to draw and build three-dimensional objects and how to calculate their surface areas.

What You Will Learn

- ❑ to label and draw views of 3-D objects
- ❑ to draw and build nets for 3-D objects
- ❑ to calculate the surface area for prisms and cylinders
- ❑ to solve problems using surface area

Key Words

- face
- edge
- vertex
- rectangular prism
- net
- triangular prism
- right prism
- surface area
- cylinder

Literacy Link

You can use a Verbal Visual Chart (VVC) to help you learn and remember new terms.

Copy the blank VVC into your math journal or notebook and use it for the term, *rectangular prism*.
- Write the term in the first box.
- Draw a diagram in the second box.
- Define the term in the third box. The glossary on pages 517–521 may help you.
- In the fourth box, explain how you will remember the term and what it means. Consider using an example, a characteristic, a memory device, or a visual.

Term	Diagram
Definition	How I Will Remember It

Making the Foldable

Materials

- 11 × 17 sheet of paper
- ruler
- glue or tape
- four sheets of blank paper
- scissors
- stapler

Step 1

Fold over one of the short sides of an 11 × 17 sheet of paper to make a 2.5 cm tab. Fold the remaining portion of paper into quarters.

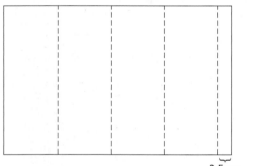

2.5 cm

Step 2

Use glue or tape to put the paper together as shown in the diagram. If you use glue, allow it to dry completely.

Step 3

Fold each of four sheets of blank paper into eighths. Trim the edges as shown so that each individual piece is 9.5 cm × 6 cm. Cut off all folded edges.

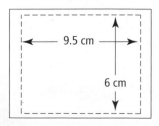

9.5 cm

6 cm

Step 4

Make the paper from Step 3 into eight booklets of four pages each.

Step 5

Collapse the Foldable. Title the faces of your Foldable. Then, staple the booklets onto each face, as shown, and add the labels shown.

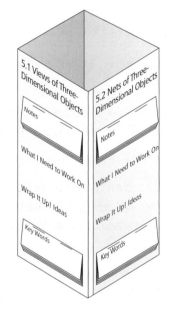

Using the Foldable

As you work through each section of Chapter 5, take notes on the appropriate face of your Foldable. Include information about the examples and Key Ideas in the Notes section. If you need more room, add sheets of paper to your booklet.

List and define the key words in the Key Words booklet. Use visuals to help you remember the terms.

Make notes under the heading What I Need to Work On. Check off each item as you deal with it.

As you think of ideas for the Wrap It Up!, record them on that section of each face of your Foldable.

MATH LINK

City Planning

When city planners design communities, they consider the purpose of the buildings, the width of the streets, the placement of street signs, the design and placement of lampposts, and many other items found in a city.

Communication and cooperation are keys to being successful, because city planners have to coordinate and work with many other people.

Imagine that you are a city planner for a miniature community.

Discuss your answers to #1 and #2 with a partner, then share with your class.

1. **a)** What buildings are essential to a new community?
   b) What different shapes are the faces of these buildings?

2. What other items are important to include in a community?

3. Using grid paper, sketch all or part of an aerial view of a community including the essential buildings your class discussed. Make sure to include roads and any other features that are important.

In this chapter, you will work in groups to create and design a miniature community.

Views of Three-Dimensional Objects

Focus on...

After this lesson, you will be able to...

❑ draw and label top, front, and side views of 3-D objects

❑ build 3-D objects when given top, front, and side views

Materials

- 20 unit blocks
- masking tape
- isometric dot paper

Literacy Link

To describe a three-dimensional (3-D) object, count its *faces*, *edges*, and *vertices*.

Face: flat or curved surface

Edge: line segment where two faces meet

Vertex: point where three or more edges meet

Sable and Josh are trying to build exactly the same three-dimensional (3-D) object. They each have the same number of blocks, but they cannot see each other's object.

Using a common vocabulary can help Sable and Josh build the same object.

Explore the Math

How can you describe and build three-dimensional objects?

1. Work with a partner. Create a 3-D object using ten unit blocks. Make sure your partner cannot see your object.

2. Describe your completed object to your partner, and have your partner try to build the same object. What key words did you use that were helpful?

3. Decide which faces will be the front and top of your object. Then determine which faces are the bottom, left side, right side, and back. You may wish to label the faces with tape. Then, describe your object to your partner again. Was it easier to describe this time?

4. Using isometric dot paper, draw what your object looks like.

Reflect on Your Findings

5. a) Do you need to know all the views to construct an object? If not, which ones would you use and why?

   b) Explain why you might need to have only one side view, if the top and front views are also given.

   c) Are any other views unnecessary? Are they needed to construct the same object?

Using isometric dot paper makes it easier to draw 3-D shapes. Follow the steps to draw a rectangular solid.

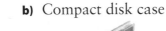

Each view shows two dimensions. When combined, these views create a 3-D diagram.

Example 1: Draw and Label Top, Front, and Side Views

Using blank paper, draw the top, front, and side views of these items. Label each view.

a) Tissue box

b) Compact disk case

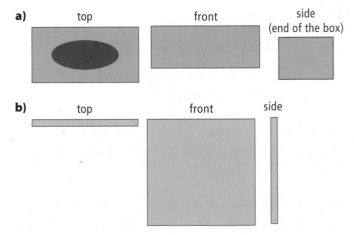

Solution

a)

top   front   side
(end of the box)

b)

top   front   side

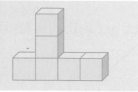
Example 2: Sketch a Three-Dimensional Object When Given Views

These views were drawn for an object made of ten blocks. Sketch what the object looks like.

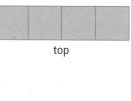

top

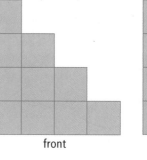

front

side

Solution

Use isometric dot paper to sketch the object.

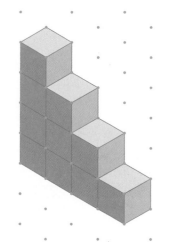

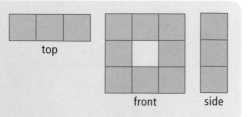

Example 3: Predict and Draw the Top, Front, and Side Views After a Rotation

The diagrams show the top, front, and side views of the computer tower.

top   front   side

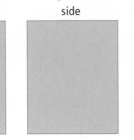

You want to rotate the computer tower 90° clockwise on its base to fit into your new desk. Predict which view you believe will become the front view after the rotation. Then, draw the top, front, and side views after rotating the tower.

This diagram shows a 90° clockwise rotation.

90°

Solution

The original side view will become the new front view after the rotation.

top   front   side

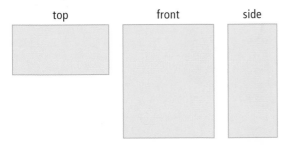

Tech 🔗 Link

You can use a Draw program to create 3-D objects.

Show You Know

Stand your *MathLinks 8* student resource on your desk. Predict what the top, front, and side views will look like if you rotate it 90° clockwise about its spine. Then, draw the top, front, and side views after rotating the book.

- A minimum of three views are needed to describe a 3-D object.
- Using the top, front, and side views, you can build or draw a 3-D object.

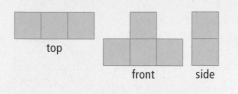

Communicate the Ideas

1. Raina insists that you need to tell her all six views so she can draw your object. Is she correct? Explain why or why not.

2. Are these views correct? Justify your answer.

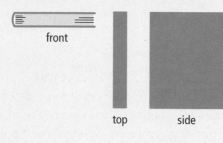 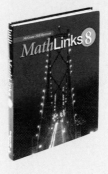

Check Your Understanding

Practise

For help with #3 and #4, refer to Example 1 on pages 165–166.

3. Sketch and label the top, front, and side views.

a)

b)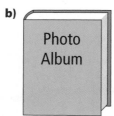

c)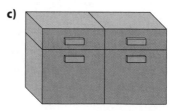

4. Choose the correct top, front, and side view for this object and label each one.

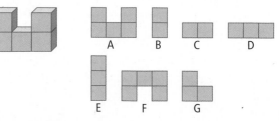

For help with #5, refer to Example 2 on page 166.

5. Draw each 3-D object using the views below.

a)

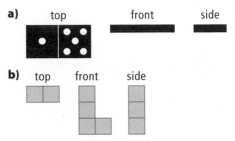

b)

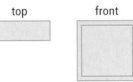

For help with #6 and #7, refer to Example 3 on page 167.

6. A television set has the following views.

If you turn the television 90° counterclockwise, how would the three views change? Sketch and label each new view.

7. Choose which object has a front view like this after a rotation of 90° clockwise onto its side.

a)

set of books

b)

CD rack

Apply

8. Choose two 3-D objects from your classroom. Sketch the top, front, and side views for each one.

9. Sketch the front, top, and right side views for these solids.

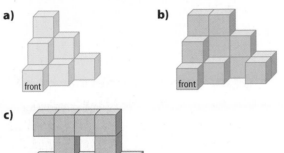

a) front

b) front

c) front

Extend

10. Describe two objects that meet this requirement: When you rotate an object 90°, the top, front, and side views are the same as the top, front, and side views of the object before it was rotated.

11. An injured bumblebee sits at a vertex of a cube with edge length 1 m. The bee moves along the edges of the cube and comes back to the original vertex without visiting any other vertex twice.
   a) Draw diagrams to show the bumblebee's trip around the cube.
   b) What is the length, in metres, of the longest trip?

MATH LINK

Choose one of the essential buildings that you discussed for your new community on page 163. Draw and label a front, side, and top view.

5.2

Nets of Three-Dimensional Objects

rectangular prism

Focus on...

After this lesson, you will be able to...

❏ determine the correct nets for 3-D objects
❏ build 3-D objects from nets
❏ draw nets for 3-D objects

rectangular prism

• a prism whose bases are congruent rectangles

Materials

• grid paper
• scissors
• clear tape
• rectangular prisms (blocks of wood, cardboard boxes, unit blocks)

net

• a two-dimensional shape that, when folded, encloses a 3-D object

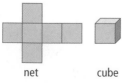

net   cube

Shipping containers help distribute materials all over the world. Items can be shipped by boat, train, or transport truck to any destination using these containers. Shipping containers are right **rectangular prisms**. Why do you think this shape is used?

Explore the Math

How do you know if a net can build a right rectangular prism?

Here are a variety of possible **nets** for a right rectangular prism.

Literacy ⊖ Link

A *right prism* has sides that are perpendicular to the bases of the prism.

1. Draw each net on grid paper.

2. Predict which nets will form a right rectangular prism.

3. Cut each net out along the outside edges and fold along the inside edges, taping the cut edges to try to form a right rectangular prism.

4. Do all the nets create right rectangular prisms?

5. Place a right rectangular prism (such as a small cardboard box) on a piece of blank paper. "Roll" the prism onto its faces, trace each face, and try to draw another correct net. Your net should be different from the examples you have already made.

Reflect on Your Findings

6. a) Compare the net you drew with those of three of your classmates. What is the same and different about your nets?

b) Is there more than one way to draw a net for a 3-D object? Explain your answer.

Example 1: Draw a Net for a Three-Dimensional Object

A company asks you to create an umbrella stand for large beach umbrellas. Draw the net for the umbrella stand.

Solution

Visualize what the umbrella stand would look like if you could cut it open and flatten it. The net has one circle and a rectangle. When the rectangle is curved around the circle, the net will form a cylinder with an open top. The width of the rectangle is equal to the circumference of the circle.

Show You Know

Draw a net for an unopened soup can.

Example 2: Build a Three-Dimensional Object From a Given Net

Before going to leadership camp, your group needs to put a tent together. Can this net be folded to form the shape of a tent?

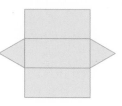

Strategies
Model It

triangular prism

- a prism with two triangular bases each the same size and shape

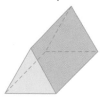

Solution

Trace the net onto paper. Cut along the outside edges and fold along the inside edges. Tape the cut edges together to try to build a right **triangular prism**.

The net can be folded to form the shape of a tent.

Show You Know

Build a 3-D object using this net. What object does it make?

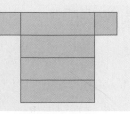

Key Ideas

- A net is a two-dimensional shape that, when folded, encloses a three-dimensional object.

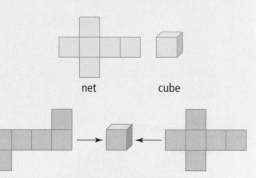

net   cube

- The same 3-D object can be created by folding different nets.

- You can draw a net for an object by visualizing what it would look like if you cut along the edges and flattened it out.

Communicate the Ideas

1. Both of these nets have six faces, like a cube. Will both nets form a cube? Justify your answer.

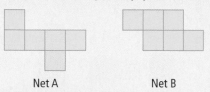

Net A   Net B

2. Patricia is playing the lead role in the school musical this year. She missed Math class while she was performing. She cannot figure out if a net will build the correct 3-D object, and asks you for help after school. Show how you would help her figure out this problem.

Check Your Understanding

Practise

For help with #3 to #5, refer to Example 1 on page 171.

3. Sketch a net for each object.

a)

hockey puck

b)

chocolate bar

c)

jewellery box

4. Draw the net for each object. Label the measurements on the net.

a)

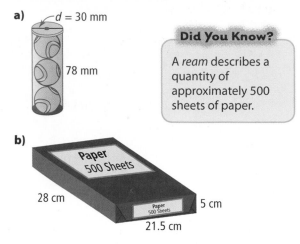

d = 30 mm

78 mm

> **Did You Know?**
>
> A *ream* describes a quantity of approximately 500 sheets of paper.

b)

Paper
500 Sheets

28 cm

5 cm

21.5 cm

5. Draw a net on grid paper for a rectangular prism with the following measurements: length is six units, width is four units, and height is two units.

For help with #6 and #7, refer to Example 2 on page 172.

6. a) Draw the net on grid paper, as shown. Cut along the outside edges of the net and fold to form a 3-D object.

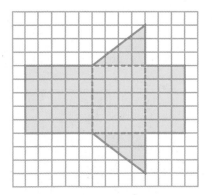

b) What is this object called?

7. Match each solid with its net. Copy the nets, then try to create the 3-D objects.

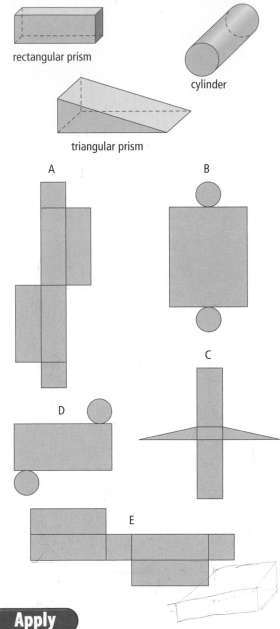

rectangular prism

cylinder

triangular prism

A   B

C

D

E

Apply

8. A box of pens measures 15.5 cm by 7 cm by 2.5 cm. Draw a net for the box on a piece of centimetre grid paper. Then, cut it out and fold it to form the box.

9. You are designing a new mailbox. Draw a net of your creation. Include all measurements.

10. Simon designed two nets.

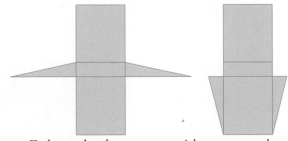

    a) Enlarge both nets on grid paper, and build the 3-D objects they form.

    b) What object does each net form?

Extend

11. Hannah and Dakota design a spelling board game. They use letter tiles to create words. Tiles may be stacked (limit of four) on top of letters already used for a word on the board to form a new word.

    a) Draw a 3-D picture of what these stacked tiles might look like.

    b) Draw a top view that illustrates the stacked tiles for people reading the instructions.

12. The six sides of a cube are each a different colour. Four of the views are shown below.

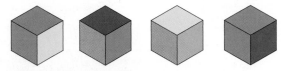

What colour is on the opposite side of each of these faces?

    a) purple

    b) blue

    c) red

13. How many possible nets can create a cube? Sketch all of them. The first one is done for you.

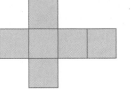

MATH LINK

When buildings are designed, it is important to consider engineering principles, maximum and minimum height requirements, and budget.

a) Create a 3-D sketch of two buildings for your miniature community, one that is a prism and one that is a cylinder.

b) Draw a net of each building, including all possible measurements needed to build your miniature.

Surface Area of a Prism

Most products come in some sort of packaging. You can help
conserve energy and natural resources by purchasing products that
• are made using recycled material
• use recycled material for packaging
• do not use any packaging

What other ways could you reduce packaging?

Explore the Math

How can you determine the surface area of a package?

1. Choose an empty cardboard box. Cut along edges of the box so it
unfolds to form a net.

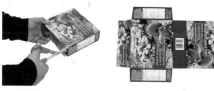

Do you need to
include the material
used in the
overlapping flaps?
Why or why not?

2. Suppose you want to design an advertisement to place on the outside
of your box. How can you determine the surface area you have to
work with?

Reflect on Your Findings

3. a) Share your method with several of your classmates. Discuss any
similarities or differences between the methods.

b) Which method do you prefer to use? Justify your response.

Example 1: Calculate the Surface Area of a Right Rectangular Prism

a) Draw the net of this right rectangular prism.

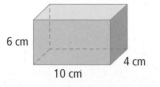

b) What is the **surface area** of the prism?

Solution

a)

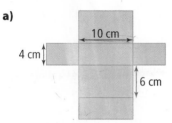

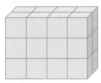
b) The right rectangular prism has faces that are three different sizes.

front or back	top or bottom	ends
6 cm [rectangle] 10 cm	4 cm [rectangle] 10 cm	4 cm [rectangle] 6 cm

$A = l \times w$ $A = l \times w$ $A = l \times w$

$A = 10 \times 6$ $A = 10 \times 4$ $A = 6 \times 4$

$A = 60$ $A = 40$ $A = 24$

The area of the front or back is 60 cm².   The area of the top or bottom is 40 cm².   The area of each end is 24 cm².

> Area is measured in square units. For example, square centimetres, square metres, etc.

The surface area is the sum of the areas of all the faces.

The front and back have the same area:
$A = 60 \times 2$
$A = 120$

The top and bottom have the same area:
$A = 40 \times 2$
$A = 80$

The two ends have the same area:
$A = 24 \times 2$
$A = 48$

Strategies

How else could you calculate the surface area?

Surface area = (area of front and back) + (area of top and bottom)
             + (area of ends)
       = 120 + 80 + 48
       = 248

> You could add the areas you calculated first. 60 + 40 + 24 = 124
>
> Each area is the same as the area of one other face, so you could then multiply the total by two. 124 × 2 = 248

The surface area of the right rectangular prism is 248 cm².

What is the surface area of this right
rectangular prism?

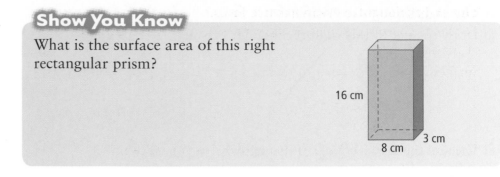

16 cm

3 cm

8 cm

Example 2: Calculate the Surface Area of a Right Triangular Prism

a) Draw the net of this right
triangular prism.

b) What is the surface area?

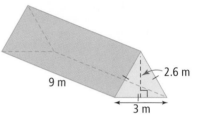

2.6 m

9 m

3 m

Solution

a)

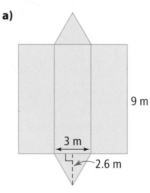

9 m

3 m

2.6 m

b) The bases of the prism are equilateral triangles.
The sides of the prism are rectangles.

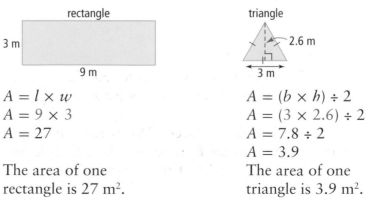

rectangle

3 m

9 m

triangle

2.6 m

3 m

$A = l \times w$
$A = 9 \times 3$
$A = 27$

The area of one
rectangle is 27 m².

$A = (b \times h) \div 2$
$A = (3 \times 2.6) \div 2$
$A = 7.8 \div 2$
$A = 3.9$

The area of one
triangle is 3.9 m².

This right triangular prism has five faces.
There are three rectangles of the same size and two triangles of the same size.

Surface area = (3 × area of rectangle) + (2 × area of triangle)
$$= (3 \times 27) + (2 \times 3.9)$$
$$= 81 + 7.8$$
$$= 88.8$$

The surface area of the right triangular prism is 88.8 m².

Find the surface area of this triangular prism.

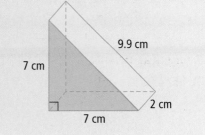

9.9 cm

7 cm

2 cm

7 cm

Key Ideas

- Surface area is the sum of the areas of all the faces of a 3-D object.

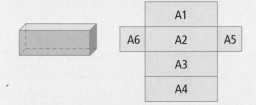

	A1	
A6	A2	A5
	A3	
	A4	

Surface Area = A1 + A2 + A3 + A4 + A5 + A6,
where A1 represents the area of rectangle 1, A2 represents the area of rectangle 2, etc.

Communicate the Ideas

1. Write a set of guidelines that you could use to find the surface area of a prism. Share your guidelines with a classmate.

2. A right rectangular prism has six faces. Why might you have to find the area of only three of the faces to be able to find the surface area? Use pictures and words to explain your thinking.

Check Your Understanding

Practise

For help with #3 and #4, refer to Example 1 on page 177.

3. Find the surface area of this right rectangular prism to the nearest tenth of a square centimetre.

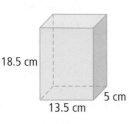

18.5 cm
13.5 cm
5 cm

4. Find the surface area of this CD case.

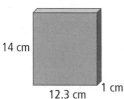

14 cm
12.3 cm
1 cm

For help with #5 to #7, refer to Example 2 on pages 178–179.

5. Calculate the surface area of this ramp in the shape of a right triangular prism. Give your answer to the nearest tenth of a square metre.

2.7 m
1.4 m
0.7 m
2.3 m

Apply

6. Cheese is sometimes packaged in a triangular box. How much cardboard would you need to cover this piece of cheese if you do not include overlapping? Calculate your answer to the nearest tenth of a square centimetre.

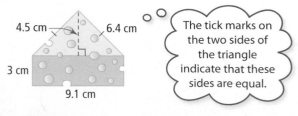

4.5 cm   6.4 cm
3 cm
9.1 cm

The tick marks on the two sides of the triangle indicate that these sides are equal.

7. Given the area of each face of a right rectangular prism, what is the surface area?

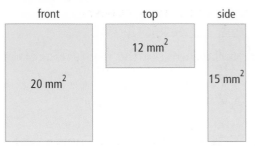

front
20 mm^2
top
12 mm^2
side
15 mm^2

8. Paco builds a glass greenhouse.

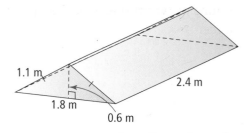

1.1 m
2.4 m
1.8 m
0.6 m

a) How many glass faces does the greenhouse have?

b) How much glass does Paco need to buy?

9. What is the minimum amount of material needed to make the cover of this textbook if there is no overlap? Give your answer to the nearest square millimetre.

10. Jay wants to make a bike ramp. He draws the following sketch. What is the surface area of the ramp?

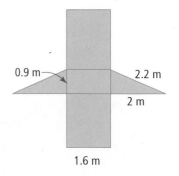

0.9 m   2.2 m
2 m
1.6 m

11. Dallas wants to paint three cubes. The cubes measure 1 m × 1 m × 1 m, 2 m × 2 m × 2 m, and 3 m × 3 m × 3 m, respectively. What total surface area will Dallas paint if he decides not to paint the bottoms of the three cubes?

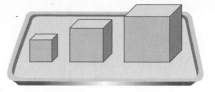

12. Tadika has a gift to wrap. Both of these containers will hold her gift. Which container would allow her to use the least amount of wrapping paper? Explain your choice.

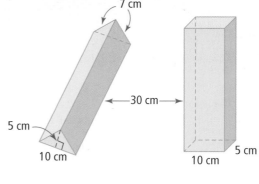

Extend

13. A square cake pan measures 30 cm on each side and is 5 cm deep. Cody wants to coat the inside of the pan with non-stick oil. If a single can of non-stick oil covers an area of 400 000 cm², how many pans can be coated with a single can?

14. Ethan is hosting games night this weekend. He bought ten packages of playing cards. Each package measures 9 cm × 6.5 cm × 1.7 cm. He wants to build a container to hold all ten packages of cards.

  a) What are the minimum inside dimensions of the container?

  b) Is there more than one kind of container that would work? Draw diagrams to help explain your answer.

15. a) If the edge length of a cube is doubled, find the ratio of the old surface area to the new surface area.

  b) What happens if the edge length of a cube is tripled? Is there a pattern?

16. Shelby wants to paint the walls and ceiling of a rectangular room.

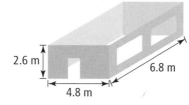

Type of Paint	Size of Paint Can	Cost
Wall paint	4 L	$24.95
	1 L	$7.99
Ceiling paint	4 L	$32.95

One litre of paint covers 9.5 m².

  a) What is the least amount of paint Shelby can buy to paint the room (subtract 5 m² for the door and windows)?

  b) How much will the paint cost, including the amount of tax charged in your region?

MATH LINK

For the prism-shaped building you created in the Math Link on page 175, how much material do you need to cover the exterior walls and the roof of the building?

Surface Area of a Cylinder

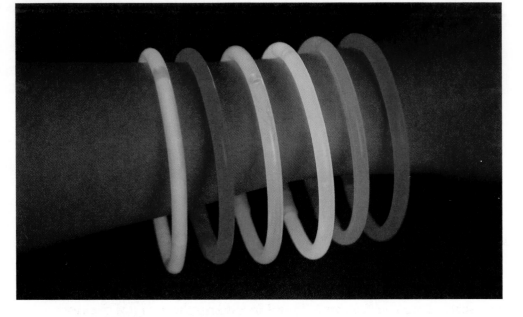

Glow sticks work because of a chemical reaction. There are two solutions in separate compartments inside the stick. Once you bend the stick, the two solutions mix. This mixture creates a new solution that gives off light. The colour of the glow stick depends on the dye in the mixture. How might you determine how much plastic would be needed to make a glow stick to fit around your wrist?

Explore the Math

How do you find the surface area of a right cylinder?

Work with a partner.

1. a) Draw the net of a glow stick. Use the actual dimensions from the diagram shown.

b) Describe each face of your net.

2. How can you use what you know about circles to help you find the surface area of the glow stick?

---

cylinder

• a three-dimensional object with two parallel and congruent circular bases

cylinder

3. What is the surface area of the glow stick, to the nearest hundredth of a square centimetre? Include the units in your final answer.

4. Share your strategies with another group.

Reflect on Your Findings

5. Would your method work for any right cylinder? Explain your reasoning.

Example 1: Determine the Surface Area of a Right Cylinder

a) Estimate the surface area of the can.

b) What is the surface area of the can? Express your answer to the nearest hundredth of a square centimetre?

11 cm

7.5 cm

Solution

The surface area of the can is found by adding the areas of the two circular bases and the rectangular side that surrounds them.

The width, w, of the rectangle is the height of the can.

The length, l, of the rectangle is equal to the circumference of the circle.

a) To estimate, use approximate values:
$d \approx 8$ cm, $w \approx 10$ cm, $\pi \approx 3$.

Area of circle $= \pi \times r^2$

r^2 means $r \times r$

$\approx 3 \times 4 \times 4$
≈ 48

There are two circles:
$2 \times 48 = 96$

How is the radius related to the diameter?

The area of the two circles is approximately 96 cm².

Area of rectangle $= l \times w$
$\qquad\qquad\qquad = (\pi \times d) \times w$
$\qquad\qquad\qquad \approx 3 \times 8 \times 10$
$\qquad\qquad\qquad \approx 240$

What formulas could you use to find the circumference of a circle?

The area of the rectangle is approximately 240 cm².

Estimated surface area $=$ area of two circles $+$ area of rectangle
$\qquad\qquad\qquad\qquad\qquad \approx 96 + 240$
$\qquad\qquad\qquad\qquad\qquad \approx 340$

The estimated surface area is 340 cm².

Literacy Link

circle
radius
centre
diameter

b) *Method 1: Use a Net*

Draw the net and label the measurements.

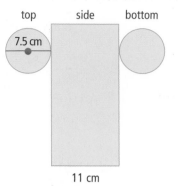

The diameter of the circle is 7.5 cm.
Determine the radius.
$7.5 \div 2 = 3.75$
The radius of the circle is 3.75 cm.

Find the area of one circle.
$A = \pi \times r^2$
$A \approx 3.14 \times 3.75^2$
$A \approx 44.15625$

> Use 3.14 as an approximate value for π.

The area of one circle is approximately 44.15625 cm².

Find the area of two circles.
$2 \times 44.15625 = 88.3125$
The area of both circles is approximately 88.3125 cm².

Find the area of the rectangle using the circumference of the circle.
$A = l \times w$
$A = (\pi \times d) \times w$
$A \approx 3.14 \times 7.5 \times 11$
$A \approx 259.05$
The area of the rectangle is approximately 259.05 cm².

> Round your answer at the end of the calculation.

Calculate the total surface area.
Surface area $= 88.3125 + 259.05$
$= 347.3625$
The total surface area is approximately 347.36 cm².

Method 2: Use a Formula.

Use this formula to find the total surface area of any cylinder.

$S.A. = 2 \times (\pi \times r^2) + (\pi \times d \times h)$
$S.A. \approx 2 \times (3.14 \times 3.75^2) + (3.14 \times 7.5 \times 11)$
$S.A. \approx 88.3125 + 259.05$
$S.A. \approx 347.3625$

The total surface area is 347.36 cm², to the nearest hundredth.

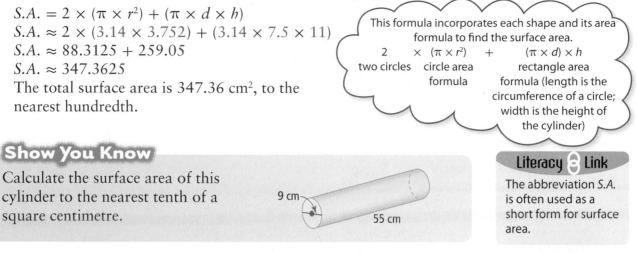

This formula incorporates each shape and its area formula to find the surface area.

2 $\times$ $(\pi \times r^2)$ $+$ $(\pi \times d) \times h$
two circles   circle area   rectangle area
formula   formula (length is the circumference of a circle; width is the height of the cylinder)

Show You Know

Calculate the surface area of this cylinder to the nearest tenth of a square centimetre.

9 cm

55 cm

Example 2: Use the Surface Area of a Cylinder

Calculate the surface area of this totem pole, including the two circular bases. The pole stands 2.4 m tall and has a diameter of 0.75 m. Give your answer to the nearest hundredth of a square metre.

Solution

The cylinder has two circular bases. The area of one circle is:
$A = \pi \times r^2$
$A \approx 3.14 \times 0.375^2$
$A \approx 0.4415625$
The area of the circle is approximately 0.4415625 m².

$r = d \div 2$

There are two circles, so the area of both circles is approximately 0.883125 m².

The side of the cylinder is a rectangle.
The area of the rectangle is:
$A = (\pi \times d) \times h$
$A \approx 3.14 \times 0.75 \times 2.4$
$A \approx 5.652$
The area of the rectangle is approximately 5.652 m².

Replace one dimension with the formula for the circumference of a circle.

Calculate the total surface area.
$S.A. \approx 0.883125 + 5.652$
$S.A. \approx 6.535125$
The total surface area is approximately 6.54 m².

This metal totem pole was created by Todd Baker, Squamish Nation. It represents the Birth of the Bear Clan, with the princess of the clan on the top half and the bear on the bottom half.

Show You Know

Calculate the surface area of a cylindrical waste bucket without a lid that measures 28 cm high and 18 cm in diameter. Give your answer to the nearest square centimetre.

Key Ideas

- The surface area of a cylinder is the sum of the areas of its faces.
- A net of a cylinder is made up of one rectangle and two circles.
- To find one of the dimensions of the rectangle, calculate the circumference of the circle.

The length of this side is the circumference of the circle $C = \pi \times d$ or $C = 2 \times \pi \times r$

Communicate the Ideas

1. What are the similarities and differences between finding the surface area of a prism and finding the surface area of a cylinder?

2. Explain why you need to find the circumference of a circle to find the surface area of a cylinder?

Check Your Understanding

Practise

For help with #3 to #7, refer to Examples 1 and 2 on pages 183–185.

3. a) Draw a net for this cylinder.
   b) Sketch a different net for this cylinder.

4. Estimate the surface area of each cylinder. Then, calculate each surface area to the nearest tenth of a square centimetre.

   a) $d = 7$ cm
   30 cm

   b) $r = 10$ cm
   22 cm

5. Find the surface area of each object to the nearest tenth of a square unit.

   a) $d = 2.5$ cm
   16 cm
   wooden rod

   b) $d = 0.003$ m
   16 m
   flag pole

   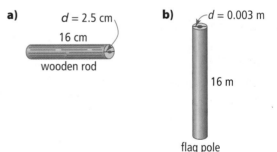

6. Use the formula
   $S.A. = 2 \times (\pi \times r^2) + (\pi \times d \times h)$ to calculate the surface area of each object. Give each answer to the nearest hundredth of a square unit.

   a) $d = 2.5$ cm
   10 cm

   b) $d = 5$ cm
   7 cm

   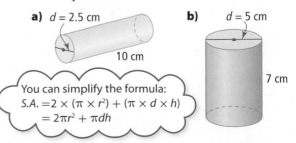

   You can simplify the formula:
   $S.A. = 2 \times (\pi \times r^2) + (\pi \times d \times h)$
   $= 2\pi r^2 + \pi dh$

7. Do you prefer to find the surface area of a cylinder by using the sum of the area of each face or by using a formula? Give at least two reasons for your choice.

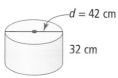
Apply

8. Anu wants to re-cover the cylindrical stool in his bedroom. How much material does he need if there is no overlap and he does not cover the bottom of the stool?

d = 42 cm

32 cm

9. Kaitlyn and Hakim each bought a tube of candy. Both containers cost the same amount. Which container required more plastic to make?

d = 7 cm — CANDY
122 cm

d = 11 cm — CANDY
85 cm

10. Paper towel is rolled around a cardboard tube. Calculate the outside surface area of the tube.

r = 2 cm

27.5 cm

> **Did You Know?**
>
> Each person produces about 1.59 kg of trash each day. Most of this is paper products.

Extend

11. If each tennis ball has a diameter of 7 cm, calculate the amount of material needed to make a can that holds three tennis balls.

12. Coins can be stored in a plastic wrapper similar to a cylinder. A roll of dimes contains 50 coins. Each dime has a diameter of 17.5 mm and a thickness of 1 mm. Calculate the minimum surface area of the plastic wrapper.

13. A paint roller in the shape of a cylinder with a radius of 4 cm and a length of 21 cm is rolled vertically on a wall.
   a) What is the length and width of the wet path after ten complete rolls?
   b) What area does the paint cover?

MATH LINK

For the cylindrical building you created in the Math Link on page 175, how much material do you need to cover the exterior walls and the roof of the building?

> **Did You Know?**
>
> Douglas J. Cardinal, one of the world's most acclaimed architects, uses his European, Blackfoot, and Ojibwa roots when designing buildings. He is known for his design of The Canadian Museum of Civilization in Gatineau, Québec, as well as a number of buildings in Western Canada, such as Telus World of Science in Edmonton and First Nations University of Canada in Regina.

5 Chapter Review

Key Words

Unscramble the letters for each puzzle in #1 to #6. Use the clues to help you solve the puzzles.

1. E T N
   a flat diagram that you can fold to make a 3-D object

2. U S F A R E C E R A A
   the sum of the areas of the faces of an object (2 words)

3. I R H T G R P M S I
   a prism whose sides are perpendicular to its bases (2 words)

4. E C N I Y D R L
   a 3-D object with two parallel circular bases

5. I R A G N R U A L T S I M R P
   a 3-D object with two parallel triangular bases (2 words)

6. L E U C A A N R G T R I R M S P
   a 3-D object with two parallel rectangular bases (2 words)

5.1 Views of Three-Dimensional Objects, pages 164–169

7. Draw and label the top, front, and side views for these objects.

   a)    b)

8. Using isometric paper, draw each 3-D object from the views given.

   a)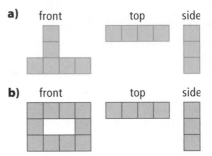

   b)

9. A filing cabinet is in the far corner of an office. Shay is redecorating the room and wants to turn the cabinet 90° clockwise. Here are the views before the turn:

   a) How does each view change after the turn?

   b) Draw and label the top, front, and side views of the filing cabinet after it is turned.

5.2 Nets of Three-Dimensional Objects, pages 170–175

10. Name the object formed by each net.

   a)   b)

   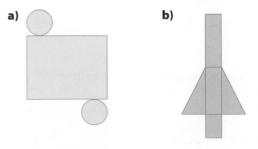

c)

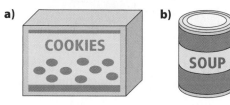

11. Draw the net for each object.

a) 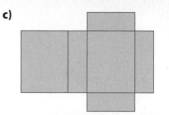 **b)**

12. Using two pieces of grid paper, create a pencil box and lid. Draw a net, cut it out, fold it, and build your pencil box. Make sure new pencils fit in it!

5.3 Surface Area of a Prism, pages 176–181

For #13 to #16, calculate the surface area to the nearest tenth of a square unit.

13. What is the surface area of each object?

a)

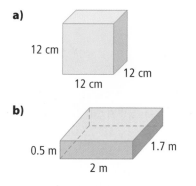

12 cm
12 cm
12 cm

b)

0.5 m
1.7 m
2 m

14. Using the measurements shown on the net of the rectangular prism, calculate the surface area.

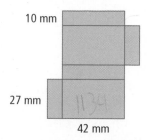

10 mm
27 mm
42 mm

15. Find the surface area of each triangular prism.

a)

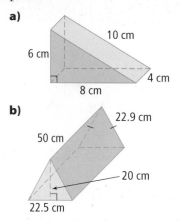

10 cm
6 cm
4 cm
8 cm

b)

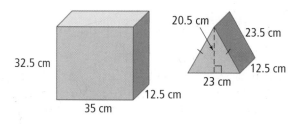

22.9 cm
50 cm
20 cm
22.5 cm

16. Liza had two more gifts left to wrap when she ran out of paper. Approximately how much more wrapping paper does she need to finish wrapping her gifts? Assume no overlap.

20.5 cm
23.5 cm
32.5 cm
12.5 cm
23 cm
12.5 cm
35 cm

5.4 Surface Area of a Cylinder, pages 182–187

For #17 to #19, calculate the surface area to the nearest tenth of a square unit.

17. Determine the surface area of the cylinder.

2.5 m
5.5 m

18. The pencil sharpener on Kay's desk has a diameter of 3.4 cm and is 7 cm tall. Calculate the surface area.

19. The circumference of a container's lid is 157 cm. If the container is 102 cm tall, what is the surface area of the container?

5 Practice Test

For #1 to #5, choose the best answer.

1. The top view of this container shows a

   A circle

   B square

   C triangle

   D rectangle

2. One face on a cube has an area of 49 cm². What is the surface area of the cube?

   A 343 cm²

   B 294 cm²

   C 196 cm²

   D 154 cm²

3. What three-dimensional object has a net like this one?

   A cube

   B cylinder

   C triangular prism

   D rectangular prism

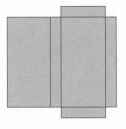

4. What is the surface area of this box?

   A 550 mm²

   B 900 mm²

   C 1100 mm²

   D 1800 mm²

5 mm

20 mm

18 mm

5. What is the surface area of a cylinder that is 30.5 cm long and has a radius of 3 cm, to the nearest hundredth of a square centimetre?

   A 274.50 cm²   B 603.19 cm²

   C 631.14 cm²   D 688.01 cm²

Short Answer

6. Sketch the top, front, and side views of this building.

7. An object may have more than one net. Draw three different nets for this cube.

8. A DVD case is made of a plastic covering that measures 19 cm long, 13.5 cm wide, and 1.4 cm thick. Calculate the surface area to the nearest tenth of a square centimetre.

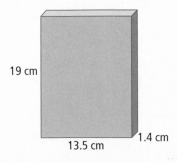

19 cm

13.5 cm

1.4 cm

9. The surface area of a cube is 1014 cm². Find the length of any side of the cube.

Extended Response

10. a) Sketch a three-dimensional object you can build using two of these triangular prisms.

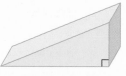

b) Draw the front view, top view, and side view of your object.

c) Draw a net for your object.

11. Ken and Arika are comparing their cylinders. Arika's cylinder is twice as tall as Ken's, but is only half the diameter. Ken's cylinder has a height of 18 cm and a diameter of 9 cm. Whose cylinder has the greater surface area? Explain.

12. Single-serving juice boxes measure 10 cm by 7 cm by 5 cm. A manufacturer wants to shrink wrap four boxes together for sale. Which of the following arrangements of the boxes will use the least amount of plastic wrap? Show how you know.

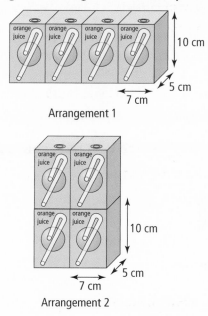

Arrangement 1

Arrangement 2

WRAP IT UP!

It is time to create your miniature community!

Work together to finalize one aerial view for your community. You may choose to start with one that you created on page 163.

Include the following in your diagram and description:

• All the buildings designed by you and your group members.
• A 3-D sketch, net, and surface area calculations for one new building for each member of your group. The new designs should include at least one prism and cylinder. Check each other's work before submitting.
• Streets to navigate through the city.
• Environmental considerations such as water source, parks, etc.

Math Games

Let's Face It!

1. Play Let's Face It! with a partner or in a small group. These are the rules:
   - Remove the jacks, queens, kings, aces, and jokers from the deck of cards.
   - Take turns dealing the cards. It does not matter who deals first.
   - Shuffle the cards and deal three cards, face up, to each player.
   - Use the values of the cards as the dimensions, in centimetres, of a rectangular prism.
   - Calculate the surface area of your rectangular prism using pencil and paper.
   - Each player who calculates the surface area of their prism correctly scores a point. (You will need to check each other's work.)
   - The player with the rectangular prism that has the greatest surface area scores an extra point for that round. If there is a tie, each of the tied players scores an extra point.
   - The first player to reach ten points wins the game. If more than one player earns ten points in the same game, these players continue playing until one of them pulls ahead.

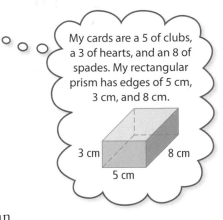

My cards are a 5 of clubs, a 3 of hearts, and an 8 of spades. My rectangular prism has edges of 5 cm, 3 cm, and 8 cm.

3 cm   8 cm
5 cm

2. Play a different version of Let's Face It! by modifying the rules as follows:
   - Deal only two cards to each player and use them to describe the size of a right cylinder. The first card gives the radius of each circle, in centimetres. The second card gives the height of the cylinder, in centimetres.
   - Use a calculator to determine the surface area of your cylinder, to the nearest hundredth of a square centimetre.
   - Award points and decide the winner in the same way as before.

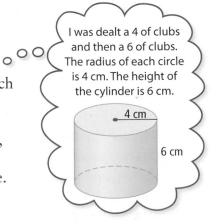

I was dealt a 4 of clubs and then a 6 of clubs. The radius of each circle is 4 cm. The height of the cylinder is 6 cm.

4 cm

6 cm

Design a Bedroom

Have you ever wondered what it would be like to completely design a room? Suppose you were given the opportunity to create the kind of space that a person your age would appreciate and make good use of.

You be the interior designer. Your first project is to create a design for a bedroom that is 4 m wide by 5 m long, and is 2.5 m high.

1. **a)** Draw the top view of the room and place at least three objects in the room.

   b) Draw the top, front, and side views of at least three objects you put in the room. Identify the 3-D shape that each object closely resembles.

2. **a)** Painting your room is the next step. Determine the amount of paint you need to cover the walls and ceiling of your room.

   b) One can of the paint you are going to use covers 10 m²/L. How many cans do you need?

6

Fraction Operations

Canada is divided into 20 ecozones. Each one has its own distinctive mix of geography, climate, animals, plants, and human activities. Because Canada is such a vast country, the ecozones have a wide variety of characteristics.

In this chapter, you will learn more about Canada's ecozones and about how you can use fractions to describe them.

What You Will Learn

❑ to multiply and divide fractions and mixed numbers using manipulatives, diagrams, and symbols

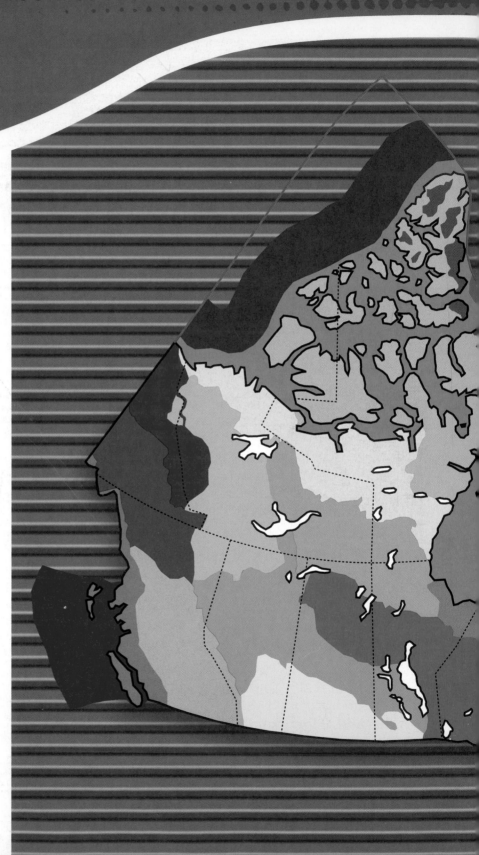

Key Words

- proper fraction
- improper fraction
- mixed number
- reciprocal
- order of operations

TERRESTRIAL ECOZONES
- ◼ Arctic Cordillera
- ◻ Northern Arctic
- ◻ Southern Arctic
- ◻ Taiga Plains
- ◻ Taiga Shield
- ◼ Taiga Cordillera
- ◻ Hudson Plains
- ◻ Boreal Plains
- ◻ Boreal Shield
- ◻ Boreal Cordillera
- ◼ Pacific Maritime
- ◻ Montane Cordillera
- ◻ Prairies
- ◻ Atlantic Maritime
- ◼ Mixedwood Plains

MARINE ECOZONES
- ◼ Pacific Marine
- ◼ Arctic Basin
- ◼ Arctic Archipelago
- ◼ Northwest Atlantic
- ◻ Atlantic Marine

Literacy 🔗 Link

Before starting the chapter, copy the following KWL chart into your math journal or notebook. Brainstorm with a partner what you already know about fraction operations.

- Record your ideas in the first column.
- List any questions you have about fraction operations in the second column.
- As you complete each section of the chapter, list what you have learned in the third column.

Fraction Operations

What I *Know*	What I *Want* to Know	What I *Learned*

Making the Foldable

Materials

- eight sheets of notebook paper
- scissors
- stapler

Step 1

Fold eight sheets of notebook paper in half, as shown in Step 2.

Step 2

With the holes to the left and the fold up, cut along the margin line of the top part of each folded paper, stopping at the fold.

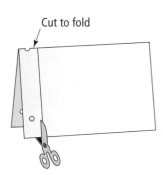

Cut to fold

Step 3

Stack the eight sheets of paper together, positioning the fold to the top and the cut margins to the left, as shown. Staple the stacked sheets along the left side.

Staple here

Step 4

Label the front of the top folded sheet as shown. Label the following six folded sheets with the section number and title for Sections 6.1 to 6.6. Label the last folded sheet "Math Links."

Chapter 6
Fraction Operations

Math Link Introduction

Step 5

Label the inside of the folded sheets for each section as shown

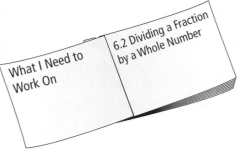

Key Words

Notes

Step 6

Label the back of the folded sheets for each section as shown.

What I Need to Work On

6.2 Dividing a Fraction by a Whole Number

Step 7

Label the back of the Foldable "Ideas for Wrap It Up!"

Using the Foldable

Record your work for the Math Link introduction on page 197 on the first part of your Foldable.

As you work through each section of Chapter 6, keep track of the Key Words and examples on the inside of the folded sheet for each section.

On the back of each section, make notes under the heading What I Need to Work On. Check off each item as you deal with it.

Use the last folded sheet to keep track of your answers for the Math Link for each section. Record your ideas for the Wrap It Up! on the back of the Foldable.

MATH LINK

Canada's Ecozones

Refer to the map of Canada's ecozones on pages 194–195. Identify the location of each ecozone that is named in this Math Link.

The boundaries between ecozones depend on variations in geography, climate, animals, plants, and human activities. Therefore, ecozones have irregular shapes. Their boundaries do not generally coincide with borders between provinces and territories. Ecozones also vary in size. For example, the Boreal Shield ecozone has over nine times the area of the Pacific Maritime ecozone.

1. **a)** About $\frac{1}{10}$ of the length of Canada's coastline is in the Pacific Marine ecozone. About $\frac{1}{5}$ of the length of Canada's coastline is in the Northwest Atlantic ecozone. Use diagrams to represent these fractions and their sum. What is the sum? What does the sum represent?

   b) The Montane Cordillera ecozone covers $\frac{1}{21}$ of Canada. The Northern Arctic ecozone covers $\frac{1}{7}$ of Canada. What total fraction of Canada do these two ecozones cover? Show your thinking.

Strategies
Draw a Diagram

2. The Prairies ecozone covers parts of three provinces. About $\frac{1}{2}$ of the area of this ecozone is in Saskatchewan, and about $\frac{1}{3}$ of the area of this ecozone is in Alberta. The rest of this ecozone is in Manitoba. What fraction of the area of this ecozone is in Manitoba? Show two ways to get your answer.

In this chapter, you will learn how to use multiplication and division of fractions to solve problems that involve Canada's ecozones.

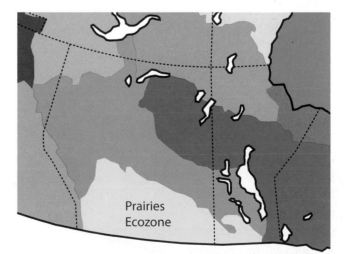

Prairies Ecozone

Multiplying a Fraction and a Whole Number

Chess is one of the most popular board games. It has been estimated that about $\frac{1}{5}$ of adult Canadians play chess at least once a year. The chess board shown has black and white squares. What fraction of the total number of squares are black? If you were told the total area of all the squares, how could you determine the total area of the black squares?

Explore the Math

How can you model the multiplication of a fraction and a whole number?

1. a) How do the pattern blocks model an addition? Describe it.

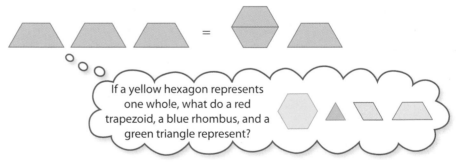

If a yellow hexagon represents one whole, what do a red trapezoid, a blue rhombus, and a green triangle represent?

b) How do the pattern blocks also model a multiplication? Describe it.

c) Work with a partner to explore other manipulatives you could use to model the multiplication.

2. a) Work with a partner to explore how you could use diagrams to model $4 \times \frac{1}{6}$.

b) Write an equation to represent your model.

3. a) Model $2 \times \dfrac{4}{3}$ using the method of your choice.

b) Write an equation to represent your model.

Reflect on Your Findings

4. a) Share your models with your classmates.

b) Suggest other manipulatives or diagrams you could use. How would you use them?

Example 1: Multiply Using A Model

Determine $3 \times \dfrac{5}{6}$. Express the product in lowest terms.

Solution

You can express the multiplication as a repeated addition.

$3 \times \dfrac{5}{6} = \dfrac{5}{6} + \dfrac{5}{6} + \dfrac{5}{6}$

Model the fractions using fraction strips.

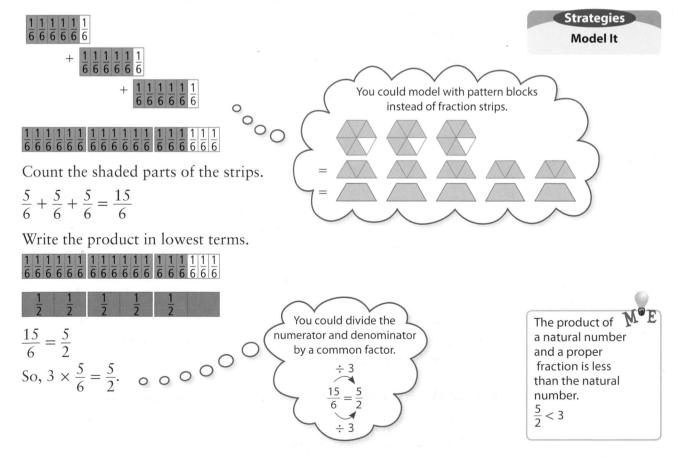

Count the shaded parts of the strips.

$\dfrac{5}{6} + \dfrac{5}{6} + \dfrac{5}{6} = \dfrac{15}{6}$

Write the product in lowest terms.

$\dfrac{15}{6} = \dfrac{5}{2}$

So, $3 \times \dfrac{5}{6} = \dfrac{5}{2}$.

You could model with pattern blocks instead of fraction strips.

You could divide the numerator and denominator by a common factor.

$$\dfrac{15}{6} \overset{\div 3}{\underset{\div 3}{=}} \dfrac{5}{2}$$

Literacy ⊖ Link

Classifying Fractions

In a *proper fraction*, such as $\dfrac{1}{2}$ or $\dfrac{5}{6}$, the denominator is greater than the numerator.

In an *improper fraction*, such as $\dfrac{5}{2}$ or $\dfrac{4}{3}$, the numerator is greater than the denominator.

A *mixed number*, such as $1\dfrac{1}{4}$ or $4\dfrac{3}{5}$, includes a whole number and a proper fraction.

Strategies

Model It

The product of a natural number and a proper fraction is less than the natural number.

$\dfrac{5}{2} < 3$

Determine each product using models. Express the product in lowest terms.

a) $2 \times \dfrac{5}{6}$ **b)** $4 \times \dfrac{2}{3}$

Example 2: Multiply Using a Diagram

Determine $3 \times \dfrac{2}{5}$. Express the product in lowest terms.

Strategies

Draw a Diagram

Solution

$3 \times \dfrac{2}{5} = \dfrac{2}{5} + \dfrac{2}{5} + \dfrac{2}{5}$

Model the fractions using a number line.

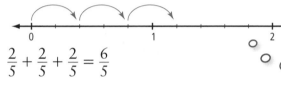

$\dfrac{2}{5} + \dfrac{2}{5} + \dfrac{2}{5} = \dfrac{6}{5}$

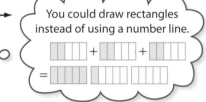

You could draw rectangles instead of using a number line.

The answer is already in lowest terms.

So, $3 \times \dfrac{2}{5} = \dfrac{6}{5}$.

Determine each product using a diagram. Express the product in lowest terms.

a) $2 \times \dfrac{3}{2}$ **b)** $4 \times \dfrac{5}{8}$

Example 3: Apply Multiplication With Fractions

A spider has eight legs. An ant has $\dfrac{3}{4}$ as many legs as a spider. How many legs does an ant have?

Literacy Link

In mathematics, the word **of** often indicates multiplication.

Solution

An ant has $\dfrac{3}{4}$ of the number of legs that a spider has.

$\dfrac{3}{4}$ of 8 means $\dfrac{3}{4} \times 8$.

Multiplying $\frac{3}{4} \times 8$ gives the same answer as multiplying $8 \times \frac{3}{4}$.

Determine $8 \times \frac{3}{4}$.

Model the multiplication as a repeated addition on a number line.

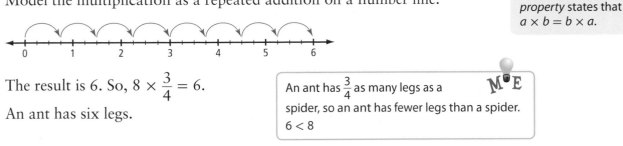

The result is 6. So, $8 \times \frac{3}{4} = 6$.

An ant has six legs.

An ant has $\frac{3}{4}$ as many legs as a spider, so an ant has fewer legs than a spider. $6 < 8$

Literacy 🔗 Link

Commutative Property

The *commutative property* states that $a \times b = b \times a$.

Show You Know

Jenelle is making a recipe that calls for six scoops of flour. She wants to make only $\frac{2}{3}$ of the recipe. How many scoops will she need to use?

Key Ideas

- You can show the multiplication of a fraction and a whole number using models and diagrams.

$3 \times \frac{1}{6} = \frac{1}{2}$

$2 \times \frac{3}{4} = \frac{3}{2}$

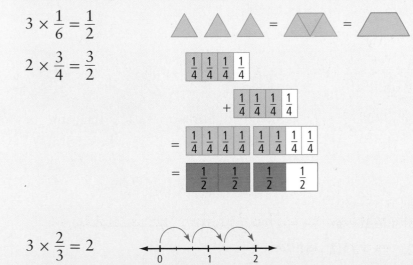

$3 \times \frac{2}{3} = 2$

- Multiplying a fraction and a whole number in either order gives the same result.

$10 \times \frac{2}{5} = 4$ $\frac{2}{5} \times 10 = 4$

1. The diagram models $3 \times \frac{6}{5}$.

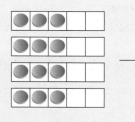

a) What equation does the diagram represent?

b) If a hexagon represents one whole, could you use pattern blocks to model the same multiplication? Explain.

2. Makoto found his own way to model $4 \times \frac{3}{5}$ by using counters on grids.

a) Why did he use 5-by-1 grids?

b) Why did he use four grids?

c) How does Makoto's model show the product?

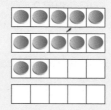

3. Nadine said that she had her own method for determining $4 \times \frac{3}{5}$. She first multiplied 4 and 3 to get 12. She then wrote the product as $\frac{12}{5}$. Do you agree with Nadine's method for multiplying a whole number and a fraction? Explain using other examples.

Check Your Understanding

Practise

For help with #4 to #7, refer to Examples 1 and 2 on pages 199–200.

4. What equation does each model represent? For pattern blocks, assume that a hexagon represents one whole.

a)

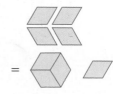

b)

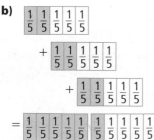

5. What equation does each diagram represent?

a)

b)

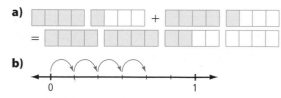

6. Determine each product using manipulatives or diagrams.

a) $4 \times \frac{1}{2}$

b) $3 \times \frac{7}{10}$

c) $5 \times \frac{2}{3}$

d) $3 \times \frac{3}{8}$

7. Determine each product.

a) $3 \times \dfrac{1}{8}$ **b)** $6 \times \dfrac{1}{4}$

c) $2 \times \dfrac{6}{5}$ **d)** $2 \times \dfrac{4}{3}$

Apply

For help with #8 to #9, refer to Example 3 on page 200.

8. The width of a Canadian flag is $\dfrac{1}{2}$ of its length. What is the width of a Canadian flag that is 4 m long?

9. A minibus that seats 12 people is $\dfrac{3}{4}$ full. How many people are seated in the minibus?

10. a) What fraction of the surface area of a cube is the area of one face?

b) What is the area of each face of a cube of surface area 6 cm²?

11. Ron's car uses 12 L of gasoline per 100 km of highway driving. Asma's car uses only $\dfrac{5}{6}$ as much fuel. How much fuel does Asma's car use per 100 km of highway driving?

12. Nunavut covers about $\dfrac{1}{5}$ of the area of Canada. The area of Canada is about ten million square kilometres. What is the approximate area of Nunavut?

13. Suppose a friend knows how to multiply whole numbers, but not fractions.

a) How could you use the following pattern to show your friend how to calculate $\dfrac{1}{2} \times 10$?

$4 \times 10 = 40$
$2 \times 10 = 20$
$1 \times 10 = 10$
$\dfrac{1}{2} \times 10 = \blacksquare$

b) Make up a pattern to show your friend how to calculate $\dfrac{1}{3} \times 9$.

14. Write a word problem that you can solve using the expression $\dfrac{1}{4} \times 8$.

Extend

15. There are 30 students in a class. Four fifths of them have brown eyes. How many students have brown eyes?

16. The perimeter of an isosceles triangle is 15 cm. The shortest side equals $\dfrac{1}{5}$ of the perimeter. What are the side lengths of the triangle?

17. A ball dropped to the ground bounces back to $\dfrac{2}{3}$ of its previous height. If the ball is dropped straight down from a height of 81 cm, how far does it travel altogether by the time it hits the ground for the fifth time?

MATH LINK

A quarter of Canada's 20 ecozones are marine ecozones, which include parts of oceans. The rest of Canada's ecozones are terrestrial ecozones. They include parts of the land, and may contain rivers, lakes, and wetlands.

a) How many marine ecozones does Canada have?

b) How many terrestrial ecozones does Canada have?

6.2 Dividing a Fraction by a Whole Number

Focus on...

After this lesson, you will be able to...

❏ divide a fraction by a whole number

❏ solve problems involving the division of fractions by whole numbers

Iqaluit, the capital of Nunavut, has frost on about $\frac{3}{4}$ of the days in a year. Iqaluit has frost on five times as many days as Vancouver, British Columbia. Work with a partner to explore how you might determine the fraction of the days in a year that Vancouver has frost.

Materials

• pattern blocks
• fraction strips

Literacy ⊝ Link

Understanding Division

In the equation $6 \div 2 = 3$, the dividend is 6, the divisor is 2, and the quotient is 3.

The equation $6 \div 2 = 3$ means that in 6 there are 3 groups of 2. This division statement also means that if 6 is separated into 2 equal groups, there are 3 in each group.

Explore the Math

How can you model the division of a fraction by a whole number?

1. a) The long rectangle in the following diagram represents one whole. The diagram models a division. Describe it.

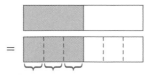

b) Work with a partner to explore other diagrams you could use to model the division.

2. a) Work with a partner to explore how you could use manipulatives to model $\frac{2}{3} \div 2$.

b) Write an equation to represent your model.

Reflect on Your Findings

3. a) Share your models with your classmates.

b) Can you think of other manipulatives or diagrams you could use? If so, explain how you would use them.

Example 1: Divide Using a Model

Determine $\frac{1}{4} \div 3$.

Solution

Use a fraction strip to represent $\frac{1}{4}$.

$\frac{1}{4}$	$\frac{1}{4}$	$\frac{1}{4}$	$\frac{1}{4}$

$\frac{1}{12}$	$\frac{1}{12}$	$\frac{1}{12}$	$\frac{1}{12}$	$\frac{1}{12}$	$\frac{1}{12}$	$\frac{1}{12}$	$\frac{1}{12}$	$\frac{1}{12}$	$\frac{1}{12}$	$\frac{1}{12}$	$\frac{1}{12}$

Identify the fraction strip that shows $\frac{1}{4}$ cut into three equal parts.

The fraction strip shows that $\frac{1}{4}$ is equivalent to $\frac{3}{12}$.

Each of the three equal parts of $\frac{1}{4}$ is $\frac{1}{12}$.

$\frac{1}{12}$	$\frac{1}{12}$	$\frac{1}{12}$	$\frac{1}{12}$	$\frac{1}{12}$	$\frac{1}{12}$	$\frac{1}{12}$	$\frac{1}{12}$	$\frac{1}{12}$	$\frac{1}{12}$	$\frac{1}{12}$	$\frac{1}{12}$

$\frac{1}{4} \div 3 = \frac{1}{12}$

Strategies

Model It

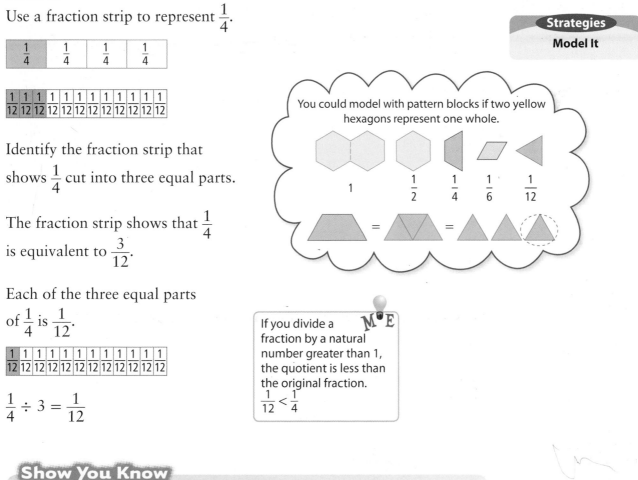

You could model with pattern blocks if two yellow hexagons represent one whole.

1 $\frac{1}{2}$ $\frac{1}{4}$ $\frac{1}{6}$ $\frac{1}{12}$

If you divide a fraction by a natural number greater than 1, the quotient is less than the original fraction.
$\frac{1}{12} < \frac{1}{4}$

Show You Know

Determine each quotient using models.

a) $\frac{3}{4} \div 3$ **b)** $\frac{5}{6} \div 2$

Example 2: Divide Using Diagrams

Determine $\frac{2}{3} \div 4$. Express the quotient in lowest terms.

Strategies

Draw a Diagram

Solution

Draw and label a number line that shows thirds.

To model division by 4, cut each third into four equal parts.

There are 12 parts in the whole, so each part is $\frac{1}{12}$.

Use brackets to cut $\frac{2}{3}$ into four equal parts.

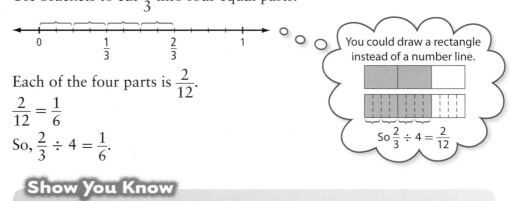

You could draw a rectangle instead of a number line.

So $\frac{2}{3} \div 4 = \frac{2}{12}$

Each of the four parts is $\frac{2}{12}$.

$$\frac{2}{12} = \frac{1}{6}$$

So, $\frac{2}{3} \div 4 = \frac{1}{6}$.

Show You Know

Determine each quotient using a diagram. Express the quotient in lowest terms.

a) $\frac{1}{2} \div 5$ **b)** $\frac{3}{5} \div 3$

Example 3: Apply Division With Fractions

Mustafa used $\frac{3}{4}$ of a jar of pasta sauce on six servings of pasta. He used the same amount of sauce on each serving. What fraction of the jar of pasta sauce did he use on each serving?

Solution

Determine $\frac{3}{4} \div 6$.

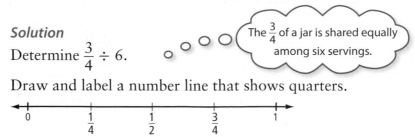

The $\frac{3}{4}$ of a jar is shared equally among six servings.

Draw and label a number line that shows quarters.

To model division by 6, cut each quarter into six equal parts.

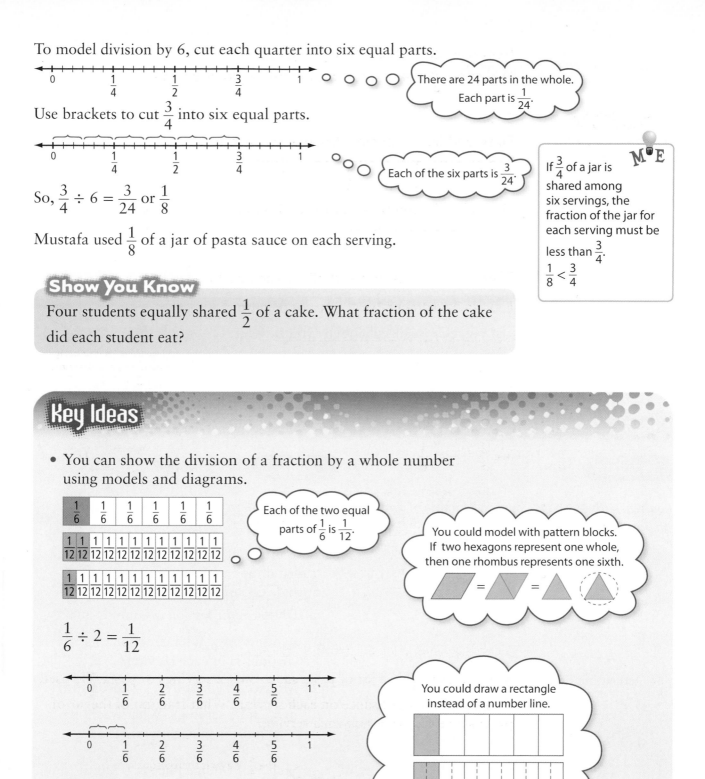

There are 24 parts in the whole. Each part is $\frac{1}{24}$.

Use brackets to cut $\frac{3}{4}$ into six equal parts.

Each of the six parts is $\frac{3}{24}$.

So, $\frac{3}{4} \div 6 = \frac{3}{24}$ or $\frac{1}{8}$

Mustafa used $\frac{1}{8}$ of a jar of pasta sauce on each serving.

If $\frac{3}{4}$ of a jar is shared among six servings, the fraction of the jar for each serving must be less than $\frac{3}{4}$.

$\frac{1}{8} < \frac{3}{4}$

Show You Know

Four students equally shared $\frac{1}{2}$ of a cake. What fraction of the cake did each student eat?

Key Ideas

• You can show the division of a fraction by a whole number using models and diagrams.

Each of the two equal parts of $\frac{1}{6}$ is $\frac{1}{12}$.

You could model with pattern blocks. If two hexagons represent one whole, then one rhombus represents one sixth.

$\frac{1}{6} \div 2 = \frac{1}{12}$

You could draw a rectangle instead of a number line.

$\frac{1}{6} \div 2 = \frac{1}{12}$

1. Lana decided to model the division $\frac{2}{3} \div 3$ using a fraction strip divided into sixths. Could you use this fraction strip to solve the problem? Explain.

2. **a)** If you use four hexagons to represent one whole, show how you can model $\frac{3}{4} \div 6$ using pattern blocks.

   b) Can you model $\frac{3}{4} \div 6$ by using two hexagons to represent one whole? Explain.

3. **a)** Model the division $\frac{1}{2} \div 2$ using manipulatives or diagrams.

   b) Which method did you choose? Explain why you chose it.

Check Your Understanding

Practise

For help with #4 and #5, refer to Examples 1 and 2 on pages 205–206.

4. Determine each quotient using manipulatives or diagrams.

   a) $\frac{1}{4} \div 2$ **b)** $\frac{1}{3} \div 3$

   c) $\frac{1}{5} \div 2$ **d)** $\frac{5}{6} \div 4$

5. Determine each quotient.

   a) $\frac{3}{5} \div 2$ **b)** $\frac{1}{5} \div 3$

   c) $\frac{1}{2} \div 4$ **d)** $\frac{2}{3} \div 6$

Apply

For help with #6 to #8, refer to Example 3 on pages 206–207.

6. Two different South Indian fish curries, called dhopa and molee curry, both include coconut.

   a) Dhopa requires $\frac{1}{2}$ a coconut to make two servings. What fraction of a coconut is in each serving?

   b) Molee curry requires $\frac{1}{2}$ a coconut to make four servings. What fraction of a coconut is in each serving?

7. A pitcher of orange juice is $\frac{2}{3}$ full. If four students equally share the juice, what fraction of the full pitcher does each student get?

8. The areas of Alberta, Saskatchewan, and Manitoba are approximately equal. The sum of their areas is about $\frac{1}{5}$ of the area of Canada. Express the area of each of these provinces as a fraction of the area of Canada.

9. Ingrid runs three laps of a track in $\frac{1}{4}$ h.

On average, how much time does she take to run one lap? Express your answer

a) as a fraction of an hour

b) in minutes

10. Mark uses $\frac{1}{3}$ of a tank of gasoline in a five-day work week driving to work and back. On average, what fraction of a tank does he use for each round trip?

11. Iqaluit has frost on about $\frac{3}{4}$ of the days in a year. It has frost on five times as many days as Vancouver. On what fraction of the days of the year does Vancouver have frost?

12. It takes $\frac{4}{5}$ of a roll of ribbon to wrap six packages. What fraction of a roll does it take to wrap three packages?

13. Create your own word problem that involves the division of a proper fraction by a whole number. Make sure that you can solve your problem. Give your problem to a classmate to solve.

Extend

14. Two fractions are equally spaced between $\frac{2}{5}$ and $\frac{4}{5}$. Determine the two fractions.

15. a) Model the division $\frac{2}{3} \div 4 = \frac{1}{6}$ using manipulatives or diagrams.

b) Explain how your method shows that $\frac{2}{3} \div \frac{1}{6} = 4$.

MATH LINK

The Montane Cordillera and Boreal Cordillera ecozones have approximately equal areas. The total area of these two ecozones equals about $\frac{1}{10}$ of the area of Canada. What fraction of the area of Canada does each of these ecozones cover?

Multiplying Proper Fractions

A two-toed sloth sleeps for 20 h per day. A chimpanzee sleeps $\frac{1}{2}$ that much. A horse sleeps $\frac{1}{2}$ as much as a chimpanzee. In a day, what fraction of the time that a two-toed sloth sleeps does a horse sleep? How do you know?

Explore the Math

Materials
• six sheets of plain paper
• yellow and blue coloured pencils or crayons

How can you multiply two proper fractions?

1. You can determine $\frac{1}{2}$ of $\frac{2}{3}$ using paper folding.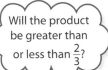

> Will the product be greater than or less than $\frac{2}{3}$?

• Fold a rectangular piece of paper into thirds along its length. Open the paper and shade $\frac{2}{3}$ of it yellow.

• Fold the paper in half across its width. Open the paper and shade half of it blue.
  How does the model show $\frac{1}{2}$ of $\frac{2}{3}$?

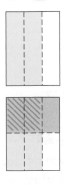

2. Copy the table. Complete the table by using the method from #1. Do not write the products in lowest terms.

Multiplication	Product
$\frac{1}{2} \times \frac{2}{3}$	
$\frac{1}{3} \times \frac{1}{2}$	
$\frac{3}{4} \times \frac{1}{3}$	
$\frac{3}{4} \times \frac{2}{3}$	
$\frac{3}{4} \times \frac{3}{4}$	

3. For each row of the table, describe the relationship between

a) the numerators   **b)** the denominators

Strategies

Look for a Pattern

4. Use your answers from #3 to write a rule for multiplying two proper fractions.

5. a) Test your rule on the product $\frac{3}{4} \times \frac{1}{2}$.

b) Check your answer to part a) by paper folding.

Reflect on Your Findings

6. a) How can you multiply two proper fractions by paper folding or using a rule?

b) Which method do you prefer? Explain.

Example 1: Multiply Using Paper Folding

Determine $\frac{1}{2} \times \frac{3}{5}$.

Solution

Fold a rectangular piece of paper into fifths along its length. Open the paper and shade three fifths of it yellow. Fold the paper in half across its width.

Open the paper and shade half of it blue. The folds make ten equal rectangles. Three of them are shaded both yellow and blue, so they appear green.

$\frac{1}{2} \times \frac{3}{5} = \frac{3}{10}$

The numerator in the product is the number of green rectangles. The denominator in the product is the total number of equal rectangles.

Determine each product using paper folding.

a) $\dfrac{1}{4} \times \dfrac{1}{2}$ b) $\dfrac{2}{3} \times \dfrac{2}{3}$

Example 2: Multiply Using Diagrams

Determine $\dfrac{2}{3} \times \dfrac{1}{2}$.

Solution

Draw a rectangle. Draw line segments to cut its length into thirds.

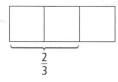

Draw a line segment to cut the width of the rectangle into halves.

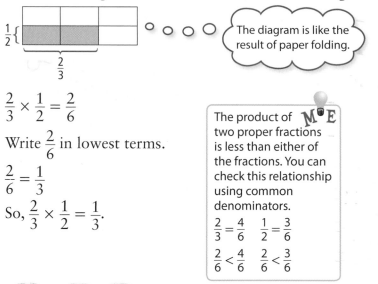

The diagram is like the result of paper folding.

$\dfrac{2}{3} \times \dfrac{1}{2} = \dfrac{2}{6}$

Write $\dfrac{2}{6}$ in lowest terms.

$\dfrac{2}{6} = \dfrac{1}{3}$

So, $\dfrac{2}{3} \times \dfrac{1}{2} = \dfrac{1}{3}$.

> **Literacy Link**
>
> **Understanding Common Denominators**
> For $\dfrac{1}{2}$ and $\dfrac{2}{3}$, a common denominator is 6, which is a common multiple of 2 and 3.

The product of two proper fractions is less than either of the fractions. You can check this relationship using common denominators.

$\dfrac{2}{3} = \dfrac{4}{6}$ $\dfrac{1}{2} = \dfrac{3}{6}$

$\dfrac{2}{6} < \dfrac{4}{6}$ $\dfrac{2}{6} < \dfrac{3}{6}$

Determine each product using diagrams.

a) $\dfrac{1}{2} \times \dfrac{1}{2}$ b) $\dfrac{1}{3} \times \dfrac{3}{4}$

Example 3: Multiply Using a Rule

Estimate and calculate $\dfrac{8}{15} \times \dfrac{5}{6}$.

Solution

Decide whether each fraction is closer to 0, $\dfrac{1}{2}$, or 1.

$\dfrac{8}{15} \approx \dfrac{1}{2}$ $\qquad \dfrac{5}{6} \approx 1$

Then estimate the product.

$$\dfrac{8}{15} \times \dfrac{5}{6} \approx \dfrac{1}{2} \times 1$$
$$\approx \dfrac{1}{2}$$

To multiply fractions, multiply the numerators and multiply the denominators.

$$\dfrac{8}{15} \times \dfrac{5}{6} = \dfrac{40}{90}$$
$$= \dfrac{4}{9}$$

The answer seems reasonable, because it is close to the estimate of $\dfrac{1}{2}$.

Show You Know

Estimate and calculate.

a) $\dfrac{3}{5} \times \dfrac{2}{9}$ **b)** $\dfrac{5}{6} \times \dfrac{4}{5}$

Key Ideas

- You can multiply two proper fractions using paper folding.

$$\dfrac{1}{4} \times \dfrac{1}{3} = \dfrac{1}{12}$$

- You can multiply two proper fractions using diagrams.

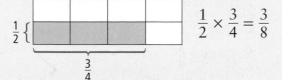

$$\dfrac{1}{2} \times \dfrac{3}{4} = \dfrac{3}{8}$$

- A rule for multiplying two proper fractions is to multiply the numerators and multiply the denominators.

$$\dfrac{3}{5} \times \dfrac{5}{6} = \dfrac{15}{30} \text{ or } \dfrac{1}{2}$$

- You can estimate the product of two proper fractions by first deciding whether each fraction is closer to 0, $\dfrac{1}{2}$, or 1.

$$\dfrac{3}{7} \approx \dfrac{1}{2} \qquad \dfrac{4}{7} \approx \dfrac{1}{2} \qquad \dfrac{3}{7} \times \dfrac{4}{7} \approx \dfrac{1}{4}$$

1. a) Model $\frac{2}{3} \times \frac{1}{3}$ using manipulatives or diagrams.

   b) Which method did you choose? Explain why you chose it.

2. Brendan calculated $\frac{3}{5} \times \frac{2}{5}$ as follows:
   $$\frac{3}{5} \times \frac{2}{5} = \frac{6}{5}$$

   a) What mistake did he make?

   b) How could you use estimation to show Brendan that he made a mistake?

   c) What is the correct product?

Check Your Understanding

Practise

For help with #3 and #4, refer to Examples 1 and 2 on pages 211–212.

3. Determine each product using paper folding or diagrams.

   a) $\frac{5}{6} \times \frac{1}{2}$ b) $\frac{3}{4} \times \frac{5}{6}$

4. Use paper folding or diagrams to determine each product.

   a) $\frac{1}{4} \times \frac{2}{3}$ b) $\frac{7}{10} \times \frac{1}{2}$

For help with #5 and #6, refer to Example 3 on page 213.

5. Estimate and calculate each product. Express your answer in lowest terms.

   a) $\frac{3}{8} \times \frac{2}{3}$ b) $\frac{3}{7} \times \frac{1}{6}$ c) $\frac{3}{4} \times \frac{3}{4}$

6. Estimate and calculate each product. Express your answer in lowest terms.

   a) $\frac{2}{5} \times \frac{4}{5}$ b) $\frac{7}{8} \times \frac{4}{5}$ c) $\frac{3}{4} \times \frac{4}{9}$

Apply

7. Tamar had $\frac{1}{2}$ of an apple pie in her refrigerator. She ate $\frac{1}{4}$ of this piece of pie. What fraction of a whole pie did she eat?

8. Marius spends $\frac{1}{3}$ of his time sleeping. While he is asleep, he dreams for $\frac{1}{4}$ of the time.

   a) For what fraction of his time is Marius dreaming?

   b) For how many hours a day is Marius dreaming?

9. About $\frac{1}{20}$ of the people in the world live in Canada or the United States. Of the people who live in Canada or the United States, about $\frac{1}{10}$ live in Canada. What fraction of the people in the world live in Canada?

10. At the age of four, the average person is about $\frac{3}{5}$ as tall as they will be as an adult. At birth, the average person is about $\frac{1}{2}$ as tall as they will be at the age of four. For the average person, what fraction is their height at birth of their height as an adult?

11. When the Summer Olympic and Paralympic Games were held in Athens, Greece, paralympic athletes won $\frac{6}{7}$ of Canada's total medals. Of the medals that Canadian paralympic athletes won, $\frac{7}{18}$ were gold medals.

a) What fraction of Canada's total medals were gold medals won by paralympic athletes?

b) Canada won a total of 84 medals. How many gold medals did Canadian paralympic athletes win?

12. Write a word problem that you can solve using the expression $\frac{3}{4} \times \frac{1}{2}$.

Extend

13. For a standard deck of 52 playing cards, the probability of randomly drawing a red card is $\frac{1}{2}$. The probability of randomly drawing a face card (jack, queen, or king) is $\frac{12}{52}$. What is the probability of randomly drawing a face card that is red?

14. Calculate. Express the product in lowest terms.

a) $\frac{1}{2} \times \frac{1}{2} \times \frac{1}{2}$

b) $\frac{2}{3} \times \frac{1}{4} \times \frac{2}{5}$

c) $\frac{3}{4} \times \frac{3}{4} \times \frac{2}{9}$

d) $\frac{5}{6} \times \frac{3}{8} \times \frac{7}{10}$

15. Copy each equation. Complete it using a fraction in lowest terms.

a) $\frac{\blacksquare}{\blacksquare} \times \frac{1}{2} = \frac{5}{16}$

b) $\frac{\blacksquare}{\blacksquare} \times \frac{3}{7} = \frac{1}{3}$

c) $\frac{2}{3} \times \frac{\blacksquare}{\blacksquare} = \frac{1}{2}$

d) $\frac{3}{4} \times \frac{\blacksquare}{\blacksquare} = \frac{5}{8}$

16. Use the sum and the product of two fractions to identify the fractions.

a) sum $\frac{1}{2}$; product $\frac{1}{16}$

b) sum $\frac{5}{6}$; product $\frac{1}{6}$

c) sum $\frac{2}{3}$; product $\frac{1}{12}$

MATH LINK

The area of British Columbia is about $\frac{1}{10}$ of the area of Canada. The Pacific Maritime ecozone covers about $\frac{1}{5}$ of the area of British Columbia. What fraction of the area of Canada does the Pacific Maritime ecozone cover?

Multiplying Improper Fractions and Mixed Numbers

The length of the flag of British Columbia is $1\frac{2}{3}$ times its width.

How would you determine the length of a flag that is 90 cm wide?

Explore the Math

How can you multiply two improper fractions or mixed numbers?

1. The diagram shows a way to model the multiplication $1\frac{1}{2} \times 1\frac{1}{2}$.

   a) What is the total area of the large square? Show your method. Express the total area as a mixed number in lowest terms.

   b) Write an equation to represent the multiplication.

	1	$\frac{1}{2}$
1	A	B
$\frac{1}{2}$	C	D

2. Model each of the following multiplications using a similar model to the one used in #1. Express each total as a mixed number in lowest terms.

   a) $2\frac{1}{2} \times 2\frac{1}{2}$

   b) $1\frac{1}{4} \times 1\frac{1}{4}$

   c) $1\frac{1}{2} \times 1\frac{1}{4}$

3. a) Copy the table. Use your results from #1 and #2 to complete it. The first line is partially completed for you.

Multiplication of Mixed Numbers	Product Expressed as a Mixed Number	Multiplication of Improper Fractions	Product Expressed as an Improper Fraction
$1\frac{1}{2} \times 1\frac{1}{2}$		$\frac{3}{2} \times \frac{3}{2}$	
$2\frac{1}{2} \times 2\frac{1}{2}$			
$1\frac{1}{4} \times 1\frac{1}{4}$			
$1\frac{1}{2} \times 1\frac{1}{4}$			

b) Write a rule to multiply two improper fractions?

c) How is your rule the same or different from the rule you developed for multiplying two proper fractions? Explain.

Literacy 🔗 Link

Converting Improper Fractions and Mixed Numbers

Convert by using the denominator to decide the number of parts in one whole.

In $\frac{11}{4}$, one whole is $\frac{4}{4}$.

$\frac{11}{4} = \frac{4}{4} + \frac{4}{4} + \frac{3}{4}$

$\frac{11}{4} = 2\frac{3}{4}$

In $3\frac{2}{5}$, one whole is $\frac{5}{5}$.

$3\frac{2}{5} = \frac{5}{5} + \frac{5}{5} + \frac{5}{5} + \frac{2}{5}$

$3\frac{2}{5} = \frac{17}{5}$

Reflect on Your Findings

4. How can you multiply two improper fractions or mixed numbers by using a model or a rule?

Example 1: Multiply Mixed Numbers Using a Model

Determine $2\frac{1}{2} \times 1\frac{3}{4}$.

Solution

Draw a rectangle.

Draw a line segment to separate each dimension into a whole number and a proper fraction.

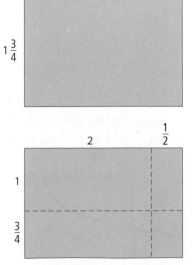

Strategies

Model It

Literacy Link

A whole number can be written as a fraction with a denominator of 1.

For example, $2 = \frac{2}{1}$

Show the area of each of the four regions in the diagram.

$2 \times \frac{3}{4} = \frac{2}{1} \times \frac{3}{4}$

$= \frac{6}{4}$

$= \frac{3}{2}$

$= 1\frac{1}{2}$

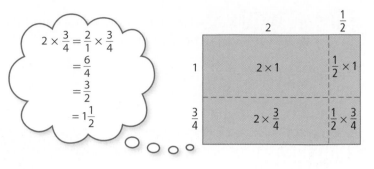

Calculate the area of each region and add the areas.

$2 \times 1 = 2 \qquad 2 \times \frac{3}{4} = 1\frac{1}{2} \qquad \frac{1}{2} \times 1 = \frac{1}{2} \qquad \frac{1}{2} \times \frac{3}{4} = \frac{3}{8}$

$2 + 1\frac{1}{2} + \frac{1}{2} + \frac{3}{8} = 4\frac{3}{8}$

So, $2\frac{1}{2} \times 1\frac{3}{4} = 4\frac{3}{8}$

Show You Know

Determine each product using a model.

a) $1\frac{3}{4} \times 1\frac{3}{4}$ **b)** $2\frac{1}{4} \times 2\frac{1}{4}$ **c)** $1\frac{1}{4} \times 1\frac{1}{3}$

Example 2: Multiply Mixed Numbers Using a Rule

Estimate and calculate $4\frac{1}{2} \times 2\frac{1}{3}$.

Solution

Estimate the product by multiplying the whole numbers closest to each mixed number.

$4\frac{1}{2} \times 2\frac{1}{3} \approx 5 \times 2$

≈ 10

To calculate $4\frac{1}{2} \times 2\frac{1}{3}$, write the mixed numbers as improper fractions.

$4\frac{1}{2} \times 2\frac{1}{3} = \frac{9}{2} \times \frac{7}{3}$

$4\frac{1}{2} = \frac{2}{2} + \frac{2}{2} + \frac{2}{2} + \frac{2}{2} + \frac{1}{2} \qquad 2\frac{1}{3} = \frac{3}{3} + \frac{3}{3} + \frac{1}{3}$

$= \frac{9}{2} \qquad\qquad = \frac{7}{3}$

To multiply the fractions, multiply the numerators and multiply the denominators.

$\frac{9}{2} \times \frac{7}{3} = \frac{63}{6}$

Write this fraction in lowest terms.

$= \frac{21}{2}$

$= 10\frac{1}{2}$

The answer is close to the estimate.

The product of two mixed numbers or improper fractions is greater than either of them.

$10\frac{1}{2} > 4\frac{1}{2} \qquad 10\frac{1}{2} > 2\frac{1}{3}$

Estimate and calculate.

a) $1\frac{1}{10} \times 3\frac{1}{2}$ **b)** $1\frac{1}{4} \times 3\frac{2}{3}$

$\frac{5}{4} \times \frac{11}{3} = \frac{55}{12} = 4\frac{7}{12}$.

Key Ideas

- You can model the multiplication of two mixed numbers or improper fractions using partial areas of a rectangle.

$$2\frac{1}{2} \times 1\frac{1}{4} = 2 + \frac{1}{2} + \frac{1}{2} + \frac{1}{8}$$
$$= 3\frac{1}{8}$$

	2	$\frac{1}{2}$
1	2×1	$\frac{1}{2} \times 1$
$\frac{1}{4}$	$2 \times \frac{1}{4}$	$\frac{1}{2} \times \frac{1}{4}$

- You can estimate the product of two mixed numbers or improper fractions by multiplying the whole numbers closest to them.

$$3\frac{1}{4} \times 1\frac{3}{4} \approx 3 \times 2$$
$$\approx 6$$

- A rule for multiplying two mixed numbers is to express them as improper fractions and then multiply the numerators and multiply the denominators.

$$1\frac{2}{3} \times 2\frac{1}{5} = \frac{5}{3} \times \frac{11}{5}$$
$$= \frac{55}{15} \text{ or } \frac{11}{3}$$

Communicate the Ideas

1. Henri multiplied $2\frac{1}{2} \times 3\frac{1}{4}$ as follows: $2 \times 3 = 6$ and $\frac{1}{2} \times \frac{1}{4} = \frac{1}{8}$, so $2\frac{1}{2} \times 3\frac{1}{4} = 6\frac{1}{8}$.

   a) What mistake did Henri make?

   b) What is the correct product?

2. To express $4\frac{2}{3}$ as an improper fraction, Naomi determined the numerator by calculating $3 \times 4 + 2$.

   a) Explain why Naomi's method works.

   b) Use your explanation to write a rule for expressing a mixed number as an improper fraction. Test your rule.

   c) Write a rule for expressing an improper fraction as a mixed number. Test your rule.

3. Moira multiplied $2\frac{1}{3} \times 2\frac{1}{2}$ as follows:

$$2\frac{1}{3} \times 2\frac{1}{2} = \frac{7}{3} \times \frac{5}{2}$$
$$= \frac{14}{6} \times \frac{15}{6}$$
$$= \frac{210}{36}$$
$$= \frac{35}{6}$$
$$= 5\frac{5}{6}$$

a) Was her final answer correct?

b) How did she make the calculation longer than necessary

Check Your Understanding

Practise

4. Express each improper fraction as a mixed number.

   a) $\frac{11}{3}$ b) $\frac{17}{6}$ c) $\frac{25}{2}$ d) $\frac{8}{5}$

5. Express each mixed number as an improper fraction.

   a) $4\frac{3}{4}$ b) $2\frac{7}{8}$ c) $6\frac{1}{3}$ d) $3\frac{4}{7}$

For help with #6 and #7, refer to Example 1 on pages 217–218.

6. Use a model to determine each product.

   a) $1\frac{1}{3} \times \frac{3}{4}$ b) $2\frac{1}{2} \times 1\frac{3}{5}$

   c) $1\frac{1}{3} \times 1\frac{1}{2}$ d) $2\frac{1}{2} \times 2\frac{1}{4}$

7. Determine each product using a model.

   a) $\frac{1}{2} \times 2\frac{1}{2}$ b) $2\frac{1}{3} \times 2\frac{1}{3}$

   c) $1\frac{1}{2} \times 2\frac{1}{3}$ d) $1\frac{1}{5} \times 1\frac{1}{2}$

For help with #8 and #9, refer to Example 2 on page 218.

8. Estimate and calculate.

   a) $\frac{4}{5} \times \frac{10}{7}$ b) $5 \times 3\frac{3}{4}$ c) $2\frac{1}{5} \times 1\frac{2}{3}$

9. Estimate and calculate.

   a) $\frac{8}{3} \times \frac{11}{6}$ b) $2\frac{5}{6} \times 4$ c) $6\frac{1}{2} \times 3\frac{1}{2}$

Apply

10. Two and a half laps of a running track equal 1 km. How many laps equal 3 km?

11. Earth turns on its axis once every 24 h. How many hours does Earth take to complete $2\frac{1}{4}$ turns?

12. On a day in Winnipeg with $10\frac{1}{2}$ h of daylight, it was sunny for $\frac{1}{3}$ of that time. For how many hours was it sunny that day?

13. Alexa takes $\frac{1}{4}$ h to ride her bicycle to her friend's house. If Alexa walks instead, the trip takes her $2\frac{1}{2}$ times as long. How long does Alexa take to walk to her friend's house

a) in hours?

b) in minutes?

14. In Eric's apartment, the living room is $1\frac{3}{4}$ times as long and $2\frac{1}{2}$ times as wide as the den. Eric is buying the same type of carpet for both rooms. How many times as much will the carpet cost for the living room as for the den?

15. Andreas has $18. Bonnie has $1\frac{2}{3}$ times as much as Andreas. Cheryl has $1\frac{3}{5}$ times as much as Bonnie. How much money do they have altogether?

16. A corner store buys goods at the wholesale price and sells them for $\frac{7}{5}$ of the wholesale price. The wholesale price of a case of 12 cans of stew is $15. For how much does the store sell one can of stew?

17. If you multiply a mixed number and a proper fraction, how does each value compare with the value of the product?

18. Create your own word problem that involves the multiplication of two mixed numbers. Make sure that you can solve your problem. Give your problem to a classmate to solve.

Extend

19. Describe each pattern. Then write the next three terms in each pattern.

a) $4\frac{1}{3}, 2\frac{1}{6}, 1\frac{1}{12}, \frac{13}{24}, \dots$ **b)** $4, 6, 9, 13\frac{1}{2}, \dots$

20. Calculate.

a) $4 \times 1\frac{1}{2} \times 2\frac{1}{2}$ **b)** $\frac{2}{3} \times 3\frac{1}{3} \times 4\frac{1}{2}$

c) $2\frac{3}{4} \times 1\frac{1}{3} \times 3\frac{1}{2}$ **d)** $1\frac{1}{6} \times 1\frac{2}{5} \times 2\frac{2}{7}$

21. Copy each equation. Use a mixed number to complete it.

a) $1\frac{2}{3} \times \blacksquare = 2\frac{1}{2}$ **b)** $\blacksquare \times 2\frac{1}{6} = 2\frac{3}{5}$

c) $\blacksquare \times 1\frac{1}{4} = 3\frac{1}{8}$ **d)** $2\frac{1}{3} \times \blacksquare = 5\frac{5}{6}$

MATH LINK

The Hudson Plains ecozone contains most of Canada's wetlands. This ecozone covers about $\frac{1}{26}$ of the area of Canada. The Northern Arctic ecozone is one of the world's largest Arctic ecosystems. This ecozone is about $3\frac{9}{10}$ times as big as the Hudson Plains ecozone. What fraction of the area of Canada does the Northern Arctic ecozone cover?

6.5 Dividing Fractions and Mixed Numbers

Focus on...

After this lesson, you will be able to...

❏ divide two fractions or mixed numbers

❏ solve problems involving the division of fractions or mixed numbers

Russia and Canada are the two countries with the largest areas in the world. How are the fraction and the mixed number in the following two statements related?

The area of Canada is about $\frac{3}{5}$ of the area of Russia.

The area of Russia is about $1\frac{2}{3}$ times the area of Canada.

Explore the Math

How can you divide a fraction by a fraction?

Work with a partner.

1. When you divide 8 by 4, you determine how many 4s there are in 8. $8 \div 4 = 2$.

   a) Show how you could determine how many $\frac{1}{2}$s there are in 3.

   b) Copy and complete the equation $3 \div \frac{1}{2} = \blacksquare$.

2. a) Show how you could determine how many $\frac{1}{4}$s there are in 2.

   b) Copy and complete the equation $2 \div \frac{1}{4} = \blacksquare$.

3. a) Show how you could determine how many $\frac{1}{4}$s there are in $\frac{3}{4}$.

   b) Copy and complete the equation $\frac{3}{4} \div \frac{1}{4} = \blacksquare$.

4. a) Show how you could determine how many $\frac{1}{6}$s are in $\frac{2}{3}$.

b) Copy and complete the equation $\frac{2}{3} \div \frac{1}{6} = \blacksquare$.

5. a) Copy the table. Complete the divisions in the first column.

Division	Division With Equal Denominators
$\frac{3}{4} \div \frac{1}{4} = \blacksquare$	$\frac{3}{4} \div \frac{1}{4} = \blacksquare$
$\frac{2}{3} \div \frac{1}{3} = \blacksquare$	$\frac{2}{3} \div \frac{1}{3} = \blacksquare$
$\frac{8}{9} \div \frac{2}{9} = \blacksquare$	$\frac{8}{9} \div \frac{2}{9} = \blacksquare$
$\frac{2}{3} \div \frac{1}{6} = \blacksquare$	$\frac{4}{6} \div \frac{1}{6} = \blacksquare$
$\frac{1}{2} \div \frac{1}{12} = \blacksquare$	$\frac{6}{12} \div \frac{1}{12} = \blacksquare$
$\frac{3}{4} \div \frac{3}{8} = \blacksquare$	$\frac{6}{8} \div \frac{3}{8} = \blacksquare$

b) How are the divisions in the second column related to the divisions in the first column? Explain.

c) Complete the second column.

d) Write a rule for dividing two fractions using common denominators.

6. a) Copy the table. Complete the divisions in the first column.

Division	Multiplication
$\frac{3}{4} \div \frac{1}{4} = \blacksquare$	$\frac{3}{4} \times \frac{4}{1} = \blacksquare$
$\frac{2}{3} \div \frac{1}{3} = \blacksquare$	$\frac{2}{3} \times \frac{3}{1} = \blacksquare$
$\frac{8}{9} \div \frac{2}{9} = \blacksquare$	$\frac{8}{9} \times \frac{9}{2} = \blacksquare$
$\frac{2}{3} \div \frac{1}{6} = \blacksquare$	$\frac{2}{3} \times \frac{6}{1} = \blacksquare$
$\frac{1}{2} \div \frac{1}{12} = \blacksquare$	$\frac{1}{2} \times \frac{12}{1} = \blacksquare$
$\frac{3}{4} \div \frac{3}{8} = \blacksquare$	$\frac{3}{4} \times \frac{8}{3} = \blacksquare$

Strategies

Look for a Pattern

b) Complete the multiplications in the second column.

c) How are the multiplications in the second column related to the divisions in the first column? Explain.

d) Write a rule for dividing by a fraction using multiplication.

Reflect on Your Findings

7. Which method do you prefer to use to divide a fraction by a fraction? Why?

Example 1: Divide Using Diagrams

Determine $\frac{2}{3} \div \frac{1}{4}$.

Solution

Use diagrams to determine how many $\frac{1}{4}$s are in $\frac{2}{3}$.

The diagram shows that the number

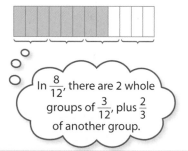

of $\frac{1}{4}$s in $\frac{2}{3}$ is between 2 and 3.

A common denominator for $\frac{1}{4}$ and $\frac{2}{3}$

is 12. So use a rectangle divided into twelfths.

$$\frac{2}{3} \div \frac{1}{4} = 2\frac{2}{3} \text{ or } \frac{8}{3}$$

In $\frac{8}{12}$, there are 2 whole groups of $\frac{3}{12}$, plus $\frac{2}{3}$ of another group.

Show You Know

Determine using diagrams.

a) $\frac{3}{4} \div \frac{1}{3}$ b) $1\frac{1}{4} \div \frac{3}{8}$ c) $\frac{1}{10} \div \frac{1}{5}$

Example 2: Divide Using a Rule

Estimate and calculate.

a) $\frac{7}{8} \div \frac{1}{4}$ b) $2\frac{1}{2} \div 3\frac{3}{4}$

Solution

a) The diagram shows that the number of $\frac{1}{4}$s in $\frac{7}{8}$ is between 3 and 4.

You can calculate the quotient using either of the following methods.

Method 1: Divide Using a Common Denominator

To divide fractions, write them with a common denominator and divide the numerators.

$$\frac{7}{8} \div \frac{1}{4} = \frac{7}{8} \div \frac{2}{8}$$
$$= \frac{7}{2} \text{ or } 3\frac{1}{2}$$

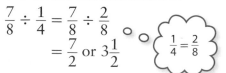

$\frac{1}{4} = \frac{2}{8}$

Method 2: Divide Using Multiplication

To divide by a fraction, multiply by its **reciprocal**.

$$\frac{7}{8} \div \frac{1}{4} = \frac{7}{8} \times \frac{4}{1}$$
$$= \frac{28}{8}$$
$$= \frac{7}{2} \text{ or } 3\frac{1}{2}$$

reciprocal

- the multiplier of a number to give a product of 1
- $\frac{3}{2}$ is the reciprocal of $\frac{2}{3}$, because $\frac{3}{2} \times \frac{2}{3} = 1$
- the result of switching the numerator and denominator in a fraction

b) You can estimate the quotient by dividing the whole numbers closest to the mixed numbers.

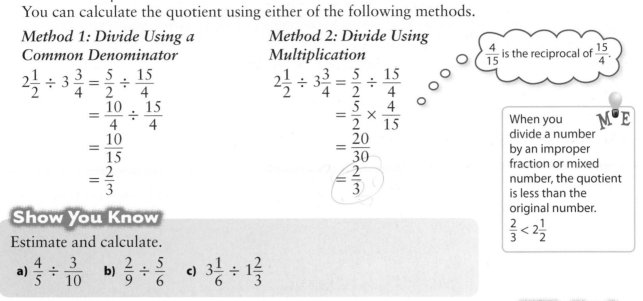

$$2\frac{1}{2} \div 3\frac{3}{4} \approx 3 \div 4$$
$$\approx \frac{3}{4}$$

You can calculate the quotient using either of the following methods.

Method 1: Divide Using a Common Denominator

$$2\frac{1}{2} \div 3\frac{3}{4} = \frac{5}{2} \div \frac{15}{4}$$
$$= \frac{10}{4} \div \frac{15}{4}$$
$$= \frac{10}{15}$$
$$= \frac{2}{3}$$

Method 2: Divide Using Multiplication

$$2\frac{1}{2} \div 3\frac{3}{4} = \frac{5}{2} \div \frac{15}{4}$$
$$= \frac{5}{2} \times \frac{4}{15}$$
$$= \frac{20}{30}$$
$$= \frac{2}{3}$$

$\frac{4}{15}$ is the reciprocal of $\frac{15}{4}$.

When you divide a number by an improper fraction or mixed number, the quotient is less than the original number.
$$\frac{2}{3} < 2\frac{1}{2}$$

Show You Know

Estimate and calculate.

a) $\dfrac{4}{5} \div \dfrac{3}{10}$ **b)** $\dfrac{2}{9} \div \dfrac{5}{6}$ **c)** $3\dfrac{1}{6} \div 1\dfrac{2}{3}$

Example 3: Apply Division With Fractions

The baby teeth, or milk teeth, that develop in childhood are replaced by larger teeth as people mature. A full set of teeth for a child has $\frac{5}{8}$ as many teeth as a full set of teeth for an adult. There are 20 teeth in a full set for a child. How many teeth are there in a full set for an adult?

Solution

Divide 20 by $\frac{5}{8}$ to determine the number of adult teeth.

$$20 \div \frac{5}{8} = \frac{20}{1} \div \frac{5}{8}$$
$$= \frac{20}{1} \times \frac{8}{5}$$
$$= \frac{160}{5}$$
$$= 32$$

There are 32 teeth in a full set for an adult.

Instead of multiplying, you could divide using common denominators.
$$20 \div \frac{5}{8} = \frac{20}{1} \div \frac{5}{8}$$
$$= \frac{160}{8} \div \frac{5}{8}$$

Check:
Use multiplication to check the division.
$$\frac{5}{8} \times 32 = \frac{160}{8}$$
$$= 20$$

Did You Know?

A beaver, like other rodents, has only one set of teeth in its lifetime. A beaver's front teeth can grow by over a metre a year. The gnawing that the beaver does to cut trees and to eat wears down its teeth and keeps them the right length.

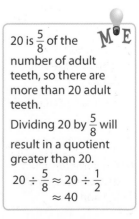

20 is $\frac{5}{8}$ of the number of adult teeth, so there are more than 20 adult teeth.

Dividing 20 by $\frac{5}{8}$ will result in a quotient greater than 20.
$$20 \div \frac{5}{8} \approx 20 \div \frac{1}{2}$$
$$\approx 40$$

If one serving is $\frac{1}{6}$ of a tray of lasagna, how many servings are in three trays of lasagna?

Key Ideas

- You can estimate and determine the quotient of two fractions using diagrams.

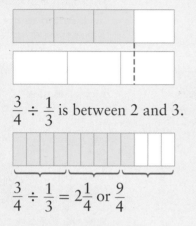

$\frac{3}{4} \div \frac{1}{3}$ is between 2 and 3.

$\frac{3}{4} \div \frac{1}{3} = 2\frac{1}{4}$ or $\frac{9}{4}$

- You can estimate the quotient of two improper fractions or mixed numbers by dividing the whole numbers closest to them.

$$5\frac{1}{4} \div 3\frac{1}{2} \approx 5 \div 4$$
$$\approx \frac{5}{4} \text{ or } 1\frac{1}{4}$$

- To divide two fractions, you can write them with a common denominator and divide the numerators.

$$\frac{7}{10} \div \frac{3}{5} = \frac{7}{10} \div \frac{6}{10} \qquad 1\frac{3}{4} \div 2\frac{1}{2} = \frac{7}{4} \div \frac{5}{2}$$
$$= \frac{7}{6} \text{ or } 1\frac{1}{6} \qquad\qquad = \frac{7}{4} \div \frac{10}{4}$$
$$= \frac{7}{10}$$

- To divide by a fraction, you can multiply by its reciprocal.

$$\frac{7}{10} \div \frac{3}{5} = \frac{7}{10} \times \frac{5}{3} \qquad 1\frac{3}{4} \div 2\frac{1}{2} = \frac{7}{4} \div \frac{5}{2}$$
$$= \frac{35}{30} \qquad\qquad = \frac{7}{4} \times \frac{2}{5}$$
$$= \frac{7}{6} \text{ or } 1\frac{1}{6} \qquad\qquad = \frac{14}{20}$$
$$= \frac{7}{10}$$

1. Anna divided $\frac{5}{6}$ by $\frac{1}{2}$ and stated that the quotient is $\frac{5}{12}$.

   a) What was Anna's mistake?

   b) What is the correct quotient? Use a diagram to show how you know.

2. Mike carried out the division $\frac{3}{4} \div \frac{2}{3}$ as follows.

   $$\frac{3}{4} \div \frac{2}{3} = \frac{4}{3} \times \frac{2}{3}$$
   $$= \frac{8}{9}$$

   Do you agree with Mike's method and answer? Explain.

3. Explain how the diagram shows that the quotient of $\frac{3}{5} \div \frac{1}{7}$ is between 4 and 5.

   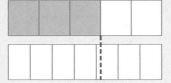

4. a) Does $2\frac{1}{2} \div 1\frac{1}{2}$ equal $1\frac{1}{2} \div 2\frac{1}{2}$?

   b) If the quotients in part a) are not equal, how are they related?

Check Your Understanding

Practise

For help with #5 and #6, refer to Example 1 on page 224.

5. Determine each quotient using diagrams.

   a) $\frac{5}{8} \div \frac{1}{4}$ b) $\frac{1}{4} \div \frac{1}{3}$

   c) $1\frac{1}{2} \div \frac{2}{3}$ d) $2\frac{1}{3} \div \frac{5}{6}$

6. Use diagrams to determine each quotient.

   a) $\frac{9}{10} \div \frac{1}{5}$ b) $\frac{1}{4} \div \frac{3}{8}$

   c) $1\frac{2}{3} \div \frac{1}{2}$ d) $2\frac{3}{4} \div \frac{2}{3}$

For help with #7 to #10, refer to Example 2 on pages 224–225.

7. Divide using a common denominator.

   a) $\frac{3}{5} \div \frac{9}{10}$ b) $1\frac{1}{2} \div \frac{5}{6}$ c) $3\frac{1}{3} \div 1\frac{5}{6}$

8. Divide using multiplication.

   a) $\frac{5}{12} \div \frac{3}{4}$ b) $4\frac{1}{2} \div 1\frac{1}{4}$ c) $10 \div 2\frac{1}{2}$

9. Divide.

   a) $\frac{3}{4} \div \frac{4}{5}$ b) $1\frac{2}{3} \div 2\frac{5}{6}$ c) $12 \div \frac{3}{4}$

10. Divide.

a) $1\frac{1}{12} \div 2\frac{1}{2}$ b) $\frac{8}{11} \div \frac{4}{5}$ c) $1\frac{3}{8} \div 2\frac{3}{4}$

Apply

For help with #11 to #13, refer to Example 3 on page 225.

11. In a comedy review, each performer has a $\frac{1}{4}$-h slot. How many performers are there in a 2-h show?

12. It takes $2\frac{1}{2}$ scoops of flour to make one cake. How many cakes do 15 scoops of flour make?

13. Three quarters of a can of apple juice fills six glasses. How many glasses will a whole can of apple juice fill?

14. An incandescent light bulb uses about $4\frac{1}{2}$ times as much energy as a compact fluorescent light bulb to produce the same amount of light. What fraction of the energy used by the incandescent bulb does the fluorescent light bulb use?

15. Shana and Zack painted their rooms using paint in cans of the same size. Shana used $1\frac{1}{2}$ cans of paint. Zack used $2\frac{3}{4}$ cans of paint. How many times as much paint did Zack use as Shana?

16. Of all the land on Earth, about $\frac{3}{10}$ is in Asia and about $\frac{3}{25}$ is in South America. How many times as big as South America is Asia?

17. The average wind speed in Calgary is $\frac{4}{5}$ of the average wind speed in Regina. The average wind speed in Calgary is 16 km/h. What is the average wind speed in Regina?

18. Use examples to explain your answer to each of the following.

a) Can the reciprocal of a proper fraction be a proper fraction?

b) Can the product of two proper fractions be greater than 1?

c) Can the quotient of two proper fractions be greater than 1?

19. a) The world's longest river is the Nile in Africa, with a length of 6825 km. This is about $1\frac{5}{8}$ times a long as the Mackenzie River, which is Canada's longest river.

a) How long is the Mackenzie River?

b) The Mackenzie River is about $2\frac{1}{10}$ times as long as the Columbia River. How long is the Columbia River?

20. Russia covers about $\frac{1}{30}$ of the Earth's surface. The area of Russia is about $1\frac{2}{3}$ times the area of Canada. What fraction of the Earth's surface does Canada cover?

21. Suppose a friend knows how to divide by whole numbers, but not by fractions.

a) How could you use the following pattern to show your friend how to calculate $4 \div \frac{1}{2}$?

$$4 \div 8 = \frac{1}{2}$$
$$4 \div 4 = 1$$
$$4 \div 2 = 2$$
$$4 \div 1 = 4$$
$$4 \div \frac{1}{2} = \blacksquare$$

b) Make up a pattern to show your friend how to calculate $9 \div \frac{1}{3}$.

22. Write a word problem that you can solve using the expression $3\frac{3}{4} \div 2\frac{1}{4}$.

Extend

23. It took Svend $9\frac{3}{4}$ min to ski up a slope on a cross-country ski trail and only $2\frac{1}{4}$ min to ski back down the same slope. How many times as fast did he ski down the slope as he skied up it?

24. The three largest islands in Canada are all north of the Arctic Circle. Baffin Island has about $2\frac{1}{3}$ times the area of Victoria Island. Baffin Island has about $2\frac{3}{5}$ times the area of Ellesmere Island. What fraction of the area of Victoria Island is the area of Ellesmere Island?

MATH LINK

The Prairies ecozone includes the Manitoba Plain and the grasslands of southwest Saskatchewan and southeast Alberta. The wettest part of this ecozone is the Manitoba Plain, which has an average annual precipitation of about 70 cm. This amount of precipitation is $2\frac{4}{5}$ of the amount in the dry grasslands.

What is the average annual precipitation in these grasslands?

Did You Know?

The Prairies ecozone contains much of Canada's farmland, but it is vulnerable to droughts.

Applying Fraction Operations

Gold has been valued since ancient times because of its beauty and its short supply. Canada is one of the world's leading gold producers.

About $\frac{17}{20}$ of the world's gold production is used to make jewellery.

About $\frac{1}{40}$ of the world's gold production is used to make coins. What operation would you use to determine how many times as much gold is used to make jewellery as is used to make coins?

Focus on...

After this lesson, you will be able to...

❑ decide when to multiply fractions and when to divide fractions in solving problems

❑ apply the order of operations to solve problems involving fractions

Did You Know?

A *gold rush* is a sudden movement of many people to an area where gold has been discovered. Canada's biggest gold rush was the Klondike Gold Rush of 1897–1898 in Yukon Territory. Large amounts of gold were discovered there in 1896 by a group led by Keish, who was a member of the Tagish First Nation. He was also known as Skookum Jim Mason.

Explore the Math

How can you decide which operations to use when solving problems involving fractions?

Many objects that appear to be made of pure gold are actually made from mixtures of gold and cheaper metals. The purity of the gold is measured using a unit called the karat. This unit represents the fraction $\frac{1}{24}$. The table shows the fraction of gold and the fraction of other metals in gold objects with two different purities.

Purity of Gold (karats)	Fraction of Gold	Fraction of Other Metals
20	$\frac{5}{6}$	$\frac{1}{6}$
14	$\frac{7}{12}$	$\frac{5}{12}$

1. How would you calculate the fraction of gold from the purity of gold? Explain.

2. How would you calculate the fraction of other metals from the fraction of gold? Explain.

3. For a gold object with a purity of 18 karats, what is

   a) the fraction of gold, in lowest terms?

   b) the fraction of other metals, in lowest terms?

4. Use the meaning of a karat to explain why pure gold is described as 24-karat gold.

5. How would you calculate the purity of gold from the fraction of gold? Explain.

6. What is the purity of gold, in karats, if the fraction of gold is

   a) $\frac{1}{2}$?   **b)** $\frac{5}{12}$?

WWW Web Link

To find out more about Canada's gold rushes and the life of Keish, go to www.mathlinks8.ca and follow the links.

Reflect on Your Findings

7. How did you decide which operations to use in #1, #2, and #5? Discuss your ideas with your classmates.

Example 1: Use the Order of Operations

Calculate.

a) $2 \div \frac{1}{4} + 3 \times \frac{1}{2}$ **b)** $\frac{1}{3} \times (9 - 2) - \frac{5}{6}$ **c)** $2\frac{1}{4} \div \left(1\frac{3}{4} + 1\frac{1}{4}\right)$

Solution

a) $2 \div \frac{1}{4} + 3 \times \frac{1}{2}$ Divide.

   $= 8 + 3 \times \frac{1}{2}$ Multiply.

   $= 8 + \frac{3}{2}$ Add.

   $= \frac{16}{2} + \frac{3}{2}$

   $= \frac{19}{2}$ or $9\frac{1}{2}$

b) $\frac{1}{3} \times (9 - 2) - \frac{5}{6}$ Brackets.

   $= \frac{1}{3} \times 7 - \frac{5}{6}$ Multiply.

   $= \frac{7}{3} - \frac{5}{6}$ Subtract.

   $= \frac{14}{6} - \frac{5}{6}$

   $= \frac{9}{6}$

   $= \frac{3}{2}$ or $1\frac{1}{2}$

c) $2\frac{1}{4} \div \left(1\frac{3}{4} + 1\frac{1}{4}\right)$ Brackets.

   $= 2\frac{1}{4} \div 3$ Divide.

   $= \frac{9}{4} \times \frac{1}{3}$

   $= \frac{9}{12}$

   $= \frac{3}{4}$

> **Literacy Link**
>
> The *order of operations* for fractions is the same as for whole numbers and decimals.
> - Brackets first.
> - Multiply and divide in order from left to right.
> - Add and subtract in order from left to right.

Literacy Link

To earn time-and-a-half means to be paid for $1\frac{1}{2}$ h for each hour of work done.

Example 2: Apply Fraction Operations

Bev earns $25/h as a machine operator in a sawmill. For time worked above 40 h in a week, she earns time-and-a-half. How much does Bev earn for working 46 h in a week?

Solution

Method 1: Calculate in Stages
Bev's regular rate of pay is $25/h. In 46 h, Bev works 40 h at her regular rate of pay and 6 h at time-and-a-half.

Amount earned at regular rate:
$40 \times 25 = 1000$

Bev works 6 h at time-and-a-half. Multiply to determine the number of hours Bev is paid for.
$6 \times 1\frac{1}{2} = 9$
Amount earned at time-and-a-half:
$9 \times 25 = 225$

Total earnings $= 1000 + 225$
$ = 1225$
Bev earns $1225 for working 46 h in a week.

Method 2: Evaluate One Expression
Bev's regular rate of pay is $25/h. In 46 h, Bev works 40 h at her regular rate of pay and 6 h at time-and-a-half.

For 6 h at time-and-a-half, Bev is paid for $1\frac{1}{2} \times 6$ h.

An expression that represents her total earnings is:
$25 \times \left(40 + 1\frac{1}{2} \times 6\right)$

Evaluate the expression using the order of operations.

$25 \times \left(40 + 1\frac{1}{2} \times 6\right)$ Brackets.
$= 25 \times 49$ Multiply.
$= 1225$
Bev earns $1225 for working 46 h in a week.

Ron earns $15/h as a security guard. For time worked above 35 h in a week, he earns time-and-a-third. How much does Ron earn for working 41 h in a week?

Key Ideas

- You need to decide which operation(s) to perform on fractions to solve problems.
- Some fraction problems can involve the order of operations.
- The order of operations for fractions is the same as for whole numbers and decimals.
  - Brackets first.
  - Multiply and divide in order from left to right.
  - Add and subtract in order from left to right.

Communicate the Ideas

1. Ranjeet is entering a competition to win some gold coins. She must answer the following skill-testing question.

   What is the value of $10 - 2 \times \frac{1}{2}$?

   She is unsure if the correct answer is 4 or 9.

   a) How could Ranjeet determine a possible answer of 4?

   b) How could Ranjeet determine a possible answer of 9?

   c) What is the correct answer? Explain.

2. Dave and Manuel were comparing their solutions to the following problem.

   Three quarters of a number is 6. What is the number?

   Dave evaluated $\frac{3}{4} \times 6$ to get an answer of $4\frac{1}{2}$.

   Manuel evaluated $6 \div \frac{3}{4}$ to get an answer of 8.

   Which answer is correct? Explain.

3. Mia evaluated the expression $\left(\frac{1}{2} + \frac{1}{4}\right) \times \frac{5}{3}$ to equal $\frac{11}{12}$.

   a) What mistake did she make?

   b) What is the correct value?

Practise

For help with #4 and #5, refer to Example 1 on page 231.

4. Calculate.

a) $\dfrac{3}{4} - \dfrac{1}{2} \times \dfrac{2}{3}$

b) $2\dfrac{1}{5} \div \left(\dfrac{4}{5} - \dfrac{1}{4}\right)$

c) $3\dfrac{1}{2} + 2\dfrac{1}{2} \times \left(1\dfrac{1}{4} - \dfrac{3}{4}\right)$

5. Calculate.

a) $\left(\dfrac{5}{6} + \dfrac{2}{3}\right) \times \dfrac{3}{7}$

b) $\dfrac{1}{2} + \dfrac{3}{5} \div \dfrac{3}{4} \div \dfrac{2}{5}$

c) $1\dfrac{2}{5} \times 2\dfrac{1}{2} \div \left(1\dfrac{1}{8} - \dfrac{2}{3}\right)$

Apply

For help with #6, refer to Example 2 on page 232.

6. Leo earns \$16/h as a gardener in a city park. For time worked above 35 h in a week, he earns time-and-a-half. How much does he earn for each of the following numbers of hours worked in a week?

a) 36 h   b) 39 h   c) 42 h   d) $37\dfrac{1}{2}$ h

7. Two thirds of the land on a farm is used for grazing beef cattle. The rest of the land is used to grow crops. Half of the land for crops is used to grow corn. What fraction of the land on the farm is used to grow corn?

8. Melissa and Shinzo found $\dfrac{1}{2}$ a pitcher of iced tea in the fridge. They equally shared $\dfrac{3}{4}$ of the iced tea.

a) What fraction of a pitcher of iced tea did each of them drink?

b) What fraction of a pitcher of iced tea was left over?

9. Five sevenths of the 28 students in a grade 8 class visited a science museum on a field trip. How many students did not go on the trip? Solve the problem in two different ways.

10. Brass is an alloy that contains the metals copper and zinc. Copper typically accounts for $\dfrac{3}{5}$ of the mass of a piece of brass.

a) What is the mass of copper in 175 g of brass?

b) What mass of brass contains 90 g of copper?

c) What mass of brass contains 50 g of zinc?

11. The advertising space in a hockey team's yearbook is sold in fractions of a page. The advertising space sold in one edition of the yearbook is shown in the table.

Size of Advertisement	Price	Number Sold
$\dfrac{1}{2}$ page	\$110	3
$\dfrac{1}{4}$ page	\$60	5
$\dfrac{1}{8}$ page	\$35	12

Calculate the following.

a) the total number of pages of advertising sold

b) the total revenue from advertising

c) the average revenue per page of advertising sold

12. One week, Marjorie spent $\frac{1}{2}$ of her allowance on a music video, $\frac{1}{4}$ of her allowance on a T-shirt, and $\frac{1}{8}$ of her allowance on bus fares. She had $5 of her allowance left at the end of the week. How much was her allowance that week?

13. Add one pair of brackets to the left side of each equation to make the equation true.

a) $\frac{5}{2} \times \frac{3}{5} - \frac{2}{5} + \frac{1}{2} = 1$

b) $1\frac{1}{2} + 2\frac{1}{2} \div \frac{3}{4} - \frac{1}{8} = 5\frac{1}{2}$

c) $\frac{2}{3} - \frac{1}{6} + \frac{5}{6} \div \frac{16}{9} = \frac{3}{4}$

14. Here is a way of using four $\frac{1}{2}$s and the order of operations to write an expression that equals 2.

$$\frac{1}{2} \div \frac{1}{2} + \frac{1}{2} \div \frac{1}{2}$$

Use four $\frac{1}{2}$s and the order of operations to write expressions with each of the following values. Compare your expressions with your classmates' expressions.

a) 0   **b)** 1   **c)** $\frac{1}{4}$

d) 3   **e)** $\frac{1}{2}$ **f)** 4

g) $\frac{5}{8}$ **h)** $\frac{5}{4}$ **i)** $2\frac{1}{2}$

Extend

15. The mean of four fractions is $\frac{2}{3}$. Three of the fractions are $\frac{1}{3}, \frac{1}{2}$, and $\frac{3}{4}$. What is the fourth fraction?

Literacy ⊖ Link

The mean of a set of fractions is their sum divided by the number of fractions.

The mean of $\frac{1}{4}, \frac{1}{2}$, and $\frac{1}{8}$ is $\left(\frac{1}{4} + \frac{1}{2} + \frac{1}{8} \right) \div 3$, which equals $\frac{7}{24}$.

16. There are $1\frac{4}{9}$ times as many white notes as black notes on a full-sized piano keyboard. There are 88 notes altogether. Determine the number of white notes and the number of black notes.

17. Pedro's CDs are stored in three full racks of different sizes. The small rack holds $\frac{1}{2}$ as many CDs as the medium rack. The medium rack holds $\frac{1}{2}$ as many CDs as the large rack. There are 224 CDs altogether. How many are in each rack?

MATH LINK

About $\frac{1}{4}$ of the species of mammals that live in Canada can be found in the Taiga Shield ecozone. About 50 species of mammals can be found in this ecozone. How many species of mammals in Canada live outside the Taiga Shield ecozone?

Key Words

For #1 to #3, match each example to the correct term.

1. $3\frac{1}{4}$ **A** improper fraction

2. $\frac{8}{9}$ **B** mixed number

3. $\frac{11}{3}$ **C** proper fraction

4. **a)** Unscramble the letters to make a key word.

   C I R C L O P E R A

   b) Define this key word.

5. Unscramble the letters to complete the following statement.

   The correct sequence of calculations for evaluating an expression is the ▮▮▮ .
   F R O A N O P O R E R T O S I D E

   froordes

6.1 Multiplying a Fraction and a Whole Number, pages 198–203

6. Determine each product using manipulatives or diagrams.

   a) $5 \times \frac{1}{4}$ **b)** $4 \times \frac{2}{3}$ **c)** $2 \times \frac{5}{2}$

7. The average mass of a porcupine is about 12 kg. The average mass of a raccoon is about $\frac{3}{4}$ of that. What is the average mass of a raccoon?

8. The length of a rectangle is 6 cm. The width is $\frac{2}{3}$ of the length. What is the width?

6.2 Dividing a Fraction by a Whole Number, pages 204–209

9. Determine each quotient using manipulatives or diagrams.

   a) $\frac{3}{4} \div 2$ **b)** $\frac{2}{3} \div 4$

10. A Polish recipe for making six servings of potato salad includes $\frac{1}{2}$ an onion. What fraction of an onion is in each serving?

11. Regina has wet weather on about $\frac{3}{10}$ of the days in a year. It has wet weather on about four times as many days as it has fog. On what fraction of the days of the year does Regina have fog?

6.3 Multiplying Proper Fractions, pages 210–215

12. Use a diagram to explain why the following expressions have the same value.

    $\frac{1}{2}$ of $\frac{3}{4}$ $\frac{3}{4}$ of $\frac{1}{2}$

13. Estimate and calculate.

    a) $\frac{3}{5} \times \frac{3}{5}$ **b)** $\frac{4}{5} \times \frac{5}{12}$ **c)** $\frac{1}{8} \times \frac{4}{7}$

14. Three fifths of a school class is made up of girls. One third of the girls walk to school. What fraction of the class is made up of girls who walk to school?

6.4 Multiplying Improper Fractions and Mixed Numbers, pages 216–221

15. Estimate and calculate.

a) $\dfrac{8}{3} \times \dfrac{6}{5}$ **b)** $1\dfrac{3}{4} \times 2\dfrac{1}{3}$ **c)** $4\dfrac{1}{2} \times 2\dfrac{1}{9}$

16. The driving distance from Winnipeg to Regina is 570 km. The driving distance from Winnipeg to Calgary is $2\dfrac{1}{3}$ times the driving distance from Winnipeg to Regina. What is the driving distance from Winnipeg to Calgary?

17. Calculate the number of hours in $3\dfrac{1}{2}$ days.

18. The value of pi can be approximated by the fraction $\dfrac{22}{7}$. Use this value and the formula $C = \pi \times d$ to calculate the approximate circumference of a circle with a diameter of 14 cm.

6.5 Dividing Fractions and Mixed Numbers, pages 222–229

19. Chris calculated $\dfrac{2}{3} \div 3$ and got an answer of 2.
a) What mistake did Chris make?
b) What is the correct answer?

20. Divide.

a) $\dfrac{2}{3} \div \dfrac{5}{6}$ **b)** $3\dfrac{1}{2} \div 2\dfrac{1}{4}$ **c)** $9 \div \dfrac{9}{10}$

21. A horse eats $\dfrac{1}{2}$ of a bale of hay per day. How long will 15 bales of hay last?

22. Marsha takes $\dfrac{3}{4}$ h to paint the first $\dfrac{1}{10}$ of a garden fence. How long will she take to paint the whole fence?

23. Vince usually takes $5\dfrac{1}{2}$ h to drive from Kamloops to Banff. Because of a snowfall, the drive took Vince $8\dfrac{1}{4}$ h one day. How many times as long as usual was the drive that day?

6.6 Applying Fraction Operations, pages 230–235

24. Calculate.

a) $\dfrac{1}{2} \times \dfrac{3}{4} + \dfrac{3}{2} \times \dfrac{1}{3}$

b) $1\dfrac{1}{2} \div \left(1\dfrac{1}{2} - \dfrac{2}{3}\right)$

25. Ari works as a chef. He has to cook a pasta dinner for 16 guests. He has $3\dfrac{1}{2}$ packages of pasta. If a pasta dinner uses $\dfrac{1}{4}$ of a package of pasta, does he have enough pasta? Solve the problem in two different ways.

26. The gas tank of a car is $\dfrac{2}{3}$ full. A trip uses up $\dfrac{1}{4}$ of the gas in the tank. How full is the tank at the end of the trip?

27. A piece of string is cut in half, so that one half can be used to bundle newspapers for recycling. One third of the remaining string is cut off and used to tie a parcel. The leftover string is 2 m long. How long was the whole piece of string?

6 Practice Test

For #1 to #5, select the correct answer.

1. Which expression does not equal $4 \times \frac{1}{3}$?

A $1\frac{1}{3}$ B $\frac{4}{3}$

C $\frac{1}{3} \times 4$ D $\frac{1}{3} \times \frac{1}{3} \times \frac{1}{3} \times \frac{1}{3}$

2. Which expression equals $\frac{4}{5} \div \frac{2}{3}$?

A $\frac{4}{5} \times \frac{2}{3}$ B $\frac{5}{4} \times \frac{3}{2}$

C $\frac{4}{5} \times \frac{3}{2}$ D $\frac{5}{4} \times \frac{2}{3}$

3. Which expression equals the reciprocal of $\frac{2}{3}$?

A $1 - \frac{2}{3}$ B $1 \div \frac{2}{3}$

C $1 + \frac{2}{3}$ D $1 \times \frac{2}{3}$

4. What is the value of the expression $\frac{1}{2} \times \left(\frac{4}{3} - \frac{1}{6}\right) + \frac{3}{4}$?

A $\frac{7}{16}$ B $\frac{23}{24}$

C $1\frac{1}{3}$ D $1\frac{1}{4}$

5. The quotient $\frac{3}{4} \div \frac{5}{12}$ expressed in lowest terms is

A $\frac{9}{5}$ B $\frac{5}{16}$

C $\frac{36}{20}$ D $\frac{15}{48}$

Complete the statements in #6 to #8.

6. The product of a fraction and its reciprocal is ■ .

7. The value of the quotient $2\frac{2}{3} \div 4\frac{2}{3}$ is ■ .

8. The value of the product $2\frac{1}{4} \times 1\frac{1}{3}$ is ■ .

Short Answer

9. Evaluate.

a) $\frac{3}{8} \times \frac{5}{6}$ b) $\frac{6}{5} \div \frac{7}{10}$

c) $3\frac{3}{5} \times \frac{3}{8}$ d) $\frac{9}{10} \div 2\frac{1}{2}$

e) $\left(1\frac{1}{4} + \frac{3}{4}\right) \div 1\frac{1}{2} - 1\frac{1}{3}$

10. Leisha worked $6\frac{1}{2}$ h for \$14/h. How much did she earn?

11. Chad likes to eat granola for breakfast every day. He eats $\frac{3}{4}$ of a box per week.

a) What fraction of a box of granola does he eat per day?

b) How many boxes of granola does he eat per year?

12. In computer terminology, a bit is $\frac{1}{8}$ of a byte. How many bits equal 16 bytes?

13. Printer paper is sold in packages of 500 sheets. If a printing job uses $1\frac{3}{4}$ packages of paper, how many sheets is that?

Extended Response

14. Lianne is saving to buy a DVD player that costs $2\frac{1}{2}$ times her weekly allowance. If she spends $\frac{3}{4}$ of her allowance on other things, how long will she take to save the money for the DVD player?

15. Airports around the world have carousels for the luggage of arriving passengers. About $\frac{3}{10}$ of the carousels always turn clockwise. About $\frac{9}{20}$ of the carousels always turn counterclockwise. The rest of the carousels may turn either way.

   a) Of every 100 carousels, how many always turn counterclockwise?

   b) Of every 100 carousels, how many may turn either way?

   c) How many times the number of carousels that always turn clockwise is the number of carousels that always turn counterclockwise?

   d) A random survey identified 75 carousels that always turned clockwise. How many carousels do you think were included in the survey? Explain.

Wrap It Up!

Most of the Boreal Plains ecozone is covered by woods and forests. The total area of the Boreal Plains ecozone is about 750 000 km², including both land and fresh water. The table shows the approximate fraction of this ecozone found in different locations.

a) Using the information given above, develop three original word problems that can be answered using division or multiplication of fractions. Include at least one division question and one multiplication question. Write solutions for your questions on a separate sheet.

b) Exchange your questions with a partner. Solve your partner's questions. Show your thinking.

Province/Territory	Fraction of the Boreal Plains Ecozone in the Province/Territory
Alberta	$\frac{13}{25}$
British Columbia	$\frac{1}{20}$
Manitoba	$\frac{17}{100}$
Northwest Territories	$\frac{1}{50}$
Saskatchewan	$\frac{6}{25}$

WWW Web Link

To find out more about Canada's ecozones, go to www.mathlinks8.ca and follow the links.

Math Games

Fabulous Fractions

1. Play Fabulous Fractions with a partner. The rules are as follows:
   - Each player spins the spinner once to decide who will play first. If there is a tie, spin again.
   - For each turn, spin the spinner four times and record the four results.
   - Use the four results to create two fractions with the greatest product. Record the fractions on your multiplication sheet.
   - Record the greatest product in lowest terms.
   - The player with the greater product scores a point.
   - If the products are equal, each player scores a point.
   - The winner is the first player with ten points.

2. a) Play the game in #1 again, but record the result of each spin on your multiplication sheet before you spin again.

   b) Does the new rule in part a) makes the game harder to play? Explain.

3. Repeat #1, but use the four results to create two fractions with the greatest quotient. Record the fractions on your division sheet.

4. Play the game in #3 again, but record the result of each spin on your division sheet before you spin again.

Materials
- spinner with nine sectors numbered 1 to 9 per pair of students
- paper clip (to make a spinner) per pair of students
- Fabulous Fractions multiplication sheet per student
- Fabulous Fractions division sheet per student

I spun 6, 7, 1, and 4. An expression for the greatest product is $\frac{6}{4} \times \frac{7}{1}$, or $\frac{7}{1} \times \frac{6}{4}$, or $\frac{7}{4} \times \frac{6}{1}$, or $\frac{6}{1} \times \frac{7}{4}$.

The result of my first spin is 5. I must decide where to record 5 in the expression $\frac{\blacksquare}{\blacksquare} \times \frac{\blacksquare}{\blacksquare}$ before my second spin.

I spun 6, 7, 1, and 4. An expression for the greatest quotient is $\frac{6}{4} \div \frac{1}{7}$, or $\frac{7}{1} \div \frac{4}{6}$, or $\frac{7}{4} \div \frac{1}{6}$, or $\frac{6}{1} \div \frac{4}{7}$.

Challenge in Real Life

Rock, Paper, Scissors

Two students played 16 rounds of rock paper, scissors. The recorder used the following symbols to mark each winning result: rock (R), paper (P), scissors (S).

Each student was then asked to create fractions from the chart to use in a fraction multiplication and division challenge. For example, one student created the fractions $\frac{3}{16}$ and $\frac{11}{16}$. What do these fractions represent? What is their product? What is their quotient?

You be the fraction expert. Try the challenge and see what fractions you can multiply to get the greatest product or divide to get the smallest quotient.

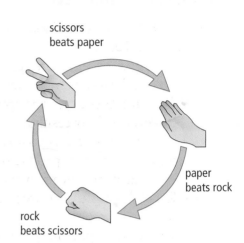

scissors beats paper

paper beats rock

rock beats scissors

R	P	S	S
R	P	P	R
R	S	S	S
R	R	R	R

1. **a)** Create two fractions from the chart and multiply them. These could be either proper or improper fractions.

   b) Create another two fractions and multiply them.

   c) Compare the products in parts a) and b). Which is bigger?

2. **a)** Create two fractions from the chart and divide them.

   b) Create and divide two other fractions from the chart.

   c) Compare the quotients in parts a) and b). Which is smaller?

3. **a)** Create a similar chart using some data from your own game of rock, paper, scissors. Play 16 rounds. Write the winning item in each square until the grid is full.

   b) What would you look for in the numerator and denominator of fractions to produce the greatest product and smallest quotient? Explain your thinking. You can use examples from the chart that you created in your explanation.

7

Volume

You live in a three-dimensional world. Ideas such as length, width, and area are not enough for you to understand some objects. To make sense of size in a three-dimensional world, you need the concept of volume, or how much space an object takes up.

Volume is used when you pour yourself a glass of milk. Volume is used in waste management to track how much recycling reduces waste. Volume is used in engineering and construction to determine the amount of concrete required for a project.

What You Will Learn
- [ ] to calculate the volume of a cube
- [ ] to calculate the volume of a right prism
- [ ] to calculate the volume of a right cylinder

- base of a prism
- height
- volume
- orientation

Literacy Link

You can use a Verbal Visual Chart (VVC) to help you learn and remember new terms.

Copy the blank VVC into your math journal or notebook and use it for the term *volume*.

- Write the term in the first box.
- Draw a diagram in the second box.
- Define the term in the third box. The glossary on pages 517–521 may help you.
- In the fourth box, explain how you will remember the term and what it means. Consider using an example, a characteristic, a memory device, or a visual.

Term	Diagram
Definition	**How I Will Remember It**

Making the Foldable

Materials

- two sheets of 11 × 17 paper
- ruler
- stapler
- large index cards (or several sheets of notebook paper cut into quarters)
- scissors (optional)

Step 1

Fold two sheets of 11 × 17 paper into thirds lengthwise.

Step 2

Unfold both sheets of paper. Fold the bottom edge of each paper upward approximately 8 cm. Staple the outer edges and along each crease to make three pockets.

Step 3

Place one sheet of paper over the other so that the pockets all face the same direction. Staple at the creases to make a booklet, as shown.

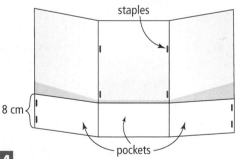

Step 4

Close the Foldable right side first so that the pockets are on the inside. Write the chapter number and title on the left cover.

Step 5

Open the left front cover. Label the pages as shown.

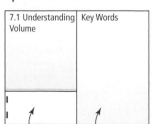

Step 6

Open to the centre of the Foldable. Label the three sections as shown.

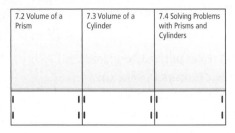

Step 7

Close the left side and open the right side of the Foldable. Label the sections as shown.

Using the Foldable

Place your answers to the Math Link introduction on page 245 and your plans and calculations for the other Math Links in the pocket on the inside back page. Keep track of your ideas for the Wrap It Up! on the back of the Foldable.

As you work through each section of Chapter 7, make notes about examples and Key Ideas on quarter sheets of paper or index cards and put them in the appropriate pocket.

Write and define the Key Words inside the first fold on the left. Use visuals to help you remember the Key Words.

On the left side of the inside back page, keep track of what you need to work on. Check off each item as you deal with it.

MATH LINK

Park Design

What is your favourite park? Where is it? What kinds of activities do people enjoy there? What structures are in the park?

People who develop parks often build benches, tables, planters, and paths. As you work through this chapter, you will have an opportunity to design an eating area for a park.

1. **a)** Why do communities spend money creating parks?
   b) What is that money spent on?

2. Describe 2-D shapes and 3-D objects that might be used in making benches, tables, planters, and paths.

3. **a)** Sketch a table that you might use for a picnic in a park.
   b) Estimate the dimensions of its tabletop.
   c) What is the area of the tabletop?

4. **a)** Sketch a cylindrical garbage can for a park.
   b) Estimate the dimensions of the cylinder.
   c) What is the area of its base?

Bruce has just taken on a part-time job at a local shipping company. He is packing boxes into a shipping container. He knows how many boxes he can fit on the bottom of the container. How can he use this information to figure out how many boxes the shipping container will hold?

Materials
• centimetre cubes

base (of a prism or cylinder)

• any face of a prism that shows the named shape of the prism
• the base of a rectangular prism is any face
• the base of a triangular prism is a triangular face.
• the base of a cylinder is a circular face

height (of a prism or cylinder)

• the perpendicular distance between the two bases of a prism or cylinder

Explore the Math

How does the area of the base of a right prism relate to its volume?

1. **a)** Use centimetre cubes to build models of four different right rectangular prisms.

   b) What is the area of the **base** for each model? Record your data.

   c) What is the **height** of each model? Record your data.

2. How does the number of cubes help to determine the **volume** of each rectangular prism? What is the volume of each prism? Record your data.

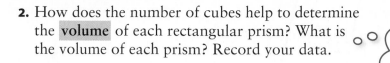

One centimetre cube is equal to 1 cm³.

volume
- the amount of space an object occupies
- measured in cubic units

Reflect on Your Findings

4. a) What is the relationship between the area of the base, the height of the prism, and the volume of a rectangular prism?

b) Do you think this same relationship exists for the volume of a right triangular prism? Explain your reasoning.

Literacy Link

Read 1 cm³ as "one cubic centimetre."

Example 1: Determine the Volume Using the Base and the Height

Determine the volume of each right prism or cylinder.

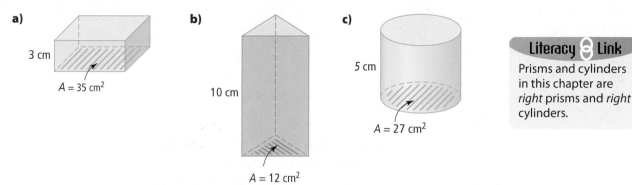

a)

3 cm

$A = 35$ cm²

b)

10 cm

$A = 12$ cm²

c)

5 cm

$A = 27$ cm²

Literacy Link

Prisms and cylinders in this chapter are *right* prisms and *right* cylinders.

Solution

a) The prism is a right rectangular prism.
The area of the rectangular base is 35 cm².
The height of the prism is 3 cm.
Volume = area of base × height of prism
$$V = 35 \times 3$$
$$V = 105$$
The volume of the right rectangular prism is 105 cm³.

Why are the units for volume in cm³?

b) The prism is a right triangular prism.
The area of the triangular base is 12 cm².
The height of the prism is 10 cm.
Volume = area of base × height of prism
$$V = 12 \times 10$$
$$V = 120$$
The volume of the right triangular prism is 120 cm³.

c) The cylinder is a right cylinder.
The area of the circular base is 27 cm².
The height of the cylinder is 5 cm.
Volume = area of base × height of cylinder
$$V = 27 \times 5$$
$$V = 135$$
The volume of the right cylinder is 135 cm³.

Show You Know

What is the volume of the right cylinder?

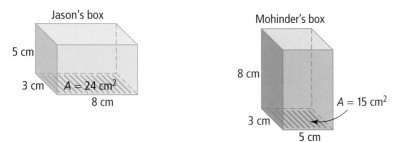

$A = 40$ cm²

22 cm

Example 2: Determine the Volume Using Different Orientations

Jason and Mohinder have two boxes with the same dimensions,
5 cm × 3 cm × 8 cm. Jason's box is short, with a height of 5 cm.
Mohinder's box is taller; its height is 8 cm. Mohinder says his box
has a larger volume than Jason's box. Is he correct?

Jason's box

5 cm

3 cm $A = 24$ cm²

8 cm

Mohinder's box

8 cm

$A = 15$ cm²

3 cm

5 cm

orientation

* the different position of
  an object formed by
  translating, rotating, or
  reflecting the object

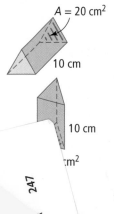

$A = 20$ cm²

10 cm

10 cm

:m²

Solution

Determine the volume of each rectangular prism.

Jason's box: Base area of 24 cm²
Volume = area of base × height
$$V = 24 \times 5$$
$$V = 120$$
The volume of the rectangular
prism is 120 cm³.

Mohinder's box: Base area of 15 cm²
Volume = area of base × height
$$V = 15 \times 8$$
$$V = 120$$
The volume of the rectangular
prism is 120 cm³.

Mohinder is not correct. Both boxes have the same volume.

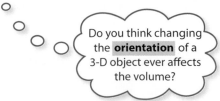

Do you think changing
the **orientation** of a
3-D object ever affects
the volume?

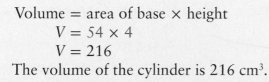

Show You Know

Which box has the greater volume? Explain your reasoning.

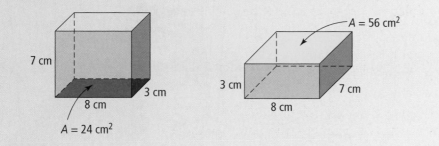

7 cm
3 cm
8 cm
A = 24 cm²

A = 56 cm²
3 cm
7 cm
8 cm

Key Ideas

- The volume of a right cylinder or a right prism can be determined by multiplying the area of the base by the height of the cylinder or prism.

Volume = area of base × height of cylinder
$$V = 20 \times 8$$
$$V = 160$$
The volume of the cylinder is 160 cm³.

8 cm
A = 20 cm²

Volume = area of base × height of prism
$$V = 17 \times 10$$
$$V = 170$$
The volume of the triangular prism is 170 cm³.

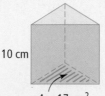

10 cm
A = 17 cm²

- Changing the orientation of a 3-D object does not affect its volume.

Volume = area of base × height
$$V = 54 \times 4$$
$$V = 216$$
The volume of the cylinder is 216 cm³.

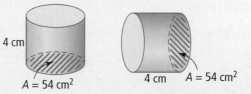

4 cm
A = 54 cm²
4 cm
A = 54 cm²

Communicate the Ideas

1. Evan calculated the volume of a right cylinder. Charlotte calculated the volume of a right rectangular prism. Did either of them make an error in their solutions? Explain how you know.

Volume = area of base × height

$V = 15 \times 2$

$V = 30$

The volume of the cylinder is 30 cm³.

2 cm

$A = 15$ cm²

$A = 63$ cm²

Volume = area of base × height

$V = 63 \times 7$

$V = 441$

The volume of the rectangular prism is 441 cm³.

3 cm

9 cm

7 cm

2. Does the volume of a right prism depend on which face is used as the base in the calculations? Use examples to support your position.

Check Your Understanding

Practise

For help with #3 and #4, refer to Example 1 on pages 247–248.

3. Determine the volume of each right prism or cylinder.

a)

4 cm

$A = 15$ cm²

b)

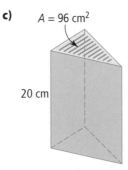

12 cm

$A = 18$ cm²

c)

$A = 96$ cm²

20 cm

4. What is the volume of each right prism?

a) area of base = 12 cm², height = 8 cm

b) area of base = 18 cm², height = 4 cm

c) height = 9 cm, area of base = 14 cm²

For help with #5 and #6, refer to Example 2 on page 248.

5. Determine the volume of each right rectangular prism.

a)

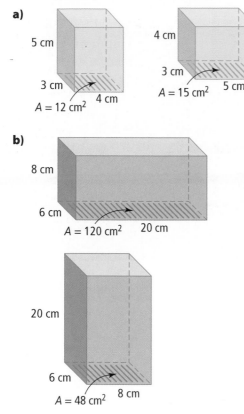

5 cm

3 cm

4 cm

$A = 12$ cm^2

4 cm

3 cm

5 cm

$A = 15$ cm^2

b)

8 cm

6 cm

$A = 120$ cm^2

20 cm

20 cm

6 cm

8 cm

$A = 48$ cm^2

6. What is the volume of each right rectangular prism?

a)

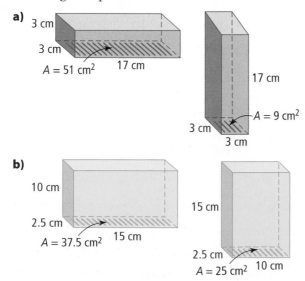

3 cm

3 cm

$A = 51$ cm^2

17 cm

17 cm

3 cm

$A = 9$ cm^2

3 cm

b)

10 cm

2.5 cm

$A = 37.5$ cm^2

15 cm

15 cm

2.5 cm

$A = 25$ cm^2

10 cm

7. What is the height of each of the following right rectangular prisms?

a) volume = 32 cm^3, area of base = 8 cm^2

b) volume = 35 cm^3, area of base = 5 cm^2

c) area of base = 9 cm^2, volume = 36 cm^3

8. Nina uses 15 centimetre cubes to make the base of a rectangular prism. Determine the volume if the prism has a total of 5 layers of cubes. Show your thinking.

9. How many ways can you build a rectangular prism from 16 centimetre cubes? Use diagrams or centimetre cubes to show your designs.

10. A water trough is in the shape of a right triangular prism with base area of 1250 cm^2 and a height of 100 cm. How much water can be put in before it overflows?

11. José is having vegetable soup. The area of the base of the soup can is 10.4 cm^2, and the height is 10 cm. When José opens the can, he sees that the soup comes up to a height of only 9 cm. What volume of soup is in the can?

Vegetable Soup

12. Bill is building a wooden sandbox with a base area of 8 m² for his granddaughters. He does not want to order more than 1.5 m³ of sand to fill it. He has enough wood to build the sandbox up to 0.22 m deep. What is the minimum height he should build the sandbox to allow the sand to be spread evenly? Justify your answer.

13. Ocean City Aquarium is building a new tank for its coral reef fish. The area of the base is 18 750 cm² and the height is 90 cm.

a) What is the volume of the tank in cubic centimetres?

b) What is the volume in litres?

1 L = 1000 cm³

14. One of the solar arrays on the International Space Station is a rectangular prism with a base area of 892 m² and a thickness of 27.5 m. What is the volume of one solar array?

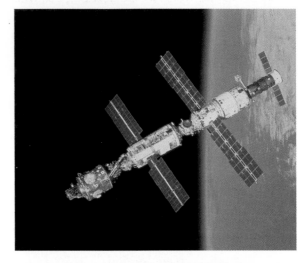

Literacy ⊖ Link

The word *thick* is sometimes used to describe the height of an object.

2 cm thick

15. The International Space Station is shaped like a cylinder that has a cross-sectional area of 615 m² and a length of 44.5 m. The living space for the astronauts is 425 m³. What percent of the volume of the space station is used for living?

The cross-sectional area is the area of the circle you see if you cut across the cylinder.

WWW Web Link

To learn more about the International Space Station, go to www.mathlinks8.ca and follow the links.

16. In the structures below, each small cube has a base area of 4 cm² and a height of 2 cm. In the first two structures, assume the side facing away from you is solid.

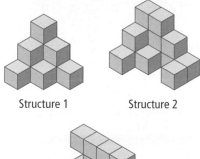

Structure 1   Structure 2

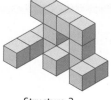

Structure 3

a) How many cubes are in each structure?

b) What is the least number of small cubes needed to complete each structure so that it becomes a rectangular prism?

c) What is the total number of cubes in each completed structure?

d) What is the volume of each completed rectangular prism?

17. Callie's rectangular fish tank has a base area of 800 cm² and contains water to a depth of 15 cm. She adds a solid decoration in the shape of a rectangular prism to the bottom of the tank. The decoration has a base area of 40 cm² and a height of 5 cm. What is the new level of water in the tank?

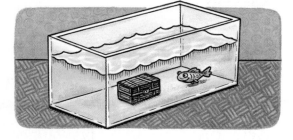

18. A cube with a base area of 4 cm² and a height of 2 cm is inside a box with a base area of 16 cm² and a height of 4 cm.

a) What is the ratio of the volume of the cube to the volume of the box?

b) What is the ratio of the area of the base of the cube to the area of the base of the box?

c) What is the ratio of the height of the cube to the height of the box?

d) What relationship exists among these three ratios?

MATH LINK

Some parks have shelters around the eating areas. These shelters consist of two or three walls. The area of the end of each wall is 0.48 m².

a) Sketch and label the dimensions of a sheltered eating area. Keep in mind that the picnic table that will go inside is about 1.8 m long and 0.74 m wide.

b) Calculate the volume of concrete used to make the walls.

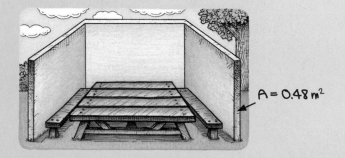

A = 0.48 m²

Volume of a Prism

Recycling bins are located in most schools. Students and staff members fill them with paper, aluminum cans, plastic and glass bottles, and other recyclables. Schools probably recycle more paper than anything else. What would you need to know about a bin for recycled paper in order to determine how much paper was recycled?

Explore the Math

How can you use the dimensions to calculate the volumes of right prisms?

1. How is volume related to the area of the base and the height of a prism?

2. Show how would you could determine the volume of the right rectangular prism shown?

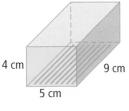

3. Show how you could determine the volume of the right triangular prism shown?

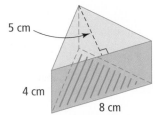

Reflect on Your Findings

4. a) If you know only the dimensions of a right rectangular prism, how can you determine the volume? Test your method using an example.

b) If you know only the dimensions of the triangular base and the height of the prism, how can you determine the volume of a right triangular prism? Test your method using an example.

c) How are the formulas for the volume of a right rectangular prism and a right triangular prism different? How are they the same?

Example 1: Use a Formula to Determine the Volume of a Right Rectangular Prism

a) Determine the volume of the right rectangular prism.

b) Determine the volume of the cube.

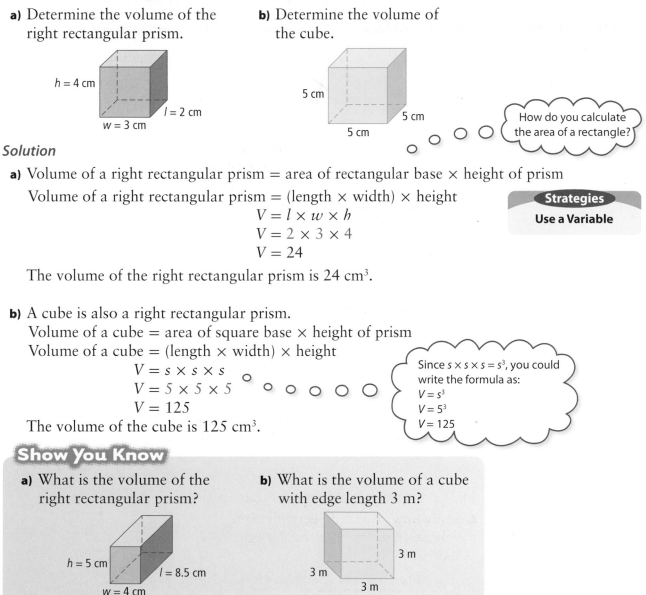

How do you calculate the area of a rectangle?

Solution

a) Volume of a right rectangular prism = area of rectangular base × height of prism

Volume of a right rectangular prism = (length × width) × height

$$V = l \times w \times h$$
$$V = 2 \times 3 \times 4$$
$$V = 24$$

Strategies

Use a Variable

The volume of the right rectangular prism is 24 cm³.

b) A cube is also a right rectangular prism.

Volume of a cube = area of square base × height of prism
Volume of a cube = (length × width) × height

$$V = s \times s \times s$$
$$V = 5 \times 5 \times 5$$
$$V = 125$$

The volume of the cube is 125 cm³.

Since $s \times s \times s = s^3$, you could write the formula as:
$V = s^3$
$V = 5^3$
$V = 125$

Show You Know

a) What is the volume of the right rectangular prism?

b) What is the volume of a cube with edge length 3 m?

Example 2: Use a Formula to Determine the Volume of a Right Triangular Prism

Determine the volume of the right triangular prism.

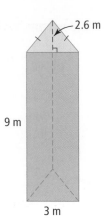

Solution

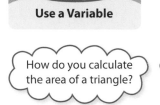

Volume of a triangular prism = area of triangular base
$$\times \text{ height of prism}$$
Volume of a triangular prism = (base × height ÷ 2)
$$\times \text{ height of prism}$$
$$V = (3 \times 2.6 \div 2) \times 9$$
$$V = 35.1$$

The volume of the right triangular prism is 35.1 m³.

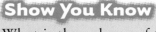

Show You Know

What is the volume of the right triangular prism?

5 mm

8 mm

9 mm

Example 3: Use Volume to Solve a Problem

When Katie opened a new box of Oat Crunchies, she noticed that the box was only $\frac{5}{6}$ full.

a) How much space was empty?

b) Why do you think packages often seem to have empty space when first opened?

30 cm

Oat
CRUNCHIES

18 cm

8 cm

Solution

a) The cereal box is a right rectangular prism.
$$V = l \times w \times h$$
$$V = 18 \times 8 \times 30$$
$$V = 4320$$

The volume of the cereal box is 4320 cm³.

The package is $\frac{5}{6}$ full. Therefore, $\frac{1}{6}$ of the package is empty.

Amount of empty space $= \frac{1}{6} \times 4320$

$$= \frac{4320}{6}$$

$$= 720$$

(thought bubble) $\frac{6}{6} - \frac{5}{6} = \frac{1}{6}$

There was 720 cm³ of empty space.

b) Packages often seem to have empty space because the contents settle when being shipped.

Show You Know

Mr. Chin bought a box of small building blocks for his four children. He will give an equal number to each of them. What volume of blocks will each child get?

20 cm 24 cm 40 cm

MINI BUILDING BLOCKS

Key Ideas

- The volume of a right rectangular prism can be determined using the formula:
  $V = l \times w \times h$

- The volume of a cube can be determined using the formula:
  $V = s \times s \times s$
  $V = s^3$

- The volume of a right triangular prism can be determined using the formula:
  $V = (\text{base of triangle} \times \text{height of triangle} \div 2) \times \text{height of prism}$

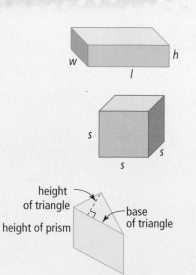

1. Grace tells Dakota that the volume of a cube can be found using the formula: $V = l \times w \times h$. Do you agree? Explain.

2. Kwan wants to build a concrete ramp to his back door. He wants to determine the volume of concrete needed for the ramp. What measurements does he need to know? Justify your response.

3. Jack's family opened a full carton of frozen yogurt for dessert. After they ate, there was $\frac{3}{4}$ left. Jack wants to know what volume of frozen yogurt they ate. He does the following calculation.

Volume of carton:
$V = 12 \times 9 \times 18$
$V = 1944$
The volume of the carton is 1944 cm³.

Volume of frozen yogurt eaten:
$V = 1944 \times \frac{3}{4}$
$V = \frac{1944 \times 3}{4}$
$V = \frac{5832}{4}$
$V = 1458$
They ate 1458 cm³ of frozen yogurt.

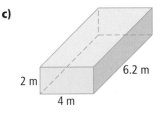

a) What mistake did Jack make?
b) Show the correct calculation.
c) Show an alternative way to calculate the answer.

Check Your Understanding

Practise

For help with #4 to #6, refer to Example 1 on page 255.

4. Determine the volume of each right rectangular prism.

a)

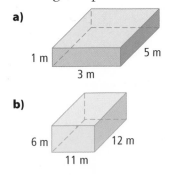

c)

5. What is the volume of each right rectangular prism?
   a) $l = 2$ m, $w = 2$ m, $h = 10$ m
   b) $l = 8$ cm, $w = 7$ cm, $h = 9$ cm
   c) $l = 11.7$ mm, $w = 6.3$ mm, $h = 2.9$ mm
   d) $l = 6.2$ cm, $w = 6.4$ cm, $h = 6.4$ cm

6. Determine the volume of each cube.

a)
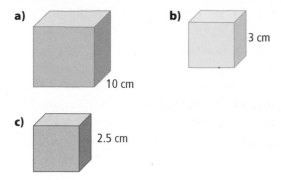
10 cm

b)
3 cm

c)
2.5 cm

For help with #7 and #8, refer to Example 2 on page 256.

7. Determine the volume of each right triangular prism.

a)
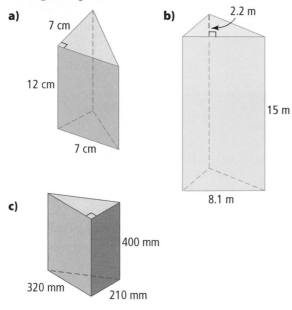
7 cm
12 cm
7 cm

b)
2.2 m
15 m
8.1 m

c)
400 mm
320 mm
210 mm

8. What is the volume of each right triangular prism?

a) base of triangle = 3 m
height of triangle = 7 m
height of prism = 8 m

b) base of triangle = 15 cm
height of triangle = 8 cm
height of prism = 20 cm

c) base of triangle = 10 mm
height of triangle = 9.1 mm
height of prism = 11.3 mm

For help with #9 and #10, refer to Example 3 on pages 256–257.

9. Determine the volume of the contents of each right prism.

a) $\frac{1}{3}$ full
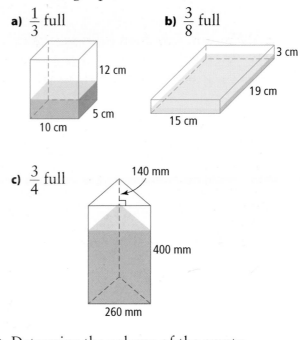
12 cm
5 cm
10 cm

b) $\frac{3}{8}$ full
3 cm
19 cm
15 cm

c) $\frac{3}{4}$ full
140 mm
400 mm
260 mm

10. Determine the volume of the empty space in each object.

a) $\frac{4}{5}$ full of facial tissues
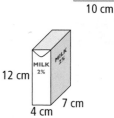
10 cm
10 cm
10 cm

b) $\frac{3}{4}$ full of milk
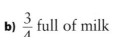
MILK 2%
MILK 2%
12 cm
4 cm
7 cm

c) $\frac{1}{6}$ full of water
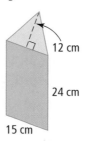
12 cm
24 cm
15 cm

Apply

11. Copy and complete the following table.

Right Rectangular Prism

	Length (cm)	Width (cm)	Height (cm)	Volume (cm³)
a)	7	2		70
b)	12		10	1080
c)		15	5	1200

12. Copy and complete the following table.

Right Triangular Prism

	Base (cm)	Height of Triangle (cm)	Height of Prism (cm)	Volume (cm³)
a)	7	2		70
b)	18		10	1080
c)		14	5	700

13. A landscaper has 0.5 m³ of gravel to use as the base of a patio. If the gravel base must be 10 cm deep and the patio is 2.6 m wide and 2.8 m long, does she have enough gravel? How much extra gravel does she have, or how much more will she need?

The word *deep* is sometimes used to describe the height.

14. A glass vase in the shape of a right triangular prism is filled with coloured sand as a decoration in a living room. What is the volume of the vase?

8 cm
80 cm
15 cm

15. Calculate the volume of concrete used to make a sidewalk 1.5 m wide and 120 m long. The concrete is poured 0.1 m thick.

16. Cindy's aquarium stands 75 cm tall and has a base that measures 1.2 m × 80 cm. At one point during the initial filling, the aquarium has a 12-cm depth of water in it. Cindy needs to fill it to 15 cm from the top before she adds the fish. Draw a diagram and label the dimensions of the aquarium. Determine how much more water Cindy must add before she puts in the fish.

17. A contractor is excavating a rectangular hole 10 m × 12 m × 3 m to pour the foundation for a house. A dump truck with a capacity of 9 m³ is used to haul away the excavated soil. How many trips does the truck need to make?

Literacy ❸ Link

Capacity refers to the greatest volume that a container such as a tank, a truck, or a measuring cup can contain.

18. Suki has 30 small linking cubes.

a) She wants to use 18 of them to make a large cube. Is this possible? Why or why not?

b) What number of linking cubes would she use to construct the largest cube she can possibly make?

19. Melissa has three glass vases. She wants to use one as a decorative fish tank for Harvey the guppy. Which will give Harvey the most water to swim in?

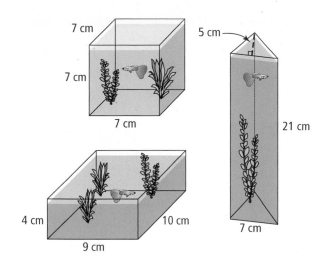

20. The ratio of length : width : height of a box is 6 : 3 : 2. What is its volume if the height is 5 cm?

21. Sketch and label all possible rectangular prisms with dimensions that are whole numbers of centimetres that have a volume of 120 cm³. Do not consider a change of orientation as a new figure; for example, 4 cm × 5 cm × 6 cm is the same as 6 cm × 4 cm × 5 cm.

22. A tank made of concrete has outside dimensions measuring 6 m × 3 m × 1 m. It has no lid. The concrete is 8 cm thick. What is the maximum volume the concrete tank can hold? What assumptions did you make?

Extend

23. Rectangular Prism A and Rectangular Prism B have the same length. The width of A is half the width of B. The height of A is twice the height of B. What is the difference in volume?

24. A rectangular tank, 40 m long by 30 m wide, is filled with 960 m³ of water.

a) Determine the depth of water.

b) If the water drains out at a rate of 60 m³/h, how much water is left after 2.5 h? What is the new depth of water?

c) Later, the depth of the water is 0.2 m. For how long has the tank been draining?

MATH LINK

The Parks Committee is considering putting 12 of these recycling bins throughout the park. If the bins are filled to the brim and emptied twice weekly, what volume of waste is recycled each week?

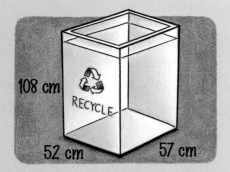

Volume of a Cylinder

Focus on...

After this lesson, you will be able to...

❑ determine the volume of a cylinder

How much water do you use? You might be surprised. The water storage tank shown has a height of about 21.6 m and a diameter of about 10.5 m. If the tank is completely filled, predict how long the water would last in your city or town.

Did You Know?

On average, each person in Canadian municipalities uses 604 L of water every day.

Explore the Math

Materials

• centimetre grid paper

• a variety of empty cylindrical cans
• ruler
• measuring cups
• sand or rice

How can you use area to develop a formula for the volume of a cylinder?

Work with a partner.

1. Choose a can. Estimate the volume of your can.

2. Calculate the volume of your can. Explain your method.

3. Share your results with three other groups. Compare the estimated and calculated volumes for each cylinder to verify the methods used.

Reflect on Your Findings

4. If you know only the radius of the base and the height of a cylinder, how can you determine the volume of the cylinder? Explain and verify your formula using an example.

Example 1: Determine the Volume of a Cylinder Given the Radius

a) Estimate the volume of the cylinder.

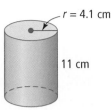

r = 4.1 cm

11 cm

b) Calculate the volume of the cylinder. Express your answer to the nearest tenth of a cubic centimetre.

Solution

a) Use 10 as an approximate value for the height of the cylinder.
Use 4 as an approximate value for the radius of the circular base.

Volume of a cylinder = Area of circular base × height of cylinder
$$V = (\pi \times r^2) \times h$$
$$V \approx (3 \times 4^2) \times 10$$
$$V \approx 3 \times 16 \times 10$$
$$V \approx 48 \times 10$$
$$V \approx 480$$

An estimate for the volume of the cylinder is 480 cm³.

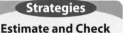

Strategies
Estimate and Check

b) Volume of a cylinder = Area of circular base × height of cylinder
$$V = (\pi \times r^2) \times h$$
$$V \approx (3.14 \times 4.1^2) \times 11$$
$$V \approx 580.6174$$

The volume of the cylinder is 580.6 cm³ to the nearest tenth of a cubic centimetre.

Show You Know

a) Estimate the volume of the cylinder.

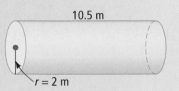

10.5 m

r = 2 m

b) Calculate the volume of the cylinder.

Example 2: Determine the Volume of a Cylinder Given the Diameter

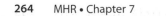

Did You Know?

Vulcanization refers to a curing process for rubber that involves high heat and the addition of sulfur.

A hockey puck is made of vulcanized rubber. What is the volume of rubber required to manufacture one puck? Express your answer to the nearest cubic centimetre.

2.5 cm
7.6 cm

Solution

The diameter is 7.6 cm.
$r = 7.6 \div 2$
$ = 3.8$
The radius is 3.8 cm.

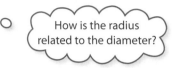

How is the radius related to the diameter?

Volume = Area of base × height
$V = (\pi \times r^2) \times h$
$V \approx (3.14 \times 3.8^2) \times 2.5$
$V \approx 113.354$

The volume of the hockey puck is 113 cm³ to the nearest cubic centimetre.

Show You Know

What volume of recyclable waste will fit into one of these bins?

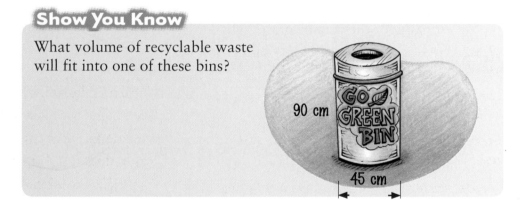

90 cm

45 cm

Key Ideas

- The base of a cylinder is a circle. The formula for the area of the base of a cylinder is $A = \pi \times r^2$.
- The volume of a cylinder can be found using the formula:
  Volume = Area of base × height
  $V = (\pi \times r^2) \times h$

r

h

1. a) List the steps you would use to find the volume of this dime.

   b) What information would you need to calculate the volume of a roll of dimes?

$d = 18.03$ mm
$h = 1.22$ mm

2. Hanna wants to calculate the volume of the cylinder shown but she does not know which measurement is the height.

   a) What is the height?

   b) Explain to Hanna how you know this is the height.

$d = 3.2$ m

2.8 m

3. Jethro calculated the volume of the cylinder shown.

$V = (\pi \times r^2) \times h$
$V \approx (3.14 \times 8^2) \times 10$
$V \approx 3.14 \times 64 \times 10$
$V \approx 2009.6$
The volume of the cylinder is 2009.6 cm³.

$d = 8$ cm

10 cm

Has he made an error in his solution? Explain how you know.

Check Your Understanding

Practise

For help with #4 to #5, refer to Example 1 on page 263.

4. Determine the volume of each cylinder.

   a) 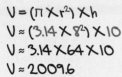 $r = 5$ cm

   23 cm

   b) $r = 14$ cm

   12 cm

   c) $r = 0.5$ m

   1.5 m

5. What is the volume of each cylinder?

   a) radius = 5 cm, height = 8 cm

   b) radius = 11 cm, height = 11 cm

   c) radius = 1.1 m, height = 2.6 m

   d) height = 25 cm, radius = 4.5 cm

For help with #6 to #7, refer to Example 2 on page 264.

6. Determine the volume of each cylinder.

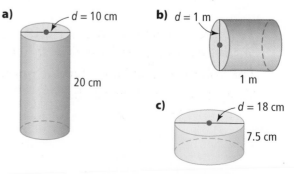

   a) $d = 10$ cm

   20 cm

   b) $d = 1$ m

   1 m

   c) $d = 18$ cm

   7.5 cm

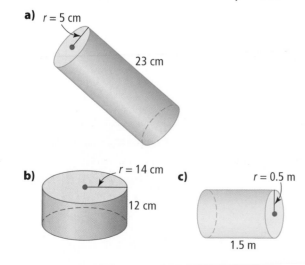

7. What is the volume of each cylinder?
   a) diameter = 8 cm, height = 12 cm
   b) height = 7 m, diameter = 2 m
   c) height = 37.5 cm, diameter = 12 cm
   d) diameter = 4.5 m, height = 19.5 m

Apply

8. The volume of a cylinder is 150 cm³ and the area of its base is 48 cm². What is the height to the nearest centimetre?

9. The Canadarm has a cylinder called a *capture envelope* that is used to catch objects floating in space. The capture envelope is 20.3 cm in diameter and 10 cm deep. What is the maximum volume of the capture envelope?

WWW Web Link

To learn more about the Canadarm, go to www.mathlinks8.ca and follow the links.

10. As of early 2006, the International Space Station consisted of several cylindrical elements.

Element	Length (m)	Diameter (m)
Zarya FGB	12.6	4.1
Unity Node 1	5.5	4.6
Zvezda service module	13.1	4.2
Z1 Truss	4.9	4.2
P6 Truss solar array	73.2	10.7
Destiny	8.5	4.3

a) Which element has the greatest volume? What is its volume?

Science ⊜ Link

The International Space Station takes about 92 min to orbit Earth once.

b) Estimate and calculate the total volume of the International Space Station.

11. Some of the largest drill pipes used in extracting oil have a length of 20 m and an inside diameter of 0.5 m. As oil flows through such a pipe, what is the maximum volume of oil in one pipe at any given time?

12. Martha has a choice of two different popcorn containers at a movie. Both containers are the same price. Which container should Martha buy if she wants more popcorn for her money? Explain.

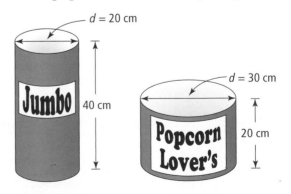

13. A company uses cardboard tubes like the one shown to make concrete posts for the foundation of a building. If a building requires 35 tubes, what is the volume of concrete required? Give your answer to the next highest cubic metre to make sure that there is enough concrete.

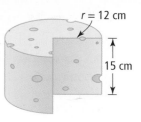

d = 0.26 m

2.4 m

14. Determine the volume of the semi-circular trough.

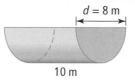

d = 8 m

10 m

Extend

15. a) What happens to the volume of a cylinder when its radius is doubled? Show how you know.

b) What happens to the volume of a cylinder when its height is doubled? Show how you know.

16. A piece of cheese was cut from a cylindrical block of cheddar. What volume of cheese was cut from the block? What assumptions did you make?

r = 12 cm

15 cm

17. Some Japanese bathtubs are in the shape of a cylinder.

1 m

2 m

a) Calculate the volume of water if the tub is filled to a depth of 0.6 m.

b) If the volume of water is 1.256 m³, how deep is the water?

c) If the water is already 0.5 m deep, how much more water is needed to fill it to a depth of 0.7 m?

18. A cylindrical water storage tank has a height of 21.6 m and a diameter of 10.5 m. If the tank is completely full, how long would the water last in a community of 10 000 people? Assume the average daily water use in the community is 604 L per person. Give your answer to the nearest hour.

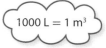

1000 L = 1 m³

MATH LINK

Picnic tables can have either a circular or a rectangular concrete top. The top is held up by a solid concrete column in the shape of a cylinder.

a) Design two concrete tables.
   - Each table has a column with a diameter of 60 cm and a height of your choice.
   - One table must have a circular top. The other table must have a rectangular top.
   - The tabletops cannot exceed a thickness of 10 cm.

b) Determine the volume of concrete needed to make both picnic tables. Show your calculations.

Solving Problems Involving Prisms and Cylinders

Focus on...

After this lesson, you will be able to...

❏ solve problems involving right rectangular prisms, right triangular prisms, and right cylinders

Danielle works at a toy store that sells remote control cars. She wants to fit 60 car boxes into a large crate. The car boxes have dimensions of 50 cm × 30 cm × 20 cm. The crate has dimensions of 140 cm × 120 cm × 110 cm. Predict whether all 60 boxes fit in the crate.

Explore the Math

Materials

• centimetre cubes
• centimetre grid paper

How can you solve a problem involving volume?

1. Calculate the volume of one car box and the volume of the crate described above.

2. Estimate the number of boxes that could fit into the crate.

3. Model the problem to determine how many boxes you can fit in the crate.

4. a) Share your model with your classmates. What was the greatest number of boxes that fit into the crate?

   b) Could you arrange your boxes differently to improve the modelled number of boxes that would fit in the crate? Explain.

Reflect on Your Findings

5. How did the estimated number of boxes compare with the modelled number of boxes that would fit in the crate? Explain any differences.

Example 1: Solve a Problem Involving Right Triangular Prisms

Marcus is making a display of packages of Prism Chocolates in his candy shop. He will stack 64 packages to form a shape that is a triangular prism, using eight packages in the bottom layer. What is the volume of the display? Show your thinking.

5 cm

5.6 cm

20 cm

Solution

The packages are triangular prisms.

The best way to stack the packages is to
place Layer 1 on the table, then invert
Layer 2 in the cavities between the packages in the first layer. In order
to maintain a triangular shape, Layer 3 must have the same number
of packages as Layer 2.

Determine the volume of one package:
Volume = (base of triangle × height of triangle ÷ 2) × height of prism
$$V = (5.6 \times 5 \div 2) \times 20$$
$$V = 14 \times 20$$
$$V = 280$$
The volume of one package is 280 cm³.

The number of packages used in the display is 64.

The volume of the display = 280 × 64
                          = 17 920
The volume of the display is 17 920 cm³.

Example 2: Solve a Problem Involving Cylinders

A cylinder with a radius of 0.6 m and a height of 15 m needs to be
replaced with a cylinder of equal volume. However, the new cylinder
has a radius of 0.5 m. How high must the new cylinder be?

Solution

Determine the volume of the original cylinder.
$$V = \pi \times r^2 \times h$$
$$V \approx 3.14 \times 0.6^2 \times 15 \qquad \boxed{C} \; 3.14 \; \boxed{\times} \; .6 \; \boxed{\times} \; .6 \; \boxed{\times} \; 15 \; \boxed{=} \; 16.956$$
$$V \approx 16.956$$
The original cylinder has a volume of 16.956 m³.

To determine the new height, replace all variables in the formula with
values except for *h*.

> The radius is now 0.5 m.
> The volume of 16.956 m³
> is the same.

$$V = \pi \times r^2 \times h$$
$$16.956 \approx 3.14 \times 0.5^2 \times h$$
$$16.956 \approx 0.785h \qquad \text{Divide both sides of the equation by 0.785 to isolate the variable.}$$
$$\frac{16.956}{0.785} \approx \frac{0.785}{0.785} h \qquad \boxed{C} = 16.956 \; \boxed{\div} \; .785 \; \boxed{=} \; 21.6$$
$$21.6 \approx h$$

The new cylinder must have a height of 21.6 m to contain the same
volume as the original cylinder.

Workers must replace a cylindrical pipe with a radius of 0.4 m and a length of 12 m. The new pipe has a radius of 0.6 m. The volume must remain the same. How long must the new pipe be?

Example 3: Solve a Problem Involving Right Prisms and Cylinders

Engineers Rob and Kyla have designed rectangular culverts to carry water under a new highway. They estimate that the distance under the highway is 45 m. Determine the volume of concrete they need to make the required number of culvert pieces. Give your answer to the next highest tenth of a cubic metre.

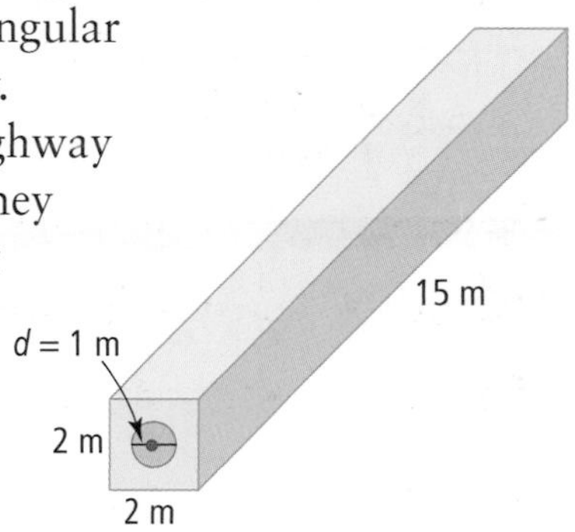

Solution

Draw a diagram of the culvert under the highway.

Determine the volume of the rectangular prism.

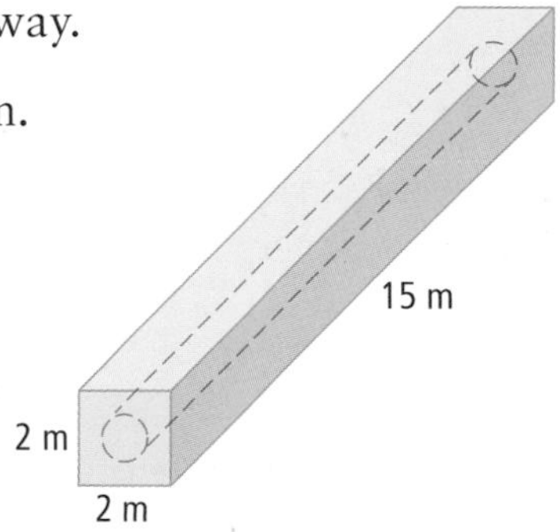

$V = l \times w \times h$
$V = 2 \times 2 \times 15$
$V = 60$

The volume of the rectangular prism is 60 m³.

Strategies

Draw a Diagram

Determine the volume of the cylindrical space.
$V = (\pi \times r^2) \times h$
$V \approx 3.14 \times 0.5^2 \times 15$ $\boxed{C}$ **3.14** $\boxed{\times}$ **.5** $\boxed{\times}$ **.5** $\boxed{\times}$ **15** $\boxed{=}$ 11.775
$V \approx 11.775$
The volume of the cylindrical space is 11.775 m³.

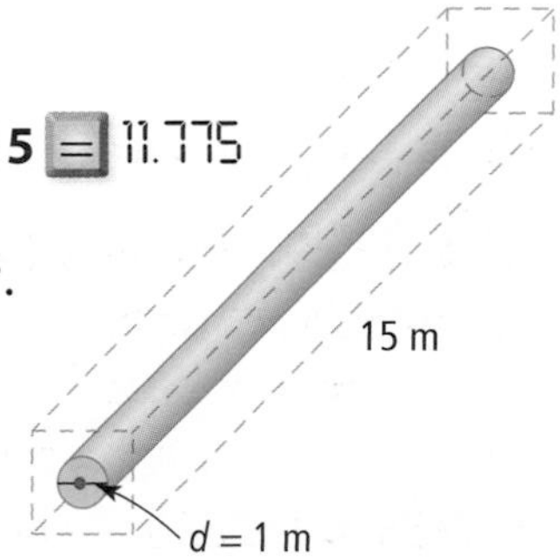

Volume of concrete required = volume of prism − volume of cylindrical space
$\approx 60 - 11.775$
≈ 48.225
The volume of concrete required for one culvert piece is 48.225 m³.

Determine how many culvert pieces Rob and Kyla will need.
The distance under the highway is 45 m. The length of each culvert is 15 m.
$45 \div 15 = 3$
They will need three culvert pieces.

Calculate the volume of concrete required for three culvert pieces.
$3 \times 48.225 = 144.675$
The volume of concrete required for three culvert pieces is 144.7 m³
to the nearest tenth of a cubic metre.

Show You Know

A cube has edges 40 cm long. A cylindrical section with a radius of 15 cm is removed from the cube. What is the remaining volume of the cube, to the nearest tenth of a cubic metre?

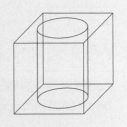

Key Ideas

- There are different types of problems involving volumes of prisms and cylinders.
  - You may need to decide which formula to use.
  - It may help to draw a diagram.
- Some problems may involve more than one set of calculations.

Communicate the Ideas

1. The triangular prism shown has a volume of 264 cm³. Explain how you could find its height.

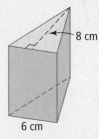

8 cm

6 cm

2. The object shown is hollow. Explain how you would determine its volume.

Check Your Understanding

Practise

For help with #3, refer to Example 1 on pages 269–270.

3. An artist has 20 triangular prisms like the one shown. He decides to use them to build a giant triangular prism with a triangular base of length 5.6 m and height 6.8 m.

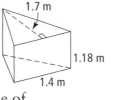
1.7 m
1.18 m
1.4 m

a) Does he have enough small prisms?

b) What is the volume of the new prism to the nearest hundredth of a metre?

For help with #4 to #6, refer to Example 2 on pages 270–271.

4. Two cylinders have the same volume. The first cylinder has a diameter of 10 cm and a height of 30 cm. The second cylinder has a diameter of 8 cm. What is the height of the second cylinder, to the nearest tenth of a centimetre?

5. A concrete culvert that is 10 m long has an outside diameter of 1 m and an inside diameter of 0.8 m. Determine the volume of concrete required to make the culvert, to the nearest tenth of a cubic centimetre.

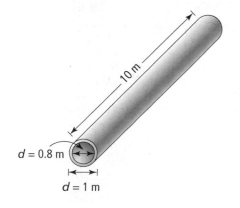
10 m
d = 0.8 m
d = 1 m

6. A pipe has an outside diameter of 10 cm, an inside diameter of 8 cm, and a height of 40 cm. What is the capacity of the pipe, to the nearest tenth of a cubic centimetre?

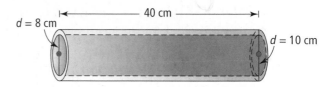
d = 8 cm
40 cm
d = 10 cm

For help with #7, refer to Example 3 on pages 271–272.

7. A clay planter has the shape of a right triangular prism as shown. Inside the planter is a cylindrical hole. Calculate the volume of clay needed to make the planter, to the nearest tenth of a cubic centimetre.

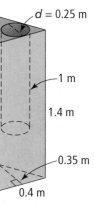
d = 0.25 m
1 m
1.4 m
0.35 m
0.4 m

Apply

8. Manuel's company uses shipping crates with dimensions 3 m × 3 m × 7 m. He has to ship 25 000 boxes with dimensions 10 cm × 10 cm × 20 cm. Calculate whether one crate will be enough.

9. Laura, an office manager, has purchased a carton that is 300 cm × 400 cm × 600 cm to store 9000 boxes of files. Each box has dimensions 30 cm × 26 cm × 10 cm. Calculate whether all of the files will fit in the carton.

10. In the cafeteria at Prairietown School, the garbage can is filled up twice every lunch hour. The garbage can is a cylinder with a radius of 25 cm and a height of 95 cm.

   a) Determine the volume of garbage produced each day in the cafeteria.

   b) Determine the volume of garbage produced in a 5-day week.

   c) The school's environment club wants to reduce the weekly garbage to below 470 000 cm³ by encouraging students to recycle. To reach this goal, how many times should the garbage can be filled each lunch hour?

11. A cylinder has a diameter of 80 cm and a length of 45 cm. Another cylinder has the same volume but is 80 cm long. What is the diameter of the longer cylinder?

12. A rectangular tub with dimensions 2 m × 1 m × 0.5 m is filled with water using a pail of radius 0.1 m and height 0.35 m. How many pails of water will be required? Give your answer to the nearest whole pail.

13. A manufacturer makes right triangular prisms like the one shown for refracting light. They will be packed in boxes 12.5 cm long, 2.5 cm wide, and 22.5 cm high. How many prisms can fit in a box?

2.2 cm

7.5 cm

2.5 cm

Science ⊖ Link

When a prism refracts light, it divides light into the colours of the spectrum.

14. Ted sells his homemade peanut butter for $1.60 a jar at the local Farmers' Market. The jar is 8 cm in diameter and 10 cm high. He decides he will also sell peanut butter in jars that are 16 cm in diameter and 20 cm high. What should he charge if he uses the same price per cubic centimetre?

15. a) A wooden block is formed in the shape shown by cutting a right rectangular solid from a larger one. What is the volume of the solid shown?

   b) Check your calculations by using a second method to solve the problem.

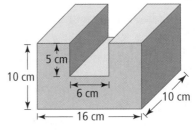

5 cm

10 cm

6 cm

10 cm

16 cm

16. Fatima wants to fill a circular wading pool. She does not have a hose, so she uses a rectangular pail that she fills from a tap. The inside diameter of the pool is 120 cm and it is 25 cm deep. The inside dimensions of the pail are 30 cm × 22 cm × 24 cm deep.

   a) Fatima wants to fill the pool to a depth of 18 cm. What volume of water does she have to carry?

   b) Each time she goes to the tap, Fatima fills the pail to a height of 20 cm. What is the volume of water in the pail?

   c) Calculate how many pails of water Fatima has to carry to fill the pool to a depth of 18 cm.

17. A sheet of paper that is 22 cm by 28 cm can be used to make a cylinder by rolling it in two different ways. Which way produces the larger volume? Show your work.

Extend

18. The volume of the triangular prism shown is 48 cm³. What is the value of the missing measurement? Show your work.

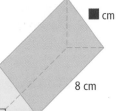

4 cm   8 cm   ■ cm

19. A cylindrical vase fits perfectly in a cube-shaped box. If the box has a volume of 8000 cm³, what is the volume of the vase?

Volume of a cube
= s × s × s
So, 8000 is the product of three equal numbers. What number is it?

20. Kevin and Jasjot plan to install a culvert that is 8 m long and holds a volume of 40 m³ of water. What diameter of culvert should they use?

21. The end of a car tunnel has the shape of a semi-circle on top of a rectangle. The tunnel is exactly 4 km long.

a) Calculate the volume of air in the tunnel with no cars in it.

b) The air in a car tunnel must be exchanged frequently. If the exhaust system pumps the air out at a rate of 10 m³ per second, how long does it take to replace the stale air with fresh air in the entire tunnel? Give your answer in hours and minutes.

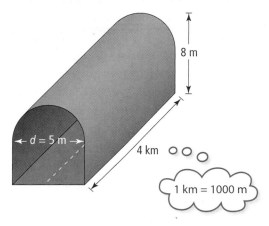

8 m

d = 5 m   4 km

1 km = 1000 m

MATH LINK

Shrub and flower planters have a variety of shapes. Some of the shapes could be connected to create a more interesting appearance.

a) Design two different planters. One must be a right triangular prism.

b) If the walls of the planters are 7 cm thick, determine the volume of concrete needed to construct one of your planters.

c) What volume of dirt do you need to fill the planter from part b) to 2 cm from the top?

Key Words

For #1 to #4, choose the letter representing the term that best matches each statement.

1. the amount of space an object occupies

   A height
   B volume
   C base of a prism
   D orientation

2. a particular view of an object

3. the distance between the two bases of a prism

4. the face that is perpendicular to the height of a prism

7.1 Understanding Volume, pages 246–253

5. What is the volume of each right prism or cylinder?

   a)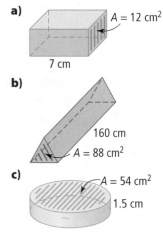
      $A = 12$ cm²
      7 cm

   b)
      160 cm
      $A = 88$ cm²

   c)
      $A = 54$ cm²
      1.5 cm

6. Determine the volume of each right prism.
   a) area of base = 6 cm², height = 4 cm
   b) area of base = 20 cm², height = 2 cm
   c) height = 10 cm, area of base = 15 cm²

7. Stephan uses 28 centimetre cubes to make the base of a rectangular prism. What is the volume if the prism has seven layers of cubes?

8. Determine the volume of each right rectangular prism.

   a)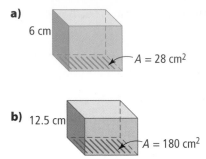
      6 cm
      $A = 28$ cm²

   b) 12.5 cm
      $A = 180$ cm²

7.2 Volume of a Prism, pages 254–261

9. What is the volume of each cube?
   a) edge length = 10 cm
   b) edge length = 8.5 cm

10. What is the volume of each right rectangular prism?
    a) $l = 12$ cm, $w = 2$ cm, $h = 5$ cm
    b) $l = 2.5$ cm, $w = 8$ cm, $h = 3.5$ cm

11. What is the volume of each right triangular prism?

    a)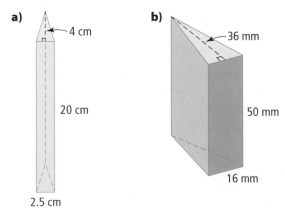
       4 cm
       20 cm
       2.5 cm

    b) 36 mm
       50 mm
       16 mm

12. A cube-shaped tank of 1 m by 1 m by 1 m contains water to a depth of 0.4 m. Determine the volume of the air in the tank.

13. On a construction site, earth is being excavated to a depth of 12 m from a rectangular pit measuring 85 m by 54 m. The earth is being removed by dump trucks that have a capacity of 42 m³ of earth, and can transport five loads each hour.

a) Calculate the volume of earth being excavated.

b) How many truckloads will be needed to remove the earth?

c) If four trucks work non-stop for a 6-h day, how many days are needed to remove all the earth? Express your answer to the nearest whole day.

7.3 Volume of a Cylinder, pages 262–267

14. What is the volume of each cylinder?

a) $r = 20$ cm

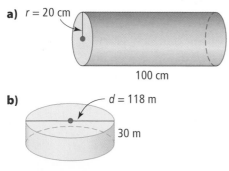

100 cm

b) $d = 118$ m

30 m

15. What is the volume of each cylinder?

a) $r = 6$ cm, $h = 20.5$ cm

b) $d = 18$ cm, $h = 18$ cm

16. What is the volume of a cylindrical pipe that is 20 m long and has an inside diameter of 3 m?

17. Jane wants to fill her circular pool to a depth of 2 m. Determine the volume of water she needs, to the nearest cubic metre.

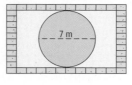

7 m

18. Fibre optic filaments are very small. An R Sensor Probe is 152.4 mm long with a diameter of 1.587 mm. What is its volume? Give your answer to the nearest tenth of a cubic millimetre.

7.4 Solving Problems Involving Prisms and Cylinders, pages 268–275

19. A cylinder with a radius of 0.28 m and a length of 7 m is to be replaced with a cylinder of radius 0.25 m. The volume must remain the same. How long must the new cylinder be? Give your answer to the nearest hundredth of a metre.

20. At Wacky Water Park, a large trough fills with water at a rate of 0.6 m³ per minute. When it is full, it tips over and dumps its contents.

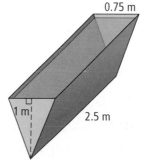

0.75 m

1 m

2.5 m

a) What is the volume of water when the trough is full?

b) How long does it take for the trough to fill with water? Give your answer in minutes and seconds.

For #1 to #5, choose the best answer.

1. What is the volume of the right rectangular prism shown?

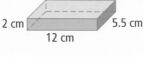

   A 101 cm³ **B** 126 cm³

   C 132 cm³ **D** 144 cm³

2. What is the volume of the right triangular prism shown?

   A 91.8 m³ **B** 183.6 m³

   C 367.2 m³ **D** 734.4 m³

3. What is the volume of a cube with edge length 8 cm?

   A 64 cm³ **B** 72 cm³

   C 384 cm³ **D** 512 cm³

4. What is the volume of a cylinder with a diameter of 7.5 cm and a height of 24 cm?

   A 282.6 cm³ **B** 565.2 cm³

   C 1059.75 cm³ **D** 4239.0 cm³

5. A rectangular watering trough measures 30 cm × 25 cm × 12 cm. In winter, a small cylindrical heater with a radius of 5 cm and a height of 12 cm is kept in the trough. What is the maximum volume of water in the trough in winter?

   A 6074 cm³ **B** 8058 cm³

   C 8700 cm³ **D** 9000 cm³

Complete the statements in #6 and #7.

6. The area of the base of a right cylinder is 20 cm². The volume of the cylinder is 140 cm³. The height of the cylinder is ■.

7. A right rectangular prism has dimensions of 3 cm by 4 cm by 6 cm. The volume of the prism is ■.

Short Answer

8. Determine the volume of oil in one full barrel. Write your answer to the nearest tenth of a cubic centimetre.

9. Ying sees this advertising flyer. She decides to buy 12 of these boxes for her shoes. What total volume will these boxes occupy in her closet?

Clear Shoeboxes

Now you can quickly and easily see every pair of shoes you own. Clearly, a better way to store your shoes!

9.5 cm 18 cm 29.5 cm

10. Ian knocked over an open can of apple juice. If it was filled to the top when it spilled, what volume of apple juice did Ian have to clean up?

$d = 10$ cm 17.5 cm

11. Leanna uses a cylinder to store jelly beans. She wonders if she could store more jelly beans if she used a triangular prism of the same height. Which container is larger? Explain.

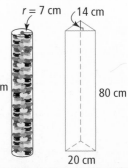

$r = 7$ cm 14 cm 80 cm 80 cm 20 cm

12. Calculate the volume of a cube with a cylindrical hole through it.

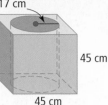

r = 17 cm

45 cm

45 cm

13. The garbage bin outside the school measures 2.5 m × 2 m × 2 m. The garbage cans in the school are cylinders 0.75 m in diameter and 1.2 m high. How many garbage cans can be emptied into the bin before it is full? Give your answer to the nearest full can.

Extended Response

14. a) Calculate how many litres of water the aquarium tank shown will hold when filled to the top.

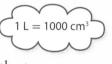

1 L = 1000 cm³

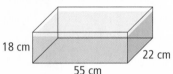

18 cm

22 cm

55 cm

b) The tank is filled with water up to 5.4 cm from the top. How many litres of water are in the tank?

15. Yuri is building a concrete patio 6 m wide by 6 m long. The concrete will be 0.15 m thick.

a) What volume of concrete does Yuri need?

b) Concrete costs \$110.00/m³. How much does Yuri have to pay before tax?

16. Twelve glass jars of salad dressing are to be shipped in a box.

r = 5 cm

Salad Dressing

25 cm

a) Give at least three possible sets of dimensions for this box.

b) What is the volume of each box?

c) The packers will add foam chips in the empty spaces to reduce breakage. What is the volume of empty space in each box?

d) The cost of shipping increases as the surface area increases. Which box would you use? Explain.

Wrap It Up!

Your local Parks Committee has asked you to create a design for an eating area.

a) Draw a plan of your eating area. It must have at least
   • one shelter
   • one table with two benches
   • one garbage container or planter
   Your design must include at least a rectangular prism, a triangular prism, and a cylinder. Clearly label all of the dimensions on your diagram.

b) Assume all your items will be molded from concrete. Determine the total volume of concrete needed for your design. Calculate the cost of the concrete, to the nearest dollar. Show your calculations.

c) Put together a cost sheet, based on your eating area plan, to present to the Parks Committee.

Math Games

The rules of this game are similar to those for Let's Face It! on page 192 in Chapter 5.

Turn Up the Volume!

The rules of this game are similar to those for Let's Face It! on page 192 in Chapter 5.

Materials
- deck of playing cards per pair or small group
- calculator per student

1. Play Turn Up the Volume! with a partner or in a small group. These are the rules:
   - Remove the jacks, queens, kings, aces, and jokers from the deck of cards.
   - Take turns dealing the cards. It does not matter who deals first.
   - Shuffle the cards and deal three cards, face up, to each player.
   - Use the values of the cards as the dimensions, in centimetres, of a rectangular prism.
   - Calculate the volume of your rectangular prism using pencil and paper.
   - Each player who calculates the volume correctly wins a point. (You will need to check each other's work.)
   - The player with the rectangular prism that has the greatest volume wins an extra point for that round. If there is a tie, each of the tied players wins an extra point.
   - The first player to reach ten points wins the game. If more than one player earns ten points in the same round, these players continue playing until one of them pulls ahead.

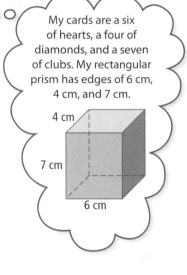

My cards are a six of hearts, a four of diamonds, and a seven of clubs. My rectangular prism has edges of 6 cm, 4 cm, and 7 cm.

2. Play a different version of the game by modifying the rules as follows:
   - Deal only two cards to each player and use them to describe the size of a right cylinder. The first card gives the radius, in centimetres, of each circle. The second card gives the height, in centimetres, of the cylinder.
   - Use a calculator to determine the volume of your cylinder, to the nearest tenth of a cubic centimetre.
   - Award points and decide the winner in the same way as before.

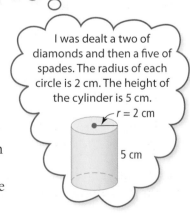

I was dealt a two of diamonds and then a five of spades. The radius of each circle is 2 cm. The height of the cylinder is 5 cm.

$r = 2$ cm

5 cm

3. In the version of the game in #2, suppose you could choose which of your two dealt cards gives the radius and which card gives the height. How would you make that choice to stand the best chance of winning? Explain using examples.

Create a Storage Container

What things do you keep in storage? What do you store them in?

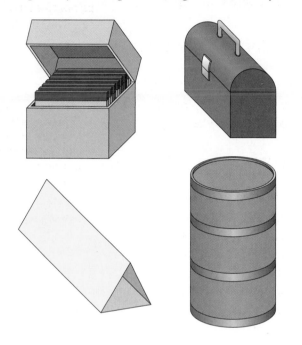

Many shops design and sell special storage containers. You be the designer. Design two storage containers for a specialty store. Your two designs should have different shapes (e.g., prism, cylinder) but hold approximately the same volume.

1. Sketch and label the top, side, and front views of each 3-D object.

2. Calculate the volume of each container showing all formulas and calculations.

3. Suggest two possible uses for your containers. Justify your choices mathematically.

4. Design an ad for your containers advertising why they are the best design for storing the items you recommend.

8

Integers

Canadian weather patterns tend to move from west to east. Winds from the west coast may carry air over the Rockies to Alberta, and then across the Prairies. The air cools as it climbs the western side of the mountains. The air warms again as it comes down the eastern side.

In this chapter, you will learn more about temperature changes including those that occur with changing altitude.

What You Will Learn

❑ to multiply and divide integers using concrete materials,
   diagrams, and symbols
❑ to solve problems using integers

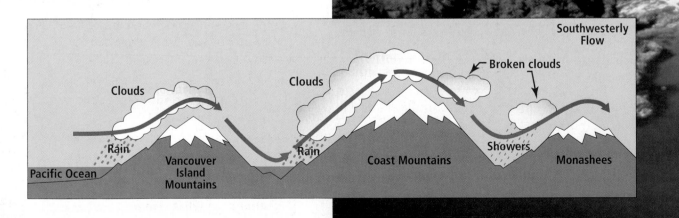

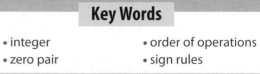

Literacy Link

Copy the following KWL chart into your math journal or notebook. Brainstorm what you already know about integers.

- Record your ideas in the first column.
- List any questions you have about integers in the second column.
- At the end of the chapter, complete the final column.

Integers

What I *Know*	What I *Want* to Know	What I *Learned*

Making the Foldable

Materials

- 11 × 17 sheet of paper
- four sheets of notebook paper
- scissors
- stapler

Step 1

Fold an 11 × 17 sheet of paper in half. Instead of creasing it, just pinch it at the midpoint. Unfold the paper then fold the outer edges of the paper to meet at the pinch or midpoint.

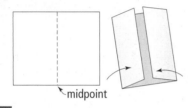

midpoint

Step 2

Fold four sheets of notebook paper in half along the long axis.

Step 3

Insert two of the sheets of notebook paper into the left crease of the folded sheet from Step 1.

Step 4

Cut one of the remaining folded sheets of paper in two along the fold. Insert one half sheet and the other folded sheet into the right crease of the folded sheet from Step 1.

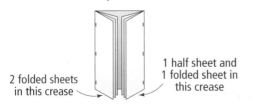

2 folded sheets in this crease

1 half sheet and 1 folded sheet in this crease

Step 5

Staple the outside edges to create multiple pages.

Step 6

Label the outside of your Foldable as shown.

Chapter 8   Integers

Integer Multiplication   Integer Division

Step 7

Put the following labels on the inside of your Foldable

Fold on the Left

- First two pages: Math Link introduction
- Next two sets of pages: 8.1 Exploring Integer Multiplication 8.2 Multiplying Integers
- Next two pages: 8.2 Math Link

Fold on the Right

- First two sets of pages: 8.3 Exploring Integer Division 8.4 Dividing Integers
- Next two pages: 8.4 Math Link

Across the Inside Back

- 8.5 Applying Integer Operations
- Wrap It Up!

Using the Foldable

As you work through Chapter 8, make notes about Key Words, examples, and Key Ideas in the appropriate section.

Record your answers to the Math Link Introduction on page 285 and the Math Link for each section in the appropriate location.

On the back of the Foldable, make notes under the heading What I Need to Work On. Check off each item as you deal with it.

MATH LINK

Temperature Changes

You often need to deal with temperatures and temperature changes in your daily life, especially in relation to the weather. The temperature affects what you wear and what you do with your time. You make use of temperature changes at home when you boil water to make a hot drink, turn up the heat in the winter, or put food in the refrigerator.

1. The diagram models a temperature increase of 8 °C from a starting temperature of −3 °C.

   a) How does the diagram model the situation?
   b) What is the final temperature? Show how you know.

2. The diagram models a temperature decrease of 9 °C from a starting temperature of +4 °C.

   a) How does the diagram model the situation?
   b) What is the final temperature? Show how you know.
   c) Draw a different diagram that models the same situation. How does your diagram model the final temperature?

```
+5
+4
+3
+2
+1
 0
−1
−2
−3
−4
−5
```

3. Suppose a temperature change from +5 °C to −15 °C occurred over a 4-h period. How could you determine the temperature change per hour?

In this chapter, you will learn how to use multiplication and division of integers in problems that involve temperature changes in the atmosphere.

Exploring Integer Multiplication

Focus on...

After this lesson, you will be able to...

❏ multiply integers using integer chips

The Columbia Icefield is the largest mass of ice in North America below the Arctic Circle. The icefield lies across the Alberta–British Columbia border in the Rockies. Six large glaciers flow from the icefield. One of them, the Athabasca Glacier, is a popular tourist destination in Jasper National Park.

The Athabasca Glacier has been melting for over a century. The front edge or "snout" of the glacier has been receding at an average of approximately 12 m per year. At that rate, how far would it recede in four years?

Explore the Math

Materials

• red and blue integer chips

How can you use integer chips to multiply two integers?

1. Multiplication can be expressed as a repeated addition.

$$(+3) \times (+2) = (+2) + (+2) + (+2)$$

a) Use red integer chips to model the addition $(+2) + (+2) + (+2)$.

b) Copy and complete the multiplication statement $(+3) \times (+2) = \blacksquare$.

2. a) Express $(+4) \times (+3)$ as a repeated addition.

b) Use red integer chips to model the addition.

c) Copy and complete the multiplication statement $(+4) \times (+3) = \blacksquare$.

3. a) Express $(+3) \times (-5)$ as a repeated addition.

b) Use blue integer chips to model the addition.

c) Copy and complete the multiplication statement $(+3) \times (-5) = \blacksquare$.

4. Use integer chips to model each multiplication. Copy and complete each multiplication statement.

a) $(+3) \times (+5) = $ ■   **b)** $(+2) \times (+3) = $ ■

c) $(+4) \times (-3) = $ ■   **d)** $(+3) \times (-4) = $ ■

5. Can you use the same method as in #1 to #4 to complete the multiplication $(-2) \times (+3)$ or the multiplication $(-3) \times (-4)$? Explain.

6. a) The diagrams show how to model the multiplications from #5 by using zero pairs. Describe each model.

Use enough zero pairs so that there are two groups of three red chips available to remove.

$(-2) \times (+3)$ $(-3) \times (-4)$

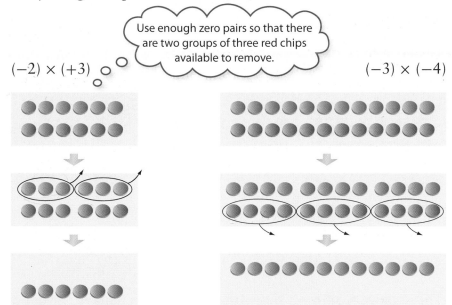

b) Copy and complete each multiplication statement.

$(-2) \times (+3) = $ ■

$(-3) \times (-4) = $ ■

7. Use integer chips to model each multiplication. Copy and complete each multiplication statement.

a) $(-4) \times (-3) = $ ■   **b)** $(-5) \times (+2) = $ ■

c) $(-2) \times (+4) = $ ■   **d)** $(-1) \times (-4) = $ ■

Reflect on Your Findings

8. How can you use integer chips to multiply two integers? In your description, state when you use zero pairs. How do you determine the number of zero pairs to use?

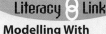

Understanding Multiplication

The product of 4 and 2 is 8, because $4 \times 2 = 8$.

The multiplication statement $4 \times 2 = 8$ means that 4 groups of 2 make 8. You can also think of 4×2 as the repeated addition $2 + 2 + 2 + 2$.

Modelling With Zero Pairs

A zero pair is a pair of integer chips, with one chip representing $+1$ and one chip representing -1.

+1   −1
zero pair

A zero pair represents zero because $(+1) + (-1) = 0$.

Any whole number of zero pairs represents zero.

Example 1: Multiply Using Integer Chips

Determine each product using integer chips. Copy and complete each multiplication statement.

a) $(+5) \times (+2)$ **b)** $(+6) \times (-2)$ **c)** $(-3) \times (+2)$ **d)** $(-2) \times (-4)$

Solution

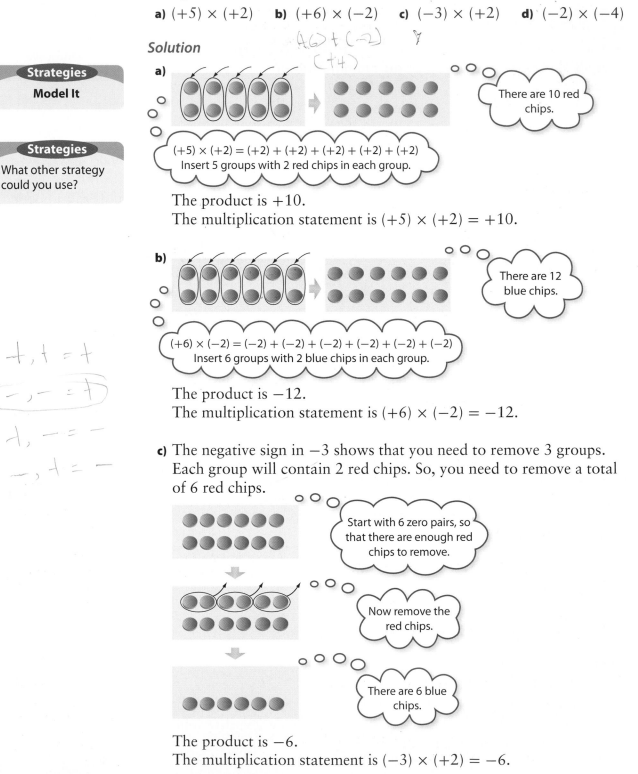

a)

(+5) × (+2) = (+2) + (+2) + (+2) + (+2) + (+2)
Insert 5 groups with 2 red chips in each group.

There are 10 red chips.

The product is +10.
The multiplication statement is $(+5) \times (+2) = +10$.

b)

(+6) × (−2) = (−2) + (−2) + (−2) + (−2) + (−2) + (−2)
Insert 6 groups with 2 blue chips in each group.

There are 12 blue chips.

The product is −12.
The multiplication statement is $(+6) \times (-2) = -12$.

c) The negative sign in −3 shows that you need to remove 3 groups. Each group will contain 2 red chips. So, you need to remove a total of 6 red chips.

Start with 6 zero pairs, so that there are enough red chips to remove.

Now remove the red chips.

There are 6 blue chips.

The product is −6.
The multiplication statement is $(-3) \times (+2) = -6$.

Strategies
Model It

Strategies
What other strategy could you use?

d) The negative sign in −2 shows that you need to remove 2 groups. Each group will contain 4 blue chips. So, you need to remove a total of 8 blue chips.

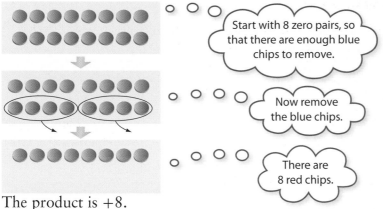

Start with 8 zero pairs, so that there are enough blue chips to remove.

Now remove the blue chips.

There are 8 red chips.

The product is +8.
The multiplication statement is $(-2) \times (-4) = +8$.

> ### Show You Know
>
> Determine each product using integer chips. Use diagrams to show your thinking.
>
> **a)** $(+4) \times (+2)$ **b)** $(+5) \times (-2)$ **c)** $(-4) \times (+2)$ **d)** $(-6) \times (-1)$

Example 2: Apply Integer Multiplication

For 5 h, the temperature in Flin Flon fell by 3 °C each hour. What was the total change in temperature?

Solution

Use the multiplication of two integers to represent the situation.
Represent the time of 5 h by the integer +5.
Represent the 3 °C decrease in each hour by the integer −3.
The total change in temperature can be represented
by the expression $(+5) \times (-3)$.

Multiply $(+5) \times (-3)$ using integer chips.

The number of hours times the change per hour gives the total change.

The product is −15.
The total change in temperature was a decrease of 15 °C.

> ### Show You Know
>
> For 4 h, the temperature in Victoria fell by 2 °C each hour. What was the total change in temperature?

Did You Know?

Flin Flon lies along the Manitoba–Saskatchewan border. The town is named after a fictional character called Professor Josiah Flintabbatey Flonatin. He was the hero of a science fiction novel called *The Sunless City*. In this novel, Josiah explored a bottomless lake in a submarine and discovered a tunnel lined with gold. Flin Flon was named after him because of the large mineral deposits discovered there.

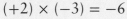

Key Ideas

- To model the multiplication of an integer by a positive integer, you can insert integer chips of the appropriate colour.

$$(+2) \times (-3) = -6$$

- To model the multiplication of an integer by a negative integer, you can remove integer chips of the appropriate colour from zero pairs.

$$(-2) \times (-3) = +6$$

Communicate the Ideas

1. David said that he could model the multiplication $(+3) \times (-7)$ using 3 red chips and 7 blue chips.

   a) Do you agree with David? Explain.

   b) What chips would you use to model $(+3) \times (-7)$? Explain.

2. To model $(-3) \times (-5)$, Raini places 15 zero pairs on her desk.

   a) Why did she use 15 zero pairs?

   b) What should she do next?

3. a) Paolo models $(-2) \times (+3)$ as shown in the diagram. He determines the correct product, -6. Explain why his method works.

   b) Could Paolo model the product if he started with 4 zero pairs? Explain.

4. Jasmine said that she did not need any integer chips to multiply $0 \times (+2)$ or to multiply $(-3) \times 0$. Explain her thinking.

Check Your Understanding

Practise

For help with #5 to #14, refer to Example 1 on pages 288–289.

5. Write each repeated addition as a multiplication.
   a) $(+1) + (+1) + (+1) + (+1) + (+1)$
   b) $(-6) + (-6)$

6. Write each expression as a multiplication.
   a) $(+7) + (+7) + (+7)$
   b) $(-4) + (-4) + (-4) + (-4)$

7. Write each multiplication as a repeated addition.
   a) $(+3) \times (+8)$ **b)** $(+5) \times (-6)$

8. Write each expression as a repeated addition.
   a) $(+7) \times (+2)$ **b)** $(+4) \times (-9)$

9. What multiplication statement does each set of diagrams represent?
   a)

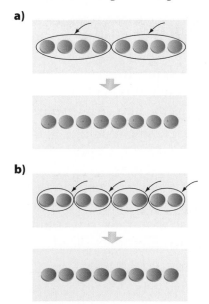

   b)

10. What multiplication statement does each set of diagrams represent?
   a)

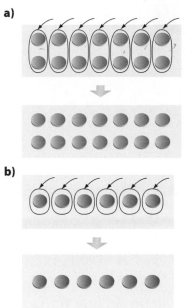

   b)

11. What multiplication statement does each set of diagrams represent?
   a)

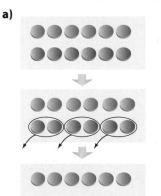

   b)

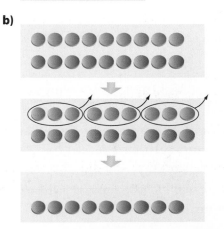

12. What multiplication statement does each set of diagrams represent?

a)

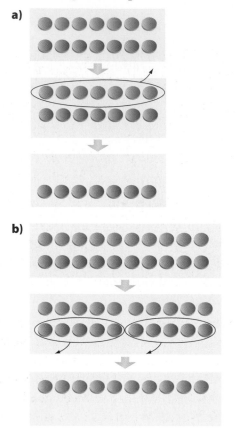

b)

13. Copy and complete each multiplication statement.

a) $(+4) \times (+6)$ **b)** $(+7) \times (-2)$

c) $(-1) \times (+5)$ **d)** $(-8) \times (-2)$

Apply

For help with #14 to #17, refer to Example 2 on page 289.

14. Use the multiplication of two integers to represent each situation. Then determine the product and explain its meaning.

a) The temperature increased for 6 h at 2 °C per hour.

b) Ayesha repaid some money she owed in 4 instalments of $8 each.

15. An aircraft descends at 3 m/s for 12 s. Use the multiplication of two integers to represent the situation. How far does the aircraft descend?

16. A building has 10 storeys above ground and 3 storeys below ground. Each storey has a height of 4 m.

a) What is the total height of the building above ground?

b) What is the total depth of the building below ground?

17. An oil rig is drilling a well at 2 m/min. How deep is the well after the first 8 min?

18. Does doubling an integer always result in an integer of greater value? Explain.

Extend

19. In a magic square, the numbers in each row, column, and diagonal have the same sum. This is called the magic sum.

a) What is the magic sum for this magic square?

+2	+3	−2
−3	+1	+5
+4	−1	0

b) Multiply each integer in the square by −2. Is the result another magic square? If so, what is the new magic sum?

c) Create a magic square with a magic sum of −12.

20. Arrange the following numbers of +1s and −1s in the small squares on a three-by-three grid so that each row, column, and diagonal has a product of −1.

a) six +1s, three −1s

b) four +1s, five −1s

Multiplying Integers

Focus on...

After this lesson, you will be able to...

❏ determine integer products using a number line

❏ apply a sign rule when multiplying integers

Birds called sooty shearwaters have the longest known migration of any animal. Huge flocks of these birds leave their breeding grounds in New Zealand as winter approaches. They fly across and around the Pacific Ocean to take advantage of summer in the Northern Hemisphere. Some of them visit the coastal waters of British Columbia. The birds head south again as winter approaches in the North. Scientists have measured the birds' annual migration at about 70 000 km.

Sooty shearwaters feed by diving into the ocean to catch fish, squid, and krill. The birds dive to an average depth of 14 m. Their deepest dives are about five times as deep as that. How could you use integers to determine the depth of their deepest dives?

Did You Know?

For many years, scientists thought that the arctic tern was the distance champion of bird migration. This bird breeds in the Arctic and migrates to Antarctica and back each year. The distance that it covers is at least 35 000 km.

Explore the Math

Materials

• red and blue integer chips

How can you multiply two integers?

1. The diagram shows how you can model the multiplication $(+3) \times (+2)$ using a number line.

$$\begin{array}{c} \xrightarrow{+2} \ \xrightarrow{+2} \ \xrightarrow{+2} \\ \hline -1 \quad 0 \quad +1 \quad +2 \quad +3 \quad +4 \quad +5 \quad +6 \end{array}$$

a) How are the two integers in the multiplication $(+3) \times (+2)$ shown in the diagram?

b) Model $(+3) \times (+2)$ using integer chips. What is the product?

c) How does the number line show the product?

2. a) Model the multiplication $(+4) \times (-3)$ using a number line. Explain your reasoning.

b) What is the product? Explain how you know.

3. Can you use the same method as in #1 or #2 to model $(-3) \times (+2)$ or $(-4) \times (-3)$ using a number line? Explain.

4. a) Copy the table. Use a suitable model to help you complete each multiplication statement.

$(+6) \times (+2) = \blacksquare$	$(+2) \times (+6) = \blacksquare$
$(+4) \times (-5) = \blacksquare$	$(-5) \times (+4) = \blacksquare$
$(-4) \times (-3) = \blacksquare$	$(-3) \times (-4) = \blacksquare$

b) Compare the two multiplication statements on each row of the completed table. What can you conclude about the order in which you can multiply two integers? Test your conclusion on some other integer multiplications.

c) From your answer to part b), describe a way to determine $(-3) \times (+2)$ using a number line.

5. a) Copy each of the following statements. Use your results from the table in #4 to complete each statement using the word "positive" or the word "negative."

The product of two integers with the same sign is ▬▬▬.
The product of two integers with different signs is ▬▬.

b) Test your statements from part a) on some other integer multiplications.

Reflect on Your Findings

6. a) How can you use a number line to multiply two integers? In your description, state any limitations of your method.

b) How can you use the signs of two integers to help determine their product?

Example 1: Multiply Integers

Calculate.

a) $(+3) \times (+4)$ **b)** $(+2) \times (-9)$ **c)** $(-5) \times (+6)$ **d)** $(-6) \times (-4)$

sign rule

(for multiplication)
• the product of two integers with the same sign is positive
• the product of two integers with different signs is negative

Solution

Multiply the numerals and then apply a **sign rule.**

a) $3 \times 4 = 12$
The integers $+3$ and $+4$ have the same sign, so the product is positive.
$(+3) \times (+4) = +12$

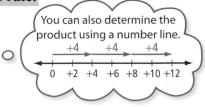

You can also determine the product using a number line.

b) $2 \times 9 = 18$

The integers $+2$ and -9 have different signs, so the product is negative.
$(+2) \times (-9) = -18$

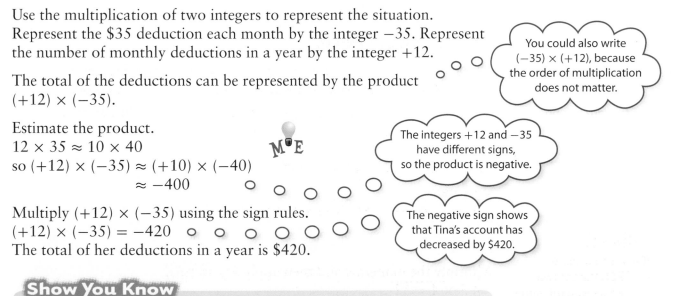

c) $5 \times 6 = 30$

The integers -5 and $+6$ have different signs, so the product is negative.
$(-5) \times (+6) = -30$

d) $6 \times 4 = 24$

The integers -6 and -4 have the same sign, so the product is positive.
$(-6) \times (-4) = +24$

Show You Know

Calculate.

a) $(+4) \times (+7)$ **b)** $(+3) \times (-10)$ **c)** $(-8) \times (-2)$ **d)** $(-4) \times (+9)$

Example 2: Apply Integer Multiplication

Tina supports her favourite charity with an automatic deduction of $35/month from her bank account. Estimate and then calculate the total of her deductions in a year?

Solution

Use the multiplication of two integers to represent the situation. Represent the $35 deduction each month by the integer -35. Represent the number of monthly deductions in a year by the integer $+12$.

> You could also write $(-35) \times (+12)$, because the order of multiplication does not matter.

The total of the deductions can be represented by the product $(+12) \times (-35)$.

Estimate the product.
$12 \times 35 \approx 10 \times 40$
so $(+12) \times (-35) \approx (+10) \times (-40)$
≈ -400

M E

> The integers $+12$ and -35 have different signs, so the product is negative.

Multiply $(+12) \times (-35)$ using the sign rules.
$(+12) \times (-35) = -420$
The total of her deductions in a year is $420.

> The negative sign shows that Tina's account has decreased by $420.

Show You Know

Duane instructs his bank to deduct $65 per month from his bank account and transfer the money into an investment account. What is the total of his deductions in 18 months?

- You can model the multiplication of a positive integer by an integer on a number line.

$(+3) \times (-2) = -6$

- You can multiply two integers by multiplying the numerals and applying the sign rules:

  - The product of two integers with the same sign is positive.
    $(+2) \times (+5) = +10$
    $(-2) \times (-5) = +10$

  - The product of two integers with different signs is negative.
    $(+2) \times (-5) = -10$
    $(-2) \times (+5) = -10$

- Multiplying two integers in either order gives the same result.
  $(-5) \times (+3) = -15$
  $(+3) \times (-5) = -15$

Communicate the Ideas

1. Darcy modelled $(+7) \times (+3)$ on a number line by drawing seven arrows. Ishnan modelled $(+7) \times (+3)$ on a number line by drawing only three arrows. Explain Ishnan's thinking.

2. Justin said, "When I multiply $+5$ by a negative integer, the product is less than $+5$. If I multiply -5 by a negative integer, I think the product should be less than -5." Do you agree with him? Explain.

3. Without doing any calculations, Wei said that -19 and $+27$ have the same product as $+19$ and -27. How did she know?

Check Your Understanding

Practise

For help with #4 to #9, refer to Example 1 on pages 294–295.

4. What multiplication statement does each diagram represent?

a)

-1 0 +1 +2 +3 +4 +5 +6 +7 +8

b)

-16 -14 -12 -10 -8 -6 -4 -2 0 +2

5. What multiplication statement does each diagram represent?

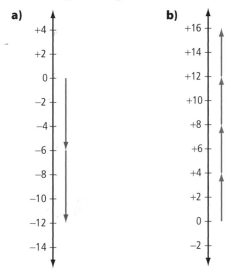

6. Determine each product using a number line.

a) $(+5) \times (+5)$ **b)** $(+3) \times (-6)$

7. Determine each product.

a) $(+4) \times (-7)$ **b)** $(+2) \times (+9)$

8. Determine each product using the sign rules.

a) $(+10) \times (+4)$ **b)** $(+6) \times (-5)$

c) $(-7) \times (+5)$ **d)** $(-8) \times (-4)$

9. Determine each product.

a) $(-6) \times (-6)$ **b)** $(+9) \times (+6)$

c) $(-12) \times (+2)$ **d)** $(+11) \times 0$

For help with #10 to #15, refer to Example 2 on page 295.

10. Estimate and then calculate.

a) $(+17) \times (-24)$

b) $(+37) \times (+22)$

c) $(-72) \times (+15)$

d) $(-28) \times (-47)$

11. Estimate and then calculate.

a) $(-18) \times (-14)$

b) $(-51) \times (+26)$

c) $(+99) \times (+12)$

d) $(+55) \times (+55)$

Apply

For #12 to #15, use the multiplication of two integers to represent each situation.

12. A telephone company offers its customers a $15 discount per month if they also sign up for Internet service. How much is the annual discount?

13. A hot-air balloon is descending at 60 m/min. How far does it descend in 25 min?

14. Ana owns 75 shares of the Leafy Greens Company. One week, the value of each share dropped by 60¢. The next week, the value of each share grew by 85¢. What was the total change in the value of Ana's shares

 a) in the first week?

 b) in the second week?

 c) over the two-week period?

15. To prepare for the weightlessness of space, astronauts train using steep dives on an aircraft. In one dive, the aircraft can descend at 120 m/s for 20 s. How far does the aircraft descend?

16. In the following list of integers, identify the two integers that have the greatest product.

$$+21, -18, +12, +14,$$
$$-23, -15, +19, -13$$

17. Without evaluating the products, identify the least product. Explain your reasoning.

$(+99) \times (+82)$
$(-99) \times (-82)$
$(+99) \times (-82)$

18. Suppose a friend knows how to multiply positive integers but has never multiplied negative integers.

 a) How could you use the following pattern to show your friend how to calculate $(+5) \times (-3)$?

$(+5) \times (+3) = +15$
$(+5) \times (+2) = +10$
$(+5) \times (+1) = +5$
$(+5) \times 0 = 0$
$(+5) \times (-1) = \blacksquare$
$(+5) \times (-2) = \blacksquare$
$(+5) \times (-3) = \blacksquare$

 b) Make up a pattern to show your friend how to calculate $(+6) \times (-2)$.

19. a) Can $+4$ be written as the product of two equal integers? Explain.

 b) Can -4 be written as the product of two equal integers? Explain.

20. Copy and complete each multiplication statement.

 a) $(+6) \times \blacksquare = +18$

 b) $\blacksquare \times (-2) = -10$

 c) $\blacksquare \times (+3) = -12$

 d) $(-4) \times \blacksquare = +16$

21. Complete each statement in as many ways as possible using integers.

 a) $\blacksquare \times \blacksquare = +10$

 b) $\blacksquare \times \blacksquare = -16$

 c) $\blacksquare \times \blacksquare = -24$

22. The sum of two integers is -5. The product of the same two integers is -36. What are the two integers?

23. Write a word problem that you can solve using the expression $(+5) \times (-6)$.

24. Create your own word problem that involves integer multiplication. Make sure that you can solve your problem. Give your problem to a classmate to solve.

Extend

25. Describe each pattern. Then write the next three terms in each pattern.

 a) $+1, +3, +9, +27, \ldots$

 b) $-1, +2, -4, +8, \ldots$

 c) $-2, -4, -8, -16, \ldots$

 d) $+2, -8, +32, -128, \ldots$

26. For each statement, describe a situation in which the statement is true.

a) The product of two integers equals one of the integers.

b) The product of two integers equals the opposite of one of the integers.

c) The product of two integers is less than both integers.

d) The product of two integers is greater than both integers.

27. a) Identify three consecutive integers whose sum and product both equal zero.

b) Repeat part a) for five consecutive integers.

c) Can you repeat part a) for two consecutive integers or for four consecutive integers? Explain.

28. In a magic multiplication square, the numbers in each row, column, and diagonal have the same product. This is called the magic product.

a) What is the magic product of this square?

+12	−1	+18
−9	−6	−4
+2	−36	+3

b) Multiply each number in the square from part a) by −2. Is the result a magic multiplication square? If so, what is the magic product?

c) Add −5 to each number in the square from part a). Is the result a magic multiplication square? If so, what is the magic product?

29. Write a sign rule for the product of each of the following.

a) an even number of positive integers

b) an odd number of positive integers

c) an even number of negative integers

d) an odd number of negative integers

MATH LINK

The temperature of still, dry air decreases by about 6 °C for each kilometre increase in altitude. A weather balloon was launched from The Pas, Manitoba, on a still, dry day.

a) If the temperature on the ground was +4 °C, what was the approximate temperature 11 km above the ground?

b) If the balloon then descended to 5 km above ground, about how much did the temperature change during the descent?

8.3 Exploring Integer Division

Grizzly bears lose much of their body mass during their winter sleep. A large male bear may enter his den at 300 kg in November. He may lose 75 kg by the time he emerges five months later. How would you represent a loss of 75 kg with an integer? What operation would you use to find the average loss of mass in one month?

Focus on...

After this lesson, you will be able to...

☐ divide integers using integer chips

Explore the Math

Materials
• red and blue integer chips

How can you use integer chips to divide two integers?

1. The diagram shows a way to model the division $(+8) \div (+2)$ using red integer chips.

a) Explain how the diagram shows the quotient $(+8) \div (+2)$.
b) Copy and complete the division statement $(+8) \div (+2) = \blacksquare$.
c) Explain how the same diagram can also model $(+8) \div (+4)$.
d) Copy and complete the division statement $(+8) \div (+4) = \blacksquare$.

2. **a)** Use red integer chips to model the division $(+15) \div (+5)$.
b) Copy and complete the division statement $(+15) \div (+5) = \blacksquare$.
c) Write the other division statement that the model can represent.

Literacy ⊝ Link

Understanding Division

In the division statement $6 \div 2 = 3$, the dividend is 6, the divisor is 2, and the quotient is 3.

This division statement means that in 6 there are 3 groups of 2. It also means that when 6 is separated into 2 equal groups, there are 3 in each group.

3. The diagram shows a way to model the division $(-8) \div (-2)$ using blue integer chips.

  a) Explain how the diagram shows the quotient $(-8) \div (-2)$.
  b) Copy and complete the division statement $(-8) \div (-2) = $ ■.
  c) Explain how the same diagram can also model $(-8) \div (+4)$.
  d) Copy and complete the division statement $(-8) \div (+4) = $ ■.

4. a) Use blue integer chips to model the division $(-15) \div (-5)$.
  b) Copy and complete the division statement $(-15) \div (-5) = $ ■.
  c) Write the other division statement that the model can represent.

5. a) Model the division $(-8) \div (+2)$ using integer chips. Explain your method.
  b) Copy and complete the division statement $(-8) \div (+2) = $ ■.

Reflect on Your Findings

6. How can you use integer chips to divide two integers?

Example 1: Divide Using Integer Chips

Determine each quotient using integer chips. Copy and complete each division statement.
  a) $(+12) \div (+3) = + +$
  b) $(-12) \div (-3) = + +$ $+ 2.$ 9 q q q q
  c) $(-12) \div (+4) = -4$

Solution

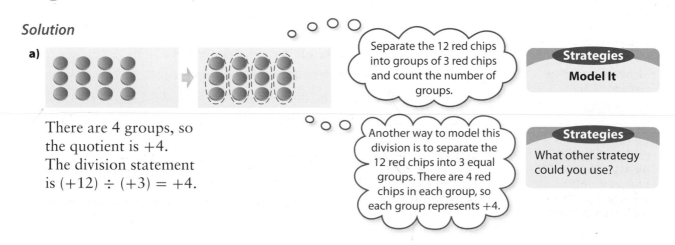

There are 4 groups, so the quotient is $+4$.
The division statement is $(+12) \div (+3) = +4$.

Separate the 12 red chips into groups of 3 red chips and count the number of groups.

Strategies
Model It

Another way to model this division is to separate the 12 red chips into 3 equal groups. There are 4 red chips in each group, so each group represents $+4$.

Strategies
What other strategy could you use?

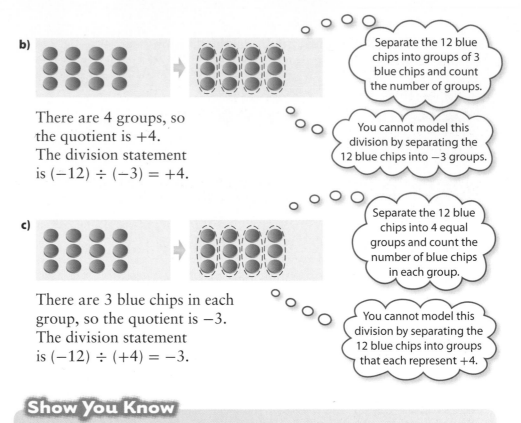

b)

There are 4 groups, so the quotient is +4.
The division statement is $(-12) \div (-3) = +4$.

Separate the 12 blue chips into groups of 3 blue chips and count the number of groups.

You cannot model this division by separating the 12 blue chips into −3 groups.

c)

There are 3 blue chips in each group, so the quotient is −3.
The division statement is $(-12) \div (+4) = -3$.

Separate the 12 blue chips into 4 equal groups and count the number of blue chips in each group.

You cannot model this division by separating the 12 blue chips into groups that each represent +4.

Show You Know

Determine each quotient using integer chips. Use diagrams to show your thinking.

a) $(+14) \div (+7)$　　**b)** $(-9) \div (-3)$　　**c)** $(-16) \div (+2)$

Example 2: Apply Integer Division

@WWW Web Link

The name *Wetaskiwin* comes from the Cree term *wi-ta-ski-oo cha-ka-tin-ow*, which means "place of peace" or "hill of peace." To find out more about Aboriginal sources of Canadian place names, go to www.mathlinks8.ca and follow the links.

One night, the temperature in Wetaskiwin, Alberta, was falling by 2 °C each hour. How many hours did it take for the temperature to fall 10 °C altogether? Show how you found your answer using integer chips.

Solution

Use the division of two integers to represent the situation.
Represent the 2 °C decrease each hour by the integer −2.
Represent the total decrease of 10 °C by the integer −10.
The number of hours taken can be represented by the expression $(-10) \div (-2)$.
Divide $(-10) \div (-2)$ using integer chips.

The total change divided by the change per hour gives the number of hours.

Separate the 10 blue chips into groups of 2 blue chips. Count the number of groups.

There are 5 groups, so the quotient is +5.
It took 5 h for the temperature to fall 10 °C altogether.

The temperature in Buffalo Narrows, Saskatchewan, was falling by 3 °C each hour. How many hours did it take for the temperature to fall 12 °C altogether? Show how you found your answer using integer chips.

Key Ideas

• You can use integer chips to model integer division.

$(-6) \div (-2) = +3$
$(-6) \div (+3) = -2$

Communicate the Ideas

1. a) Allison modelled the division $(+12) \div (+6)$ by separating 12 red chips into groups of 6. Tyler modelled the same division by separating 12 red chips into 6 equal groups. Explain how they each determined the correct quotient.

b) Explain how each of their methods also models the division $(+12) \div (+2)$.

c) Using blue chips, could you use Tyler's method to model $(-12) \div (+6)$? Explain.

d) Using blue chips, could you use Allison's method to model $(-12) \div (+6)$? Explain.

2. a) Wing modelled the division $0 \div (+4)$ by separating 8 zero pairs into 4 groups. There were 2 zero pairs in each group. Explain how his model shows the quotient.

b) Could you model the same division with a different number of zero pairs? Explain.

c) Would you use integer chips to divide 0 by a positive or negative integer? Explain.

Check Your Understanding

Practise

For help with #3 to #8, refer to Example 1 on pages 301–302.

3. Copy each division statement. Use the diagrams to complete it.

a) $(+10) \div (+2) = \blacksquare$

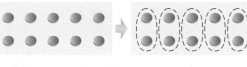

b) $(-16) \div (-4) = \blacksquare$

c) $(-14) \div (+2) = \blacksquare$

4. Copy each division statement. Use the diagrams to complete it.

a) $(-4) \div (-2) = \blacksquare$

b) $(+9) \div (+3) = \blacksquare$

c) $(-12) \div (+6) = \blacksquare$

5. Copy both division statements. Use the diagrams to complete them.

a) $(+14) \div (+2) = \blacksquare$
$(+14) \div (+7) = \blacksquare$

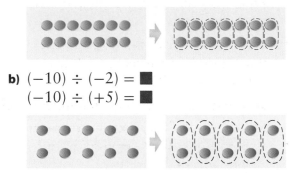

b) $(-10) \div (-2) = \blacksquare$
$(-10) \div (+5) = \blacksquare$

6. Copy both division statements. Use the diagrams to complete them.

a) $(+15) \div (+5) = \blacksquare$
$(+15) \div (+3) = \blacksquare$

b) $(-18) \div (-9) = \blacksquare$
$(-18) \div (+2) = \blacksquare$

7. Determine each quotient using integer chips. Have a partner check your chips. Then copy and complete the division statement

a) $(+16) \div (+4) = \blacksquare$

b) $(-7) \div (+7) = \blacksquare$

c) $(-12) \div (-6) = \blacksquare$

8. Divide using integer chips. Then copy and complete the division statement.

a) $(-20) \div (-10) = \blacksquare$

b) $(-10) \div (+2) = \blacksquare$

c) $(+4) \div (+2) = \blacksquare$

For help with #9 to #11, refer to Example 2 on page 302. Use the division of two integers to represent each situation and solve the problem.

9. A submarine was diving at 3 m/min. How long did it take to dive 21 m?

10. From 11:00 p.m. to 5:00 a.m., the temperature in Saskatoon fell from $-1\,°C$ to $-19\,°C$.

   a) What was the change in temperature?

   b) What was the change in temperature per hour? What assumption did you make?

11. Gary takes four bus trips on each day of the weekend. He spends $16 each weekend on bus fares. How much does each trip cost?

12. Copy the pattern.

$(-12) \div (-3) = \blacksquare$
$(-9) \div (-3) = \blacksquare$
$(-6) \div (-3) = \blacksquare$
$(-3) \div (-3) = \blacksquare$
$0 \div (-3) = \blacksquare$
$(+3) \div (-3) = \blacksquare$
$(+6) \div (-3) = \blacksquare$

   a) Use integer chips to complete the first four lines. Describe the pattern.

   b) Extend the pattern to determine the quotient $(+6) \div (-3)$.

13. Copy the pattern.

$(-8) \div (-2) = \blacksquare$
$(-6) \div (-2) = \blacksquare$
$(-4) \div (-2) = \blacksquare$
$(-2) \div (-2) = \blacksquare$
$0 \div (-2) = \blacksquare$
$(+2) \div (-2) = \blacksquare$
$(+4) \div (-2) = \blacksquare$

   a) Use integer chips to complete the first four lines. Describe the pattern.

   b) Extend the pattern to determine the quotient $(+4) \div (-2)$.

14. The deepest recorded dive is 500 m for an emperor penguin and 2000 m for a sperm whale.

   a) Use the division of two integers to represent how many times as deep a sperm whale can dive as an emperor penguin.

   b) How can you model the division using only 20 integer chips?

   c) What is the quotient?

Extend

15. Divide each of the following using integer chips or diagrams of chips. Explain your reasoning.

   a) $(+15) \div (+5) \div (+3)$

   b) $(-24) \div (-2) \div (+4)$

   c) $(-20) \div (+2) \div (-5)$

   d) $(-18) \div (+2) \div (+3)$

16. Since sunset 6 h ago, the temperature in Brandon, Manitoba, has decreased from $+1\,°C$ to $-11\,°C$. Predict what the temperature will be 3 h from now. What assumptions did you make?

8.4

Dividing Integers

After this lesson, you will be able to...

❑ determine integer quotients using a number line
❑ apply a sign rule when dividing integers

Farmers around the world use fertilizers made from potash mined in Saskatchewan. The province produces over 40% of the world's supply of potash.

To reach the potash, miners are lowered down a vertical mineshaft in a cage. Typical mineshafts are 900 m to 1100 m deep. The cage descends at about 6 m/s. How could you use integer chips to determine the time it takes to descend 900 m? Describe any difficulty you see in using integer chips to determine the time.

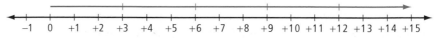

How can you divide two integers?

• red and blue integer chips

1. The diagram shows how you can model the division $(+15) \div (+3)$ using a number line.

```
      ──┬──┬──┬──┬──┬──┬──┬──┬──┬──┬──┬──┬──┬──┬──┬──┬──→
        −1  0  +1 +2 +3 +4 +5 +6 +7 +8 +9 +10 +11 +12 +13 +14 +15
```

a) How are the two integers in the division $(+15) \div (+3)$ shown in the diagram?

b) Model $(+15) \div (+3)$ using integer chips. What is the quotient?

c) How does the number line show the quotient?

d) Explain how the diagram can also model the division $(+15) \div (+5)$.

2. The diagram shows how you can model the division $(-15) \div (-3)$ using a number line.

-16 -15 -14 -13 -12 -11 -10 -9 -8 -7 -6 -5 -4 -3 -2 -1 0 +1

a) How are the two integers in the division $(-15) \div (-3)$ shown in the diagram?

b) Model $(-15) \div (-3)$ using integer chips. What is the quotient?

c) How does the number line show the quotient?

d) Explain how the diagram can also model the division $(-15) \div (+5)$.

3. a) Model the division $(-15) \div (+3)$ using a number line. Explain your reasoning.

b) Copy and complete the division statement $(-15) \div (+3) = \blacksquare$.

c) Explain how your diagram can also model the division $(-15) \div (-5)$.

4. Can you use the same methods as in #1 to #3 to model the division $(+15) \div (-3)$? Explain.

5. The first row of the table shows a multiplication statement and the two division statements related to it. Copy and complete the table.

Multiplication Statement	Related Division Statements	
$(+2) \times (+4) = +8$	$(+8) \div (+4) = +2$	$(+8) \div (+2) = +4$
$(+6) \times (+2) = +12$		
$(+3) \times (-5) = -15$		
$(-3) \times (+6) = -18$		
$(-5) \times (-4) = +20$		
$(-1) \times (-9) = +9$		

6. Copy each of the following statements. Use your results from the table to complete each statement using the word "positive" or the word "negative."

The quotient of two integers with the same sign is $\blacksquare$.
The quotient of two integers with different signs is $\blacksquare$.

Reflect on Your Findings

7. a) How can you use a number line to divide two integers? In your description, state any limitations of your method.

b) How can you use the signs of two integers to help determine their quotient?

Example 1: Divide Integers

Calculate.

a) $(+6) \div (+2)$ **b)** $(-12) \div (-6)$
c) $(-20) \div (+4)$ **d)** $(+42) \div (-14)$

Solution

sign rule

(for division)
- the quotient of two integers with the same sign is positive
- the quotient of two integers with different signs is negative

Divide the numerals and then apply a **sign rule.**

a) $6 \div 2 = 3$
The integers $+6$ and $+2$ have the same sign, so the quotient is positive.
$(+6) \div (+2) = +3$

You can also determine the quotient using a number line.

b) $12 \div 6 = 2$
The integers -12 and -6 have the same sign, so the quotient is positive.
$(-12) \div (-6) = +2$

c) $20 \div 4 = 5$
The integers -20 and $+4$ have different signs, so the quotient is negative.
$(-20) \div (+4) = -5$

d) $42 \div 14 = 3$
The integers $+42$ and -14 have different signs, so the quotient is negative.
$(+42) \div (-14) = -3$

C 42 ÷ 14 +⁄− = -3.

Check:
$(-3) \times (-14) = +42$

You can use multiplication to check your division.

Tech Link

To enter a positive integer on your calculator, you do not need to enter the positive sign. You do need to enter the negative sign for a negative integer. On most calculators, the key used to enter a negative sign is not the subtraction key. Check that the key sequence shown in Example 1d) works correctly on your calculator. Modify the sequence, if necessary.

Show You Know

Calculate.

a) $(+24) \div (+8)$ **b)** $(+30) \div (-10)$
c) $(-48) \div (-12)$ **d)** $(-66) \div (+11)$

Example 2: Apply Integer Division

Daria and four of her friends went out for lunch. They agreed to split the cost equally. The total bill came to $85, which Daria paid on her credit card. How much did each of her friends owe Daria?

Solution

Use the division of two integers to represent the situation.
Represent the total cost of $85 by the integer -85.
Represent the 5 people by the integer $+5$.
Each person's share can be represented by the expression $(-85) \div (+5)$.
$(-85) \div (+5) = -17$
Each of her friends owed Daria $17.

> $85 \div 5 = 17$. The integers -85 and $+5$ have different signs, so the quotient is negative.

Check.
Use multiplication to check the division.
$(-17) \times (+5) = -85$

Show You Know

Pierre paid $42 to admit himself and two of his friends into a science museum. What was the cost of each admission?

Key Ideas

- You can model some integer divisions on a number line.

$(-12) \div (-4) = +3 \qquad (-12) \div (+3) = -4$

- You can divide two integers by dividing the numerals and applying the sign rules.
  - The quotient of two integers with the same sign is positive.
    $(+6) \div (+2) = +3 \qquad (-6) \div (-2) = +3$
  - The quotient of two integers with different signs is negative.
    $(+6) \div (-2) = -3 \qquad (-6) \div (+2) = -3$

Communicate the Ideas

1. To model the division $(+15) \div (+3)$ on a number line, you first draw an arrow that represents $+15$. You then have two choices:
   - You can cut the arrow into parts that each represent $+3$ and count how many parts there are.
   - You can cut the arrow into three equal parts and determine the value that each part represents.

   Which choice do you prefer? Explain.

2. Aziza used a number line to model the division $(-12) \div (-2)$. Yuri used a number line to model the division $(-12) \div (+6)$. They drew the same diagram. What was the diagram?

3. Michel said, "When I divide $+6$ by $+3$, $+2$, or $+1$, the quotient is less than or equal to $+6$. If I divide -6 by $+3$, $+2$, or $+1$, I think the quotient should be less than or equal to -6." Do you agree with him? Explain.

4. Without doing any calculations, Stefani said that the quotients $(-252) \div (-18)$ and $(+252) \div (+18)$ must be the same. How did she know?

Check Your Understanding

Practise

For help with #5 to #10, refer to Example 1 on page 308.

5. Write two division statements that each diagram could represent.

a)

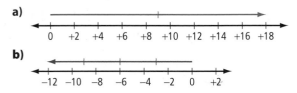

b)

6. Write two division statements that each diagram could represent.

a)

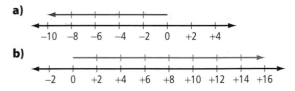

b)

7. Determine each quotient using a number line.
  a) $(+12) \div (+6)$ **b)** $(-20) \div (-4)$
  c) $(-8) \div (+4)$ **d)** $(-10) \div (-5)$

8. Determine each quotient using a number line.
  a) $(-14) \div (-7)$ **b)** $(+16) \div (+4)$
  c) $(-22) \div (+2)$ **d)** $(-15) \div (-5)$

9. Calculate and check.
  a) $(+20) \div (+5)$ **b)** $(+36) \div (-6)$
  c) $(-57) \div (+19)$ **d)** $(-84) \div (-42)$

10. Calculate.
  a) $(-26) \div (-26)$ **b)** $(+95) \div (-5)$
  c) $0 \div (-33)$ **d)** $(-68) \div (+17)$

Apply

For help with #11 to #15, refer to Example 2 on page 309. Use the division of two integers to represent each situation and solve the problem.

11. Raoul borrowed $15 per month from his mother to pay for the art supplies he needed for an evening class. At the end of the course, he owed his mother $60. How long was the course?

12. a) A submarine took 16 min to dive 96 m from the surface. How far did it dive per minute?

  b) The submarine took 12 min to climb back to the surface. How far did it climb per minute?

13. A scuba diver was collecting water samples from a lake. He collected samples at 5-m intervals starting at 5 m below the surface. He collected the final sample at a depth of 35 m. How many samples did he collect?

14. Mina was drilling down through a 21-cm thick concrete floor to install a new plumbing pipe. She drilled for 5 min, took a break, and then finished drilling in another 2 min. At what rate did the drill cut through the floor, in centimetres per minute? What assumptions did you make?

15. A school spent $384 to buy a set of 32 calculators. What was the cost of each calculator?

16. Without evaluating the quotients, identify the quotient with the least value. Explain your reasoning.

$(+2408) \div (+43)$
$(-2408) \div (-43)$
$(+2408) \div (-43)$

17. If 28 times an integer is −448, what is the integer?

18. Copy and complete each statement.

a) $(+72) \div (\blacksquare) = +9$

b) $(\blacksquare) \div (+12) = -10$

c) $(\blacksquare) \div (-13) = -11$

d) $(-84) \div (\blacksquare) = +6$

19. Write a word problem that you can solve using the expression $(-80) \div (+16)$.

20. Create your own word problem that involves integer division. Make sure that you can solve your problem and that the calculation results in an integer. Give your problem to a classmate to solve.

Extend

21. Describe each pattern. Then write the next three terms in each pattern.

a) $+125\,000, +25\,000, +5000, +1000, \ldots$

b) $-512, +256, -128, +64, \ldots$

c) $-1\,000\,000, -100\,000, -10\,000, -1000, \ldots$

d) $+1458, -486, +162, -54, \ldots$

22. The sum of two integers is +20. Dividing the larger integer by the smaller integer gives a quotient of −3. What are the two integers?

MATH LINK

The temperature of still, dry air decreases by about 6 °C for each kilometre increase in altitude. On a still, dry day, the temperature in Yellowknife, Northwest Territories, was −11 °C. The air temperature outside a plane flying above Yellowknife was −53 °C.

a) Approximately how much lower was the temperature outside the aircraft than the temperature in Yellowknife?

b) How high was the aircraft above Yellowknife?

8.5 Applying Integer Operations

Focus on...

After this lesson, you will be able to...

❑ apply the order of operations to solve problems involving integers

Did You Know?

The *Ben Franklin* is named after the American scientist and diplomat Benjamin Franklin, 1706—1790. While a passenger on transatlantic voyages, he spent his time measuring ocean temperatures. Franklin mapped a stream of warm water about 70 km wide flowing across the cold Atlantic. He named this stream the Gulf Stream.

A famous submersible, the *Ben Franklin*, is at the Vancouver Maritime Museum. This submersible was built to study the currents and sea life along the east coast of North America in the Gulf Stream.

The *Ben Franklin* explored the Gulf Stream at depths from 200 m to 600 m. How would you represent these depths with integers? What operation would you use to find how many times as great a depth of 600 m is as a depth of 200 m?

Explore the Math

Why is it important to know the order of operations when solving problems involving integers?

Laura, Abeni, and Rob were discussing the following problem.

A submersible dives from the surface at 15 m/min for 6 min and then at 25 m/min for 20 min. What is the depth of the submersible after the dive?

They worked together to write the following expression to solve the problem.
$6 \times (-15) + 20 \times (-25)$

Then they evaluated the expression independently.
Laura evaluated the expression as $+1750$.
Abeni evaluated the expression as -590.
Rob evaluated the expression as -750.

1. Explain how the expression represents the problem.

2. Which student evaluated the expression correctly? How do you know?

3. What errors did the other two students make?

4. What is the depth of the submersible after the dive?

Reflect on Your Findings

5. Why is it important to know the order of operations when solving problems involving integers?

Example 1: Use the Order of Operations

Calculate. $+5 -(-8) = +13$

a) $(-15) \div (-3) - (+4) \times (-2)$

b) $(-6) - (-9) + (-14) \div (+2)$

c) $-8 + (-2) \times [4 + (-1)]$

Solution

a) $(-15) \div (-3) - (+4) \times (-2)$ Multiply and divide in order, from left to right.

$= (+5) - (+4) \times (-2)$

$= (+5) - (-8)$ Subtract.

$= +13$

b) $(-6) - (-9) + (-14) \div (+2)$ Divide.

$= (-6) - (-9) + (-7)$ Add and subtract in order, from left to right.

$= (+3) + (-7)$

$= -4$

c) $-8 + (-2) \times [4 + (-1)]$ Brackets.

$= -8 + (-2) \times 3$ Multiply.

$= -8 + (-6)$ Add.

$= -14$

Grouping is shown using square brackets, because −1 is already in round brackets.

Show You Know

Calculate.

a) $(+4) + (-7) \times (-3) - (+5)$

b) $(-16) \div [(+5) - (+6) + (-7)]$

c) $-2 \times [5 + (-3)] + (-15)$

WWW Web Link

Submersibles are still used to explore the world's oceans. The ROPOS submersible operates out of Sidney, British Columbia. ROPOS can reach a depth of 5000 m.

To learn more about the *Ben Franklin* and ROPOS submersibles, go to www.mathlinks8.ca and follow the links.

Literacy Link

Omitting Positive Signs or Brackets

A positive integer can be written without the positive sign or brackets. For example, $(+3) \times (+4)$ can be written as 3×4.

Negative integers must include the negative sign. The brackets can be omitted from a negative integer that does not follow an operation symbol. For example, $(-9) \div (-3)$ can be written as $-9 \div (-3)$.

Example 2: Apply Integer Operations

One week in March in Peguis, Manitoba, the daily high temperatures were −2 °C, −6 °C, +1 °C, +2 °C, −5 °C, −8 °C, and +4 °C. What was the mean daily high temperature for that week?

Solution

The mean temperature is the sum of the temperatures divided by the number of temperatures.

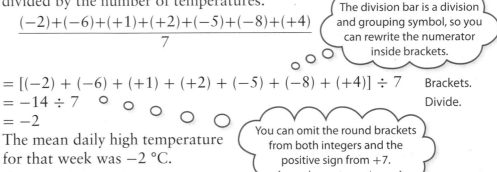

$$\frac{(-2)+(-6)+(+1)+(+2)+(-5)+(-8)+(+4)}{7}$$

The division bar is a division and grouping symbol, so you can rewrite the numerator inside brackets.

$$= [(-2) + (-6) + (+1) + (+2) + (-5) + (-8) + (+4)] \div 7 \quad \text{Brackets.}$$
$$= -14 \div 7 \qquad\qquad\qquad\qquad\qquad\qquad\qquad\quad \text{Divide.}$$
$$= -2$$

The mean daily high temperature for that week was −2 °C.

You can omit the round brackets from both integers and the positive sign from +7.

Show You Know

On four days in June in Resolute, Nunavut, the daily low temperatures were −6 °C, 0 °C, +1 °C, and −7 °C. What was the mean daily low temperature for those four days?

Key Ideas

- When solving a problem, you need to decide which operation(s) to perform on integers.
- Some integer problems involve the order of operations.
- The order of operations for integers is the same as for whole numbers and decimals.
  - Brackets.
  - Multiply and divide in order, from left to right.
  - Add and subtract in order, from left to right.

Communicate the Ideas

1. Lance evaluated the expression $-2 \times (4 + 5) + 3$ to equal 0.
   a) What mistake did he make?
   b) What is the correct value of the expression?

2. Ivan said that the mean of −18, −16, +11, and +15 is positive. Without calculating the value of the mean, Norah disagreed with him. How did she know that the mean is not positive?

3. If 15 times an integer is −255, would it be easier to determine the integer using multiplication or division? Explain.

Check Your Understanding

Practise

For help with #4 to #7, refer to Example 1 on page 313.

4. Calculate using the order of operations.
   a) $(+30) \div (-10) + (-20) \div (-1)$
   b) $(-2) \times [(+10) - (+8)] + (-7)$
   c) $(+6) + (+9) \times (-5) \div (-3)$

5. Calculate using the order of operations.
   a) $(-4) - (+8) \times (-2) - (+15)$
   b) $(-3) + (-18) \div (+2) \div (-3)$
   c) $(+16) \div [(+4) - (+2)] + (-4)$

6. Calculate.
   a) $(4 - 7) \times 2 + 12$
   b) $-10 \div 5 + 3 \times (-4)$
   c) $3 \times [14 + (-18)] - 8 \div (-4)$

7. Calculate.
   a) $-16 \div 2 \times (3 + 1)$
   b) $5 + (-9) \times 4 \div (-1)$
   c) $25 + (-10) - 3 \times [2 - (-2)]$

Apply

For help with #8 to #12, refer to Example 2 on page 314.

8. The daily low temperatures in Prince Rupert, British Columbia, for five days in January were −4 °C, +1 °C, −2 °C, +1 °C, and −6 °C. What is the mean of these temperatures?

9. The table shows changes in the number of subscribers to a community newsletter over a six-month period.

Month	Change in the Number of Subscribers
1	+8
2	+6
3	−12
4	+5
5	−9
6	−10

   a) What was the mean change per month in the number of subscribers?
   b) There were 207 subscribers at the beginning of this period. How many were there at the end?

10. Over a ten-year period, the population of Saskatchewan decreased from 989 000 to 979 000. What was the mean population change per year?

11. The mean of five integers is −11. What is the sum of the integers?

12. A golfer had a mean score of −3 for the 4 rounds of a golf tournament.

   a) What was the golfer's score for the whole tournament?

   b) If par for the course is 72 strokes, how many strokes did the golfer take to complete the tournament?

Sports ⊖ Link

Golf Scores

Par for a golf course is the total number of strokes an expert golfer should take to complete the course. An integer shows a golfer's performance for each round of golf. Using 68 strokes to complete a round on a par 70 course gives a score of 2 below par or −2 for that round. Using 74 strokes to complete a round on a par 70 course gives a score of 4 over par or +4 for that round.

13. The average temperature of Earth's surface is about 15 °C. The temperature of Earth's crust increases by about 25 °C for each kilometre below the surface. What is the average temperature 3 km below Earth's surface?

Did You Know?

The high temperatures below Earth's surface can create hot springs. Water is heated underground and then runs to the surface before it can cool down. The water that feeds the Miette Hot Springs in Jasper National Park is at 54 °C when it reaches the surface. Hot springs support many forms of life. Dr. Kathleen Londry of the University of Manitoba studies an endangered species of snail that lives in the Cave and Basin Hot Springs in Banff National Park.

14. Ahmed had $100 in his savings account at the start of his summer job. For the next eight weeks, he added $70 to his savings each week. After he went back to school, he withdrew $55 per week from his savings. For how many weeks did he make withdrawals until his savings were gone?

15. A new freezer is at a room temperature of 22 °C. When the freezer is turned on, the temperature inside drops by 4 °C per hour. How long does it take the freezer to reach −10 °C?

16. A hang glider descends at 50 m/min for 3 min. The glider then catches an updraft and rises at 100 m/min for 2 min.

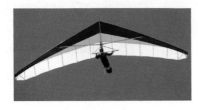

   a) What is the overall change in the hang glider's altitude over this 5-min period?

   b) What is the mean rate of change in the altitude over this period?

17. Because the batteries are low, Darren's watch is losing 9 min every hour. At 8:00 p.m., he sets the watch correctly. What time will his watch show when the correct time is 10:00 a.m. the next day?

18. a) A store that sells ski equipment lost a total of $18 000 in June, July, and August. What was the mean loss per month?

   b) The store broke even in April, May, and September. The store owner wants to make a profit of $54 000 for the year. To meet this target, what mean profit per month does the store need to make in the other six months?

19. Rohana earns $50 a week from babysitting. She spends $25, saves $15, and uses the rest to repay a loan of $100 from her sister.

   a) After six weeks, how much has Rohana spent, how much has she saved, and how much does she still owe her sister?

   b) How many more weeks will Rohana take to pay off the loan?

20. Write and evaluate an expression that represents each statement.

a) Subtract the product of 3 and −8 from 20.

b) Add the product of 4 and 5 to the product of −2 and −3.

c) Divide −62 by the sum of −11 and 9.

d) Multiply the sum of −3 and −5 by 3, then divide by −4 and subtract 13.

Extend

21. Copy each statement. Complete it by including operation symbols.

a) 2 ■ 3 ■ 4 ■ 5 = −14

b) 3 ■ [14 ■ (−2)] ■ 30 = 6

22. The mean of two integers is −17. The product of the two integers is 273. What are the two integers?

23. A multiple-choice test with 50 questions has five possible choices for each question. There are 4 marks for each correct answer, −1 mark for each incorrect answer, and 0 marks for each unanswered question.

a) What is the total score of a student with 35 correct answers, 10 incorrect answers, and 5 unanswered questions?

b) Express the student's score as a percent.

24. Here is one way of using four −2s and the order of operations to write an expression that equals 1.

$$(-2) \div (-2) + (-2) - (-2)$$

Use four −2s and the order of operations to write expressions that equal 2, 3, 4, 5, 6, and 8.

Sports ⊖ Link

Scoring System in the Modern Pentathlon

Monica Pinette from Langley, British Columbia, is a successful Canadian athlete. She has won gold medals at both the Canadian and the Pan American championships in the modern pentathlon. This sport includes five events: shooting, fencing, swimming, show jumping, and running. The events are all held on the same day. The winner is decided using a points system that involves integer operations.

The running event is a 3000-m cross-country race. A male athlete scores 1000 points for finishing this event in 10-min. A female athlete scores 1000 points for finishing in 11 min 20 s. Each whole second below these times is worth 4 extra points. Each whole second above these times results in a 4-point deduction.

1. Show how the following points are calculated.

a) 920 points for a male with a time of 10 min 20 s

b) 1060 points for a female with a time of 11 min 5 s

2. Calculate the points earned by each of the following athletes.

a) a female with a time of 11 min 43 s

b) a male with a time of 9 min 51 s

3. Calculate the time taken by each of the following athletes.

a) a female who scores 1100 points

b) a male who scores 892 points

Did You Know?

Another sport that includes several events is the decathlon. Dave Steen from New Westminster, British Columbia, won a bronze medal in the decathlon at the summer Olympics in Seoul, South Korea. He competed in ten events over two days.

 WWW Web Link

To learn more about the modern pentathlon, including the scoring of the other four events, go to www.mathlinks8.ca and follow the links.

Key Words

Copy and complete each statement in #1 to #3.

1. Integers include positive and negative whole numbers and ▊▊▊▊.

2. When following the order of operations to evaluate $-2 + (4 - 9) \div 5 \times 3$, do ▊▊▊▊ first.

3. An integer chip representing $+1$ and an integer chip representing -1 are together called a(n) ▊▊▊▊.

8.1 Exploring Integer Multiplication, pages 286–292

4. What multiplication statement does each set of diagrams represent?

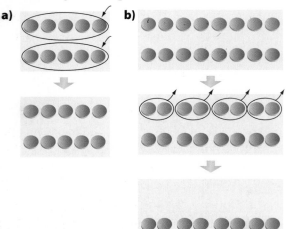

a) b)

5. Determine each product.

   a) $(+3) \times (+3)$
   b) $(+4) \times (-5)$
   c) $(-2) \times (-1)$
   d) $(-5) \times (+3)$

6. A sloth took 9 min to climb down a tree at 2 m/min. How far did the sloth climb down?

8.2 Multiplying Integers, pages 293–299

7. Determine each product using a number line.

   a) $(+3) \times (-6)$
   b) $(+4) \times (+2)$

8. Calculate.

   a) $(+7) \times (-8)$
   b) $(-12) \times (-9)$

9. Estimate and then calculate.

   a) $(+22) \times (+35)$
   b) $(-49) \times (+13)$

10. The product of two integers is -99. What could the integers be? Give four possible answers.

11. Kenji spends $5 per week to buy a sports magazine.

    a) Represent the amount he spends in a year by an integer multiplication.
    b) Determine the amount he spends in a year.

8.3 Exploring Integer Division, pages 300–305

12. Copy both division statements. Use the diagrams to complete them.

a)

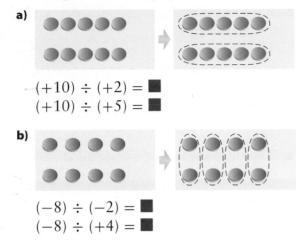

$(+10) \div (+2) = \blacksquare$
$(+10) \div (+5) = \blacksquare$

b)

$(-8) \div (-2) = \blacksquare$
$(-8) \div (+4) = \blacksquare$

13. Determine each quotient.

a) $(+16) \div (+8)$

b) $(-14) \div (-2)$

c) $(-2) \div (+2)$

14. Write a word problem that you can solve using the expression $(-14) \div (+7)$.

8.4 Dividing Integers, pages 306–311

15. Determine $(-18) \div (-3)$ using a number line.

16. Without evaluating the quotients, identify the greatest quotient. Explain your reasoning.

$(-247) \div (+13)$
$(-247) \div (-13)$
$(+247) \div (-13)$

17. Calculate.

a) $(+75) \div (+25)$

b) $(+64) \div (-8)$

c) $(-85) \div (+5)$

d) $(-88) \div (-11)$

18. If two integers have a quotient of -1, how are the integers related?

19. Six friends visited a zoo. The total cost of admission was $90. One of the group was celebrating his birthday, so the others agreed that he should not pay. How much did each of the others pay?

8.5 Applying Integer Operations, pages 312–317

20. Calculate.

a) $-3 \times [(-4) - (-10)] + 12$

b) $12 \div (5 - 8) - 4 \times (-2)$

21. The sum of six integers is -42.

a) What is their mean?

b) Do you have enough information to determine the six integers? Use examples to help explain your answer.

22. Over a five-year period, the number of Manitobans living on farms decreased from 79 840 to 68 135. What was the mean change per year?

23. A small aircraft descended 90 m at 3 m/s and then descended 80 m at 2 m/s. For how much time did it descend altogether?

24. A fitness club charges its members $250/year. If a member makes a single payment to pay for the next three years, there is a discount of $5/month. How much is the single payment?

For #1 to #6, select the correct answer.

1. Which expression is equivalent to $(-5) + (-5) + (-5) + (-5)$?

   A $(+3) \times (-5)$ B $(-3) \times (-5)$

   C $(+4) \times (-5)$ D $(-4) \times (-5)$

2. Which multiplication do the integer chips represent?

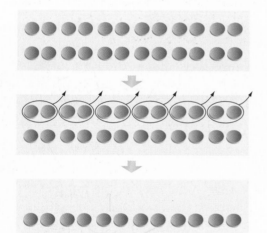

   A $(+6) \times (+2)$ B $(-6) \times (-2)$

   C $(+6) \times (-2)$ D $(-6) \times (+2)$

3. Which expression does not equal $+3$?

   A $(-3) \times (-1) \div (+1)$

   B $(+3) \div (-1)$

   C $(+27) \div (+9)$

   D $(+27) \div (-3) \div (-3)$

4. Which expression equals $(-3) \times (+8)$?

   A $(-12) \times (-2)$

   B $(-24) \div (-1)$

   C $(+4) \times (+6)$

   D $(+72) \div (-3)$

5. What is the greatest product of any two integers in this list?

$$+12, -22, +18, +15,$$
$$-13, -15, +19, -16$$

   A $+37$ B $+342$

   C $+352$ D $+418$

6. What is the value of the expression $(+2) \times [(+5) - (-3)] + (-6)$?

   A $+10$ B $+7$

   C $+4$ D -2

Complete the statements in #7 and #8.

7. Dividing any integer by its opposite results in a quotient of ■.

8. The temperature in Grande Prairie, Alberta, was $+3\,°C$ at midnight. The temperature dropped by $2\,°C/h$ until 6:00 a.m. to reach the overnight low temperature of ■ $°C$.

Short Answer

9. How can one diagram on a number line be used to model both $(-12) \div (+3)$ and $(-12) \div (-4)$? Explain your reasoning.

10. Calculate.

    a) $(-65) \times (+18)$ b) $(-24) \times (-31)$

11. Calculate.

    a) $(-64) \div (-16)$ b) $(+99) \div (-11)$

12. Calculate.

    a) $(-6) \times (+5) + (-27) \div (-9)$

    b) $[8 + (-6)] \div (-2) - 4 \times (-3)$

13. The daily high temperatures in Whitehorse, Yukon Territory, one week in March were −6 °C, +3 °C, +1 °C, −1 °C, −3 °C, −2 °C, and −6 °C. What was the mean daily high temperature that week?

14. Write a word problem that you can solve using the expression (+4) × (−8).

Extended Response

15. How can you tell by looking at two integers if their product is positive, negative, or zero? Use examples to help explain your answer.

16. A submarine dives from the surface at 12 m/min for 6 min and then at 7 m/min for 4 min. What is the depth of the submarine after the dive?

17. Peter had a $200 balance in his bank account. In the next two months, he made four $95 deposits and eight cash withdrawals of $50 each. The bank also made two $10 withdrawals to pay monthly account fees.

a) Determine the account balance at the end of the two months.

b) If Peter continued in the same way, how long after this two-month period would the account be empty?

WRAP IT UP!

The effect of altitude on air temperature is different for rising or falling air than for still air. The amount of moisture in the air can change the effect.

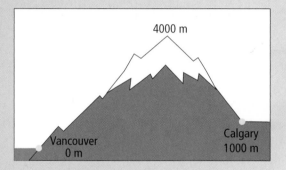

Damp air at 18 °C is blown east at sea level from Vancouver Island. It rises to about 4000 m to clear the mountains on the mainland. It then descends to Calgary, which is about 1000 m above sea level.

- For the first 1000 m of the climb up the mountains, the air cools at 10 °C/km.
- Condensation begins to form as the damp air reaches the 1000-m level, and so it rains.
- The air cools at 5 °C/km as it rises above the 1000-m level, and soon the rain turns to snow.
- The air is now drier, and the snow stops. As the air flows down the mountains to Calgary, the air warms up at 10 °C/km.

a) Draw a diagram similar to the one shown to model the temperature changes at 1000-m altitude intervals as the air travels from Vancouver to Calgary.

b) What is the temperature of the air when it reaches Calgary?

c) Use your understanding of integer multiplication or division to show how you could determine the answer for part b) without using a diagram.

d) Suppose the temperature when the air reaches Calgary is 30 °C. What was the starting temperature in Vancouver? Show your solution in two different ways.

Math Games

Integer Race

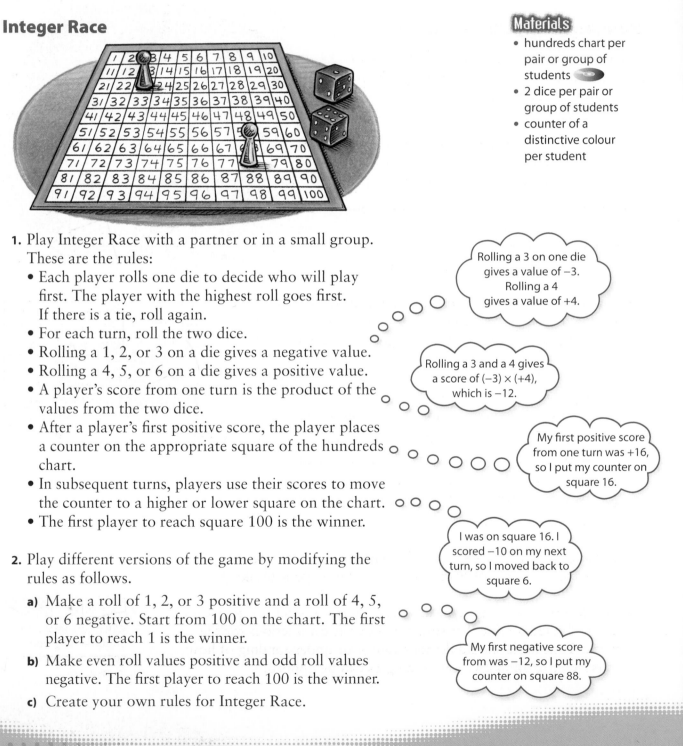

Materials
- hundreds chart per pair or group of students
- 2 dice per pair or group of students
- counter of a distinctive colour per student

1. Play Integer Race with a partner or in a small group. These are the rules:
   - Each player rolls one die to decide who will play first. The player with the highest roll goes first. If there is a tie, roll again.
   - For each turn, roll the two dice.
   - Rolling a 1, 2, or 3 on a die gives a negative value.
   - Rolling a 4, 5, or 6 on a die gives a positive value.
   - A player's score from one turn is the product of the values from the two dice.
   - After a player's first positive score, the player places a counter on the appropriate square of the hundreds chart.
   - In subsequent turns, players use their scores to move the counter to a higher or lower square on the chart.
   - The first player to reach square 100 is the winner.

2. Play different versions of the game by modifying the rules as follows.
   a) Make a roll of 1, 2, or 3 positive and a roll of 4, 5, or 6 negative. Start from 100 on the chart. The first player to reach 1 is the winner.
   b) Make even roll values positive and odd roll values negative. The first player to reach 100 is the winner.
   c) Create your own rules for Integer Race.

Rolling a 3 on one die gives a value of −3. Rolling a 4 gives a value of +4.

Rolling a 3 and a 4 gives a score of $(-3) \times (+4)$, which is −12.

My first positive score from one turn was +16, so I put my counter on square 16.

I was on square 16. I scored −10 on my next turn, so I moved back to square 6.

My first negative score from was −12, so I put my counter on square 88.

Challenge in Real Life

Running a Small Business

Small business owners need to keep track of their finances—both the money they take in from customers and the money they pay out to suppliers.

You be the small business owner! Assume that you own a games store. Part of your job is to keep track of your financial accounts.

The table below the visual shows information about some of the games you carry.
• You buy them from a supplier at one price.
• You sell them to customers at a higher price.

1. Choose a + or − sign to place beside each value in the table. Choose the sign by considering how each value affects your account (money in or money out). Justify your choice of signs.

Buy from Supplier	Game X $14
	Game Y $10
	Game Z $6
Sell to Customers	Game X $24
	Game Y $15
	Game Z $11

2. Show how the multiplication or division of integers can be used to model each situation below. Justify your choices.
   a) You buy 12 copies of Game Z from the supplier.
   b) You spend $72 to buy these copies of Game Z from the supplier.
   c) You sell three copies of Game Y to customers.
   d) A customer returns two copies of Game X for a refund.
   e) You find that four copies of Game Y have defects. You return them to the supplier.

3. If you buy 36 copies of Game X from the supplier, how many will you have to sell to *break even* on them? Show your thinking.

4. Create a scenario for a typical week of buying, selling, returns, and so on. Design a table that summarizes your transactions for the week. Your table should demonstrate your understanding of how multiplication and division of integers can be applied.

Literacy Link

When you *break even* on something, you neither gain nor lose money.

Chapters 5-8 Review

Chapter 5 Surface Area

1. Sketch the front, top, and side views.

   a) 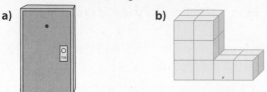 **b)**

2. Draw a net on grid paper for a right rectangular prism with the following measurements: length is 6 units, width is 3 units, and height is 4 units.

3. An official hockey puck has a diameter of 7.6 cm and is 2.5 cm high. Find the surface area of the puck.

4. Cho and her dad are building a skateboard launch ramp. They decide on the following measurements: the base of the ramp will be 1.2 m wide and 2.1 m long; the ramp will be 2.3 m long and 0.9 m high. They are undecided about building the base of the ramp.

   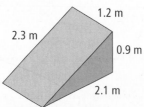

   1.2 m
   2.3 m
   0.9 m
   2.1 m

   a) How much plywood will they need to make the entire ramp?
   b) Calculate the amount of plywood needed without the base of the ramp.

5. Determine the number of square metres of vinyl needed to line the inside of a right rectangular swimming pool. The pool is 7 m long, 4 m wide, and has a uniform depth of 2.5 m.

6. Each side of a wooden cube is 5 cm long. Riley drills a cylindrical hole with a diameter of 4 cm through the cube. What is the total surface area of the remaining part if Riley wants to spray paint all the surfaces including inside the hole?

7. The radius of cylinder A is 30 cm. The radius of cylinder B is 60 cm. Both cylinders have a height of 45 cm. Determine the surface area of each cylinder.

Chapter 6 Fraction Operations

8. The time from when a bird lays an egg to when the egg hatches is called the incubation time. For a pigeon egg, the incubation time is 18 days.

   a) For a chicken egg, the incubation time is $\frac{7}{6}$ of the incubation time for a pigeon egg. Determine the incubation time for a chicken egg.

   b) For a warbler egg, the incubation time is $\frac{7}{9}$ of the incubation time for a pigeon egg. Determine the incubation time for a warbler egg.

9. At the end of a party, half of a cake is left over. Five people decide to share the leftover cake equally and take their share home. What fraction of a cake does each person take home? Show your solution using a diagram and using fraction operations.

10. The maximum lifespan of a moose is $\frac{2}{3}$ of the maximum lifespan of a bison. The maximum lifespan of a white-tailed deer is $\frac{3}{4}$ of the maximum lifespan of a moose. What fraction is the maximum lifespan of a white-tailed deer of the maximum lifespan of a bison?

11. The Indian Ocean covers about $\frac{1}{7}$ of Earth's surface. The area of the Pacific Ocean is about $2\frac{1}{3}$ times the area of the Indian Ocean. What fraction of Earth's surface does the Pacific Ocean cover?

12. The length of a flag of Nunavut Territory is $1\frac{7}{9}$ times the width. If a flag of Nunavut is 96 cm long, how wide is it?

13. In Saskatoon, it snowed for $3\frac{1}{2}$ h on Wednesday and $2\frac{1}{2}$ h on Thursday.
    a) How many times as long did it snow on Wednesday as on Thursday?
    b) How many times as long did it snow on Thursday as on Wednesday?

14. In a writing competition run by a local newspaper, the three prize winners shared a total of $900. The winner got $\frac{1}{2}$ of the total, the runner-up got $\frac{1}{3}$ of the total, and the third-place finisher got $\frac{1}{6}$ of the total. How much money did each prize winner win?

15. Mei can usually drive home at an average speed of 60 km/h. One day, a winter storm caused Mei to reduce her speed so that her average speed was two thirds her normal speed. What was her average speed on her drive home that day?

16. A flagpole is installed so that $\frac{1}{5}$ of its height is below the ground. If 2 m of the flagpole is below the ground, what is the height of the flagpole above the ground? Solve the problem in two different ways.

Chapter 7 Volume

17. Find the total volume of oil in the cylindrical drum.

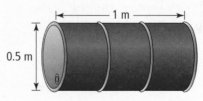

18. A solid cube has a side length of 11 cm. A cylindrical section with a radius of 3 cm is removed from the cube.
    a) Calculate the volume of the cube before the cylinder is removed.
    b) What is the total remaining volume of the cube?

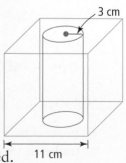

19. Jojo's waterbed is 2.15 m long, 1.53 m wide, and 0.23 m thick. If water has a mass of 1000 kg per cubic metre, what is the mass of water in Jojo's bed when it is filled?

20. Pop cans are often sold in paperboard boxes of 12 cans as shown. A pop can has a radius of approximately 3.2 cm and a height of approximately 12 cm.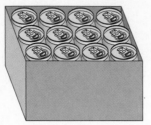

   a) What is the volume of 12 pop cans?

   b) What is the minimum volume of the box?

21. Find the volume of the L-shaped metal bracket.

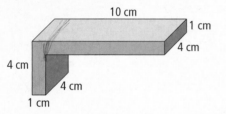

Chapter 8 Integers

22. Copy and complete each statement.

   a) $(+5) \times (\blacksquare) = +15$

   b) $(\blacksquare) \times (-2) = +28$

   c) $(\blacksquare) \times (+8) = -32$

   d) $(-6) \times (\blacksquare) = -24$

23. Estimate and then calculate.

   a) $(+22) \times (-14)$

   b) $(-46) \times (-13)$

24. List the pairs of integers that have a product of -20.

25. Copy and complete each statement.

   a) $(+20) \div (\blacksquare) = +5$

   b) $(\blacksquare) \div (-11) = +2$

   c) $(\blacksquare) \div (+8) = -3$

   d) $(-21) \div (\blacksquare) = +7$

26. What is the quotient of two opposite integers? Explain.

27. a) Does the multiplication of two integers always result in an integer? Explain.

   b) Does the division of two integers always result in an integer? Explain.

28. Dave is paying off a $350 loan at $25/month. After paying for six months, how much does he still owe?

29. The temperature in Inuvik, Northwest Territories, increased at the same rate from $-22\,°C$ at 9:00 a.m. to $-8\,°C$ at 4:00 p.m. one day. What was the temperature at 2:00 p.m.?

30. Len's car uses 11 L of gasoline per 100 km of city driving and 8 L of gasoline per 100 km of highway driving. One month, he drove 600 km in the city and 1500 km on highways. How much gasoline did he use that month?

31. Calculate.

   a) $-2 \times [-6 - (-12)] + 10$

   b) $14 \div (5 - 7) - 3 \times (-4)$

32. If you divide an integer by 4, then add 14, and then multiply by 5, your result is 45. What is the integer?

Task

Fraction Cubes

1. Create nets for two sets of two cubes (four cubes in all). As you develop the nets for your cubes, remember to include tabs so that you can glue the cubes together. Make an extra copy of your net to hand in to your teacher.

Materials
• centimetre grid paper
• glue
• scissors

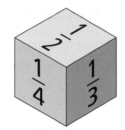

2. **a)** On the nets for both sets of cubes, print a different fraction for each face.

   • The fractions on the cubes can be proper fractions, improper fractions, or mixed numbers.
   • Use the following guidelines for your fractions.

   Set 1: When you multiply the fractions on these two cubes, you get a product between zero and one.

   Set 2: When you divide the fractions on these two cubes, you get a quotient greater than two. Decide and identify in your work which cube is the dividend and which is the divisor.

   b) Glue your nets into cubes.

3. Record the fractions you use for multiplying and dividing. Organize your results. Use them to justify your choice of fractions. Make generalizations about your findings when deciding what fractions to use for the product and quotient.

9

Linear Relations

Do you prefer a holiday that has an extra element of excitement? You may enjoy adventure travel tours, such as mountain biking, horseback riding, kayaking, or polar bear watching.

Whenever you travel, it is important to plan ahead. You need to think about such factors as the length of the trip, the cost, and the supplies you will need. One factor may be related to another—for example, a longer trip may cost you more. Sometimes you can show the relationship between these two factors mathematically.

What You Will Learn

- ❏ to recognize patterns and analyse data in a table of values
- ❏ to graph two-variable linear relations
- ❏ to solve problems using linear relations

Key Words

- relationship
- table of values
- expression
- linear relation
- variable
- formula
- equation

Literacy Link

Before starting the chapter, copy the following KWL chart into your math journal or notebook. Brainstorm with a partner what you already know about linear relations.

- Record your ideas in the first column.
- List any questions you have about linear relations in the second column.
- As you complete each section of the chapter, list what you have learned in the third column.

For more information about how to use a KWL chart, go to Chapter 1 Literacy Link on page 3.

Linear Relations

What I *Know*	What I *Want* to Know	What I *Learned*

Making the Foldable

Materials

- 11 × 17 sheet of paper
- seven sheets of centimetre grid paper or 0.5 cm grid paper
- stapler
- scissors

Step 1

Fold an 11 × 17 sheet of paper in half. Instead of creasing it, just pinch it at the midpoint. Fold the outer edges of the paper to meet at the midpoint.

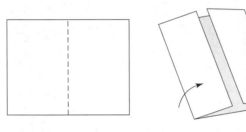

Step 2

Staple two sheets of grid paper to the inside back of the Foldable. Label them 9.3 Linear Relationships, as shown.

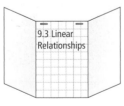

Step 3

Fold five sheets of grid paper lengthwise in half. Cut one of the folded sheets in half.

Step 4

Insert two and a half of the sheets into the left crease of the Foldable. Insert two of the sheets into the right crease of the Foldable. Staple them into place.

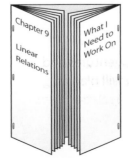

Step 5

Label the outside of your Foldable with the labels Chapter 9 Linear Relations and What I Need to Work On, as shown in the diagram in Step 4.

Step 6

Put the following labels on the inside of your Foldable.

Fold on the Left

- First half page: Key Words.
- Front and back of second half page: Math Link introduction
- Third half page: 9.1 Analysing Graphs of Linear Relations
- Last two half pages: 9.1 Math Link

Fold on the Right

- First three half pages: 9.2 Patterns in a Table of Values
- Last half page: 9.2 Math Link

Using the Foldable

As you work through Chapter 9, make notes about the Key Words on the first half page inside the left flap.

Record your answers to the Math Link introduction on page 331 on the half page after the Key Words. Draw your graph on the back of that half page.

Record the examples and Key Ideas in the appropriate section. Use the grid paper to show examples of linear relations.

Place your answers to the Math Links in sections 9.1 and 9.2 in the appropriate sections. List your ideas for the Wrap It Up! on the back of the Foldable.

On the front of the right flap, keep track of what you need to work on. Check off each item as you deal with it.

MATH LINK

Adventure Travel

Have you ever wanted to climb a mountain? Via Ferrata is a mountain experience for adventurers who want to climb to the summit of Whistler Peak in British Columbia. It features a vertical pathway with cables and metal ladders that lead climbers to the top.

Paulette decides to climb to Whistler Peak on the Via Ferrata trail. She times the last eight 100-m sections of her climb. Here are her times: 10 min, 9 min, 10 min, 11 min, 10 min, 30 min, 10 min, and 10 min.

1. Describe patterns you see in Paulette's data.

2. Give two reasons why you think her sixth time was so different from all the others.

3. Copy and complete the following table of values.

Total Distance (m)	Total Time (min)
100	10
200	19
300	
400	
500	
600	
700	
800	

4. Draw a graph showing Paulette's total distance compared with the total time over the last 800 m of the climb. Label the axes.

5. Describe patterns you see on your graph.

Throughout this chapter, you will explore a variety of adventures and eco-travel opportunities. At the end of the chapter, you will plan an adventure or eco-travel package, showing mathematical relationships between quantities such as time, cost, and supplies.

What adventure do you want to go on?

Analysing Graphs of Linear Relations

Graphs have been around for a long time. The pictorial writings of Aboriginal peoples and the drawings in the tombs of ancient Egypt are two examples. Graphs have gone through significant changes. Many graphs are now used to show relationships between sets of data.

A table of values also shows a relationship between two quantities. What is an advantage of a graph compared with a table of values?

Explore the Math

How can you represent a linear relation?

Tony's Pizzeria sells medium pizzas for $9 each. You can order extra toppings for $1 per topping.

TONY'S PIZZERIA

medium pizza $9

each extra topping $1

The graph shows the cost of Tony's medium pizzas.

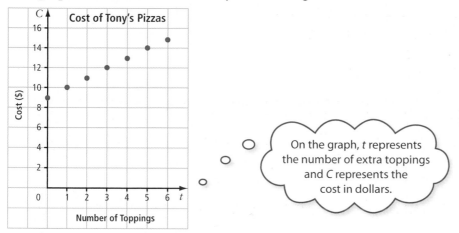

On the graph, *t* represents the number of extra toppings and *C* represents the cost in dollars.

1. a) Use a cardboard circle and coloured counters to model a medium pizza with extra cheese, pineapple, and ham.

b) Explain how your model could represent the cost of a medium pizza with three toppings. What cost does your model show?

Strategies

Model It

2. Look at the graph. What is the cost of a medium pizza with three toppings? How does this compare with your answer in #1b)?

3. a) From the graph, make a table of values that shows the cost of a medium pizza with zero to six toppings.

b) What headings did you use for your table? Why?

Literacy Link

A *table of values* is a chart showing two sets of related numbers.

Reflect on Your Findings

4. a) What are three ways you can represent data?

b) Which way do you prefer? Why?

You can arrange a table of values horizontally or vertically. In a horizontal table, the top row should show the *x*-coordinates from a graph.

x	1	2	3	4
y	5	10	15	20

In a vertical table, the first column should show the *x*-coordinates from a graph.

x	**y**
1	5
2	10
3	15
4	20

Example 1: Make a Table of Values From a Graph

The graph shows the total cost in relation to the number of baseballs you buy.

a) Describe patterns you see on the graph.

b) Make a table of values from the graph.

c) If the relationship continues, what is the cost of 14 baseballs?

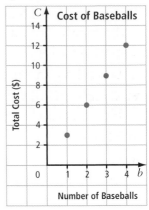

Tech Link

You can use a spreadsheet program to create a table.

Solution

a) The patterns can be described in the following ways:
  - The graph provides data on the cost of baseballs. One ball costs $3, two balls cost $6, three balls cost $9, …
  - The points appear to lie in a straight line.
  - The graph shows that to move from one point to the next, you go one unit horizontally and three units vertically.

b)

Number of Baseballs, b	1	2	3	4
Total Cost, C ($)	3	6	9	12

Strategies

Solve an Equation

c) The graph shows that the cost increases by $3 for each baseball purchased.

Let b represent the number of baseballs. The cost could be represented by $3b$.

Cost of 14 baseballs = 3(14)
= 42

The cost of 14 baseballs is $42.

Show You Know

The graph shows the number of triangles in relation to the figure number in a pattern.
a) Describe patterns you see on the graph.
b) Draw a triangle pattern that matches the graph.
c) Make a table of values from the graph.
d) If the pattern continues, how many triangles are in Figure 99?

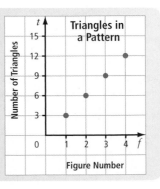

Example 2: Analyse Data on a Graph of a Linear Relation

The graph shows Nicole's rate of pay based on the number of hours she has worked at her part-time job.

a) Describe patterns you see on the graph.

b) What is Nicole's hourly rate of pay? How do you know?

c) Make a table of values from the graph.

d) Is it possible to have points between the ones on the graph? Explain.

Solution

a) The patterns can be described in the following ways:

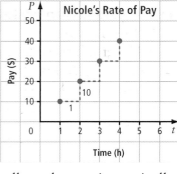

- The graph provides data on the pay Nicole receives for each hour worked. The pay for 1 h is $10, the pay for 2 h is $20, the pay for 3 h is $30, …
- The points appear to lie in a straight line. The graph shows a linear relation.
- The graph shows that to move from one point to the next, you go one unit horizontally and ten units vertically.

b) Nicole's hourly rate of pay is $10. The graph shows that Nicole's pay increases by $10 for each hour that she works.

c)

Time, t (h)	0	1	2	3	4
Pay, P ($)	0	10	20	30	40

d) It may be possible to have points between the ones on the graph. For example, Nicole could get paid for working for $3\frac{1}{2}$ h, and then a point could be shown between (3, 30) and (4, 40) on the graph.

> **Literacy Link**
>
> A *linear relation* is a pattern made by a set of points that lie in a straight line.
>
>

Show You Know

Chad is buying notebooks at Bob's Bargain Store. The graph shows the cost of notebooks.

a) Describe patterns you see on the graph.

b) What is the cost per notebook? How do you know?

c) Make a table of values from the graph.

d) Is it possible to have points between the ones on the graph? Explain.

- You can use the coordinates of the points on a graph to make a table of values.
- The top row or left column in a table of values has the same label as the horizontal axis. The second row or right column has the same label as the vertical axis.

Time Worked, *t* (h)	1	2	3
Pay, *P* ($)	12	24	36

Time Worked, *t* (h)	Pay, *P* ($)
1	12
2	24
3	36

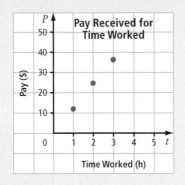

- When you describe a pattern, tell what it relates to, where it starts, and how it changes.

- A linear relation is a pattern made by a set of points that lie in a straight line.

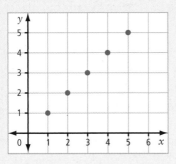

- Sometimes, it is possible to have points between the ones on a graph. Ask yourself, "Does it make sense to have other values between those on the graph?"

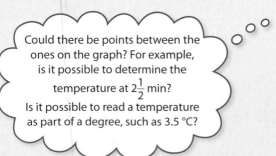

Could there be points between the ones on the graph? For example, is it possible to determine the temperature at $2\frac{1}{2}$ min?
Is it possible to read a temperature as part of a degree, such as 3.5 °C?

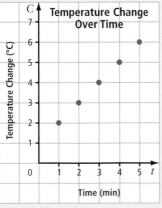

Communicate the Ideas

1. Tell whether you think it is reasonable to have points between the ones on each graph. Explain your answer.

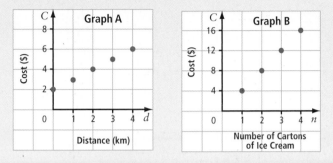

2. Draw a graph of a linear relation. Use integer values only. Label your graph. Write a brief description that matches the information on your graph.

3. Use an example to show one way that a graph and a table of values are different and one way that they are similar.

Check Your Understanding

Practise

For help with #4 and #5, refer to Example 1 on page 334.

4. The graph shows the increase in total height for each step of a staircase.

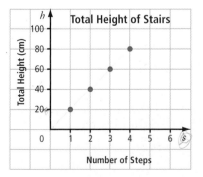

a) Describe patterns you see on the graph.
b) Make a table of values from the graph.
c) If the pattern continues, what is the total height on step 10?

5. The graph shows the maximum number of students allowed on a field trip based on the number of teachers available to supervise.

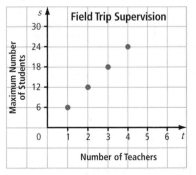

a) Describe three patterns on the graph.
b) Make a table of values from the graph.
c) If there are eight teachers available for a field trip, what is the maximum number of students who can go?

For help with #6 and #7, refer to Example 2 on page 335.

6. Tessa and Vince go shopping at Bulk Bin. The graph shows the cost of banana chips.

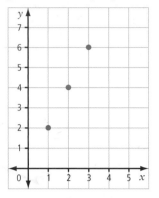

a) Describe patterns shown on this graph. Does the graph show a linear relation? Explain.

b) Make a table of values from the graph.

c) Is it reasonable to include a point on the graph that shows the cost of 250 g of banana chips? Explain.

7. The graph shows the height of a stack of cubes in relation to the number of cubes.

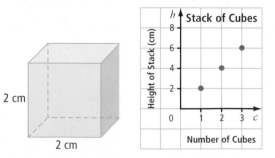

a) Describe patterns on the graph. Does the graph show a linear relation? Explain.

b) Make a table of values from the graph.

c) Is it reasonable to include a point for $c = 2.5$? Explain.

Apply

8. a) Make a table of values for the ordered pairs on the graph.

b) Assume the pattern continues. Extend your table, using the next three whole number values for x.

c) Describe the patterns on the graph.

d) What is the value of y when the value of x is 9?

9. The graph shows the rate of pay based on the number of hours worked.

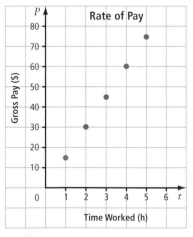

a) Make a table of values from the graph.

b) What is the hourly rate of pay shown on this graph?

c) Do you think it is reasonable to include a point for $t = 3.5$ h?

10. The graph shows part of a linear relation that represents the cost to purchase sugar flowers for a cake.

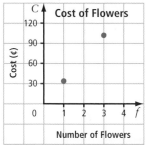

a) Is it reasonable to have points between the ones on the graph? Explain your answer.

b) How many points could there be between the two shown on the graph? Explain your answer.

11. The graph shows the simple interest for one year at 5% for different dollar amounts invested.

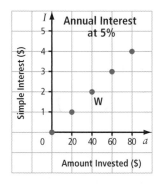

a) What are the coordinates for point W?

b) What does each coordinate for point W represent?

c) Describe patterns on the graph.

d) If the pattern continues, what is the simple interest earned on $180 after one year?

12. The graph shows the perimeter of a square in relation to the length of its side.

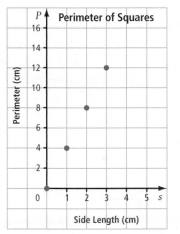

a) Copy the table and fill in the missing values for s and P.

Side Length, s (cm)	Perimeter, P (cm)
0	0
1	4
2	
	12
4	
5	
	32
28	
	124

b) Describe the patterns on the graph.

c) Are any other points possible between those shown on the graph? Explain.

d) Does the graph represent a linear relation? Explain.

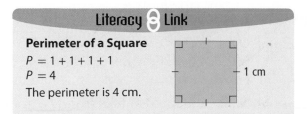

Literacy Link

Perimeter of a Square

$P = 1 + 1 + 1 + 1$
$P = 4$

The perimeter is 4 cm.

— 1 cm

13. The graph shows the cost of dried apricots at Bulk N Save.

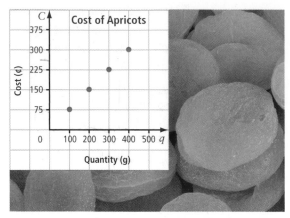

a) Make a table of values from the graph.

b) Describe patterns on the graph.

c) Use the graph to estimate the cost of 350 g of dried apricots.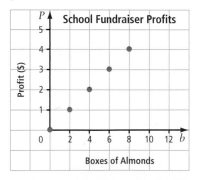

d) What is the actual cost of 350 g of dried apricots? Round your answer to the nearest cent.

e) Compare your answers in parts c) and d).

14. The graph below represents the relationship between the number of boxes of almonds a student sells for a school fundraiser and the profit in dollars for the school.

a) Make a table of values from the graph.

b) Describe three patterns on the graph.

c) How much profit does the school make on two boxes of almonds?

d) What is the value of P when the value of b is 2? How does this answer relate to your answer in part c)?

15. The following graph represents the number of words Tom can type in relation to the time in minutes.

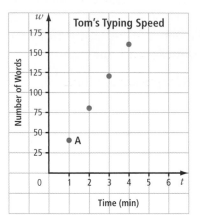

a) For the ordered pair (2, 80) tell what each coordinate represents.

b) What is the typing speed in words per minute for point A?

c) Does this graph represent a linear relation? Explain.

d) Would most people's typing speed result in a linear graph? Explain.

16. Alena gathered data comparing the amount of time she spent studying for her tests and the marks she received.

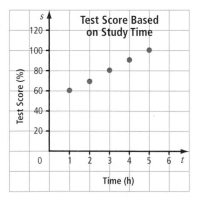

a) Make a table of values from this graph.

b) Does the graph appear to be a linear relation? Why?

c) Will Alena's scores continue increasing at this same rate with more and more time spent studying? Why?

17. At Ciao Restaurant, Mario works in the kitchen for $10 an hour. Susie works as a server. She gets $30 monthly clothing allowance plus $8 an hour.

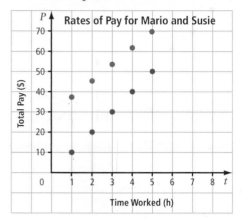

a) Which colour of points provides information about Susie's wages?

b) Make a table of values with three columns showing Time Worked (h) and Total Pay ($) for Susie and Mario.

c) If the pattern continues, at what point will the two sets of points meet?

18. Mark begins saving $15 a day to buy a three-month gym membership for $90. Kendal has $105 in the bank and spends $5 a day to go to the gym. The graph shows how much money they have over the first three days.

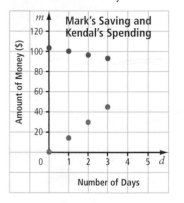

a) Which colour of points provides information about Mark?

b) When will Kendal run out of money?

c) When will Mark have saved enough money to buy the membership?

MATH LINK

Whatever adventure you are looking for, it can be found in Western and Northern Canada. Adventures include polar bear tours in Churchill, Manitoba, aurora borealis adventures in the Northwest Territories, and white-water rafting in Yukon Territory.

You are going on a polar bear adventure tour. The graph shows the cost of the trip.

a) Describe any patterns on the graph.

b) Make a table of values from the graph.

c) Assume the pattern continues. Extend your table of values to include the cost of a tour for eight days.

d) Suppose it is possible to upgrade to better accommodations for a one-time fee of $300 plus the regular $400 per day. Make a new table of values for deluxe tours that last from one to eight days.

e) Compare the data in the two tables of values. How are they similar? How are they different?

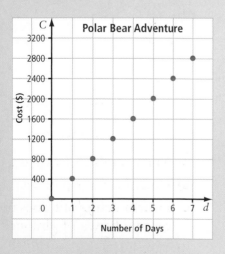

Patterns in a Table of Values

Focus on...

After this lesson, you will be able to...

❏ identify relationships in a table of values

❏ decide if a table of values represents a linear relation

❏ graph points represented by values in a table

As humans, we see patterns all around us. It is a way for us to make sense of our world. However, different people may see patterns in different places and in different ways. In the picture, Kendra describes a pattern she sees in the wallpaper. What patterns can you identify?

Explore the Math

Materials
• grid paper

How can you represent patterns?

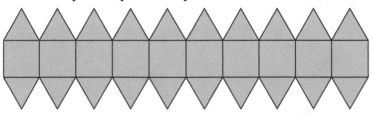

1. What are three patterns you see in the design?

2. How many squares and triangles are in this design?

3. The design can be lengthened or shortened. Each section of the design must have only complete squares and triangles. If this design has ten sections, what does one section of the design look like?

4. Make a table of values like the one shown. Complete your table for one to four sections in the design.

Number of Sections	Number of Vertical Segments	Number of Horizontal Segments	Number of Slanting Segments
1			
2			
3			
4			

 vertical | horizontal — slanting / or \

5. a) Use words to describe the relationship between the number of sections and the number of vertical segments.

b) Choose variables to represent the number of sections and the number of vertical segments. Why did you choose these letters?

c) Draw a graph to show the relationship between the number of sections and the number of vertical segments. Label the axes with the variables you chose in part b), and with the titles Number of Sections and Number of Vertical Segments.

d) Describe in words the relationship between the variables.

e) What is an expression for the number of vertical segments in terms of the number of sections?

6. a) Draw a graph to show the relationship between the number of sections in the design and the data in one of the other columns in the table. Label each axis with a variable and a title.

b) What is an expression that represents the data in the column you chose in terms of the number of sections in the design?

Reflect on Your Findings

7. a) What ways did you use to represent patterns in this activity?

b) Which parts of the activity did you find most challenging? Why?

WWW Web Link

To practise your graphing skills, go to **www.mathlinks8.ca** and follow the links.

Literacy Link

A *variable* is a letter that represents an unknown quantity. For example, in $3a - 5$, the variable is a.

It can be helpful to choose variables that are meaningful. For example, t for time and s for score.

Literacy Link

An *expression* is any single number or variable, or a combination of operations (+, −, ×, ÷) involving numbers and variables. An expression does not include an equal sign. The following are examples of expressions:

$5 \qquad r \qquad 8t$
$x + 9 \qquad 2y - 7$

Example 1: Identify the Relationship in a Table of Values

The pattern in the table of values represents a linear relation.

A	B
0	0
1	3
2	6
3	9
4	12

a) Graph the ordered pairs in the table of values.

b) What is the difference in value for consecutive *A*-values? for consecutive *B*-values?

c) Describe in words the relationship between the values for *A* and *B*.

d) What is an expression for *B* in terms of *A*?

Solution

a)

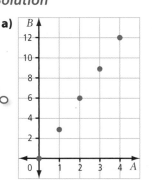

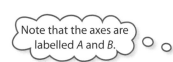

Note that the axes are labelled *A* and *B*.

b) The difference in consecutive *A*-values is 1. Find the difference in consecutive *B*-values.

$3 - 0 = 3$ $9 - 6 = 3$
$6 - 3 = 3$ $12 - 9 = 3$

The difference in consecutive *B*-values is 3.

c) When *A* increases by 1, *B* increases by 3.

The relationship can be written in different ways:
• in words   *B* is 3 times *A*.
• as an ordered pair   (*A*, 3*A*)
• as an expression   3*A*

d) Use the difference in *B*-values of 3. Each *B*-coordinate is 3 times its *A*-coordinate.
An expression for *B* is 3 × *A*, or 3*A*.

Mentally check with values for *A* in the table.

$3 \times 1 = 3$
$3 \times 2 = 6$
$3 \times 3 = 9$
$3 \times 4 = 12$

Show You Know

The table of values represents a linear relation.

x	1	2	3	4	5	6	7
y	5	10	15	20	25	30	35

a) Graph the ordered pairs in the table of values.
b) What is the difference in value for consecutive *x*-values? What is the difference in value for consecutive *y*-values?
c) Describe in words the relationship between the *x*-values and *y*-values.
d) What is an expression for *y* in terms of *x*?

Tech **Link**

You can use a spreadsheet program to make the graph.

Example 2: Use a Table to Determine a Linear Relation

For each table of values below, answer the following questions:

a) What is the pattern in the values for the first variable in each table?

b) What is the difference in consecutive values for the second variable in each table? Is the difference within each table the same?

c) Graph each set of ordered pairs. Which relations are linear?

d) How does your answer in part c) compare with your answer in part b)?

Table 1

x	2	4	6	8
y	3	7	11	15

Table 2

m	1	2	3	4
n	1	4	7	8

Solution

a) Table 1: The *x*-coordinates differ by 2.
Table 2: The *m*-coordinates differ by 1.
The consecutive values of the first variables differ by the same amount within each table.

Strategies

Look for a Pattern

b) Table 1: The *y*-coordinates differ by 4. The difference is the same.
Table 2: The *n*-coordinates differ by 3, 3, and 1. The difference is not the same.

c)

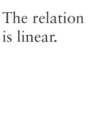

The relation is linear.

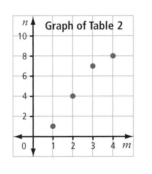

The relation is not linear.

d) Table 1: The difference in the *y*-coordinates is the same and the relation is linear.
Table 2: The difference in the *n*-coordinates is not the same and the relation is not linear.

Literacy Link

If consecutive values for the first variable do not have the same difference, it is difficult to tell from the table whether the relationship is linear. You may be able to tell by drawing a graph.

Show You Know

Determine whether each table represents a linear relation. Explain how you know. Check each answer by graphing the ordered pairs.

Table 1

A	1	4	7
B	1	10	19

Table 2

p	0	1	2	3
q	0	1	3	6

Example 3: Use a Table of Values in Solving a Problem

Photo World charges $3 for the first enlargement and $2 for each additional enlargement.

a) Make a table of values showing the cost in relation to the number of enlargements for one to five enlargements.

b) Is this a linear relation? Why?

c) What is an expression for the cost in relation to the number of enlargements?

d) What is the cost of 15 enlargements?

Solution

a)

Number of Enlargements, n	1	2	3	4	5
Cost, C ($)	3	5	7	9	11

b) The difference between consecutive numbers of enlargements is 1. Determine the difference for consecutive costs.

$5 - 3 = 2$
$7 - 5 = 2$
$9 - 7 = 2$
$11 - 9 = 2$

Consecutive costs differ by 2.
Each consecutive number of enlargements differs by the same value.
Each consecutive cost differs by the same value.
The relation is linear.

c) The cost increases by $2 for each additional enlargement.
Let n represent the number of enlargements.
$2n$ will be part of an expression for the cost.
Check using a value for n from the table: $n = 4$.
$2(4) = 8$
The value of 8 is not the same as the value of 9 in the table.
You need to add 1 to get from 8 to 9.
An expression for the cost is $2n + 1$, where n is the number of enlargements.

d) Substitute $n = 15$ into the expression $2n + 1$.
$2(15) + 1 = 31$
The cost of 15 enlargements is $31.

Mentally check $2n + 1$ with other values for n in the table.
$2(1) + 1 = 3$
$2(2) + 1 = 5$
$2(3) + 1 = 7$
$2(5) + 1 = 11$

Show You Know

Sky sells magazine subscriptions. She receives $20 for every five subscriptions she sells. The table shows the relationship between the number of subscriptions she sells and the pay she receives.

Number of Subscriptions, n	0	5	10	15	20	25
Pay, P ($)	0	20	40	60		

a) Copy and complete the table.

b) Is this a linear relation? How can you tell?

c) What is an expression for Sky's pay in relation to the number of subscriptions she sells?

d) How much does Sky receive for selling 40 subscriptions?

Key Ideas

- The following are some ways that you can represent a linear relation.
  - Table of values:

Mass, m (g)	0	100	200	300
Cost , C (¢)	0	200	400	600

  - Graph:

    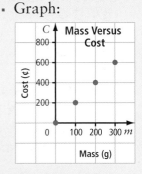

  - Words: The cost in cents is 2 times the mass in grams.
  - Ordered pair: $(m, 2m)$
  - Expression: The cost in cents is $2m$, where m is the mass in grams.

- You can sometimes tell from a table whether the relationship is linear.

    Table 1

p	2	3	4	5
q	7	13	19	25

    Table 2

p	q
20	31
40	27
60	23
80	19

  You can tell that the relationships in the above tables are linear because both of the following statements are true:
  - Each consecutive value for p changes by the same amount.
  - Each consecutive value for q changes by the same amount.

1. Giselle and Tim are discussing the table of values shown.

m	3	5	7	9
a	1	3	5	7

Who is correct? How do you know?

2. a) Describe a real-life situation that matches the pattern in the table of values.

n	1	2	3	4
p	1	3	5	7

b) What do n and p represent in your situation?

The table does not represent a linear relation.

I think it does.

3. You are given a table of values. Can you sometimes, always, or never tell whether the relationship is linear without drawing the graph? Use examples to support your answer.

Check Your Understanding

Practise

For help with #4 to #7, refer to Example 1 on page 344.

4. Graph the ordered pairs in the table of values.

a	d
1	5
2	8
3	11
4	14

5. Draw a graph using the ordered pairs in the table of values.

w	t
1	1
4	7
7	13
10	19

6. The table of values represents a linear relation.

x	0	1	2	3	4	5
a	0	4	8	12	16	20

a) Graph the ordered pairs.

b) What is the difference in value for consecutive x-values? What is the difference in value for consecutive a-values?

c) In words, describe the relationship between x and a.

d) What is an expression for a in terms of x?

7. The table of values shows a linear relation.

n	3	4	5	6	7
d	18	24	30	36	42

a) Graph the ordered pairs.

b) What is the difference in value for consecutive n-values? What is the difference in value for consecutive d-values?

c) In words, describe the relationship between n and d.

d) What is an expression for d in terms of n?

For help with #8 and #9, refer to Example 2 on page 345.

8. For each table of values, tell whether the relationship is linear. Explain your answer. Check by graphing the ordered pairs.

a)

c	d
2	7
3	10
4	13
5	16

b)

x	y
0	−3
1	1
3	9
5	17

9. Tell whether the relationship for each table of values is linear. Explain how you know.

a)

p	4	7	10	16
q	11	17	23	29

b)

x	2	3	4	5
y	3	2	1	0

For help with #10 and #11, refer to Example 3 on page 346.

10. Mara reads at a rate of 90 words per minute.

a) Make a table of values that shows the total number of words Mara reads in one to six minutes. Use whole minutes.

b) Is this a linear relation? Explain.

c) What is an expression for the number of words Mara reads in terms of time?

d) How many words does Mara read in 12 min?

11. The dosage of a certain medication to be given to a child is related to the child's mass. A 10-kg child receives 50 mg of the medication. For each increase in mass of 1 kg, the child receives an additional 10 mg of the medication.

a) Make a table showing the dosage for children with an increase of 1 kg to 10 kg over the mass of 10 kg. Use whole kilograms only.

b) Is this a linear relation? Explain how you know.

c) What is an expression for the dosage in terms of the increase in mass over 10 kg?

d) What is the dosage for a child with a mass of 27 kg?

e) Can your table of values start at 0 kg? Why or why not?

Apply

12. Evan has $6 in quarters and dimes.

a) Name five combinations of quarters and dimes that Evan might have.

b) Make a table of values showing the relationship between quarters and dimes. Include five pairs of values in your table.

c) Draw a graph. Is the relationship between quarters and dimes linear in this example? Explain.

d) What is the largest possible number of dimes? of quarters?

13. Divers experience an increase in pressure as they dive deeper below sea level. The table shows the relationship between depth in metres and pressure in atmospheres.

Depth (m)	Pressure (atm)
0	1
10	2
20	3
	4
	5
	6

a) Copy and complete the table.

b) Draw a graph for the ordered pairs in the table. How should your axes be labelled?

c) Divers sometimes become dizzy when the pressure exceeds 5 atm. Below what depth do divers tend to become dizzy?

14. The following pattern continues.

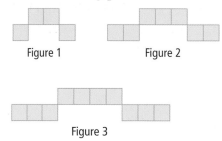

Figure 1   Figure 2

Figure 3

a) Make a table of values showing the figure number and the number of squares for the first six figures.

b) Write an expression showing the number of squares in terms of the figure number. What does your variable represent?

c) How many squares would appear in Figure 20?

d) How many more squares are in Figure 20 than in Figure 10? Show two ways to find the answer.

15. The following pattern of squares continues.

a) Copy and complete the table of values below that shows the relationship between the number of squares and the perimeter of each figure.

Number of Squares	1	2		
Perimeter (cm)	4	6		

b) Draw a graph from the table of values.

c) Describe the patterns on the graph.

d) What is an expression for the perimeter in terms of the number of squares?

e) If the pattern continues, what is the perimeter when there are 50 squares?

16. As you climb a mountain, the temperature drops 1 °C for every 150 m of increased height.

a) Copy and complete the table to show the relationship between height and temperature if the temperature at the bottom of the mountain is 20 °C.

Height (m)	0	150	300	450	600	750
Temperature (°C)	20					

b) Graph the ordered pairs.

c) Is the relationship linear?

d) How high have you climbed if the temperature is 13 °C?

17. A skydiver jumps from an airplane. The table provides data for the period of time shortly after the parachute opens, relating time in seconds to total distance descended in metres.

Time (s)	Distance (m)
10	300
11	354
12	408
13	462

a) Predict how a graph for these ordered pairs would look.

b) Graph the ordered pairs. Was your prediction correct?

c) Describe the graph in words.

18. A community centre has a new banquet hall. The centre charges $5 per person to rent the hall.

a) Make a table of values showing the rental cost for 20, 40, 60, 80, and 100 people.

b) Graph the ordered pairs.

c) What is an expression for the rental cost in terms of the number of people?

Extend

19. The community centre in #18 changes the cost for renting its banquet hall. The centre now charges $50 plus $5 per person.

a) Make a table of values showing the rental cost for 20, 40, 60, 80, and 100 people.

b) Graph the ordered pairs. How does the graph differ from the graph in #18?

c) What is an expression for the rental cost in terms of the number or letter of people? What does each number or letter in your expression represent?

20. Jamal is renting snowboard equipment.

COST TO RENT
$40 for the first day.
$35 for each additional day.
COST TO BUY $350

a) Copy and complete the table.

Number of Additional Days	0	1	2	3	4	5
Rental Cost ($)						

b) What is an expression for the rental cost in terms of the number of additional days?

c) What is the cost to rent the snowboard for a total of ten days? What might be a better option for Jamal instead of renting for ten days?

MATH LINK

Have you ever gone for a canoe trip on the waters of one of Canada's national parks? You are planning a canoe trip. The cost to rent a canoe is $40 a day. A national park pass for one week costs $36.

a) Make a table of values showing the total cost for the pass and canoe for a trip from one to seven days.

b) Graph the ordered pairs in your table of values. Is this a linear relation? Explain.

c) What is an expression for the cost based on the number of days?

d) Think of a linear relationship to do with canoeing. Show the relationship using a table of values, a graph, words, and an expression.

Linear Relationships

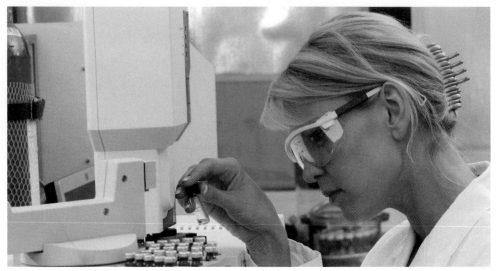

Scientists look for patterns. They collect experimental data in charts and tables. Then, they graph the data. These graphs are pictures that show mathematical relationships in the data. When scientists write a formula for the relationship, it may represent a new scientific discovery! What are some formulas that you are familiar with?

Explore the Math

How do you determine a relationship?

Work in a group.

1. Beginning in a corner, place about 2 m of masking tape horizontally on a wall at eye level. Start at the corner and mark off the masking tape in 5-cm intervals.

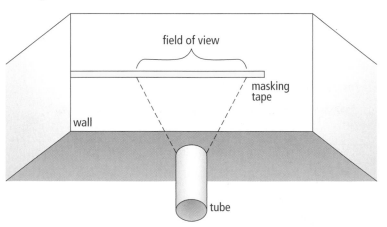

2. On the floor, measure and mark five distances from the wall. Start at 100 cm and increase the distance by 30 cm each time.

3. Copy the table into your notebook.

Distance From Wall (cm)	Width of Field of View (cm)

4. Predict how the width of your field of view through a tube will change as your distance from the wall increases.

5. For each distance from the wall, measure the width that you can see through the tube. Record the data in the table.

6. Write the results of your experiment as a set of ordered pairs. Graph the ordered pairs.

7. Compare your results with your prediction.

8. Repeat steps 3 to 7, using a different-sized tube.

Reflect on Your Findings

9. a) Do your data show a linear relation? Explain.

b) Why might the points on your graph line up as they do?

Example 1: Graph From a Linear Formula

Sound travels 1500 m/s in salt water. This relationship can be expressed by the formula $d = 1500t$, where d is the distance travelled, in metres, and t is the time, in seconds.

a) Make a table of values. Use integers only.

b) Graph the ordered pairs in your table of values.

c) Is it reasonable to have points between the ones on this graph? Explain.

d) Calculate the distance sound travels in 3.5 s.

Literacy Link

A *formula* is a mathematical statement that represents the relationship between specific quantities. An example is $C = \pi \times d$, where C is the circumference and d is the diameter of the circle.

Solution

a) Choose the numbers to use in the table of values. For example,
$t = 0, 1, 2, 3, 4, 5, 6$

Time, t (s)	0	1	2	3	4	5	6
Distance, d (m)	0	1500	3000	4500	6000	7500	9000

To determine d, substitute each t value into the formula. For example, substitute $t = 3$.
$d = 1500t$
$d = 1500(3)$
$d = 4500$

Choose at least four values for t in the table of values. Check that they are reasonable. It is not possible for t to be a negative integer since time cannot be negative. Check that $t = 0$ is reasonable in the context. When you are graphing, it is often useful to include zero as a value on the horizontal axis.

b)

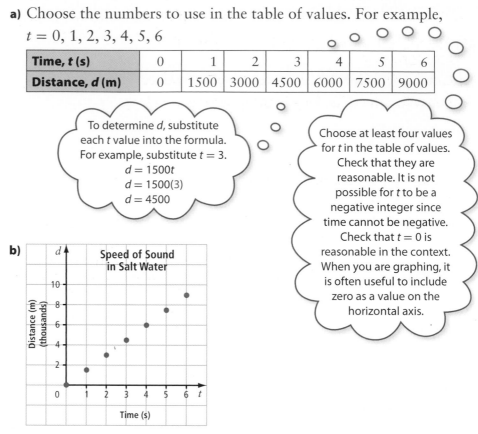

c) It is reasonable to have points between the ones on the graph. For example, it is possible to determine the distance at 2.5 s, and it is possible to determine the time at 4800 m.

d) Substitute 3.5 for t in the formula $d = 1500t$.
$d = 1500(3.5)$
$d = 5250$
The distance travelled at 3.5 s is 5250 m.
The estimate of 5000 m is close to the calculated distance of 5250 m.

Show You Know

When you rent a tool or machine, you are charged by the hour. For example, if you rent a backhoe and use it for $6\frac{1}{2}$ h, you are charged for 7 h.

Paula rents a lawnmower for $8 per hour. A formula representing this relationship is $C = 8t$, where C is the rental cost, in dollars, and t is the time, in hours.
a) Make a table of values.
b) Graph the ordered pairs in your table of values.
c) Is it reasonable to have points between those on the graph? Explain.
d) Calculate the cost to rent for 12 h.

Example 2: Graph From a Linear Equation Using Integers

Use the linear equation $y = -3x + 4$ to complete the following steps.

a) Make a table of values. Use positive and negative integers and zero for values of x.

b) Graph the ordered pairs in your table of values.

c) Determine the value for y in the ordered pair $(11, y)$.

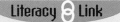

> **Literacy Link**
>
> An *equation* is a mathematical statement with two expressions that have the same value. The two expressions are separated by an equal sign. For example,
>
> $x + 2 = 3$
> $y - 7 = -4$
> $3a - 2 = a + 2$
> $b = 4$

Solution

a) Choose the numbers to use in the table of values. For example,

$x = -1, 0, 1, 2, 3, 4$

x	−1	0	1	2	3	4
y	7	4	1	−2	−5	−8

> Since no context is given, many values for x and y are possible. Choose values for x that are the same distance apart. For example, you could choose $x = -1, 0, 1, 2, 3, 4$ or $x = -2, 0, 2, 4, 6, 8$.

b)

(graph showing points for the ordered pairs on an xy-coordinate grid)

c) Substitute $x = 11$ into the equation $y = -3x + 4$.

$y = -3x + 4$
$y = -3(11) + 4$
$y = -33 + 4$
$y = -29$

The value of the y-coordinate is -29.
The ordered pair is $(11, -29)$.

> **Strategies**
>
> **Solve an Equation**

> ### Show You Know
>
> Use $y = 2x + 3$ to answer the following.
> **a)** Make a table of values. Use integers only.
> **b)** Graph the ordered pairs in your table of values.
> **c)** What are the coordinates for the point that would lie on the y-axis?

> What is the value for x of a point that lies on the y-axis?

- You can graph a linear relation represented by a formula or an equation.
  - First, make a table of values. Check that the values in the table are reasonable.
  - Then, graph using the ordered pairs in the table.

$t = 3h - 2$

h	t
0	−2
1	1
2	4
3	7

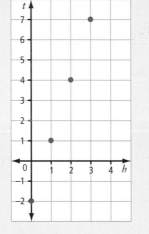

- Whenever possible, choose variables that are meaningful. For example, h for height and t for temperature.

Communicate the Ideas

1. a) What do you notice about the coordinates for points on the x-axis?

   b) What do you notice about the coordinates for points on the y-axis?

2. The equation $y = 2x - 1$ represents a linear relation. A table of values for $y = 2x - 1$ has been started below. Show two different ways to find the value of the missing y-coordinate.

x	0	1	2	3	4
y	−1	1	3	5	

3. a) When you choose values for a table of values, what considerations might influence your choice?

   b) Why is it often useful to use zero as one of your x-values?

4. a) Give an example of a linear relation found in real life. Then, give an example of a linear relation without a context.

   b) Make a table of values for each linear relation. Use integers only.

   c) Graph each set of ordered pairs.

   d) How are these graphs similar? How are they different?

Check Your Understanding

Practise

For help with #5 and #6, refer to Example 1 on pages 353–354.

5. A long-distance telephone plan can be represented as $C = 6t$, where C is the cost in cents and t is the time in minutes.

1 2 3
4 5 6
7 8 9
* 0 #

Only 6¢ per minute anytime for calls across Canada!

Call**Canada**

a) Make a table of values, using at least four whole number values for t.

b) Graph the ordered pairs.

c) If part minutes are rounded up to the next whole minute, is it reasonable to have points between the ones on your graph? Explain.

6. An animal shelter hires you to walk dogs for $5 per dog. The relationship between the money you make and the number of dogs you walk can be expressed as $W = 5d$, where W is the wage you make, in dollars, and d is the number of dogs you walk.

a) Make a table of values.

b) Graph the ordered pairs.

c) Is it reasonable to have points between the ones on your graph? Explain.

For help with #7 to #12, refer to Example 2 on page 355.

7. Evaluate each equation using the given value.

a) $y = 5x - 3$ when $x = 6$

b) $y = x - 8$ when $x = 5$

c) $y = -5x$ when $x = -2$

d) $y = x$ when $y = 25$

8. Evaluate $y = 7x + 3$ using each value.

a) $x = 1$ b) $x = -4$

c) $x = 0$ d) $y = 17$

9. Make a table of values for each equation using $x = -2, 0, 2, 4$. Draw each graph.

a) $y = 3x + 2$ b) $y = x - 5$

c) $y = -4x$ d) $y = 7 - x$

10. Make a table of values for each equation. Choose at least four integer values for x. Graph each set of ordered pairs.

a) $y = 2x$ b) $y = 3x - 1$

c) $y = -4x + 5$ d) $y = 5 - x$

11. The graph below represents part of the linear relation $y = -2x$.

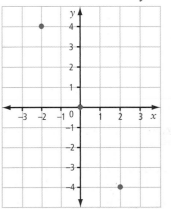

a) Use the equation to calculate the y-coordinate when $x = -1$.

b) What is the value of y in $(-4, y)$?

12. The graph represents part of the linear relation $y = \dfrac{x}{3}$.

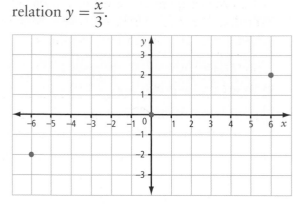

a) What are the coordinates for the point that lies on the y-axis?

b) Use the equation to calculate the y-coordinate when $x = -3$.

c) For the point $(-9, y)$, what is the value of y?

Apply

13. a) Graph the ordered pairs in the table.

x	y
−2	0
1	2
4	4
7	6

b) Is it reasonable to assume there are points between the ones on your graph if you have no other information? Why?

14. You are given part of the table of values for a linear relation.

x	−3	−2	−1	0	1	2
y				6	8	10

a) How could you use a pattern to find the missing y-coordinates?

b) Identify the missing y-coordinates.

15. In a bulk food store, rice crackers sell for 80¢ per 100 g.

a) Copy and complete the table of values.

Mass of Purchase (g)	Cost (¢)
0	
100	
200	
300	

b) If you continue the table, what is the next most logical value to use for Mass of Purchase? Explain, using your knowledge of linear relations and patterns.

c) Graph the ordered pairs.

16. The graph shows Nigel's monthly earnings.

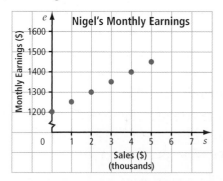

a) If Nigel does not make any sales, what are his monthly earnings?

b) Nigel has sales of $4000 in one month. How much does he earn?

c) Nigel earns $1500 in a month. What are his sales?

17. You can buy work gloves from The Fix-It Store's web site according to the formula $C = 5g + 2$, where C is the cost in dollars and g is the number of pairs of gloves.

a) Make a table to show the number of pairs of gloves purchased in relation to the total cost. Use five values for g.

b) Graph the ordered pairs.

c) Does the relation appear linear? Why?

d) Are there other points possible between the ones on the graph? Explain.

e) What might 2 represent in the formula?

18. George is a carpenter. He has a rewards card for the hardware store he uses. He receives 40 points for every $1 he spends. He can use the points to get savings on future purchases.

a) Copy and complete the table showing the dollar amount spent in relation to the number of points received.

Amount Spent ($)	Points Received
1	40
2	
3	
4	
5	

b) How many points does George receive for spending $100?

c) George can get a hammer for 100 000 points. How much money does he have to spend to get the hammer?

100 000 points

19. Shandi determined the mass of five pieces of a type of metal. The table shows her results. The relationship is linear. Shandi made one error in finding the masses.

Volume (cm³)	8	9	10	11	12
Mass (g)	88	99	110	121	144

a) Use patterns to show how to find the incorrect mass. What is the correct mass?

b) Draw points on a graph using Shandi's results in the table above.

c) How could you use your graph to show which value is incorrect?

Extend

20. A taxi company in Edmonton charges $3 for the first 210 m plus 20¢ for each additional 210 m.

a) What is the cost for a trip of length 2100 m? of length 4.41 km?

b) Make a table of values showing the relationship between the distance in metres and the cost in cents. Use integers only.

c) Graph the ordered pairs.

d) Is it a linear relation? Why?

21. Describe the pattern in each table of values. Then, graph each set of ordered pairs.

a)

t	0	1	2	3	4
d	2	3	4	5	6

b)

x	8	7	6	2
y	4	3	2	−2

22. a) Complete the table using the relationship "multiply x by 2 and then add 3 to get y."

x	−2	−1	0	1	2	3	11
y							

b) Is it a linear relation? Explain.

Key Words

Unscramble the letters for each term. Use the clues to help you.

1. P R E S E X N I O S
   an example is $n - 4$

2. E I L R A N   O T L E R A I N
   a pattern in which the points lie in a straight line (two words)

3. M A L U R O F
   an equation that represents the relationship between specific quantities

4. Q O N A T U I E
   a mathematical statement with two expressions that have the same value

5. A B E V I R A L
   in $3A + 2$, the letter A is an example

6. L E B T A   F O   S U A V L E
   a table showing two sets of related numbers (three words)

9.1 Analysing Graphs of Linear Relations, pages 332–341

7. Klaus works after school. The graph shows his rate of pay.

   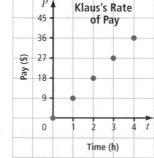

   a) Make a table of values from the graph.

   b) Does the graph represent a linear relation? Explain.

   c) Is it possible to have other points between the ones on this graph? Explain.

8. The graph shows a linear relation.

   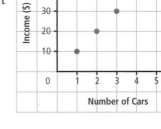

   a) Describe what the graph is about.

   b) Describe patterns on the graph.

   c) What is the cost of one car wash?

   d) Make a table of values from the graph.

   e) If 15 cars are washed, what is the income for the grade 8 class?

9. The graph shows part of a linear relation.

   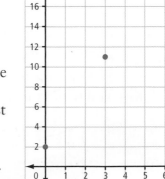

   a) Describe patterns on the graph.

   b) Make a table of values using at least five whole number values for x.

   c) What is the value of y when $x = 2$?

   d) What is the value of y when $x = 5$?

9.2 Patterns in a Table of Values, pages 342–351

10. The table of values represents a linear relation.

A	B
0	1
1	5
2	9
3	13
4	17
5	21

a) Graph the ordered pairs.

b) What is the difference in value for consecutive A-values? What is the difference in value for consecutive B-values?

c) Describe the relationship between the values for A and B. Use words and an expression.

11. For each table of values below, answer the following questions.

a) What is the difference in consecutive values for the first variable?

b) What is the difference in consecutive values for the second variable? Is the difference the same for consecutive values?

c) Graph the ordered pairs to check your answer.

Table 1

m	−2	−1	0	1	2	3
n	−4	−2	0	2	4	6

Table 2

p	q
−4	−9
−2	5
0	1
2	−3
4	−7

Table 3

d	C
1	5
2	8
3	10
4	13
5	15

12. Speedy Print Shop charges $2 for the first colour copy and $1 for each additional colour copy.

a) Make a table of values representing the number of colour copies in relation to the cost. Include zero to five colour copies.

b) Is this a linear relation? Explain.

c) What is an expression for the cost in terms of the number of colour copies?

d) What is the cost of 12 colour copies?

9.3 Linear Relationships, pages 352–359

13. Craig travels at a constant speed in kilometres per hour. The formula $d = 15t$ represents the relationship.

a) What does each variable represent?

b) What does 15 represent?

c) Make a table of values. Use five whole number values for t.

d) Graph the ordered pairs.

e) Is it reasonable to have points between the ones on the graph? Explain.

f) How far would Craig travel in 8 h?

14. For each equation, make a table of values using five positive and negative integer values for x. Graph the ordered pairs. Then, determine the value for y when $x = −7$.

Equation A: $y = 7x$
Equation B: $y = 3x − 2$
Equation C: $y = −2x + 3$

15. Dana has graphed the equations $y = 2x + 1$ and $y = −2x + 1$, using integer values.

a) How are the graphs similar?

b) How are they different?

For #1 to #5, select the best answer.

1. You can describe $2x - 1$ as a(n)

  A constant   **B** equation

  C expression   **D** variable

2. The table shows the toothpicks in the base of a triangle in relation to its perimeter.

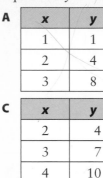

Toothpicks in Base (b)	Toothpicks in Perimeter
1	3
2	6
3	9

Which expression represents the number of toothpicks in the perimeter of any triangle in this pattern?

  A $b + 3$ **B** $3b$

  C $\dfrac{b}{3}$ **D** $b - 3$

3. Which table of values represents the linear relation shown?

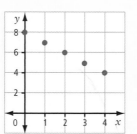

A

x	0	1	2	3	4
y	8	6	6	5	4

B

x	0	1	2	3	4
y	8	7	6	4	2

C

x	0	1	2	3	4
y	8	7	6	5	4

D

x	0	1	2	3	4
y	8	6	4	3	2

4. Which table of values represents the linear equation $y = 3x - 2$?

A

x	y
1	1
2	4
3	8

B

x	y
0	2
2	8
4	1

C

x	y
2	4
3	7
4	10

D

x	y
3	9
5	15
7	21

5. Which graph represents "a banquet room rents for $50 plus $2 per person"?

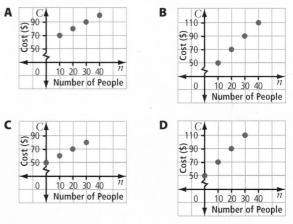

Complete the statements in #6 and #7.

6. If the equation is $s = -4t + 2$, the value for s in $(-1, s)$ is ■.

7. To describe the graph in #3, you can say that when the x-coordinate increases by 1, the y-coordinate ▬▬▬ by ■.

Short Answer

8. The graph shows the cost of a new drink called Zap.

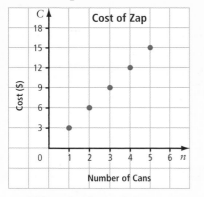

a) What is the price per can of Zap?

b) Describe three patterns on the graph.

c) If you placed a point at (0, 0), what would each coordinate represent?

9. The pattern can be represented by the formula $b = 4f$, where b is the number of black dots and f is the figure number.

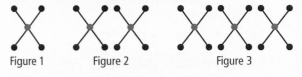

Figure 1   Figure 2   Figure 3

a) Make a table of values for the number of black dots in Figures 1 to 5.

b) Use the formula to determine the number of black dots in Figure 60.

Extended Response

10. The formula for the pattern below is $s = 2f + 1$, where s is the number of small squares and f is the figure number.

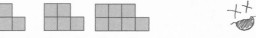

Figure 1   Figure 2   Figure 3

a) Make a table of values for the first five figures in the pattern.

b) Draw a graph to show the relationship.

c) Is the relationship linear? Explain.

WRAP IT UP!

You are going on an adventure tour. Your adventure could be hang-gliding, hiking, canoeing, white-water rafting, dog sledding, whale watching, cycling, or any other adventure that interests you. What is your adventure? Where does it take place?

Use travel brochures, the Internet, or other sources to locate information on your adventure. Then, find or create data for a linear relation that has to do with your adventure. Use integers only. Refer to the Math Links in this chapter for ideas.

a) Write one or two paragraphs giving information on your adventure.

b) Arrange the data for your linear relation in a table of values.

c) Graph the ordered pairs listed in your table values.

d) Is it reasonable to have points between the ones on your graph? Explain why or why not.

Math Games

Friends and Relations

Materials
- spinner with 9 sectors (numbered with integers from 4 to − 4)
- paper clip (to be used with the spinner)
- set of 20 Friends and Relations game cards
- Friends and Relations record sheet for each student

1. The Friends and Relations game is played by two friends and involves relations. These are the rules:
- Each player spins the spinner once to decide who will deal the cards. If there is a tie, spin again.
- The dealer shuffles and deals ten Friends and Relations game cards to each player. The other player takes the first turn.
- For each turn, flip over the top card in your stack and spin the spinner.
- Copy the linear relation from the card into the Linear Relation column of your Friends and Relations record sheet. Record the result of the spin in the x-column.
- Calculate the y-value by substituting the x-value into the linear relation. Record the y-value in the y-column of the record sheet.
- After each turn, record your total score, which is the sum of all the y-values you have recorded so far.
- Check each other's calculation of each y-value and each total score.
- The player with the higher total score after ten turns is the winner.
- If there is a tie after ten turns, shuffle the deck again and deal the cards. Take more turns until one player pulls ahead.

> My y-value was 14 in my first turn and −8 in my second turn. My total score after two turns is 14 + (−8), which equals 6.

2. Play variations on the game. Here are some possible variations to get you started:
- Determine the integer x-values in different ways. For example, you might design a different spinner or roll dice.
- Make your own cards that show linear relations. (Make sure that they will result in integer y-values for integer x-values.)

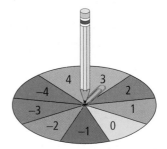

Linear Relation	x	y	Total

Challenge in Real Life

Comparing Wages

Five people work at Moy's Food Mart. One of the weekly time sheets is displayed below.

Employee	Mon	Tues	Wed	Thurs	Fri	Sat	Sun	Total Hours	Hourly Wage	Total Wage
Mr. Moy	8	8	8	8	9	–	–		$12.50	
Ms. Wong	–	8	8	7	–	9	9		$9.50	
Maria	8	5	–	–	6	9	5		$7.50	
Tom	4	4	4	4	4	8	8		$7.50	
Jacob	–	–	5	7	7	5	5		$7.50	
							Total			

1. **a)** For each employee, calculate the total hours and total wage.

   b) What total amount is paid out in wages for the week?

2. Which day is the busiest day of the week? the slowest? Justify your choices.

3. **a)** What is the average hourly wage for store employees?

   b) There is more than one way to answer part a). Show a second method.

   c) Which method gives a better indication of the average hourly wage? Explain.

4. Draw a graph showing how much Mr. Moy, Ms. Wong, and Maria would make for 0, 5, 10, 15, and 20 h of work. Use a different colour for each person.

5. Maria has been offered a 40% raise and a promotion to manager.

   a) Complete a table of values for Maria's new wage using 0, 5, 10, 15, and 20 as the number of hours worked.

   b) Plot Maria's new wage on the graph from #4 using a different colour.

   c) List the following in order according to their hourly wage, from highest to lowest: Mr. Moy, Ms. Wong, Maria before her raise, and Maria after raise.

   d) Describe, in words, how the points on the graph are plotted with respect to the employees' hourly wage.

10

Solving Linear Equations

What do a scientist, accountant, meteorologist, professional athlete, and tradesperson have in common? All of these careers involve activities that can be modelled using linear equations. In fact, you would be amazed by how linear equations can represent so much of what goes on in the world around you.

What You Will Learn

❑ to use linear equations to model problems
❑ to solve problems involving linear equations

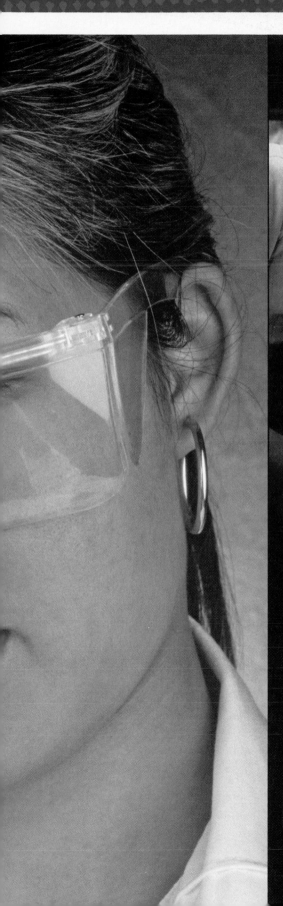

Literacy Link

Before starting the chapter, copy the following KWL chart into your math journal or notebook. Brainstorm with a partner what you already know about solving linear equations.

- Record your ideas in the first column.
- List any questions you have about solving linear equations in the second column.
- As you complete each section of the chapter, list what you have learned in the third column.

For more information about how to use a KWL Chart, go to Chapter 1 Literacy Link on page 3.

Solving Linear Equations

What I *Know*	What I *Want* to Know	What I *Learned*

Making the Foldable

Materials

- 11 × 17 sheet of paper
- stapler
- scissors
- ruler

Step 1

Fold an 11 × 17 sheet of paper in half. Instead of creasing it, just pinch it at the midpoint. Fold the outer edges of the paper to meet at this midpoint.

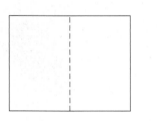 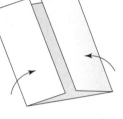

Step 2

Open the paper back up, and then fold it in half the other way so that the two horizontal edges meet.

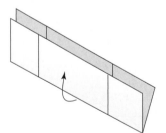

Step 3

Fold the left and right ends along the creases toward the middle to make a large central pocket with one tab on the left and one on the right. Staple the tabs along the outside edge to hold the pocket together.

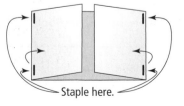

Staple here.

Step 4

Cut off the bottom crease of the left and right tabs as shown by the dashed lines in the visual with Step 5.

Step 5

Use a ruler to divide each tab in half horizontally, then cut along the lines to make two small booklets out of each tab, as shown below.

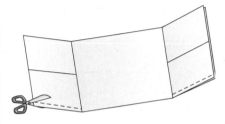

Step 6

Label the front of each small booklet as shown.

10.1 Modelling and Solving One-Step Equations: $ax = b$, $\frac{x}{a} = b$	10.2 Modelling and Solving Two-Step Equations: $ax + b = c$
10.3 Modelling and Solving Two-Step Equations: $\frac{x}{a} + b = c$	10.4 Modelling and Solving Two-Step Equations: $a(x + b) = c$

Using the Foldable

As you work through each section of Chapter 10, list and define the Key Words and record your notes about each example in the appropriate section of the Foldable.

In the large central pocket, store your work for the Math Link introduction on page 369 and the Math Links for each section. You may wish to place other examples of your work there as well. You can store your work on the Wrap It Up! in this pocket also.

On the back of the Foldable, make notes under the heading What I Need to Work On. Check off each item as you deal with it.

MATH LINK

Modelling Equations

Linear equations can be used to model everyday situations. You can even use your knowledge of linear equations to encrypt a password.

Jim's password is *weather*. He is going to encrypt this word using a two-step process.

Step 1: Jim assigns a number to represent each letter of the alphabet, as shown below.

1 = a	2 = b	3 = c	4 = d	5 = e	6 = f	7 = g
8 = h	9 = i	10 = j	11 = k	12 = l	13 = m	14 = n
15 = o	16 = p	17 = q	18 = r	19 = s	20 = t	21 = u
22 = v	23 = w	24 = x	25 = y	26 = z		

The number sequence for the password *weather* looks like 23 5 1 20 8 5 18.

Step 2: Jim uses the equation $y = 3x + 2$ to convert the number sequence to an encrypted number sequence. For example, the letter *w* was originally represented by the number 23. Substitute 23 into the equation:

$y = 3x + 2$
$y = 3(23) + 2$
$y = 71$

> 3*x* means 3 × *x*.

The number 71 represents *w* in Jim's encrypted password.

a) What encrypted number sequence represents Jim's password of *weather*?

b) Discuss with a classmate how you might decrypt the encrypted number sequence 59 29 38 38 77. What process would you follow? What password does this number sequence represent?

c) Encrypt your own password using the values in the table above and a linear equation of your choice.

d) Exchange your password from part c) with your classmate. Decrypt each other's password and tell what equation was used to create the encryption system. If your classmate needs a hint, tell what number represents *e* in your encryption system.

> Keep in mind that the most commonly used letters in the English language are, in order, E, T, A, O, I, N, S, H, R, D, and L.

Modelling and Solving One-Step Equations: $ax = b, \frac{x}{a} = b$

When Simone tried her new pair of Moon Shoes, she wondered what made them so bouncy. She discovered that they have springs inside that store energy. How do you think this energy is used to make the shoes bounce?

Explore the Math

How do you model and solve a one-step equation?

Simone decided to conduct an experiment with a spring. She wanted to determine an equation that models how much force is required to stretch a spring. She used the apparatus shown to take the measurements.

Every time Simone added a mass, the force on the spring increased and the spring stretched a further distance. The data that she collected during her experiment are shown in the table.

Trial	Force, F (newtons)	Distance Stretched, d (cm)
1	10	5
2	20	10
3	30	15
4	40	20
5	50	25

1. Draw a graph with Force on the horizontal axis and Distance Stretched on the vertical axis. Plot the values from the table.

2. a) How much more force is added for each trial?

   b) How much greater is the distance stretched each time force is added? Is the difference in the distance stretched the same for each consecutive trial?

3. What is the ratio, k, for the amount of force to the spring distance?

Reflect on Your Findings

4. What is a <mark>linear equation</mark> that models the relationship between force and distance stretched?

> The force, F, required to stretch a spring distance, d, can be modelled using the equation $F = kd$. Use the value of k that you determined in #3.

5. a) If you use a force of 60 N, what is the distance the spring would stretch?

   b) How did you get your answer?

6. a) Imagine the spring is compressed instead of stretched. What would be the linear equation?

   b) How much force would it take to compress the spring 5 cm?

> A positive force stretches a spring. A negative force compresses a spring.

Example 1: Solve an Equation

Solve each equation.

a) $3x = -12$ **b)** $\dfrac{r}{-2} = -7$

Solution

Method 1: Solve by Inspection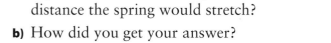

a) $3(-4) = -12$ or $\dfrac{-12}{3} = -4$

The solution is $x = -4$.

> Ask yourself, "What number multiplied by 3 equals −12?"

> Ask yourself, "What number results from dividing −12 by 3?"

b) $\dfrac{14}{-2} = -7$ or $-7 \times (-2) = 14$

The solution is $r = 14$.

> Ask yourself, "What number divided by −2 equals −7?"

> Ask yourself, "What number results from multiplying −7 by −2?"

Method 2: Solve Using Models and Diagrams

a) Use algebra tiles.

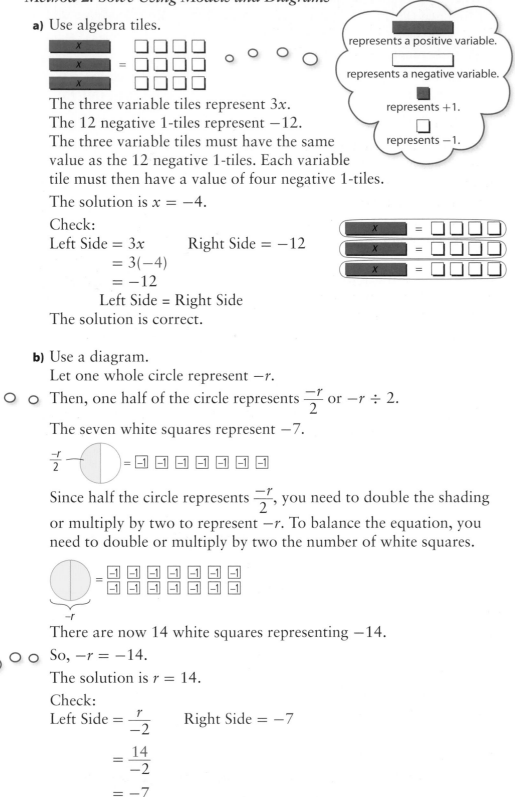

The three variable tiles represent $3x$.
The 12 negative 1-tiles represent -12.
The three variable tiles must have the same value as the 12 negative 1-tiles. Each variable tile must then have a value of four negative 1-tiles.

The solution is $x = -4$.

Check:

Left Side $= 3x$ Right Side $= -12$
$\qquad = 3(-4)$
$\qquad = -12$

Left Side = Right Side
The solution is correct.

b) Use a diagram.

Let one whole circle represent $-r$.

Then, one half of the circle represents $\dfrac{-r}{2}$ or $-r \div 2$.

The seven white squares represent -7.

Since half the circle represents $\dfrac{-r}{2}$, you need to double the shading or multiply by two to represent $-r$. To balance the equation, you need to double or multiply by two the number of white squares.

There are now 14 white squares representing -14.

So, $-r = -14$.

The solution is $r = 14$.

Check:

Left Side $= \dfrac{r}{-2}$ Right Side $= -7$

$\qquad = \dfrac{14}{-2}$

$\qquad = -7$

Left Side = Right Side
The solution is correct.

The expression $\dfrac{r}{-2}$ means the same as $\dfrac{-r}{2}$.

What operation do you need to apply to both sides of the equation to solve for r?

Example 2: Divide to Apply the Opposite Operation

Simone uses a different spring in her experiment. The equation that models this new spring is $F = 12d$, where F is the force, in newtons, needed to stretch or compress the spring a distance, d, in centimetres. Simone applies a force of 84 N to compress the spring. What distance is the spring compressed?

Solution

Since Simone compressed the spring, the force, F, is a negative number. Substitute -84 into the formula $F = 12d$. Then, isolate the variable to solve the equation.

$$F = 12d$$
$$-84 = 12d$$
$$\frac{-84}{12} = \frac{12d}{12}$$
$$-7 = d$$

The opposite of multiplying by 12 is dividing by 12.

The spring was compressed a distance of 7 cm.

Check:
Left Side $= -84$ Right Side $= 12d$
$= 12(-7)$
$= -84$

Left Side $=$ Right Side
The solution is correct.

Example 3: Multiply to Apply the Opposite Operation

For the month of January, the average afternoon temperature in Edmonton is $\frac{1}{3}$ the average afternoon temperature in Yellowknife. The average afternoon temperature in Edmonton is -8 °C. What is the average afternoon temperature in Yellowknife?

Solution

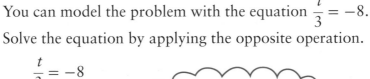
The variable represents the unknown value.

Let t represent the average afternoon temperature in Yellowknife.

The average afternoon temperature in Edmonton is $\frac{1}{3}$ the average afternoon temperature in Yellowknife, or $\frac{t}{3}$.

You can model the problem with the equation $\frac{t}{3} = -8$.

Solve the equation by applying the opposite operation.

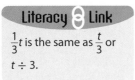
Literacy ⊖ Link
$\frac{1}{3}t$ is the same as $\frac{t}{3}$ or $t \div 3$.

$$\frac{t}{3} = -8$$
$$\frac{t}{3} \times 3 = -8 \times 3$$

The opposite of dividing by 3 is multiplying by 3.

$$t = -24$$

The average afternoon temperature in Yellowknife is -24 °C.

Check:

Left Side $= \dfrac{t}{3}$ Right Side $= -8$

$\qquad\quad = \dfrac{-24}{3}$

$\qquad\quad = -8$

The solution of -24 °C is correct.

Show You Know

Solve by applying the opposite operation. Check your answer.

a) $\dfrac{d}{-5} = 3$ b) $-6 = \dfrac{p}{7}$

- There are several ways to solve equations involving integers.

  - Solve by inspection.
    $-2w = 6$
    $-2(-3) = 6$

    or

    $\dfrac{6}{-2} = -3$

    Ask yourself, "What number multiplied by -2 equals 6?"

    Ask yourself, "What number results from dividing 6 by -2?"

    The solution is $w = -3$.

  - Model the equation using concrete materials and then balance it.
    $-2w = 6$

    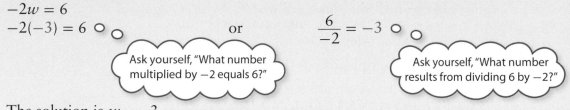

    Each negative variable tile must have a value of three positive 1-tiles.
    The positive variable tile must then have a value of three negative 1-tiles.
    The solution is $w = -3$.

  - Perform the opposite operation on both sides of the equal sign.
    $$\dfrac{w}{-2} = 6$$
    $$\dfrac{w}{-2} \times (-2) = 6 \times (-2)$$
    $$w = -12$$

    The opposite of dividing by -2 is multiplying by -2.

- Two methods you can use to check your solution are substitution and modelling:

  - Substitute your solution into the equation. Both sides should have the same value.

    Left Side $= \dfrac{w}{-2}$ Right Side $= 6$

          $= \dfrac{-12}{-2}$

          $= 6$

    Left Side $=$ Right Side
    The solution is correct.

  - Model the equation using concrete materials like algebra tiles as shown above.

Communicate the Ideas

1. Draw a diagram to show how you can model $\frac{x}{6} = -3$. Explain your diagram in words.

2. Give an example of an equation that has a variable with a negative integer value.

3. An unknown number is multiplied by 5. The result is -45.

a) Choose a variable. Write an equation to represent the situation.

b) Draw a picture to show how you might solve the equation.

4. Raj is solving the equation $\frac{n}{9} = -4$.

$$\frac{n}{9} = -4$$
$$\frac{n}{9} \times (-9) = -4 \times (-9)$$
$$n = 36$$

Is Raj's solution correct or incorrect? Explain.

Check Your Understanding

Practise

For help with #5 to #10, refer to Example 1 on pages 371–372.

5. Write the equation modelled by each diagram.

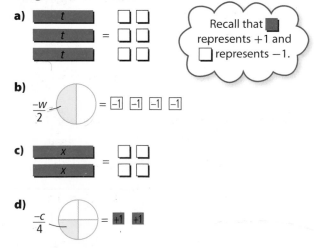

a) Recall that ■ represents $+1$ and □ represents -1.

b) $\frac{-w}{2}$

c) x

d) $\frac{-c}{4}$

6. Write the equation represented by each model.

a)
$$\boxed{-1}\ \boxed{-1} = \quad \frac{m}{3}$$

b)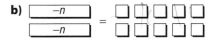
$$\frac{-n}{-n} =$$

c)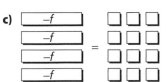
$$\frac{-f}{-f} = \frac{-f}{-f}$$

d)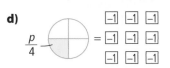
$$\frac{p}{4}$$

7. Solve by inspection.

   a) $-8j = 64$

   b) $5n = -25$

   c) $-6 = \dfrac{k}{3}$

   d) $\dfrac{x}{-11} = -4$

8. Use mental math to solve each equation.

   a) $-12 = 3r$

   b) $-16 = -4p$

   c) $-30 = \dfrac{t}{2}$

   d) $\dfrac{d}{-4} = 5$

9. Use models or diagrams to solve each equation.

   a) $2k = -8$ **b)** $-3 = \dfrac{t}{4}$

10. Solve each equation using models or diagrams.

   a) $3b = -15$ **b)** $\dfrac{x}{-3} = -3$

For help with #11 to #14, refer to Example 2 on page 373.

11. By what number would you divide both sides of the equation to solve it?

   a) $-3x = 9$

   b) $-36 = -4g$

   c) $72 = -9t$

   d) $4p = -8$

12. By what number would you divide both sides of the equation to solve it?

   a) $-10 = 5w$

   b) $-48 = -4c$

   c) $4y = -400$

   d) $-84 = -21b$

13. Solve each equation using the opposite operation. Check your answer.

   a) $4s = -12$

   b) $-156 = -12j$

   c) $-4j = 104$

   d) $-108 = -27t$

14. Use the opposite operation to solve each equation. Verify your answer.

   a) $8f = -56$ **b)** $-5q = 45$

   c) $-2h = -42$ **d)** $14k = -70$

For help with #15 to #18, refer to Example 3 on page 374.

15. By what number would you multiply both sides of the equation to solve it?

   a) $13 = \dfrac{g}{-6}$ **b)** $\dfrac{m}{3} = -25$

   c) $-6 = \dfrac{n}{-21}$ **d)** $\dfrac{z}{17} = 6$

16. By what number would you multiply both sides of the equation to solve it?

   a) $\dfrac{s}{11} = 9$ **b)** $-6 = \dfrac{y}{-12}$

   c) $\dfrac{w}{4} = -13$ **d)** $16 = \dfrac{x}{-3}$

17. Solve each equation using the opposite operation. Check your answer.

   a) $\dfrac{t}{3} = -12$ **b)** $12 = \dfrac{h}{-10}$

   c) $\dfrac{s}{-7} = 15$ **d)** $-63 = \dfrac{x}{-9}$

18. Use the opposite operation to solve each equation. Verify your answer.

   a) $\dfrac{y}{5} = -4$ **b)** $-6 = \dfrac{k}{-8}$

   c) $-1 = \dfrac{b}{10}$ **d)** $\dfrac{r}{12} = 15$

19. Show whether $x = -2$ is the solution to each equation.

    a) $-8x = 16$

    b) $10x = -20$

    c) $-5x = 10$

    d) $36 = 18x$

20. Show whether $y = 12$ is the solution to each equation.

    a) $3 = \dfrac{y}{-4}$

    b) $\dfrac{y}{-36} = -3$

    c) $2 = \dfrac{y}{24}$

    d) $\dfrac{y}{-6} = -2$

21. For the month of January, the average afternoon temperature in Calgary is $\dfrac{1}{4}$ the average morning temperature. The average afternoon temperature is $-4\ ^\circ C$. What is the average morning temperature?

    a) If m represents the average morning temperature, what equation models this problem?

    b) Solve the equation. Verify your answer.

22. Nakasuk's snowmobile can travel 13 km on a litre of gas. He is going to visit his aunt in a community 312 km away. Nakasuk wants to know how many litres of gas he needs to travel to his aunt's community.

    a) Write an equation in the form $ax = b$ to represent this problem. What does your variable represent?

    b) How many litres of gas does Nakasuk need?

23. The height of a great grey owl is five times the height of a pygmy owl. A great grey owl can grow to 85 cm.

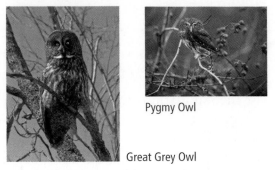

Pygmy Owl

Great Grey Owl

    a) Model this problem with an equation of the form $ax = b$. Tell what your variable represents.

    b) What is the height of the pygmy owl?

24. Lucy is making four pairs of mitts. She has 144 cm of trim to sew around the cuffs of the mitts. How much trim does she have for each mitt?

    a) Write an equation to represent this situation.

    b) Solve the equation.

25. People can be left-handed, right-handed, or ambidextrous. The number of boys in Canadian secondary schools who are left-handed is about $\dfrac{1}{7}$ of the number of boys who are right-handed. About 11% of boys are left-handed. Write and solve an equation to determine what percent of boys are right-handed.

Did You Know?

There are more ambidextrous students in Canada than there are left-handed students. *Ambidextrous* means that you are able to use your left hand and right hand with equal ability.

26. Kim works at an art gallery. An art dealer offers her a sculpture for $36 000. The dealer says the current value of the sculpture is twice its value the previous year.

   a) What was its value the previous year?

   b) If the sculpture's value increases at the same rate next year, what will the new value be?

Extend

27. The area of the triangle shown is 30 cm². Write and solve an equation to determine its height.

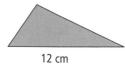

12 cm

28. Workers are repairing a section of road that is 5 km long. The speed limit has been changed from 50 km/h to 20 km/h. How many minutes does this add to the drive along this section of road?

29. The formulas that give the length of time for sound to travel underwater are

$$t = \frac{d}{149\ 700} \text{ for fresh water, and}$$

$$t = \frac{d}{150\ 000} \text{ for salt water, where } t \text{ is}$$

time, in seconds, and d is distance, in centimetres.

   a) If a sound travels for 2 s, what distance does it travel in metres in fresh water? in salt water?

   b) Two scientists are doing an underwater study of dolphin sounds. Sandra is 90 cm away from a freshwater dolphin. Donald is 1 m away from a saltwater dolphin. Who hears each sound in less time, Sandra or Donald? Show your work.

MATH LINK

Have you ever dropped Silly Putty® onto a hard surface? It bounces! The greater the height from which a ball of Silly Putty® is dropped, the higher it bounces.

a) Design and perform an experiment that allows you to record how high a ball of Silly Putty® bounces when dropped from different heights.

b) Determine an equation that models the results of your experiment. Write the equation in the form $b = kh$, where h is the height from which the Silly Putty® ball is dropped, b is the height of the first bounce, and k is a numerical coefficient that you will determine from your experiment.

WWW Web Link

For a Silly Putty® recipe, go to www.mathlinks8.ca and follow the links.

Modelling and Solving Two-Step Equations: $ax + b = c$

Cali borrowed $19 from her brother to purchase a CD. The next day, she paid back $3. She will pay back the rest at a rate of $4/week. Suggest ways that Cali might determine how long it will take to pay back her brother.

Explore the Math

How do you solve two-step equations of the form $ax + b = c$?

Example 1: Model With a Balance Scale

The city in Canada with the highest average wind speed is St. John's, Newfoundland. The city with the lowest average wind speed is Kelowna, British Columbia. The relationship between the wind speeds can be modelled using the equation $s = 4k + 3$, where s represents the wind speed in St. John's and k represents the wind speed in Kelowna. If the average wind speed in St. John's is 23 km/h, what is the average wind speed in Kelowna?

Solution

Substitute the known wind speed into the equation.
The wind speed for St. John's is 23 km/h.
$$23 = 4k + 3$$

You can model this equation using blocks and a scale.

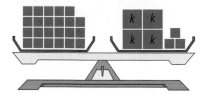

To isolate the variable, first remove the three unit blocks from the right side of the scale. To keep the scale balanced, you must remove the same number of unit blocks from the left side of the scale.

There are four k blocks on the right side of the scale. There are 20 unit blocks on the left side of the scale. For the scale to balance, each k block must have a mass of five unit blocks.

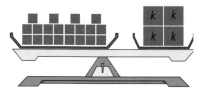

The average wind speed in Kelowna is 5 km/h.

Check:
Left Side $= 23$ Right Side $= 4k + 3$
$$= 4(5) + 3$$
$$= 20 + 3$$
$$= 23$$

Left Side $=$ Right Side
The solution is correct.

WWW Web Link

To practise solving linear equations using a balance scale, go to www.mathlinks8.ca and follow the links.

Show You Know

Solve each equation by drawing a diagram of a balance scale and blocks.

a) $6n + 6 = 12$ **b)** $13 = 9 + 2p$

Example 2: Model With Algebra Tiles

A cow sleeps 7 h a day. This amount of sleep is 1 h less than twice the amount an elephant sleeps a day. How long does an elephant sleep?

Literacy **Link**

To solve a problem, you sometimes need to translate words into an equation. For example, *two more* means you need to add 2, and *three times* means you need to multiply by 3. What other words translate into math operations?

Solution

Let *e* represent the hours an elephant sleeps.
A cow sleeps 1 h less than twice what an elephant sleeps, or $2e - 1$.
A cow sleeps 7 h.
$$2e - 1 = 7$$

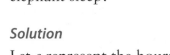

One less means you need to subtract 1, and *twice* means you need to multiply by 2.

To isolate the variable, first add one positive 1-tile to both sides.

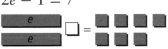

This is called a zero pair because $-1 + (+1) = 0$.

The negative 1-tile and positive 1-tile on the left side equal zero.

The two variable tiles must have the same value as the eight positive 1-tiles on the right side of the model. Each variable tile must then have a value of four positive 1-tiles.

An elephant sleeps 4 h a day.

Literacy **Link**

Order of Operations

When substituting a value into the equation, make sure to use the correct order of operations:
• first, multiply and divide in order from left to right
• finally, add and subtract in order from left to right

Check:
Left Side $= 2e - 1$ Right Side $= 7$
     $= 2(4) - 1$
     $= 8 - 1$
     $= 7$
          Left Side $=$ Right Side
The solution is correct.

Show You Know

Model each equation with algebra tiles. Then, solve.
a) $2g + 4 = -6$ **b)** $-2r - 7 = -11$

How do you represent $-2r$ using algebra tiles?

Example 3: Apply the Opposite Operations

Cali borrowed $19 from her brother. The next day, she paid back $3. To pay off the rest of the debt, she will give him $4/week. How many weeks will it take her to pay off the debt?

Solution

Let w represent the number of weeks.
Cali is paying off $4/week and has already paid $3. The total she will pay is $4w + 3$. She owes a total of $19.

$$4w + 3 = 19$$

> The amount Cali still needs to pay back is $4 times the number of weeks, or "$4w$". The amount of $3 that she has already paid back is represented by "$+ 3$."

> If you think of money owed as being negative, you can use the equation $-4w - 3 = -19$. When you solve it, the value of w is still the same.

Isolate the variable w to solve the equation.

$$4w + 3 = 19$$
$$4w + 3 - 3 = 19 - 3 \qquad \text{Subtract 3 from both sides of the equation.}$$
$$4w = 16$$
$$\frac{4w}{4} = \frac{16}{4} \qquad \text{Divide both sides of the equation by 4.}$$
$$w = 4$$

It will take Cali four weeks to pay off her debt.

Check:

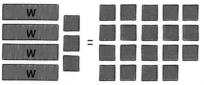

Subtract three positive 1-tiles from both sides.

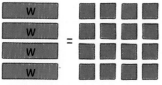

The four variable tiles must have the same value as the 16 positive 1-tiles on the right side of the model. Each variable tile must then have a value of four positive 1-tiles.

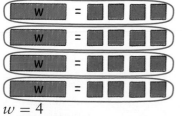

$w = 4$

The solution is correct.

Show You Know

Solve by applying the opposite operations.
  a) $4 + 26g = -48$ **b)** $-3x + 7 = 19$

- To solve an equation, isolate the variable on one side of the equal sign. When undoing the operations performed on the variable, follow the reverse order of operations:
  - add and/or subtract
  - multiply and/or divide

$$2x - 4 = 8$$
$$2x - 4 + 4 = 8 + 4$$
$$2x = 12$$
$$\frac{2x}{2} = \frac{12}{2}$$
$$x = 6$$

- Two methods you can use to check your solution are substitution and drawing a diagram:
  - Substitute your answer into the equation. Both sides should have the same value.

    Left Side $= 2x - 4$ Right Side $= 8$
    $$= 2(6) - 4$$
    $$= 12 - 4$$
    $$= 8$$
    Left Side $=$ Right Side

    The solution is correct.

  - Draw a diagram to model the equation.

    Add four positive 1-tiles to both sides.

    The four negative 1-tiles and the four positive 1-tiles on the left side equal zero. The two variable tiles must have the same value as the 12 positive 1-tiles. That means each variable tile must have a value of six positive 1-tiles .

    The solution of $x = 6$ is correct.

Communicate the Ideas

1. Draw diagrams to show how you would solve the equation $24 = 14 - 5x$ using algebra tiles. Explain each step in words.

2. a) Describe how you would isolate the variable in the equation $5x + 10 = 40$.

   b) If the equation is changed to $5x - 10 = 40$, would you use the same process to isolate the variable? Explain.

Check Your Understanding

Practise

For help with #3 and #4, refer to Example 1 on page 380–381.

3. Solve the equation modelled by each balance scale. Check your solution.

a)

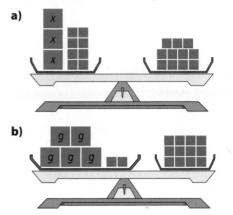

b)

4. Solve the equation represented by each balance scale. Verify your solution.

a)

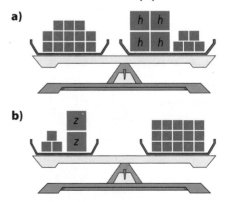

b)

For help with #5 and #6, refer to Example 2 on page 382.

5. Solve each equation modelled by the algebra tiles. Check your solution.

a)

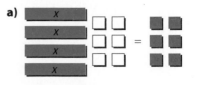

b)

6. Solve each equation represented by the algebra tiles. Verify your solution.

a)

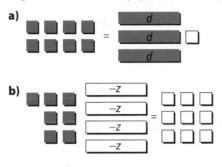

b)

For help with #7 to #10, refer to Example 3 on page 383.

7. What is the first operation you should perform to solve each equation?

  a) $4r - 2 = 14$

  b) $3 - 3x = -9$

  c) $-22 = -10 + 2m$

  d) $53 = -9k - 1$

8. What is the second operation you should perform to solve each equation in #7?

9. Solve each equation. Check your answer.

  a) $6r + 6 = 18$

  b) $4m + 8 = 12$

  c) $39 + 9g = 75$

  d) $-37 = 8f - 139$

10. Solve. Verify your answer.

  a) $-17 = 3k + 4$

  b) $29 = -14n + 1$

  c) $8x - 7 = -31$

  d) $-10 = 4n - 12$

11. Show whether $x = -3$ is the solution to each equation.

    a) $-8x - 1 = 25$

    b) $3 - 7x = -24$

    c) $29 = -10x - 1$

    d) $30 = 6x + 12$

12. Matt is saving $750 to buy a clothes dryer. If he triples the amount he has saved so far, he will have $30 more than he needs. The situation can be modelled as $3s - 30 = 750$, where s represents the amount he has saved so far.

    a) Explain how $3s - 30 = 750$ models the situation.

    b) How much money has Matt saved so far?

    c) What other strategy could you use to determine Matt's savings?

13. You are buying lunch at Sandwich Express. The cost is $4 for a sandwich and $2 each for your choice of extras. You have $10. The equation to determine how many extras you can get is $10 = 2e + 4$, where e is the number of extras. How many extras can you buy if you spend all of your money?

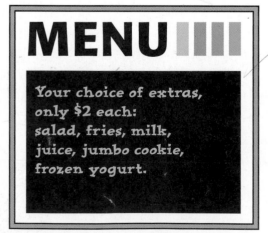

14. The percent of elementary school students who choose hockey as their favourite physical activity is 14%. This percent of students is 2% more than four times the percent who choose skiing.

    a) Let s represent the percent of students who choose skiing. What equation models this situation?

    b) Solve the equation to find the percent of students who choose skiing.

15. If Jennifer doubled the money that she has in her account now and then took out $50, she would have enough left in her account to buy a new bike that costs $299. Write and solve an equation to determine how much money Jennifer has now.

16. A classroom's length is 3 m less than two times its width. The classroom has a length of 9 m. Write and solve an equation to determine the width of the classroom.

17. An eagle is hunting a bird in flight. The eagle begins its descent from a height of 74 m. The eagle reaches its prey at a height of 3 m. This situation can be modelled using the formula $74 = 3 + 6t$, where t represents the time in seconds.

    a) What do you think the value of 6 represents in the equation?

    b) After how many seconds does the eagle reach its prey? Give your answer to the nearest tenth of a second.

18. The base of an isosceles triangle is 6 m less than two times one side. The base is 24 m. What is the area of the triangle?

19. The deck around a swimming pool has the same width all the way around. The perimeter of the pool is 50 m. The outside perimeter of the deck is 74 m. What is the width of the deck?

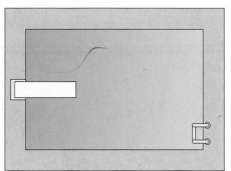

20. The variable *m* is a positive integer. The variable *n* is an integer from 0 to 9. Identify all of the values for *m* that would satisfy the equation $3m + n = 2008$.

21. Mallika walked at 2 km/h for 2 h and then cycled at *x* km/h for 3 h. If the average speed for the whole journey was 3 km/h, how fast did she cycle? Give your answer to the nearest tenth of a kilometre per hour.

MATH LINK

When any object falls, it picks up more and more speed as it falls. In fact, a falling object increases its speed by about 10 m/s for every second it falls.

Suppose a stone is dislodged from the side of a canyon and falls with an initial speed of 5 m/s. It hits the water below it at a speed of 45 m/s.

Write and solve an equation to determine the amount of time the stone fell before it hit the water.

Modelling and Solving Two-Step Equations: $\frac{x}{a} + b = c$

The mass of a Persian cat is typically 2 kg less than $\frac{1}{3}$ of the average mass of a border collie. The average mass of a Persian cat is 4 kg. Describe how you might determine the average mass of a border collie.

Explore the Math

How do you model and solve two-step equations of the form $\frac{x}{a} + b = c$?

1. Use d to represent the average mass of a border collie. What is an equation that models the relationship between the masses of the border collie and the Persian cat?

2. How could you use a model or diagram to represent your equation?

3. Use your model or diagram to help you solve this equation.
   a) What is the first thing you do to isolate d?
   b) What equation does your model or diagram represent now?
   c) What do you do next?
   d) What is the average mass of a border collie?

Reflect on Your Findings

4. a) Why is this type of equation called a two-step equation?

   b) How is solving an equation of the form $\frac{x}{a} + b = c$ similar to solving one of the form $ax + b = c$? How is it different?

Materials
• algebra tiles

Example 1: Model Equations

The elevation of Qamani'tuaq, Nunavut, is 1 m less than $\frac{1}{2}$ the elevation of Prince Rupert, British Columbia. If the elevation of Qamani'tuaq is 18 m, what is the elevation of Prince Rupert?

Solution

Let p represent the elevation of Prince Rupert.

The equation that models this situation is $\frac{p}{2} - 1 = 18$.

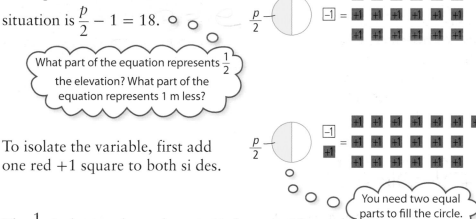

What part of the equation represents $\frac{1}{2}$ the elevation? What part of the equation represents 1 m less?

To isolate the variable, first add one red +1 square to both si des.

You need two equal parts to fill the circle.

The $\frac{1}{2}$ circle must have the same value as +19.
Multiply by 2 to fill the circle.
To balance the equation, multiply +19 by 2.
The variable p must then have a value of $2 \times 19 = 38$.
The elevation of Prince Rupert is 38 m.

Check:

$$\text{Left Side} = \frac{p}{2} - 1 \qquad \text{Right Side} = 18$$
$$= \frac{38}{2} - 1$$
$$= 19 - 1$$
$$= 18$$
$$\text{Left Side} = \text{Right Side}$$

The solution is correct.

Show You Know

Solve by modelling each equation.

a) $\frac{x}{4} - 5 = -7$ **b)** $\frac{-p}{3} + 1 = -4$

Example 2: Apply the Reverse Order of Operations

During the 2006–2007 NHL season, Kristian Huselius of the Calgary Flames had a total of 41 more than $\frac{1}{2}$ the number of shots on goal as Jarome Iginla. If Huselius had 173 shots on goal, how many did Iginla have?

> Use the reverse order of operations. Add and subtract first, then multiply and divide.

> Why would you not use models to solve this problem?

Solution

Let j represent the number of shots on goal Jarome Iginla had.

This situation can be modelled with the equation $\frac{j}{2} + 41 = 173$.

$\frac{j}{2} + 41 - 41 = 173 - 41$ Subtract 41 from both sides of the equation.

$$\frac{j}{2} = 132$$

$\frac{j}{2} \times 2 = 132 \times 2$ Multiply both sides of the equation by 2.

$$j = 264$$

Jarome Iginla had 264 shots on goal during the 2006–2007 season.

Check:

Left Side $= \frac{j}{2} + 41$ Right Side $= 173$

$\qquad\quad = \frac{264}{2} + 41$

$\qquad\quad = 132 + 41$

$\qquad\quad = 173$

Left Side $=$ Right Side

The solution is correct.

Show You Know

Solve by applying the reverse order of operations.

a) $\frac{-x}{12} - 6 = 4$ **b)** $-4 = 3 + \frac{k}{7}$

Key Ideas

- To solve an equation, isolate the variable on one side of the equal sign. When undoing the operations performed on the variable, follow the reverse order of operations:
  - subtract and/or add
  - multiply and/or divide

$$\frac{x}{-4} + 3 = 5$$

$$\frac{x}{-4} + 3 - 3 = 5 - 3$$

$$\frac{x}{-4} = 2$$

$$\frac{x}{-4} \times (-4) = 2 \times (-4)$$

$$x = -8$$

$$5 = 2 - \frac{n}{4}$$

$$5 - 2 = 2 - 2 - \frac{n}{4}$$

$$3 = -\frac{n}{4}$$

$$3 \times 4 = -\frac{n}{4} \times 4$$

$$12 = -n$$

$$12 \div (-1) = -n \div (-1)$$

$$-12 = n$$

- One method you can use to check your answer is substituting it back into the equation. Both sides of the equation should have the same value.

Left Side $= \dfrac{x}{-4} + 3$ Right Side $= 5$

$= \dfrac{-8}{-4} + 3$

$= 2 + 3$

$= 5$

Left Side $=$ Right Side

The solution is correct.

Communicate the Ideas

1. Describe a situation that can be modelled with the equation $\dfrac{x}{4} - 2 = 3$.

2. Describe how to isolate the variable when solving $12 - \dfrac{n}{5} = 6$.
   Compare your answer with a classmate's.

3. Manjit believes that the first step in solving the equation $\dfrac{x}{-4} + 7 = 9$
   is to multiply both sides of the equation by -4 as shown.

$$\frac{x}{-4} \times (-4) + 7 = 9 \times (-4)$$

Is he correct? Explain.

Check Your Understanding

Practise

For help with #4 to #7, refer to Example 1 on page 389.

4. Solve the equation modelled by each diagram. Check your solution.

a)

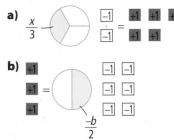

$$\frac{x}{3}$$

b)

$$\frac{-b}{2}$$

5. Solve the equation represented by each diagram. Verify your solution.

a)

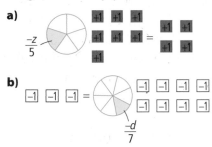

$$\frac{-z}{5}$$

b)

$$\frac{-d}{7}$$

6. Draw a model for each equation. Then, solve. Verify your answer.

a) $-5 + \dfrac{g}{-2} = 3$ b) $-3 = 7 + \dfrac{n}{5}$

7. For each equation, draw a model. Then, solve. Check your answer.

a) $\dfrac{f}{-5} + 3 = -2$ b) $-1 = \dfrac{n}{8} - 4$

For help with #8 to #11, refer to Example 2 on page 390.

8. What is the first operation you should perform to solve each equation?

a) $\dfrac{t}{-5} + 12 = 9$ b) $\dfrac{p}{13} - 2 = -3$

c) $\dfrac{-k}{12} + 6 = 15$ d) $14 = 11 - \dfrac{x}{3}$

9. What is the second operation you should perform to solve each equation in #8?

10. Solve each equation. Verify your answer.

a) $2 + \dfrac{m}{3} = 18$ b) $\dfrac{c}{-8} - 8 = -12$

c) $16 = 9 + \dfrac{b}{-8}$ d) $-3 = \dfrac{n}{-7} + 19$

11. Solve. Check your answer.

a) $4 + \dfrac{j}{-8} = 8$ b) $\dfrac{r}{2} - 12 = -12$

c) $15 = -5 + \dfrac{x}{-6}$ d) $-2 = \dfrac{n}{13} - 17$

Apply

12. Show whether $n = -72$ is the solution to each equation.

a) $6 + \dfrac{n}{9} = 14$ b) $2 = 14 + \dfrac{n}{6}$

c) $\dfrac{n}{-3} + 6 = -18$ d) $-17 = \dfrac{n}{36} - 15$

13. The amount of sleep needed each night by people 18 years old or younger can be modelled by the equation $s = 12 - \dfrac{a}{4}$, where the amount of sleep in hours is s, and the age in years is a.

a) If 10 h is the amount of sleep Brian needs, how old is he likely to be?

b) Natasha is 13. She gets 8 h of sleep each night. Is this enough? Explain your reasoning.

14. The cost of a concert ticket for a student is $2 less than one half of the cost for an adult. The cost of the student ticket is $5. Let a represent the cost of an adult ticket. Write and solve an equation to determine the cost of an adult ticket.

15. In the following formula, T is the air temperature in degrees Celsius at an altitude of h metres, and t is the ground temperature in degrees Celsius:
$$T = t - \frac{h}{150}.$$

a) If the ground temperature is 25 °C, what is the temperature outside an aircraft at an altitude of 7500 m?

b) What is the altitude of the same plane if the outside air temperature is −35 °C?

16. In Canada, the percent of secondary school students who say their favourite subject is science is 1% less than $\frac{1}{2}$ of the number of students who choose math. The percent of students who prefer science is 6%. Write and solve an equation to determine what percent of students prefer math.

Extend

17. The recommended energy requirement per day for 14-year-old boys depends on how active they are. The requirement can be modelled by the following equations, where a is the age and C is the number of Calories.

Active	Moderately Active
$a = \dfrac{C}{100} - 17$	$a = \dfrac{C}{100} - 13$

a) Tom is an active 14-year-old. What is the recommended number of Calories he should consume?

b) Juan is a moderately active 14-year-old boy. If he consumes 2831 Calories per day, is this greater or fewer Calories than the recommended amount?

c) The recommended requirement for a moderately active 14-year-old girl is 2100 Calories. Model this energy requirement by determining the value for x in the equation $a = \dfrac{C}{100} - x$.

MATH LINK

Meteorologists rely on models of our atmosphere to help them understand temperature and pressure differences, humidity, and a wide range of other variables. An important part of our atmosphere is the troposphere. It is the lowest layer of the atmosphere, where humans live and where weather occurs.

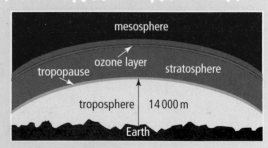

The equation that models air temperature change in the troposphere is $t = 15 - \dfrac{h}{154}$, where t is the temperature, in degrees Celsius, and h is the altitude, in metres.

a) What patterns do you see in the graph?

b) What connections do you see between the graph and the equation?

c) At what height in the troposphere is the temperature 0 °C?

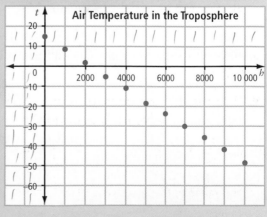

Modelling and Solving Two-Step Equations: $a(x + b) = c$

Kia plans to make a square Star Quilt for her grandmother. The quilt will have a 4-cm wide border around it. Kia wants the perimeter of the completed quilt to be 600 cm. How can Kia decide how long each side of the quilt should be before she adds the border?

Explore the Math

Materials
• algebra tiles

How do you solve equations of the form $a(x + b) = c$?

Viktor missed yesterday's math class. Jackie will show him how to model and solve the equation $3(x - 5) = -6$

1. a) Use a variable tile to represent x.

   b) How will you use negative 1-tiles to represent -5?

2. a) How many sets of $x - 5$ will you include in your model? Explain.

   b) How will you complete your model of the equation?

3. a) What is the first thing you do to isolate the variable tile?

   b) What equation does your model represent now?

   c) What do you need to do to solve the equation?

4. What is the unknown value of x?

Reflect on Your Findings

5. What steps did you take to solve the equation?

Did You Know?

The centre of a Star Quilt is in the shape of the traditional eight-pointed morning star of the Lakota and Dakota Sioux. The Star Quilt is a symbol of tradition to the Plains peoples.

Example 1: Model With Algebra Tiles

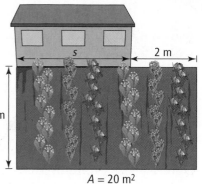

A flower garden is in the shape of a rectangle. The length of the garden is 2 m longer than the length of the shed beside it. The width of the garden is 4 m. If the area of the garden is 20 m², what is the length of the shed?

Solution

Let *s* represent the unknown length of the shed. The length of the garden can be represented by $s + 2$. The width of the garden is 4 m. The equation that models the area of the garden is $4(s + 2) = 20$. There are four groups of $(s + 2)$. That means there are four variable tiles and eight positive 1-tiles on the left side of the equation.

> What is the formula for the area of a rectangle?

To isolate the variable, subtract eight positive 1-tiles from both sides of the equal sign.

> This is the same as adding eight negative 1-tiles to both sides of the equal sign.

There are now four variable tiles on the left side and 12 positive 1-tiles on the right side.

The four variable tiles must have the same value as the 12 positive 1-tiles.

Each variable tile must then have a value of three positive 1-tiles.
The length of the shed is 3 m.

Check:
Left Side $= 4(s + 2)$ Right Side $= 20$
$\quad\quad\quad = 4(3 + 2)$
$\quad\quad\quad = 4(5)$
$\quad\quad\quad = 20$
$\quad\quad$ Left Side $=$ Right Side
The solution is correct.

Literacy ⊖ Link

When substituting a value into an equation, be sure to use the correct order of operations:
• Brackets.
• Multiply and divide in order from left to right.
• Add and subtract in order from left to right.

Show You Know

Solve by modelling the equation.
a) $2(g + 4) = -8$ **b)** $3(r - 2) = 3$

Example 2: Solve Equations

Kia is making a square quilt with a 4-cm wide border around it. She wants the completed quilt to have a perimeter of 600 cm. What must the dimensions of Kia's quilt be before she adds the border?

Solution

Strategies

Draw a Diagram

Let s represent the unknown side length of the quilt before the border is added. A border of 4 cm is added to each side. That means the side length of the quilt after the border is added is $s + 8$. Model with the equation $4(s + 8) = 600$.

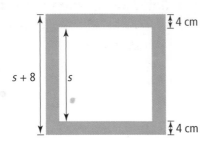

> The length must be multiplied by 4 because there are four sides to the square quilt.

Method 1: Divide First

Isolate the variable s.

$$4(s + 8) = 600$$
$$\frac{4(s + 8)}{4} = \frac{600}{4} \qquad \text{Divide by 4 to undo the multiplication.}$$
$$s + 8 = 150$$
$$s + 8 - 8 = 150 - 8 \qquad \text{Subtract 8 to undo the addition.}$$
$$s = 142$$

The quilt dimensions before adding the border should be 142 cm × 142 cm.

Method 2: Use the Distributive Property First

Isolate the variable s.

$$4(s + 8) = 600$$
$$4s + 32 = 600 \qquad \text{Multiply both } s \text{ and 8 by 4.}$$
$$4s + 32 - 32 = 600 - 32 \qquad \text{Subtract 32 from both sides of the equation.}$$
$$4s = 568$$
$$\frac{4s}{4} = \frac{568}{4} \qquad \text{Divide both sides of the equation by 4.}$$
$$s = 142$$

Literacy Link

The *distributive property* states that $a(b + c)$ equals $a \times b + a \times c$.

> To use the distributive property, multiply the terms in the brackets by 4.
>
> $4(s + 8) = 4 \times (s + 8)$
> $= (4 \times s) + (4 \times 8)$
> $= 4s + 32$

The quilt dimensions before adding the border should be 142 cm × 142 cm.

Check:

Left Side $= 4(s + 8)$ Right Side $= 600$
$= 4(142 + 8)$
$= 4(150)$
$= 600$
Left Side $=$ Right Side

The solution is correct.

Show You Know

Solve each equation.

a) $-2(x - 3) = 12$ **b)** $-20 = 5(3 + p)$

- To solve an equation, isolate the variable on one side of the equal sign.
- When undoing the operations performed on the variable, use opposite operations.
- Solve an equation of the form $a(x + b) = c$ by dividing first or by using the distributive property first.

Divide First:

$$-4(x - 7) = 16$$
$$\frac{-4(x - 7)}{-4} = \frac{16}{-4}$$ Divide by -4 to undo the multiplication.
$$x - 7 = -4$$
$$x - 7 + 7 = -4 + 7$$ Add 7 to undo the subtraction.
$$x = 3$$

Use the Distributive Property First:

$$-4(x - 7) = 16$$
$$-4x + 28 = 16$$ Use the distributive property.
$$-4x + 28 - 28 = 16 - 28$$ Subtract 28 to undo the addition.
$$-4x = -12$$
$$\frac{-4x}{-4} = \frac{-12}{-4}$$ Divide by -4 to undo the multiplication.
$$x = 3$$

- One method you can use to check your answer is substituting it back into the equation. Both sides of the equation should have the same value.

Left Side $= -4(x - 7)$ Right Side $= 16$
$$= -4(3 - 7)$$
$$= -4(-4)$$
$$= 16$$
Left Side $=$ Right Side

The solution is correct.

Communicate the Ideas

1. Draw diagrams to show how you would solve the equation $4 = 2(v - 3)$ using algebra tiles. Explain each step in words.

2. Julia and Chris are solving the equation $-18 = -6(x + 2)$. Is either strategy correct? Explain.

Julia: ○ ○ ○ First, I subtract 2 from both sides. Then, I divide both sides by -6.

Chris: ○ ○ ○ I start by dividing $-6(x + 2)$ by -6. Then, I subtract 2 from both sides.

3. Describe a situation that can be modelled with the equation $2(r + 3) = -6$.

Practise

For help with #4 to #7, refer to Example 1 on page 395.

4. Solve the equation modelled by each diagram. Check your solution.

a)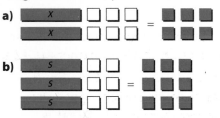

b)

5. Solve the equation represented by each diagram. Verify your answer.

a)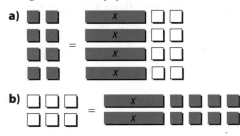

b)

6. Model and then solve each equation. Check your answer.

   a) $3(t - 2) = 12$ **b)** $6(j - 1) = -6$

7. Model and then solve each equation. Verify your solution.

   a) $2(3 + p) = 8$ **b)** $0 = 7(n - 2)$

For help with #8 and #9, refer to Example 2 on page 396.

8. Solve each equation. Check your answer.
   a) $6(r + 6) = -18$
   b) $4(m - 3) = 12$
   c) $3(1 + g) = -75$
   d) $36 = 6(f + 13)$

9. Solve. Verify your solution.
   a) $-21 = 3(k + 3)$
   b) $42 = -14(n - 11)$
   c) $8(x - 7) = -32$
   d) $-10 = -5(w + 13)$

Apply

10. Show whether $x = -4$ is the solution to each equation.
   a) $-8(x - 1) = 24$
   b) $3(-8 - x) = -24$
   c) $25 = -5(x - 1)$
   d) $66 = 6(x + 7)$

11. The fence around Gisel's new tree is in the shape of an equilateral triangle. Gisel wants to increase the length of each side by 7 cm. The perimeter of her new fence will be 183 cm.

   a) Let s represent the side length of the old fence. What equation models this situation?
   b) Determine the length of each side of the old fence.

12. The amount of food energy per day required by hikers is modelled by the equation $e = -125(t - 122)$, where e is the amount of food energy, in kilojoules (kJ), and t is the outside temperature, in degrees Celsius.
   a) If the outside temperature is $-20\ °C$, how much food energy is required per day?
   b) If a hiker consumes 19 000 kJ of food energy based on the outside temperature, what is the temperature?

13. Barney wants to frame a square picture of his dog. The frame he bought fits a picture with a perimeter no greater than 96 cm. He plans to put a 2-cm blue border around the picture.

a) What equation models this situation?

b) Determine the maximum dimensions that the picture can have.

Extend

14. A computer rental company charges by the hour: $5 for the first hour and $4 for every hour after that. The fee rate can be modelled with the equation $4(n - 1) = T - 5$, where n is a number of hours greater than zero and T is the rental fee, in dollars. Candy's rental fee was $17. For how many hours did she rent the computer?

15. A parking lot charges by the hour: $2 for the first hour and $3 for every hour after that. The formula used to calculate the number of hours someone has parked is $3(h - 1) = T - 2$, where h represents a number of hours greater than zero and T represents the total amount of the parking fee, in dollars. If Mark's parking fee is $8, how long did he park in the lot?

16. The distance between Andrew's house and his grandfather's apartment is 42 km.

a) If Andrew rides his bike 2 km/h faster than his current speed, he could get there in 3 h. What is Andrew's current speed?

b) If Andrew wants to get there in 2 h, how much faster than his current speed should he ride his bike?

c) Do you think Andrew can get there in 2 h? Explain.

MATH LINK

Some jobs require working the night shift, such as from midnight to 8:30 a.m. Other jobs require working in isolated areas or under hazardous conditions. Depending on the job, the wage may be increased by a certain amount per hour or per month. This increase is called a premium.

a) Research and describe three different jobs that pay hourly or monthly wages plus a premium.

b) For each job, model the pay using an equation.

Key Words

For #1 to #7, choose the word from the list that goes in each blank.

variable   distributive property   equation
linear equation   constant   numerical coefficient
opposite operations

1. A letter that represents an unknown number is called a(n) ▨▨▨.

2. A mathematical statement with two expressions that have the same value is called a(n) ▨▨▨.

3. Multiplication and division are ▨▨▨ ▨▨▨.

4. A number that multiplies the variable is called a(n) ▨▨▨ ▨▨▨.

5. $5(b + 3) = 5 \times b + 5 \times 3$ is an example of how you use the ▨▨▨ ▨▨▨.

6. A number that does not change and that is added or subtracted from the value of an expression is called a(n) ▨▨▨.

7. An equation that, when graphed, results in points that lie along a straight line is called a(n) ▨▨▨ ▨▨▨.

10.1 Modelling and Solving One-Step Equations: $ax = b$, $\frac{x}{a} = b$, pages 370–379

8. Solve the equation modelled by each diagram. Check your solution.

a)
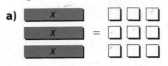

b)
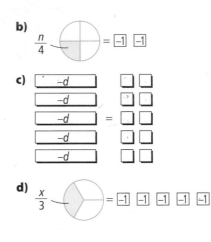

c)

$-d$	☐☐
$-d$	☐☐
$-d$ =	☐☐
$-d$	☐☐
$-d$	☐☐

d) $\frac{x}{3}$ ⬯ = $\boxed{-1}$ $\boxed{-1}$ $\boxed{-1}$ $\boxed{-1}$ $\boxed{-1}$

9. Solve by inspection.

   a) $-22 = -11x$ b) $6r = -18$
   c) $-8 = 2z$ d) $-5t = 15$

10. Solve each equation. Check your answer.

   a) $-5 = \dfrac{p}{3}$ b) $\dfrac{n}{-11} = 3$
   c) $-9 = \dfrac{x}{-4}$ d) $\dfrac{a}{-2} = -7$

11. Write two different equations that have a solution of 5 and that can be solved using multiplication or division.

10.2 Modelling and Solving Two-Step Equations: $ax + b = c$, pages 380–387

12. Write and solve the equation modelled by each diagram. Check your solution.

a)
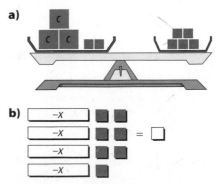

b)

13. Show whether $x = -5$ is the solution to each equation.

   a) $-7x - 2 = 33$ **b)** $4 - 3x = 19$

   c) $-28 = 5x - 3$ **d)** $30 = 2x + 20$

14. Solve each equation. Check your solution.

   a) $-3t + 8 = 20$ **b)** $5j - 2 = -127$

   c) $-12 + 9p = 24$ **d)** $130 = 12n - 5$

15. Zoë has a collection of CDs and DVDs. The number of CDs she has is three fewer than four times the number of DVDs. Zoë has 25 CDs.

   a) Choose a variable to represent the number of DVDs Zoë has. Write an equation that represents this situation.

   b) How many DVDs does Zoë have?

10.3 Modelling and Solving Two-Step Equations: $\frac{x}{a} + b = c$, pages 388–393

16. Solve the equation modelled by each diagram. Check your solution.

   a)

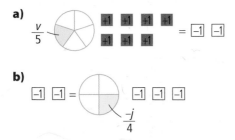

   b)

17. Identify the first operation and the second operation you should perform to solve each equation.

   a) $\dfrac{t}{-3} + 13 = 9$ **b)** $\dfrac{r}{15} - 7 = -11$

   c) $2 - \dfrac{x}{22} = 17$ **d)** $13 = -16 - \dfrac{h}{4}$

18. Solve. Verify your answer.

   a) $3 - \dfrac{v}{-3} = 7$ **b)** $\dfrac{d}{3} - 13 = -8$

   c) $17 = -4 + \dfrac{x}{-2}$ **d)** $-2 = \dfrac{n}{4} - 11$

19. According to the Canadian Soccer Association, in 2006, Saskatchewan's number of registered players was 1120 fewer than $\frac{1}{5}$ the number of soccer players registered in British Columbia. Saskatchewan had 23 761 registered soccer players that year. Write and solve an equation to determine how many players British Columbia had.

10.4 Modelling and Solving Two-Step Equations: $a(x + b) = c$, pages 394–399

20. Solve the equation modelled by each diagram. Check your solution.

   a)

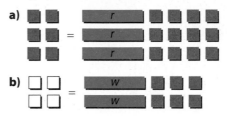

   b)

21. Solve. Verify your solution.

   a) $6(q - 13) = -24$ **b)** $-14 = 2(g + 4)$

   c) $-18 = -6(k + 17)$ **d)** $16 = -4(x - 5)$

22. Diane wishes to create a square Star Quilt like the one shown. There will be a 3-cm border around the quilt and the perimeter of the completed quilt will be 372 cm. Write and solve an equation to determine the dimensions of the quilt before she adds the border.

23. Each side of a regular octagon is decreased by 3 cm. If the perimeter of the new octagon is 48 cm, what was the measure of each side of the original octagon?

For #1 to #5, choose the best answer.

1. What is the solution to $\dfrac{x}{3} = -12$?

   A $x = 36$ **B** $x = 4$

   C $x = -4$ **D** $x = -36$

2. The force, F, in newtons, required to stretch a spring a distance, d, in centimetres, is represented by the equation $F = 15d$. If a force of 38 N is used, how far will the spring stretch, to the nearest tenth of a centimetre?

   A 0.3 cm   **B** 0.4 cm

   C 2.5 cm   **D** 2.6 cm

3. What is the solution to $5n - 7 = -4$?

   A $n = \dfrac{3}{5}$ **B** $n = \dfrac{4}{5}$

   C $n = \dfrac{11}{5}$ **D** $n = \dfrac{31}{5}$

4. Which of these equations has the solution $p = -6$?

   A $\dfrac{p}{3} - 4 = -2$ **B** $\dfrac{p}{3} + 4 = -2$

   C $\dfrac{p}{-3} - 4 = -2$ **D** $\dfrac{p}{-3} + 4 = -2$

5. Wanda solved the equation $4(x - 3) = 2$ like this:

              $4(x - 3) = 2$

   Step 1 $4x - 12 = 8$

   Step 2 $4x = 20$

   Step 3 $x = 5$

   At which step did Wanda make her first mistake?

   A Step 1   **B** Step 2

   C Step 3   **D** No mistake was made.

Complete the statements in #6 and #7.

6. The opposite operation of division is ▉.

7. The solution to $-4(y + 10) = 24$ is $y = ▉$.

Short Answer

8. a) Draw a diagram that models the equation $-3x - 4 = 2$.

   b) What is the solution to this equation?

9. Dillon used algebra tiles to model a problem.

   a) What equation is being modelled?

   b) What is the first step that Dillon should take to solve the equation using the algebra tiles?

10. Solve each equation. Verify your solution.

   a) $4x = 48$ **b)** $\dfrac{t}{-5} = -8$

   c) $2k - 6 = 31$ **d)** $\dfrac{d}{7} - 5 = 16$

   e) $3 - \dfrac{n}{4} = 8$ **f)** $12 = 4(x - 2)$

11. a) Describe the steps you would take to solve the equation $-3(b + 3) = -15$.

   b) How are these steps different from the steps you would take to solve the equation $-3b + 3 = -15$?

12. The surface elevation of Lake Louise is 1536 m. This elevation is 45 m higher than seven times the elevation of Lake Athabasca.

   a) Choose a variable to represent the elevation of Lake Athabasca. Write an equation to model this situation.

   b) What is the elevation of Lake Athabasca?

13. The length of a rectangular vegetable garden is to be increased by 3 m. The new garden will have an area of 90 m². Write and then solve an equation to determine the length of the original garden.

5 m

Extended Response

14. a) What is wrong with the method used to solve the following equation?

$$-6 = 18 + 3x$$
$$-6 + 18 = 18 - 18 + 3x$$
$$12 = 3x$$
$$4 = x$$

   b) What is the correct method?

15. The formula for the perimeter of a rectangle is $P = 2(l + w)$, where P is the perimeter, l is the length, and w is the width of the rectangle. The perimeter of the rectangle shown is 14 cm.

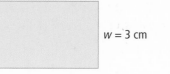

$w = 3$ cm

   a) What is the length of the rectangle? Check your solution.

   b) Another rectangle has the same length as the rectangle shown but a perimeter of 12 cm. What is the area of this rectangle?

Wrap It Up!

Report on how different linear equations could be used in everyday situations. Include all five of these types of linear equations:

$ax = b$ $\frac{x}{a} = b, a \neq 0$ $ax + b = c$

$\frac{x}{a} + b = c, a \neq 0$ $a(x + b) = c$

In your report,
• describe a different situation or job for each of the five linear equations
• identify what each variable, constant, and numerical coefficient represents in each of your equations
• solve each of your linear equations, using values appropriate for the situation or job
• identify how one of your equations may change based on the circumstances

Math Games

Rascally Riddles

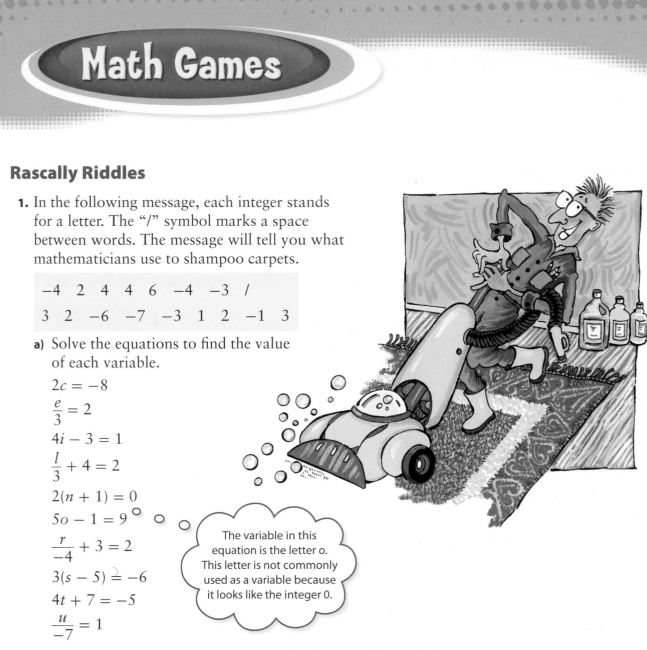

1. In the following message, each integer stands for a letter. The "/" symbol marks a space between words. The message will tell you what mathematicians use to shampoo carpets.

−4	2	4	4	6	−4	−3	/
3	2	−6	−7	−3	1	2	−1	3

a) Solve the equations to find the value of each variable.

$2c = -8$

$\dfrac{e}{3} = 2$

$4i - 3 = 1$

$\dfrac{l}{3} + 4 = 2$

$2(n + 1) = 0$

$5o - 1 = 9$

$\dfrac{r}{-4} + 3 = 2$

$3(s - 5) = -6$

$4t + 7 = -5$

$\dfrac{u}{-7} = 1$

> The variable in this equation is the letter o. This letter is not commonly used as a variable because it looks like the integer 0.

b) Replace each integer in the message by the variable with this value. What do mathematicians use to shampoo carpets?

2. a) As a class or in a group, brainstorm how you would write a riddle like the one in #1.

b) Write a riddle of your own. It must include
   • a short message made with integers that stand for letters
   • a set of equations that can be solved to determine the letters that will replace the integers

c) Check that your equations give your intended message.

d) Have a classmate solve your riddle.

Challenge in Real Life

The Earth's Core

Earth is made up of several distinct layers. The deeper layers are hotter and denser because the temperature and pressure inside Earth increases with depth. The table below provides information concerning how the temperature increases with depth.

• grid paper

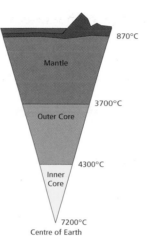

Layer	Depth (km)	Temperature (°C)
Crust	−90	870
Mantle	−2921	3700
Outer core	−5180	4300
Inner core	−6401	7200

1. Graph the data from the table. Label your graph. Note: Make sure that your y-axis goes to at least 9000 °C, since you will need this value to complete #3b).

2. a) Calculate the total temperature change moving from the lower part of the crust to the centre of Earth.

   b) What is the total depth change moving from the lower part of the crust to the centre of Earth? Show your work.

   c) What is the approximate change in temperature for every kilometre you go into Earth? Justify your answer.

3. The approximate temperature by depth can be modelled using the linear equation $T = d + 870$, where d is the depth, in kilometres, and T is the temperature, in degrees Celsius.

   a) Use the equation to calculate the approximate temperature at a depth of 3400 km. Show your calculations. Verify your solution by placing an x on your graph from #1.

   b) Use the equation to identify the depth at which the temperature is approximately 9000 °C. Show your calculations and verify your solution by placing a y on your graph from #1.

   c) How does your answer to #3b) compare to your answer in #2c)? Explain why there may be some differences.

Probability

People often want to know how to determine the likelihood of events. The probability that snow will fall tomorrow is of interest to meteorologists, climatologists, and the general public.

Meteorologists base their predictions on the current weather patterns. Climatologists work from climate data that show the weather trends over many years.

In this chapter, you will continue your study of probability in order to assess the likelihood of events more accurately.

What You Will Learn

❏ to calculate probabilities for several events occurring together
❏ to develop quicker ways to calculate probability

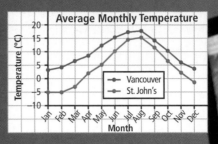

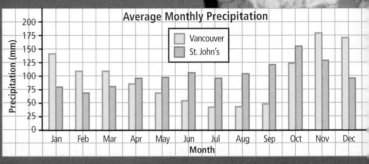

Literacy ⊖ Link

You can use a concept map to visually organize your understanding of a math concept such as probability.

Copy the concept map below into your math journal or notebook. Make each shape large enough to write in. Write what you already know about probability.

- Definition: What is probability?
- Comparisons: What can you compare probability to?
- Facts: Outline some facts about or characteristics of probability.
- Examples: Provide examples of different types of probability.

Share your ideas with a peer. You may wish to add to or correct what you have written.

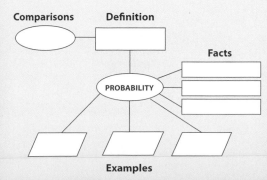

Making the Foldable

Materials

- 11 × 17 sheet of paper
- two sheets of notebook paper
- scissors
- stapler

Step 1

Fold an 11 × 17 sheet of paper in half from bottom to top. Instead of creasing it, just pinch it at the midpoint. Fold the outer edges of the paper to just meet at the pinch or midpoint.

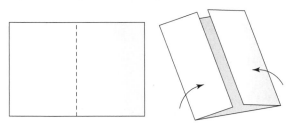

Step 2

Fold it in half from top to bottom.

Step 3

Open up the Foldable and cut the creases shown to create four doors. Label each door as shown in Step 4.

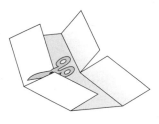

Step 4

Fold two sheets of notebook paper into quarters. Cut each paper to make two folded half sheets. Place the half sheets inside the fold for each door. Staple each door along the outside edge to hold the booklet together.

Step 5

Open the 11.1, 11.2, and 11.3 booklets to the back page. Label that page for the section Math Link.

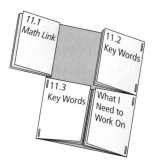

Using the Foldable

When you start Chapter 11, do the Math Link introduction on page 409 on the back of the Foldable.

As you work through the chapter, list and define the Key Words on the door for each section. Use the section booklet for your notes and examples.

Do the Math Link for each section on the last page of each booklet, and on that part of the inside back of the Foldable.

In the fourth booklet, make notes under the heading What I Need to Work On. Include notes about how to solve any problems you are having. Check off each item as you deal with it.

MATH LINK

Probability Games

Many card games and board games involve chance. In these games, your likelihood of winning is based on the outcomes of rolling dice or dealing cards. These games involve probability.

1. Explain, in your own words, what the word *likelihood* means in the previous paragraph.

2. List two or three games that you have played using cards or dice.

3. Choose one game from #2 and explain how the outcomes of rolling dice or dealing cards affect the probability of winning the game.

4. Compare your answers with those of a classmate.

One game that involves probability is a stick game. Throughout this chapter, you will learn how to play this game. At the end of the chapter, you will determine whether the scoring system is fair and suggest modifications, if necessary.

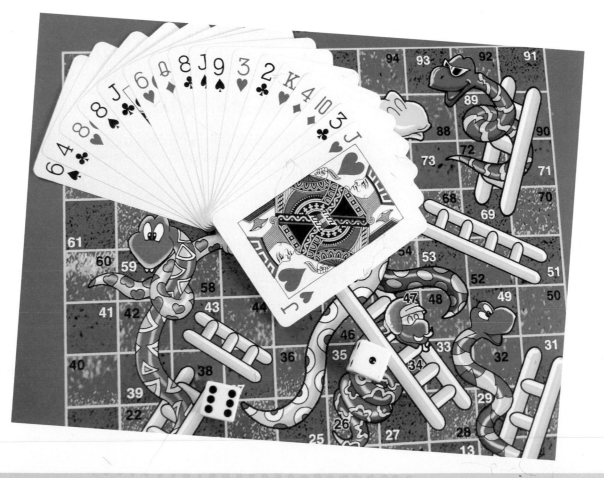

Determining Probabilities Using Tree Diagrams and Tables

Focus on...

After this lesson, you will be able to...

❏ determine the sample space of a probability experiment with two independent events

❏ represent the sample space in the form of a tree diagram or table

❏ express the probability of an event as a fraction, a decimal, and a percent

At the end of a unit on probability, Ms. Pascal decided to allow her students to determine what kind of test the class would write. All the students' names were put into a hat. Owen was chosen to spin a spinner divided into three equal regions to determine the kind of test: multiple choice (MC), short answer (SA), or a combination (MC & SA). Ava was chosen to roll a four-sided die to determine the number of questions on the test: 5, 10, 15, or 20.

Ms. Pascal explained that spinning the spinner and rolling the die are **independent events**. How does she know that these events are independent?

independent events

• results for which the outcome of one event has no effect on the outcome of another event

Explore the Math

How can you use the outcomes of an experiment to determine probabilities?

Materials

• ruler

1. Show how you could represent the possible outcomes of this experiment.

probability

• the likelihood or chance of an event occurring

2. What is the **probability** that the test will have multiple-choice questions only? How did you determine your answer?

3. What is the probability that the test will consist of ten questions? Explain your reasoning.

4. List the **sample space** for this experiment.

sample space

• all possible outcomes of a probability experiment

Reflect on Your Findings

5. Show your answers to parts b), c), and d) as a fraction, a percent, and a decimal.

a) How many different tests are possible for the students in Ms. Pascal's class?

b) What is the probability that the students will write a combined multiple-choice/short-answer test with 20 questions? Show how you arrived at your answer.

c) What is the probability that students will write a multiple-choice test with at least ten questions?

d) What is the probability that the students will not write a short-answer test with 15 questions? Explain how you found your answer.

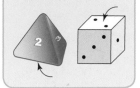

Did You Know?

When you roll a four-sided die, you read the number that is on the bottom. When you roll a six-sided die, you read the number on top.

Example 1: Determine Probabilities From a Tree Diagram

A spinner is divided into three equal regions as shown. The spinner is spun twice. For each probability you determine, express the answer as a fraction, a decimal, and a percent.

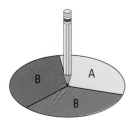

a) What is the probability of spinning A on the first spin?

b) Draw a tree diagram to represent the sample space for both spins.

c) What is the probability of spinning A followed by B: P(A then B)?

d) What is the probability of getting the same letter on both spins: P(A, A) or P(B, B)?

Solution

a) The spinner has three equal regions: A, B, and B. There is only one **favourable outcome**, A, out of the three regions.

$$\text{Probability} = \frac{\text{number of favourable outcomes}}{\text{total number of possible outcomes}}$$

$$P(A) = \frac{1}{3}$$
$$= 0.\overline{3} \qquad \boxed{\text{C}}\ 1\ \boxed{\div}\ 3\ \boxed{=}\ 0.333333333$$

The probability of spinning an A is $\frac{1}{3}$, $0.\overline{3}$, or $33.\overline{3}\%$.

Strategies

Draw a Diagram

b) The following tree diagram displays all possible outcomes.

Spin 1	Spin 2	Outcome
A	A	A, A
A	B	A, B
A	B	A, B
B	A	B, A
B	B	B, B
B	B	B, B
B	A	B, A
B	B	B, B
B	B	B, B

c) The tree diagram shows nine possible outcomes. There are two favourable outcomes (shaded blue).

$$\text{Probability} = \frac{\text{number of favourable outcomes}}{\text{total number of possible outcomes}}$$

$$P(A \text{ then } B) = \frac{2}{9}$$
$$= 0.\overline{2} \qquad \boxed{\text{C}}\ 2\ \boxed{\div}\ 9\ \boxed{=}\ 0.222222222$$

Since $\frac{2}{10}$ is 20%, the answer should be slightly greater than 20%.

The probability of spinning A on the first spin and B on the second spin is $\frac{2}{9}$, $0.\overline{2}$, or $22.\overline{2}\%$.

d) The favourable outcomes (shaded orange) in the tree diagram are (A, A), (B, B), (B, B), (B, B), (B, B). The probability that the same letter will appear on both spins is $\frac{5}{9}$, $0.\overline{5}$, or $55.\overline{5}\%$.

Ellen flips a coin and rolls a
four-sided die numbered 1, 2, 3, and 4.

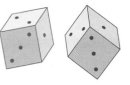

a) What is the sample space? Use a tree
diagram to show how you got your answer.

b) What is $P(H, 4)$?

Example 2: Determine Probabilities From a Table

Two standard six-sided dice are rolled. One die is
blue and the other is red. For each probability you
determine, express the answer as a fraction, a
decimal, and a percent.

a) Create a table to represent the sample space.

b) What is the probability of rolling a sum greater than ten?

c) What is the probability that the number on the red die is one larger
than the number on the blue die?

d) What is the probability that the sum of the two numbers is less
than 11?

Solution

a) The following table represents the sample space. The numbers from
the red die are shown in red and the numbers from the blue die are
shown in blue.

Strategies

Make a Table

		Blue Die					
		1	**2**	**3**	**4**	**5**	**6**
	1	1, 1	1, 2	1, 3	1, 4	1, 5	1, 6
	2	2, 1	2, 2	2, 3	2, 4	2, 5	2, 6
Red Die	**3**	3, 1	3, 2	3, 3	3, 4	3, 5	3, 6
	4	4, 1	4, 2	4, 3	4, 4	4, 5	4, 6
	5	5, 1	5, 2	5, 3	5, 4	5, 5	5, 6
	6	6, 1	6, 2	6, 3	6, 4	6, 5	6, 6

b) The probability of rolling a sum greater than ten can be found by adding the two numbers in each cell of the table. There are three cells in the table with a sum greater than ten. So, there are three favourable outcomes.

		Blue Die					
		1	**2**	**3**	**4**	**5**	**6**
	1	1, 1	1, 2	1, 3	1, 4	1, 5	1, 6
	2	2, 1	2, 2	2, 3	2, 4	2, 5	2, 6
Red	**3**	3, 1	3, 2	3, 3	3, 4	3, 5	3, 6
Die	**4**	4, 1	4, 2	4, 3	4, 4	4, 5	4, 6
	5	5, 1	5, 2	5, 3	5, 4	5, 5	5, 6
	6	6, 1	6, 2	6, 3	6, 4	6, 5	6, 6

$$P(\text{sum} > 10) = \frac{3}{36}$$
$$= 0.08\overline{3}$$

C 3 ÷ 36 = 0.083333333

The probability of a sum greater than ten is $\frac{3}{36}$, $0.08\overline{3}$, or $8.\overline{3}\%$.

c) The probability that the number on the red die will be one larger than the number on the blue die can be found by counting favourable outcomes in the table.

		Blue Die					
		1	**2**	**3**	**4**	**5**	**6**
	1	1, 1	1, 2	1, 3	1, 4	1, 5	1, 6
	2	2, 1	2, 2	2, 3	2, 4	2, 5	2, 6
Red	**3**	3, 1	3, 2	3, 3	3, 4	3, 5	3, 6
Die	**4**	4, 1	4, 2	4, 3	4, 4	4, 5	4, 6
	5	5, 1	5, 2	5, 3	5, 4	5, 5	5, 6
	6	6, 1	6, 2	6, 3	6, 4	6, 5	6, 6

$$P(\text{number on red die is one larger than number on blue die}) = \frac{5}{36}$$
$$= 0.13\overline{8}$$

C 5 ÷ 36 = 0.138888889

The probability that the number on the red die is one larger than the number on the blue die is $\frac{5}{36}$, $0.13\overline{8}$, or $13.\overline{8}\%$.

d) You can find the probability that the sum of the two numbers will be less than 11 by counting favourable outcomes.

				Blue Die			
		1	**2**	**3**	**4**	**5**	**6**
	1	1, 1	1, 2	1, 3	1, 4	1, 5	1, 6
	2	2, 1	2, 2	2, 3	2, 4	2, 5	2, 6
Red Die	**3**	3, 1	3, 2	3, 3	3, 4	3, 5	3, 6
	4	4, 1	4, 2	4, 3	4, 4	4, 5	4, 6
	5	5, 1	5, 2	5, 3	5, 4	5, 5	5, 6
	6	6, 1	6, 2	6, 3	6, 4	6, 5	6, 6

Sometimes it is quicker to count the number of non-favourable outcomes and then subtract this number from the total number of possible outcomes. In this example, a non-favourable outcome is a sum greater than 10. There are three non-favourable outcomes. $36 - 3 = 33$ favourable outcomes.

$$P(\text{sum} < 11) = \frac{33}{36}$$
$$= 0.91\overline{6}$$

[C] 33 [÷] 36 [=] 0.916666666

The probability that the sum of the two numbers is less than 11 is $\frac{33}{36}$, $0.91\overline{6}$, or $91.\overline{6}\%$.

Show You Know

A spinner is divided into four equal regions as shown. You spin this spinner and roll a standard six-sided die once each.

a) Create a table to show the sample space.

b) What is $P(4, 4)$?

c) What is $P(\text{sum} > 5)$?

Key Ideas

- Probability = $\dfrac{\text{number of favourable outcomes}}{\text{total number of possible outcomes}}$

- The probability of both A and B occurring can be expressed as $P(A, B)$.

- The probability of event A occurring followed by event B can be expressed as $P(A \text{ then } B)$.

- You can use tree diagrams and tables to show the sample space for a probability experiment.

- Probabilities can be determined from tree diagrams and tables by direct counting of favourable outcomes and comparing the number of favourable outcomes with the total number of outcomes.

1. John flips a coin and rolls a standard six-sided die.

   a) What does the notation $P(H, 3)$ mean?

   b) Explain how you could use a tree diagram to determine $P(H, 3)$.

2. Monique missed class today. Explain to her how you could use this tree diagram to determine the probability of flipping a coin three times and getting exactly two heads and one tail.

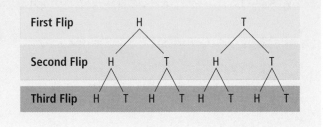

Check Your Understanding

Practise

Express all probabilities as a fraction, a decimal, and a percent.

For help with #3 and #4, refer to Example 1 on pages 411–412.

3. A spinner is divided into three equal regions as shown. Damien flips a coin and spins the spinner once.

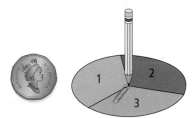

   a) Draw a tree diagram to represent the sample space.

   b) List the sample space.

   c) What is the probability of $P(H, 2)$?

4. The following tree diagram represents the sample space for a probability experiment.

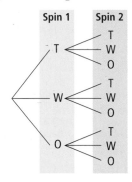

   a) What is the sample space for this experiment?

   b) What is $P(T, W)$?

   c) What is the probability that both letters are identical?

For help with #5 and #6, refer to Example 2 on pages 413–415.

5. Two four-sided dice are each rolled once. Each die is numbered 1, 2, 3, and 4.

   a) Create a table to represent the sample space.

   b) What is the probability that the sum is greater than five?

   c) What is the probability that the same number is the outcome on both dice?

6. Ali draws a card at random from the set of five cards pictured and rolls a standard six-sided die once.

   a) Create a table to show the sample space.

   b) What is the probability that the same number is the outcome on both the card and die?

   c) What is the probability that the sum of the two numbers is even?

   d) What is the probability that the number on the die is equal to or larger than the number on the card?

Apply

7. Lucy is jigging for fish through the ice. She has an equal chance of catching a whitefish, a trout, an arctic char, or losing the fish. If she pulls her hook out twice, what might she catch?

   a) Draw a table showing the results of Lucy's fishing.

   b) What is *P*(whitefish, char) in either order?

   c) What is *P*(char, char)?

   d) What is the probability she will catch nothing at all?

8. The sample space for the flip of a coin and a randomly picked card from five playing cards is (H, 6), (H, 7), (H, 8), (H, 9), (H, 10), (T, 6), (T, 7), (T, 8), (T, 9), and (T, 10).

   a) Draw a tree diagram to show the sample space.

   b) Construct a table to show the sample space.

   c) What is the probability that the result of this experiment includes an even-numbered card?

9. Two babies were born today.

   a) Construct a table to show the possible genders for the two babies.

   b) What is the probability that there is one boy and one girl?

   c) What assumption did you make about the likelihood of a boy or girl being born?

10. A spinner is divided into four equal regions. The spinner is spun twice.

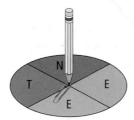

   a) Create a table to show the sample space.

   b) What is the probability of spinning a T and then an E: *P*(T then E)?

   c) What is *P*(E, E)?

   d) What is *P*(same letter on both spins)?

11. Nick and Manny are snowboarding in the Rockies. On one run down the mountain, they decide to flip a coin to choose which of two paths they will take at each of the three places where the ski runs branch. They will go down the left ski run if the coin is a head and the right ski run if the coin is a tail.

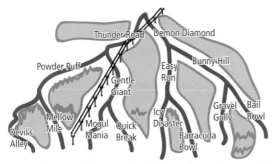

a) What is the probability that they will take Thunder Road?

b) What is the probability that Nick and Manny will finish on a run containing the name *Bowl*?

c) What is the probability that they will take Thunder Road and Quick Break? Explain your answer.

12. A spinner is divided into four equal regions. The spinner is spun three times.

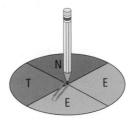

a) Draw a tree diagram to show the sample space.

b) What is the probability of $P(E, E, E)$?

c) What is the probability of spinning three different letters in alphabetical order?

d) What is the probability that one letter appears exactly twice?

13. Alena rolls two standard six-sided dice.

a) What is the probability that the difference between the two numbers is two?

b) What is the probability that the sum is a multiple of three?

c) What is the probability that the product is a multiple of four?

MATH LINK

The stick game uses four flat sticks. One side of each stick is bare and the other side is decorated. The four sticks are tossed in the air and allowed to fall to the ground. The score depends on the number of decorated sides that land facing up.

a) Draw a tree diagram or create a table to show the possible outcomes.

b) At the end of each branch or in each cell, record the total number of decorated sides showing.

c) What is the probability of exactly three sticks landing decorated side up?

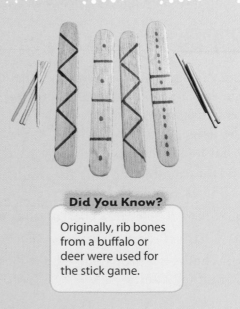

Did You Know?

Originally, rib bones from a buffalo or deer were used for the stick game.

11.2 Outcomes of Independent Events

Lunch Special: $5.95
Choose one appetizer, one main meal, and one drink.
Appetizers: chicken soup or salad
Main meals: cheeseburger, turkey hot dog, or vegetable lasagna
Drinks: milk, chocolate milk, apple juice, or sparkling water

Focus on...

After this lesson, you will be able to...

- ❑ determine the outcomes of two or more independent events
- ❑ verify the total number of possible outcomes using a different strategy

You make many choices every day. Ethan's decision is simple when he looks at today's cafeteria menu. He loves soup, cheeseburgers, and chocolate milk. But Sarah likes all the items listed on the menu. How many choices does she have? A lunch special consists of one appetizer, one main meal, and one drink. How many different lunch specials can you create for her to choose from?

Explore the Math

How do you determine the total number of possible outcomes?

1. Use a method of your choice to show Sarah's possible choices. You may wish to use abbreviations for the choices, such as CB for cheeseburger.

2. Compare your method of showing Sarah's choices to those of other classmates. What other methods were used? Which method is the most efficient? Justify your choice.

3. How many possible outcomes did Sarah have?

Literacy ⊜ Link

The order is not important in a combination. For example, (juice, cookie) is the same combination as (cookie, juice).

4. Determine the number of possible outcomes for each combination given in the table.

Number of Choices for Item 1	Number of Choices for Item 2	Number of Choices for Item 3	Outcomes
2 types of ice-cream cones	3 flavours of ice cream	none	
5 shirts	4 pants	none	
5 models of sports cars	3 different colours	none	
4 models of computers	4 models of monitors	none	
3 models of computers	4 models of monitors	2 models of printers	

5. Study the numbers in each row of the table, looking for any patterns. How could you calculate the total number of outcomes using the number of choices for each item?

Reflect on Your Findings

6. a) Use your conclusion from #5 to calculate the number of different lunch specials available to Sarah. Explain your reasoning. Compare your result with your answer to #3.

b) At another school's cafeteria, Martha has two choices of soup, four choices of main dish, two choices of dessert, and three choices of a beverage. Determine the number of possible lunch specials she can choose from. Show that you are correct by using another method.

c) Suggest a rule for determining the total number of possible outcomes in a series of independent events without creating a tree diagram or table.

Example 1: Determine the Total Number of Outcomes From Two Events

Carrie flips a coin and rolls a standard six-sided die. How many possible outcomes are there?

Solution

Method 1: Create a Table

Coin Flip	Number on Die					
	1	**2**	**3**	**4**	**5**	**6**
H (head)	H, 1	H, 2	H, 3	H, 4	H, 5	H, 6
T (tail)	T, 1	T, 2	T, 3	T, 4	T, 5	T, 6

Strategies

Make a Table

The table shows 12 possible outcomes.

Method 2: Use Multiplication
Number of possible outcomes on die: 6
Number of possible outcomes on coin: 2
Total number of possible outcomes = 6 × 2
                                  = 12

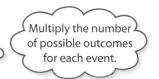

Multiply the number of possible outcomes for each event.

There are 12 possible outcomes.

Show You Know

A café offers four types of sandwiches (egg salad, tuna, ham, or turkey) on one of three types of bread (white, rye, or whole wheat).

a) Use a table to determine the number of sandwich combinations offered by the café.

b) Check your answer using a different strategy.

Example 2: Determine the Total Number of Outcomes From Three or More Events

A coin is flipped, a spinner divided into three equal regions is spun, and a four-sided die numbered 1, 2, 3, and 4 is rolled.

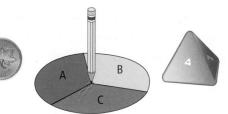

a) How many possible outcomes are there?

b) Why could you not easily represent the sample space for this probability experiment with a table?

Solution

a) *Method 1: Use a Tree Diagram*

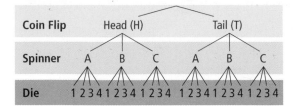

The tree diagram shows 24 possible outcomes.

Method 2: Use Multiplication

Number of possible outcomes for coin flip: 2
Number of possible outcomes for spinner: 3
Number of possible outcomes for die: 4
Total number of possible outcomes = $2 \times 3 \times 4$
$= 24$

There are 24 possible outcomes.

b) A table is ideal for experiments that involve two events, because you can show one event in the columns and one event in the rows. You could not easily represent the sample space for this experiment in a table. For three events, you would need a three-dimensional table or more than one table in order to display all of the outcomes.

Show You Know

A café offers three types of sandwiches (cheese, chicken salad, or tuna) on one of the three types of bread (white, whole wheat, or spelt) with one of two choices of side orders (carrots or chips).

a) How many possible combinations are offered by the café?

b) Check your answer using a different strategy.

Key Ideas

- The total number of possible outcomes can be determined by counting outcomes shown in a table or tree diagram.

Coin Flip	Number on Spinner				
	1	**2**	**3**	**4**	**5**
H (head)	H, 1	H, 2	H, 3	H, 4	H, 5
T (tail)	T, 1	T, 2	T, 3	T, 4	T, 5

Total number of possible outcomes from the table: 10

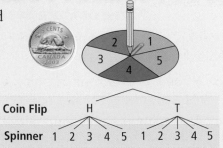

Total number of possible outcomes from the tree diagram: 10

- The total number of possible outcomes can also be determined by multiplying the number of possible outcomes for each event.

Number of possible outcomes from coin flip: 2
Number of possible outcomes from spinner: 5
Total number of possible outcomes $= 2 \times 5$
$$= 10$$

Communicate the Ideas

1. Jasmine wrote a different number from one to ten on each of ten small pieces of paper and put them in a bag. She drew one number from the bag. At the same time, she flipped a coin. Using three different methods, show another student how to determine the total number of possible outcomes.

2. **a)** Three flights travel from Lethbridge to Calgary each morning. Four flights go from Calgary to Edmonton in the afternoon. Show two methods for finding how many different ways you could fly from Lethbridge to Edmonton on a given day.

   b) Which method is more efficient? Explain your thinking.

Check Your Understanding

Practise

For help with #3 and #4, refer to Example 1 on pages 420–421.

3. A bag contains four marbles: one green, one red, one blue, and one yellow. A spinner has three equal sections numbered 1, 2, and 3. A marble is randomly chosen from the bag and the spinner is spun.

   a) Display the sample space in a table.

   b) How many possible outcomes does the table show?

   c) Check your answer to part b) using another strategy.

4. Wei flips a coin and randomly draws a card from the set of six cards shown.

a) Use a method of your choice to determine the total number of possible outcomes.

b) Verify your answer using a different strategy.

For help with #5 and #6, refer to Example 2 on pages 421–422.

5. A coin is flipped, a six-sided die is rolled, and a marble is randomly selected from a bag containing one black, one yellow, and one red marble.

a) Draw a tree diagram to organize the outcomes of these three events.

b) How many possible outcomes are there?

c) Use multiplication to verify the answer to part b).

6. Greta, Joe, and Jared do a probability experiment. Greta flips a coin, Joe spins a spinner divided into four equal regions, and Jared rolls a four-sided die.

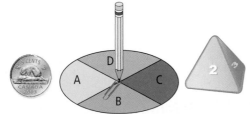

a) Use a tree diagram to organize the outcomes of these three events.

b) How many possible outcomes are there for this probability experiment?

c) Verify the answer to part b) by using multiplication.

7. Tony has four different pairs of pants and six different shirts. How many shirt–pant combinations can he make?

8. The map shows possible routes between three towns. How many possible routes could you take from Leftsville to Right City?

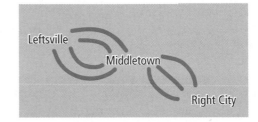

9. The birthday menu at Blue Bird Restaurant gives you one choice from each category:

Drink: four choices
Meal: five choices
Dessert: three choices

How many different combinations are possible?

10. Michaela has a nickel, a dime, and a loonie in her left jacket pocket. She has a penny and a quarter in her right pocket. She randomly picks one coin from each pocket.

a) How many combinations of coins could she get?

b) Use a second method to verify your answer to part a).

c) What is the largest sum possible for these two coins?

d) What is the smallest possible sum?

11. Make up a question that would give the following number of possible outcomes:
$2 \times 4 \times 5 = 40$

12. An ice-cream store has 31 flavours of ice cream and three types of cones (waffle, sugar, and plain).

    a) Determine the number of possible single-scoop ice-cream cones.

    b) How many two-scoop ice-cream cones are possible if waffle–chocolate–strawberry is considered different from waffle–strawberry–chocolate? Hint: You could have two scoops of the same flavour if you desired.

    c) How many two-scoop cones are possible if both flavours of ice cream must be different? Explain your reasoning.

13. A set meal consists of a choice of drink, main dish, and dessert. There are four different desserts, 36 possible meals in total, and more than one choice in each category. Determine the possible number of drink and main dish choices. Explain your reasoning.

14. Alikut is planning to make a beaded yoke for her new parka. She has five colours of beads: red, blue, black, white, and yellow. She wants to use only six shapes of beads: square, circle, star, triangle, rectangle, and heart. Alikut plans to use only one colour of bead in each shape.

    a) How many colour–shape combinations could she use?

    b) Use a second method to verify your answer to part a).

    c) Suppose Alikut decides to use two colours of beads in each shape. How many colour–shape combinations could she use now?

15. Determine the number of four-digit numbers that contain only the digits 1, 2, 3, and 4. A digit can be repeated. Two valid numbers are 1423 and 4442.

16. How many car license plates can be made if the first three characters are letters and the last three characters are digits from 2 through 9 inclusive?

MATH LINK

In the stick game, each stick can land in one of two ways—decorated or plain side up.

a) Use a different method than you used in section 11.1 to confirm the total number of possible outcomes for a game with four sticks.

b) Sometimes the game uses different numbers of sticks. What is the total number of possible outcomes for three sticks? five sticks?

c) If there are 128 possible outcomes, how many sticks are being used?

Determining Probabilities Using Fractions

Focus on...

After this lesson, you will be able to...

❑ solve probability problems

❑ verify your answers using a different method

Erv and his friend Al have been chosen as contestants in a new TV reality program called Wheel of Thrills. Five contestants start the game. A wheel is divided into five equal sectors and labelled with each person's name. The wheel is spun once to determine who will be the potential winner for the 30-minute show. Once a person is selected, a standard six-sided die is rolled to determine what kind of thrill he or she will experience.

Erv and Al both love to swim. How likely do you think it is that one of these boys will be chosen and will get to swim with dolphins or scuba-dive on a coral reef?

How can you determine probabilities using fractions?

Materials
• ruler
• red and yellow pencils

1. a) Copy the table into your notebook.

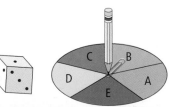

		Number on Die					
		1	**2**	**3**	**4**	**5**	**6**
Name of Contestant	**Al**						
	Beatrice						
	Cherie						
	Denise						
	Erv						

b) Use a red pencil to shade the rows that correspond to the spinner landing on Al or Erv's name. What fraction of the five rows did you shade?

c) Use a yellow pencil to shade the columns that correspond to the die roll showing swimming with dolphins or scuba-diving on a coral reef. What fraction of the six columns did you shade?

2. a) What fraction of the total number of cells in the table are shaded both red and yellow? Do not write this fraction in lowest terms.

b) How could you use the fractions from #1 to determine the fraction of the total number of cells that are shaded both red and yellow?

c) What probability does this fraction represent?

Reflect on Your Findings

3. a) How could you use multiplication to calculate the total number of possible outcomes for this experiment?

b) How is the total number of possible outcomes related to your answer to #2c)?

c) How is the number of outcomes that thrill Al or Erv related to your answer to #2c)?

d) How can you use the probabilities of single events to determine the probability of two independent events happening?

Example 1: Calculating Probabilities Using a Table and Multiplication

Mackenzie spins a spinner divided into five equal regions and rolls a four-sided die once each.

a) Construct a table to represent the sample space. How many possible outcomes are there?

b) From the table, what is P(blue, 2) expressed as a fraction?

c) Use multiplication to determine P(blue, 2).

d) From the table, what is P(red or blue, < 4) expressed as a fraction. ○

e) Use the method from part c) to calculate P(red or blue , < 4).

> The < symbol means *less than*. In part d), rolling less than a four means rolling a one, two, or three.

Solution

Strategies

Make a Table

a)

Spinner	Four-Sided Die			
	1	**2**	**3**	**4**
Blue	blue, 1	blue, 2	blue, 3	blue, 4
Red	red, 1	red, 2	red, 3	red, 4
Green	green, 1	green, 2	green, 3	green, 4
Yellow	yellow, 1	yellow, 2	yellow, 3	yellow, 4
Purple	purple, 1	purple, 2	purple, 3	purple, 4

Number of possible outcomes: 20

b) Label the Blue row in blue. Shade the column labelled 2. Identify the part of the table that is both labelled in blue and shaded.

Spinner	Four-Sided Die			
	1	**2**	**3**	**4**
Blue	blue, 1	blue, 2	blue, 3	blue, 4
Red	red, 1	red, 2	red, 3	red, 4
Green	green, 1	green, 2	green, 3	green, 4
Yellow	yellow, 1	yellow, 2	yellow, 3	yellow, 4
Purple	purple, 1	purple, 2	purple, 3	purple, 4

The table shows one favourable outcome.

$$P(\text{blue, 2}) = \frac{1}{20}$$

Multiply the probabilities of the single events to determine the probability of the two independent events happening.

c) The probability of spinning blue is $\frac{1}{5}$. The probability of rolling a 2 is $\frac{1}{4}$.

$$P(\text{blue, 2}) = \frac{1}{5} \times \frac{1}{4}$$
$$= \frac{1}{20}$$

d) Colour your table to determine the probability of landing on red or blue and rolling 1, 2, or 3.

Spinner	Four-Sided Die			
	1	**2**	**3**	**4**
Blue	blue, 1	blue, 2	blue, 3	blue, 4
Red	red, 1	red, 2	red, 3	red, 4
Green	green, 1	green, 2	green, 3	green, 4
Yellow	yellow, 1	yellow, 2	yellow, 3	yellow, 4
Purple	purple, 1	purple, 2	purple, 3	purple, 4

The table shows six favourable outcomes.

$$P(\text{red or blue}, < 4) = \frac{6}{20}$$

e) The probability of spinning red or blue is $\frac{2}{5}$.

The probability of rolling a 1, 2, or 3 is $\frac{3}{4}$.

$$P(\text{red or blue}, < 4) = \frac{2}{5} \times \frac{3}{4}$$

$$= \frac{6}{20}$$

Example 2: Calculating Probabilities Using a Tree Diagram and Multiplication

Jason rolls a standard six-sided die and Rachel spins a spinner with three equal sections. What is the probability of rolling an even number and spinning a B? Verify your answer using another method.

Solution

For the die: $P(\text{even number}) = \frac{3}{6}$

For the spinner: $P(B) = \frac{1}{3}$

$$P(\text{even number}, B) = P(\text{even number}) \times P(B)$$

$$= \frac{3}{6} \times \frac{1}{3}$$

$$= \frac{3}{18}$$

Use a tree diagram to verify your answer.

The tree diagram shows that there are 18 possible outcomes and three favourable outcomes.

$$P(\text{even number}, B) = \frac{3}{18}$$

The tree diagram agrees with the result of the multiplication. The probability of rolling an even number and spinning a B is $\frac{3}{18}$ or $\frac{1}{6}$.

Die	Spinner	Outcome
1	A	1, A
	B	1, B
	C	1, C
2	A	2, A
	B	2, B
	C	2, C
3	A	3, A
	B	3, B
	C	3, C
4	A	4, A
	B	4, B
	C	4, C
5	A	5, A
	B	5, B
	C	5, C
6	A	6, A
	B	6, B
	C	6, C

Show You Know

A blue, standard six-sided die and a red, four-sided die numbered 1, 2, 3, and 4 are each rolled once. Determine the following probabilities, and then verify your calculations using a second method.

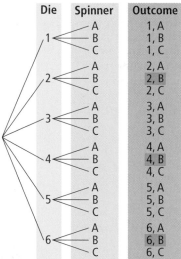

a) $P(\text{blue} = 4, \text{red} = 4)$ **b)** $P(\text{blue} < 4, \text{red} < 4)$

c) $P(\text{blue} = 4, \text{red} < 4)$

Example 3: Simulations

Gina is planning the time needed to get to her soccer game. There are two traffic lights between her house and the soccer field. These lights are red (or yellow) 60% of the time. Gina wonders how likely it is that both lights will be red on her way to the game.

Model this situation by spinning a spinner divided into five equal regions twice. The table shows the results for ten trials.

Trial	Experimental Results		
	First Light (Green or Red)	Second Light (Red or Green)	Both Lights Red?
1	R	R	yes
2	G	G	no
3	R	G	no
4	G	R	no
5	R	R	yes
6	R	G	no
7	R	R	yes
8	G	G	no
9	G	R	no
10	G	G	no

a) What is the experimental probability that both lights are red?

b) What is the theoretical probability that both lights are red?

c) Compare the experimental probability with the theoretical probability. How could Gina improve the accuracy of the experimental probability?

Solution

a) From the table, there are three favourable outcomes.

$$P(\text{both lights red}) = \frac{3}{10}$$
$$= 0.3$$

The experimental probability that both lights are red is $\frac{3}{10}$, 0.3, or 30%.

b) The probability that one traffic light is red is 60% or $\frac{3}{5}$.

$$P(\text{both lights red}) = \frac{3}{5} \times \frac{3}{5}$$
$$= \frac{9}{25}$$
$$= 0.36$$

The theoretical probability that both lights are red is $\frac{9}{25}$, 0.36, or 36%.

c) The experimental probability is lower than the theoretical probability. If Gina performed more trials of the experiment, the two probabilities would likely be closer in value.

Andrew flips two coins to simulate the genders of the children in families with two children. He decides that heads indicates a girl and tails indicates a boy. The following chart shows his results for 100 simulations. Express your answers to parts a) and b) as a decimal and a percent.

Coin Outcomes	HH	HT	TH	TT
Child Outcomes	two girls	girl, boy	boy, girl	two boys
Number of Results	27	24	27	22

a) What is Andrew's experimental probability of getting two boys?

b) What is the theoretical probability of getting two boys? Use multiplication to determine your answer.

b) Compare the experimental probability with the theoretical probability. Why are the two values different?

Key Ideas

• For probability experiments involving two or more independent events, the probability can be found by multiplying the probabilities of success for each single event.

A spinner with three equal regions labelled 1, 2, and 3 is spun and a coin is flipped. What is the probability of spinning a 2 and flipping tails?

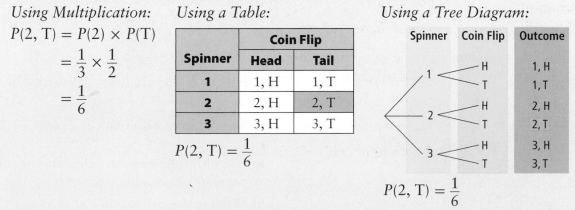

Using Multiplication:
$$P(2, T) = P(2) \times P(T)$$
$$= \frac{1}{3} \times \frac{1}{2}$$
$$= \frac{1}{6}$$

Using a Table:

	Coin Flip	
Spinner	Head	Tail
1	1, H	1, T
2	2, H	2, T
3	3, H	3, T

$$P(2, T) = \frac{1}{6}$$

Using a Tree Diagram:

Spinner	Coin Flip	Outcome
1	H	1, H
	T	1, T
2	H	2, H
	T	2, T
3	H	3, H
	T	3, T

$$P(2, T) = \frac{1}{6}$$

• A simulation is an experiment that can be used to model a real situation. The results of a simulation are called experimental results.

1. A bag contains three red marbles and two black marbles. A second bag contains two pennies and four dimes. A marble and a coin are drawn from each bag at random. Explain to a classmate who missed the lesson how to calculate P(red, penny) using multiplication.

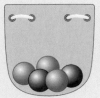

2. Catherine gives the following explanation for how to calculate P(black, dime). She says that there are two choices for marbles (red and black) and two choices for coins (pennies and dimes).

$$P(\text{black, dime}) = \frac{1}{2} \times \frac{1}{2}$$
$$= \frac{1}{4}$$

What mistake did Catherine make?

3. Explain the difference between experimental probability and theoretical probability.

Check Your Understanding

Practise

Express all probabilities as fractions in lowest terms unless otherwise specified.

For help with #4 and #5, refer to Example 1 on pages 427–429.

4. Brittany spins a spinner divided into four equal regions and rolls a standard die once.

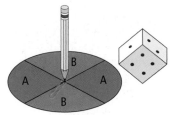

   a) Construct a table to organize the sample space.

   b) What is the probability of spinning an A and rolling a two?

   c) Use a second method to determine P(A, 2).

5. Joe takes one marble from the first bag and Ron takes one marble from the second bag.

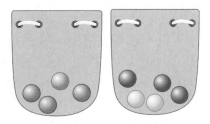

   a) Use multiplication to calculate the total number of possible outcomes.

   b) What is the probability of P(blue, red)? Show two different strategies for determining the answer.

For help with #6 and #7 refer to Example 2 on page 429.

6. A coin is flipped twice.

   a) What is the probability that a head is flipped on the first flip, *P*(H)?

   b) What is the probability that a head is flipped on both flips, *P*(H, H)?

   c) Check both answers by using another method.

7. Levi rolls two dice, a six-sided one numbered from 1 to 6 and a four-sided one labelled A, B, C, and D.

   a) Calculate *P*(2, B).

   b) Calculate *P*(even number, consonant).

   c) Check your answers by using another method.

For help with #8 and #9 refer to Example 3 on pages 430–431.

8. Students in grade 8 are each given one flower seed from a package of mixed flower seeds. The package contains an equal number of daisy, marigold, poppy, and snapdragon seeds. The students roll a four-sided die to find out where each will plant the seed. On the die, 1 means in the front garden at the school, 2 means by the back fence, 3 means in the garden of the senior citizens' home near the school, and 4 means in a flower pot to take home.

   a) Design a simulation to find the probability that Bianca will plant a marigold in a flower pot. Perform ten trials of the simulation. What is the experimental probability of *P*(marigold, flower pot)?

   b) Use multiplication to determine the theoretical probability of *P*(marigold, flower pot).

   c) Compare your experimental probability with your theoretical probability.

9. Boxes of Oatie Smacks cereal contain a toy racing car in one of five colours: green, purple, black, blue, and red. The likelihood of each colour car is the same, 20%. Trevor uses a five-section spinner to simulate the minimum number of boxes of cereal he will have to buy to make sure he gets at least one car of each colour. The tally chart shows his results.

Green	Purple	Black	Blue	Red

   a) Which car colour was spun last? How do you know?

   b) What is the experimental probability of the spinner landing on blue? Express your answer as a decimal.

   c) What is the theoretical probability of the spinner landing on blue? Express your answer as a decimal.

   d) What is the theoretical probability of getting two blue cars in two consecutive boxes?

Apply

10. The weather forecaster predicts that the chance of rain today is 75% in Victoria and 20% in Calgary. What is the probability that it will rain in both cities today?

11. What is *P*(red, blue) if one marble is randomly selected from each bag? Express the answer as a fraction, a decimal, and a percent.

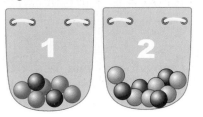

12. The following tree diagram represents the outcomes when two spinners are each spun once.

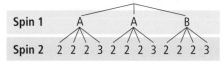

a) Draw a picture of both spinners.

b) What is the probability that the first spinner will land on an A?

c) What is the probability that the second spinner will land on two?

13. The following diagram shows five water pumping stations between Lowtown and Highville. Water is pumped from Lowtown to Highville through pipes that are connected to the pumping stations as illustrated. With the pumps getting old, the likelihood that a specific pumping station is working at any given time is $\frac{2}{3}$.

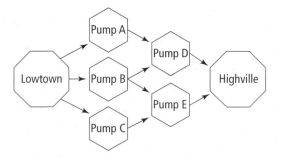

a) In how many different pathways can water be transported from Lowtown to Highville?

b) How can you use a standard six-sided die to simulate whether a specific pumping station is working?

c) From the data collected in the table below and the diagram of pumping stations, determine the experimental probability that at least one pathway is available to carry water between the two towns.

Trial #	Pump A	Pump B	Pump C	Pump D	Pump E
1	working	no	working	working	no
2	working	working	working	working	no
3	no	working	no	no	working
4	working	working	no	no	no
5	no	no	working	working	no
6	working	working	no	working	working
7	working	no	working	no	working
8	no	no	no	working	working
9	working	working	working	no	working
10	no	working	no	working	no

Extend

14. It is Random Menu night at the Guess Grill restaurant. You do not order your own meal! For $3.99 you are given one of four possible appetizers and one of six possible main courses. Jeremy figures that he would be happy with three of the appetizers and three of the main courses.

a) What is the probability that Jeremy will be happy with both his appetizer and main course?

b) What is the probability that he will be unhappy with both his appetizer and main course?

c) Explain why the answers to parts a) and b) do not add to one.

15. The next two batters for the Okotoks Wanderers have batting averages of .313 and .289, respectively. For the first batter, this means that for every 1000 at-bats in the past, he hit the ball and got on base 313 times.

   a) What is the probability that both players will hit a fair ball and get on base? Express your answer as a decimal to the nearest thousandth.

   b) What is the probability that the first player gets a hit and the second player does not? Express your answer as a decimal to the nearest thousandth.

16. From a deck of 52 playing cards, a card is drawn at random. Then the card is placed back in the deck, the deck is shuffled, and a second card is drawn at random. Determine the following probabilities and express each one as a decimal to the nearest thousandth. Consider an ace to be the number one.

   a) $P(4, 7)$?

   b) $P(4, \text{not } 4)$?

   c) $P(4, \text{number less than } 4)$?

17. A probability experiment consists of three independent events, A, B, and C. Two of these events have the probabilities $P(A) = \frac{1}{2}$ and $P(B) = \frac{3}{7}$. The probability of all three events occurring is $\frac{9}{70}$. What is the probability of event C, $P(C)$? Express your answer as a fraction and explain your reasoning.

WWW **Web Link**

Computers are often used to conduct simulations. To try an on-line simulation, go to www.mathlinks8.ca and follow the links.

MATH LINK

   a) The four sticks are tossed. Two of them land on the table with the decorated side up. The other two fall under the table. What is the theoretical probability that both sticks under the table are decorated side up?

   b) What if three sticks fall under the table? What is the theoretical probability that all three sticks land decorated side up?

   c) Set up a simulation to show the experimental probability for part b).

Key Words

For #1 to #5, unscramble the letters for each puzzle. Use the clues to help you solve the puzzles.

1. E N I T P D E N E D N T S V E E N

   results for which the outcome of one event has no effect on the outcome of another event (two words)

2. M E L A P S P E A C S

   represents all possible outcomes of a probability experiment (two words)

3. O N M I S U L I A T

   a real situation modelled using an experiment

4. Y P O R B T L I B I A

   the chance of an event occuring

5. V F A B E A L O U R C M O E T U O

   a successful result in a probability experiment (two words)

11.1 Determining Probabilities Using Tree Diagrams and Tables, pages 410–418

6. Two standard six-sided dice are rolled.

   a) Organize the sample space in a table.

   b) What is the probability that the sum of the two numbers is ten?

   c) What is the probability that the two numbers are identical?

   d) What is the probability that the product of the two numbers is a multiple of ten?

7. A coin is flipped three times.

   a) Display the sample space in a tree diagram.

   b) What is the probability that all three flips result in heads?

   c) What is the probability of flipping exactly two heads and one tail in any order?

8. One card is chosen at random from a set consisting of the three to the nine of clubs. One standard six-sided die is rolled.

   a) Show the sample space in a tree diagram or table.

   b) What is the probability that the number on the card matches the number on the die?

   c) What is the probability that the number on the card is larger than the number on the die?

   d) What is the probability that both numbers are even?

11.2 Outcomes of Independent Events, pages 419–425

9. A coin is flipped and the spinner is spun once.

   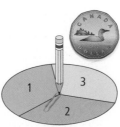

   a) List all possible outcomes.

   b) What is the total number of possible outcomes?

   c) How can you find the answer to part b) using multiplication?

10. Janessa wins a contest on the radio. Her prize is her choice of one item from each category:
  • six T-shirts
  • four CDs
  • tickets to two upcoming concerts

How many combinations of choices does she have?

11. A travel company is selling a get-away ski package to Whistler that includes a choice of three hotels, ski passes to either Blackcomb or Whistler, and dinner at one of several restaurants. The newsprint advertisement is smudged where the number of restaurants is listed. However, the ad boasts that there are 42 different combinations with this package. How many restaurants are listed in the ad? Explain your reasoning.

11.3 Determining Probabilities Using Fractions, pages 426–435

12. A bag contains three red marbles and two black marbles. A box contains four green marbles and one yellow marble. One marble each is selected randomly from the bag and the box.

  a) What is P(red marble)?
  b) What is P(green marble)?
  c) What is P(red marble, green marble)?

13. The probabilities of snow today in Abbotsford, Lethbridge, and Estevan are:
$P(A) = 0.1$
$P(L) = 0.4$
$P(E) = 0.5$
Find the following probabilities and express your answers in decimal form.
  a) $P(A, E)$
  b) $P(A, L, E)$
  c) Explain what you calculated in part b).

14. A standard six-sided die is rolled three times. Use multiplication to determine the probability that a one or two appears on the first roll, a three appears on the second roll, and an odd number appears on the third roll.

15. A spinner is divided into four equal regions as shown. The spinner is spun 20 times and the results are shown in a tally chart.

Red	Purple	Green	Blue
IIII	HHII	HHI III	III

  a) What is the theoretical probability of the spinner landing on blue on a single spin? Express your answer as a percent.
  b) From the tally chart, what is the experimental probability of the spinner landing on blue? Express your answer as a percent.
  c) Give a possible explanation for why the answers to parts a) and b) are not the same.
  d) If the spinner was spun 1000 times instead of 20 times, would you expect the experimental probability for the spinner landing on blue to change? If so, how?

For #1 to #3, choose the best answer.

Two four-sided dice (one red, one blue) are rolled. The following table represents the sample space for the possible outcomes. Use the table to answer #1 to #3.

Blue Four-Sided Die	Red Four-Sided Die			
	1	2	3	4
1	1, 1	1, 2	1, 3	1, 4
2	2, 1	2, 2	2, 3	2, 4
3	3, 1	3, 2	3, 3	3, 4
4	4, 1	4, 2	4, 3	4, 4

1. What is the probability that the same number appears on each die?

   A $\frac{1}{4}$ B $\frac{1}{5}$ C $\frac{2}{16}$ D $\frac{1}{16}$

2. What is the probability that the sum of the two dice is less than four?

   A $\frac{13}{16}$ B $\frac{1}{2}$ C $\frac{1}{4}$ D $\frac{3}{16}$

3. What is the probability that neither die has a two showing?

   A $\frac{9}{16}$ B $\frac{1}{2}$ C $\frac{7}{16}$ D $\frac{1}{4}$

A coin is flipped once. A spinner, divided into six equal regions, is spun once. Use the diagram to help complete the statements in #4 and #5.

4. The total number of possible outcomes is ■.

5. An expression that calculates the probability that the coin lands heads up and the spinner stops on a vowel is ■ × ■.

Short Answer

6. Determine the total number of possibilities if one item is selected from each of the categories on the menu shown.

CAFETERIA
Drink choices: milk
apple juice
Meal choices: burger
pizza
chicken strips
Dessert: ice cream
chocolate cake
fresh fruit

7. A marble is selected randomly from a bag containing five orange marbles and three purple marbles. A jellybean is randomly chosen from a jar containing two red jellybeans and three blue jellybeans.

   a) What is the probability of selecting a red jellybean? Express your answer as a fraction and a percent.

   b) What is the probability of selecting an orange marble and a blue jellybean? Express your answer as a fraction and a decimal.

8. David decides to survey the next 30 people who walk into the library at school to see who they are going to vote for in the school elections next week. His results are summarized in the following table. What is the experimental probability that a student will vote for Maria in the election? Express your answer as a decimal and a percent.

Candidates	Jesse	Maria	Marcus	Angela
Votes	11	7	4	8

Extended Response

9. Jamie is going camping this weekend. She is hoping that it does not rain either Saturday or Sunday. The forecast calls for a 70% chance of rain on Saturday and a 50% chance of rain on Sunday.

   a) What is the probability that it will rain both days?

   b) What is the probability that no rain will fall for the entire weekend?

   c) Jamie has ten cards, each labelled with a number from one to ten. Explain how she could perform a simulation to see if it will rain on both days.

   d) She does not know whether to perform 10 trials or 100 trials. Explain which number of trials is likely to be more accurate.

10. Explain how you could use a coin to determine the experimental probability that a family with four children has four girls. Determine the theoretical probability of four girls. Describe any assumptions that you make.

WRAP IT UP!

- With a partner, make a set of four sticks for a stick game. Use tongue depressors or something similar; make sure each stick has two flat surfaces.
- Decorate one side of each of the four sticks.
- Taking turns, each person holds the sticks in one hand and lets them fall to the ground. Record your experimental results.
- The scoring is shown in the table. Keep a running score.

All four decorated sides up	5 points
Three up and one down	2 points
Two up and two down	1 point
One up and three down	2 points
All four down	5 points

- The game can finish after a certain length of time, or when someone reaches a certain score (for example, 50).

a) Determine the theoretical probability for each of the five possible outcomes. You may wish to draw the sample space as a tree diagram.

b) Is the scoring system fair? Explain your reasoning.

c) How close is the scoring system to your theoretical results?

d) How close are your experimental results to your theoretical results?

Math Games

Play Fair!

Each player in a fair game has an equal probability of winning. The following games are based on rolling two dice and using the results in different ways. Some of the ways may be fair but others may not be.

Materials
- 2 standard six-sided dice of different colours per pair of students
- coin per pair of students

1. Play this version of the game with a partner. The rules are:
   - Each player rolls one die to decide who will play first. If there is a tie, roll again.
   - In each turn, roll two dice and add the values.
   - Use a coin toss to decide who is Player A and who is Player B. Player A scores a point for each even total. Player B scores a point for each odd total.
   - Record the points scored by each player.
   - The first player to reach ten points is the winner.

2. Is the game in #1 fair? Explain.

3. Repeat the game in #1. This time, Player A scores a point for each total of seven or less. Player B scores a point for each total of eight or more.
   a) Is this game fair? Explain.
   b) If the game is not fair, suggest a way to modify it to make it fair.

4. Suppose you repeat the game in #1, but this time you multiply the values instead of adding them. Player A scores a point for each even product. Player B scores a point for each odd product. Is this game fair? Explain.

5. Suppose you repeat the game in #1, but this time you determine the difference in the results from the two dice instead of the sum. Player A scores a point for each difference of zero, two, or four. Player B scores a point for each difference of one, three, or five.
   a) Is this game fair? Explain.
   b) Would the game be fair if Player A scored a point for each difference of zero, one, or two, and Player B scored a point for each difference of three, four, or five? Explain.

Challenge in Real Life

Treasure Hunt

Materials
• centimetre grid paper
• coloured pencils
• red marker

A group of Canadian treasure hunters found a map on a sunken ship. The map shows treasure scattered on Resolution Island in an area that is 10 km by 10 km. It is not clear exactly where the treasure is.

You be the treasure hunter. What are your chances of finding treasure?

1. a) On a 10 by 10 grid, randomly colour the squares using the ratio yellow : white : brown = 2 : 5 : 3

   b) Yellow represents treasure. White represents ice. Brown represents sand. What is the theoretical probability of each colour on the grid? Express each answer as a percent.

2. a) Use a red marker to divide the 10 by 10 grid into four sections as outlined below:
   • Draw a vertical line that divides the vertical distance into $\frac{3}{10}$ and $\frac{7}{10}$.
   • Draw a horizontal line that divides the horizontal distance into $\frac{2}{5}$ and $\frac{3}{5}$.
   • Label the largest zone as Zone 1, the second-largest zone as Zone 2, the third-largest zone as Zone 3, and the smallest zone as Zone 4.

   b) What is the theoretical probability of choosing each zone in the grid? Express each answer as a fraction, a decimal, and a percent.

   c) Using your answers from #1b) and #2b) and the following formula, what is the theoretical probability of each colour appearing in each zone? Justify your thinking.

$$\begin{array}{ccc} \text{theoretical probability} \\ \text{of each colour in each zone} \end{array} = \begin{array}{c} \text{theoretical probability} \\ \text{of each colour on the grid} \end{array} \times \begin{array}{c} \text{theoretical probability} \\ \text{of each zone} \end{array}$$

3. a) You have time to search only two zones. Using the theoretical probability, which two zones will you search? Explain why.

   b) How might your answer to part a) change if you used an experiment to decide what zones to search? Justify your response.

12

Tessellations

The Dutch artist M.C. Escher was fascinated by tiling patterns, also called tessellations. Escher made these tiling patterns by starting with a basic shape and then transforming the shape using translations, rotations, and reflections. These tessellations were very complex and many of them looked like animals and humans.

Escher created this tessellation by translating a parallelogram with griffins drawn on it. A griffin (or gryphon) is a legendary creature with the body of a lion and the head and wings of an eagle. Since the lion was considered the "king of beasts" and the eagle the "king of the air," the griffin was thought to be an especially powerful and majestic creature.

In this chapter, you will learn how to describe and create tessellations.

What You Will Learn

☐ to describe and create tessellations
☐ to explore and describe tessellations in the environment

Key Words

- plane
- tiling pattern
- tessellation
- tiling the plane
- transformation

Literacy Link

A Frayer model can help you understand new terms. Copy the following Frayer model in your math journal or notebook. Make it large enough to write in each box. Record the following information for each new word.

- Write the term in the middle.
- Define the term in the first box. The glossary on pages 517–521 may help you.
- Write some facts in the second box.
- Give some examples in the third box.
- Give some non-examples in the fourth box.

Definition	Facts
Examples	Non-examples

Tessellation

Making the Foldable

Materials

- 11 by 17 sheet of paper
- three sheets of 0.5-cm grid paper
- scissors
- stapler
- glue (optional)

Step 1

Fold an 11 × 17 sheet of paper in half lengthwise and pinch the centre to show the midpoint.

Step 2

Fold the outside edges toward the centre.

Step 3

Fold the paper in half again the other way.

Step 4

Cut along the crease to create four doors.

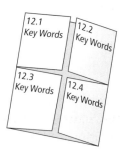

Step 5

Label each door as shown.

> 12.1 Key Words   12.2 Key Words
> 12.3 Key Words   12.4 Key Words

Step 6

Cut pieces of 0.5-cm grid paper the size of each door flap and glue or staple them on the inside of each flap.

Step 7

Cut a full sheet of 0.5-cm grid paper in half. Label the pieces as shown. Place the pieces in the middle section behind the doors you labelled in Step 5.

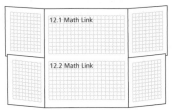

> 12.1 Math Link
> 12.2 Math Link

Step 8

Cut a full sheet of blank notebook paper in half. Staple each piece on top of the Math Link grids for 12.1 and 12.2, as shown.

> Math Link Introduction

Step 9

Cut another sheet of 0.5-cm grid paper in half horizontally. Staple these to the back of the Foldable and label them as shown.

> 12.3 Math Link
> 12.4 Math Link

Using the Foldable

As you work through each section of Chapter 12, list and define the Key Words on the outside of the flap for each section. Place and label examples on the inside of the flap for each section.

Record your answers to the Math Link introduction on page 445 on the blank sheets inside the Foldable. Use the grids inside the Foldable and on the back to keep track of the designs you develop for each Math Link during the chapter.

In the space underneath each Math Link grid, make notes under the heading What I Need to Work On. Check off each item as you deal with it.

MATH LINK

Mosaic Designs

Mosaics can be used to decorate shelves, table tops, mirrors, floors, walls, and other objects. In this chapter, you will learn how to design and make your own mosaic.

1. Irregularly shaped triangular pieces can be used to create mosaics. What makes a triangle *irregular* in shape?

2. **a)** If triangular tiles are congruent, they can be used to make a mosaic. How can you tell if the triangular tiles labelled ABC and XYZ are congruent or not? Explain your reasoning.

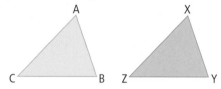

   b) Copy the shape of one of the triangles onto a piece of cardboard or construction paper. Cut out the triangle. Create a design on half of a blank sheet of paper by repeatedly tracing the triangle. Make sure that the sheet of paper is covered and there are no spaces left between the triangles.

   c) Colour your design.

Did You Know?

A tile used to make a mosaic is called a *tessera*. This word comes from the ancient Greek word *tessares*, which means *four*. The tiles used to make ancient mosaics had four corners.

3. **a)** Regular polygons can also be used to create interesting mosaics. What characteristics make a polygon *regular*?

   b) Copy the shape of this regular hexagon onto a piece of cardboard or construction paper. Cut out the hexagon. Create a new design using the same process you used for the irregular triangles in #2b).

   c) Write a brief paragraph explaining what geometric transformations you used to create your design in part b) of this question. For example, did you use translations, rotations, or reflections to make your design? Did you use a combination of transformations? If so, what steps did you follow to create your design?

Exploring Tessellations With Regular and Irregular Polygons

Focus on...

After this lesson, you will be able to...

- ❏ identify regular and irregular polygons that can be used to create tessellations
- ❏ describe why certain regular and irregular polygons can be used to tessellate the plane
- ❏ create simple tessellating patterns using polygons

Mosaics are often made of repeating patterns of tiles. What patterns do you see in the design?

Many mosaic tile designs are made from shapes that cover the area, or the plane, without overlapping or leaving gaps. These patterns are called tiling patterns or tessellations. Covering the plane in this way is called tiling the plane.

tiling pattern

- a pattern that covers an area or plane without overlapping or leaving gaps
- also called a **tessellation**

tiling the plane

- using repeated congruent shapes to cover an area without leaving gaps or overlapping
- also called tessellating the plane

Explore the Math

Which shapes can you use to tile or tessellate the plane?

1. Copy the following table into your notebook.

Shape	Regular or Irregular Polygon?	Measure of Each Interior Angle	*Prediction:* Will the shape tile the plane?	*Result:* Does the shape tile the plane?
Equilateral triangle				
Isosceles triangle				
Square				
Regular pentagon				
Regular hexagon				
Regular octagon				
Irregular quadrilateral				
Irregular pentagon				
Irregular hexagon				

2. a) Select an equilateral triangle block. Is this a regular or irregular polygon? Record your answer in the table.

   b) Measure each interior angle and record your measurements in the table.

   c) Predict whether the shape will tile the plane. Record your prediction in the table.

3. Trace the outline of the equilateral triangle. Move the triangle to a new position, so that the two triangles share a common side. Trace the outline of the triangle again. Continue to see if the shape tiles the plane. Record your conclusion in the table.

Materials
- set of pattern blocks, or cardboard cutouts of pattern block shapes
- protractor
- cardboard cutouts of an isosceles triangle, a regular pentagon, and a regular octagon
- cardboard
- scissors
- ruler

4. Use the same method to find out if the isosceles triangle, square, regular pentagon, regular hexagon, and regular octagon tile the plane. Record your results in the table.

penta means 5
hexa means 6
octa means 8

5. Cut out the shape of an irregular quadrilateral.

   a) Predict whether the shape will tile the plane.

   b) Try to tile the plane with the shape. Record your results in the table.

   c) Repeat steps 5a) and 5b) using an irregular pentagon and an irregular hexagon of your own design.

Reflect on Your Findings

6. a) What regular shapes tile the plane? Explain why some regular shapes tile the plane but others do not. Hint: Look at the interior angle measures. Is there a pattern?

   b) Explain why some irregular shapes tile the plane but others do not.

Literacy Link

The term *plane* means a two-dimensional flat surface that extends in all directions.

Example: Identify Shapes That Tessellate the Plane

Do these polygons tessellate the plane? Explain why or why not.

a)

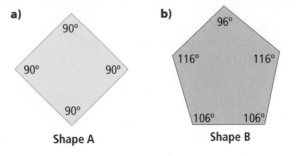

Shape A

b)

Shape B

Solution

a) Arrange the squares along a common side. The rotated squares do not overlap or leave gaps when you try to form them into a tessellation. Shape A can be used to tessellate the plane.

Check:
Each of the interior angles where the vertices of the polygons meet is 90°. The sum of the four angles is 90° + 90° + 90° + 90° = 360°. This is equal to a full turn. The shape can be used to tessellate the plane.

b) Arrange the pentagons along a common side. The irregular pentagons overlap or leave gaps when you try to form them into a tessellation. Shape B cannot be used to tessellate the plane.

What other possible arrangements of the pentagons can you find? Do they overlap or leave gaps?

Check:
Each of the interior angles where the vertices of the polygons meet is 96°. The sum of the four angles is 96° + 96° + 96° + 96° = 384°. This is more than a full turn. The shape cannot be used to tessellate the plane.

Which of the following shapes can be used to tessellate the plane?
Explain your reasoning.

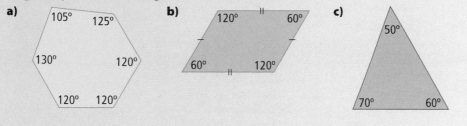

a) 105° 125° 130° 120° 120° 120°

b) 120° 60° 60° 120°

c) 50° 70° 60°

Key Ideas

- A tiling pattern or tessellation is a pattern that covers a plane without overlapping or leaving gaps.
- Only three types of regular polygons tessellate the plane.
- Some types of irregular polygons tessellate the plane.
- Regular and irregular polygons tessellate the plane when the interior angle measures total exactly 360° at the point where the vertices of the polygons meet.

90° 90°
90° 90°

105° 75°
105° 75°

90° + 90° + 90° + 90° = 360°

105° + 75° + 75° + 105° = 360°

Communicate the Ideas

1. Draw three types of regular polygons that tessellate the plane. Justify your choices.

2. What are two types of irregular polygons that can be used to tessellate the plane? Explain your choices to a friend.

3. Megan is tiling her kitchen floor. Should she choose ceramic tiles in the shape of a regular octagon? Explain how you know.

Practise

For help with #4 to #7, refer to the Example on page 448.

4. Do these regular polygons tessellate the plane? Explain why or why not.

a)

b)

5. Use this shape to tessellate the plane. Show and colour the result on grid paper.

6. Tessellate the plane with an isosceles triangle. Use colours or shading to create an interesting design on grid paper.

7. Describe three tessellating patterns that you see at home or at school. What shapes make up the tessellation?

Apply

8. Jared is painting a mosaic on one wall of her bedroom that is made up of tessellating equilateral triangles. Describe two different tessellation patterns that Jared could use. Use triangular dot paper to help you describe the tessellations.

9. Patios are often made from interlocking rectangular bricks. The pattern shown below is called herringbone.

On grid paper, create two different patio designs from congruent rectangular bricks.

10. Some pentagons can be used to tessellate the plane.

a) Describe a pentagon that will tessellate the plane. Explain how it tessellates the plane.

b) Compare your pentagon with those of your classmates. How many different tessellating pentagons did you and your classmates find?

11. A pentomino is a shape made up of five squares. Choose two of the following pentominoes and try to make a tessellation with each one. Do each of your pentominoes make a tessellation? Explain why or why not.

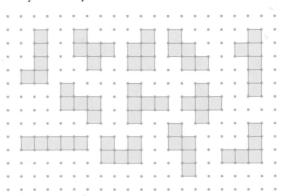

12. Sarah is designing a pattern for the hood and cuffs of her new parka. She wants to use a regular polygon in the design and three different colours. Use grid paper to create two different designs that Sarah might use. Colour your designs.

Extend

13. The diagram shows a tessellation of squares. A dot has been added to the centre of each square. The dots are joined by dashed segments perpendicular to common sides. The result is another tessellation, which is called the *dual* of the original tessellation.

a) Describe the dual of the original square tessellation.

b) Draw a tessellation of regular hexagons. Draw and describe its dual.

c) Draw a tessellation of equilateral triangles. Draw and describe its dual.

14. Identify two different regular polygons that can be used together to create a tessellating pattern. Draw a tessellation on grid paper using the two polygons.

Did You Know?

Many Islamic artists make very intricate geometric decorations and are experts at tessellation art.

MATH LINK

This tiling pattern is from Alhambra, a Moorish palace built in Granada, Spain. Four different tile shapes are used to create this pattern.

a) Describe the four shapes. Are they regular or irregular polygons?

b) Use templates to trace the shapes onto cardboard or construction paper.

c) Cut out ten of each shape and use some or all of them to create at least two different tile mosaics. Use each of the four shapes in your mosaics.

WWW Web Link

To generate tessellations on the computer, go to www.mathlinks8.ca and follow the links.

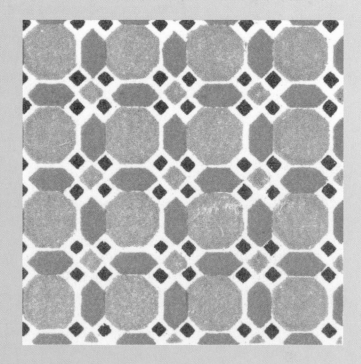

Constructing Tessellations Using Translations and Reflections

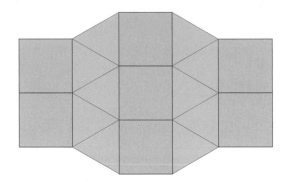

Focus on...

After this lesson, you will be able to...

❑ identify how translations and reflections can be used to create a tessellation

❑ create tessellating patterns using two or more polygons

transformation

• a change in a figure that results in a different position or orientation

Materials

• set of pattern blocks, or cardboard cutouts of pattern block shapes
• ruler
• scissors
• glue stick
• tape
• cardboard or construction paper

In section 12.1 you created simple tessellating patterns using regular and irregular polygons. Tessellations can also be made by combining regular or irregular polygons and then transforming them. Do you recognize the polygons used in this tessellation? What **transformations** were used to create the pattern?

Explore the Math

How can you create a tessellation using transformations?

1. Draw a regular hexagon on a piece of paper using a pattern block or cardboard cutout. Cut out the hexagon and glue it to a sheet of cardboard or construction paper.

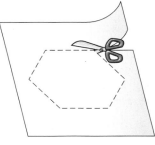

2. Draw two equilateral triangles on a piece of paper using a pattern block or cardboard cutout. Make sure that the side lengths of the triangles are the same as the side lengths of the hexagon. Cut out the triangles and glue them to a sheet of cardboard or construction paper so that they are attached to the sides of the hexagon as shown.

3. Cut out the combined shape. Trace the shape on a new sheet of paper.

4. Translate the shape so that the hexagon fits into the space formed by the two triangles. Trace around the translated shape and repeat two more times. What other ways can you translate the shape?

5. Translate the combined piece vertically and horizontally so that the base of the hexagon is now at the top of one of the triangles.

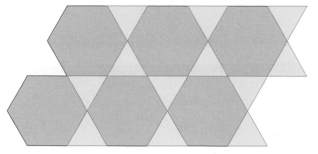

Reflect on Your Findings

6. a) Describe how to use translations to create tessellations.

   b) What other transformations could you use to get the same pattern as in #5? Explain the difference.

Example: Identify the Transformation

a) What polygons and what transformations are used to create this tessellation?

b) Does the area of the tessellating tile change during the tessellation?

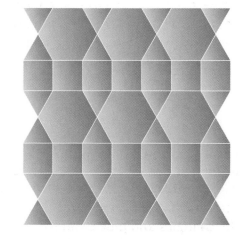

Solution

a) The tessellation is made from a tessellating tile consisting of a hexagon with two squares and two equilateral triangles. The tessellating tile is then translated vertically and horizontally. This tessellation is created using translations.

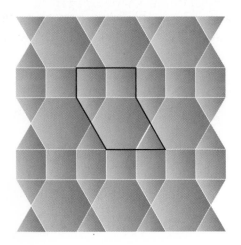

b) The area of the tessellating tile remains the same throughout the tessellation. There are no gaps or overlapping pieces.

Show You Know

What transformation was used to create this tessellation? Explain your reasoning.

Key Ideas

- Tessellations can be made with two or more polygons as long as the interior angles where the vertices of the polygons meet total exactly 360°.
- Two types of transformations commonly used to create tessellations are
  - translations
  - reflections
- The area of the tessellating tile remains the same after it has been transformed to create a tessellation.

Communicate the Ideas

1. Brian missed today's class. How would you explain to him why some tessellating patterns made using translations could also be made using reflections?

2. Ashley and Vijay are trying to figure out how this tessellation was made. Whose answer is correct? Explain.

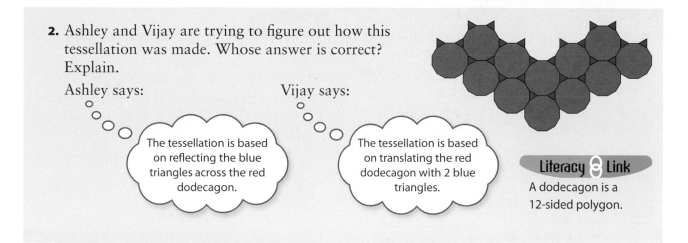

Ashley says:

> The tessellation is based on reflecting the blue triangles across the red dodecagon.

Vijay says:

> The tessellation is based on translating the red dodecagon with 2 blue triangles.

Literacy Link

A dodecagon is a 12-sided polygon.

Check Your Understanding

Practise

For help with #3 and #4, refer to the Example on pages 453–454.

3. Identify the two regular polygons used to create each tessellation.

a)

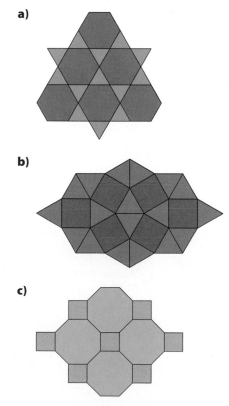

b)

c)

4. What type of transformation could be used to create each tessellation in #3?

Apply

5. The diagram shows a garden path made from irregular 12-sided bricks.

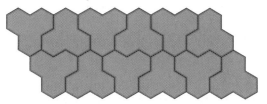

a) Explain why the 12-sided brick tessellates the plane.

b) Use grid paper to design an irregular ten-sided brick that could be used to make a path.

c) Explain why your ten-sided brick tessellates the plane.

d) Use grid paper to design an irregular six-sided brick that could be used to tessellate the plane.

e) Explain why your six-sided brick tessellates the plane.

6. Simon is designing a wallpaper pattern that tessellates. He chooses to use the letter "T" as the basis of his pattern. Create two tessellations using the three coloured letters shown.

7. Priya is designing a kitchen tile that uses two different regular polygons. She then uses two different translations to create a tessellation. Use grid paper to design a tile that Priya could use. Show how it tiles the plane.

8. Barbara wants to make a quilt using the two polygons shown. Will she be able to create a tessellating pattern using these shapes? Explain.

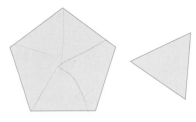

Extend

9. An equilateral triangle is called a reptile (an abbreviation for "repeating tile") because four equilateral triangles can be arranged to form a larger equilateral triangle.

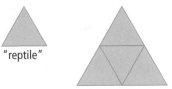

"reptile"

Which of these figures are reptiles? Use grid paper to draw the larger figure for each reptile.

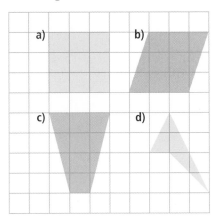

MATH LINK

Many quilt designs are made using tessellating shapes. This quilt uses fabric cut into triangles that are sewn together to form squares. The squares are then translated vertically and horizontally.

Design your own quilt square using one or more regular tessellating polygons. Create an interesting design based on patterns or colours.

12.3 Constructing Tessellations Using Rotations

Focus on...

After this lesson, you will be able to...

- ☐ identify how rotations can be used to create a tessellation
- ☐ create tessellating patterns using two or more polygons

Pysanky is the ancient Eastern European art of egg decorating. The Ukrainian version of pysanky is the most well known. The name comes from the verb *to write*, because artists use a stylus to write with wax on the eggshell. Can you see how rotations are used to make the patterns on these eggs?

Explore the Math

How can you create tessellations using rotations?

1. Draw an equilateral triangle with side lengths of 4 to 5 cm on a piece of paper. Cut out the triangle and glue it to a sheet of cardboard or construction paper to create a tile.

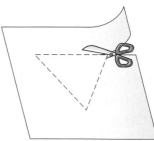

2. Trace around your tile on a piece of paper.

Materials

- tracing paper
- scissors
- glue stick
- tape
- cardboard or construction paper
- coloured pencils

3. Rotate the tile 60° about one vertex until the edge of the tile falls along the edge of the previous tracing as shown. Trace around the tile again.

4. Repeat #3 until a full turn has been made.
   a) What shape did you create?
   b) How many times did you have to rotate the tile to create this shape?

5. Add colour and designs to the tessellation to make a piece of art.

6. How could you continue to use rotations to make a larger tessellation?

Reflect on Your Findings

7. a) Describe how to use rotating polygons to create tessellations.
   b) What types of polygons can be used to make tessellations based on rotations? Explain.

Example: Identify the Transformation

What polygons and what transformation could be used to create this tessellation?

Solution

The tessellating tile is made up of a regular hexagon that has been rotated three times to make a complete turn. The three hexagons forming this tile can be translated horizontally and diagonally to enlarge the tessellation.

> What other transformation(s) could create this tessellation?

What polygons and transformations could be used to create this tessellation? Explain how you know.

- Tessellations can be made with two or more polygons as long as the interior angles where the polygons meet total exactly 360°.
- Rotations can be used to create tessellations.

Communicate the Ideas

1. When creating a tessellation using rotations, why is it important for the sum of the angle measures at the point of rotation to equal 360°? Explain.

2. Describe to a partner how to use rotating polygons to create tessellations.

Check Your Understanding

Practise

For help with #3 and #4, refer to the Example on page 458.

3. Identify the polygons used to create each tessellating tile.

a)

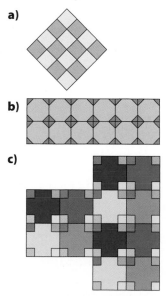

b)

c)

4. What transformations could be used to create each tessellation in #3?

Apply

5. Examine the piece of stained glass.

a) Describe the transformation(s) used to make this pattern.

b) If you were using this pattern to tile the plane, what modifications would you have to make?

6. Design your own stained-glass window on grid paper. Describe the steps you followed to create the pattern.

7. Create a tessellation using two different regular polygons and rotations.

8. Which of the following shapes tessellate? Explain how you know a shape will or will not tessellate.

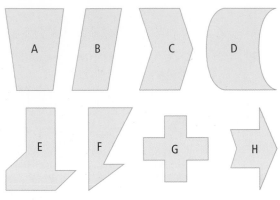

9. The diagram shows one arrangement of three or more polygons that can be used to create tessellations using rotations. One triangle and two dodecagons can be used because the angles at each vertex total 360° where they join. This is represented as (3, 12, 12). The table shows the features of this tessellation, for Shape 1.

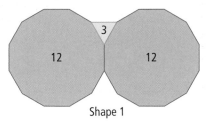

Shape 1

Tessellations Involving Three Regular Polygons	Shape 1	Shape 2	Shape 3	Shape 4
Triangle (60°)	1			
Square (90°)	0			
Pentagon (108°)	0			
Hexagon (120°)	0			
Octagon (135°)	0			
Dodecagon (150°)	2			
Number of Sides	(3, 12, 12)			
Sum of Angles	60 + 2(150) = 360°			

a) Copy the table into your notebook. Complete the table for Shape 2 for the diagram shown.

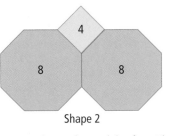

Shape 2

b) Complete the table for Shapes 3 and 4, using different combinations of three or more regular polygons that total 360°.

c) Create construction paper or cardboard cutouts of the regular polygons from part b). Try to tessellate the plane using the combinations that you believe will work.

MATH LINK

Create your own pysanka design based on tessellating one or more polygons. Use at least one rotation in your design. Trace your design on grid paper, and colour it. Make sure it is the correct size to fit on an egg. If you have time, decorate an egg with your pysanka design.

WWW Web Link

To see examples of pysankas, go to www.mathlinks8.ca and follow the links.

Creating Escher-Style Tessellations

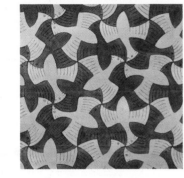

In the previous sections, you created tessellating patterns using regular and irregular polygons. When Escher created his tessellations, he did so in a variety of ways. Look at the two Escher works. What is different about the tessellations?

Explore the Math

How do you make Escher-style tessellations?

1. Draw an equilateral triangle with 6-cm sides on a blank piece of paper. Cut out the triangle and glue it to a sheet of cardboard or construction paper. Cut out the triangle again.

2. Inside the triangle, draw a curve that connects two adjacent vertices. Cut along the curve to remove a piece from one side of the triangle.

3. Rotate the piece you removed 60° counterclockwise about the vertex at the top end of the curve. This rotation moves the piece to another side of the triangle. Tape the piece in place to complete your tile.

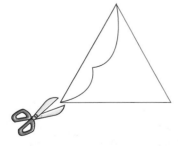

4. To tessellate the plane, draw around the tile on a piece of paper. Then, rotate and draw around the tile over and over until you have a design you like.

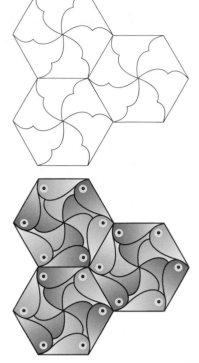

5. Add colour and designs to the tessellation to make a piece of art.

6. Repeat steps 1 through 5 using a parallelogram and translations to create another Escher-style drawing.

Reflect on Your Findings

7. You can use transformations to create Escher-style tessellations just as you did with regular and irregular polygons.

a) Describe how to use rotations to create Escher-style tessellations.

b) What do you notice about the sum of the angle measures at the vertices where the tessellating tiles meet?

c) How does the area of the modified tile compare with the area of the original polygon? Explain.

Example: Identify the Transformation Used in a Tessellation

What transformation was used to create each of the following tessellations?

Tessellation A

Tessellation B

Solution

Tessellation A is made up of triangles that have been rotated to form a hexagon. This tessellation is made using rotations.

Tessellation B is made up of figures that alternate gold to black and then repeat horizontally across the drawing. This tessellation is made using translations.

Show You Know

What transformation was used to create this tessellation? Explain your answer.

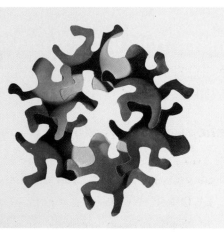

Key Ideas

- You can create Escher-style tessellations using the same methods you used to create tessellations from regular or irregular polygons:
  - Start with a regular or irregular polygon.
  - The area of the tessellating tile must remain unchanged—any portion of the tile that is cut out must be reattached to the tile so that it fits with the next tile of the same shape.
  - Make sure there are no overlaps or gaps in the pattern.
  - Make sure interior angles at vertices total exactly 360°.
  - Use transformations to tessellate the plane.

1. When creating a tile for an Escher-style tessellation, the original polygon is cut up. How do you know the area of the original polygon is maintained?

2. Rico believes that he can use this tile to create an Escher-style tessellation. Is he correct? Explain.

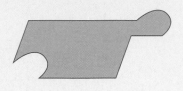

3. Tessellations must have no gaps or overlaps. What other two properties must be maintained when creating Escher-style tessellations?

Check Your Understanding

Practise

For help with #4 to #7, refer to the Example on pages 462–463.

4. Identify the transformations used to create each tessellation.

   a)

   b)
   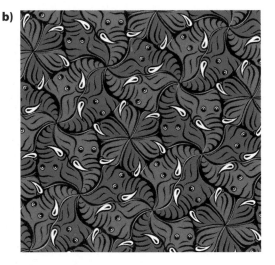

5. Identify the original shape from which each tile was made for each tessellation in #4.

6. Identify the transformations used to create each tessellation.

a)

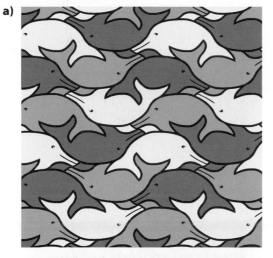

b)

7. Identify the original shape from which each tile was made for each tessellation in #6.

8. Create an Escher-style tessellation using a scalene triangle with translations.

9. Create an Escher-style tessellation using an equilateral triangle with rotations.

10. Create an Escher-style tessellation using squares with rotations and translations.

Extend

11. Escher also used impossible figures in his art, as shown.

a) What impossible figures were used in the drawing?

b) Research other examples of Escher's art that include impossible figures.

MATH LINK

Use an Escher-style tessellation to create a design for a binder cover, wrapping paper, a border for writing paper, or a placemat.

WWW Web Link

To see examples of Escher's art, go to www.mathlinks8.ca and follow the links.

Key Words

For #1 to #4, unscramble the letters for each puzzle. Use the clues to help you solve the puzzles.

1. L I T G I N   H T E   E P A L N

using repeated congruent shapes to cover a region without leaving gaps or overlapping

2. L E N A P

a 2-D flat surface that extends in all directions

3. S L T I O E E T A N L S

a pattern that covers a plane without overlapping or leaving gaps

4. R M T S A I N F N O T A O R

examples include translations, rotations, and reflections

12.1 Exploring Tessellations With Regular and Irregular Polygons, pages 446–451

5. What different types of polygons are used to create each tiling pattern?

a)

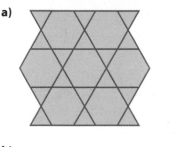

b)

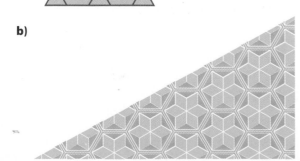

c)

d)

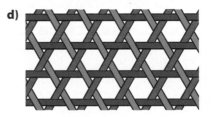

6. Which of the polygons in #5 are regular polygons and which are not? Explain how you know.

7. Can a regular octagon be used to tile the plane? Explain.

12.2 Constructing Tessellations Using Translations and Reflections, pages 452–456

8. What transformation or transformations could be used to create the following patterns?

a)

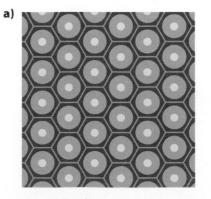

b)

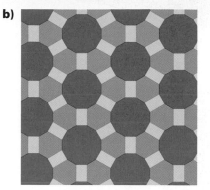

9. Create a tiling pattern using equilateral triangles and squares. Use one translation and one reflection to create the pattern.

10. Create a tessellation using three regular polygons and two different translations.

12.3 Constructing Tessellations Using Rotations, pages 457–460

11. What transformations could be used to create the following patterns?

a)

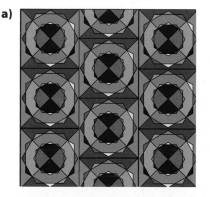

b)

12. Create a tessellation using this irregular polygon. What additional polygon is needed to complete the pattern?

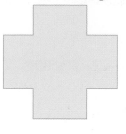

12.4 Creating Escher-Style Tessellations, pages 461–465

13. What original shape was used to create this tessellation?

14. What transformations were used to create the tessellation in #13?

15. Create two different Escher-style tessellations from the same square tile design. Use a different transformation for each tessellation.

For #1 to #5, select the best answer.

1. Which one of these regular polygons cannot be used to tile the plane?

   A square

   B triangle

   C hexagon

   D pentagon

2. When polygons can be used to create a tessellation, what is the sum of the interior angles where the vertices of the polygons meet?

   A 90°

   B 180°

   C 270°

   D 360°

3. Which statement below is false?

   A Any regular quadrilateral can be used to tessellate the plane.

   B Any irregular quadrilateral can be used to tessellate plane.

   C Any regular hexagon can be used to tessellate plane.

   D Any irregular hexagon can be used to tessellate plane.

4. Which polygon can be used to create a tessellation?

   A regular pentagon

   B regular hexagon

   C regular heptagon

   D regular octagon

5. How many different polygons were used to create this tessellation?

   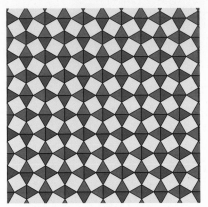

   A 1

   B 2

   C 3

   D 4

Short Answer

6. Can the regular octagon and two squares be used to tile the plane? Explain.

7. Can Jamie create a tessellation using this triangle? Explain.

8. Describe how this pattern can be created. What type of polygon is being used to create the pattern?

9. Square tiles have been arranged in an F-shape. Use grid paper to find out if the F-shape will tile the plane.

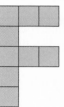

10. Describe how you could create this tessellation.

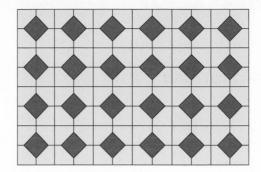

Extended Response

11. Create an Escher-style tessellation using an equilateral triangle or a square and rotations.

WRAP IT UP!

Mosaic designs can be used on tiles, wallpaper, carpets, furniture, and fabrics.

a) Create a mosaic design that incorporates at least two different shapes and two different transformations.

b) Construct your mosaic using available materials, such as coloured construction paper, coloured transparencies, tile pieces, paints, etc.

c) Write a brief paragraph describing the different shapes *and* transformations you used to create your mosaic.

d) Work with other students to connect the patterns together to make a class mosaic.

Math Games

Playing at Tiling

Many game boards, such as chess boards, are made from squares. Squares tessellate, so the board can be made without overlapping the squares or leaving gaps between them.

Materials

• one Playing at Tiling game board per pair of students or small group

• two standard 6-sided dice per pair of students or small group

• one coloured counter for each student

1. Game boards can be made from other polygons, or combinations of polygons, that tessellate. The board shown here includes squares and regular octagons.

   Play a game on this board with a partner or in a small group.

   These are the rules:

   • Each player rolls one die to decide who will play first. If there is a tie, roll again.

   • For each turn, roll the two dice and identify the greater value. On the board, move your coloured counter that number of places ahead.

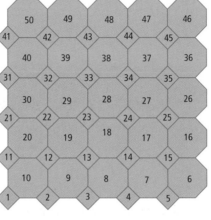

   • If you roll a double, move ahead to the next place that has a different shape from your present place. Then move ahead the number of places equal to the value from either die.

   • The first player to reach 50 wins.

   > I rolled a 3 and a 5. The greater value is 5, so I moved my counter ahead 5 places on the board.

2. Design a game board using a shape, or combination of shapes, that tessellates. Create the rules for a dice game to be played on this board. You might want to consider bonus points or penalty points for landing on a particular colour. Play the game with a partner or in a small group. Modify the rules to make the game better.

   > I rolled two 4s when my counter was on square 13. I moved ahead to the next octagon, number 16. I then moved ahead 4 places to position 20.

Challenge in Real Life

Border Design

Designers create patterns and border designs for such uses as tiles, wallpaper borders, upholstery, fabrics, and rugs. You have been commissioned to design and paint a border on the wall at the skateboard park. Using your knowledge of tessellations, create a design for a border 12 cm wide.

Materials
- construction paper
- scissors
- coloured pencils or markers

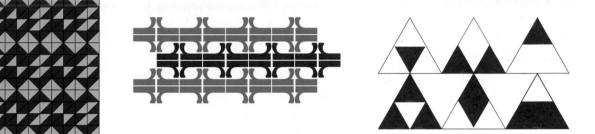

1. On construction paper, design and cut out a regular polygon such as an equilateral triangle, a square, a pentagon, or a polygon with more than five sides. This is your template.

2. Use your template to create a reflection, rotation, and translation of your shape. Label each transformation.

3. Using your knowledge of transformations and your work from #2, create a border design on a piece of paper that is 12 cm × 28 cm. The design must use at least two different types of transformations.

4. Colour your design to emphasize the two types of transformations.

Chapters 9–12 Review

Chapter 9 Linear Relations

1. The table of values shows the number of triangles in an increasing pattern.

Figure Number	1	2	3	4
Number of Triangles	3	5	7	

   a) How many triangles are in Figure 4?

   b) Graph the table of values. Label your axes.

   c) Does your graph represent a linear relation? Explain.

2. You buy a quantity of something according to the linear relation shown on the graph.

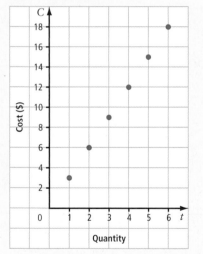

   a) Describe what you might have purchased. What is the cost if you purchase one item?

   b) Describe patterns you see in the graph.

   c) Make a table of values for the data on the graph. What variables might you use to label your table? Explain what the variables represent.

   d) What is an expression for the cost in terms of the quantity?

   e) If the quantity is eight, what is the cost?

3. A farmer is building a post-and-rail fence around his yard. The number of rails in relation to the number of posts can be represented by $r = 3p - 3$ where r is the number of rails and p is the number of posts.

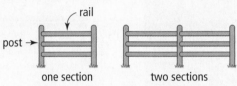

   a) Copy and complete the table of values.

Number of Posts, p	2	3	4	5	6	7
Number of Rails, r						

   b) Draw a labelled graph. Does the relationship appear to be linear? Explain.

4. Each of the following represents a linear relation.

   $$y = 2x - 3$$
   $$y = 2x + 1$$

   a) Make a table of values for each equation. Use at least five positive and five negative integer values for x. Why did you choose those x-values?

   b) Graph both linear relations on the same grid.

   c) What is similar about the graphs? What is different?

Chapter 10 Solving Linear Equations

5. The diagram represents an equation.

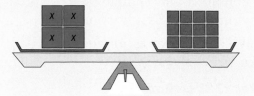

   a) What equation does this diagram represent?

   b) What is the solution to the equation?

6. Use models or diagrams to solve each equation.

   a) $\dfrac{s}{2} = -5$

   b) $-3x + 6 = -3$

   c) $10 = 6 + \dfrac{v}{4}$

   d) $2(x - 5) = -4$

7. Solve each equation. Check your answers.

   a) $\dfrac{x}{7} = -4$

   b) $14 = -26 + 5x$

   c) $11 - \dfrac{x}{3} = 17$

   d) $4(x - 9) = -16$

8. Jason's age is three years fewer than $\dfrac{1}{3}$ his father's age. Jason is ten years old.

   a) What equation models this situation?

   b) How old is Jason's father?

9. Elijah works in a diamond mine. When he works the late shift, $2/h is added to his regular hourly wage. Last week, he worked the late shift for a total of 40 h and made $960. Write and solve an equation to determine Elijah's regular hourly wage.

Chapter 11 Probability

10. Two six-sided dice are rolled.

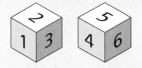

   a) Draw a tree diagram or table to represent the sample space.

   b) What is the probability that an even number is rolled on both dice? Express the probability as a fraction.

   c) What is the probability that the sum of the two numbers is greater than or equal to six, $P(\text{sum} \geq 6)$? Express the probability as a fraction.

11. A spinner is divided into five equal regions and labelled with the whole numbers zero to four.

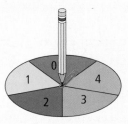

   a) What is the probability of spinning an odd number?

   b) What is the probability of spinning an even number?

   c) If you spin the spinner twice, what is the probability of spinning an odd number on the first spin and an even number on the second spin?

12. An online computer company has a sale in which customers choose one of four different computers and one of three different printers. How many computer–printer options are available?

13. Gillian flips a disk labelled H on one side and T on the other side. She spins a spinner divided into three equal regions once.

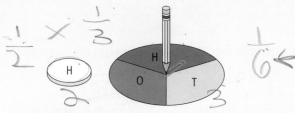

a) What is the probability that an H is flipped on the disk? What is the probability that an H is spun on the spinner? Express the probabilities as fractions.

b) What is the probability of H appearing on both the disk and spinner? Express the probability as a fraction.

c) Check your answer to part b) using another method.

14. Ria and Renata are identical twins. They like the same kind of cereal and their favourite colour is blue. The cereal company that makes their favourite cereal is having a promotion—each box of cereal includes a spinning top toy that comes in one of four colours, including blue. The girls want to run a simulation.

a) Describe a simulation that the twins could run to determine the probability that the next two boxes of cereal they open will each contain a blue spinning top.

b) What assumption(s) do Ria and Renata need to make regarding the spinning tops?

c) In a set of 20 trials, two blue tops resulted only once. What is the experimental probability for this experiment? Express your answer as a fraction and as a percent.

d) What is the theoretical probability that the next two boxes of cereal will contain a blue spinning top? Express your answer as a fraction and as a percent.

Chapter 12 Tessellations

15. Which of the following polygons cannot be used to tile the plane? Explain how you know.

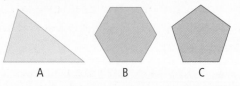

16. Create a tiling pattern using a square and one other shape. Describe the transformation(s) you used to create your pattern.

17. Describe how this tessellation can be created.

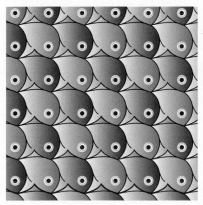

18. Create an Escher-style tessellation using a parallelogram as the original shape. Describe the transformation(s) you used for your tessellation.

Task

Put Out a Forest Fire

One effective way to fight a forest fire is to drop water and fire retardant on it from an airplane. A number of factors influence how effective this is, including wind direction and speed, speed of the airplane, and temperature of the fire. You are training as a pilot of a firefighting airplane. Create a simulation to observe how effective you can be at putting out the fire.

Materials
- shape to tessellate
- ruler
- coloured pencils (orange, green, blue)
- modelling clay or bingo chips

1. Do the following to prepare your simulation.
   - Draw a rectangle that is 14 cm by 16 cm on a blank sheet of paper.
   - Cut out the shape you have been given. The full triangle counts as two shapes. In order to fill your rectangle, you will sometimes use half of the triangle. Each half triangle counts as one shape.
   - Using transformations and the shape provided, tile your paper until the rectangle is completely full.
   - Colour the shapes in your tessellation using the ratio of 1 blue : 3 orange : 4 green.
   - Cut out the rectangle.
   - Work with a group of at least three other students. Join your tessellated paper with those of the other group members. This larger tessellation represents the map of a forest fire. Orange represents the area that is burning, green is the forest, and blue is the lakes.

2. The object of the simulation is to put out the entire fire by dropping water on each of the orange areas.
   - One at a time, stand beside the tessellated map and drop three pieces of modelling clay or three chips onto it. Each drop represents a water drop.
   - Record what colour each drop lands on.

3. **a)** Hitting an orange shape puts out the fire in that part of the tessellation, including all of the orange shapes that are attached to the orange shape that was hit. What is the experimental probability of hitting an orange shape?

   b) How much did the simulation help you improve your understanding of experimental probability versus theoretical probability? Explain why.

   c) What is the theoretical probability of randomly hitting an orange shape?

Answers

Chapter 1

1.1 Advantages and Disadvantages of Different Graphs, pages 13–17

4. a) Ravi spends $10 more on food than on movies. The pictograph better shows how much more he spent on food than movies because each symbol in the pictograph represents $10, and no partial symbols were used. In the circle graph the percents must be multiplied by $200 to determine the amounts spent on food and movies. **b)** The circle graph shows that half of the circle is made up of the categories *Food* and *Clothing*. **c)** One advantage of the circle graph is that the categories are represented as percents of his total spending. One advantage of the pictograph is that it is a precise way of presenting each amount since the amounts are all multiples of ten. One disadvantage of the circle graph is that it is necessary to perform calculations to determine the dollar amounts spent on each category. One disadvantage of the pictograph is that the percent of his money spent on each category must be calculated.

5. Answers may vary. Example: **a)** The circle graph shows the percent of time out of a total of 40 h that each person practises each week. The bar graph shows the number of hours of practice each person does each week. **b)** "Which two people together use 75% of the practice time?" Min and Ann together use 75% of the practice time. **c)** "How much longer does Ann spend practising than Sara each week?" Ann spends 6 h more practising than Sara each week.

6. a) The line graph shows the change of growth from week 1 to week 4. The pictograph shows the height of the plant at the end of weeks 1, 2, 3, and 4. **b)** The plant grew at the same rate between weeks 1 and 2, and weeks 2 and 3. **c)** The plant changed the most in height between weeks 3 and 4. The line graph shows this change more clearly. **d)** One advantage of the line graph is that it shows the rate of change of the growth of the plant. One advantage of the pictograph is that it shows the height of the plant after each week. One disadvantage of the pictograph is that it does not show the rate of change in height.

7. a)

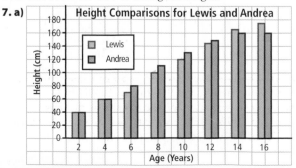

b) The trends are similar in that both friends' heights are increasing from age 2 to age 14. The trends are different in that Andrea's height stops increasing after age 14, but Lewis' height continues to increase after age 14. **c)** The line graph shows their height trends more clearly because it shows changes in their heights over time. **d)** Because the heights are not parts of a whole, circle graphs would not be effective.

8. a)

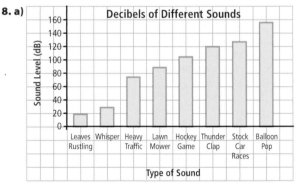

A bar graph allows for an accurate comparison of sound levels. **b)** Because the data are not a comparison over a period of time, a line graph would not be a good choice of graph. **c)** Because the data do not represent a comparison of parts to a whole, a circle graph would not be a good choice of graph. **d)** A pictograph could be used, but it would not be as accurate as a bar graph because of the fractions of pictures required to represent these data.

9. a) Science fiction books are 3.4 times as popular as history books. **b)** The circle graph shows the relationship between the different categories of books. **c)** The number of mystery books signed out is about the same as the total number of history and sports books because 10% + 13% = 23%. **d)** Because the circle graph shows the percent of the total for each category, the answer is more apparent. **e)** Science fiction: $4080, Mystery: $2760, Teen romance: $2400, Sports: $1560, History: $1200 **f)** The circle graph is easier to use because the percents are given, and they can be multiplied by $12 000.

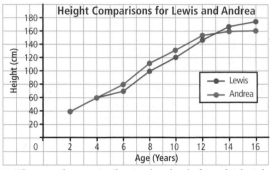

10. a)

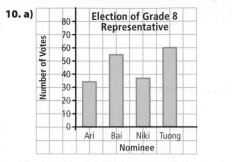

b) The bar graph allows you to better estimate the actual number of votes. **c)** A line graph would not be the best choice because the data do not show a change over time. **d)** An advantage of using a circle graph is that you can show the percent of votes that each person received. A disadvantage is that you must calculate the number of votes each candidate received.

11. a) Answers may vary. Example:

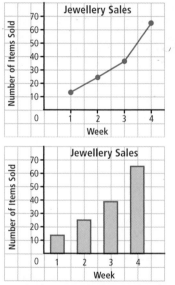

b) The line graph shows the change of sales over the four weeks, while the bar graph shows the number of items sold for each of the four weeks. Both graphs are equally effective.

c) The store should continue to sell the jewellery because the line graph shows that the number of sales is steadily increasing over time.

12. a) Answers may vary. Example: **b)** A bar or circle graph would be most appropriate. **c)** A bar graph would give the number of scores in each range.

Math Test Scores	
Range	**Frequency**
40 to 49	4
50 to 59	4
60 to 69	5
70 to 79	8
80 to 89	5
90 to 99	4
Total	30

13. a) Answers may vary. Example:

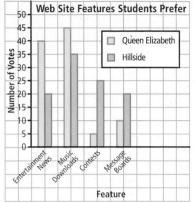

The double bar graph shows a comparison of both schools across the four different categories.
b) *Entertainment News* and *Music Downloads*
14. a) A bar graph or circle graph would be more appropriate for the data. **b)** A line graph is best for showing changes in data over time.
15. Answers may vary according to research. Example:
a)

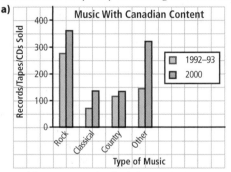

Possible questions include, "How many more *Rock* albums with Canadian content were sold in 2000 than in 1992–93?" and "How have sales of *Classical* vs. *Country* albums with Canadian content changed from 1992–93 to 2000?" Answer to first question: Approximately 85. Answer to second question: In 1992–1993, more *Country* than *Classical* albums were sold. In 2000, more *Classical* albums were sold than *Country*.

b)

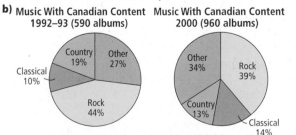

c) "What types of music with Canadian content increased in popularity between 1992–93 and 2000?" and "What type of music with Canadian content was the most popular in 1992–93?" Answer to first question: *Classical* and *Other*. Answer to second question: *Rock*.

d) An advantage to the double bar graph is that you can compare each type of music in each of the years. A disadvantage of the double bar graph is that you do not see what percent of the albums sold each year were a specific type. An advantage of the circle graph is that you can see what percent of the albums sold were each type of music. A disadvantage of the circle graph is that you must have two separate graphs to illustrate the data.

16. Answers may vary. Example: **a)** The graph could represent the number of days that Cassandra babysat for her neighbour in each month from January to December.

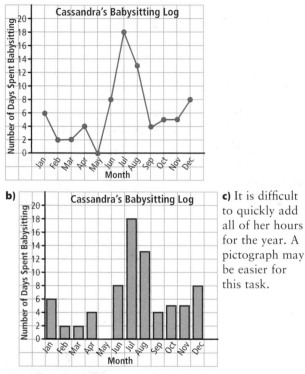

b)

c) It is difficult to quickly add all of her hours for the year. A pictograph may be easier for this task.

17. a) Answers may vary. Example: A survey question to ask members of your class could be, "What is your favourite season of the year: winter, spring, summer, or fall?" There are four choices, and there is a good chance that there will be a different number of people responding with each option. **b)** Since the total number of people responding to the question will be known, the percent for each response can be calculated. **c)** Answers may vary. Example: A survey question to ask members of your class could be, "How many hours a week do you spend watching television?" A bar graph or pictograph may be more suitable.

1.2 Misrepresenting Data, pages 23–27

4. a) The scale of the y-axis is misleading because it contains a break. **b)** The graph suggests that the temperature increased by a significant amount between 8 a.m. and 2 p.m. **c)** The graph should be redrawn with a consistent scale on the vertical axis from 0 °C to 32 °C, with no break.

5. a) 3 **b)** 2 **c)** Answers may vary. Example: It appears that candidate B received 3 times as many votes as candidate A. **d)** The graph could be redrawn with the vertical axis showing values from 0 to 200, with no break.
6. a) Apples seem to sell the best because the line containing the apple symbols is longer than the lines for the other fruit. **b)** Answers may vary. Example: It appears that about the same number of each fruit was sold because the line representing each type of fruit is approximately the same length. **c)** The pictograph should be redrawn so that each symbol is the same size, and the symbols should be spaced the same distance apart.
7. a) The Big Cheese appears to be the favourite burger because it is larger than the Bonzo Burger. **b)** Answers may vary. Example: The sizes of the burgers suggest a significant difference in the taste test results. **c)** Use a pictograph, with each symbol the same size, and space each symbol equally on the line.
8. Answers may vary. Example: **a)** The horizontal scale has a break from levels 0 to 10. Also, the width of each bar is not equal. **b)** Scott's progress appears to be more than twice as much as Bryce's progress. **c)** Start the scale at zero with no break between levels 0 and 10, and make Scott's and Bryce's bars have equal widths.
9. Answers may vary. Example: **a)** The vertical axis in Graph A has a uniform scale from 0 to 160 by units of 20. The vertical axis in Graph B has a break between 0 and 140, after which the scale increases uniformly by units of 2. **b)** In Graph A it appears that the sales were very near the same amount for each student. In Graph B it appears that Chris sold twice as many bars as Megan. **c)** Graph A is more accurate because the vertical scale has no break.
10. Answers may vary. Example: **a)** The vertical scale has a break between 0 and 200. **b)** The profits seem to be four times as high in June as they were in January.

Profits are two and a half times as high in June as they were in January.

11. Answers may vary. Example: **a)**

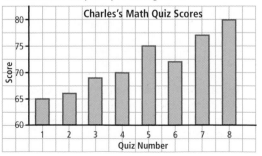

b)

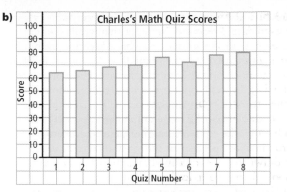

Charles's Math Quiz Scores

c) In Graph A it appears that Charles' scores have been increasing by a large amount. In Graph B the increase in scores does not seem as large.

12. a) The vertical scale goes from 0 to 500, but the greatest number of votes was less than 200. Therefore, it appears that all three candidates were close to winning, and the title implies that all three candidates tied. **b)** Answers may vary. Example: Candidate B barely won the election. **c)** No, the votes were not divided evenly three ways. Answer may vary. Example: A new title could be *Election Results*.

13. a) Answers may vary. Example: The information does not appear to be the same because the sector sizes in the graphs are different. **b)** The sizes of the sectors in Graph A do not appear to coincide with their percents.

14. Answers may vary. Example: **a)** There is no scale or legend for comparison purposes. Also, the number of cans in each box is equal **b)** Mr. Rajwani's class appears to have collected 4 times the amount of food that was collected by Ms. Chan's class.

c)

Food Drive

Ms. Chan's Class

Mr. Rajwani's Class

represents 50 cans of food

15. a) The beach appears to be about three and a half times as popular as the pool. **b)** No, the majority did not choose the beach. Only 50 out of the 115 votes cast were for the beach.

c) Answers may vary. Example:

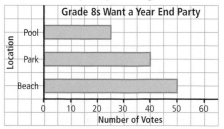

Grade 8s Want a Year End Party

16. a) *Cool Flavours* probably created this graph because it appears that they sell twice as much ice cream as *Dairy Tasty*. **b)** Answers may vary. Example: There is no scale for comparison purposes.

17. a)

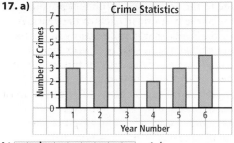

Crime Statistics

b)

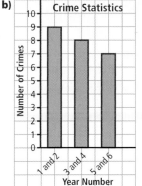

Crime Statistics

c) Answers may vary. Example: It appears from the second bar graph that the number of crimes is consistently decreasing. This does not support the data in the table. The number of crimes went down for year 4, but the number of crimes increased in the last two years. **d)** The second graph is misleading because the data for each year are not represented separately.

18. Answers may vary. Example:

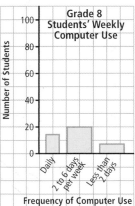

Grade 8 Students' Weekly Computer Use

19. a) Health **b)** Answers may vary. Example: The Health sector is at the front of the diagram and appears much larger than the Energy and Education sectors.

c) Answers may vary. Example:

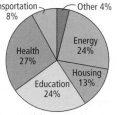

Provincial Budget (2008–2009)

20. Answers may vary. Example: A possible question is, "How many apples do you eat each week?"

a)

Number of Apples	Tally
Less than 3	ＨＨ
3 to 4	ＨＨ ＩＩＩ
5 to 6	ＨＨ
More than 6	ＨＨ Ｉ

b) See bar graph.

c) The wider bar in the "3 to 4" category and the break in the vertical axis make it appear that there are 8 times as many students eating 3 to 4 apples each week than there are eating less than 3 each week. There are actually less than twice as many students eating 3 to 4 apples each week than there are eating less than 3 each week.

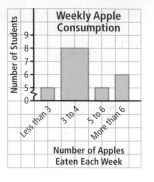

Weekly Apple Consumption

Number of Students (vertical axis)
Number of Apples Eaten Each Week (horizontal axis: Less than 3, 3 to 4, 5 to 6, More than 6)

21. Answers may vary. Example: **a)** The scale on the horizontal axis of the line graph does not increase by units of 1 year. The 3-D circle graph distorts the size of the sections. Sales have increased by a large amount from 2004 to 2007, but the annual change is not shown. There are no percent labels on the circle graph. The data on the circle graph may not represent a typical day's sales.

b) Scale the horizontal axis on the line graph by units of 1 year. Change the 3-D circle graph to a 2-D circle graph. Include percent labels in the circle graph.

22. Answers may vary. Example:

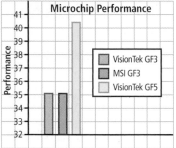

Microchip Performance

Performance (vertical axis: 32–41)
VisionTek GF3, MSI GF3, VisionTek GF5

a) See bar graph on right.

b) In the original graph, it looked like the VisionTek GF5 chip performed twice as well as the other two chips, but the performance among the chips is relatively similar, as shown in the second graph.

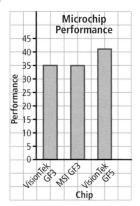

Microchip Performance

Performance (vertical axis: 0–45)
Chip (horizontal axis: VisionTek GF3, MSI GF3, VisionTek GF5)

1.3 Critiquing Data Presentation, pages 32–35

4. a) Madison used a double bar graph to compare each type of communication by gender. **b)** The graph is not misleading because it is scaled uniformly with no breaks, and the bars are a consistent width. **c)** Answers may vary. Example: More girls use the Internet than boys. Boys and girls both prefer to communicate in person or on the Internet. **d)** The data do not show a change over time.

5. Answers may vary. Example: **a)** More grade 9 students spend less than 1 h on the Internet than grade 8 students. Twenty-four grade 8 students spend 2 h to less than 3 h on the Internet. **b)** No, the graph is not misleading. The scale is uniform, there are no breaks, and both axes are clearly labelled. **c)** No improvements are recommended. **d)** A comparison of time spent on the Internet of both grades can be shown on one graph. **e)** Two circle graphs (one for grade 8 students, one for grade 9 students) would show the percent of the students in each grade that use the Internet for each time interval. The circle graphs may be more informative.

6. a) Answers may vary. Example: Eighteen cars in the parking lot were sedans. Forty-eight percent of the cars in the parking lot were either SUVs or minivans. **b)** The graph is not misleading. The sections of the circle are labelled with the category name and percent. The title contains the total number of cars in the lot. **c)** Answers may vary. Example: A circle graph shows a comparison of each car type as a percent of the total number of cars. **d)** Answers may vary. Example: A bar graph could have been used to show a comparison of the number of cars of each type in the lot, but it would not have shown what percent of the cars in the lot was each type of car.

7. Answers may vary. Example: The bar graph shows that *Health* had almost twice as many votes as any other type of organization.

8. a) The size of the blue bar appears to be about three times as large as the orange one, but Truong is not correct. The scale indicates that 56 blue calculators were sold and that 25 orange calculators were sold.

b)

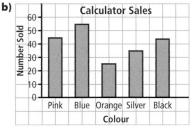

Calculator Sales

Number Sold (vertical axis: 0–60)
Colour (horizontal axis: Pink, Blue, Orange, Silver, Black)

Answers may vary. Example: About twice as many blue calculators as orange calculators were sold.

c) Calculator Sales (205 sold)

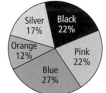

Silver 17%, Black 22%, Orange 12%, Pink 22%, Blue 27%

d) Answers may vary. Example: A circle graph shows the percent of the calculators sold for each colour.

9. Answers may vary. Example:
a) See circle graph on the right
b) Almost half of the rentals were of *Freerider*. **c)** The circle graph allows you to clearly see what percent of each type of board was rented. **d)** The type of graph should be a good choice for displaying the data, the graph should be designed in a way that represents the data accurately, and the graph should be informative.

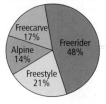

Snowboard Rentals

Freecarve 17%, Freerider 48%, Alpine 14%, Freestyle 21%

10. a) Although the graph shows that in each two-day period there is an increase in time spent, Chloe has not been increasing the time she spends doing homework over the last 6 days because she only spent 0.5 h doing homework on Friday, but 6 h on Saturday.
b) Yes, the graph is misleading.

Time Spent on Homework (13.5 h)

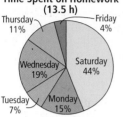

c) Answers may vary. Example: Almost half of her homework time was spent on Saturday. Chloe spent the least amount of time doing homework on Friday.

d)

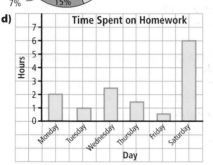

e) Answers may vary. Example: Chloe spent three times as long doing homework on Saturday as she did on Monday. She spent six times as long doing homework on Saturday as she did on Tuesday.
f) Answers may vary. Example: The bar graph is better if a comparison of number of hours is required. A circle graph is better if a comparison of percents is required.
11. Answers may vary. Example: **a)** Graph A makes it appear that there was a small change in minimum wage from 2001 to 2007. Graph B makes it appear that there was a large change in minimum wage from 2001 to 2007.
b) Graph A would support such a claim. Minimum wages have only increased from just over $6 to $8 in 7 years.
c) An employer would use Graph B because it appears that there has been a large increase in the minimum wage over the 7-year period.
12. Answers may vary. Example: **a)** *Connor's Cars* probably developed the bar graph because the drop in sales is not as obvious as it is in the line graph. **b)** *Amy's Autos'* sales have steadily increased. *Connor's Cars'* sales dropped significantly from March to April.

Chapter Review, pages 36–37

1. E **2.** A **3.** F **4.** C **5.** B
6. a) Answers may vary. Example: The circle graph allows you to determine the exact number of each type of book because it states the total number of books and the percent of each type. The bar graph also shows the number of books of each type, but the exact number is more difficult to read. **b)** The circle graph makes the distribution of the funds easier. Fiction: $500, Sports: $190, History: $60, Science Fiction: $250.

7. Answers may vary. Example:
a) The data could be displayed in a bar graph, a circle graph, or a pictograph.
b) **Michelle's Saturday Activities (24 h)**

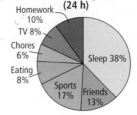

c) An advantage of a circle graph is that it shows what percent of Michelle's time is spent on each activity. A disadvantage of a pictograph is that it is difficult to show exact amounts.

8. Answers may vary. Example: **a)** A bar graph could display the population of the western provinces and territories. **b)** A double bar graph could display the number of boys and girls in each of the grades 7, 8, and 9 at a school. **c)** A circle graph could be used to display how Ross spends his weekly allowance of $20. **d)** A line graph could show the monthly change in Internet usage over a period of one year.
9. a) False. The break in the horizontal axis makes it appear that the number of computers compared to the number of cell phones and MP3 players is much greater than it actually is.

b)

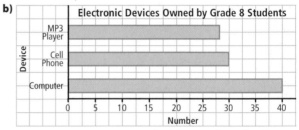

c) Answers may vary. Example: The number of cell phones is 75% of the number of computers.
10. Answer may vary. Example: **a)** It appears that *Mega Pizza* is twice as popular as *Mr. Pizza*.

b) **Pizza Taste Test**

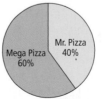

11. Answers may vary. Example:

a)

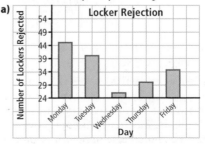

b)

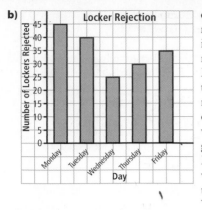
Locker Rejection

c) The first graph makes it appear as if the number of rejected lockers on Monday is more than 20 times the number rejected on Wednesday, while the second graph shows that Monday's rejections were less than twice as many as Wednesday's.

12. a) Answers may vary. Example: The majority of the students are right-handed. There are approximately as many left-handed students as ambidextrous students. **b)** Yes, a circle graph is appropriate because it shows the percent of students in each category. **c)** Answers may vary. Example: A bar graph could be used. An advantage of a bar graph is that the number of students in each category would be displayed.

13. a) Graph A shows a comparison of all seasons' ratings. Graph B shows a comparison of season 4 ratings only. **b)** Answer may vary. Example: A title for Graph A could be *Open Mike Comics Gains Popularity* and a title for Graph B could be *Laughing Out Loud Is the Best Comedy*. **c)** Graph A was created by the producer of *Open Mike Comics* because it shows a steady increase in popularity of *Open Mike Comics*. **d)** Graph B appears to show that *Laughing Out Loud* is more than twice as popular as *Open Mike Comics*, so this graph was probably created by the producers of *Laughing Out Loud*.

Chapter 2

2.1 Two-Term and Three-Term Ratios, pages 51–54

5. a) $2:8$ **b)** $21:26$ **c)** $16:14:30$
d) Answers may vary. Example: $13:28$.
6. a) $1:4$ **b)** $21:26$ **c)** $8:7:15$
d) Answers may vary. Example: $13:28$.
7. a) $\frac{4}{10}$ **b)** $\frac{3}{9}$ **c)** $\frac{3}{15}$ **d)** $\frac{27}{60}$
8. a) 4 **b)** 15 **c)** 6 **d)** 1 **e)** 7 **f)** 5
9. a) Hockey and baseball have equivalent win-loss ratios. Express each ratio in decimal form and compare them.
b) $\frac{9}{15}$, 0.6, 60%

10. a)

b) 9 cars **c)** $1:4:6$ **d)** $6:20 = \frac{3}{10} = 30\%$

11. a) blue to white **b)** blue to red to white **c)** red to all **d)** red and white to all
12. a) $\frac{8}{32}$, 25% **b)** $24:8$ or $3:1$
13. a) 12 games lost **b)** $16:12$ or $4:3$; The team lost 12 games. If they played 28 games, they won $28 - 12$ or 16 games. The ratio $16:12$ is equivalent to $4:3$. **c)** 15 losses
14. a)

b) 36 adults. Answers may vary. Example: The ratio $3:8$ is equivalent to the ratio $36:96$. **c)** 60 adults. There are 96 adults in total minus 36 adults who are less than 150 cm tall equals 60 adults who are 150 cm or taller.

15. a) $2:6:5$ of Romano to mozzarella to cottage cheese. **b)** 300 g of Romano and 750 g of cottage
16. a) $1:2$ **b)** $1:2$ **c)** Each length is $\frac{1}{2}$ of what it originally was.
17. a) $16:48$ or $1:3$ **b)** $12:44 = \frac{3}{11} = 0.\overline{27} = 27.\overline{27}\%$
18. a) 24 cm **b)** 1.5 m
19. a) $\frac{1608}{1800} = \frac{67}{75}$ **b)** 1.02
c) 0.56; Answers may vary. Example: The Churchill River is about twice as long as the Thelon River.
20. 4.5 kg of nitrogen, 6 kg of phosphorus, and 3 kg of potassium, for a total of 13.5 kg
21. a) 24 m × 38.9 m and 348 mm × 565 mm **b)** 10.4 m
22. a) $\frac{1}{4}$ **b)** $\frac{1}{4} = 0.25 = 25\%$ **c)** increase the slope; decrease the slope; decrease the slope; increase the slope

2.2 Rates, pages 60–62

4. a) 55 km/h **b)** 64 km/h **c)** 90 daffodils/h
5. a) 4 t/day **b)** 19.3 km/h **c)** 6 bellows/h
6. Gina: $\frac{\$78}{6 \text{ h}} = \$13/\text{h}$; Asad: $\frac{\$192.50}{14 \text{ h}} = \$13.75/\text{h}$. Asad has the greater hourly rate of pay.
7. a) Pkg 1: $\$0.73/100$ g; Pkg 2: $\$0.62/100$ g; Pkg 3: $\$0.69/100$ g **b)** Pkg 2 is the best buy because the cost per 100 g was the least. This is assuming the quality of mixed nuts is the same in all packages.
8. a) small size: $\frac{\$0.59}{250 \text{ mL}} = \$0.00236/\text{mL}$;
medium size: $\frac{\$1.09}{500 \text{ mL}} = \$0.00218/\text{mL}$;
large size: $\frac{\$1.99}{1000 \text{ mL}} = \$0.00199/\text{mL}$
b) $\$0.199/100$ mL **c)** The large carton is the best buy because its unit rate is the least.

9. a) Answers may vary. There are four 250 mL small jars in one 1000 mL jar. Since 2.79×4 is greater than $9.59, four smaller jars would be more expensive for the equivalent amount of honey. This means the bigger jar is the better buy. **b)** small size: $\frac{\$2.79}{250 \text{ mL}} = \$0.01116/\text{mL}$; large size: $\frac{\$9.59}{1000 \text{ mL}} = \$0.00959/\text{mL}$. Therefore, the large size is the better buy.

10. Trevor: $\frac{84 \text{ km}}{3 \text{ h}} = 28 \text{ km/h}$; Jillian: $\frac{70 \text{ km}}{2.5 \text{ h}} = 28 \text{ km/h}$. They both rode at the same rate; therefore, neither is the fastest cyclist.

11. a) $\frac{\$9.96}{12 \text{ bars}} = \$0.83/\text{bar}$ **b)** Answers may vary. Example: The answer to part a) is a rate because it is a comparison of two quantities in different units. A ratio is a comparison of quantities in the same units.

12. Saskatchewan Glacier: $\frac{1500 \text{ m}}{75 \text{ year}} = 20 \text{ m/year}$; Peyto Glacier: $\frac{1320 \text{ m}}{70 \text{ year}} = 18.86 \text{ m/year}$. The Saskatchewan Glacier has the greater annual rate of melting.

13. a) $\frac{60 \text{ L}}{840 \text{ km}} = 0.0714 \text{ L/km}$ **b)** Answers may vary. Example: Multiply the answer by 100. **c)** Joe's vehicle has the lowest fuel consumption.

14. a) 416.4 euros **b)** 332.14 US dollars **c)** 518.72 Australian dollars

15. a) 1000 m race: 73.11 s; 1500 m race: 111.79 s; 3000 m race: 233.34 s **b)** 13.4 m/s **c)** 128.57 m

16. a) Daniel: 1.50 lawns/h; Grace: 1.33 lawns/h **b)** The difference is 0.17 lawn/h

17.

Planet	Radius (km)	Circumference (km)	Length of Day (h)	Rotation Rate (km/h)
Venus	6051	38 000	2808	13.5
Earth	6378	40 054	24	1669.8
Saturn	60 268	378 483	10 233	37

18. a) 0.8823; It represents that one Canadian dollar is equivalent to 0.8823 US dollar. **b)** $617.61 **c)** 1.1158 **d)** $627.35 US

19. 16.67 m/s

2.3 Proportional Reasoning, pages 67–69

4. a) 33¢/roll **b)** 2 kg/object

5. a) 47¢/pen **b)** 6 cm/block

6. $21.00

7. $\frac{\$35}{5 \text{ h}} = \frac{\$x}{3 \text{ h}}$ or $\frac{\$7}{1 \text{ h}} = \frac{\$x}{3 \text{ h}}$; $21.00

8. a) 10 **b)** 2 **c)** 9 **d)** 9

9. a) 120 km **b)** 20 cans **c)** 89 beats **d)** $64.00

10. a) $\frac{10 \text{ beans}}{17 \text{ g}} = \frac{30 \text{ beans}}{51 \text{ g}}$ **b)** $\frac{13 \text{ boys}}{15 \text{ girls}} = \frac{65 \text{ boys}}{75 \text{ girls}}$ **c)** $\frac{1 \text{ cm}}{25 \text{ km}} = \frac{6.4 \text{ cm}}{160 \text{ km}}$

11. Answers may vary. Example:

$\frac{18 \text{ small gear turns}}{4 \text{ large gear turns}} = \frac{54 \text{ turns}}{x \text{ turns}}$; 12 times or turns.

12. a) $\frac{175 \text{ mL}}{50 \text{ mL}} = \frac{300 \text{ mL}}{x \text{ mL}}$ **b)** $\frac{3 \text{ home runs}}{17 \text{ strikeouts}} = \frac{x \text{ home runs}}{187 \text{ strikeouts}}$

13. 25 nickels

14. Answers may vary. Example: As a unit rate: $\frac{30 \text{ cm}}{6 \text{ h}} = 5 \text{ cm/h}$, so $\frac{45}{5} = 9$ h. As a proportion: $\frac{30 \text{ cm}}{6 \text{ h}} = \frac{45 \text{ cm}}{x \text{ h}}$, which results in $x = 9$ h.

15. Answers may vary. Example: $\frac{1 \text{ figure}}{2 \text{ squares}} = \frac{7 \text{ figures}}{x \text{ squares}}$.

16. $50.00

17. a) $52.80 **b)** $\frac{\$17.60}{2000 \text{ g}} = \frac{\$x}{1600 \text{ g}}$; $x = \$14.08$

18. a) $2.50/ride **b)** $45.00; Answers may vary. Example: Using unit rate: $2.50 \times 18 = \$45.00$. Using a proportion: $\frac{\$2.50}{\text{ride}} = \frac{\$x}{18 \text{ rides}}$, where $x = \$45.00$.

19. a) 4, 9 **b)** $48, 192 km

20. 150 g of rice

21. 17.5 min

22. a) 1.8 m **b)** 48 cm or 0.48 m

23. 0.33 kg

24. a) Answers may vary. Example: The numerators consist of the whole numbers in consecutive order; the denominators consist of the even whole numbers in consecutive order. **b)** Answers may vary. Example: The numerators are multiples of 5 and the denominators are multiples of 6. **c)** Answers may vary. Example: The products are equal. **d)** Answers may vary. Example: The cross-products will be the same. Example: In the equivalent pair $\frac{7}{8} = \frac{14}{16}$, the cross-products are both 112.

25. a) Frog: 96 insects/day; dragonfly: 99 insects/day. The dragon fly eats 3 more insects per day. **b)** 693 insects **c)** 2976 insects

26. a) $1:2$ **b)** $1:4$

27. $20:35$ or $4:7$

28. 13.75 mL

Chapter Review, pages 70–71

1. D **2.** B **3.** E **4.** A **5.** G

6. a) $6:6$ **b)** $6:12$ **c)** $\frac{1}{2} = \frac{3}{6}$ **d)** 50%

7. a) $6:16$ **b)** $\frac{3}{8}$ **c)** $8:4$

8. a) $1:2:5$ **b)** 8 **c)** blue cars to total **d)** silver to (non-silver, non-blue, non-red, and non-yellow) **e)** $\frac{1}{4}$, 25%

9. a) 8 **b)** $10:8$

10. a) $24:6$ **b)** $48:12$ **c)** 4

11. a) 50 steps/min **b)** $0.90/L **c)** 624 km/h **d)** 50 kg/year
12. a) Answers may vary. Example: 4.98 : 13.95
b) Answers may vary. Example: $4.98/3 kg **c)** The unit price in Winnipeg is $1.66/kg. The unit price in Little Grand Rapids is $4.65/kg. The difference in price/kg is $2.99/kg.
13. a) fridge: 5.0¢/h; computer and monitor: 3.6¢/h; television: 1.9¢/h; treadmill: 26.6¢/h **b)** The television has the lowest rate of electricity consumption.
14. a) Shelley travelled farther. **b)** The difference is 2.5 km.
15. a) 16 kg **b)** $10.50 **c)** 18 min
16. a) $7.84 **b)** 5.3 cm
17. a) 8.40 cm **b)** 10.7 g **c)** 33 g
18. a) 5 m **b)** 51 cm

Chapter 3

3.1 Squares and Square Roots, pages 85–87

5. a) $4 = 2 \times 2$ **b)** Yes, the prime factor, 2, appears an even number of times. **c)**

6. a) $64 = 2 \times 2 \times 2 \times 2 \times 2 \times 2$ **b)** Yes, 64 is a perfect square. The prime factor, 2, appears an even number of times. **c)**

8 cm — $A = 64$ m^2

7. a) $42 = 2 \times 3 \times 7$; 42 is not a perfect square.
b) $169 = 13 \times 13$; 169 is a perfect square.
c) $256 = 2 \times 2 \times 2 \times 2 \times 2 \times 2 \times 2 \times 2$; 256 is a perfect square.
8. a) $144 = 2 \times 2 \times 2 \times 2 \times 3 \times 3$; 144 is a perfect square.
b) $60 = 2 \times 2 \times 3 \times 5$; 60 is not a perfect square.
c) $40 = 2 \times 2 \times 2 \times 5$; 40 is not a perfect square.
9. a) 100 square units **b)** 256 square units
10. a) 400 square units **b)** 289 square units
11. a) 81 **b)** 121
12. a) 9 **b)** 324
13. 7 mm
14. 30 cm
15. a) 7 **b)** 8 **c)** 25
16. a) 3 **b)** 5 **c)** 40
17. $54 = 2 \times 3 \times 3 \times 3$; No, 54 is not a perfect square because it has an odd number of factors of 2 and 3.
18. 196 m^2
19. 1360 m
20. a) 36 m^2 **b)** 6 m
21. a) 56 m^2 **b)** Answers may vary. Example: 7 m by 8 m is one set of dimensions for the patio. **c)** No, it is not possible to make a patio with the same area that is a square since 56 is not a perfect square.
22. a) 630 m by 630 m **b)** 395 641 m^2 **c)** 622 m by 622 m or 623 m by 623 m or 624 m by 624 m or 625 m by 625 m or 626 m by 626 m or 627 m by 627 m.
23. 20 m

24. a) 10, 15, 21 **b)** The sum of any two consecutive triangular numbers is a perfect square.
25. a) 12 cm **b)** 1296 cm^2 **c)** 9 times **d)** 3 times **e)** To find the number of times the side length is enlarged, calculate the square root of the times that the area has been enlarged.
26. a) perfect squares: 100 and 10 000 **b)** $\sqrt{100} = 10$ and $\sqrt{10\ 000} = 100$ **c)** Answers may vary. Example: The number 1000 is not a perfect square. The prime factorization of 1000 is $2 \times 2 \times 2 \times 5 \times 5 \times 5$. There is an odd number of factors of 2 and 5.
d) Any power of 10 with an even number of trailing zeros will be a perfect square.
e) No, 1 000 000 000 is not a perfect a square because it has an odd number of trailing zeros.
27. a) $\sqrt{6400} = 80$, $\sqrt{640\ 000} = 800$, $\sqrt{64\ 000\ 000} = 8000$ **b)** Take the square root of 64 and then "add" half the number of trailing zeros from the original number.
c) There is an odd number of trailing zeros.
d) 800 000; Calculate the square root of 64, which is 8. Then count the number of trailing zeros, which is 10. Take half of that number of trailing zeros, which is 5, and attach that many zeros to 8.

3.2 Exploring the Pythagorean Relationship, pages 92–94

4. 900 mm^2; 1600 mm^2; 2500 mm^2
5. a)

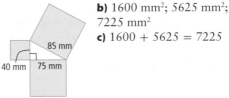

b) 1600 mm^2; 5625 mm^2; 7225 mm^2
c) $1600 + 5625 = 7225$

6. a) $25 + 144 = 169$ **b)** 5 cm; 12 cm; 13 cm
c) The sum of the areas of the two smaller squares is equal to the area of the largest square: $5^2 + 12^2 = 13^2$.
7. a) 81 cm^2; 144 cm^2; 225 cm^2 **b)** $81 + 144 = 225$ **c)** The sum of the areas of the two smaller squares is equal to the area of the largest square: $9^2 + 12^2 = 15^2$.
8. No, the triangle is not a right triangle. The sum of the areas of the smaller squares is not equal to the area of the largest square: $20^2 + 40^2 \neq 50^2$
9. a) 4 cm^2; 9 cm^2; 16 cm^2 **b)** No, the triangle is not a right triangle. The sum of the areas of the smaller squares is not equal to the area of the largest square: $2^2 + 3^2 \neq 4^2$.
10. Yes, the triangle is a right triangle. The sum of the areas of the two smaller squares is equal to the area of the largest square: $120^2 + 160^2 = 200^2$.
11. Answers may vary. Example: No, the triangle is not a right triangle. The sum of areas of the squares of the two shorter sides does not equal the area of the square of the longest side, the hypotenuse. $5^2 = 25$, $6^2 = 36$, and $8^2 = 64$; $25 + 36 \neq 64$.
12. a) 52 cm^2 **b)** 676 mm^2 **c)** 65 cm^2 **d)** 24 cm^2
13. No, the garden is not a right triangle. The sum of the areas of the smaller squares is not equal to the area of the largest square: $4800 + 4800 \neq 9800$.

14. Triangle A is a right triangle: $9^2 + 12^2 = 15^2$.
Triangle B is not a right triangle: $7^2 + 8^2 \neq 11^2$.
Triangle C is a right triangle: $7^2 + 24^2 = 25^2$.
Triangle D is a right triangle: $16^2 + 30^2 = 34^2$.
Triangle E is not a right triangle: $10^2 + 11^2 \neq 14^2$.

15. No, the angle is not a right angle. The diagonal would have to be 10 m for the angle to be right angled.
$6^2 + 8^2 = 100; \sqrt{100} = 10$

16. Answers may vary. Example: Baldeep should ensure that the sum of the areas of the squares for the width and the length of the rectangle equals the area of the square that can be drawn on the diagonal of the rectangle: $144 + 400 = 544$.

17. a) 1225 cm² **b)** 169 mm²

18. a) 28 m² **b)** 16 m²

19. 5 cm² and 25 cm²;

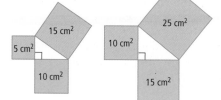

20. Answers may vary. Example: The sum of the areas of the two smaller semicircles is equal to the area of the semicircle attached to the hypotenuse of the triangle.

21. a) 6, 8, and 10 form a Pythagorean triple: $6^2 + 8^2 = 10^2$. **b)** Answers may vary. Example: Multiply each number by 10: $60^2 + 80^2 = 100^2$. The results form a Pythagorean triple. **c)** No, there is no natural number that does not make a Pythagorean triple when 3, 4, and 5 are multiplied by it.

3.3 Estimating Square Roots, pages 99–100

4. Answers may vary for the estimates. **a)** 8.5 **b)** 10.1 **c)** 7.4

5. Answers may vary for the estimates. **a)** 3.7 **b)** 9.3 **c)** 11.7

6. Answers may vary. Example: 90

7. Answers may vary. Example: 130

8. 5, 6, 7, and 8

9. 17, 18, 19, 20, 21, 22, 23, 24

10. Answer may vary. Example: 5.2 m

11. a) Answers may vary. Example: 4.5 cm **b)** 4.5 cm

12. a) Answers may vary. Example: An estimate is 3.2 m. **b)** 3.3 m **c)** Yes, the rug will fit since its side length, 3.3 m, is smaller than the shorter side of the room.

13. a) 10.7 m **b)** Answers may vary. Example: 10 m or 11 m **c)** 100 m² or 121 m² **d)** She will choose the 121 m² dance floor since it is much closer to her desired size.

14. a) 60 **b)** No, there is only one answer. The number must be between 49 and 64. The only multiple of 12 in this range is 60.

15. $\sqrt{27}$, 5.8, 6.3, $\sqrt{46}$, 7

16. a) 27 m² **b)** Answers may vary. Example: The fitness centre should order dimensions of 5.1 m by 5.1 m so that the area does not exceed 75% of the space available.

17. a) 324 cm² **b)** 1296 cm² **c)** 36 cm by 36 cm

18. a) 3 **b)** Answers may vary. Example: 1.7 **c)** 1.73 **d)** Answers may vary. Example: 0.03

19. Answers may vary. Example: A reasonable estimate for the square root of 160 100 is 400. $16 \times 10\,000 = 160\,000$. The square root of 16 is 4. The square root of 10 000 is 100. The square root of 160 100 is approximately $4 \times 100 = 400$.

20. 14

21. 106 500 and 106 800

3.4 Using the Pythagorean Relationship, pages 104–105

3. a) 20 cm **b)** 34 m

4. a) 9.2 cm **b)** 13.6 cm

5. a) 36 cm²; 64 cm² **b)** 100 cm² **c)** 10 cm

6. a) 24 cm **b)** 10 cm

7. a) 7.5 mm **b)** 10.2 mm

8. 206 cm

9. 13.4 m

10. 38.2 m

11. 72.2 cm

12. 8.6 cm

13. 12 mm

14. $b = 4$ m; $c = 7.2$ m

15. 4.5 cm

16. 14.8 mm

3.5 Applying the Pythagorean Relationship, pages 110–111

3. a) 420 m **b)** 323 m **c)** Maria walked further by 97 m.

4. 9.8 m

5. Yes, these dimensions could form a rectangle. Square both sides of the rectangle and then sum the values: $9^2 + 22^2 = 565$. Calculate the square root of 565, which is 23.8 cm. This length is equal to the length of the diagonal.

6. No, there is not a right angle at first base because $27^2 + 27^2 = 38.2^2$. Since the distance between home plate and second base is 37.1 m and not 38.2 m, the triangle is not a right triangle.

7. 12.6 cm

8. Answers may vary. Example: Shahriar is correct. The diagonal is 39.1 cm when calculated with the Pythagorean relationship, which is smaller than the advertised 42 cm diagonal.

9. a) 4.2 cm **b)** 34 cm

10. Yes, she will have enough room. The diagonal of the mat is $\sqrt{12^2 + 12^2} \approx 17.0$ m, according to the Pythagorean relationship. The gymnast requires 16 m for the tumbling run and she will have one metre to spare.

11. maximum of 291.7 cm, minimum of 279.1 cm

12. a) 9.65 m **b)** $19.30

13. 235 km

14. 15.6 mm

Chapter Review, pages 112–113

1. square root **2.** perfect square
3. hypotenuse **4.** Pythagorean relationship
5. prime factorization
6. a) 36 **b)** 121 **c)** 625
7. a) 7 **b)** 16 **c)** 10 000
8. No, the fabric has an area of 4×4 or 16 m². Lisa needs 17 m².
9. a) No, the triangle is not a right triangle. The sum of the two smaller squares is 16 cm² + 16 cm² = 32 cm². This does not equal the area of the largest square, which is 36 cm². **b)** 4 cm; 4 cm; 6 cm
10. Yes, the triangle is a right triangle since the sum of the squares of the two smaller sides is 225 + 1296 = 1521, which is equal to the square of the largest side.
11. Triangles A, C, and D are right triangles.
12. a) Answer may vary. Example: 30 cm² **b)** 5 cm, 6 cm
c) Answer may vary. Example: 5.5 cm
d) Answer may vary. Example: 5.5 cm
13. a) 3.2 **b)** $\sqrt{6}$ is closer to 2 than 3 because 6 is closer to 4 (2²) than 9 (3²). **c)** When 3.61 is squared the result is 13.0321, which is closest to 13.
14. a) $d = 13$ m **b)** $v = 12$ cm
15. a) 5.4 cm; 6.7 cm **b)** 15.7 cm
16. No, the ladder will not reach the window. The length the ladder needs to reach is greater than 4 m: $1^2 + 3.9^2 \approx 4.03^2$.
17. 99.0 cm

Chapter 4

4.1 Representing Percents, pages 128–129

4. a) 112% **b)** $\frac{2}{10}$% **c)** $85\frac{1}{3}$%

5. a) $\frac{3}{8}$% **b)** $125\frac{1}{2}$% **c)** 282%

6. a)

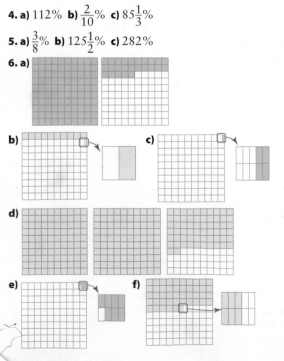

7. a)

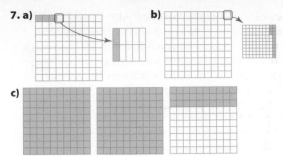

b)

c)

8. a) 3 **b)** 5 **c)** 12
9. Answers may vary. Example: Two situations where the percent will be greater than 100% are a mother's mass compared to her newborn child, and the volume of water in the Pacific Ocean in relation to a lake in Canada.
10. A scientist may need to relate the measurement of something that is less than 1% of its size. Example: The percent of different pollutants in the water will likely be between 0% ands 1%.
11. Saskatchewan   Alberta

12. Answers may vary.

One glass of milk: 30% of the RDV of calcium $3\frac{1}{3}$ of milk: 100% of the RDV of calcium

13. a)   **b)** Answers may vary. You must know how to convert a repeating decimal to fraction form.

14. a)

b)

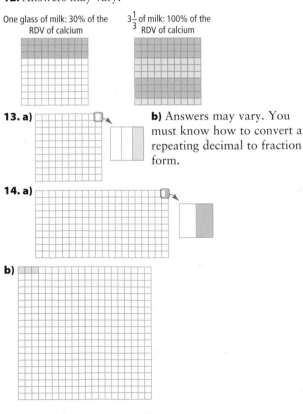

15. Since one square on a hundred grid is equal to 1%, then one square on a thousand grid (10 hundred grids placed together) would be equal to 0.1%. If this pattern is continued, then very small percents can be expressed on larger grids. If a ten million grid was used, then 0.0000125% would be represented by 1.25 squares.

Grid Type (number of squares)	Value of One Square as a Percent
Hundred	1%
Thousand	0.1%
Ten thousand	0.01%
Hundred thousand	0.001%
Million	0.0001%
Ten million	0.000 01%

16. a) 1.7% **b)** 130%

c) $87\frac{1}{2}\%$; $56\frac{1}{4}\%$

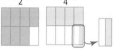

4.2 Fractions, Decimals, and Percents, pages 135–137

4. a) 0.004 or 0.4% **b)** 0.405 or 40.5% **c)** 1.4 or 140%

5. a) 1.7 or 170% **b)** 0.105 or 10.5% **c)** 0.006 or 0.6%

6. a) 0.72% or $\frac{72}{10\,000} = \frac{9}{1250}$ **b)** 54.8% or $\frac{548}{1000} = \frac{137}{250}$

c) 345% or $\frac{345}{100} = \frac{69}{20}$

7. a) 25.6% or $\frac{256}{1000} = \frac{32}{125}$ **b)** 0.05% or $\frac{5}{10\,000} = \frac{1}{2000}$

c) 650% or $\frac{650}{100} = \frac{13}{2}$

8. a) 2.48 or $\frac{248}{100} = \frac{62}{25}$ **b)** 0.0056 or $\frac{56}{10\,000} = \frac{7}{1250}$

c) 0.7575 or $\frac{7575}{10\,000} = \frac{303}{400}$

9. a) 0.059 or $\frac{59}{1000}$ **b)** 5.5 or $\frac{550}{100} = \frac{11}{2}$

c) 0.008 or $\frac{8}{1000} = \frac{1}{125}$

10.

Percent	Fraction	Decimal
165%	$\frac{165}{100}$	1.65
230%	$\frac{230}{100}$	2.3
0.38%	$\frac{38}{10\,000}$	0.0038
19.9%	$\frac{199}{1000}$	0.199

11. a) $\frac{17}{25}$ or 0.68 or 68% **b)** $\frac{9}{24} = \frac{3}{8}$ or 0.375 or 37.5%

12. a) $\frac{33}{25}$ or 1.32 or 132% **b)** $\frac{47}{20}$ or 2.35 or 235%

13. 2000%

14. 2.25% or 0.0225 or $\frac{225}{10\,000} = \frac{9}{400}$

15. smallest to largest: 0.6%, $\frac{5}{8}$%, 33.5%, 0.65, 1.32, 145%

16. approximately 0.4% or $0.00\overline{4}$ or $\frac{4}{900} = \frac{1}{225}$

17. Answers may vary. Example: **a)** "Ticket sales are $\frac{13}{10}$ of what they were this time last year." The number 1.3 sounds like a small number. **b)** "We are already at 0.605 of our target and we just started!" The decimal 0.605 is easily recognizable as more than half. **c)** "We have managed to cut our costs by $\frac{75}{10\,000}$." The large denominator makes this number sound large.

18.

Species	Number	Percent of Total	Fraction of Total	Decimal Equivalent
Chinook	143	53.56%	$\frac{143}{267}$	0.5356
Coho	122	45.69%	$\frac{122}{267}$	0.4569
Steelhead	2	0.75%	$\frac{2}{267}$	0.0075

19. 600% or 6.0 or $\frac{600}{100} = \frac{6}{1}$

20. 90 beats per minute: 120% or $\frac{6}{5}$ or 1.2;

125 beats per minute: $166.\overline{6}$% or $\frac{5}{3}$ or $1.\overline{6}$;

150 beats per minute: 200% or $\frac{200}{100} = \frac{2}{1}$ or 2.0

21.

	Percent	Decimal	Fraction
a)	1000	10.00	$\frac{10}{1}$
b)	500	5.00	$\frac{5}{1}$
c)	250	2.50	$\frac{5}{2}$
d)	125	1.25	$\frac{5}{4}$
e)	62.5	0.625	$\frac{5}{8}$

4.3 Percent of a Number, pages 142–143

3. a) 6000 **b)** 0.75 **c)** 0.04

4. a) 12 **b)** 1000 **c)** 10.5

5. a) 1.3 **b)** approximately 144.88 **c)** $219.63

6. a) 3.25 **b)** 150.8 **c)** $191.25

7. a) 0.5% **b)** 5

8. $21.42

9. 5957.73 m

10. a) 75 mL **b)** 825 mL

11. approximately 649 004 km²

12. 1100 km

13. a) Commission is the portion of the sale price that the real estate agent earns. **b)** $18 700

14. 50; 4% is half of 8%, and 50 is half of 100

15. Answer may vary. Example: $572.15, with an assumption that no rounding occurred after each bid.

16. 8

4.4 Combining Percents, pages 148–149

4. $38.04

5. $66.57

6. $38.25

7. a) 132 caribou **b)** The increase is not 30% because the 20% increase in the second year is based on the new population after the 10% increase in the first year.

8. Answers may vary based on the PST rate in your province. Example: Based on a total tax of 12% (GST = 5% and PST = 7%):

Item Purchased	Price	Total Tax (12%)	Total Cost
a) Boots	$119.99	$14.40	$134.39
b) Pants	$89.99	$10.80	$100.79
c) Gloves	$39.99	$4.80	$44.79
d) Helmet	$189.99	$22.80	$212.79

9. a) $23 736 **b)** $26 109.60
10. $362.10
11. a) $1060.90 **b)** 6.09%
12. a) swim: approximately 2.9%; bike: approximately 77.7%; run: approximately 19.4%
b) approximately 97.1%
13. 70%
14. 8%

Chapter Review, pages 150–151

1. percent   **2.** fractional   **3.** combined
4. a) 2 **b)** 6 **c)** 15
5. a) $\frac{7}{10}$% **b)** $\frac{3}{5}$% **c)** $50\frac{1}{4}$% **d)** 245%

6.
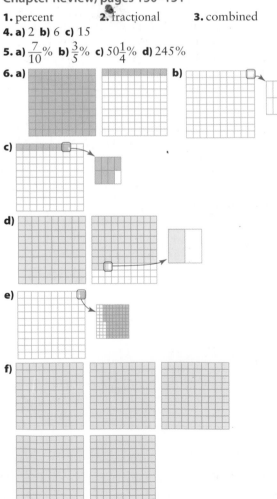

7.
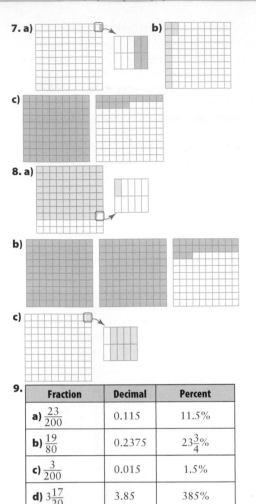

9.

Fraction	Decimal	Percent
a) $\frac{23}{200}$	0.115	11.5%
b) $\frac{19}{80}$	0.2375	$23\frac{3}{4}$%
c) $\frac{3}{200}$	0.015	1.5%
d) $3\frac{17}{20}$	3.85	385%

10. a) $\frac{110}{100} = \frac{11}{10}$ or 1.1 **b)** Answer may vary. Example: It means that you must give more of an effort than you would normally.

11. a) 0.955 or $\frac{955}{1000} = \frac{191}{200}$; Kyle scored $\frac{191}{200}$ on his practice test. **b)** 1.4 or $\frac{140}{100} = \frac{7}{5}$; The store's sales increased by a factor of 1.4. **c)** 0.009 or $\frac{9}{1000}$; By getting your car tuned up, you can reduce emissions by 0.009 times the original amount.

12. a) 264.5 **b)** 40.4 **c)** 0.1 **d)** 0.8 **e)** 7656 **f)** 500
13. 6.25 cm
14. $5.50
15. a) 1814 trees **b)** fir: approximately 31%; pine: approximately 18%; larch: approximately 9%; cedar: approximately 5%; hemlock: approximately 37%
16. $329.31
17. a) No, the populations did not increase by the same amount. In the second year, the 7% increase in Cedarville is applied to the new population after the initial year increase of 7%. In Pinedale, the 15% increase is applied to the initial population of 1200.
b) Cedarville: 1387 people; Pinedale: 1380 people

Chapters 1–4 Review, pages 156–158.

1. Answers may vary. Example: **a)** bar graph: compares data across categories **b)** double bar graph: compares two sets of data across categories **c)** circle graph: compares categories to the whole using percents **d)** line graph: shows changes in data over time

2. a) Answers may vary. Example: A pictograph uses symbols to compare the number of people who prefer different types of food. It would show more clearly that people prefer Italian and Chinese food.

b)

Food Preferences

c) The data do not show changes over time.

3. a) Answers may vary. Example: Game system 1 is more popular than game system 2; more game system 1s and game system 2s were sold in December than in the other months; sales of game system 1 and game system 2 both increase each month.

b)

Game System Sales

c) Answers may vary. Example: Sales of game system 1 are increasing faster than sales of game system 2; Sales of game systems 1 and 2 both increased from July to December. **d)** Answers may vary. Example: the bar graph; It is easier to see the increases in the bar graph. **e)** Answers may vary. Example: A bar graph's strength is that it is easy to compare two sets of data; a bar graph's limitation is that it is harder to see that one set of data is increasing faster than the other. A line graph's strength is that it is easy to see changes over time; a line graph's limitation is that it is harder to compare sales in a particular month.

4. a) Answers may vary. Example: This graph is misleading because computers appear to be the favourite; the line for computers is the longest one and the symbol for computers is much larger.

b)

Favourite Items for a Long Car Trip

Book		represents 10 books
Cell Phone		represents 10 cell phones
Computer		represents 10 computers
MP3 Player		represents 10 mp3 players

c)

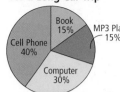
Favourite Items for a Long Car Trip

Book 15% MP3 Player 15% Cell Phone 40% Computer 30%

d) Answers may vary. Example: One advantage of using a circle graph is that each section can be easily compared so you know which items are the most and least popular.

5. Answers may vary. Example:
a) See graph on right.
b) His pulse rate increases for the first 3 min and then levels off.
c) A line graph shows change over time, so you can see how Calvin's pulse rate changes over 5 min.

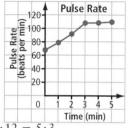
Pulse Rate

6. a) 12 **b)** $\frac{20}{32} = \frac{5}{8}$; 62.5% **c)** 20 : 12 = 5 : 3

7. Answers may vary. Example: They should charge less than $10.39 for their 4-kg bag of cat food. Calculate the price for 1 kg and multiply it by four.

8. a) Answers may vary. Example: Pasta Supreme appears to be the better buy because it is a much larger quantity for just a little bit more cost. **b)** Super Choice: $0.14/100 g; Pasta Supreme: $0.10/100 g **c)** Pasta Supreme is a better buy because it costs less per 100 g. **d)** Answers may vary. Example: Estimating unit costs is useful because it can help you determine the cheapest brand and help you save money.

9. a) Vehicle 1: 10.63 L/100 km; Vehicle 2: 9.72 L/100 km; Vehicle 3: 10.63 L/100 km **b)** Vehicle 2 has the lowest fuel consumption because it uses the least amount of fuel for 100 km.

10. a) $2.56 **b)** 4.4 cm

11. 25

12. a) 64 **b)** 169 **c)** 289 **d)** 6400

13. a) 11 **b)** 30 **c)** 7 **d)** 16

14. a) 36; 49 **b)** 121; 144 **c)** 196; 225

15. a) 7.6 **b)** 11.8 **c)** 2.4 **d)** 5.4

16. 9.5

17. Yes; $11^2 + 60^2 = 61^2$; $121 + 3600 = 3721$

18. a) 118.6 m **b)** $1779

19. 25 m

20.

21. 0.9%

22. a) $0.6\overline{6}$; $\frac{2}{3}$ **b)** 300

23. $28.35

24. 18 000
25. $13.54
26. a) 800 **b)** 196

Chapter 5

5.1 Views of Three-Dimensional Objects, pages 168–169

3. a) top   front   side   **b)** top   front   side

c) top   front   side

4. top view: D; front view: A; side view: B

5. a) 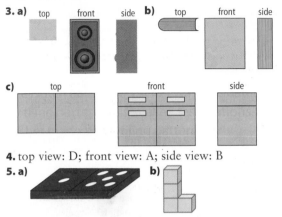   **b)**

6. The new front view is the same as the original side view. The new top view is the same as the original top, but rotated 90° counterclockwise.

top   front   side

7. CD rack

8. Answers may vary. Example: a chair and a bookcase:
Chair: top   front   side

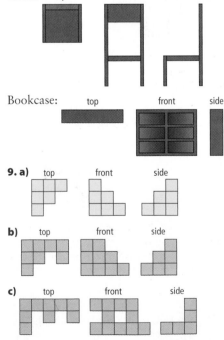

Bookcase: top   front   side

9. a) top   front   side

b) top   front   side

c) top   front   side

10. Answers may vary. Example: a cube and a square-based rectangular prism.

11. a) Answers may vary. Example:
b) 8 m

1 m

5.2 Nets of Three-Dimensional Objects, pages 173–175

3. a) Answers may vary. Example: **b)** Answers may vary. Example:

c) Answers may vary. Example:

4. a) Answers may vary. Example:
30 mm
94 mm
78 mm

b) Answers may vary. Example:
28 cm
21.5 cm   5 cm

5. Answers may vary. Example:

6. a) and **b)** triangular prism
7. rectangular prism: E; cylinder: B; triangular prism: C
8. Answers may vary. Example:
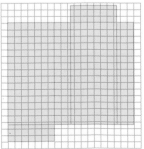

9. Answer may vary. Example:

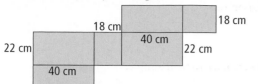

10. a) and **b)** Both nets form the same triangular prism.

11. a) Answers may vary.
Example:

b) Answers may vary.
Example:

12. a) yellow **b)** green **c)** brown

13. There are 11 possible nets:

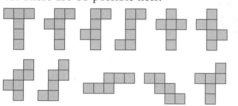

5.3 Surface Area of a Prism, pages 180–181

3. 819.5 cm²
4. 397.0 cm²
5. 7.7 m²
6. 106.7 cm²
7. 94 mm²
8. a) 4 **b)** 6.36 m²
9. Answers may vary. Example: 115 700 mm² (book cover of length 26 cm, width 21 cm, and thickness 2.5 cm)
10. 9.96 m²
11. 70 m²
12. The triangular prism would require less wrapping paper because its surface area of 770 cm² is less than the surface area of 1000 cm² of the rectangular prism.
13. 266 pans
14. a) 9 cm × 13.0 cm × 8.5 cm
b) Yes, these two sets of dimensions are possible: 9 cm × 6.5 cm × 17 cm and 9 cm × 32.5 cm × 3.4 cm.

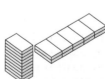

15. a) 1 : 4 **b)** The ratio of the old surface area to the new surface area is 1 : 9. Yes, there is a pattern. The surface area is increased by a factor equal to the square of the multiplier of the edge length.
16. a) one 4-L can and two 1-L cans of wall paint plus one 4-L can of ceiling paint **b)** Answer may vary. Example: The paint costs $73.88. At a tax rate of 12% (GST and PST), the total cost would be $82.75.

5.4 Surface Area of a Cylinder, pages 186–187

3. Answers may vary. Example:

a)   **b)**

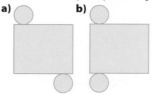

4. a) 736.3 cm² **b)** 2009.6 cm²
5. a) 135.4 cm² **b)** 0.2 m²
6. a) 88.31 cm² **b)** 149.15 cm²
7. Answers may vary. Example: Use a formula. It is quicker, and you are less likely to miss part of the calculation.
8. 5604.9 cm²
9. The 85-cm long container required more plastic. Its surface area of 3125.87 cm² is greater than the surface area of 2758.49 cm² of the other container.
10. 345.4 cm²
11. 538.51 cm²
12. 3228.31 mm²
13. a) length: 251.2 cm; width: 21 cm **b)** 5275.2 cm²

Chapter Review, pages 188–189

1. net   **2.** surface area
3. right prism   **4.** cylinder
5. triangular prism   **6.** rectangular prism
7. a) Answers may vary. Example:

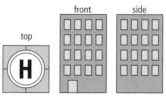

b) Answers may vary. Example:

8. a) Answers may vary.
Example:

b) Answers may vary.
Example:

9. a) The new front view will be the same as the original side view. The new side view will be the same as the original front view. The new top view will be a 90° turn of the original top view.
b)

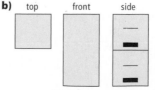

10. a) cylinder **b)** triangular prism **c)** rectangular prism
11. a) Answers may vary. **b)** Answers may vary.
Example: Example:

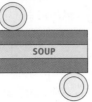

12. Answers may vary. Example:

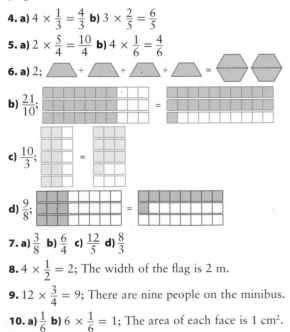

13. a) 864 cm² **b)** 10.5 m²
14. 3648 mm²
15. a) 144 cm² **b)** 3865 cm²
16. 5309 cm²
17. 125.6 m²
18. 92.9 cm²
19. 19 939 cm²

Chapter 6

6.1 Multiplying a Fraction and a Whole Number, pages 202–203

4. a) $4 \times \frac{1}{3} = \frac{4}{3}$ **b)** $3 \times \frac{2}{5} = \frac{6}{5}$

5. a) $2 \times \frac{5}{4} = \frac{10}{4}$ **b)** $4 \times \frac{1}{6} = \frac{4}{6}$

6. a) 2;

b) $\frac{21}{10}$;

c) $\frac{10}{3}$;

d) $\frac{9}{8}$;

7. a) $\frac{3}{8}$ **b)** $\frac{6}{4}$ **c)** $\frac{12}{5}$ **d)** $\frac{8}{3}$

8. $4 \times \frac{1}{2} = 2$; The width of the flag is 2 m.

9. $12 \times \frac{3}{4} = 9$; There are nine people on the minibus.

10. a) $\frac{1}{6}$ **b)** $6 \times \frac{1}{6} = 1$; The area of each face is 1 cm².

11. $12 \times \frac{5}{6} = 10$; Asma's car uses only 10 L of gasoline per 100 km.

12. $10\ 000\ 000 \times \frac{1}{5} = 2\ 000\ 000$; Nunavut is about 2 000 000 km².

13. a) 5; Example: Divide the previous product by two to continue the pattern. **b)** Answer may vary.
Example: $9 \times 9 = 81$, $3 \times 9 = 27$, $1 \times 9 = 9$, $\frac{1}{3} \times 9 = 3$

14. Answers may vary. Example: Jane spends $\frac{1}{4}$ of her allowance on books. If Jane's allowance is $8 each week, how much does she spend on books? Answer: $\frac{1}{4} \times 8 = 2$; She spends $2 each week on books.

15. $30 \times \frac{4}{5} = 24$; Twenty-four students have brown eyes.

16. $15 \times \frac{1}{5} = 3$; The shortest side measures 3 cm.
$15 - 3 = 12$, $12 \div 2 = 6$; The other two sides measure 6 cm each.

17. 341 cm

6.2 Dividing a Fraction by a Whole Number, pages 208–209

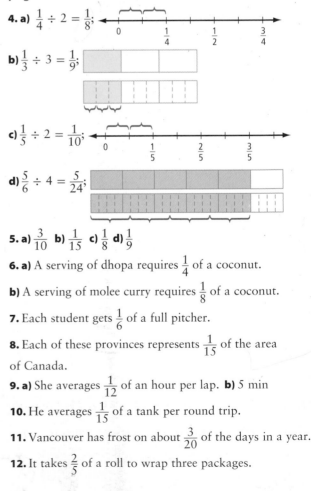

4. a) $\frac{1}{4} \div 2 = \frac{1}{8}$;

b) $\frac{1}{3} \div 3 = \frac{1}{9}$;

c) $\frac{1}{5} \div 2 = \frac{1}{10}$;

d) $\frac{5}{6} \div 4 = \frac{5}{24}$;

5. a) $\frac{3}{10}$ **b)** $\frac{1}{15}$ **c)** $\frac{1}{8}$ **d)** $\frac{1}{9}$

6. a) A serving of dhopa requires $\frac{1}{4}$ of a coconut.

b) A serving of molee curry requires $\frac{1}{8}$ of a coconut.

7. Each student gets $\frac{1}{6}$ of a full pitcher.

8. Each of these provinces represents $\frac{1}{15}$ of the area of Canada.

9. a) She averages $\frac{1}{12}$ of an hour per lap. **b)** 5 min

10. He averages $\frac{1}{15}$ of a tank per round trip.

11. Vancouver has frost on about $\frac{3}{20}$ of the days in a year.

12. It takes $\frac{2}{5}$ of a roll to wrap three packages.

13. Answers may vary. Example: Ryan divides three quarters of a watermelon among himself and five friends. What fraction of the watermelon does each person receive? Answer: $\frac{1}{8}$

14. $\frac{8}{15}$, $\frac{10}{15}$ or $\frac{2}{3}$

15. a)

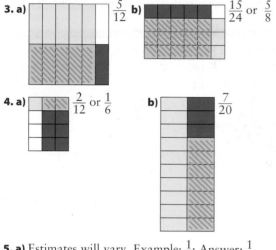

b) Answers may vary. Example: The number line shows that there would be four sections of $\frac{1}{6}$.

6.3 Multiplying Proper Fractions, pages 214–215

3. a) $\frac{5}{12}$ **b)** $\frac{15}{24}$ or $\frac{5}{8}$

4. a) $\frac{2}{12}$ or $\frac{1}{6}$ **b)** $\frac{7}{20}$

5. a) Estimates will vary. Example: $\frac{1}{4}$; Answer: $\frac{1}{4}$

b) Estimates will vary. Example: 0; Answer: $\frac{3}{42}$ or $\frac{1}{14}$

c) Estimates will vary. Example: $\frac{1}{2}$; Answer: $\frac{9}{16}$

6. a) Estimates will vary. Example: $\frac{1}{2}$; Answer: $\frac{8}{25}$

b) Estimates will vary. Example: 1; Answer: $\frac{7}{10}$

c) Estimates will vary. Example: $\frac{1}{4}$; Answer: $\frac{12}{36}$ or $\frac{1}{3}$

7. $\frac{1}{8}$ of a pie

8. a) $\frac{1}{12}$ **b)** 2 h

9. approximately $\frac{1}{200}$

10. $\frac{3}{10}$

11. a) $\frac{1}{3}$ **b)** 28

12. Answers may vary. Example: A bottle is $\frac{3}{4}$ full of juice. If Karen drinks $\frac{1}{2}$ of the juice in the bottle, what fraction of a full bottle did she drink? Answer: $\frac{3}{8}$

13. $\frac{6}{52}$ or $\frac{3}{26}$

14. a) $\frac{1}{8}$ **b)** $\frac{1}{15}$ **c)** $\frac{1}{8}$ **d)** $\frac{7}{32}$

15. a) $\frac{5}{8}$ **b)** $\frac{7}{9}$ **c)** $\frac{3}{4}$ **d)** $\frac{5}{6}$

16. a) $\frac{1}{4}$ and $\frac{1}{4}$ **b)** $\frac{1}{3}$ and $\frac{1}{2}$ **c)** $\frac{1}{6}$ and $\frac{1}{2}$

6.4 Multiplying Improper Fractions and Mixed Numbers, pages 220–221

4. a) $3\frac{2}{3}$ **b)** $2\frac{5}{6}$ **c)** $12\frac{1}{2}$ **d)** $1\frac{3}{5}$

5. a) $\frac{19}{4}$ **b)** $\frac{23}{8}$ **c)** $\frac{19}{3}$ **d)** $\frac{25}{7}$

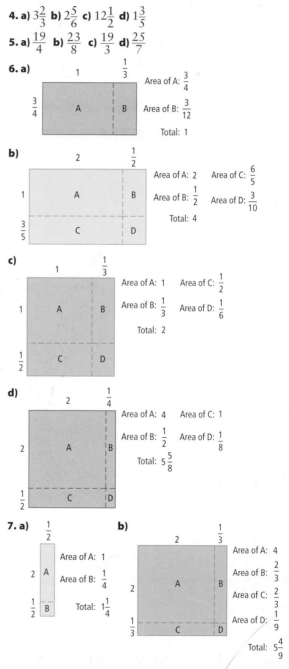

6. a)
Area of A: $\frac{3}{4}$
Area of B: $\frac{3}{12}$
Total: 1

b)
Area of A: 2   Area of C: $\frac{6}{5}$
Area of B: $\frac{1}{2}$ Area of D: $\frac{3}{10}$
Total: 4

c)
Area of A: 1   Area of C: $\frac{1}{2}$
Area of B: $\frac{1}{3}$ Area of D: $\frac{1}{6}$
Total: 2

d)
Area of A: 4   Area of C: 1
Area of B: $\frac{1}{2}$ Area of D: $\frac{1}{8}$
Total: $5\frac{5}{8}$

7. a)
Area of A: 1
Area of B: $\frac{1}{4}$
Total: $1\frac{1}{4}$

b)
Area of A: 4
Area of B: $\frac{2}{3}$
Area of C: $\frac{2}{3}$
Area of D: $\frac{1}{9}$
Total: $5\frac{4}{9}$

c)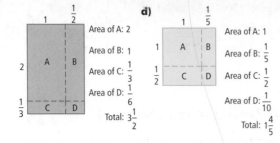

Area of A: 2
Area of B: 1
Area of C: $\frac{1}{3}$
Area of D: $\frac{1}{6}$
Total: $3\frac{1}{2}$

d)

Area of A: 1
Area of B: $\frac{1}{5}$
Area of C: $\frac{1}{2}$
Area of D: $\frac{1}{10}$
Total: $1\frac{4}{5}$

8. a) Estimates may vary. Example: 1; Answer: $1\frac{1}{7}$

b) Estimates may vary. Example: 20; Answer: $18\frac{3}{4}$

c) Estimates may vary. Example: 4; Answer: $3\frac{2}{3}$

9. a) Estimates may vary. Example: 4; Answer: $4\frac{8}{9}$

b) Estimates may vary. Example: 12; Answer: $11\frac{1}{3}$

c) Estimates may vary. Example: 24; Answer: $22\frac{3}{4}$

10. $7\frac{1}{2}$ laps

11. 54 h

12. $3\frac{1}{2}$ h

13. a) $\frac{5}{8}$ h **b)** $37\frac{1}{2}$ min

14. $4\frac{3}{8}$ times as much as the den

15. $96 altogether

16. $1.75

17. Answers may vary. Example: The product is smaller than the mixed fraction. The product is larger than the proper fraction.

18. Answers may vary. Example: It took Mary $3\frac{1}{3}$ h to finish her project. Roger spent $1\frac{1}{2}$ times as long as Mary to complete his project. How many hours did it take Roger to complete his project? Answer: 5 h

19. a) If each fraction is changed to its improper fraction form, the numerator is 13, and the denominator is twice the denominator of the previous term; $\frac{13}{48}, \frac{13}{96}, \frac{13}{192}$

b) Each term is multiplied by $\frac{3}{2}$ to get the next term; $20\frac{1}{4}, 30\frac{3}{8}, 45\frac{9}{16}$

20. a) 15 **b)** 10 **c)** $12\frac{5}{6}$ **d)** $3\frac{11}{15}$

21. a) $1\frac{1}{2}$ **b)** $1\frac{1}{5}$ **c)** $2\frac{1}{2}$ **d)** $2\frac{1}{2}$

6.5 Dividing Fractions and Mixed Numbers, pages 227–229

5. a) 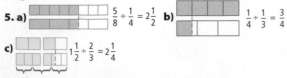 $\frac{5}{8} \div \frac{1}{4} = 2\frac{1}{2}$ **b)** $\frac{1}{4} \div \frac{1}{3} = \frac{3}{4}$

c) $1\frac{1}{2} \div \frac{2}{3} = 2\frac{1}{4}$

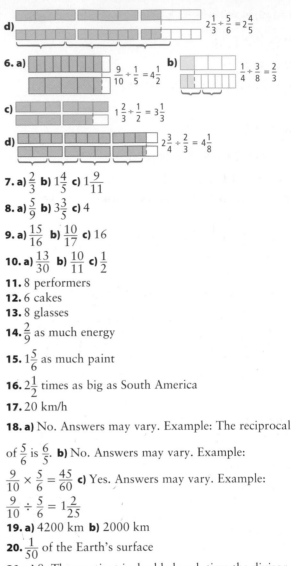

d) $2\frac{1}{3} \div \frac{5}{6} = 2\frac{4}{5}$

6. a) $\frac{9}{10} \div \frac{1}{5} = 4\frac{1}{2}$ **b)** $\frac{1}{4} \div \frac{3}{8} = \frac{2}{3}$

c) $1\frac{2}{3} \div \frac{1}{2} = 3\frac{1}{3}$

d) $2\frac{3}{4} \div \frac{2}{3} = 4\frac{1}{8}$

7. a) $\frac{2}{3}$ **b)** $1\frac{4}{5}$ **c)** $1\frac{9}{11}$

8. a) $\frac{5}{9}$ **b)** $3\frac{3}{5}$ **c)** 4

9. a) $\frac{15}{16}$ **b)** $\frac{10}{17}$ **c)** 16

10. a) $\frac{13}{30}$ **b)** $\frac{10}{11}$ **c)** $\frac{1}{2}$

11. 8 performers

12. 6 cakes

13. 8 glasses

14. $\frac{2}{9}$ as much energy

15. $1\frac{5}{6}$ as much paint

16. $2\frac{1}{2}$ times as big as South America

17. 20 km/h

18. a) No. Answers may vary. Example: The reciprocal of $\frac{5}{6}$ is $\frac{6}{5}$. **b)** No. Answers may vary. Example: $\frac{9}{10} \times \frac{5}{6} = \frac{45}{60}$ **c)** Yes. Answers may vary. Example: $\frac{9}{10} \div \frac{5}{6} = 1\frac{2}{25}$

19. a) 4200 km **b)** 2000 km

20. $\frac{1}{50}$ of the Earth's surface

21. a) 8; The quotient is doubled each time the divisor is halved.

b) $9 \div 9 = 1, 9 \div 3 = 3, 9 \div 1 = 9, 9 \div \frac{1}{3} = 27$

22. Answers may vary. Example: Mac can ride his scooter to his grandmother's house in $3\frac{3}{4}$ h. If he takes the bus, he can make the trip in $2\frac{1}{4}$ h. How many times longer does it take him to ride his scooter than it takes him to ride the bus? Answer: It takes Mac $1\frac{2}{3}$ times longer to ride his scooter.

23. $4\frac{1}{3}$ times as fast

24. $\frac{35}{39}$ of the area of Ellesmere Island

6.6 Applying Fraction Operations, pages 234–235

4. a) $\frac{5}{12}$ **b)** 4 **c)** $4\frac{3}{4}$

5. a) $\frac{9}{14}$ **b)** $2\frac{1}{2}$ **c)** $7\frac{7}{11}$

6. a) \$584 **b)** \$656 **c)** \$728 **d)** \$620

7. $\frac{1}{6}$

8. a) $\frac{3}{16}$ **b)** $\frac{1}{8}$

9. $\left(1 - \frac{5}{7}\right) \times 28 = 8; \frac{5}{7} \times 28 = 20, 28 - 20 = 8$

10. a) 105 g **b)** 150 g **c)** 125 g

11. a) $4\frac{1}{4}$ pages **b)** \$1050 **c)** approximately \$247.06

12. \$40

13. a) $\frac{5}{2} \times \left(\frac{3}{5} - \frac{2}{5}\right) + \frac{1}{2} = 1$ **b)** $1\frac{1}{2} + 2\frac{1}{2} \div \left(\frac{3}{4} - \frac{1}{8}\right)$

c) $\left(\frac{2}{3} - \frac{1}{6} + \frac{5}{6}\right) \div \frac{16}{9} = \frac{3}{4}$

14. Answers may vary. Example: **a)** $\frac{1}{2} \times \frac{1}{2} - \frac{1}{2} \times \frac{1}{2}$

b) $\frac{1}{2} + \frac{1}{2} \div \frac{1}{2} - \frac{1}{2} \times \frac{1}{2}$ **c)** $\left(\frac{1}{2} + \frac{1}{2}\right) \times \frac{1}{2} \times \frac{1}{2}$ **d)** $\left(\frac{1}{2} + \frac{1}{2} + \frac{1}{2}\right) \div \frac{1}{2}$

e) $\frac{1}{2} \times \frac{1}{2} + \frac{1}{2} \times \frac{1}{2}$ **f)** $\frac{1}{2} \div \frac{1}{2} \div \frac{1}{2} \div \frac{1}{2}$ **g)** $\frac{1}{2} \times \frac{1}{2} \times \frac{1}{2} + \frac{1}{2}$

h) $\left(\frac{1}{2} + \frac{1}{2}\right) + \left(\frac{1}{2} \times \frac{1}{2}\right)$ **i)** $\left(\frac{1}{2} + \frac{1}{2}\right) \div \frac{1}{2} + \frac{1}{2}$

15. $\frac{13}{12}$

16. There are 36 black notes and 52 white notes.

17. The racks hold 128, 64, and 32 CDs.

Chapter Review, pages 236–237

1. B **2.** C **3.** A

4. a) reciprocal **b)** Answer may vary. Example: The multiplier of a number to give a product of 1.

5. order of operations

6. Answer may vary. Example: **a)**

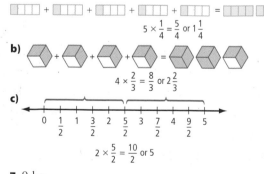

$5 \times \frac{1}{4} = \frac{5}{4}$ or $1\frac{1}{4}$

b)

$4 \times \frac{2}{3} = \frac{8}{3}$ or $2\frac{2}{3}$

c)

$2 \times \frac{5}{2} = \frac{10}{2}$ or 5

7. 9 kg

8. 4 cm

9. a) Answer may vary. Example:

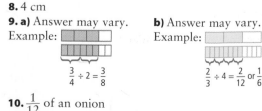

$\frac{3}{4} \div 2 = \frac{3}{8}$

b) Answer may vary. Example:

$\frac{2}{3} \div 4 = \frac{2}{12}$ or $\frac{1}{6}$

10. $\frac{1}{12}$ of an onion

11. $\frac{3}{40}$ of the days of the year

12.

$\frac{1}{2}$ of $\frac{3}{4} = \frac{3}{8}$

$\frac{3}{4}$ of $\frac{1}{2} = \frac{3}{8}$

13. a) Estimates will vary. Example: $\frac{1}{4}$; Answer: $\frac{9}{25}$

b) Estimates will vary. Example: $\frac{1}{2}$; Answer: $\frac{1}{3}$

c) Estimates will vary. Example: 0; Answer: $\frac{1}{14}$

14. $\frac{1}{5}$ of the class

15. a) Estimates will vary. Example: 3; Answer: $\frac{48}{15}$ or $3\frac{1}{5}$

b) Estimates will vary. Example: 4; Answer: $\frac{49}{12}$ or $4\frac{1}{12}$

c) Estimates will vary. Example: 8; Answer: $\frac{19}{2}$ or $9\frac{1}{2}$

16. 1330 km

17. 84 h

18. approximately 44 cm

19. a) He multiplied the two numbers rather than dividing them. **b)** $\frac{2}{9}$

20. a) $\frac{4}{5}$ **b)** $1\frac{5}{9}$ **c)** 10

21. 30 days

22. $7\frac{1}{2}$ h

23. $1\frac{1}{2}$ times as long

24. a) $\frac{7}{8}$ **b)** $1\frac{4}{5}$

25. $3\frac{1}{2} \div \frac{1}{4} = 14; 16 \times \frac{1}{4} = 4$; He only has enough pasta to cook 14 dinners. He would need four full packages of pasta to cook 16 dinners.

26. $\frac{1}{2}$ full

27. 6 m

Chapter 7

7.1 Understanding Volume, pages 250–253

3. a) 60 cm³ **b)** 216 cm³ **c)** 1920 cm³

4. a) 96 cm³ **b)** 72 cm³ **c)** 126 cm³

5. a) 60 cm³; 60 cm³ **b)** 960 cm³; 960 cm³

6. a) 153 cm³; 153 cm³ **b)** 375 cm³; 375 cm³

7. a) 4 cm **b)** 7 cm **c)** 4 cm

8. 75 cm³

9. There are four ways to build a rectangular prism from 16 centimetre cubes.

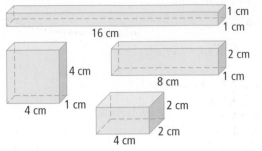

Changing the orientation of each figure does not form a new figure.

Length (cm)	Width (cm)	Height (cm)	Volume (cm³)
16	1	1	16
4	4	1	16
2	8	1	16
2	2	4	16

10. 125 000 cm³
11. 93.6 cm³
12. 0.1875 m
13. a) 1 687 500 cm³ **b)** 1687.5 L
14. 24 530 m³
15. 1.6%
16. a) Structure 1: 10 cubes; Structure 2: 14 cubes; Structure 3: 15 cubes **b)** Structure 1: 17 cubes; Structure 2: 22 cubes; Structure 3: 30 cubes **c)** Structure 1: 27 cubes; Structure 2 : 36 cubes; Structure 3: 45 cubes **d)** volume of Structure 1: 216 cm³, volume of Structure 2: 288 cm³, volume of Structure 3: 360 cm³
17. level of water in the tank: 15.25 cm
18. a) volume of cube to volume of box = 1 to 8 **b)** area of base of cube to area of base of box = 1 to 4 **c)** height of cube to height of box = 1 to 2 **d)** When the side length of a cube is doubled, the area of the base is four times as large and the volume of the cube is eight times as large.

7.2 Volume of a Prism, pages 258–261

4. a) 15 m³ **b)** 792 m³ **c)** 49.6 m³
5. a) 40 m³ **b)** 504 cm³ **c)** 213.759 mm³ **d)** 253.952 cm³
6. a) 1000 cm³ **b)** 27 cm³ **c)** 15.625 cm³
7. a) 294 cm³ **b)** 133.65 m³ **c)** 13 440 000 mm³
8. a) 84 m³ **b)** 1200 cm³ **c)** 514.15 mm³
9. a) 200 cm³ **b)** 320.625 cm³ **c)** 5 460 000 mm³
10. a) 200 cm³ **b)** 84 cm³ **c)** 1800 cm³
11.

Length (cm)	Width (cm)	Height (cm)	Volume (cm³)
7	2	5	70
12	9	10	1080
16	15	5	1200

12.

Base (cm)	Height of Triangle (cm)	Height of Prism (cm)	Volume (cm³)
7	2	10	70
18	12	10	1080
20	14	5	700

13. The landscaper does not have enough gravel. She needs 0.728 m³ of gravel and has 0.5 m³ of gravel. She will need 0.228 m³ more gravel.
14. 4800 cm³
15. 18 m³
16. 460 800 cm³

17. 40 trips
18. a) No. There is no whole number that can be cubed that will equal 18. **b)** Suki would need 27 cubes to make a 3 × 3 × 3 cube.
19. volume of cube: 343 cm³; volume of rectangular prism: 360 cm³; volume of triangular prism: 367.5 cm³. Harvey the guppy will have the most water in the triangular prism.
20. 562.5 cm³
21. 16 rectangular prisms with the dimensions shown in the table can be sketched.

Length (cm)	Width (cm)	Height (cm)
1	1	120
2	60	1
3	40	1
4	30	1
5	24	1
6	20	1
8	15	1
10	12	1
2	2	30
2	3	20
4	2	15
5	2	12
2	6	10
6	4	5
8	3	5
4	10	3

22. maximum volume of cement: 16.59 m³, assuming the tank is 1 m high
23. Both prisms have the same volume.
24. a) depth of water: 0.8 m **b)** water left after 2.5 h: 810 m³; new depth of water: 0.675 m **c)** length of time: 12 h

7.3 Volume of a Cylinder, pages 265–267

4. a) 1805.5 cm³ **b)** 7385.28 cm³ **c)** 1.1775 m³
5. a) 628 cm³ **b)** 4179.34 cm³ **c)** 9.87844 m³ **d)** 1589.625 cm³
6. a) 1570 cm³ **b)** 0.785 m³ **c)** 1907.55 cm³
7. a) 602.88 cm³ **b)** 21.98 m³ **c)** 4239 cm³ **d)** 309.976875 m³
8. 3 cm

9. 3234.9065 cm^3

10. a) P6 Truss solar array; volume: 6578.82438 m^3.
b) Estimate of the total volume is 7000 m^3. Total volume: 7209.078115 m^3

11. 3.925 m^3

12. Martha should buy the "Popcorn Lover's' container because it has a larger volume. The volume of the "Jumbo" popcorn container is 12 560 cm^3. The volume of the "Popcorn Lover's" container is 14 130 cm^3.

13. 5 m^3

14. 251.2 m^3

15. a) The volume of the cylinder is four times as large. The volume of the cylinder is calculated using the formula $V = (\pi \times r^2) \times h$. If the radius is doubled, the formula will be $V = (\pi \times (2r)^2) \times h$
$$V = (\pi \times 4r^2) \times h$$
$$V = 4(\pi \times r^2) \times h$$

b) The volume of the cylinder is twice as large. The volume of the cylinder is calculated using the formula $V = (\pi \times r^2) \times h$. If the height is doubled, the formula will be $V = (\pi \times r^2) \times 2h$
$$V = 2(\pi \times r^2) \times h$$

16. 1695.6 cm^3; Assume that one quarter of the block of cheese was cut away.

17. a) 1.884 m^3 **b)** 0.4 m^3 **c)** 0.628 m^3

18. 7 h

7.4 Solving Problems Involving Prisms and Cylinders, pages 273–275

3. a) To build a giant prism with a triangular base of length 5.6 m and height 6.8 m requires four prisms on the bottom layer. $4 + 3 + 3 + 2 + 2 + 1 + 1 = 16$
The artist would need 16 small prisms to build the large prism. With 20 prisms, he has enough. **b)** 22.47 m^3

4. 46.9 cm

5. 2.826 m^3

6. 2.0 cm^3

7. 48 937.5 cm^3

8. One crate will be enough. The volume of the crate is 63 m^3 and the volume of the 25 000 boxes is 50 m^3.

9. All of the files will fit in the carton. The volume of the carton is 72 000 000 cm^3 and the volume of 9000 boxes is 70 200 000 cm^3.

10. a) 372 875 cm^3 **b)** 1 864 375 cm^3 **c)** To reach this goal the garbage can should be 0.5 full on each lunch hour on each of the five school days.

11. 60 cm

12. 91 pails

13. 27 prisms

14. $12.78 per jar

15. a) 1300 cm^3 **b)** You can check your calculations by dividing the shape into a different set of rectangular prisms.

16. a) 203 472 cm^3 **b)** 13 200 cm^3 **c)** 15.4 pails

17. Answers may vary. Example: Rolling the cylinder so that the circumference is 28 cm and the height is 22 cm will produce the larger volume. The cylinder with a circumference of 22 cm and a height of 28 cm has a

volume of 1077 cm^3. The cylinder with a circumference of 28 cm and a height of 22 cm has a volume of 1373 cm^3.

18. 5 cm

19. 6280 cm^3

20. 2.5 m

21. a) 149 250 m^3 **b)** 4 h and 9 min

Chapter Review, pages 276–277

1. B **2.** D **3.** A **4.** C

5. a) 84 cm^3 **b)** 14 080 cm^3 **c)** 81 cm^3

6. a) 24 cm^3 **b)** 40 cm^3 **c)** 150 cm^3

7. 196 cm^3

8. a) 168 cm^3 **b)** 2250 cm^3

9. a) 1000 cm^3 **b)** 614.125 cm^3

10. a) 120 cm^3 **b)** 70 cm^3

11. a) 100 cm^3 **b)** 14 400 mm^3

12. 0.6 m^3

13. a) 55 080 m^3 **b)** 1311.4 truck loads **c)** 11 days

14. a) 125 600 cm^3 **b)** 327 910.2 m^3

15. a) 2317.32 cm^3 **c)** 4578.12 cm^3

16. 141.3 m^3

17. 76.93 m^3 or 77 m^3

18. 301.3 mm^3

19. 8.79 m

20. a) volume of water: 0.9375 m^3
b) length of time: 1 min 34 s

Chapter 8

8.1 Exploring Integer Multiplication, pages 291–292

5. a) $(+5) \times (+1)$ **b)** $(+2) \times (-6)$

6. a) $(+3) \times (+7)$ **b)** $(+4) \times (-4)$

7. a) $(+8) + (+8) + (+8)$
b) $(-6) + (-6) + (-6) + (-6) + (-6)$

8. a) $(+2) + (+2) + (+2) + (+2) + (+2) + (+2)$
b) $(-9) + (-9) + (-9) + (-9)$

9. a) $(+2) \times (+4)$ **b)** $(+4) \times (-2)$

10. a) $(+7) \times (+2)$ **b)** $(+6) \times (-1)$

11. a) $(-3) \times (-2)$ **b)** $(-3) \times (+3)$

12. a) $(-1) \times (+7)$ **b)** $(-2) \times (-5)$

13. a) $(+4) \times (+6) = 24$ **b)** $(+7) \times (-2) = -14$
c) $(-1) \times (+5) = -5$ **d)** $(-8) \times (-2) = 16$

14. a) $(+6) \times (+2) = 12$; The temperature increased 12 °C in 6 h. **b)** $(+4) \times (+8) = 32$; Ayesha repaid a total of $32.

15. $(+12) \times (-3) = -36$; The aircraft descends 36 m.

16. a) 40 m **b)** 12 m

17. 16 m

18. No. Doubling a negative integer results in an integer of lesser value.

19. a) 3 **b)** Yes; -6 **c)** The easiest solution is to multiply each integer in part a) by -4. Many other solutions are possible. Example:

-4	-22	14
-4	4	-12
-4	6	-14

20. Many solutions are possible. Example:

a)

1	1	−1
1	−1	1
−1	1	1

b)

1	−1	1
−1	−1	−1
1	−1	1

8.2 Multiplying Integers, pages 297–298

4. a) $(+2) \times (+4)$ **b)** $(+3) \times (-5)$

5. a) $(+2) \times (-6)$ **b)** $(+4) \times (+4)$

6. a)

; 25

b)

; −18

7. a) −28 **b)** +18

8. a) 40 **b)** −30 **c)** −35 **d)** 32

9. a) 36 **b)** 54 **c)** −24 **d)** 0

10. Estimates may vary. **a)** −408 **b)** 814 **c)** −1080 **d)** 1316

11. Estimates may vary. **a)** 252 **b)** −1326 **c)** 1188 **d)** 3025

12. $180

13. 1500 m

14. a) The first week, the value of her shares dropped by 4500¢ or $45.00. **b)** The second week, the value of her shares rose by 6375¢ or $63.75. **c)** Over the two-week period her shares rose by 1875¢ or $18.75.

15. 2400 m

16. −23 and −18

17. The least product is $(+99) \times (-82)$. The first two products have factors with like signs. Therefore, only the third product is negative.

18. Answers may vary. Example: **a)** Explain to your friend that the products are decreasing by five. So, as the pattern continues, the missing numbers are −5, −10, −15, and so on. **b)** Change the order of the factors to $(+6) \times (-2)$. Then, use the following pattern: $(+6) \times (+3) = 18$, $(+6) \times (+2) = 12$, $(+6) \times (+1) = 6$, $(+6) \times 0 = 0$, $(+6) \times (-1) = -6$, $(+6) \times (-2) = -12$.

19. a) Yes; $(+2) \times (+2) = 4$ and $(-2) \times (-2) = 4$. **b)** No. Since −4 is negative, the two factors must have opposite signs. Therefore, these factors cannot be equal.

20. a) $(+6) \times (+3) = +18$ **b)** $(+5) \times (-2) = -10$ **c)** $(-4) \times (+3) = -12$ **d)** $(-4) \times (-4) = +16$

21. a) $(-1) \times (-10)$, $(-2) \times (-5)$, $(+1) \times (+10)$, $(+2) \times (+5)$, $(-10) \times (-1)$, $(-5) \times (-2)$, $(+10) \times (+1)$, $(+5) \times (+2)$ **b)** $(-1) \times (+16)$, $(+16) \times (-1)$, $(+1) \times (-16)$, $(-16) \times (+1)$, $(+2) \times (-8)$, $(-8) \times (+2)$, $(-2) \times (+8)$, $(+8) \times (-2)$, $(+4) \times (-4)$, $(-4) \times (+4)$ **c)** $(+1) \times (-24)$, $(-1) \times (+24)$, $(+2) \times (-12)$, $(-2) \times (+12)$, $(+3) \times (-8)$, $(-3) \times (+8)$, $(+4) \times (-6)$, $(-4) \times (+6)$, $(-24) \times (+1)$, $(+24) \times (-1)$, $(-12) \times (+2)$, $(+12) \times (-2)$, $(-8) \times (+3)$, $(+8) \times (-3)$, $(-6) \times (+4)$, $(+6) \times (-4)$

22. −9 and 4

23. Answers may vary. Example: The temperature dropped 6 °C/h over a 5-h period. What was the temperature at the end of the 5-h period if the original temperature was 0 °C?

24. Answers may vary. Example: A mine elevator descends at a rate of 2 m/s. How far would it descend in 5 min? Answer: $(-2) \times (+5) \times (+60) = -600$. The elevator would descend 600 m.

25. Descriptions may vary. Example: **a)** Each number is the previous number multiplied by 3. The next three numbers are 81, 243, and 729. **b)** Each number is the previous number multiplied by −2. The next three numbers are −16, +32, and −64. **c)** Each number is the previous number multiplied by 2. The next three numbers are −32, −64, and −128. **d)** Each number is the previous number multiplied by −4. The next three numbers are 512, −2048, and 8192.

26. a) One of the integers is 1. **b)** One of the integers is −1. **c)** The two integers have different signs, and neither integer is a 1, 0, or −1. **d)** Both integers are less than −1 or both integers are greater than +1.

27. a) −1, 0, 1 **b)** −2, −1, 0, 1, 2 **c)** No. Explanations may vary. Example: The sum of consecutive integers is zero only if the integers include zero and pairs of integers with opposite signs. Therefore, the number of integers must be odd.

28. a) −216 **b)** Yes; −1728 **c)** No.

29. a) The product of an even number of positive integers is positive. **b)** The product of an odd number of positive integers is positive. **c)** The product of an even number of negative integers is positive. **d)** The product of an odd number of negative numbers is negative.

8.3 Exploring Integer Division, pages 304–305

3. a) $(+10) \div (+2) = +5$ **b)** $(-16) \div (-4) = +4$ **c)** $(-14) \div (+2) = -7$

4. a) $(-4) \div (-2) = +2$ **b)** $(+9) \div (+3) = +3$ **c)** $(-12) \div (+6) = -2$

5. a) $(+14) \div (+2) = +7$; $(+14) \div (+7) = +2$ **b)** $(-10) \div (-2) = +5$; $(-10) \div (+5) = -2$

6. a) $(+15) \div (+5) = +3$; $(+15) \div (+3) = +5$ **b)** $(-18) \div (-9) = +2$; $(-18) \div (+2) = -9$

7. a)

$(+16) \div (+4) = +4$

b)

$(-7) \div (+7) = -1$

c)

$(-12) \div (-6) = +2$

8. a)

$(-20) \div (-10) = +2$

b)

$(-10) \div (+2) = -5$

c)

$(+4) \div (+2) = +2$

9. 7 min

10. a) The temperature fell −18 °C **b)** −3 °C/ h; Assume that the rate of change was constant.

11. $2

12. a)

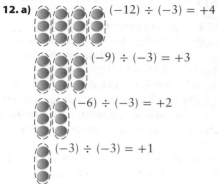

$(-12) \div (-3) = +4$

$(-9) \div (-3) = +3$

$(-6) \div (-3) = +2$

$(-3) \div (-3) = +1$

Descriptions may vary. Example: The quotients are decreasing consecutive integers starting with +4.
b) $(+6) \div (-3) = -2$

13. a)

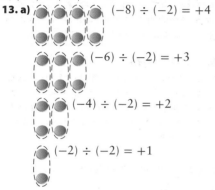

$(-8) \div (-2) = +4$

$(-6) \div (-2) = +3$

$(-4) \div (-2) = +2$

$(-2) \div (-2) = +1$

Descriptions may vary. Example: The quotients are decreasing consecutive integers starting with +4.
b) $(+4) \div (-2) = (-2)$

14. a) $(-2000) \div (-500) = (+4)$ **b)** Answers may vary. Example: Let each chip represent 100 m. **c)** +4

15. a) 15 positive chips are grounped by 5s into 3 groups. 3 positive chips are grouped by 3s into 1 group. Quotient is 1.

b) 24 negative chips are grouped by 2s into 12 groups. These 12 groups represent $(-24) \div (-2) = 12$. 12 positive chips are grouped by 4s into 3 groups. Quotient is 3.

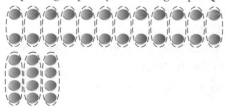

c) 20 negative chips are separated into 2 groups of 10 chips. These 10 chips are grouped by 5s into 2 groups. Quotient is 2.

d) 18 negative chips are separated into 2 groups of 9 chips. These 9 chips are grouped by 3s into 3 groups. Quotient is −3.

16. In 3 h, the temperature will be −17 °C. Assume that the temperature continues to drop at the constant rate of 2 °C/h.

8.4 Dividing Integers, pages 310–311

5. a) $(+18) \div (+9) = +2$; $(+18) \div (+2) = +9$
b) $(-12) \div (-3) = +4$; $(-12) \div (+4) = -3$
6. a) $(-10) \div (+5) = -2$; $(-10) \div (-2) = +5$
b) $(+16) \div (+2) = +8$; $(+16) \div (+8) = +2$
7. a)

The quotient is +2.
b)

The quotient is +5.
c)

The quotient is −2.
d)

The quotient is +2.
8. a)

The quotient is +2.
b)

The quotient is +4.
c)

The quotient is −11.
d)

The quotient is +3.
9. a) +4; $(+4) \times (+5) = +20$ **b)** −6; $(-6) \times (-6) = +36$
c) −3; $(-3) \times (+19) = -57$ **d)** +2; $(+2) \times (-42) = -84$
10. a) +1 **b)** −19 **c)** 0 **d)** −4
11. 4 months
12. a) 6 m/min **b)** 8 m/min
13. 7
14. The drill cut through the floor at a rate of 3 cm/min. Assume that the cutting rate was constant.

15. $12

16. $(+2408) \div (-43)$. In the first two expressions, the two integers have the same sign, so both these quotients are positive. In the third expression, the two integers have different signs, so the quotient is negative.

17. -16

18. a) $(+72) \div (+8) = +9$ **b)** $(-120) \div (+12) = -10$
c) $(+143) \div (-13) = -11$ **d)** $(-84) \div (-14) = +6$

19. A pump draws 80 L of water from a storage tank in 16 s. By how much does the volume of water in the tank change in 1 s?

20. Answers may vary. Example: Yvette borrows $80 from her brother and pays him back in 16 equal weekly payments. How much does she pay her brother each week?

21. a) Each number in the sequence is the previous number divided by 5. The next three terms are $+200$, $+40$, and $+8$. **b)** Each number in the sequence is the previous number divided by -2. The next three terms are -32, $+16$, and -8. **c)** Each number in the sequence is the previous number divided by 10. The next three numbers are -100, -10, and -1. **d)** Each number in the sequence is the previous number divided by -3. The next three numbers are $+18$, -6, and $+2$.

22. $+30$ and -10.

8.5 Applying Integer Operations, pages 315–317

4. a) $+17$ **b)** -11 **c)** $+21$

5. a) -3 **b)** 0 **c)** $+4$

6. a) 6 **b)** -14 **c)** -10

7. a) -32 **b)** 41 **c)** 3

8. $-2\ °C$

9. a) a decrease of two subscribers per month **b)** 195

10. a decrease of 1000 people

11. -55

12. a) 12 strokes below par, or -12 **b)** 276

13. $90\ °C$

14. 12 weeks

15. 8 h

16. a) an increase of 50 m **b)** 10 m/min

17. 7:54 a.m.

18. a) $6000/month **b)** $12\ 000/month.

19. a) Rohana spent $150, saved $90, and still owes her sister $40. **b)** 4

20. a) $20 - 3 \times (-8) = 44$ **b)** $4 \times 5 + (-2) \times (-3) = 26$
c) $-62 \div (-11 + 9) = 31$
d) $[-3 + (-5)] \times 3 \div (-4) - 13 = -7$

21. a) $2 \times 3 - 4 \times 5 = -14$ **b)** $3 \times [14 + (-2)] - 30 = 6$

22. -21 and -13

23. a) 130 **b)** 65%

24. Answers may vary. Example:
$(-2) \div (-2) + (-2) \div (-2) = 2$;
$[-2 + (-2) + (-2)] \div (-2) = 3$;
$-2 \times (-2) \times (-2) \div (-2) = 4$;
$-2 \times (-2) + (-2) \div (-2) = 5$;
$-2 - (-2) \times (-2) \times (-2) = 6$;
$-2 \times (-2) + (-2) \times (-2) = 8$

Chapter Review, pages 318–319

1. zero

2. the operation (subtraction) within the brackets

3. zero pair

4. a) $(+2) \times (-5)$ **b)** $(-4) \times (+2)$

5. a)   The product is $+9$.

b)

The product is -20.

c)   The product is $+2$.

d)

The product is -15.

6. The sloth climbed down 18 m.

7. a)

The product is -18.

b)

The product is $+8$.

8. a) -56 **b)** 108

9. Estimates may vary. **a)** 770 **b)** -637

10. Possible answers are -3 and $+33$, $+3$ and -33, -9 and 11, 9 and -11, -1 and 99, and 1 and -99.

11. a) 5×52 **b)** $260

12. a) $(+10) \div (+2) = +5$; $(+10) \div (+5) = +2$
b) $(-8) \div (-2) = +4$; $(-8) \div (+4) = -2$

13. a)   The quotient is $+2$.

b)   The quotient is $+7$.

c)   The quotient is -1.

14. Answers may vary. Example: The value of a share of Orange Computers Limited fell $14 in 7 h. How much did the value fall per hour if the rate of fall was constant?

15.

The quotient is $+6$.

16. $(-247) \div (-13)$. The quotient of two integers with the same sign is positive. The quotient of two integers with different signs is negative. Therefore, only $(-247) \div (-13)$ is positive.

17. a) $+3$ **b)** -8 **c)** -17 **d)** $+8$

18. Answers may vary. Example: The two integers are identical except for having different signs.

19. $18

20. a) -6 **b)** 4

21. a) −7 **b)** No. Different sets of integers can have the same mean. Example: {−20, −16, 18, −25, 22, −21} and {−62, 9, −2, 1, 6, 6} both have a sum of −42 and a mean of −7.

22. a decrease of 2341 people per year

23. 70 s

24. $570

Chapters 5–8 Review, pages 324–326

1. a) 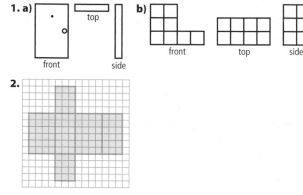 **b)**

2.

3. 150.4 cm²

4. a) area with bottom: 8.25 m²

b) area without bottom: 5.73 m²

5. 83 m²

6. 187.68 cm²

7. cylinder A: about 14 130 cm²; cylinder B: about 39 564 cm²

8. a) 21 days **b)** 14 days

9. $\frac{1}{10}$ of a cake

10. $\frac{1}{2}$ of the lifespan of a bison

11. $\frac{1}{3}$ of Earth's surface

12. 54 cm

13. a) $1\frac{2}{5}$ **b)** $\frac{5}{7}$

14. winner: $450; runner-up: $300; third-place: $150

15. 40 km/h

16. *Method 1:* Since $\frac{1}{5}$ of the flagpole is 2 m long, the remaining $\frac{4}{5}$ must be four times as long, which is 8 m.

Method 2: Since $\frac{1}{5}$ of the flagpole is 2 m long, the length of the whole flagpole is 5 × 2 m, which equals 10 m. The length of portion above ground is 10 m − 2 m, which equals 8 m.

17. 0.196 m³

18. a) 1331 cm³ **b)** about 1020 cm³

19. 756.6 kg

20. a) 4630 cm³ **b)** 5898 cm³

21. 52 cm³

22. a) (+5) × (+3) = +15 **b)** (−14) × (−2) = +28

c) (−4) × (+8) = −32 **d)** (−6) × (+4) = −24

23. Estimates may vary. **a)** −308 **b)** 598

24. 1 and −20; −1 and 20; 2 and −10; −2 and 10; 4 and −5; −4 and 5

25. a) (+20) ÷ (+4) = +5 **b)** (−22) ÷ (−11) = +2

c) (−24) ÷ (+8) = −3 **d)** (−21) ÷ (−3) = +7

26. −1

27. a) Yes. Multiplication is repeated addition. Since the sum of any set of integers is an integer, the product of two integers is also an integer. **b)** No. Division of an integer by most other integers gives parts that do not contain a whole number of units. For example, the quotient of 5 divided by any integer greater than 5 or less than −5 is not an integer.

28. $200

29. −12 °C

30. 186 L

31. a) −2 **b)** 5

32. −20

Chapter 9

9.1 Analysing Graphs of Linear Relations, pages 337–341

4. a) The points appear to lie in a straight line. The total height increases by 20 cm for each additional step.

b)

Number of Steps	Total Height of Steps
1	20
2	40
3	60
4	80
5	100

c) total height on step 10: 200 cm

5. a) The points appear to lie in a straight line. The number of students increases by six for each additional teacher. The pattern starts with one teacher and increases to four teachers.

b)

Number of Teachers	Maximum Number of Students
1	6
2	12
3	18
4	24

c) maximum number of students: 48

6. a) The quantities of banana chips range from 0 g to 400 g. The graph is linear because the points appear to lie in a straight line.

b)

Quantity (g)	Cost (¢)
0	0
100	60
200	120
300	180
400	240

c) Yes, it is possible to buy amounts of banana chips that are not exactly multiples of 100 g.

7. a) Yes, the points appear to lie in a straight line, so the graph shows a linear relation. The number of cubes varies from one to three. For every increase of one cube, the height increases by 2 cm.

b)

Number of Cubes	Height (cm)
1	2
2	4
3	6

c) No, it is not possible to include a point for $c = 2.5$. The number of cubes must be whole numbers.

8. a)

x	y
1	2
2	4
3	6

b)

x	y
1	2
2	4
3	6
4	8
5	10
6	12

c) The points appear to lie in a straight line. For every increase of one in the x-value, there is an increase of two in the y-value. **d)** value of y when $x = 9$: 18

9. a)

Hours Worked	Gross Pay ($)
1	15
2	30
3	45
4	60
5	75

b) hourly rate of pay: $15 **c)** Yes, it is reasonable to include a point for $h = 3.5$. An employee could work for three and a half hours.

10. a) Yes, it should be possible to purchase two flowers. **b)** There should be one point between the two points.
11. a) coordinates of point W: (40, 2) **b)** The number 40 represents the amount of money invested in dollars. The number 2 represents the amount of interest earned by the $40 investment after two years, in dollars. **c)** The points lie in a straight line. For every increase in $20 invested there is an increase in $1 in the interest earned. **d)** simple interest earned on $180 after one year: $9

12. a)

Side Length, s (cm)	0	1	2	3	4	5	8	28	31
Perimeter, P (cm)	0	4	8	12	16	20	32	112	124

b) The points lie on a line. For every increase of 1 cm in the side length of the square, there is an increase of 4 cm in its perimeter. **c)** Yes, it is possible to have other points between those shown on the graph. It is possible to have squares with side lengths that are not whole numbers. Example: A square might have a side length of 1.7 cm. **d)** Yes, the graph represents a linear relationship because the points lie in a straight line.

13. a)

Quantity (g)	Cost (¢)
100	75
200	150
300	225
400	300

b) The points appear to lie in a straight line. The cost ranges from 75¢ to 300¢. **c)** estimated cost of 350 g of dried apricots: 260¢. **d)** actual cost of 350 g of dried apricots: 263¢.
e) The difference in values was 263¢ − 260¢ = 3¢.

14. a)

Boxes of Almonds	Profit ($)
0	0
2	1
4	2
6	3
8	4

b) The points appear to lie in a straight line. There is an increase in profit of $1 for every two boxes of almonds sold. The profits range from $1 to $4.

c) profit on the sale of two boxes of almonds: $1
d) value of P when the value b is 2: $1
This is the same value as in part c), since both questions refer to the same point on the graph.
15. a) The number 2 refers to the number of minutes that Tom typed; 80 refers to the number of words that he typed in the two minutes. **b)** The typing speed for point A is 40 words per minute. **c)** Yes, it is a linear relation because the points appear to lie in a straight line. **d)** Answer may vary. Example: No. Fatigue, error correcting, or distractions can affect typing speed.

16. a)

Time (h)	Test Score (%)
1	60
2	70
3	80
4	90
5	100

b) Yes, the graph is a linear relation. The points appear to lie in a straight line. **c)** No, the rate cannot continue to increase at this same rate with more and more studying. Alana's test scores will reach 100% after five hours of studying. It is not possible for her success rate to improve beyond 100%.
17. a) Susie's wages: red points
b)

Time (h)	Total Pay for Mario ($)	Total Pay for Susie ($)
1	10	38
2	20	46
3	30	54
4	40	62
5	50	70

c) The two sets of points will meet at the point (15, 150).
18. a) Mark: red points **b)** Kendal will run out of money in 21 days. **c)** 6 days

9.2 Patterns in a Table of Values, pages 348–351

4.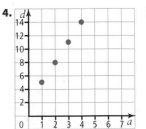

5.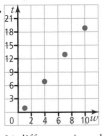

6. a)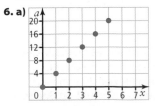

b) difference in value for consecutive x-values: 1; difference in value for consecutive a-values: 4 **c)** The value of a is equal to four times the value of x. **d)** $a = 4x$

7. a)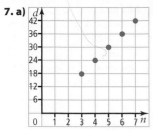

b) difference in value for consecutive *n*-values: 1; difference in value for consecutive *d*-values: 6 **c)** The value of *d* is six times the value of *n*. **d)** $d = 6n$

8. a) The relationship is linear because the difference between consecutive values of each variable is constant. The graph confirms that the relationship is linear.

b) The relationship may be linear because the difference between three of the consecutive values of each variable is constant. The graph confirms that the relationship is linear.

9. a) The relationship is not linear. The difference between successive *q*-values is the same but the difference between successive *p*-values is not the same. **b)** The relationship is linear. The difference between successive *x*-values is the same and the difference between successive *y*-values is the same.

10. a)

Time, *t* (min)	1	2	3	4	5	6
Number of Words, *w*	90	180	270	360	450	540

b) Yes, the relation is linear because the consecutive values for each variable have the same difference.
c) $w = 90t$ where *w* is the number of words and *t* is the time in minutes. **d)** 1080 words.

11. a)

Increase in Mass Over 10 kg, *m* (kg)	Dosage, *d* (mg)
1	60
2	70
3	80
4	90
5	100
6	110
7	120
8	130
9	140
10	150

b) Yes. Consecutive values of *m* increase each time by 1, and consecutive values of *d* increase each time by 10.
c) $10m + 50$
d) $10(17) + 50 = 220$. The dosage is 220 mg.
e) Yes. The value of 0 kg represents a child with a mass of 10 kg.

12. a) The following five combinations of quarters and dimes each equal $6.00: 4 quarters and 50 dimes, 8 quarters and 40 dimes, 12 quarters and 30 dimes, 16 quarters and 20 dimes, and 20 quarters and 10 dimes.

b)

Number of Quarters, *q*	Number of Dimes, *d*
4	50
8	40
12	30
16	20
20	10

c)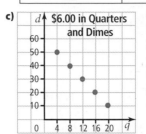

Yes, the relation is linear because the points appear to lie in a straight line. **d)** largest possible number of dimes: 55 (2 quarters); largest possible number of quarters: 22 (5 dimes)

13. a)

Depth (m)	Pressure (atm)
0	1
10	2
20	3
30	4
40	5
50	6

b)

Label the horizontal axis *d* for the depth and label the vertical axis *p* for pressure.
c) Divers tend to become dizzy at depths greater than 40 m.

14. a)

Figure Number	Number of Small Squares
1	4
2	7
3	10
4	13
5	16
6	19

b) $s = 3n + 1$ where *n* is the figure number and *s* is the number of squares. **c)** Figure 20: 61 squares **d)** 30 squares

15. a)

Number of Squares, *n*	1	2	3	4
Perimeter, *P* (cm)	4	6	8	10

b)

c) The perimeter increases by 2 cm for each additional small square that is added to the pattern.
d) $P = 2n + 2$ **e)** Perimeter of 50 squares: 102 cm

16. a)

Height (m)	0	150	300	450	600	750
Temperature (°C)	20	19	18	17	16	15

b)

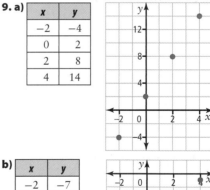

Height and Temperature

c) Yes, the relationship is linear. There is a common difference between the consecutive values for both variables.
d) Height climbed if the temperature is 13 °C: 1050 m

17. a) There is a common difference between consecutive values for both variables. The prediction is that the graph will be linear.

b)

Distance Travelled by Skydiver

Yes, the prediction was correct.
c) The parachutist descends about 54 m per second after the parachute opens.

18. a)

Number of People, n	20	40	60	80	100
Rental Cost, C ($)	100	200	300	400	500

b)

Rental Cost of Banquet Hall

c) $C = 5n$

19. a)

Number of People, n	20	40	60	80	100
Rental Cost, C ($)	150	250	350	450	550

b)

Rental Cost of Banquet Hall

The points on the graph are moved up an equal distance from each of the points on the graph in #18. **c)** $C = 5n + 50$; The variable n represents the number of people and the variable C represents the cost of renting the banquet hall.

20. a)

Number of Additional Days	0	1	2	3	4	5
Rental Cost ($)	40	75	110	145	180	215

b) $C = 35n + 40$ **c)** $390; A better option would be to buy the snowboard equipment for $350.

9.3 Linear Relationships, pages 357–359

5. a)

Time, t (min)	1	2	3	4	5	6
Cost, C (¢)	6	12	18	24	30	36

b)

Cost of Long Distance Phone Plan

c) No. Any part minutes will be rounded up to the nearest minute.

6. a)

Number of Dogs, d	1	2	3	4	5	6
Wage, W ($)	5	10	15	20	25	30

b)

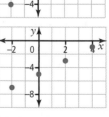

Wages Earned for Dog Walking

c) No, it is not reasonable to have points between the ones on the graph. The number of dogs walked will be a whole number.

7. a) $y = 27$ **b)** $y = -3$ **c)** $y = 10$ **d)** $x = 25$
8. a) $y = 10$ **b)** $y = -25$ **c)** $y = 3$ **d)** $x = 2$

9. a)

x	y
−2	−4
0	2
2	8
4	14

b)

x	y
−2	−7
0	−5
2	−3
4	−1

c)

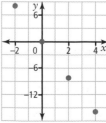

x	y
−2	8
0	0
2	−8
4	−16

d)

x	y
−2	9
0	7
2	5
4	3

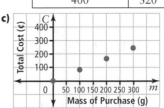

10. a) Answers may vary. Example:

x	y
−1	−2
0	0
1	2
2	4
3	6

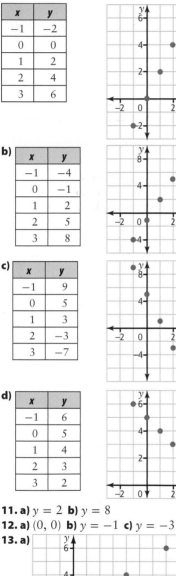

b)

x	y
−1	−4
0	−1
1	2
2	5
3	8

c)

x	y
−1	9
0	5
1	3
2	−3
3	−7

d)

x	y
−1	6
0	5
1	4
2	3
3	2

11. a) $y = 2$ **b)** $y = 8$

12. a) $(0, 0)$ **b)** $y = −1$ **c)** $y = −3$

13. a)

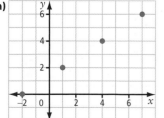

b) Yes, it is reasonable to assume that there are points between the values given. Without any restrictions in the question, numbers with decimal values can be evaluated in linear relations.

14. a) Since the x-values are consecutive integers, consecutive y-values will have the same difference in the linear relation. The difference for this linear relation is two.

b)

x	−3	−2	−1	0	1	2
y	0	2	4	6	8	10

15. a)

Mass of Purchase (g)	Cost (¢)
0	0
100	80
200	160
300	240
400	320

b) Answers may vary. Example: The most logical value is 400 g because the common difference between consecutive values of mass is 100 g.

c)

16. a) $1200 **b)** $1400 **c)** $6000

17. a)

Number of Pairs of Gloves, g	1	2	3	4	5	6
Total Cost, C ($)	7	12	17	22	27	32

b)

c) Yes, the points appear to lie in a straight line on the graph.
d) No. The values for g must be whole numbers because they represent the number of pairs of gloves.
e) This number could represent the cost of shipping or administrative charges.

18.

Amount Spent ($)	Points Received
1	40
2	80
3	120
4	160
5	200

b) 4000 **c)** $2500

19. a) The difference between consecutive masses is 11 g except for the metal with a volume of 12 cm³, which has a mass of 144 g in the given table. The correct mass is 132 g.

b)

c) A straight line could be drawn through the first four points and extended to show that the correct mass associated with a volume of 12 cm³ is 132 g.

20. a) $4.80; $7.00

b)

Distance Travelled, d (m)	210	420	630	840	1050	1260
Taxi Cost, C (¢)	300	320	340	360	380	400

c)

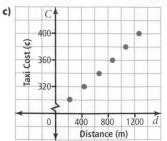

d) Yes, the relation is linear. The increase in cost for each 210 m travelled after the first segment is constant.

21. a) The value of *d* is 2 more than the value of *t*.

b) The *y*-value is four less than the *x*-value.

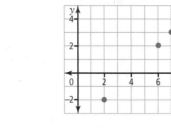

22. a)

x	−2	−1	0	1	2	3	11
y	−1	1	3	5	7	9	25

b) Yes, the relation is linear. The difference between consecutive *x*-values and the consecutive *y*-values is constant.

Chapter Review, pages 360–361

1. expression
2. linear relation
3. formula
4. equation
5. variable
6. table of values

7. a)

Time (h)	Pay ($)
0	0
1	9
2	18
3	27
4	36

b) Yes, the graph represents a linear relation. The points on the graph lie in a straight line and rate of pay is $9 for each hour worked. **c)** Yes, it is possible that Klaus works for part of an hour and is paid a portion of his hourly salary.

8. a) The graph shows the amount of money earned at a grade 8 car wash based on the number of cars washed.
b) For every car that is washed $10 is collected. The points appear to lie in a straight line. **c)** cost of one car wash: $10

d)

Number of Cars	Income ($)
1	10
2	20
3	30
4	40

e) $150

9. a) The points lie in a straight line. The *x*-values range between 0 and 6. The *y*-values range between 2 and 20.

b)

x	1	2	3	4	5	6
y	5	8	11	14	17	20

c) *y* = 8 when *x* = 2 **d)** *y* = 17 when *x* = 5

10. a)

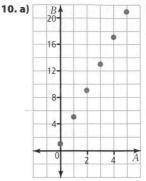

b) The difference in consecutive *A*-values is one. The difference in consecutive *B*-values is four. **c)** In words: For every increase of one unit in the *A*-value there is a corresponding increase of four units in the *B*-value. As an expression: $B = 4A + 1$

11. a) Table 1: the *m*-variable increases by one unit; Table 2: the *p*-variable increases by two units; Table 3: the *d*-variable increases by one unit **b)** Table 1: the *n*-variable increases by two units; Table 2: the *q*-variable decreases by four units; Table 3: the *C*-variable increases alternately—by 3 units then by 2 units.

c) Table 1   Table 2

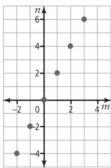   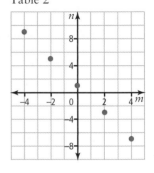

Table 3

12. a)

Number of Copies, n	0	1	2	3	4	5
Total Cost, C ($)	0	2	3	4	5	6

b) Yes, this is a linear relation for one or more copies. The consecutive values for both variables for one or more copies have a common difference. **c)** For one or more copies: $C = n + 1$ where *C* is the cost in dollars and *n* is the number of colour copies. **d)** $13

13. a) The variable *t* represents the time the cyclist travels in hours. The variable *d* represents the distance the cyclist travels in kilometres. **b)** 15 represents the constant speed of 15 km/h travelled by the cyclist.

c)

Time (h)	Distance (km)
1	15
2	30
3	45
4	60
5	75

d)

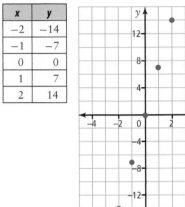

e) Yes, it is reasonable to have points between the ones in the graph. The cyclist can travel for times that are not whole numbers of hours. **f)** 120 km

14. Equation A: $y = 7x$

x	y
−2	−14
−1	−7
0	0
1	7
2	14

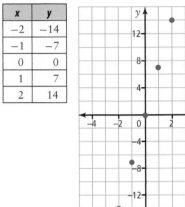

$y = -49$ when $x = -7$
Equation B: $y = 3x - 2$

x	y
−2	−8
−1	−5
0	−2
1	1
2	4

$y = -23$ when $x = -7$
Equation C: $y = -2x + 3$

x	y
−2	7
−1	5
0	3
1	1
2	−1

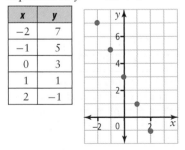

$y = 17$, when $x = -7$

15. a) Both graphs are linear relations and both graphs cross the y-axis at $(0, 1)$. **b)** The points on the graph lie on straight lines that slant in different directions. The graph of $y = 2x + 1$ increases from left to right and the graph of $y = -2x + 1$ decreases from left to right.

Chapter 10

10.1 Modelling and Solving One-Step Equations: $ax = b$, $\frac{x}{a} = b$, pages 376–379

5. a) $3t = -6$ **b)** $-\frac{w}{2} = -4$ **c)** $2x = -4$ **d)** $-\frac{c}{4} = 2$

6. a) $-2 = \frac{m}{3}$ **b)** $-2n = -10$ **c)** $-4f = -12$ **d)** $\frac{p}{4} = -9$

7. a) $j = -8$ **b)** $n = -5$ **c)** $k = -18$ **d)** $x = 44$

8. a) $r = -4$ **b)** $p = 4$ **c)** $t = -60$ **d)** $d = -20$

9. a) $k = -4$ **b)** $t = -12$

10. a) $b = -5$ **b)** $x = 9$

11. a) -3 **b)** -4 **c)** -9 **d)** 4

12. a) 5 **b)** -4 **c)** 4 **d)** -21

13. a) $s = -3$ **b)** $j = 13$ **c)** $j = -26$ **d)** $t = 4$

14. a) $f = -7$ **b)** $q = -9$ **c)** $h = 21$ **d)** $k = -5$

15. a) -6 **b)** 3 **c)** -21 **d)** 17

16. a) 11 **b)** -12 **c)** 4 **d)** -3

17. a) $t = -36$ **b)** $h = -120$ **c)** $s = -105$ **d)** $x = 567$

18. a) $y = -20$ **b)** $k = 48$ **c)** $b = -10$ **d)** $r = 180$

19. a) Yes. **b)** Yes. **c)** Yes. **d)** No.

20. a) No. **b)** No. **c)** No. **d)** Yes.

21. a) $\frac{m}{4} = -4$ **b)** $m = -16\ °C$

22. a) $13n = 312$; n is the number of litres. **b)** 24 L

23. a) $5p = 85$; p is the height of the pygmy owl in centimetres. **b)** 17 cm

24. a) $8m = 144$ **b)** $m = 18$ cm

25. Let x be the percent of right-handed boys.

$\frac{1}{7}x = 11$

$x = 77$

Therefore, 77% of boys are right-handed.

26. a) \$18 000 **b)** \$72 000

27. $\frac{12h}{2} = 30$; $h = 5$ cm

28. 9 min

29. a) 2994 m in fresh water; 3000 m in salt water **b)** Sandra

10.2 Modelling and Solving Two-Step Equations: $ax + b = c$, pages 385–387

3. a) $x = 1$ **b)** $g = 2$

4. a) $h = 2$ **b)** $z = 6$

5. a) $x = 3$ **b)** $t = -7$

6. a) $d = 3$ **b)** $z = 4$

7. a) Add 2 to both sides of the equation.
b) Subtract 3 from both sides of the equation.
c) Add 10 to both sides of the equation.
d) Add 1 to both sides of the equation.
8. a) Divide both sides of the equation by 4.
b) Divide both sides of the equation by -3.
c) Divide both sides of the equation by 2.
d) Divide both sides of the equation by -9.

9. a) $r = 2$ **b)** $m = 1$ **c)** $g = 4$ **d)** $f = 12.75$
10. a) $k = -7$ **b)** $n = -2$ **c)** $x = -3$ **d)** $n = 0.5$
11. a) No. **b)** No. **c)** Yes. **d)** No.
12. a) $3s$ represents triple his current savings. By subtracting 30 from $3s$, Matt will have the amount he needs: $750. **b)** savings: $260 **c)** Answers may vary. Example: Algebra tiles could be used to determine Matt's savings.
13. 3 extras
14. a) $4s + 2 = 14$
b) Percent of students who choose skiing: 3%
15. $2m - 50 = 299$; Jennifer has $174.50 in her account now.
16. $2w - 3 = 9$; width of the classroom: 6 m
17. a) The value of 6 represents the number of metres that the eagle drops every second. **b)** 11.8 s
18. 108 m^2
19. 3 m
20. There are three possible values for m: 667, 668, and 669.
21. 3.7 km/h

10.3 Modelling and Solving Two-Step Equations: $\frac{x}{a} + b = c$, pages 392–393

4. a) $x = 21$ **b)** $b = -18$
5. a) $z = 15$ **b)** $d = -35$
6. a) $g = -16$ **b)** $n = -50$
7. a) $f = 25$ **b)** $n = 24$
8. a) Subtract 12 from both sides of the equation.
b) Add 2 to both sides of the equation.
c) Subtract 6 from both sides of the equation.
d) Subtract 11 from both sides of the equation.
9. a) Multiply both sides of the equation by -5.
b) Multiply both sides of the equation by 13.
c) Multiply both sides of the equation by 12.
d) Multiply both sides of the equation by 3.
10. a) $m = 48$ **b)** $c = 32$ **c)** $b = -56$ **d)** $n = 154$
11. a) $j = -32$ **b)** $r = 0$ **c)** $x = -120$ **d)** $n = 195$
12. a) No. **b)** Yes. **c)** No. **d)** Yes.
13. a) Brian's age: 8 years old **b)** Answers may vary. Example: Natasha is not getting enough sleep according to the formula. She needs 8.75 h of sleep.
14. $\frac{a}{2} - 2 = 5$; Cost of an adult ticket: $14
15. a) -25 °C **b)** 9000 m
16. $\frac{m}{2} - 1 = 6$; 14% of students prefer math.
17. a) 3100 Calories **b)** 2831 is greater than the recommended amount of Calories, which is 2700.
c) $x = 7$

10.4 Modelling and Solving Two-Step Equations: $a(x + b) = c$, pages 398–399

4. a) $x = 6$ **b)** $s = 5$
5. a) $x = 4$ **b)** $x = -7$
6. a) $t = 6$ **b)** $j = 0$

7. a) $p = 1$ **b)** $n = 2$
8. a) $r = -9$ **b)** $m = 6$ **c)** $g = -26$ **d)** $f = -7$
9. a) $k = -10$ **b)** $n = 8$ **c)** $x = 3$ **d)** $w = -11$
10. a) No. **b)** No. **c)** Yes. **d)** No.
11. a) $3(s + 7) = 183$
b) Length of each side of old fence: 54 cm
12. a) 17 750 kJ **b)** -30 °C
13. a) $4(x + 4) = 96$ **b)** Maximum dimensions of the square picture: 20 cm by 20 cm
14. Rental time: 4 h
15. Parking time: 3 h
16. a) Andrew's current speed: 12 km/h **b)** 9 km/h
c) Answers may vary. Example: Andrew would not be able to get to his grandfather's apartment in two hours if he was riding his bicycle through a city with several traffic lights and several steep hills. It would also depend on the types of roads and the terrain that he would have to bicycle over, and on his athletic ability.

Chapter Review, pages 400–401

1. variable **2.** equation
3. opposite operations **4.** numerical coefficient
5. distributive property **6.** constant
7. linear equation
8. a) $x = -3$ **b)** $n = -8$ **c)** $d = 2$ **d)** $x = -15$
9. a) $x = 2$ **b)** $r = -3$ **c)** $z = -4$ **d)** $t = -3$
10. a) $p = -15$ **b)** $n = -33$ **c)** $x = 36$ **d)** $a = 14$
11. Answers may vary. Example: Two equations which would result in an answer of five are $-3p = -15$ and $20 = 4x$.
12. a) $3c + 2 = 5$; $c = 1$ **b)** $-4x + 7 = -1$; $x = 2$
13. a) Yes. **b)** Yes. **c)** Yes. **d)** No.
14. a) $t = -4$ **b)** $j = -25$ **c)** $p = 4$ **d)** $n = 11.25$
15. a) $4d - 3 = 25$ **b)** Zoë has seven DVDs.
16. a) $v = -50$ **b)** $j = -4$
17. a) Subtract 13 from both sides of the equation. Then multiply both sides of the equation by -3. **b)** Add 7 to both sides of the equation. Then multiply both sides of the equation by 15. **c)** Subtract 2 from both sides of the equation. Then multiply both sides of the equation by -22. **d)** Add 16 to both sides of the equation. Then multiply both sides of the equation by -4.
18. a) $v = 12$ **b)** $d = 15$ **c)** $x = -42$ **d)** $n = 36$
19. $\frac{b}{5} - 1120 = 23\ 761$; British Columbia had 124 405 soccer players in 2006.
20. a) $r = -2$ **b)** $w = -5$
21. a) $q = 9$ **b)** $g = -11$ **c)** $k = -14$ **d)** $x = 1$
22. $4(x + 6) = 372$; Without the border, the quilt is 87 cm by 87 cm.
23. The sides of the original octagon were 9 cm long.

Chapter 11

11.1 Determining Probabilities Using Tree Diagrams and Tables, pages 416–418

3. a)

Coin Flip	Spin	Outcome
H	1	H, 1
	2	H, 2
	3	H, 3
T	1	H, 1
	2	H, 2
	3	H, 3

b) (H, 1), (H, 2), (H, 3), (T, 1), (T, 2), (T, 3)

c) $P(\text{H, 2}) = \frac{1}{6}$ or $0.1\overline{6}$ or $16.\overline{6}\%$

4. a) (T, T), (T, W), (T, O), (W, T), (W, W), (W, O), (O, T), (O, W), (O, O) **b)** $P(\text{T, W}) = \frac{1}{9}$ or $0.\overline{1}$ or $11.\overline{1}\%$

c) $P(\text{that both letters are identical}) = \frac{1}{3}$ or $0.\overline{3}$ or $33.\overline{3}\%$

5. a)

		Blue Die			
		1	2	3	4
Green Die	1	1, 1	1, 2	1, 3	1, 4
	2	2, 1	2, 2	2, 3	2, 4
	3	3, 1	3, 2	3, 3	3, 4
	4	4, 1	4, 2	4, 3	4, 4

b) $P(\text{sum} > 5) = \frac{3}{8}$ or 0.375 or 37.5%

c) $P(\text{both numbers are identical}) = \frac{1}{4}$ or 0.25 or 25%

6. a)

		Die					
		1	2	3	4	5	6
Cards	3	3, 1	3, 2	3, 3	3, 4	3, 5	3, 6
	4	4, 1	4, 2	4, 3	4, 4	4, 5	4, 6
	5	5, 1	5, 2	5, 3	5, 4	5, 5	5, 6
	6	6, 1	6, 2	6, 3	6, 4	6, 5	6, 6
	7	7, 1	7, 2	7, 3	7, 4	7, 5	7, 6

b) $P(\text{both numbers are identical}) = \frac{2}{15}$ or $0.1\overline{3}$ or $13.\overline{3}\%$

c) $P(\text{sum of the two numbers is even}) = \frac{1}{2}$ or 0.5 or 50%

d) $P(\text{number on die} \geq \text{number on card}) = \frac{1}{3}$ or $0.\overline{3}$ or $33.\overline{3}\%$

7. a)

		Second Catch			
		W	T	C	Lost
First Catch	W	W, W	W, T	W, C	W, Lost
	T	T, W	T, T	T, C	T, Lost
	C	C, W	C, T	C, C	C, Lost
	Lost	Lost, W	Lost, T	Lost, C	Lost, Lost

b) $P(\text{whitefish, char}) = \frac{1}{8}$ or 0.125 or 12.5%

c) $P(\text{char, char}) = \frac{1}{16}$ or 0.0625 or 6.25%

d) $P(\text{she will catch nothing at all}) = \frac{1}{16}$ or 0.0625 or 6.25%

8. a)

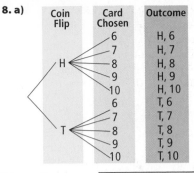

Coin Flip	Card Chosen	Outcome
H	6	H, 6
	7	H, 7
	8	H, 8
	9	H, 9
	10	H, 10
T	6	T, 6
	7	T, 7
	8	T, 8
	9	T, 9
	10	T, 10

b)

		Card Chosen				
		6	7	8	9	10
Coin Flipped	H	H, 6	H, 7	H, 8	H, 9	H, 10
	T	T, 6	T, 7	T, 8	T, 9	T, 10

c) $P(\text{outcome includes an even-numbered card}) = \frac{3}{5}$ or 0.6 or 60%

9. a)

		Second Baby	
		B	G
First Baby	B	B, B	B, G
	G	G, B	G, G

b) $P(\text{one boy and one girl}) = \frac{1}{2}$ or 0.5 or 50%

c) Assume that it is equally likely that a boy or girl is born for any birth.

10. a)

		Second Spin			
		T	E	E	N
First Spin	T	T, T	T, E	T, E	T, N
	E	E, T	E, E	E, E	E, N
	E	E, T	E, E	E, E	E, N
	N	N, T	N, E	N, E	N, N

b) $P(\text{T then E}) = \frac{1}{8}$ or 0.125 or 12.5%

c) $P(\text{E, E}) = \frac{1}{4}$ or 0.25 or 25%

d) $P(\text{same letter on both spins}) = \frac{3}{8}$ or 0.375 or 37.5%

11. a) $P(\text{Thunder Road}) = \frac{1}{2}$ or 0.5 or 50%

b) $P(\text{skiing on a run containing the name "Bowl"}) = \frac{1}{4}$ or 0.25 or 25%

c) $P(\text{skiing on Thunder Road and Quick Break}) = \frac{1}{8}$; or 0.125 or 12.5%

12. a)

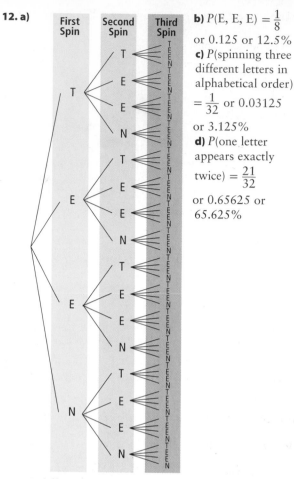

b) $P(E, E, E) = \dfrac{1}{8}$ or 0.125 or 12.5%

c) P(spinning three different letters in alphabetical order) $= \dfrac{1}{32}$ or 0.03125 or 3.125%

d) P(one letter appears exactly twice) $= \dfrac{21}{32}$ or 0.65625 or 65.625%

13. a) P(difference between the two numbers is two) $= \dfrac{2}{9}$ or $0.\overline{2}$ or $22.\overline{2}$%

b) P(the sum is a multiple of three) $= \dfrac{1}{3}$ or $0.\overline{3}$ or $33.\overline{3}$%

c) P(the product is a multiple of four) $= \dfrac{5}{12}$ or $0.41\overline{6}$ or $41.\overline{6}$%

11.2 Outcomes of Independent Events, pages 423–425

3. a)

	Spinner		
	1	**2**	**3**
G	G, 1	G, 2	G, 3
R	R, 1	R, 2	R, 3
B	B, 1	B, 2	B, 3
Y	Y, 1	Y, 2	Y, 3

(Marble)

b) Possible outcomes: 12 **c)** Using the multiplication method, the number of possible outcomes is $4 \times 3 = 12$.

4. a) Answers may vary. Example: Using the multiplication method, the number of possible outcomes is $2 \times 6 = 12$ **b)** Answers may vary. Example: Using a tree diagram, the number of possible outcomes is 12.

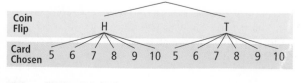

5. a)

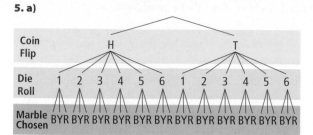

b) Total number of possible outcomes: 36 **c)** Using multiplication, the total number of possible outcomes is $2 \times 6 \times 3 = 36$.

6. a)

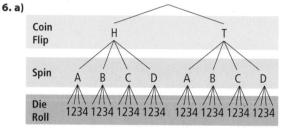

b) Total number of possible outcomes: 32 **c)** Using multiplication, the total number of possible outcomes is $2 \times 4 \times 4 = 32$.

7. Shirt-pant combinations: 24

8. Possible routes: 12

9. Possible different combinations: 60

10. a) Using the multiplication method, the number of combinations of coins she could get is $3 \times 2 = 6$.

b)

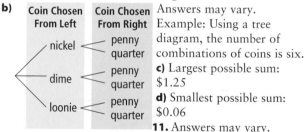

Answers may vary. Example: Using a tree diagram, the number of combinations of coins is six. **c)** Largest possible sum: $1.25 **d)** Smallest possible sum: $0.06

11. Answers may vary. Example: Jim has two pairs of shoes, four pairs of pants, and five dress shirts from which to choose. If he selects one item from each of the three types of clothing, how many combinations of clothing are possible?

12. a) Number of possible single-scoop ice-cream cones: 93 **b)** Number of possible two-scoop ice-cream cones: 2883 **c)** Number of possible two-scoop ice-cream cones with both flavours different: 2790. The number of double cones could be subtracted from the answer to part b): $2883 - (3 \times 31) = 2790$.

13. There are three drink choices and three main dish choices. Divide the total number of possible meal combinations, 36, by the number of desserts, 4. The quotient, 9, is equal to the product of the choices for the drink and main menu. The factor pairs of 9 are 3×3 and 1×9. Since there must be more than one choice in each category, the only choice of factor pairs is 3×3.

14. a) Possible colour-shape combinations: 30
b) Using a table

Beads		Shapes					
		Square (SQ)	Circle (C)	Star (S)	Triangle (T)	Rectangle (RE)	Heart (H)
	Red (R)	R, SQ	R, C	R, S	R, T	R, RE	R, H
	Blue (BL)	BL, SQ	BL, C	BL, S	BL, T	BL, RE	BL, H
	Black (BLK)	BLK, SQ	BLK, C	BLK, S	BLK, T	BLK, RE	BLK, H
	White (W)	W, SQ	W, C	W, S	W, T	W, RE	W, H
	Yellow (Y)	Y, SQ	Y, C	Y, S	Y, T	Y, RE	Y, H

the number of possible colour-shape combinations is 30.
c) Possible colour-shape combinations: 120
15. 256
16. 8 998 912

11.3 Determining Probabilities Using Fractions, pages 432–434

4. a)

Spinner		Die					
		1	2	3	4	5	6
	A	A, 1	A, 2	A, 3	A, 4	A, 5	A, 6
	A	A, 1	A, 2	A, 3	A, 4	A, 5	A, 6
	B	B, 1	B, 2	B, 3	B, 4	B, 5	B, 6
	B	B, 1	B, 2	B, 3	B, 4	B, 5	B, 6

b) P(spinning an A and rolling a two) $= \frac{1}{12}$

c) $P(A, 2) = \frac{1}{2} \times \frac{1}{6} = \frac{1}{12}$

5. a) Total number of possible outcomes: $4 \times 5 = 20$
b) Answers may vary. Example:
Method 1: Using multiplication,
P(blue, red) $= \frac{3}{4} \times \frac{3}{5} = \frac{9}{20}$
Method 2: Using a table,

Bag 1		Bag 2				
		Yellow	Yellow	Red	Red	Red
	Blue	B, Y	B, Y	B, R	B, R	B, R
	Blue	B, Y	B, Y	B, R	B, R	B, R
	Blue	B, Y	B, Y	B, R	B, R	B, R
	Green	G, Y	G, Y	G, R	G, R	G, R

P(blue, red) $= \frac{9}{20}$

6. a) $P(H) = \frac{1}{2}$ **b)** $P(H, H) = \frac{1}{4}$

c) Using a tree diagram,
$P(H, H) = \frac{1}{4}$

First Coin Flip	Second Coin Flip
H	H
	T
T	H
	T

7. a) $P(2, B) = \frac{1}{24}$ **b)** P(even number, consonant) $= \frac{3}{8}$

c) Use a tree diagram to determine that $P(2, B) = \frac{1}{24}$ and
P(even number, consonant) $= \frac{9}{24} = \frac{3}{8}$.

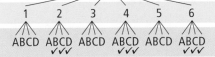

8. a) Answers may vary. Example: Use two 4-sided dice to simulate the type of seed chosen and the location. Roll the two dice ten times and record the seed type and location in a tally chart. A possible experimental probability is P(marigold, flower pot) $= \frac{1}{10}$.

b) P(marigold, flower pot) $= \frac{1}{4} \times \frac{1}{4} = \frac{1}{16}$

c) Answers may vary. Example: The experimental probability of $\frac{1}{10}$ is larger than the theoretical probability of $\frac{1}{16}$.

9. a) Red was the car colour that was spun last. There is only one tally mark for red and Trevor has to have at least one car of each colour.

b) Experimental probability P(blue) $= \frac{4}{13} = 0.\overline{307692}$

c) Theoretical probability P(blue) $= 20\% = 0.2$

d) Theoretical probability P(blue, blue) $= \frac{1}{25} = 0.04$

10. P(rain in Victoria, rain in Calgary) $= \frac{3}{4} \times \frac{1}{5} = \frac{3}{20}$

11. P(red, blue) $= \frac{3}{7} = 0.\overline{428571} = 42.\overline{857142}\%$

12. a)

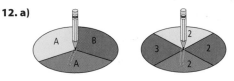

b) $P(A) = \frac{2}{3}$ **c)** $P(2) = \frac{3}{4}$

13. a) Different pathways: 4 **b)** Answers may vary. Example: Numbers 1, 2, 3, and 4 on the die simulate the pump is working, and numbers 5 and 6 simulate the pump is not working. Roll the die ten times and determine the experimental probability that a specific pumping station is working.
c) P(at least one pathway is available to carry water between the two towns) $= \frac{7}{10} = 0.7$

14. a) P(happy with appetizer, happy with main course) $= \frac{3}{8}$ **b)** P(unhappy with appetizer, unhappy with main course) $= \frac{1}{8}$ **c)** The outcome where Jeremy is happy with only one of his food items has not been considered.
15. a) P(both players with hit a fair ball and get on base) $= 0.090$ **b)** P(first player gets a hit and the second player does not) $= 0.223$

16. a) $P(4, 7) = 0.006$ **b)** $P(4, \text{not } 4) = 0.071$
c) $P(4, \text{number less than } 4) = 0.018$
17. $P(C) = \frac{3}{5}$. The probability of $P(A, B) = \frac{3}{14}$. Divide the
probability of the three events occurring,
$P(A, B, C) = \frac{9}{70}$, by the value of $P(A, B) = \frac{3}{14}$ as
follows: $\frac{9}{70} \div \frac{3}{14} = \frac{9}{70} \times \frac{14}{3} = \frac{3}{5}$.

Chapter Review, pages 436–437

1. independent events **2.** sample space
3. simulation **4.** probability
5. favourable outcome
6. a)

		Red Die					
		1	**2**	**3**	**4**	**5**	**6**
	1	1, 1	1, 2	1, 3	1, 4	1, 5	1, 6
	2	2, 1	2, 2	2, 3	2, 4	2, 5	2, 6
Blue	**3**	3, 1	3, 2	3, 3	3, 4	3, 5	3, 6
Die	**4**	4, 1	4, 2	4, 3	4, 4	4, 5	4, 6
	5	5, 1	5, 2	5, 3	5, 4	5, 5	5, 6
	6	6, 1	6, 2	6, 3	6, 4	6, 5	6, 6

b) $P(\text{the sum of the two numbers is } 10) = \frac{1}{12}$

c) $P(\text{the two numbers are identical}) = \frac{1}{6}$

d) $P(\text{the product of the two numbers is a multiple of } 10)$
$= \frac{1}{6}$

7. a)

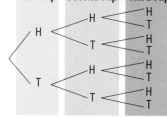

First Flip Second Flip Third Flip **b)** $P(H, H, H) = \frac{1}{8}$

c) $P(\text{two heads and one tail in any order}) = \frac{3}{8}$

8. a)

		Die					
		1	**2**	**3**	**4**	**5**	**6**
	3	3, 1	3, 2	3, 3	3, 4	3, 5	3, 6
	4	4, 1	4, 2	4, 3	4, 4	4, 5	4, 6
	5	5, 1	5, 2	5, 3	5, 4	5, 5	5, 6
Card	**6**	6, 1	6, 2	6, 3	6, 4	6, 5	6, 6
	7	7, 1	7, 2	7, 3	7, 4	7, 5	7, 6
	8	8, 1	8, 2	8, 3	8, 4	8, 5	8, 6
	9	9, 1	9, 2	9, 3	9, 4	9, 5	9, 6

b) $P(\text{number on the card matches number on the die})$
$= \frac{2}{21}$ **c)** $P(\text{number on the card is larger than number}$
$\text{on the die}) = \frac{16}{21}$ **d)** $P(\text{both numbers are even}) = \frac{3}{14}$

9. a) (H, 1), (H, 2), (H, 3), (T, 1), (T, 2), (T, 3)
b) Total number of outcomes: 6
c) Total number of outcomes $= 2 \times 3 = 6$
10. Combinations of choices: 48
11. Number of restaurants: 7. Multiply the number of
hotel choices, 3, by the number of ski pass choices, 2.
Then divide the total number of combinations by the
product that was calculated: $42 \div 6 = 7$.

12. a) $P(\text{red marble}) = \frac{3}{5}$ **b)** $P(\text{green marble}) = \frac{4}{5}$

c) $P(\text{red marble, green marble}) = \frac{12}{25}$

13. a) $P(A, E) = 0.05$ **b)** $P(A, L, E) = 0.02$
c) The probability that it will snow in Abbotsford,
Lethbridge, and Estevan today.

14. $P(1 \text{ or } 2, 3, \text{ odd number}) = \frac{1}{36}$

15. a) Theoretical probability, $P(\text{blue}) = 25\%$
b) Experimental probability, $P(\text{blue}) = 15\%$
c) Answers may vary. Example: The experimental
probability is often different from the theoretical
probability. **d)** Yes, the two probabilities would become
closer to each other in value.

Chapter 12

12.1 Exploring Tessellations With Regular and Irregular Polygons, pages 450–451

4. a) Yes. Each angle of a regular hexagon is 120°. The
sum of three vertices of a regular hexagon is 360°.
b) No. Each angle of a regular heptagon is about 128.6°.
Any number of vertices of this shape will not have the
interior angle measures total exactly 360°.
5. Answers may vary. Example:

6. Answers may vary. Example:

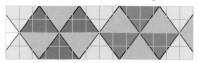

7. Answers may vary. Example: The tessellations of
rectangular bricks on walls, of rectangular shingles on
roofs, and of square tiles on floors.
8. Answers may vary. Example: One tessellation is drawn
on triangular dot paper and the other is drawn on the
same triangular dot paper rotated 90°.

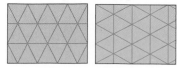

9. Answers may vary. For example,

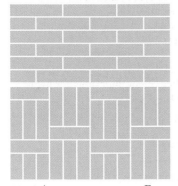

10. a) Answers may vary. Example: A pentagon made of a rectangle and a triangle can tessellate the plane. At the point where the vertices meet, the sum of the interior angles measures is the sum of the three angles of the triangle (180°) and the two right angles of the rectangle (180°), which is 360°.

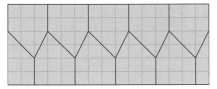

11. Answers may vary. Example:

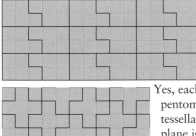

Yes, each of these two pentominos makes a tessellation because the plane is completely covered by repeated patterns of each shape without any overlap or gaps.

12. Answers may vary. Example: Using a square on grid paper:

Use an equilateral triangle on triangular dot paper:

13. a) The dual is a translation of the original tessellation, so it also tessellates the plane. If the square is a unit square, the translation is half unit right and half unit down.

b) The dual is a tessellation of congruent equilateral triangles.

c) The dual is a tessellation of congruent regular hexagons.

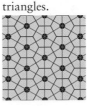

14. Answers may vary. Example: A regular octagon and a square can be used together to create a tessellation.

12.2 Constructing Tessellations Using Translations and Reflections, pages 455–456

3. a) regular hexagon and equilateral triangle **b)** square and equilateral triangle **c)** regular octagon and square

4. Answers may vary. Example: **a)** translation or reflection **b)** reflection **c)** translation or reflection

5. a) The sum of the interior angle measures at the point where the vertices of the dodecagons meet is 360°.

b) Answers may vary. Example:

c) The sum of the interior angle measures at the point where the vertices of the decagons meet is 360°.

d) Answers may vary. Example:

e) The sum of the interior angle measures at the point where the vertices of the hexagons meet is 360°.

6. Answers may vary. Example:

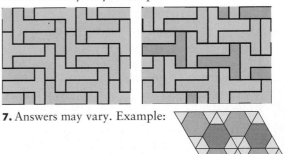

7. Answers may vary. Example:

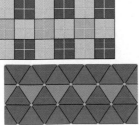

8. No. Each angle of the regular pentagon is 108° and each angle of the equilateral triangle is 60°. There is no combination of 108° vertices and 60° vertices that will have the interior angle measures total 360°.

9. The shapes a) and b) are reptiles. Answer may vary. Example:

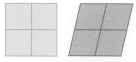

12.3 Constructing Tessellations Using Rotations, pages 459–460

3. a) square **b)** regular octagon and triangle
c) a cross shape and square
4. Answers may vary. Example: **a)** Rotate the square 90° about one of its vertices until a full turn is made. Then, rotate the larger square formed 90° about one of its vertices until a full turn is made. **b)** Rotate the square shape formed by a regular octagon and four isosceles triangles 90° about one of its vertices until a full turn is made. Then, translate the larger square horizontally to the right two times.
c) Rotate the shape formed by the cross shape with 4 small squares 90° about the free corner of the small square until a full turn is made. Then, translate the resulting shape horizontally to the right and vertically up and down.
5. a) Answers may vary. Example:
• Start with the top piece of the stained glass that is a 45° sector, or one-eighth, of the circle. Reflect it along a line making 45° with the horizontal.
• Reflect the resulting larger piece along the x-axis.
• Reflect the resulting larger piece along the y-axis.
b) Answers may vary. Example: Trim the edge of the 45° sector to make a right-angled triangle with the right angle touching the line of reflection. The resulting shape will be a square that tiles the plane.
6. Answers may vary. Example: Translate the combined shape of 4 squares and 4 isosceles triangles in four different colours horizontally to form the pattern.

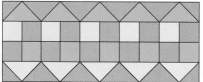

7. Answers may vary. Example: The following tessellation is made using regular hexagons and equilateral triangles.

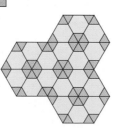

8. Shapes A, B, C, D, and G tessellate. Answers may vary. Example: A and B are quadrilaterals and all quadrilaterals tessellate the plane. C and D can tessellate by horizontal translation, fitting the part sticking out of the shape into the space going into the shape. G can tessellate by horizontal and vertical translations, fitting the parts sticking out into spaces going in.

9. a) and **b)** Answers may vary. Example: A combination of three regular hexagons (6, 6, 6) and a combination of one square, one regular hexagon, and one dodecagon will work.

Tessellations Involving Three Regular Polygons	Shape 1	Shape 2	Shape 3	Shape 4
Triangle (60°)	1	0	0	0
Square (90°)	0	1	0	1
Pentagon (108°)	0	0	0	0
Hexagon (120°)	0	0	3	1
Octagon (135°)	0	2	0	0
Dodecagon (150°)	2	0	0	1
Number of sides	(3, 12, 12)	(4, 8, 8)	(6, 6, 6)	(4, 6, 12)
Sum of angles	60° + 2(150°) = 360°	90° + 2(135°) = 360°	3(120°) = 360°	90° + 120° + 150° = 360°

c) Answers may vary. Example:

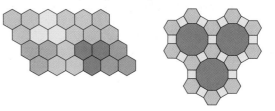

12.4 Creating Escher-Style Tessellations, pages 464–465

4. a) translation **b)** rotation
5. a) hexagon **b)** triangle
6. a) rotation and reflection **b)** rotation and translation
7. a) parallelogram **b)** square
8. Answers may vary. Example:

9. Answers may vary. Example:

10. Answers may vary. Example:

11. a) Answers may vary. Example: Staircases that appear to be upside down, people that appear to be walking right side up and upside down and sideways.

Chapter 12 Review, pages 466–467

1. tiling the plane   **2.** plane
3. tessellation   **4.** transformation
5. a) regular hexagon and equilateral triangle
b) rhombus, isosceles triangle, and regular hexagon
c) regular hexagon and equilateral triangle
d) regular hexagon, parallelogram, and equilateral triangle
6. The regular hexagons and equilateral triangles in #5 are regular polygons, while the isosceles triangles, rhombuses, and parallelograms are not. Regular polygons have equal interior angle measures and equal side lengths.
7. No. Answers may vary. Example: Each interior angle of a regular octagon is 135°, which is not a factor of 360°. However, two octagons and a square can tile the plane.
8. Answers may vary. Example: **a)** Translation or rotation of the combined shape. **b)** Translation of the dodecagon and reflections of the hexagon and rectangle.
9. Answers may vary. For example,

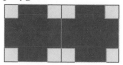

10. Answers may vary. Example:

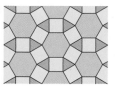

11. Answers may vary. Example: **a)** translation and reflection **b)** translation and reflection
12. Answers may vary. Example: A square that has the same side length as the shorter side of the irregular polygon.

13. a quadrilateral
14. a rotation about the centre of the regular hexagon

15. Answers may vary. Example:
Translation: Rotation:

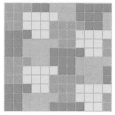 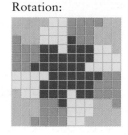

Chapters 9–12 Review, pages 473–475

1. a) 9 triangles
b)

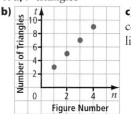

c) Yes. When the four points are connected, they form a straight line.

2. Answers may vary. Example: **a)** I might have purchased hamburgers or sandwiches. The cost of one item is $3.
b) For every additional item purchased, the cost increases by $3.
c)

Quantity	2	3	4	5	6	7
Cost ($)	3	6	9	12	15	18

Use q for quantity and c for cost; q represents the quantity purchased and c represents the cost of purchase.
d) $c = 3q$ **e)** The cost is $24.
3. a)

Number of Posts, p	2	3	4	5	6	7
Number of Rails, r	3	6	9	12	15	18

b) Answers may vary. Example:

The relationship appears to be linear because the six points seem to lie on a straight line.
4. Answers may vary. Example: **a)** $y = 2x - 3$

x	−5	−4	−3	−2	−1	0	1	2	3	4	5
y	−13	−11	−9	−7	−5	−3	−1	1	3	5	7

$y = 2x + 1$

x	−5	−4	−3	−2	−1	0	1	2	3	4	5
y	−9	−7	−5	−3	−1	1	3	5	7	9	11

These values for x are easy to graph.

b)

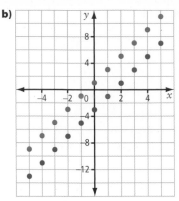

c) Similar: The points for the two graphs form parallel lines. Different: For the same x-value, the y-value on the graph of $y = 2x + 1$ is 4 greater than the corresponding y-value on the graph of $y = 2x - 3$.

5. a) $4x = 12$ **b)** $x = 3$

6. a) $s = -10$ **b)** $x = 3$ **c)** $v = 16$ **d)** $x = 3$

7. a) $x = -28$ **b)** $x = 8$ **c)** $x = -18$ **d)** $x = 5$

8. a) $10 = \frac{1}{3}x - 3$ **b)** Jason's father is 39 years old.

9. $40(x + 2) = 960$; $x = 22$
Elijah's regular hourly wage is $22/h.

10. a) Answers may vary. Example: Use a table.

		Die 2				
	1	**2**	**3**	**4**	**5**	**6**
1	1, 1	1, 2	1, 3	1, 4	1, 5	1, 6
2	2, 1	2, 2	2, 3	2, 4	2, 5	2, 6
Die 3	3, 1	3, 2	3, 3	3, 4	3, 5	3, 6
1 4	4, 1	4, 2	4, 3	4, 4	4, 5	4, 6
5	5, 1	5, 2	5, 3	5, 4	5, 5	5, 6
6	6, 1	6, 2	6, 3	6, 4	6, 5	6, 6

b) $P(\text{both even}) = \frac{9}{36} = \frac{1}{4}$

c) $P(\text{sum} \geq 6) = \frac{26}{36} = \frac{13}{18}$

11. a) $P(\text{odd number}) = \frac{2}{5}$ **b)** $P(\text{even number}) = \frac{2}{5}$

c) $P(\text{odd, then even}) = \frac{2}{5} \times \frac{2}{5} = \frac{4}{25}$

12. 12 options

13. a) $P(\text{H on disk}) = \frac{1}{2}$; $P(\text{H is spun}) = \frac{1}{3}$

b) $P(\text{H on disk, H is spun}) = \frac{1}{2} \times \frac{1}{3} = \frac{1}{6}$

c) Answers may vary. Example: Use a tree diagram.

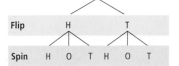

From the tree diagram, $P(\text{H on disk, H is spun}) = \frac{1}{6}$.

14. a) Answers may vary. Example: The twins could use a spinner divided into four equal regions labelled with the four colours of the spinning tops. They can spin the spinner twice in each trial for at least 20 trials to find the probability of spinning blue in both spins.
b) They need to assume that the spinning tops are identical.

c) $P(\text{experimental}) = \frac{1}{20}$ or 5%

d) $P(\text{theoretical}) = \frac{1}{4} \times \frac{1}{4} = \frac{1}{16}$ or 6.25%

15. Polygon A, a triangle, can tile the plane because two congruent triangles form a parallelogram, which is a quadrilateral. A quadrilateral can tile the plane because the sum of the interior angle measures is 360° at the point where the vertices of the quadrilaterals meet.
Polygon B, a regular hexagon, can tile the plane because each interior angle measure is 120°, which can total 360° at the point where the vertices of the hexagons meet.
Polygon C, a regular pentagon, cannot be used to tile the plane because each interior angle measure is 108°, which cannot total 360° at the point where the vertices of the pentagons meet.

16. Answers may vary. Example:

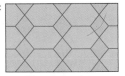

The pattern is made up of squares and irregular hexagons. Translation is used to create the pattern.

17. Answers may vary. Example: A tessellating tile is made from a square by removing a piece from the bottom and left side of the square and translating these pieces to the opposite sides of the square. The tessellating tile is then translated horizontally and vertically to create the tessellation.

18. Answers may vary. Example:

A tessellating tile is made by removing a piece from the left side of a parallelogram and adding the piece to the other side. The tessellation is created by translating the tessellating tile horizontally and vertically.

Glossary

B

bar graph A graph that uses horizontal or vertical bars to represent data visually.

base of a prism Any face of a prism that reflects the general shape of the prism.

C

circle graph A graph that represents data using sections of a circle. The sum of the percents in a circle graph is 100%.

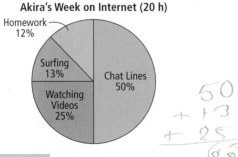

combined percents Adding individual percents together.

commutative property The order of adding or multiplying quantities does not affect the result.
$$a + b = b + a$$
$$a \times b = b \times a$$

constant A number that does not change.

cylinder A three-dimensional object with two parallel and congruent circular bases.

D

distort To change the appearance or twist the meaning of something in a way that is misleading.

distributive property Multiplication of each term inside the brackets of an expression by the term outside the brackets:
$$a(b + c) = a \times b + a \times c$$
$$= ab + ac$$

double bar graph A graph that uses two sets of horizontal or vertical bars to compare two sets of data across categories.

double line graph A graph that uses two lines to represent changes of two sets of data over time.

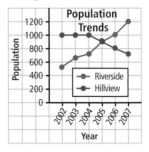

E

edge A line segment where two faces meet.

← edge

equation A mathematical statement with two expressions that have the same value. The two expressions are separated by an equal sign. $3a - 2 = 4$ is an equation.

expression Any single number, single variable, or combination of operations $(+, -, \times, \div)$ involving numbers and variables. An expression does not include an equal sign. $x + 9$, $2y - 7$, $8t$, and 5 are expressions.

F

face A flat or curved surface.

face

favourable outcome A successful result in a probability experiment.

formula A mathematical statement that represents the relationship between specific quantities. An example is $C = \pi \times d$, where C is the circumference and d is the diameter of a circle.

fractional percent A percent that includes a portion of a percent, such as $\frac{1}{2}\%$, 0.42%, $7\frac{3}{8}\%$.

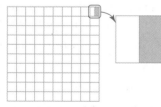

H

height The perpendicular distance from the base to the opposite side. Common symbol is h.

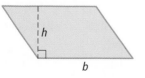

hypotenuse The longest side of a right angle triangle. Opposite the right angle.

hypotenuse

I

improper fraction A fraction in which the numerator is greater than the denominator. $\frac{4}{3}$ is an improper fraction.

independent events Results in which the outcome of one event has no effect on the outcome of another event.

integer Any of the numbers ..., $-3, -2, -1, 0$, $+1, +2, +3, ...$

interval The spread between the smallest and the largest numbers in a range of numbers.

L

line graph A graph that uses a line to represent changes in data over time.

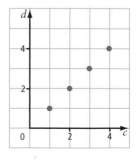

linear equation An equation that, when graphed, results in points that lie along a straight line.

linear relation A pattern made by a set of points that lie in a straight line.

M

mixed number A number made up of a whole number and a fraction, such as $3\frac{1}{2}$.

N

net A two-dimensional figure that, when folded, encloses a 3-D object.

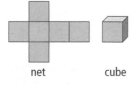

net   cube

numerical coefficient A number that multiplies the variable. In $2x + 4$, the number 2 is the numerical coefficient.

O

opposite operation A mathematical operation that undoes another operation. Subtraction and addition are opposite operations; multiplication and division are opposite operations. Also called inverse operation.

order of operations The correct sequence of steps for a calculation. Brackets first, then multiply and divide in order from left to right, and then add and subtract in order from left to right.

orientation The different position of an object formed by translating, rotating, or reflecting the object.

P

part-to-part ratio Compares different parts of a group to each other.

part-to-whole ratio Compares one part of a group to the whole group. Can be written as $a:b$ or $\frac{a}{b}$.

percent Means out of 100 and is another way of saying hundredths. 30% means $\frac{30}{100}$ or 0.30.

perfect square A number that is the product of two identical factors. It has an even number of prime factors. $2 \times 2 = 4$, so 4 is a perfect square. $2 \times 2 \times 3 \times 3 = 36$, so 36 is a perfect square.

pictograph A graph that illustrates data using pictures and symbols.

Varieties of Apples Sold

Fuji	
Golden Delicious	
Jonagold	
MacIntosh	
Red Delicious	

🍎 represents 10 apples

plane A two-dimensional flat surface that extends in all directions.

prime factorization A number written as the product of its prime factors. The prime factorization of 6 is 2×3.

probability The likelihood or chance of an event occurring. Probability can be expressed as a ratio, a fraction, or a percent.

proper fraction A fraction in which the denominator is greater than the numerator. $\frac{5}{8}$ is a proper fraction.

proportion An equation that says that two ratios or two rates are equal. It can be written in fraction form as $\frac{1}{4} = \frac{4}{16}$, or in ratio form as $1:4 = 4:16$.

Pythagorean relationship The relationship between the lengths of the sides of a right triangle. The sum of the areas of the squares attached to the legs of the triangle equals the area of the square attached to the hypotenuse.

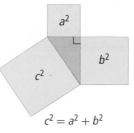

$c^2 = a^2 + b^2$

R

rate A comparison of two quantities measured in different units. $1.69 per 100 grams or $1.69/100 g is a rate for purchasing bulk food. 72 beats per minute or 72 beats/min is a heart rate.

reciprocal The multiplier of a number to give a product of 1. $\frac{3}{4}$ is the reciprocal of $\frac{4}{3}$ because $\frac{3}{4} \times \frac{4}{3} = 1$.

rectangular prism A prism whose bases are congruent rectangles.

right prism A prism that has sides that are perpendicular to the bases of the prism.

S

sample space All possible outcomes of a probability experiment.

sign rules In division, the quotient of two integers with the same sign is positive, and with different signs is negative. In multiplication, the product of two integers with the same sign is positive, and with different signs is negative.

square root A number that when multiplied by itself equals a given value. The symbol is $\sqrt{\ }$. 9 is the square root of 81 because $9 \times 9 = 81$.

surface area The number of square units needed to cover a 3-D object. The sum of the areas of all the faces of an object.

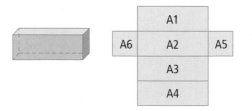

T

table of values A chart showing two sets of related numbers.

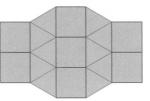

x	1	2	3	4
y	5	10	15	20

tessellation A pattern that covers an area or plane without overlapping or leaving gaps. Also called a tiling pattern.

three-term ratio Compares three quantities measured in the same units. Can be written as $a:b:c$, or a to b to c.

blue : red : yellow is 6 : 4 : 2

tiling pattern A pattern that covers an area or plane without overlapping or leaving gaps. Also called a tessellation.

tiling the plane Using repeated congruent figures to cover an area without leaving gaps or overlapping.

transformation A change in a figure that results in a different position or orientation. Examples are translations, reflections, and rotations.

trend The general direction in which a line graph is going.

triangular prism A prism with two triangular faces that are the same size and shape.

two-term ratio Compares two quantities measured in the same units. Can be written as $a:b$ or a to b.

blue:red is 6:4

U

unit price A unit rate that involves prices. Often shown per 100 g or 100 mL. $5.00 per 100 g is a unit price.

unit rate A rate in which the second term is 1. 64 beats/min is a unit rate.

V

variable A letter that represents an unknown number. In $3a - 5$, the variable is a.

vertex The point where three or more edges of a figure meet. The plural is vertices.

vertex

volume The amount of space an object occupies. Measured in cubic units.

Z

zero pair A pair of integer chips with one chip representing $+1$ and one chip representing -1. The pair represents zero because $(+1) + (-1) = 0$. Any whole number of zero pairs represents zero.

+1   −1

Index

F

face, 164
favourable outcome, 412, 428–429
formulas
  area of a circle, 263, 264
  defined, 353
  linear, 353–354, 356
  surface area of cylinder, 185
  volume of cube, 255, 257
  volume of cylinder, 262–264
  volume of prism, 255, 256, 257
fraction operations
  applying, 230–235
  division, *see* division
  multiplication, *see* multiplication
fractional percent, 126, 127
fractions
  converting to decimals and percents, 131
  decimals as, 132
  percents as, 130–131, 133, 135
  and probabilities, 426–435
Frayer model, 43, 443

G

golden rectangle, 54
graphs
  advantages of types, 12
  analysing data on, 335
  data relations, 332, 333, 336
  from equation, 355, 356
  from formula, 353–354, 356
  key considerations, 31
  misleading, 18–22
  summary of types, 7
  table of values, 334, 336
grids, 122–127
GST and PST, 145–146

H

halving, 139, 141
height of prism or cylinder, 247

hypotenuse
  defined, 89
  length, 102, 103, 106
  Pythagorean relationship, 90, 101–102, 103

I

improper fractions
  converting, 217
  explained, 199
  multiplying, 216–221
independent events, 410
  outcomes, 419–425
integer chips
  model for multiplication, 286–292
  model for division, 300–305
  zero pairs, 287
integers, 282–323
  division, 300–311
  multiplication, 286–299
interval, 6
isolating the variable, 373, 384

K

KWL chart, 3, 195, 283, 329, 367

L

line graph, 7, 12
  double line graph, 7, 13
  misrepresentation, 18–19, 25
linear equation, 355, 356
  defined, 371
  solving, 366–405
linear formula, 353–354, 356
linear relations, 328–365
  analysing, 332–341
  defined, 336
  graph from equation, 355, 356
  graph from formula, 353–354, 356
  representing, 332–336, 344–347
  table of values and, 344–347

M

magic square, 292
manipulatives
  division, 205, 207
  multiplication, 199–200, 201
mean
  fractions, 235
  whole numbers, 314
mental math for percents, 139–140, 141
misrepresenting data, 18–27
mixed numbers
  converting, 217
  division with fractions, 222–229
  explained, 199
  in lowest terms, 216
  multiplying, 216–221
mosaics, 445, 469
multiplication
  diagrams, 200, 201, 212, 213
  fraction and whole number, 198–203
  improper fractions, 216–221
  integer chips as model, 286–292
  manipulatives, 199–200, 201
  mixed numbers, 216–221
  number line, 293–294, 296
  paper folding, 210, 211–212, 213
  proper fractions, 210–215
  repeated addition, 198, 199, 201
  rule for, 213
  sign rule, 294–295, 296
  table, probabilities, 427–429, 431
  tree diagram, probabilities, 429, 431
  understanding, 198, 287
  whole numbers, 198–203
multiplication statement, 198

Credits

Photo Credits

p vi Bill Ivy; p vii Charlie Munsey/CORBIS; p viii Photo courtesy of Hayley Wickenheiser, In The Game, Inc; Adrian Wyld/CP; bottom left Robert Dall/CP, W. Lynch/IVY Images; bottom right Jeff Greenberg/Alamy; p x Will Ivy/IVY Images; p2–3 Photo courtesy of Hayley Wickenheiser, In The Game, Inc; p5 Adrian Wyld/CP; p6 David Tanaka; p8 Vasko Miokovic/Istock; p17 Bill Ivy; p39 Jeff Greenberg/Alamy; p40 David Tanaka; p42–43 Leo Mason/CORBIS, COC/Cromby McNeil/CP, top left, Photo courtesy of Schockmoele Stables; p44 Don Ford; p45 David Tanaka; p46 top, Robert Dall/CP, W. Lynch/IVY Images; p54 Keith Binns/Istock; p55 Helen Mason; p56 Bill Ivy; p58 David Tanaka; p61 left, Will Ivy/IVY Images, Jeff McIntosh/CP; p62 Stock Food/Maxx Images; p63 Istock; p69 David Tanaka; p73 D. Trask/IVY Images; p79 Colleen Harrington/CORBIS; p80 David Tanaka; p85 Tribune Media Services; p86 left, Galina Barskaya/Istock, Jon Arnold/Alamy; p87 Martin Pernter/Istock; pp101, 104 Rick Friedman/Corbis; p106 Bill Ivy; p110 Galina Barskaya/Istock; p116 David Tanaka; pp118–119 Planetary Visions Ltd/Photo Researchers, Inc; p120 Don Ford; p121 Jeff McIntosh/CP; p122 David Tanaka; p138 REUTERS/Zohra Bensemra; p142 W. Fraser/IVY Images; p143 Car Culture/Corbis; p149 Reuters/CORBIS; p151 Will Ivy/IVY Images; p153 left, Christina Ivy, TORTEL/CORBIS SYGMA; p154 David Tanaka; p160–161 B. Lowry/IVY Images; p163 top, J. DeVisser/IVY Images, Ron Garnett/Airscapes International Inc.; p165 David Tanaka; p167 Bill Ivy; p168 David Tanaka; p170 Istock; pp171, 172 David Tanaka; p175 Bill Ivy; p176 top, Richard Buchan/CP, David Tanaka; p182 Bill Ivy; p183 left, Stuart Pitkin/Istock, Photo courtesy of K. Nolan; p185 Photo courtesy of the artist Todd Baker; p187 Bill Ivy; p190 Nicole K. Cioe/Istock; p191 IVY Images; p197 Evgeniya Lazareva/Istock; p198 David Tanaka; p204 O. Bierwagon/IVY IMAGES; p209 left, Myles Dumas/Istock, Will Ivy/IVY Images; p215 PA/Gareth Copley/CP, W. Fraser/IVY Images; p216 B. Lowry/IVY Images; p221 top, Christina Ivy/IVY Images, W. Lynch/IVY Images; p222 D. Trask/IVY Images; p228 left, Andrew Lambert Photography/Science Photo Library, John Foster/Masterfile; p229 top, Loic Bernard/Istock, Alan & Sandy Carey/IVY Images; p230 Stefan Hermans/Istock; p234 D. Trask/IVY Images; p235 top, Pali Rao/Istock, Bill Ivy; p237 W. Sproul/IVY Images; p239 Niko Vujevic/Istock; p242 top left clockwise, Bill Ivy, Dusan Ponist/Istock, Bill Ivy, Robert Estall/CORBIS, Bill Ivy; p245 top, Juan Monino, Fred Hall/Istock; p252 left, Paul Erickson/Istock, NASA Marshall Space Flight Center (NASA-MSFC); p254 David Tanaka; p260 Don Ford; p262 Bill Ivy; p264 David Tanaka; p266 NASA; p274 Roger Antrobus/CORBIS; p275 Bill Ivy; p277 left, IVY Images, Charles O'Rear/CORBIS; p279 Claudio Arnese/Istock; p282–283 Neil Rabinowitz/CORBIS; p285 Guelph Mercury/Darren Calabrese/CP; p286 Will Ivy/IVY Images; p294 Richard R. Hansen/Photo Researchers, Inc.; p297 D. Trask/IVY Images; p299 D. Nowlan/IVY Images; p300 Bill Ivy; p305 left, David Tanaka, W. Lowry/IVY Images; p306 O. Bierwagon/IVY Images; p311 D. Trask/IVY Images; p312 Vancouver Maritime Museum; p316 Dan Eckert/Istock; p317 AP/Armando Franca/CP; p318 Istock; p319 J. Whyte/IVY Images; p328–329 Charlie Munsey/CORBIS; p331 B. Lowry/IVY Images; p332 Istock; pp338, 339, 340 Bill Ivy; p346 Jason Lugo/Istock; p350 B. Lowry/IVY Images; p351 T. Parker/IVY Images; p352 Istock;

p357 Bill Ivy; p358 Tom Brown/Istock; p360 Patricia Edel/Istock; p361 Istock; p363 B.Lowry/IVY Images; p366–367 left, D. Trask/IVY Images, O. Bierwagen/IVY Images, Lisa F. Young/Istock; p378 top left, Bill Ivy, Allan & Sandy Carey/IVY Images, B. Lowry/IVY Images; p379 David Tanaka; p386 Andrew Howe/Istock; p387 W. Ivy/IVY IMAGES; p390 Larry MacDougall/CP; p393 Ken Babione/Istock; p399 Istock; p406–407 left, Bill Ivy, Visuals Unlimited/CORBIS; pp409, 418, 423, 435, 440 David Tanaka; p442–443 M.C.Escher © 2007 The M.C. Escher Company-Holland. All Rights Reserved. *www.mcescher.com*; p445 Bill Ivy; p446 Hugh MacDougall/Istock; p451 Professor Steven Edwards, Department of Mathematics, Southern Polytechnic State University, Marietta, GA USA.; p456 Judith Nickol & David Tanaka; p457 top, David Tanaka, Jim Sugar/CORBIS; p459 Nick Inverso/Istock; pp461, 462, 463 top and middle, M.C.Escher © 2007 The M.C. Escher Company-Holland. All Rights Reserved. *www.mcescher.com*; p463 bottom, Bill Ivy; p465 left top and bottom, Dr. Andrew Crompton, School of Architecture, Manchester University, right M.C.Escher © 2007 The M.C. Escher Company-Holland. All Rights Reserved. *www.mcescher.com*; p475 B. Lowry/IVY Images.

Text Credits

p10 Edmonton Oilers data: www.nhl.com; p12 climate data: *www.worldclimate.com*; p15 decibel levels data: The Canadian Hearing Society, *Hear to Stay: Make Noise about Noise – Book #1: Noise Facts.* Reprinted with permission. Also from *www.nshsc.ns.ca/icathreshold.html* (accessed on November 16, 2007) and *www.canada.com/victoriatimescolonist* (April 15, 2007); p28 The Vancouver Sun, August 16, 2006, p. B1; p37 handedness data: Adapted from Statistics Canada, Census at School, Right-handed, left-handed or ambidextrous? from *www19.statcan.ca/04/04_0506/04_0506_013_e.htm* (accessed on April 15, 2007); p38 population data: adapted from Statistics Canada, Population and dwelling counts, for Canada provinces and territories, 2006 and 2001 censuses from *www12.statcan.ca/english/census06/data/popdwell/Table.cfm?T=101* (accessed on April 15, 2007); pp194–195 map adapted from Natural Resources Canada, Data Management and Dissemination Branch; p378 handedness data: Adapted from Statistics Canada, Census at School, Right-handed, left-handed or ambidextrous? from *www19.statcan.ca/04/04_0506/04_0506_013_e.htm* (accessed on May 4, 2007); p386 physical activity data: Adapted from Statistics Canada, Census at School, What is your favourite physical activity? from *www19.statcan.ca/04/04_0607/04_0607_021_e.htm* (accessed on April 23, 2007); p393 favourite school subject data: Adapted from Statistics Canada, What is your favourite subject? from *www19.statcan.ca/04/04_0506/04_0506_026_e.htm* (accessed on April 23, 2007); energy requirements data: adapted from *www.hc-sc.gc.ca*; p477 music with Canadian content graph: adapted from Statistics Canada, Music With Canadian Content from *www.statcan.gc.ca/english/kits/winner/2003/grade8/music/graph2.png* (accessed on September 18, 2007); p480 graph: Adapted from *www.pcstats.com*

Illustration Credits

Allure Illustrations: 210, 236, 388

Ben Hodson: xiv, 74, 75, 76–77, 87, 88, 95, 111, 115, 130, 155, 193, 246, 253 (top), 253 (bottom), 257, 261, 264, 267 (top), 267 (bottom), 274, 322, 323, 351, 365, 369, 374, 382, 421, 429, 437, 441

Tina Holdcroft Enterprises Inc.: vi, 41, 80, 98, 100, 103, 108, 137, 144, 164, 250, 252, 268, 269, 342, 348, 370 (top), 370 (bottom), 373, 380 (top), 380 (bottom), 404, 410, 419, 423, 426, 439

www.mikecarterstudio.com: 18, 194–195, 197, 464 (left), 464 (right)

Technical Art

Tom Dart, Luciano Sebastion De Monte, Kim Hutchinson, and Adam Wood of First Folio Resource Group, Inc.

Mathematics
for Retail Buying

4th Edition

Bette K. Tepper
Fashion Institute of Technology

Newton E. Godnick
Fashion Institute of Technology

Fairchild Publications
New York